ILLUMINATIONS
ON THE
SYNOPTIC GOSPELS

AN ANTHOLOGY

COMPILED AND EDITED BY

LEILA WHITNEY GALBRAITH

C.S.S. Publishing Co., Inc.

Lima, Ohio

"... a beam in the darkness.
Let it grow." - Tennyson

November 1
Leila Whitney Galbraith

ILLUMINATIONS ON THE SYNOPTIC GOSPELS

FIRST EDITION
Copyright © 1989 by
Leila Whitney Galbraith

PRINTED IN U.S.A.
by The C.S.S. Publishing Co., Inc.

7666 / ISBN 1-55673-120-5

Acknowledgments

The following publishers and authors have granted permission for the inclusion of copyrighted material in the present volume.

Abingdon Press: From *Jesus and Logotherapy* by Robert Leslie. Copyright © 1965 by Abingdon Press. Used by permission. From *Abingdon Bible Commentary*. Copyright renewal © 1956 by Abingdon Press. Used by permission.

The Anglican Digest: Mellick Belshaw, "Spirit Holy or Unholy?", copyright © Pentecost 1983.

Augsburg Fortress Publishers: Reprinted by permission from *The Resurrection* by Norman Perrin, copyright © 1977, Fortress Press. Reprinted by permission from *In Debt to Christ* by Douglas Webster, copyright © 1957, Fortress Press.

The Balkin Agency: Nahum Glatzer (ed.), *Martin Buber: On the Bible*, copyright © 1982.

Bethany House Publishers: Reprinted by permission from *Speaking in Tongues* by Larry Christianson, published and copyrighted © 1968 by Bethany House Publishers, Minneapolis, MN 55438.

Cambridge University Press: T. W. Manson, *The Teaching of Jesus*, © 1935.

Christian Literature Crusade: Amy Carmichael, *Thou Givest . . . They Gather*, Copyright © 1958 Dohnavur Fellowship. Roy Hession, *We Would See Jesus*, copyright © 1958. Roy Hession, *Calvary Road*, copyright © 1950. Frank L. Houghton, *Amy Carmichael of Dohnavur*, copyright © 1953 Dohnavur Fellowship. F. B. Meyer, *Elijah*.

Collins Fount: 8 Grafton St, London, W1X 3LA, England. C. S. Lewis, *The Problem of Pain, The Great Divorce, The Trouble With X, The Weight of Glory, Mere Christianity, Miracles , Screwtape Letters, An Experiment in Criticism, Epilogue.*

The Crossroad Publishing Company: From *Voices on Fire* by John Walchars, S. J. Copyright © 1981 by John Walchars, S. J. From *In the Stillness Dancing* by Neil McKenty. Copyright © 1986 by Neil McKenty. Reprinted by permission of **The Crossroad Publishing Company**.

Crossway Books: From *The Real Presence* by Leanne Payne, Copyright © 1979. Used by permission of **Good News Publishers/Crossway Books**, Westchester, Illinois 60153.

Desclee Publishing Company: Rue de Vaugirard, 75006, Paris, France. Monk of the Eastern Church, *Jesus: A Dialogue With the Saviour*, copyright © 1963.

Dimension Books Inc.: From *The Woman at the Well* by Adrian van Kaam, C.S.Sp., P.O. Box 811, Denville, NJ 07834. From *As Bread That is Broken* by Peter G. van Breemen, S. J. Published by **Dimension Books Inc.**, P.O. Box 811, Denville, NJ 07834.

Dominican Publications: Wilfrid Harrington, *Explaining the Gospels*, copyright © 1963.

Doubleday: Reprinted by permission of **Doubleday**, a division of Bantam, Doubleday, Dell Publishing Group, Inc. for the following books: Fulton Oursler, *The Greatest Story Ever Told*, © 1949. [fair use; U.S. & Canada]. St. Teresa of Avila, *Interior Castle*, 1961 Avila. Donald Senior, *Invitation to Matthew*, © 1977. Fulton Sheen, *The Life of Christ*, © 1977. Fulton Sheen, *Go To Heaven. Peace of Soul* © 1949.

Gerald Duckworth & Co. Ltd.: 43 Gloucester Crescent, London, NW1 7DY. S. H. Hooke, *The Kingdom of God*, copyright © 1949.

Edward England Booke: Hugh Evan Hopkins, *Charles Simeon of Cambridge*, copyright © 1977. Margaret Duggan, *Through the Year With Michael Ramsey*, copyright © 1975.

Eerdmans Publishing Company: Richard Holloway, *Beyond Belief*, copyright © 1981. Rosamond Sprague, *A Matter of Eternity*, copyright © 1973. John Stott, *Basic Christianity*, copyright © 1958. William Neil, *Difficult Sayings of Jesus*, copyright © 1975. Patrick Grant, *A Dazzling Darkness*, copyright © 1985. Richard Holloway, *A New Heaven*, © 1978.

Faber and Faber Limited: D. M. Baillie, *God Was in Christ*, copyright © 1961. Theophan the Recluse, *Unseen Warfare*, copyright © 1963. (translated by E. Kadloubovsky and G. E. H. Palmer). Dag Hammarskjold, *Markings*, copyright © 1964. (translated by W. H. Auden and Leif Sjoberg).

Forward Movement Publications: Mark A. Beaufoy, *The Parables*, copyright © 1971. Frederick Dillistone, *The Holy Spirit*. Brother Lawrence, *His Letters and Conversations on the Practice of the Presence of God*, copyright © 1941.

Harcourt Brace Jovanovich, Inc.: Excerpt from *Surprised By Joy*, copyright © 1955 by C. S. Lewis, renewed by Arthur Owen Barfield, Executor of the Estate of C. S. Lewis, reprinted by permission of **Harcourt Brace Jovanovich, Inc.** Scattered excerpts from *Reflections on the Psalms*, copyright © 1958 by C. S. Lewis, renewed 1986 by Arthur Owen Barfield, Executor of the Estate of C. S. Lewis, reprinted by permission of **Harcourt Brace Jovanovich, Inc.** Excerpts from *Letters to Malcolm: Chiefly on Prayer*, copyright © 1963, 1964 by the Estate of C. S. Lewis and/or C. S. Lewis, reprinted by permission of **Harcourt Brace Jovanovich, Inc.** Excerpts from *Letters of C. S. Lewis*, copyright © 1966 by W. H. Lewis and Executors of C. S. Lewis, reprinted by permission of **Harcourt Brace Jovanovich, Inc.**

Harper Row: Permission granted for inclusion from: Gunther Bornkamm, *Jesus of Nazareth*, copyright © 1975. Gunther Bornkamm, *Paul*, copyright ©1971. Marguerite Harmon Bro, *Every Day a Prayer*, copyright © 1943. Marguerite Harmon Bro, *More Than We Are*, copyright © 1948. Teilhard de Chardin, *The Divine Milieu*, copyright © 1960. Robert Dentan, *First Reader in Biblical Theology*, copyright © 1961. Edmund Fuller (ed.), *The Showing Forth of Christ: Sermons of John Donne*, copyright © 1964. Monica Furlong, *Merton*, copyright © 1980. Reuel Howe, *Man's Need and God's Action* copyright © 1954. F. W. Kates (ed.), *A Bishop Brent Anthology*, copyright © 1949. John M. Krumm, *The Art of Being a Sinner*, copyright © 1967. Paul L. Maier, *First Christians*, copyright © 1976. T. R. Milford, *Foolishness to the Greeks*, copyright © 1953. William Neil, *Can We Trust the Old Testament*, copyright © 1979. Michael Ramsey, *Sacred and Secular*, copyright © 1965. Dorothy Sayers, *A Man Born to Be King*, copyright © 1943. J. W. Stevenson, *God in My Unbelief*, copyright © 1960. Helmut Thielicke, *The Waiting Father*, copyright © 1959. Thomas Traherne, *Centuries*, copyright © 1959. Shirwood Wirt, *Love Song*, copyright © 1971. Weld and Sydnor, *The Son of God*, copyright © 1957.

Verlag Herder Freiburg: Postfach, 07800, Freiburg im Breisgau, West Germany. Rudolf Schnackenburg, *God's Rule and Kingdom*, copyright © 1963.

David Higham Associates Limited: Dorothy L. Sayers, *The Mind of the Maker*, published by Methuen, copyright © 1941.

Holy Cross Monastery: Ralph Milligan (ed.), *All For the Love of God: A Holy Cross Omnibus*, copyright © 1957. Allan Whittemore, *Joy in Holiness*, copyright © 1964.

Zola Levitt: Zola Levitt, *The Seven Feasts of Israel*, copyright © 1972.

With grateful acknowledgment for personal permission from the following authors for use of their material:

✠ ✠ ✠ ✠
**This book is dedicated
to the memory of Nick,
his faith and support.**
✠ ✠ ✠ ✠

Appreciations

✠ ✠ ✠ ✠ ✠ ✠

   This book would not have been conceived without the fellowship of beloved class members who shared learning experiences through Bible discussion illuminated by the inspiration of exegetes, some of whose words are here under one cover. My love and gratitude to all of my classmates and to The Reverend William Pounds, The Reverend Robert Hewitt, The Reverend Kenneth Burton, Professor Joseph Pickle and Father John Walchars, S. J. for stimulating and supporting my initial efforts. I thank the following for lovingly helping to prepare this publication: Sally Hopkins, Rita Nielson, Nancy Nesavich, Rose Michael Weber, S. C., Betty Boyd and Helen Johnson for essential secretarial help; Cindy McMahon for creative and tireless organizational support; The Reverend Donald Armstrong for his effective enthusiasm as our new rector; James Cunningham for his generosity of spirit and professionalism during endless hours of proof reading; Nicoll Galbraith and Whitney Galbraith, my two sons, for their support and encouragement; Sydney Schults and my daughter, Leila Galbraith Delger, whose confidence in the *Illuminations* prompted their counselling and working out of my publication weals and woes.

   We all have praised the Lord for giving us the C.S.S. Publishing Company as His co-workers. I am deeply appreciative of the advice, cooperation and patience extended to me by Pastor Wesley Runk, the company president; by Michael Sherer, Dawn Lausa, Ellen Shockey, the editors; and by their staff members.

   I recognize with special appreciation and affection the many writers and publishers who, in generously granting my permission to use their readings, have made it possible for these illuminations to "make disciples."

Leila Whitney Galbraith

Sequence of Units

✠　✠　✠　✠　✠　✠

PREFACE

✠　✠　✠　✠　✠　✠

After retiring from teaching literature in secondary schools, I sought a Bible study which would require an academic preparation by the student and an inspired clarification of the word of God by its leaders. As the recipient of such a study, I did have the enthusiasm and didactic skills with which to meet the ultimate invitation to lead classes, but I certainly did not have the inspiration nor in-depth understanding of the Bible. My one resource was my alphabetized notebook of references to the Bible, chapters and verses, and of topical annotations. These I had been recording during thirty-five years as I read the works of inspired scholars, writers and exegetes.

Because I, as a neophyte Bible discussion leader, found the use of these passages effective in the preparation of my presentations and as stimulation for class discussion, I feel at least constrained, and at most inspired, to share these illuminations as a didactic tool.

This anthology is neither exhaustive nor inclusive. Limited selectivity has been my prevailing discipline. A reflection of C. S. Lewis has been a helpful guide: "An author simply and solely tries to embody in his own art some reflection of eternal beauty and wisdom. . . . And always of every idea and every method, the Christian will ask, 'Not is it mine?' but is it good?" How well have the many writers whose clarifications and commentary are included in this anthology met that standard!

Subsequent to writing this statement of incentive and purpose, I found encouragement in the message of Bishop William Frey in the May-June, 1984, *Colorado Episcopalian*: "Don't wait until you know everything about the Lord before you begin sharing what you do know. Don't wait until you feel totally prepared to share the good news of the Gospel with other people or to invite them to church with you. The Lord is apparently willing to take a chance on us just as we are. And there's no better way to learn than to learn while doing."

Leila Whitney Galbraith

On the Preparation for the Advent of the Gospel

"The first race of mankind, launched into the world and into the world's history, fails. But not because of the sin against God. The sin against God led only to the expulsion from Paradise. It is the sin of men against each other, the way of strife, beginning with fratricide and ending with filling the earth with 'violence'; it is the wickedness of men 'corrupting' the earth itself that leads to the Deluge. . . . And then the second race of men also fails; this time by sinning against God. . . . This race wanted to be united in a common humanity — by rising up against God. They shared work centers in the tower, its spires pointed to heaven, against heaven. The second race suffered precisely the fate it had sought to prevent without having been actually threatened by it: the fate of dispersal. . . . The humanity which was none because it sought union against God is 'scattered' into nations. . . .

The basic assumption is this: after men in two successive ages thwarted, time and again, the Lord's intention that they grow into one human community of their own free will and human obedience, a third beginning is to be made. . . . But how is this aim to be reached? A new people must arise, one that will come not only out of the natural begetting of generations but will be helped into being by the revelation, the promise and the commandment from above. . . .

The man Abram is singled out, and sent out. . . . The entire history of the road from Ur of the Chaldees to Sinai is a consequence of choices and partings, events of history — tribal history and national history. But above them stands revelation and gives them their meaning, points out to them their goal. For the end of all these partings is a future community of all men.''

Nahum Glatzer, ed.
Martin Buber: On the Bible
pp. 26-29

"The Old Testament Law, including the ceremonial law, had been given the Jews by God for a purpose. The Jews were the Chosen People, the race of men chosen by God to be prepared for His Incarnation. When God became man, He had to become a member of some specific race. It was essential that at least some members of that race know enough about God to recognize him when he came. Centuries of teaching about the nature of God were needed to prepare the Jews for the coming of Christ. This could be accomplished only by accumulated tradition handed down from generation to generation. During the process the Jews had to be a race apart, cut off from the surrounding nations, in order that their special revelation might not be dissipated by contact with pagan religions. The ceremonial law was that which made the Jew so different from his neighbors that he could live, even in a pagan city, as a member of a separate and uncontaminated race.''

Ralph Milligan, ed.
All For the Love of God: Holy Cross Omnibus
p. 174

There has never been a nobler or more complete religion than the Jewish one, yet its very sublimity and nobility was its greatest weakness. It was, for one thing, extremely elitist. The proper observance of the minutely detailed tradition was something which the common man found impossible, and to the Gentile who was outside the Law, it was, in many of its requirements, incomprehensible. It thus seemed to place a vast and complicated minefield between man and God, which man must cross with extreme care if he would make his way to God. This minefield consisted of hundreds of commandments and ordinances which covered everything, from circumcision and the cleaning of vessels and the ritual washing of hands, to exclusive prohibitions against whole classes of technically unclean people. While it exalted some, others it reduced to despair. What could you do if you were, say, a tax collecter following a trade which was itself beyond the spiritual pale, unclean, impermissible? Or if you were a prostitute? Or a half-caste? To these spiritual proletarians, the Jewish Law was a way, not to God, but to despair and hopelessness and a sense that they were without God in the world.''

Richard Holloway
A New Heaven
p. 20

"Ezekiel's later prophecies are very interesting because they combine old elements with the new, and the priestly outlook with the prophetic. He goes further than Jeremiah in regard to the individual, not only in maintaining that in the long run it is the sinner himself who suffers for his sins, but in his insistence on the need of personal faith and repentance. He takes up the old prophetic hope of the messianic kingdom. . . . The establishment and maintenance of this ideal kingdom is pre-eminently the work of Yahweh himself. By it he will declare his holiness to the nations, though there is as yet no thought that the nations will have a share in it. The deliverer through whom the kingdom is to be set up is spoken of as Yahweh himself and as the Davidic prince, almost in a breath, though the two are never specifically identified."

Sister Penelope
The Wood
p. 79

"The fact is that the Gospel itself is only the Gospel in so far as it is the true, and the only, fulfilling of the Law. The Gospel is the power to fulfill the Law. And if there had not been first the developed experience and sense of the Law itself and of the necessity of fulfilling it; and then the no less true experience of the impossibility of the Law fulfilling itself in us, or of our fulfilling it ourselves; and then again the experience of the actual transgression and the consequent sense of sin, and if all this had not gone before, there would have been neither truth in itself nor possible meaning for us in the Gospel. The Hebrew development of the moral sense and the moral law, the Hebrew passion for righteousness and sense of sin, was the most necessary preparation for the advent of the Gospel."*

William Du Bose
The Gospel According to Saint Paul *
p. 25

"It may be a little presumptuous and it may be a little premature, but it seems to me that in this twentieth century, with the whole inhabited world awakening and opening up before our eyes, we have the chance for the first time to see the vastness of God's integrating plan. The apparent insignificance of its beginning is breath-taking. For if we strip away for a moment the romance and decoration of the Christmas story, we stand aghast at the awe-inspiring humility of God's beginning of his task of integration. The things that look romantic on a Christmas card or which sound pretty by association with delightful carols were in fact most devastatingly humble. For a pregnant woman to hunt desperately for a room when her time drew near would hardly be our choice for God's entry into the world on human terms! And yet so it was. That is how he came, right in at the human level: the Word of wholeness was born into a world of misery and strife, of suffering and sin."

J. B. Phillips
Making Men Whole
p. 18

---

*See also 116:1, Webster; 116:1 Penelope.

New Illuminations:

On the Incarnation of the Almighty Word

Matthew 1:1-25   Luke 1:1-4; 26-38   John 1:1-14

"The Christmas story is very popular; but multitudes of people think of it as something like a fairy tale, and the Christmas cards, with pretty angels and the romantic surroundings of the stable, reinforce the impression. They do not reckon with the serious fact that the Son of God was made man for us men and for our salvation. It was into this dark and sinful world of ours that the Son of God came when he was made man. . . .

"It is necessary to hold fast to the truth of God's saving purpose in history, which the Bible relates. . . . Many parts of the Old Testament seem to have little to teach us directly, yet it is profoundly impressive to think how the divine purpose is slowly moving to its climax in the advent of the Messiah. . . . The Prophets spoke God's word, but no prophet was able to see the whole vision of God's purpose. It was only when the Son of God came that God's word was heard, full and complete."

A. G. Hebert
Scripture and the Faith
pp. 64-67

"That the revelation received by Moses was incomplete (Exodus 33:19, 22, 23) is shown in his testimony to the people that 'the Lord said unto me I will raise them up a Prophet from among their brethren, like unto thee, and will put my words in his mouth, and he shall speak unto them all that I shall command him.' (Deuteronomy 18:15, 18) According to the Old Testament, all Israel lived in expectation of the coming of the Prophet of whom 'Moses wrote' (John 5:46), the Prophet *par excellence*, 'THAT Prophet' (John 1:21). The Jewish people looked for the coming of the Messiah who when he was come would tell them 'all things' (John 4:25). *Come and live among us, that we may know thee* was the constant cry of the ancient Hebrews. Hence the name 'Emmanuel, which being interpreted is 'God with us' (Isaiah 7:14; Matthew 1:23). For us Christians the focal point of the universe and the ultimate meaning of the entire history of the world is the coming of Jesus Christ, who did not repudiate the archetypes of the Old Testament but vindicated them, unfolding to us their real significance and bringing new dimensions to all things — infinite, eternal dimensions."

Archimandrite Sophrony
His Life is Mine
p. 19

"The Incarnation, the coming of Christ, is the sudden awakening on the plane of human history, the sudden change from the old order of striving for redemption through obedience to the Law to the new order of redemption through the gift of divine grace.

While all things were in quiet silence, and that night was in the midst of her silent course, thine Almighty Word, O Lord, leaped down out of thy royal throne, Alleluia!

"The Incarnation is of effect for each and all, in every time and place. . . . The predisposition and action of God towards humanity is ever the same for his nature does not change. . . . But to be communicated fully to creatures with spatial and temporal minds, it had to be projected into a spatial and temporal event, and, of necessity, into some particular place and time."

Alan Watts
Behold the Spirit
pp. 78-79, 82-83

"Through the failure of Israel, we are meant to learn that more than human resources are needed, even with divine guidance, if the world is to become the kind of place God means it to be. So God comes into the human scene directly, in the person of his son, in the mystery of the incarnation. . . . God comes down to our level to lift us up to his, to give us the power of new life through the Holy Spirit."

William Neil
The Message of the Bible
pp. 4, 12

"The Incarnation is the first of two advents, and the coming of the Spirit is the second. Because the Son of God is clothed with our flesh, he is a 'partaker' of what is ours — 'the mystery of His incarnation.' Because 'we are invested with his spirit,' we are 'partakers' of what is his — 'the mystery of our inspiration.' "

A. M. Allchin
The World Is a Wedding
pp. 35-36
Lancelot Andrewes, "Whitesun Sermon" [Paraphrase]

"The central miracle asserted by Christians is the Incarnation. They say that God became man. . . . The historical difficulty of giving for the life, sayings and influence of Jesus any explanation that is not harder than the Christian explanation, is very great. . . . The first difficulty that occurs to any critic of the doctrine lies in the very center of it. What can be meant by 'God becoming Man'? In what sense is it conceivable that eternal, self-existing Spirit should be so combined with a natural human organism as to make one person? . . . We cannot conceive how the Divine Spirit dwelled within the created and human spirit of Jesus: but neither can we conceive how his spirit, or that of any man, dwells within his natural organism. What we can understand, if the Christian doctrine is true, is that our own composite existence is not the sheer anomaly it might seem to be, but a faint image of the Divine Incarnation itself — the same theme in a very minor key. We can understand that if God so descends into a human spirit and human spirit so descends into Nature, and our thoughts into our senses and passions, and if adult minds can descend into sympathy with children, and men into sympathy with beasts, then everything hangs together and the total reality, both Natural and Supernatural, is more multifariously and subtly harmonious than we had suspected. We catch sight of a new key principle — the power of the Higher, just in so far as it is truly Higher, to come down — the power of the greater to include the less."*

C. S. Lewis
Miracles
pp. 131-34

*See also 67:2, Payne.

"In the Incarnation God the Son takes the body and the human soul of Jesus and, through that, the whole environment of Nature, all the creaturely predicament into His own being. . . . The pure light walks the earth; the darkness received into the heart of the deity is there swallowed up. Where except in the uncreated light can the darkness be drowned?"

C. S. Lewis
Letters to Malcolm
pp. 70-71

"The Incarnation was, after all, the basis for a rescue operation for fallen man. . . . When God entered the world in human form he came to a fallen world with the purpose of offering redemption from human sin; it ill becomes us to pretend that we have no sins to be redeemed from. Had God's incarnation in Christ itself obliterated sin from the human scene and restored man to his pristine innocence, then there would have been no need of a Crucifixion."

Harry Blamires
Where Do We Stand?
p. 39

New Illuminations:

On the Incarnation Within Man

"The birth of Christ in our souls is for a purpose beyond ourselves: It is because his manifestation in the world must be through us. Every Christian, as it were, is part of the dustladen air which shall radiate the glowing Epiphany of God, catch and reflect his golden light. 'Ye are the light of the world' — but only because you are enkindled, made radiant by the One Light of the World. And being kindled, we have got to get on with it, be useful. As Christ said in one of his ironical flashes: 'Do not light a candle in order to stick it under the bed.' "

Evelyn Underhill
The Light of Christ
p. 41

"Jesus brought us the Light at God's command. This new light can appear within every man, freeing him from the past, endowing him with new creative power and guiding him toward a higher and more spiritual life. Paul describes the new Light by the words 'Christ lives in me' (Galatians 2:20).* Meister Eckhardt called it the 'birth of the Son in the castle of our soul.' . . . All of them agree that this light appears 'by grace'. The human soul, as it were, is the mother; the father is the eternal spirit. It is a virgin birth of Christianity within each of us. . . . Matthew depicts the favorable as well as the unfavorable factors surrounding the great event. The three kings tending to worship and to search for the new light all over the earth, travel across the outer and inner desert and a mysterious star guides them. Joseph struggles and conquers his pride. Herod kills much potential life outside and inside himself, but misses the point. Mary in amazement and unspeakable joy accepts the new life as if it were the most natural thing in the world. And it is."

Fritz Kunkel
Creation Continues
pp. 32-33

"The incarnation is staggering to the mind. That the Creator gave himself to us in his son whom he sent into our dark world through the womb of Mary, there to grow in the form and flesh of man — that this the greatest of all myths — happens to be the true one is a thing only to be grasped as the Father gives the power (Matthew 16:17). And we, like Mary, believe in order to receive that 'Holy Thing' (Luke 1:38). It is then that we find ourselves to be the extensions of the Incarnation by the pouring out of God's Spirit upon us. . . . Christ has given us His Spirit, and His Presence therefore remains with us and in us.''*

Leanne Payne
Real Presence: The Holy Spirit in the Works of C.S. Lewis
pp. 112, 20

"If the Word of God is to intervene for the elevation, purification, vitalization of man, it must be by entering into the essence of man's organism. The higher life which shall accomplish the divine will must clothe itself with the lower life which has by death become incapable of accepting the divine will. The law sufficeth not, spoken as it was to man, so the Word must speak not only to man but in man. . . . It is impossible to invest man's feebleness with God's omnipotence. God's omnipotence must come and clothe itself with man's feebleness."

R. M. Benson
The Way of Holiness
pp. 35-36

"Make good your Christmas Day, that Christ by a worthy receiving of the Sacramant be born in you. Then he that died for you will live with you all the year, and all the years of your lives, and inspire into you and receive from you at the last gasp this blessed acclamation, 'Lord lettest now thy servant depart in peace. . . .' "

Edmund Fuller, ed.
The Showing Forth of Christ: Sermons of John Donne
p. 77

---

*See also 61:1, Penelope; 67:2, Payne.

'See also 107:1, Lewis.

"God, for St. John, is the light that shines through the darkness of our alienation. Incarnation means for him that the divine light comes into the world to dispel our darkness bringing new graced life*. . . . The life promised to the Samaritan woman is the transcendent inner life of God himself."*

Adrian Van Kaam
The Woman at the Well
p. 6

*See also 62:1, Father Andrew.

*See also 42:1, Phillips.

New Illuminations:

On Mary the Mother of the Incarnate God

"In her response in faith, Mary, the mother of Jesus, is first among the saints of the church. She was open and vulnerable to the unexpected — to the coming of the Lord. She and Elizabeth were most unlikely to become pregnant, the one a devout young woman engaged to be married and the other barren and past the age of childbearing. They bore the unexpected fruit because their ears were open to the message.

"In youth, faith and innocence, Mary said 'Yes,' not as duty of a mother but as a person of faith. Her only question being 'How?' Not asking 'Why?' evidences true response."

William Pounds
Sermon Notes

"The Blessed Virgin Mary is one of the saints, a human creature united to God in all the ways that the saints are. But there is something unique, besides, in her relation to God; her place in the Christian religion is a special one. . . . She is what she is almost wholly by grace (favor first, and then help — 'Hail thou art highly favored'; 'Hail Mary, full of grace'). The grace of God to man in the Incarnation goes beyond what was directly imparted to the human mind of the historic Jesus: He favored Mary with a mode of union of God and man which is hers alone, as the Mother of Incarnate God. . . .

"The response of Mary stands for still another way of receiving Incarnate God. . . . Sometimes, what better response can there be than just taking good care of him as a mother would, as a mother did? . . . In our meditation let us see her as having something humanly worthwhile to do in God's self-revelation. The pictures in our churches which represent the great things in our religion will not adequately represent the relation of God with us, God taking our nature, unless it does include someone who didn't discuss anything much but 'kept all these sayings and pondered them in her heart' — unless it includes Mary simply holding our Lord in her arms."

Ralph Milligan, ed.
All For the Love of God: A Holy Cross Omnibus
pp. 16-18

"The first announcement of the Gospel narrative is not a proclamation about God's nature or even his demands. The Angel Gabriel comes to tell our Lady what God is go-

ing to do. . . . God was to be revealed in action. As the primary premise of faith, we too often forget it. But we can learn from our Lady's response. Not — Behold God's creature, willing to worship him: not — Behold God's daughter, full of respect for him. No, that is too static. *Behold God's handmaid ready to be used by him in his active work.* The work is already afoot. God initiates; man fits in with his plan — or he does not fit in. . . . The perfect prayer is always our Lady's prayer. Be it unto me according to thy word."

Harry Blamires
The Will and the Way: A God Who Acts
pp. 29-30

"Consider Mary as the Second Eve. In Gabriel's message she encountered a challenge to her faith greater than that at which her prototype had failed, harder and even more momentous than the one her father Abraham had taken up. It is striking that in her acceptance of it she calls herself 'the servant of the Lord', the title of the Second Isaiah's Servant (Chapter 42) with the gender changed. With her the words were simply the expression of absolute surrender to God's will. Nevertheless, Mary was royal, both as David's daughter and as the chosen mother of the Messiah; and her vocation from the first involved the greatest suffering on her Son's account. Never has he rebuked and chastened any whom he loves as he rebuked and chastened his own blessed mother. Mary is thus the Second Eve, in that she met the crucial testing before the Second Adam. She is the Second Eve also in that as his mother she is the mother also of all who live by him."

Sister Penelope
The Coming
pp. 88-89

"Jeremy Taylor speaks of a very personal moment in the Gospel, a hidden almost silent incident: The meeting between Mary and Elizabeth, the moment called the Visitation. . . . 'It is not easy to imagine what a collision of joys was at this blessed meeting: Two mothers of two great princes, the one the greatest that was born of women, and the other was his Lord. These, made mothers by two miracles, met together with joy and mysteriousness. The mother of our Lord went to visit the mother of his servant; and the Holy Ghost made the meeting festival and descended upon

Elizabeth, and she prophesied. Never but in heaven was there more joy and ecstacy. The persons . . . meeting together to compare and unite their joys and their eucharist, and then made prophetical and inspired, must needs to have discoursed like seraphims. 'For it came to pass when Elizabeth heard the salutation of Mary, the babe leaped in her womb and Elizabeth was filled with the Holy Ghost.'

It would be a great mistake to think that the baroque elaboration of Taylor's style in such a passage were mere decoration. . . . The comparison of Mary and Elizabeth to angelic orders, for instance, takes up an idea found throughout the tradition. Man, made little lower than the angels, is in Christ crowned with a glory and honor greater than theirs, since drawn into a closer and more intimate relationship with God. Therefore she who is the mother of the Lord is rightly called more honorable than the cherubim and incomparably more glorious than the seraphim. . . .

"But this is not perhaps the primary point which Taylor wishes to make in speaking of this meeting as one characterized by 'joy and mysteriousness.' Rather he wants to tell us something about liturgy, the common prayer of the Church, the gathering together of God's people into one place. Joy and thanksgiving, he tells us, are things which grow by being shared. The united praises of men, even when two or three are gathered together, rise up before God carrying the praises of all creation with them. The liturgy is not only a meeting of man with God, it is also a meeting of man with man, a coming together into one. In this sense the meeting of Mary and Elizabeth is the beginning of Christian liturgy; two women coming together. . . . 'The Holy Ghost made the meeting festival.' In the power of the Spirit, man's coming together to praise God is transformed into a coming together of man with God in the feast of the Kingdom."

A. M. Allchin
The World Is a Wedding
pp. 60-62

New Illuminations:

On the Birth of Jesus

Matthew 1:18-25   Luke 2:1-20

"In A.D. 6 Quirinius went as legate to Syria. Between A.D. 6 and 7, he carried out a census, but this cannot be the one referred to by St. Luke since by that time Jesus was over ten years old. According to the Biblical narrative, the census decreed by Caesar Augustus took place the year Christ was born. For a long time it seemed as though St. Luke had made a mistake. It was only when a fragment of a Roman inscription was found at Antioch that the surprising fact emerged that Quirinius had been the Emperor's legate in Syria on a previous occasion, in the days of Saturninus the Proconsul. At that time his assignment had been purely military. Quirinius established his seat of government as well as his headquarters in Syria between 10 and 7 B.C. . . .

"Sometimes two planets move so close to each other that they have the appearance of a single larger and more brilliant star. . . . About the end of February in 7 B.C. the clustering began. Jupiter moved out of the constellation Aquarius toward Saturn in the constellation of Pisces. . . . On May 29, visible for fully two hours in the morning sky, the first close encounter took place. The second conjunction took place on October 3. On December 4, the third and last time, a close encounter of Jupiter and Saturn took place. 'We have seen his star in the East' (Matthew 2:2), said the Wise Men. . . .

"But why this ancient, learned expedition of the three Wise Men to Palestine when, as we know, they could see the occurrence just as well in Babylon? . . . Since Nebuchadnezzar's time, many thousands of Jews had lived in Babylon. Many of them may have studied at the School of Astrology in Sippar. This wonderful encounter of Jupiter with Saturn, guardian of Israel, in the constellation (Pisces) of the 'West Country' of the Messiah, must have deeply moved the Jewish astrologers, for, according to astrological ways of thinking, it pointed to the appearance of a mighty king in the west country, the land of their fathers. To experience that in person, to see it with their own eyes, that was the reason for the journey of the wise astronomers from the East*. . . . Travel on the caravan routes even on camels, the swiftest means of transport, was a leisurely affair. If we think in terms of a journey lasting about six weeks, the Wise Men would arrive in Jerusalem toward the end of November. . . .

"Christendom celebrates Christmas from December 24 to 25. Astronomers and historians, secular and ecclesiastical, are, however, unanimously agreed that December 25 of the year 1 was not the authentic date of the birth of Christ, as regards either the year or the day. . . . The Biblical tradition gives us this clear indication: 'Now when Jesus was born in Bethlehem of Judea, in the days of Herod the king. . . .' (Matthew 2:1). We know from numerous contemporary sources who Herod was and when he lived and reigned. In 40 B.C. Herod was designated King of Judea by the Romans. His reign ended with his death in 4 B.C. Jesus must therefore have been born before 4 B.C."

Werner Keller
The Bible As History
pp. 344-53

"Jesus could not have been born at Christmas; Bethlehem is generally intensely cold at the end of December, and no shepherds could have been 'watching over their flocks by night' then. In the winter the flocks are taken into sheepfolds or caves at night, but in late summer sheep are too languid to feed in the daytime, so the shepherds take them out at night. Everything points to the late summer or early autumn of 6 or 7 B.C. as the date of his birth."

The Abingdon Bible Commentary
p. 1034

"What is one to make of people who will believe other miracles and 'draw the line' at the Virgin Birth? In reality the miracle is no less, and no more, surprising than any others. . . . The human father is merely an instrument by which God normally creates a man. No woman ever conceived a child, no mare a foal, without him. But once, and for a special purpose, he dispensed with that long line which is his instrument. Once the great glove of Nature was taken off his hand, his naked hand touched her. There was of course a unique reason for it. That time he was creating not simply a man but the Man who was to be himself: was creating man anew: was beginning at this divine and human point, the New Creation of all things. The whole soiled and weary universe quivered at this direct injection of essential life. But we are here concerned with it simply as Miracle — that and nothing more. As far as concerns the creation of Christ's human nature (the Grand Miracle whereby his divine begotten nature enters into it is another matter) the miraculous conception is one more witness that here is Nature's Lord. He is doing now, small and close, what he does

---
*See also 7:1, Underhill.

in a different fashion for every woman who conceives. He does it this time without a line of human ancestors: but even where he uses human ancestors, it is not the less he who gives life.''

C. S. Lewis
Miracles
pp. 165-67

"To an orthodox of the old faith, an icon is a window into eternity. The gospel story of the Birth of the Christ Child may stir enough imagination in us to open such a window of our own. . . .

"Birth is never easy. I know it is difficult to let the Christ be born within me. I wonder if I have the courage and strength to stand against the world. I concentrate on Mary and Joseph and the problems they had to face so that child could be born: first in Nazareth and then the long trip to Bethlehem.

". . . The image of Mary in Nazareth, the perfect image of the human soul. Mary, young, alive, obedient, open. As the pictures begin to flow, I see her standing there thinking back to the garden and the strange appearance of the angel with the startling news that the power of the highest is to overshadow her and she is to bear a child. How can the Christ child be born in me until I am as willing as Mary . . . . as open and as ready to take whatever comes? Lord, how is it possible for me to be accepting in the way that Mary was? She knew that people of Nazareth wouldn't understand. . . .

"Even Joseph had doubted. So often the doubters and the gossips have their way. We open ourselves to the spirit and find new life and then we back away because we cannot bear the criticism, the misunderstanding, the derision and condemnation. . . . I watch as Joseph swings open the door and comes over to embrace Mary. His face is troubled and Mary senses that something is wrong. Joseph says, 'We do have seventy-five miles to get to Bethlehem, and with you about to bear your child, how can we do it?' . . . How can any of us face the trip we have to make to our spiritual home where we can allow the Christ to enter?

"It was not easy to bear the Christ child then, but Mary and Joseph make their plans. The donkey that usually carries the carpenter's heavy beams will carry her. They will gather food together and start out in two days so as to avoid the Sabbath restrictions.

"Bright and early they start, leaving the little home locked expecting to return. The sky is overcast and a cold wind blows. . . . They trudge the dusty road hour after hour. . . . Hour by hour they go on. They break at high noon for rest and then go on again. . . . This night an old villager and his wife let them sleep in a corner of their hut. It is good they say to welcome strangers. . . . Another long day, cold wind and snow on the mountains, but ahead the lights of

Bethlehem. . . . They had enough money for the inn. They had taken all their savings just for this. . . . In hope and expectation, Joseph knocks at the great door of the inn. The innkeeper opens the door. . . . 'Sorry, no room.' 'Not even a corner?' 'No not even a corner.' And, 'No I don't know what you will do.' . . . The heavy door clangs shut and the dark is even more penetrating.

"Joseph stumbles down a little hill. The time is very close. There is a cave in the hillside with a shelter built in front of it . . . some straw in the back and standing in the shadows a donkey and some oxen. . . . Not a very likely place for the birth of God, but perhaps the less likely the better. Then no one can say that his life is a less probable place. . . . The child is born. The Christ is born. They have some clothes to wrap him in. Some straw laid in the manger makes a crib for him, and the oxen are lowing softly in the background. And so the Christ child is born. It is no easy thing to bear this child. . . . and if he can be born in this stable, he can be born even in me. . . . The star is shining . . . and there is a heavenly song breaking through the cold night air.''

Morton T. Kelsey
The Other Side of Silence
pp. 239-242

This is the month and this the happy morn,
Wherein the Son of Heaven's eternal King,
Of wedded Maid and Virgin Mother born,
Our great redemption from above did bring;
For so the Holy sages once did sing,
That he our deadly forfeit should release,
And with his Father work us a perpetual peace.

John Milton
"On the Morning of Christ's Nativity"

"Luke 2 opens with a reference not to Herod the Great, but to the Emperor Augustus (2:1). The context widens. Luke begins now to be concerned not with the writings of the prophets, but with the decrees of Caesar, not with priests but with governors, not with Jerusalem and the temple, but with Rome and 'all the World.' The Holy Babe is born. It is true in Bethlehem, the City of David, and the angelic announcement is made to simple Jewish shepherds in the fields nearby. But if the Christmas gospel is for 'all the people'* (Luke 2:11), the heavenly host promises peace on earth among men with whom God is pleased (R.S.V.), and no racial reference is made. 'Glory to God in the highest,

_____
*See also 76:1, Bornkamm.

and on earth peace, good will toward men' (K. J.). When the child is brought to the temple to be presented to the Lord, the aged and Godly Simeon is inspired by the Spirit to perceive the fulfilment of Isaiah's prophecies (Luke 2:30-32). He recognizes in Jesus the salvation which God had prepared for 'all peoples' and the light which would be both revelation for the Gentiles and for the glory of his people Israel.''

John Stott
Men With a Message
pp. 38-39

"The sign by which the shepherds will recognize the Saviour is that they will find 'the infant wrapped in swaddling clothes and laid in a manger.' No sign of power accompanies the birth of Christ. On the contrary, God become Man will make himself known first of all by his poverty, his humility, his weakness. As a small child wrapped in swaddling clothes, he is at the mercy of those who press around him. He depends on them. He cannot resist anyone. He is unable to exercise his will, nor can he defend himself. As he appears in his birth, so will he appear in his passion; and that is how he wants me to be.''

Monk of the Eastern Church
Jesus: A Dialogue with the Savior
pp. 93-94

"The Incarnation reveals to us that generosity in giving, which is part of the adorable character of God. Coming to his world and making himself known to it, he willed to come in the most generous way possible, in the way which would be the greatest help and blessing. He came to lay his head in the place of poverty. He willed that his cradle should be the poorest of cradles and his quilt the cheapest of all quilts; and he lay there in the generosity of his self-oblation with the wood of the manger beneath him and the straw of the stable about him, the great God manifest under the guise of the poorest little Baby that ever was born.''*

Harry C. Griffith, ed.
*A Gift of Light: A Collection
of Thoughts from the Writings of Father Andrew*
p. 37

"The heavens open and what is disclosed? A Baby, God manifest in the flesh. The stable, the manger, the straw; poverty, cold, darkness — these form the setting of the Divine Gift. In this child, God gives his supreme message to the soul — Spirit to spirit — but in a human way. Outside in the fields, the heavens open and the shepherds look up astonished to find the music and radiance of Reality all around them. But inside, our closest contact with that same Reality is being offered to us in the very simplest, homeliest way — emerging right into our ordinary life. A baby — just that. We are not told that the Blessed Virgin Mary saw the Angels or heard the *Gloria* in the air. Her initiation had been quite different, like a quiet voice speaking in our deepest prayer — 'The Lord is with thee!' 'Behold the handmaid of the Lord.' Humble self-abandonment is quite enough to give us God.

Think of the tremendous contrast, transcendent and homely brought together here as a clue to the Incarnation — the hard life of the poor, the absolute surrender and helplessness of babyhood and the unmeasured outpouring of Divine Life.''

Evelyn Underhill
Light Of Christ
p. 37

---

*See also 84:1 Thielicke.

New Illuminations:

On Joy, Rejoice and Joyous

"The whole Gospel of Luke sheds an atmosphere of joy and peace. Joy is mentioned at the birth of John, at the annunciation to Mary, at the visitation and at the angels' message to the shepherds. The Magnificat, the prophecy of Zecharias, the Gloria in Excelsis and the Nunc Dimittis are all songs of ecstacy.

The seventy-two disciples returned rejoicing from their mission, and Jesus pointed out to them the true motive of joy, and he himself rejoiced in the Holy Spirit. The crowds rejoiced at the works they witnessed. The disciples rejoiced on the occasion of their entry into Jerusalem, and after the Ascension they returned to the city with great joy."

Wilfred Harrington
Explaining the Gospels
p. 122

"Real Joy is ecstatic (Gk. stand from, displacement). Joy draws us out from ourselves. This is almost the purest joy that life affords. Real joy is ecstatic in that it stands out from the self in the other. . . . It is always the enjoyment of something beyond the self.

Richard Holloway
A New Heaven
p. 95

"Joy is the kind of experience usually associated with the sudden impinging upon us of some aspect of transcendent reality. It is as though we were caught up in a blaze of eternity."

H. A. Williams
The Joy of God
p. 9

"Joy on the psychological level is longing and desire. Two things first taught Lewis this longing: the green Castlereagh Hills that he could see from his nursery window, and a tiny toy garden that his brother made on the lid of a biscuit tin. With these came his first sense of beauty and the longing for the apparently unattainable. . . .

The Images of Joy were not to be idolatrously mistaken for joy as Object: that is, the beauty of the flowering currant, the memory of a past memory, or the Idea of Autumn were simply the images through which that Reality could shine, and not the true object of desire. . . .

Joy is the creaturely experience of 'receiving' from the Holy Other. This joy calls one up out of the mists of self and subjectivity into an objective and suprapersonal Presence. It calls the real I forward. Lewis, closed into the world of self, was the 'receiver' of that which would never be in his power to control, for 'the wind of the Spirit blows where it wills.' When joy darted down into Lewis' soul and just as quickly left again, he began looking outward in search of the Object whence these experiences came. . . . 'Joy is distinct not only from pleasure in general but even from aesthetic pleasure. It must have the stab, the pang, the inconsolable longing.' "

Leanne Payne
*The Real Presence:
The Holy Spirit in the Works of C.S. Lewis*
pp. 133, 35, 39

"Joy itself considered simply as an event in my own mind turned out to be of no value at all. All the value lay in that of which Joy was desiring. . . . The form of the desire is in the desire. . . . And that object was quite clearly no state of my own mind or body at all. . . . I did not yet ask who is desired? Only what is it? . . . No slightest hint was vouchsafed me that there ever had been or ever would be any connection between God and Joy. If anything it was the reverse. I had hoped that the heart of reality might be best symbolized as a place; instead, I found it to be a Person."

C. S. Lewis
Surprised by Joy
p. 220-221, 230

"Joy is the spirit of selfless delight.* . . . the very character of the beatitude of heaven given here and now in our grubby little souls, provided only that they are loving little souls. . . .

"Joy has no name. Its very being is lost in the tide of selfless delight — creation's response to the infinite loving of God. But, of course, the point for us is that this selfless joy has got to go on at times when we ourselves are in the dark, obsessed by the sorrow of life, so that we can feel no joy because we cannot gaze at the beauty. . . . There is

*See also 44:1, Harton.

18

always a night shift, and sooner or later we are put on it. The praise does not cease with the fading of the light but goes on through the spiritual night as well as the spiritual day. And if you are picked for the night shift, well praise the Lord.''

Evelyn Underhill
The Fruits of the Spirit
pp. 11, 15-16

"The tension between joy and the opposite of joy is, once again, something that is viewed with a certain mistrust by an age committed to the pursuit of happiness. . . . But we must not disguise from ourselves that happiness is a gift of the heathen gods, whereas joy is a Christian duty. The command is to rejoice, not to display a placid contentment or a stoic fortitude. And happiness, whether applied to a man's fortune or his disposition, is the assessment of something extended in time along his whole career. But joy (except for those saints who live continually in the presence of God) is of its nature brief and almost instantaneous — it is an apprehension of the eternal moment. And as such it is the great invading adversary that can break open the gates of Hell.''

Rosamund Sprague, ed.
A Matter of Eternity:
Selections from the writings of Dorothy L. Sayers
Page 88

"How can our non-Christian friends — and we ought to have plenty of them — ever be expected to realize the extent of our debt to Christ or our love for him if we never talk about him or press them to consider him. . . . It is because most of us take fright at this point, that the world never recognizes what it owes to Christ and never hears his Cross proclaimed. . . . If this evangelistic witness bears fruit, we shall be drawn into the unsurpassed joy which was always with Christ, enabling him to endure the cross and despise the shame, because it is the joy of one sinner that repents.''*

Douglas Webster
In Debt to Christ
p. 157

*See also 78:2, Jeremias.

New Illuminations:

On the Magi's Coming to Worship Jesus

Matthew 2:1-12

"It is not certain just when faith in a future Redeemer arose in Israel, although it can hardly have been before the time of the Hebrew Monarchy, since the Redeemer was originally pictured as a *king*. . . . In Matthew 2:1-11 we read a story which pictures men of various nations eagerly awaiting the coming of a personal Redeemer (cf. John 4:25). The Gentiles are represented as watching for his sign in the heavens; the Jews as searching their sacred books. This is an accurate picture of a large part of the world in the days of Jesus, when multitudes of both Jews and Gentiles were searching anxiously for some kind of a religion which promised redemption from the futility of ordinary human existence. . . . The Bible tells us such hope is not vain and foolish — that God has promised a Redeemer and that, indeed, he has already come."

Robert Dentan
A First Reader in Biblical Theology
pp. 129-30

"The visitors are called *magoi* (Lat. magi). Originally the term designated the learned, priestly caste of the Persians. . . . The mention of the star shows that they are called *magoi* because of their knowledge of astrology. Nothing else is said about them. '. . . from the East . . .' suggests Mesopotamia, the home of astrology in the Hellenistic world. The story reflects the popular belief that each person is represented by a star, which appears at his birth. . . . The story of the magi, like the genealogy of Jesus, affirms that Jesus is a king Messiah. The Magi seek a king and Herod consults the religious experts of Judaism to find out where they should look. Of this there is no doubt; they should look not in Jerusalem, but in Bethlehem. Micah 5:1-3 is cited. . . . No guidance of the star is suggested for the journey prior to the arrival of the Magi in Jerusalem; but now it leads them not only to the town but to the very house."

John L. McKenzie
Jerome Biblical Commentary
43:20

"Let us take the story of the Magi. You know how sometimes on a pitch black night in the country, you see far off one glimmer of light and you follow it and it turns out to be just a candle in a cottage window — but it was enough to assure you of life ahead, to give you the lead you wanted in the dark. In the same way, when the Magi turned from their singular calculations, they did not arrive at a great mathematical result or revelation of the cosmic mind.* They found a poor little family party and were brought to their knees — because like the truly wise, they were really humble-minded — before a baby born under most unfortunate circumstances, a mystery of human life, a little living growing thing. What a paradox! The apparently rich magi coming to the apparently poor child. Then they laid down their intellectual treasures — all pure gold to them — and, better than that, offered, the spirit of adoration, the incense which alone consecrates the intellectual life and quest of truth, and that reverent acceptance of pain, mental suffering and sacrifice, that death to self which like myrrh hallows the dedicated life in all its forms. . . .

"Now take another point. The Christmas mystery has two parts: the Nativity and the Epiphany. A deep instinct made the church separate these two feasts. In the first, we commemorate God's humble entrance into human life, the emergence and birth of the Holy, and in the second, its manifestation to the world. . . .

"Christ is a Light to lighten the Gentiles as the Glory of his people Israel. Think of what the Gentile was when these words were written — an absolute outsider. All cozy religious exclusiveness falls before that thought. . . . The first point about Epiphany is that all are called and welcomed and accepted. Our own adoration and deep certitude, if God in his mercy gives us that, is never to break our brotherhood with those who come longer journeys by other paths, led by a different star. The Magi took more trouble than the shepherds. The intellectual virtues and intellectual longings of men are all blessed in Christ."

Evelyn Underhill
The Light of Christ
pp. 37-41

"Two of the kings were old and the other wise man was young. He knew that his treasury had been ransacked for rich gifts for the King of Kings, and yet he was not content. . . . He sat and thought deeply. At length he smiled and went into a high chamber to which he had not been since he was a child. Presently he came out and approached the caravan. . . . He took a toy from his hand and placed it upon the sand. It was a dog of tin, painted white and speckled with black spots. Great patches of paint had worn away. He turned a key in the side of the little black and white dog and stepped aside. The dog leaped high in the air and turned

---

*See also 5:1, Keller.

a somersault. He turned another and another and then fell over on his side and lay there. . . . The young wise man picked up the toy of tin and opened the treasure sack, placed his last gift with his own hands in the mouth of the sack so that it rested safely upon the soft bags of incense. 'What folly has seized you?' cried the eldest of the wise men. 'Is this a gift to carry to the King of Kings in the far country?' And the young man answered and said: 'For the King of Kings there are gifts of great richness, gold and frankincense and myrrh. But this,' he said, 'is for the child in Bethlehem.' ''

Heywood Broun
"Frankincense and Myrrh"

" 'Behold there came wisemen from the East to Jerusalem saying ''Where is the King of the Jews, that is born? For we have seen his star in the East, and we have come to worship him'' ' (Matthew 2:1-2). There are in these two verses two principal points: the persons that arrived at Jerusalem and their errand. . . . Their errand we may best learn from themselves — to worship him. Their errand, our errand, and the errand of this day. . . . But for conceiving it better, I will put forth these points to be used. First, their faith; faith in that they never ask *whether* he be, but, *where* he is born, for that born he is, they steadfastly believe.

"Then the work of this faith: . . . The text is of a star. St. Peter calls faith the day-star rising in our hearts (2 Peter 1:19). This sorts well with the star in the text rising in the sky — that, in the sky, manifesting itself to them; this, in their hearts, manifesting itself from below to him, to Christ. The works or service of their faith are as so many beams of their faith — the day-star risen in their hearts. . . . First, their confession of their faith ('saying'): They were no sooner come but they spoke of it so freely and to so many that it came to Herod's ear and troubled him greatly that any king of the Jews should be worshiped beside himself. So then their belief is not kept to themselves without saying anything about it to anybody. The star in their hearts cast one beam out of their mouths. . . . And though they came from the East (those peoples, to whom and their king, the Jews had long time been captives and underlings), they were not ashamed to tell that they came to seek one of the Jews' race and to seek him for the purpose of worshiping him. So neither afraid of Herod nor ashamed of Christ they confessed their errand and cared not who knew it.

Secondly, faith is said to have a foundation, to have a good reason for it. How came you to believe? We have seen a star, say the magi. And this is a well-grounded faith. We came not of our own heads, not before we saw some reason for it. Seeing the star set us on coming. . . . We must come for our Morning-light to this Book, to the word of Prophecy. Our seeing a star is as good as nothing without it. The Star is past and gone, long since. Heaven and earth shall pass but this word shall not pass. Here, on this, we are to fix our eye and ground our faith. . . . The light of the star in their eyes, the word of prophecy in their ears, the beam of his spirit in their hearts, these three made up a full 'we have seen' — the reason for their coming. . . .

"Thirdly, we shall come to 'doing.' It is not saying nor seeing that will serve St. James: 'Show me your faith by some work' (v. 2:18). And so they do. They make their faith to be seen. . . . They sat not still gazing on the star. Their seeing made them come, come a great journey. Many a wide and weary step they made before they could say 'we have come'. First the distance of the place they came from. This was riding many a hundred miles and cost them many a day's journey. Secondly we consider the way they came. It was not pleasant — through the waste and desolation of the desert. Nor was it easy, through the rocks and crags of both Arabias. It was not safe, passing through the midst of thieves and cut-throats. Last we consider the time of their coming. It was no summer progress. A cold coming they had of it. . . . All these difficulties they overcame. And for all this, they came and came cheerfully and quickly. . . . And we, what should we have done? With them it was 'we came,' with us it would have been, at most, 'we are coming.' Our fashion is to see and see again before we stir a foot. . . . Our Epiphany would have fallen in Easter week at the soonest. . . . And it must not be through a desert. Ever so little danger is enough to stop us. But if we be at this point, the wisemen would likely leave us behind. . . .

"The fourth beam of faith was their finding. 'And the star came and stood over where the child was. . . . And they came into the house and saw the child with Mary, his mother . . .' (Matthew 2:9, 11). Between coming and adoring there is a true place for 'Where is he?' . . . Regularly there is no promise of finding but to those who seek. It is not safe to presume to find him otherwise. . . . How shall we get this 'where' resolved? Where they did. They put together a convocation of scribes who resolved it out of Micah (5:2), '. . . but you Bethlehem' as the place of his birth. . . . Thus then to do it ourselves; not through others, as Herod did. For so we might never find him, no more than he did. . . .

"The end of all is neither in the seeking nor the finding. The cause of all is in the last words, 'to worship him.' That is all in all. And without it, all our seeing, coming, seeking, finding is to no purpose. The scribes could tell, and did tell but were never the nearer for it. And what is worship? . . . To tell you what it is in particular I must turn you to verse 11: falling down and offering. Thus they did. Thus we are to do. These two are all, and more than these we find not. . . . There now remains nothing but to include ourselves and bear our part with the Wise Men and with the Angels and with all who this day adore him. This was the guiding star of the Magi. And what were they? Gentiles. And so are we. But if the star is to be ours, then we must go with them in confessing their faith freely, grounding it thoroughly, coming to him speedily, finding him diligently, and worshiping him devoutly." (Transcribed — Ed.)

Lancelot Andrewes
"A Christmas Sermon"

"The Magi, divinely warned in a dream, return to their country by another road. They must avoid Herod. In a spiritual sense, he whom God has led to the crib can certainly go back home, to his own country, to his house; but it will be by another road. That is to say that the motives, attitudes, manner of existing, and means used can no longer be the same. When one has gone to Bethlehem, a radical change takes place."

Monk of the Eastern Church
Jesus: A Dialogue with the Savior
pp. 3-4

New Illuminations:

On Jesus' Presentation at the Temple

Luke 2:22-39

"At this time our Savior Christ, according to the Law by which all the first born were to be presented to God in the temple at a certain time after their birth, was presented to God in the temple and there acknowledged to be his; and then bought of him again by his parents at a certain price prescribed in the Law. . . .

"Thus our Savior was presented to God. And in this especially was that fulfilled: 'The glory of the later house shall be greater than the glory of the former' (Haggai 2:19). The later temple exceeded the former in this, that the Lord, the God of this house, was in the house bodily as one of the congregation. And the little body of a sucking child was a chapel in that temple, infinitely more glorious than the temple itself. How was the joy of Noah at the return of the dove into the ark multiplied upon Simeon at the bringing of this Dove into the temple?

"At how cheap a price was Christ tumbled up and down in this world? It does almost take off our pious scorn of the low price at which Judas sold him, to consider that his father sold him to the world for nothing; and then when he had him again, by this new title of primogeniture and presentation, he sold him to the world again, if not for a turtle or a pigeon, yet at most for five shekels. . . . If you have truly given yourself to him in the Sacrament, God has given yourself back so much mended as that you have received yourself and him too. [You have] received yourself in a holy liberty to walk in the world in a calling, and himself in giving a blessing upon all the works of your calling and imprinting in you a holy desire to do all those works to his glory."

Edmund Fuller, ed.
The Showing Forth of Christ: Sermons of John Donne
pp. 78-79

"The testimony for Simeon's competency and fitness to see his Savior was that he was a just and righteous man. This is a legal righteousness; . . . that is in the sight of the world. . . . That he was righteous and fearing God was evidence enough that the Holy Spirit was upon him. This addition is a testimony of a more particular presence and operation of the Holy Spirit, in some certain way. And the way is agreed by all to be that the Holy Spirit was upon him in the spirit of prophecy, so as that he made him at that time a prophet. There are more elements in the making up of this man, many more. He waited, says the story, for the consolation of Israel. It is not an appropriating of hopes for himself, but a charitable desire of a communication of this consolation upon all the Israel of God. . . . All that we consider in Simeon is how he was fitted to depart in peace. . . . For that was the accomplishment and fulfilling of God's word — that he should not see death before he had seen the Lord's Christ. . . . He saw not how that God was in this child and that this child was the Son of God. He saw not how this Son of God became man in a virgin's womb. . . . God had promised Simeon nothing concerning these mysteries. But the Lord's salvation and Simeon's salvation Simeon saw . . . and contented himself saying, 'Lord now lettest thou thy servant depart in peace, etc.' And so, Nicephorus says, Simeon had his wish. He prayed that he might die and actually he did die then. Neither can a man at any time be fitter to make and obtain this wish than when he has seen his salvation in the sacrament."

Edmund Fuller, ed.
The Showing Forth of Christ: Sermons of John Donne
pp. 78-79

New Illuminations:

On Herod's Infanticide, Jesus' Flight and Return

"Looking back to the wearisome genealogy and to the puzzle of Jesus' 'irregular descent,' looking forward to the bewildering stories of the three kings and the slaughter of the children in Bethlehem, we might say that Matthew's message is confusion and suffering rather than peace on earth and good will. The contradictions between Luke's sweet harmonies and Matthew's shrill discords force us into a new meditation. Did Jesus come to bring peace or the sword or both? . . .

"Luke illustrates the fascinating power which emanates from the child. He records at length the adoration of the shepherds and Simeon and Anna. Matthew gives a single instance, but a more effective one: the visit of the magi. These three astrologers from Persia have recognized in the stars the time and place of the child's birth. Though 'heathen' they were keenly aware of the signs of the time and therefore admitted to the mystery. But first they had to meet another 'King of the Jews,' Herod. Herod represents not only the irritability and selfishness of all human tyrants he also illustrates the cruelty and pettiness of the Jewish government under Roman supervision. Palestine at that time was not the idyllic land that some writers would have us believe it to be. Riots and bloody retaliations were daily occurrences. Jesus, during his childhood, probably witnessed a very large number of crucifixions. Herod's slaughter of the children in Bethlehem must be understood as a typical illustration of this reign of terror. . . .

"The terrible rage of Herod proves his helplessness. He cannot destroy the little child who frightens him. . . . The Light cannot be destroyed, but it can be forced to withdraw; it can be shut out. The three wise men as well as Joseph are servants of the Light, and are therefore able to receive and to understand its commands (Matthew 2:12-14). Herod is cheated and the child is brought to Egypt. . . . The Light withdraws. Darkness enjoys its temporary superiority, and lashes out in all its destructiveness and ugliness. . . .

"It has been said that Egypt itself stands for darkness and that Jesus in his childhood had to pass through a period of deviation and 'Egyptian errors.' It is likely that Matthew wanted to emphasize the parallelism between Jesus' childhood and the history of the Jewish nation. This outstanding child had to go through all the important experiences of Jewish history. . . . When Joseph finally received the order to return, he chose his new home not at Jerusalem but in an inconspicuous place on the outskirts of his country, Nazareth. An unknown village becomes the headquarters of the impending campaign of the Light. The decisive battle would have to be fought one day in the very center of the spiritual world (which meant at that time in the temple at Jerusalem). But the preparation of the commander and the training of the army had to be achieved behind the front."

Fritz Kunkel
Creation Continues
pp. 27-30

New Illuminations:

On the Preparatory Work of John

Matthew 3:1-12; 11:7-11   Mark 1:1-8   Luke 3:1-18

"The New Testament begins (Mark 1:1-3) by going back behind the centuries of disappointment and frustration that followed the Return; and, by quoting a nameless prophet of the Exile, it recalls to mind the whole thought-circle of the new Great Deliverance to which he then looked forward. And the beginning of this Good News from God was, for his contemporaries, John. Appearing from nowhere, for they did not know the story of his birth, he told them that God was going to *act*, to vindicate his People and himself. He was going to establish his kingdom, as the prophets and the apocalyptists had foretold. But the new kingdom carried with it a new covenant, and in the ministry of John the new peeps already from the old, like a seedling from the soil. . . . John put the person through whom the new age was to be inaugurated in the forefront of his message. Yet he himself was ignorant of that person's identity. The forerunner, busy with his work of making ready, may not look behind him to see who is coming after. Nevertheless the moment comes when the Comer catches up to the forerunner, and they stand at last face to face. That moment was the baptism of Jesus."

Sister Penelope
The Wood
pp. 108-09

"John the Baptist, according to the tradition, stands right from the beginning in the light of God's redemptive plan. He himself is part of the gospel of Jesus Christ (Mark 1:1-2). . . . Suddenly, abruptly he stands there. No story of his being called precedes his appearance. The recorders do not linger for a moment on details of his biography. . . .

John too, like Jesus, is the prophet of the coming kingdom of God. He has nothing in common with the political revolutionaries. His ascetic clothing and his scanty food remind us rather of the prophet Elijah. Significant also is the place of his appearance, the Jordan steppes in the wide valley on the southern reaches of the river. . . . Thus John calls to repentance, and this call applies to all. For no claim of an inherited membership in God's chosen people will be of any account before the coming judge of the world. . . . What is being destroyed is the assumption that God's chosen people and the visible Israel here on earth are one and the same thing. For God does not stand under the compulsion of history, under a 'must' which a presumptuous faith casts up at him. . . .

"John's call to repentance renews the message of the Old Testament prophets of judgment. What makes it different is the urgent nearness of the time of God's kingdom and the disturbing 'already' of the present hour in the world's course. Neither does our definition of repentance as 'change of mind' exhaust its meaning nor does it make clear that this conversion means not only a change of mind but also of actions. . . . About face! That means: make room in our present existence for the coming world change, the turning away from an old Godless past and toward God and his coming reign. The Messiah whom John the Baptist announces is the judge of the world, not the fulfiller of political expectations but he who gathers in the last harvest."

Gunther Bornkamm
Jesus of Nazareth
pp. 45-46

"John's appeal for repentance and baptism is only to be explained from a Messianic and eschatological standpoint. His prophetic warnings focus on a judgment of God in the immediate future, and they announced a 'stronger man' who would follow him (Luke 3:7-9). But however his relation to John be envisaged, Jesus acknowledged the person and efforts of the great Baptist, confirming them as God's appeal to his contemporaries and, in spite of notable divergencies associated himself with John's preaching (Luke 7:24-28). . . . Although the Messianic promise of salvation is by no means absent from the Baptist's preaching (Luke 3:17), the great precursor did not know that God's intention is first to offer grace and salvation and then at some future date to separate and judge. His gaze is directed toward the last things: the intervening 'year of the Lord' (Luke 4:19) was hidden from him prior to the coming of Jesus (note his question asked from prison, Luke 7:18f). He thus continues the line of prophets, even if he does surpass them as God's immediate herald before the era of salvation (Luke 7:27-28);* as the man who fulfilled the prophecy of the precursor (Elijah!); and he may thus be regarded as a living sign of the dawn of salvation. But he retains that characteristic note of the Old Testament prophecy of concentrating on the eschatological, and this prevents him from seeing the period in between."

Rudolf Schnackenburg
God's Rule and Kingdom
pp. 82, 91

---

*See also 30:2, Hooke.

"Jesus' road to the cross began when he joined other pilgrims to travel across the Judean hills to the Jordan valley to identify himself with the compelling preacher who was denouncing Israel's apostasy and demanding the dramatic act of Baptism as a symbol of repentance and the recognition of the imminence of divine judgment. So Jesus joined his ministry onto the ministry of John, and the two were linked together in the ministry of the Christian Church forever.''*

John Krumm
The Art of Being a Sinner
p. 93

*See also 101:1, Bornkamm.

New Illuminations:

On John's Baptism and Jesus' Baptism

Matthew 3:11-12	Mark 1:8, 15	Luke 3:16, 5:32; 7:29

"The Jews believed that their ancestors had been baptised before their admission to the covenant at Sinai; and in later times baptism was used not only for the cleansing of those who had contracted Levitical defilement, but also in the admission of proselytes to covenant relationship. John's baptism was therefore more than a token of forgiveness following an act of repentance or change of mind; it was a sign that those who received it were ready to be admitted to the new covenant and kingdom."

Sister Penelope
The Wood
p. 109

"And Paul said, 'John baptized with the baptism of repentance, telling the people to believe in him who was coming after him.' "

New American Standard Bible
Acts 19:4

"The preacher of penance by the Jordan began with the threat of judgment and insisted upon conversion and fruits of repentance before promising to penitents of goodwill a delivery from future Messianic judgment (Matthew 3:7-12). Even his baptism cannot be accepted as an eschatological grace, whatever significance John may have attached to it. It remains a means by which men could escape from future judgment, but it does not communicate salvation. It is a sign of membership of the redeemed won through penance (Mark 1:4) and a strengthening of the will to do penance (Luke 3:7-13). It is a preparation for the future, not yet an eschatological reality."

Rudolf Schnackenburg
God's Rule and Kingdom
pp. 90-91, 266

"John the Baptist uses a different picture in calling the work of the 'One to come' a baptism of the Holy Spirit and of fire*, for the salvation of the true people of God (the wheat) and for the destruction of those who are not prepared to repent (the chaff) (Luke 3:17). The Baptist stands

in the service of him who is to come as the one who is not worthy to loose the shoes of the stronger. His baptism is to be understood in the light of the end of the world and the judgment. . . . As a 'baptism of repentance' it is the last preparation and sealing of the baptised for the coming 'baptism' of the Messiah and preserves them from the day of wrath to come."

Gunter Bornkamm
Jesus of Nazareth
pp. 46-47

"The Gentile had to be symbolically born again: going down under the cleansing waters, washing away his old and defiled life, being buried by baptism and rising from the water as a new man, i.e. born a Jew. John required the same preparation for entry into the kingdom. It staggered Nicodemus (John 3:3-7) that Jesus was pressing the truth that if the Jew wanted to rank as a child of God and belong to the kingdom of God, he must be born again — submit to double baptism: water for pardon and cleansing of past sin and defilement, and 'of the Spirit' for the inspiration of a new life and a holy life."

The Expositors Bible, Vol. I
p. 101

"The Lord's statement to Nicodemus was clear: the new birth is not identical with baptism although baptism is its sign and seal. It is a deep, inward and revolutionary change of heart effected by the Holy Spirit.** Without it a man cannot 'see' the kingdom, let alone 'enter it.' 'Except a man be born of water and of the Spirit he cannot enter the Kingdom of Heaven' (John 3:5). Birth of water can only have meant one thing to Nicodemus. The words must refer to John's baptism, for John himself was distinguishing between his own baptism and the coming Messiah's 'Spirit baptism.' (Luke 3:16)."

John Stott
Men With a Message
p. 20

---

*See also 86:3, Chardin.
**See also 31:1, Van Kamm.

"Jesus' call to repentance has a meaning other than that of the prophets. He calls for a response to the divine offer of salvation, a reaction to God's saving activity which has already been inaugurated (Mark 1:15). . . . Jesus is conscious of himself, wholly and exclusively, as the bearer of salvation, and his innermost desire is the salvation of all men. Yet he has the obligation, imposed on him by God, of making men understand the seriousness of their personal decision by which they decide their future destiny. . . .

In the reign of the Messiah which has already begun, the graces necessary for salvation are there and are bestowed upon believers, namely forgiveness of sins and the Holy Spirit; they are communicated through the one Savior, Jesus Christ. Seen from the Gospel account this is now already an era of fulfillment. Salvation, incarnated in the Savior, is given to everyone who believes and receives baptism. The Holy Spirit, present personally and operative in Jesus since his baptism is poured out on all the faithful."

Rudolf Schnackenburg
God's Rule and Kingdom
pp. 89-90, 266

"There is a beautiful oriental rug covering the floor of an enormous baronial hall. In the middle of the rug a caterpillar is laboriously working his belly-wise way towards some destination of which he seems not too sure. Progress is slow and confused because this particular species is strangely susceptible to the influence of color. He is crawling through the midst of a seemingly endless and intricate design of many colors. His travel is, of necessity, so close to the design that he cannot possible see its contour, point, or purpose. Confusion conquers perspective. Life to him is a series of surprises, many of which are unpleasant. First he finds himself in the midst of a cobalt blue, and he responds with a spell of feeling blue; next he is in the yellow which makes him feel bright and well again; crawling on he finds himself in a patch of brown, in which he feels achey and tired all over;

now he turns to red in the design and he fairly burns up with emotional uncontrol which so overstimulates his emotional glands that his confusion soon turns to biliousness. He wanders on into a stretch of green and so life continues — a meaningless combination of confusions. In the midst of life he is in pleasure, pain, sadness, joy, sickness, and finally, in despair. . . .

"Life goes on for our friend out in the middle of the vast rug: he proceeds with heavy heart, an irritable disposition, a hyperacid stomach, and complete disillusionment. After long nights of insomnia, he finally drops off into a deep sleep — for how long he does not know. When he awakens he is suddenly aware of a change in his life; something has happened. What is it? He sits up and takes a good look at himself and wonder of wonders, he has become a butterfly. A beautiful yellow colleague swoops down over him and calls, 'Come on up here and have a look.' Our friend slowly spreads his wings. What power he feels! He takes off, uncertain at first, and then with mighty pulls he feels himself being propelled up and up. As he peers down upon the rug, he sees that all those painful colors which he kept getting into, without knowing why, are part of a great design. Now he realizes that when he had been in the midst of the rug he could do nothing but blunder from one event to another without reasoning or understanding. No wonder life on the rug was hell. In a flash life becomes clear to him and his problems are reduced to a new understanding. From above he can see where he has been; the past is full of meaning; he can see where he was just a second ago and where he is now. But what is even greater, he can see into the future. From where he is, the past, present, and future are all one great whole.* What a wonderful way to live, to be able to see where you are heading and to know why. So back he goes to the rug. Now he moves with confidence and joy. He knows that he has wings and can rise above his problems. So can everyone who is born of the Spirit."

Austin Pardue
He Lives
pp. 5-7

*See also 89:2, Underhill.

New Illuminations:

On the Baptism of Jesus

Matthew 3:13-17   Mark 1:9-11   Luke 3:21-22

''Nothing could be more illuminating of Jesus' understanding of sin or of how he believed it must be dealt with than his decision to be baptised. Sin is not to be dealt with as a matter of personally keeping oneself scrupulously clean and uncontaminated from the infections in the world around him. Like John the Baptist, Jesus conceived of sin as a poisoning of the whole atmosphere of a society which enters into the acts of all its members to defile and corrupt. Sin cannot be dealt with by trying to immunize oneself against these influences but by an entering into all the relationships and living in them penitently and redemptively. St. Paul wrote that Christ was made sin for us that he might cleanse and deliver us from sin. The burden he bore on the Cross he accepted first in the baptism in Jordan* when he joined the pilgrims thronging to hear John and to receive his washing of penitence. He said, in effect, 'I belong to the whole human community, to its failures, its blindness, its insensitivity, its sin. I claim no immunity and no innocence.' ''

John M. Krumm
The Art of Being a Sinner
p. 94

''John was a logical thinker. 'I baptize with water unto repentance. He has no sin. Therefore I should not baptize him. If anything he should baptize me!' Good reasoning. . . . But it does not conform to the Word and will of God.

''Jesus, discerning what God's will is, says, 'Let it be so now.' God's ways and plan are bigger than human logic and understanding (Isaiah 55:9). . . . It is quite possible that Jesus did not fully know what was going to happen when he was baptized by John. He simply had this word from God: 'Be baptized of John . . . for thus it is fitting to fulfill all righteousness.'

''The whole ministry of the Lord Jesus hangs in the balance on the banks of the Jordan River as long as he stood there. It is the will of God that the anointing and in-filling of the Holy Spirit shall come by way of a baptism, only by Jesus stepping down into the water**. . . . In spiritual things the pathway of understanding and truth is not by human knowledge and reason but by way of humble obedience to the word of God, which Jesus lives out before our eyes.''

Larry Christenson
Speaking in Tongues
pp. 34-35

''Jesus let the waters meet over his head. In bowing thus beneath the hostile waters, he showed that he was taking on the role of Hero-God, savior and creator. But water is ambivalent. It is not only the hostile element; it also cleanses and is essential for life; indeed it symbolizes life. John's baptism was a symbolic cleansing of the penitent; and our Lord's acceptance of it showed that he was shouldering the sin of man.* And further, as the fathers loved to teach, he cleansed the waters by thus entering them, so that the waters might become the sacramental channel of the new life he was setting out to make available for all mankind.

''Then on his emergence from the water he received the anointing of the Holy Spirit, who appeared in the form of a dove. . . . And with the Spirit came the Father's voice, 'Thou art my beloved Son.' . . . The Hebrew word *yahidh* comes from a root meaning to be united, to be one, and has the twin senses of 'only' and 'most dear.' . . . The phrase 'with thee I am well pleased' echoes Isaiah 42:1: 'Behold my servant, whom I uphold, my chosen in whom my soul delights; I have put my Spirit upon him.' ''

Sister Penelope
The Wood
pp. 110-11

''The baptism of Jesus by John the Baptist can be interpreted as the historical moment when he demonstrated the surrender of himself to the will of God. . . . That was why the early Church was reluctant to accept the obvious meaning of Christ's submission to a baptism of repentance. John was extremely reluctant to baptize one whose life dcnied the need of the ceremony to which he was submitting. . . . It was, therefore, an acting-out of the interior surrender of himself. . . .

''Before God can take us, and use us we must offer ourselves, make ourselves available. There has to be a letting go — our surrender to God. . . . We are called to some ceremony of surrender, a moment in which we express our abandonment to God. . . . As it was for Naaman (2 Kings 5:10-14), the moment of surrender may have to be intrinsically demeaning or humbling. . . . Whatever it is it has to go and cast itself into the muddy Jordan. . . .

''The exasperating thing about all of this is that it is no once-for-all event. . . . The baptism, the moment of offering and being taken is the emblem or sign of a process that

---
*See also 70:1, Hooke.
**See also 121:2, Hooke; 67:1, Perrin.

*See also 70:1, Stevenson.

is never complete but is now to be inaugurated. . . . Conversion is a dynamic in which the soul is slowly unselfed and remade, formed after the pattern of Jesus. . . .

"Ask God to show you what your Jordan is; what it is that has to be surrendered; what in you must be humbled and brought low. Then make the act of surrender, enter your Jordan, wherever you are, and allow God to take your life."

Richard Holloway
A New Heaven
pp. 79-83

———————

New Illuminations:

On the Temptations of Jesus

Matthew 4:1-11   Mark 1:12-13   Luke 4:1-13

"Our minds shrink from contemplating the mystery of our Lord's temptation; and by the same instinct that makes us give him a visible halo in pictures, we tend always to minimize its terrible, adorable reality. . . . The story must have come ultimately from him. And its form, being literal or allegorical, is that into which he put it, and the only one in which we could understand even the outermost fringes of the mystery. What does it mean? This surely: that the incarnate Word, the Second Adam, met the author of evil in single combat and, just because he resisted to the end, he experienced *the full range* of his seductive power. . . . And the devil, trying thus to re-enact in the Judean wilderness the tragedy of Eden, dealt with the new Man as he had with the old. He laid siege to just that trinity of virtues which constitute man's right relationship with God — the faith, the love, and the obedience which are religion. 'If you *are* the Son of God as you have just been told, use your miraculous powers you have just received to supply your own needs! Command allegiance by making a sensation! Take a short cut to your goal!' . . .

"Jesus, true Man, staying himself upon revealed truth, held on. And at length the devil departed. . . . Picture Jesus as he returned from the wilderness to begin his public ministry! The Hebrew word for blessed or happy comes from a root meaning *to go straight forward**; and this precisely counters the idea of sin, which means to go crookedly. Was there ever anyone as happy as Jesus rejoicing as a giant to run his course?''

> Sister Penelope
> *The Wood*
> pp. 111-12

"We can see from the readiness with which Jesus quotes the Scripture during his temptations and ministry that for him it was something that had penetrated into his very soul and colored his whole outlook.''

> William Neil
> *Can We Trust the Old Testament?*
> p. 2

"The early Christians were puzzled by the problem of why the Spirit should wish Jesus or anyone else to be tempted. James in his letter says, 'God is incapable of being tempted by evil and he tempts no one. Everyone is tempted as he is beguiled and allured by his own desire'

(James 1:13-14 Moffat). . . . There is no step forward that does not present the possibility of error, and the great step forward which Jesus had to take included so many possibilities of failure that Jesus, more than anyone else might have experienced the need of his prayer, 'Lead us not into temptation!'*

"Jesus knew that bread, the satisfaction of physical needs, would not change the character of man. Old Adam, well fed, remains as egocentric, ambitious, and cruel as he ever was. . . . We need bread, but we need more. We need dissatisfaction. And we need the nourishment of mind and spirit as much as the nourishment of the body. . . . The image of the King-Messiah arises. . . . He must have felt strong enough to conquer 'all the kingdoms of the world and the glory of them'; yet he refused this way. . . . Thus he will be immune to all the attempts of individuals and groups which offer him political leadership. He will face their disappointment and take the risk that they may feel betrayed and even cooperate with his enemies in bringing about his destruction. . . .

"If a person were to leap from the topmost pinnacle of the temple without hurting himself, the result of this event would be unique in history. Not only the Jews, but also the Greeks and Romans would have to acknowledge his divine authority. . . . Here is the weak spot in the devil's argument. God has promised that his angels will protect the Son of God. . . . If the Messiah forces God to act according to his promise, the essence of his Messianic mission, namely to bring freedom and maturity to men, will be frustrated by the very means which the Messiah applies. . . . Jesus always acted according to the principle that the nearer we come to spiritual maturity the more we are opposed to miracles and the less we need them. Whenever Jesus was forced to use his 'miraculous power,' he tried to avoid all publicity.

"Jesus rejected three powerful images which tried to lead his activity into traditional channels. He refused to be the Great Baker, the Great Conqueror, and the Great Miracle Monger. He left behind the three ideals of his time and of ours: the materialism of the Saducces, the power policy of the Romans, and the spiritual totalitarianism of the Pharisees. . . . At the end of his forty days in the desert his mission was clear to him. He turned away from the well known paths of human life and set out into the unknown future. By doing so he passed the gate of a new phase of creation.''**

> Fritz Kunkel
> *Creation Continues*
> pp. 42-50

---

*See also 59:4, Penelope.
**See also 50:2, Sheen.

---

*See also 30:2, Hooke.

"Our Lord knowing that those kingdoms could be won only by his suffering and death said, 'I don't want your world at your cheap price.' . . . It is the kingdoms of the world that are to be elevated to the Kingdom of God, not the Kingdom of God that is to be dragged down to the level of the kingdoms of the world."

Fulton Sheen
The Life of Christ
p. 43

"Man's struggle to realize his potential, and the demoniac forces that tempt him to settle for a lesser life, are vividly set forth in the record of the temptation of Jesus. When these three temptations are recognized as basic questions with which every person is confronted, and to which answers have to be given, then the scriptural account becomes far more than only a presentation of the preparation of Jesus for his wider ministry. It is the story of Man who identifies the forces struggling within himself for mastery, who makes a conscious renunciation of these common temptations, and so lays down an orientation for his life that is based on a value system which will give meaning to all he undertakes.

"However one attempts to define maturity, some kind of integrating principle must always be included. . . . The temptation experiences make clear to us the path by which Jesus reached the unshakable sense of direction which characterized his whole ministry.*

"The first temptation which came to Jesus, which is common to all of us, was to let the pleasure principle prevail, to satisfy immediate sensual desires without regard for any long term goals. . . . Viktor Frankl, who survived Nazi concentration camps, insists that the evidence is quite clear that man's need for bread must not be satisfied before he can turn to meeting other's needs. . . . Thus the first decision that Jesus made was to forego immediate gratification in the interest of what long term goals required, as seen in the light of God's will for him.** . . .

"The second temptation which Jesus faced was to put personal ambition for status and prestige above all else. The power drive leads to subservience to the devil. . . . This is the answer that Jesus gives to the devil: the position of honor is given to him who serves; please God and the status question takes care of itself.

"The third temptation, faced both by Jesus and by us, is to evade personal responsibility. . . . Over and above all conditioning influences, man's life unfolds as he exercises his freedom to make conscious decisions. Jesus would not

---

*See also 30:2, Hooke.
**See also 41:1, Lewis.

turn over to God the responsibility which rightly belonged to him. . . .

"How better could the outcome be recorded than to say that 'angels came and ministered.' When a course has been chosen that keeps one's life open to God and thus to ultimate values in life, then a sense of quiet contentment fills the heart, as different as the agony of spiritual struggle as are angels from the devil."

Robert Leslie
Jesus and Logotherapy
pp. 15-23

"The Father's love, pouring into our hearts, frees us so that we can leave behind false saviors. We see this in Luke 4:1-13. Following the baptism where the Father calls Jesus his son, his beloved, Jesus is driven into the wilderness. . . . To be called as Jesus was at his baptism is also to be sent. But how do you live relying only on the Father? How do you share that vision with others? How do you live in purity of heart? Jesus wrestled with that in the desert when he was tempted to turn stones into bread. The story symbolizes Jesus' struggle to use his charismatic gifts in the best way possible. Look at the reaction to his multiplication of the loaves in John 6:15 and following. The people tried to make him king. They saw the power and missed the point. When we read that he was invited to bow to Satan in exchange for power, is this to be taken in a literal way, or does it refer to the constant danger of collaborating with evil? The temptation is to align oneself with the power of the world. Isn't this a temptation to put one's trust in that power and not to rely on the miracle of God's love alone? The reference to 'tempting God' reflects the inner struggle which Jesus underwent in choosing crucifixion. To tempt God is to try to force his hand, to insist on his intervention as a proof that he is real. In the end the Father did intervene, raising Jesus from the dead. But was Jesus right to look for something like this? What was the essential difference between getting himself crucified and jumping from the parapet of the temple?"

Thomas Kane
"Powerless and Weak"

"For my illustration of 'stunt religion' I turn to our Lord's temptation in the wilderness, when he resisted the suggestion to cast himself down from a pinnacle of the temple and to win his way to power by substituting sensation for sacrifice. In its proper sense 'stunt means to check growth or development.' It would have been a spectacular fulfillment of the old prophecy that the Lord would suddenly come to his temple.* Had he yielded to that impulse he would have been a nine day wonder but not the Christ of the ages, the sensation of the world but not its savior.''

G. D. Rosenthal
Sins of the Saints
pp. 142-43

---

*See also 99:3, Sheen.

New Illuminations:

On Satan

"It is evident that the sin of man was not the beginning of evil. God has an enemy: personal evil walks in his good world. How did it get there? The consensus of Jewish and Christian opinion is that the original or ultimate fall consisted in the voluntary rebellion of created and finite wills against God before the appearance of man on this planet. The authors of this pre-human revolt were the spiritual beings commonly called angels, and their leader was Lucifer, who by his sin became Satan, the adversary, and the prince of darkness. . . .

"The whole subject of the origin and nature of evil is deeply mysterious: but two things are clear. Evil had a beginning and God did not make it. Lucifer as he left his maker's hand was as lovely as Gabriel or Michael. God made him an angel: he made himself a devil. Moreover, just as Genesis proclaims that evil had a beginning so does the Apocalypse almost shout at us that it will have an end. Between that beginning and that end lies the long process of Restoration; and the method of that is that the evil shall be made to serve the good."

Sister Penelope
The Wood
pp. 32-33

"There are souls that have become so accustomed to busying themselves with outside affairs that they have grown accustomed to living all the time with reptiles and other creatures. They have almost become like them. . . . These creatures are at once so venomous and so active and it is so dangerous for us to be among them that it will be a miracle if we escape stumbling over them and falling. For if a man is bitten by a viper his whole body is poisoned and swells up. . . . Let us say no more, then, of these paralysed souls, who, unless the Lord himself comes and commands them to rise, are like the man who had lain beside the pool for thirty years (John 5:5). They are unfortunate creatures and live in great peril. . . . Obviously a great deal of attention will be necessary if we are to be cured, and only the mercy of God will preserve us from death."

St. Teresa of Avila
Interior Castle
pp. 31-32, 47, 49

"Mere activity is simply diabolical — noise for the sake of noise, bustle for the sake of bustle. It is perhaps signifi-

cant that in the Vulgate version of one of the Compline Psalms, the devil is described as 'the business that prowls around in the shadows,' sheer mischief by which it can make an entry. 'Damnation,' wrote Miss Dorothy Sayers, 'is without direction or purpose. Why not? It has nothing to do and all eternity to do it in.'*"

E. L. Mascall
Grace and Glory
p. 23

" 'Is it God or is it me?' is the question we sometimes ask. But it is a nonsensical question, if we mean it seriously. The essential question is not whether it is God or me, but whether it is God or Satan. It is Satan who comes to us as an outsider, who works on us externally and can get possession of us only by constraining us. But God works within us, within our hearts and minds, within our freedom."

Simon Tugwell
The Beatitudes: Soundings in Christian Tradition
p. 96

"The commonest question is whether I really 'believe in the Devil.' Now if by 'the devil' you mean a power opposite to God and, like God, self-existent from all eternity, the answer is certainly No. There is no uncreated being except God. God has no opposite. No being could attain a 'perfect badness' opposite to the perfect goodness of God; for when you have taken away every kind of good thing (intelligence, will, memory, energy, and existence itself), there would be none of him left.

"The proper question would be whether I believe in devils. I do. That is to say, I believe in angels, and I believe that some of these, by the abuse of their free will, have become enemies to God and, as a corollary, to us. These we may call devils. They do not differ in nature from good angels, but their nature is depraved. Devil is the opposite of angel only as Bad Man is the opposite of Good Man. Satan, the leader or dictator of devils is opposite, not of God, but of Michael. I believe this not in the sense that it is part of my creed, but in the sense that it is one of my opinions. . . . It seems to me to explain a good many facts. It agrees with the plain sense of Scripture, the tradition of Christendom, and the beliefs of most men at most times. And it

_____
*See also 35:2, Thielicke.

conflicts with nothing that any of the sciences have shown to be true. . . .

"I feign that devils can, in a spiritual sense, eat one another; and us. Even in human life we have seen the passion to dominate, almost to digest, one's fellow — to make his whole intellectual and emotional life merely an extension of one's own. . . . On Earth this desire is often called 'love.' In Hell I feign that they recognize it as hunger. But there the hunger is more ravenous and the satisfaction is possible. . . . It is for this that the devils desire human souls and the souls of one another. It is for this that Satan desires all of his own followers and all the sons of Eve and all the host of Heaven. His dream is of the day when all shall be inside him and all that says 'I' can say it only through him."*

C. S. Lewis
The Screwtape Letters:
"Preface 1962"
pp. xxii-xxiii, xxvi

_____
*See also 61:2, Penelope.

"Christ definitely spoke of power of spiritual evil, and he called this power 'Satan,' 'the Devil,' or 'the Evil one.' Now whatever mystery lies behind the existence of such an evil spiritual power, there can be no blinking the fact that Christ spoke, and acted, on the assumption that there is a power of evil operating in the world. We are so accustomed by modern thought to regard evil as 'error,' as the 'growing pains' of civilization, or simply as an inexplicable problem, that once more the mind does not readily accept what is in effect God's own explanation — that there is a spirit of evil operating in the world. We find Christ speaking quite plainly of this spirit as responsible for disease and insanity as well as being the unremitting enemy of those who want to follow the new, true order. . . . Yet it would seem that Christ did not give man a full explanation of the origin and operation of the evil forces in this world. But he did recognize evil as evil, not as a mere absence of good: he did, wherever he found it possible, destroy evil."

J. P. Phillips
Your God Is Too Small
pp. 105-106

_____

New Illuminations:

On Jesus' Early Ministry

| Matthew 13:54-58 | Mark 6:1-6 | Luke 4:14-30 |

"Interpreting the life and fate of Jesus through the scriptures is a major emphasis of the evangelist Luke, as can be seen perhaps best from Luke 4:16-20, the rejection at Nazareth. In Luke's source, the Gospel of Mark, it is a transitional unit (6:1-6) bringing to an end the first major section of the gospel. In this section, Jesus is depicted as mighty in deed and word, and Mark ends the section with the theme of rejection, a theme that is to grow in importance until we reach the cross. . . . The progressively total rejection of Jesus is a major element in the suffering motif. Luke completely changes the function of the rejection pericope. First of all he transposes it to the very beginning of the first phase of the ministry of Jesus rather than at its end. Then he transforms the pericope by introducing a wholly new element (4:l6b-21).

"The effect of this redactional insertion, and of the further redactional changes which Luke introduces into his Markan source is to change the whole tenor of the pericope. Now it becomes a frontispiece, introducing and interpreting the whole ministry of Jesus as Luke understands it. Luke pursues the theme of the Isaiah quotation throughout his presentation of that ministry. But my concern at the moment is to point out that Luke's whole interpretation of the ministry of Jesus is dependent upon a quotation of scripture.

"This is perhaps the most spectacular instance of Luke's concern for the fulfillment of scripture, but it is by no means isolated. Luke pursues the theme of scriptural fulfillment throughout his gospel, so that the emphasis upon it in the Emmaus road story (24:27) is a reiteration of a major Lukan theme."

Norman Perrin
The Resurrection
p. 63-64

"After the baptism and the temptation it is 'in the power of the spirit' that Jesus returned to Galilee and began his Messianic work. And his very first words were a quotation of Isaiah 61:1f: 'The Spirit of the Lord is upon me because he has appointed me to preach the good news to the poor.' The whole public ministry is thus put under the sign of the Spirit, and all the works and teaching of Christ must be seen in the light of this introduction."

Wilfred Harrington
Explaining the Gospels
p. 120

"The cure of the deaf is not only a liberation from a bodily defect but also the opening of the ears for the words of salvation. In Isaiah 35:5f which refers to the healing of the blind and deaf, lame and dumb, the major emphasis rests upon the saving joy and happiness given by God. This thought emerges into the full light in Isaiah 61:1 seq., 'to preach to the poor the gospel of salvation.' Jesus introduced this passage in his initial discourse at Nazareth, gave it a Messianic interpretation and declared that it was fulfilled. 'This day is fulfilled this scripture in your ears.' Jesus reveals what he wishes to be and to be considered, not through any public Messianic utterance but through his understanding of the scriptures which he applies to his own advent: namely, as the Savior and Redeemer who brings God's grace and mercy, God's salvation and joy to those who accept his message, and this means the humble and the poor, those bowed beneath burdens and guilt.

"This testimony of Jesus to himself makes it obvious how closely his miracles and preaching are related. The point of the cures is to prove what he is proclaiming, the all-embracing salvific will of God; they are signs of the eschatological salvation which has come with Jesus. It is already there in so far as the blind actually see, the deaf hear, the lame walk, the lepers are cleansed. It is not completely there, in so far as all sicknesses are not yet healed and the accursed earth not yet transfigured. It is precisely this salvation, perceptible already though not yet fulfilled, that is dawning with the reign of God manifested in these cures and wonders. In this sense his preaching itself is one of the signs of the saving era. The gospel of divine mercy and forgiveness is announced to the poor. In itself, it stands beside and beneath the miracles; it is itself the miracle of God's mighty saving word. Jesus not only speaks of divine forgiveness which will be granted with the abandonment of divine punishment in the 'acceptable year of the Lord' (Luke 4:19) to all who genuinely repent. He actually imparts this forgiveness to the men he meets (Luke 5:20, 24). Here salvation is realized. The reign of God begins, in this specific sense; the miracles might be called 'kingdom of God in action.'

"It is likely that Jesus' initial discourse at Nazareth was deliberately broken off with the reference to the 'year of the Lord,' and that no mention was made of its sequel in Isaiah 61:2 and of a 'day of vengeance of our God.' His were the 'words of grace' which astonished his own people and at which they took umbrage (4:22)."

Rudolf Schnackenburg
God's Rule and Kingdom
pp. 120-21, 89

"With a brief reference to Jesus' initial preaching ministry in Galilee (4:14-15), Luke records the remarkable occasion of his visit to Nazareth. Some have thought this visit is the same that Matthew and Mark describe towards the end of the Galilean ministry. . . . Alternatively, it may be a different visit altogether, and certainly there is little verbal similarity between the account of Matthew and Mark and this by Luke. In any case the meaning of the incident to Luke is clear. The context is thoroughly Jewish (in the Synagogue, on the Sabbath with a reading from Isaiah), but the mind of Jesus reaches out to the Gentile world. The Lord reminds his listeners that although there were many widows in Israel in the days of Elijah, the prophet was only sent to the Sidonian widow at Zarephath, and that although in the days of Elisha there were many lepers in Israel, none was cleansed except Naaman, the Syrian. The starving widow was fed and the leprous general cured, despite their foreign nationality. This aroused the hostility of his audience. They cast him out of the city and led him to the brow of the hill to throw him headlong. The rejection by Nazareth foreshadows the rejection by the Jewish people and the subsequent universal mission of the church."*

John Stott
Men With a Message
pp. 39-40

"When Jesus returns from the desert, he knows he is the Father's beloved and a man who chooses to rely on that, not on the power or security he can create for himself.

---

*See also 115:1, Wright.

Grounded in his Father's love, imaginative, capable of deep human intimacy and fidelity, blessed with charismatic gifts, he chooses to proclaim the miracle of his Father's love in utter simplicity. This is a man who is strong. He knows who he is and what he will do. He invites people into fellowship with him, but he never manipulates them. If they choose to go another way, he lets them go. But he does not stop loving them."

Thomas Kane
"Powerless and Weak"

"The redeeming, liberating presence of Jesus can be communicated only by a liberating presence of those who have in their turn been redeemed by him. If we who are the church only talk about that presence instead of personally being that presence to others inside and outside the church circles, our talking will not make much sense to anyone.

We who have been reborn into the life of the Risen Jesus and who have caught the breath of the Spirit try to be the saving presence of Jesus in the world. This in a basic sense is a worldly or secular (not secularistic) task. It means supporting one another and banding together to change the quality of human life from despair to hope, from all-pervasive fear and suspicion to trust, from oppression of the poor and weak to justice for all. This is what Jesus said he had come to do, when he quoted the passage from Isaiah in his home town synagogue."

Monica Hellwig
The Meaning of the Sacraments
p. 53

New Illuminations:

Matthew 3:2, 8; 4:17   Mark 1:15   Luke 3:8-9; 5:32; 11:32

"Judaism knows of the necessity and promise of repentance. The rabbis tell of the duty to repent. They speak also of the importance of true repentance which shows itself in the renouncing of former sins and of making good wrongs committed. Nor is there any lack of words warning people against taking things too lightly, an attitude which presumes on grace and simply counts on it while continuing in sin. Therefore in the Gospels, both John and Jesus call for fruits consistent with professed repentance (Luke 3:8; 11:32). Repentance here means turning away from an old Godless past and turning towards God and his coming reign. It means not only a change of mind but also of actions. . . .

"Repent for the kingdom of heaven is at hand' (Matthew 3:2; 4:17) comprises the teaching of both. For both of them, repentance ceases to be an exercise of piety by means of which the righteous can show himself to be such. Both put an end to hypocritical play with repentance. Jesus' call to repentance does have a new meaning. The hour of salvation is different from the fiery day of the last judgment proclaimed by John. Repentance means to lay hold on the salvation that is already at hand, and to give up everything for it."

Gunter Bornkamm
Jesus of Nazareth
pp. 32, 46

"St. Mark tells us that the burden of Jesus' message during his Galilean ministry was 'repent and believe.' By repent, He obviously meant something more than regret for past peccadilloes. He meant that men should turn their backs upon their past — their sinful selfish aimless past with its record of failure, frustration, and folly — and turn their faces toward God in faith and commitment. It means a re-orientation of the whole personality, becoming God-centered instead of self-centered. It is something we do not do for ourselves but God does for us, and much of it happens unconsciously as we avail ourselves of the means of grace. Clearly then this major and decisive act of committing our lives to God involves a greater degree of repentance than repentance we feel every time we say the Lord's Prayer, or ask for forgiveness, or when we join in the general confession. . . . He would not tell us to pray for forgiveness if we had nothing to repent of. We know ourselves only too well not to be conscious of our daily failure to live as we ought to live and of how much we need the help of God, to whom all hearts are open and from whom no secrets are hid."

William Neil
The Difficult Sayings of Jesus
p. 76

"Jonah is intended as a sign in his preaching repentance to the Ninevites, who even though they were pagans were converted to God. . . . The point of the comparison is made explicit. If only 'this generation' would repent 'at the preaching' of the Son of Man (Luke 11:32)!"

Carroll Stuhlmueller
Jerome Biblical Commentary
44:107

"Penitence is the resurrection of character. If we are satisfied with our own condition, we shall certainly not try to rise to something higher. Where there is no penitence there can be no progress. The underside of the splendor of the saint's robes is the sackcloth of his penitence."

Kathleen Burne, ed.
Love's Fulfilment: From the Writings of Father Andrew
p. 52

"The sequence of Antiphons which the ancient Church ordained for the opening days of Lent — a liturgical direction, as it were, for the intention of the penitent Christian soul — shows how many-sided is our creaturely need for the pitying indulgence and redeeming action of God. 'Lord, that I may have light! . . . Wash me thoroughly from my wickedness and cleanse me from my sin.' Each phrase casts its searchlight on our condition. We need light, for the eyes of the mind are darkened so that we cannot see the reality of our state; we need cleansing, for our very self-hood is sullied and impure. . . . We end with an act of total and contrite confidence in God's restoring action — the crown of penitence: 'Say the word only and my soul shall be healed.' . . . The penitent soul accepts the jurisdiction of Charity, and Charity will have its perfect and searching work; burning up the chaff in the unquenchable fire of love. The cleansing pains of contrition are part of the mercy of God.'"*

Evelyn Underhill
Abba
pp. 61, 63

"I do not mind at all if you have no other meditations upon your own wretchedness, or upon God's goodness, than such as come through the single word SIN or GOD, or some

---
*See also 86:2, 1 Corinthians 3:12-15.

such like word of your own choosing. Do not analyse or expound these words with imaginative cleverness, as if, by considering their constituent parts, you would increase your devotion. But take the words as they are, whole. Mean by 'sin' the whole lump of it, not particularizing about any part, for it is nothing other than yourself. . . . If personal prayers are in words, as they seldom are, then they are very few words; the fewer the better. If it is a little word of one syllable, I think it is better than if it is of two, and more in accordance with the work of the Spirit.

"We can illustrate this by looking at nature. A man or woman suddenly frightened by fire, or death, or what you will, is suddenly in his extremity of spirit driven hastily and of necessity to cry or pray for help. And how does he do it? He bursts out in his terror with one little word and that of a single syllable: 'Fire!' it may be or 'Help!' Just as this little word pierces the ears of the hearers more quickly, so too does a little word of one syllable express the intention in the depth of our spirit. And it pierces the ears of Almighty God more quickly than any long Psalm churned out unthinkingly. That is why it is written 'Short prayer penetrates heaven' . . . and is so soon heard by God! Yes, even if it is a very sinful soul, who is as it were an enemy of God. If he through grace were to cry such a short syllable in the height, depth, length and breadth of his spirit he would always be heard because of this anguished cry, and be helped by God. . . .

"What should this little word be? In itself prayer is nothing more than a devout setting of our will in the direction of God in order to get good and remove evil. Since all evil is summed up in sin, when we pray with the intention for the removal of evil, we should neither say, think, nor mean any more than this little word 'sin.' And if we pray with intention for acquiring goodness, let us pray in word or thought or desire, no other word than 'God.' . . .

"And because all the while you live this wretched life you have to experience in some sort this filthy and nauseating lump of sin, part and parcel of yourself, you must constantly revert to these two words in turn, 'sin' and 'God.' With the knowledge that if you had God, you would not have sin; and if you had not sin, then you would have God! . . . Therefore lift your heart up with this blind surge of love and consider now 'sin' and now 'God.' God you want to have; sin you want to lose. You lack God; you know all about sin. Good God help you now, for it is now that you have need of him."

Clifton Wolters, trans.
The Cloud of Unknowing
pp.103-10

"Existential mistrust cannot be replaced by trust, but it can be replaced by a reborn candor. This attitude involves risk, the risk of giving oneself, of inner transformation. Inner transformation simply means that the person one is intended to be penetrates what has appeared up till now, the customary soul enlarges and transfigures itself into the surprise soul. This is what the prophets of Israel understood by the 'turning' in their language of faith: not a return to an earlier, guiltless stage of life, but a swinging around to where the wasted hither-and-thither becomes walking on a way, and guilt is atoned for in the newly arisen genuineness of existence."

Nahum N. Glatzer, ed.
Martin Buber: On the Bible
p. 186

New Illuminations:

On Jesus' Restoration of the Afflicted

"Some people are rather troubled about the amount of space the healing of the sick takes in the Gospels. . . . This is because we are apt to think of healing as getting rid of people's normal pain, disease, and distress. But healing is really restoring to the true normality, mending the breaches in our perfect humanity, and making us again what God intends us to be. It shows us his life-giving Spirit: the Lord and Giver of Life ever at work producing and restoring fullness of life. For all disease of soul or body is a subtraction from human nature, a way of being substandard. There are no colds in paradise. So healing of any kind is a kind of regenerative work, a direct expression and furtherance of God's Will. It means bringing life back to what it ought to be, giving new strength to the weak, new purity to the tainted by the action of his charity."

Evelyn Underhill
Light of Christ
p. 58

"There is a sense in which no doctor ever heals. The doctors themselves would be the first to admit this. The magic is not in the medicine but in the patient's body — the recuperative energy of Nature. What the treatment does is to stimulate natural functions or to remove what hinders them. No cut can be healed in a corpse. . . . All who are cured are cured by God. . . . in the sense that their very tissues are repaired by the far descending energy which, flowing from him, energises the whole system of nature. But once he did it visibly to the sick in Palestine, a Man meeting with men. . . . The power that always was behind all feelings put on a face and hands. Hence, of course, the apparent chanciness of the miracles. It is idle to complain that he heals those whom he happens to meet, not those whom he doesn't. To be a man means to be in one place and not in another. The world which would not know him as present everywhere was saved by his becoming local."

C. S. Lewis
Miracles
p. 168

"Clearly Jesus is thinking of the kingdom of God as the kingly rule of God present in the world in a new way,

associated with himself and evidenced by the routing of evil in all its forms, including disease. . . . His healing miracles were signs of the kingdom of God in action, restoring the broken in mind and body to health and sanity. His care and concern for the outcasts of society were living illustrations of the wideness of God's mercy; his forgiveness of sinners was absolution from God himself. . . .

"Jesus himself regarded his healing acts as evidence of the power of God at work in a new way through himself. He offered himself to God as a channel through which that power could flow, and set no bounds as to what it could accomplish."

William Neil
The Difficult Sayings of Jesus
p. 87, 36

"I have sometimes wondered why Jesus so frequently touched the people he healed, many of whom must have been unattractive, obviously diseased, unsanitary, smelly. With his power he easily could have waved a magic wand. . . . But he chose not to. Jesus' mission was not chiefly a crusade against disease (if so why did he leave so many unhealed in the world and tell followers to hush up details of healings?), but rather a ministry to individual people, some of whom happened to have a disease. He wanted those people, one by one, to feel his love and warmth and his full identification with them. Jesus usually involves touching — that incredible richness of response that a tactile loving summons up. . . .

"The ideal then is to give love to someone you can touch — a neighbor, a relative, a needy person in your community. I was able to do that in India. Now I look for people in Carville to love through touch. Touch corpuscles are located deep inside my skin, and the activities on the surface can indeed reverberate through other cells conveying the sense of touch."

Paul Brand and Phillip Yancey
Fearfully and Wonderfully Made
pp. 140, 148

"It is a perfectly correct view of things — and strictly consonant with the Gospel — to regard Providence across the ages as brooding over the world in ceaseless effort to spare that world its bitter wounds and to bind up its hurts. Most certainly it is God himself who, in the course of centuries, awakens the great benefactors of humankind, and the great physicians, in ways that agree with the general rhythm of progress. He it is who inspires, even among those furthest from acknowledging his existence, the quest for every means of comfort and every means of healing."

Teilhard de Chardin
The Divine Milieu
p. 84

New Illuminations:

On the Recognition of Jesus' Authority

Matthew 7:28-29; 8:8-9; 9:6-8   Mark 1:22   Luke 4:32, 36; 5:24; 7:7-8

"The subject of Jesus' proclamation was the coming of God's kingdom already being announced by himself in word and deed, and breaking into the present world and its holy traditions and standards with liberating and judging power. The power of the coming kingdom was the basis of Jesus' own authority."

Gunther Bornkamm
Paul
p. 178

"The passages in the Gospels which deal with Jesus' perception and penetrating insight concern a most characteristic trait in the historical Jesus, one which quite accurately is confirmed by the nature of his preaching. The Gospels call this patent immediacy of Jesus' sovereign power his 'authority.' They apply this word to his teaching; they also use it for the power of his healing word. The word 'authority' already contains the mystery of Jesus' personality and influence as understood by faith. . . .

"In his encounters with the most different people, Jesus' 'authority' is always immediately and authentically present. . . . We have repeatedly drawn attention to the 'wisdom sayings' in Jesus' preaching. Their characteristic is that they reject all necessity for outside proof, whether it be from the prescribed sphere of authority found in the scriptures or in the recognized interpretations of the fathers. . . . The immediate obviousness of Jesus' words leaves no room for an 'if' or 'but' and requires no justification from outside."

Gunther Bornkamm
Jesus of Nazareth
pp. 60, 106

"The scribes were copiers of the law, public secretaries, and such teaching as they did after the return of the Hebrew people from their tragic dispersal was an echo of what they had learned. They could quote but not create. . . . Because our Lord spoke authoritatively, some of the scribes remarked, 'This man blasphemeth.' They just couldn't 'take' the Divine Word. . . . When it comes to our private opinion about the authority of Jesus Christ, it is wise to remember Gamaliel's forthright statement: 'If this counsel or this work be of men, it will come to naught; but if it be of God you cannot overthrow it' (Acts 5:38, 39). In the very

beginning of his Galilean ministry, Jesus stated his authority in such clear and unmistakable terms that they were silenced. . . .

"None of us can do without authority of some kind. . . . In one of his essays, Charles Lamb sets forth vividly our proper attitude toward Christ's authority and person: 'If Shakespeare should come into the room, we would all rise and greet him; if that other one entered we would all fall to our knees and try to kiss the hem of his robe.' Unless we recognize the complete otherness of Christ, we feel isolated, estranged from a power on which we depend to heal and strengthen us.' "*

Richardson Wright
A Sower Went Forth
pp. 27-30

"Only one who knows who he is need not defend himself and is in command of every situation."

William Wolfrum
Sermon Notes

"The whole process of training, if it is to be fruitful, takes place under the protection of authority accepted and discipline submitted to. . . . The fellow-seeker listens to the voice of collective tradition and grants that it is authority. He is thereby able to step personally into the background, to direct eyes and attention to something other and far greater than himself. . . . Authority is the only thing that can save us from authoritarianism. Authority attaches essentially to the impersonal, to the collective tradition; while authoritarianism attaches essentially to the personal individual will. . . . In religion, in education, and in the life of society generally, it is authority that saves us from the multiplicities of intolerable, petty authoritarianisms exercised by those who have the loudest voices, the longest arms, or the most assertive egos. . . . There are two marks of the deep Christian that are essential to the rest: his sensitivity to divine Grace and his sensitivity to authority."

Harry Blamires
Where Do We Stand?
pp. 15, 72-73, 90

*See also 38:1, Bornkamm.

New Illuminations:

On the Miracles of Jesus

Matthew 8:1-17, 28; 9:8   Mark 1:21-34, 40; 2:13   Luke 4:33-41; 5:12-26; 7:1-15

"God incarnate is a God who operates among men and within man. Moving among men, to what extent does he perform actions which are openly and indisputably beyond the range of merely human capacities? We think of miracles, of course. In any consideration of God's mode of acting upon earth, the miracles must be taken into account. It is probably true to say that there is something paradoxical about the different ways in which the miracles strike believers and unbelievers. To the unbeliever the miracles are a stumbling block. What astonishes him about them is precisely their miraculousness. But the believer takes a different view. He is astonished that God in Man so consistently avoids the overt sensational miracle. . . . There is no summoning of legions of angels; lightning is not called down from Heaven; crowds are not entertained by supernatural phenomena. On the contrary, our Lord seems to be determined without resorting to concealment or subterfuge to make his miraculous acts, as nearly as can be, consonant with the natural processes of human life. . . . Even when feeding the five thousand he does not call for manna from Heaven but carefully gathers in the available resources of bread and fish. On the other hand, our Lord restrains himself from the conscious concealment: he does not resort to any pretense that what he does is purely natural and human achievement. The Man does not play the God. The God does not play the Man. The God-Man acts."

Harry Blamires
The Will and The Way: A God Who Acts
pp. 34-35

"The English word 'miracle' comes from the Latin *miraculum*, 'something to be wondered at,' but this word does not even occur in the Vulgate New Testament. . . . In the New Testament, the synoptic writer's word for miracle is *dynamis*, 'act of power,' and John uses *semeion*, 'sign,' or *ergon*, 'work.' *Teras*, 'wonder,' is never used alone to refer to a miracle of Jesus. In neither Testament does the vocabulary of the original texts give real emphasis to the marvelous. . . .

"Jesus' miracles were not only or primarily external confirmation of his message; rather the miracle was the vehicle of his message. Side by side, word and miraculous deed gave expression to the entrance of God's kingly power into time. This understanding of the miracle as an intrinsic part of the revelation is intimately associated with a theory of revelation where the emphasis on the God who acts is equal to (or even more stressed than) the emphasis on the God who speaks. . . . The ministry of Jesus, centered on the estab-

lishment of God's reign over men, involves the destruction of Satan's rule over the world. The miracles were Jesus' chief weapon in the struggle with Satan; that is why a miracle is a *dynamis* or 'act of power.' The expulsion of demons is the most obvious example of the use of miracles to destroy Satan's power. The cure of sickness is another aspect of the war against Satan. In raising the dead and even in conquering natural disasters like storms (notice in Mark 4:39, Jesus addresses the wind as if it were a demon), Jesus is showing God's power over the demonic."

R. E. Brown
Jerome Biblical Commentary
78:113, 126-27

"The value of Christ's miracles lies less in their supernatural character than in their spiritual significance. They are 'signs' as well as 'wonders.' They are never performed selfishly or senselessly but are illustrations of moral authority. They are in fact the acted parables of Jesus. They exhibit his claims visually. They are his works which dramatize his words. St. John saw this clearly and constructs his gospel around selected signs. Thus, the changing of water into wine at a wedding reception in Cana is not in itself a particularly edifying miracle. Its significance lies beneath the surface. John tells us that the water pots of stone stood ready for the Jewish rites of purification (John 2:6). This is the clue we are seeking. The water stood for the old religion. The wine stood for the religion of Jesus. As Christ changed the water into wine, so the Gospel would supersede the Law. The sign advanced the claim that he was competent to inaugurate the new order. He was the Messiah. As he was soon to say to the Samaritan woman, 'I . . . am he.' "

John Stott
Basic Christianity
p. 31

"In the miracles of the Old Creation we see the Divine Man focusing for us what the God of Nature has already done on a larger scale. In the Miracles of Dominion over the Inorganic, we find some that are of the Old Creation and some that are of the New Creation. When Christ stills the storm he does what God has often done before. . . . But when Christ walks on the water we have a miracle of the New Creation. God had not made the Old Nature, the world before the Incarnation, of such a kind that water would support a human body. The miracle is the foretaste of a nature that is still in the future. The New Creation is just breaking in. For a moment it looks as if it were going to spread. Two men are living in that new world. St. Peter also walks on the water — a pace or two: then his trust fails him and he sinks. He is back in Old Nature.* . . . The miracles of Reversal all belong to the New Creation. It is a miracle of reversal when the dead are raised. Old Nature knows nothing of this process. The one or two instances of it in the Gospel are early flowers — what we call spring flowers because they are prophetic, although they really bloom while it is still winter. And the miracles of Perfecting or of Glory, the Transfiguration, the Resurrection and the Ascension, are even more emphatically of the New Creation. These are the true spring, or even the summer of the world's new year."

C. S. Lewis
Miracles
pp. 169-170

"All those who turn to him in faith count on the power of Jesus which knows no bounds and on the miracle which he can work, where all human help fails. . . . The miracle stories in all the Gospels are meant to show that Jesus does not disappoint these expectations, and that he has been given this power. It would be difficult to doubt the physical healing powers which emanated from Jesus, just as he himself interpreted his casting out of demons as a sign of the dawning of the kingdom of God. . . .

"Faith** which Jesus demands, and which alone he recognizes as such, has to do with power and with miracle. And this is not in the general sense that God is all-powerful and can work miracles, but in a very concrete sense: faith as very definitely counting on and trusting in God's power — that it is not at an end at the point where human possibilities are exhausted. . . . This faith becomes true and capable of receiving the miracle of God. Where Jesus does not find this faith, he can not work a miracle (Mark 6:5-6). This certainly does not mean that faith itself is the power that works the miracle. What matters here is the readiness to receive the miracle. It is so indispensable for Jesus' work that he can say repeatedly to the cured and the saved — for both terms are implied by the word salvation — 'Your faith has made you whole.'

"Does faith need miracle? This question is first asked openly in the Gospel of John, and decided here quite clearly. The faith which will not believe until it has seen a miracle is no real faith. This is why Jesus withdraws from the crowd who believe because of the signs he works (John 2:23). Hence his first word to the nobleman who asks him to heal

---

*See also 41:2, Lewis.
**See also 89:1, Merton.

his son: 'Unless you see signs and wonders, you will not believe' (John 4:48). For: 'Blessed are those who have not seen and yet believe' (John 20:29). . . . Jesus would not allow miracles to be considered a proof of God's working and power which could be demanded as a prerequisite to faith. Such a demand is challenging of God. Trust and obedience have both been destroyed at the roots."

Gunther Bornkamm
Jesus of Nazareth
pp. 130-133

"All Christians agree that the Spirit continues to bestow his gifts upon the church, but they do not agree that these must be precisely the same gifts accorded the early church. Are there no differences between the miracles of Jesus and the apostles and the 'miracles' claimed today? There certainly are, as the following table illustrates:

MIRACLES CLAIMED IN THE NEW TESTAMENT	. . . AND TODAY
People were raised from the dead.	The dead are not raised.
Jesus changed water into wine, walked on water, stilled tempests, and the like.	Such supernatural control over the elements or nature is not duplicated.
Miracles attempted by Jesus succeeded in each case, as also by the Apostles in Acts.	Miracles attempted today do not succeed in so many, many instances.

". . . More contrasts could be noted. This is certainly not to say that miracles *cannot* happen today. In Christian theology, God never binds himself, and believers should be the very last to try restricting the Almighty. If someone has truly experienced healing, let him or her be grateful for it. But beyond any debate, whoever insists that today's 'miracles' are fully equal to those reported in the Gospels and the Book of Acts is actually *diminishing the latter*. The New Testament miracles were necessary to authenticate the message of Jesus and the disciples and to assist the spread of Christianity. But when, after the apostolic age, the faith was broadly established in the Mediterranean world, the great miracles seem to have ceased on any regular basis. God evidently did not feel obliged to keep supplying believers with supernatural proof after supernatural proof, necessary as these were to help launch the faith."

Paul L. Maier
First Christians
pp. 109-111

"What Nazianzen once said is most true: 'Man is of all other the greatest miracle. Should all the miracles that ever were done be drawn together, man is a miracle greater than they.' The dividing of the sea, the commanding of the sun, the making of the world is nothing to the single creation of one soul: There is so much wisdom and power expressed in its faculties and inclinations. . . . Here the dimensions of innumerable worlds are shut up in a center. . . . The consideration of one Soul is sufficient to convince all the atheists in the world."

Thomas Traherne
Centuries
p. 208

New Illuminations:

On the Call and Beginning of Discipleship

| Matthew 4:18-20 | Mark 1:16-20 | Luke 5:1-11 |

"Luke tells us that it was at a fishing incident where Jesus first made sense to Peter. . . . Peter argues with Jesus, protesting that they had fished all night and caught nothing. But grudgingly Peter obeys what he considers the foolish suggestion of Jesus. Luke records for us Peter's reaction to the great catch. 'But when Simon Peter saw it, he fell down at Jesus' knees saying, "Depart from me for I am a sinful man, O Lord." '

"Jesus had really won Peter to himself in that fishing incident. It was not so much through the words of his sermons, not even his signs. Peter needed to meet Jesus in the place that he understood as well as to hear words that he understood. This fishing incident is an important signpost in his life."

Earl F. Palmer
The Intimate Gospel
p. 177

"This incident comes out of the blue. It is the first meeting between Jesus and his future disciples. He comes up to them, calls them and immediately, without a word of explanation, they walk away from their old lives and follow him. . . . Jesus, as the baptised one, as he who has been anointed in the spirit of God, is the one sent to proclaim hope. Therefore, when he speaks, he cuts right to the heart. Peter and Andrew, James and John can't tell us exactly what happened. But what their hearts have always longed for, what they have always looked for in the wrong place, in a flash opens before them. They follow him because their hearts are so full; they can walk away from everything else.

"As we listen to the story from Peter's and Andrew's viewpoint, as that prayerful listening gradually enables us to grow into the story, it can remind us of all those times in the past when God's love has touched and filled us with an unspeakable hope. Indeed as we turn this story over in our hearts again and again, it happens now. We are Peter. We can hear that call 'Follow me.' Right now we are the ones being called."

Thomas Kane
"Inhabiting the Gospel"

"When our Lord said to Saint Peter, 'Launch out into the deep and let down your nets,' and the apostle answered, 'At thy word I will,' he was not going to do something different from what he had been doing daily, but this very commonplace thing he had been constantly doing, he did now with a sense of vocation and as an act of responsive obedience. The sense of vocation may alter the whole condition of life. It may take a man from an office to the priesthood as it took Matthew from his office to his discipleship. But it may on the other hand only change the motive and quality of his life, leaving it the same, but transfigured and vastly enriched, as it is lifted from a profession to a vocation."

Harry Griffith, ed.
*A Gift of Light: A Collection
of Thoughts from the Writings of Father Andrew*
pp. 91-92

"A familiar example chosen from the legions of examples available in every authentic account of God's relations with man is the story of the 'miraculous draught of fishes.' At the conclusion of a sermon given from a fishing boat moored a little from the shore, Christ makes a suggestion to the owner of the craft: 'Launch out into the deep and let down your nets for a draught.' . . .

"The fundamental reason this story is chosen is that in its telling it moves quickly through the invariable spiritual progression. First there is God's prevenience, or initiating suggestion — 'launch out.' In the next sentence, we note the typical human hesitancy, founded upon experience of futility, to accept God's invitation. The owner of the fishing boat, Peter, said — for all of us, so many times — 'we have toiled all the night and taken nothing,' which constitutes that 'what's the use?' However, Peter went on to add the all-important affirmation, 'Nevertheless at thy word I will let down the net.' The result was an astonishing catch of fish that filled his boat and his partner's as well. This, however, is not the end. In a swift sentence or so, the story moves to its proper climax, affording a classical expression to the truth we are exploring. This point is that, whereas Peter could see no further than catching fish when he said 'yes' (and then did so in abundance), Christ was able to open his eyes to greater possibilities by saying, 'From henceforth thou shall catch men.' God, who speaks in parables, always takes the limited literal handle we give him and then steps up the frequency. He leads not only Peter, whose whole apostolate depended upon his reluctant yes, but all of us into regions that we never dreamed existed. . . . Some of our most vivid, searching, and disquieting memories cluster around those many times when we toiled diligently all through the night of many years and still took nothing. . . .

"Early in the spiritual life, often at the time of

conversion great and astonishing 'catches of fish' usually occur. This is the very nature of things. . . . After this, however, nothing so miraculous happens. The new man is merely able to work steadily and satisfactorily at his job. Is the less dramatic less important? Are the long years of sober joy to be regarded as the failure of God? In short, the temple of one's body does not need to be so violently cleansed again, after the initial overthrowing. Increasingly after that one begins to see the hand of God in the 'little' things. The things he has yet to say to us are spoken in a quieter voice and said more slowly. . . . Increasingly, we know with increasing satisfaction, 'How silently, how silently, The wondrous gift is given.' . . .

"The fact is that there was a steady development in our Lord's human understanding of things. We are told that he 'increased in wisdom' over the years. Stages of this development can be discerned from the synoptic Gospels ranging from 'I must be about my Father's business,' through the upsurge of knowledge about himself at his baptism, through his transfiguration experience and finally at the Cross.

"At his culminating moment he was, it would seem, caught in the dilemma of knowing he was the Messiah and yet that the Messiah must die. How does a dead king bring in a kingdom? But our Lord's faith in the 'yes' to the Father held firm, of course; so he went to his death in sure and certain hope of some sort of resurrection. The multitude of fish that were enclosed by this net which was let down into the depths for a draught have not yet been counted."

Gale D. Webbe
The Night and Nothing
pp. 88-93

"The Gospels state very clearly that the fact of some-one becoming a disciple or being a disciple depends on Jesus' sovereign decision, and not on a free choice of individuals who are especially drawn to him. This is shown in all the stories concerning the call of a disciple. . . . The way in which the Gospels tell these stories makes it clear that they want to show by means of examples what a call to discipleship means. This is why they do not tell the story as the historian would, who would be concerned with the disciples as individuals. The main point is the master who calls. His word is heard: 'Follow me!' And he draws the called person into the closest personal relationship with himself.

". . . These reports record something unique and unrepeatable. Jesus calls, appoints, selects from among the people, even from among his followers, certain individuals and bids them follow him. . . . But it does not include everybody who listens to Jesus' words, who is moved and healed by them and follows him along with the crowd. . . .

"The task of the disciples is clearly expressed in the words with which Jesus calls them away from their occupation of fishing: 'I will make you become fishers of men,' a word which surprises us by its drastic nature. For to 'catch men' is in ordinary language — Hebrew as well as Greek — a vernacular expression used at times jokingly and sometimes disapprovingly, just as we might say 'to trap' a person, to 'get hold of' him, to 'hook' him. This rough startling quality of 'to catch' men coming out in Jesus' words does not have the suggestion of outwitting the other person. The prophets already use as threat the figure of fishers and hunters which Yahweh will send when the days of his judgment are come (Jeremiah 16:16f; Ezekiel 47:8f). Has this figure the same meaning when used by Jesus? As Jesus uses it it certainly means to catch men for the kingdom of God. But with Jesus it rings for the first time with a note of salvation and promise. Only for him who refuses salvation will it become judgment."

Gunther Bornkamm
Jesus of Nazareth
pp. 145-46, 148-49

New Illuminations:

On the Emergence of Pharisaism Within Traditional Judaism

"When Alexander died at the age of thirty-three, his vast empire fell to his generals: Seleucus getting Syria and Asia Minor and Ptolemy getting Egypt and Palestine. From 331 to 198 B.C. is known as the Ptolemaic period. After that the Jews were under the rule of the Seleucid kings of Syria. . . . Into the backwater of Palestine itself, Greek influence surged like a spring tide; and the result was a cleavage and a crisis. Many apostatized; others, though remaining Jews in name, caught the Greek madness. At the head of this worldly party, carefully keeping in favor with their heathen rulers, were the high priests; but as always, there was a faithful remnant, a small party which clung fiercely to their faith and the law and hated everything Greek. . . .

"In 198 B.C. the Syrian king, Antiochus Epiphanes determined to stamp out Judaism by persecution. He first issued an edict that every Jew should sacrifice to thc Gods or die. Then he profaned the temple at Jerusalem by sacrificing a sow to Zeus on the brazen altar. His action caused the saving of the faith that it was calculated to destroy. In face of the prevailing apostasy and indifference, one family — a priest named Mattathias and his five sons — raised the standard of revolt; and fleeing to the wilderness, they rallied around them the *perushim* or pious, the faithful remnant of the day. . . . Judas Maccabaeus, succeeding his father, gained such victories over the Syrians that in 165 he was able to rededicate the altar and the temple. This event was celebrated to the end of the Jewish national history as the Feast of Dedication."

Sister Penelope
The Wood
pp. 89-92

"As the Gospels themselves indicate the most influential picture of Judaism in Jesus' day is that of the Pharisees. They appear for the first time in the period of the Maccabees under the name of 'the pious' (Chassidim), who formed a sharp opposition to the secularised priestly aristocracy. Their programme is the rigorous and uncompromising keeping of the Torah in all spheres and situations of daily life. Even their name (the Separated Ones) probably points to the fact that they kept themselves apart from those they called disdainfully 'Am-aaretz' — i.e., the people from the country who were not expert in the law. The Pharisees are a lay movement joined closely together in a community of their own. . . . The entire life of the individual from morning to night was ritualised to the minutest detail, with prayer and cleansing regulations, with rules for eating and for relations with other people. Is it permissible on the Sabbath to eat an egg laid on the Sabbath day? To keep food hot on the fire? To get engaged? . . . Little as one wishes to question the considerable measure of moral wisdom and religious sincerity which is also to be found in this tradition, nevertheless there developed that formalistic legalising of the law, and a corresponding detailed technique of piety, to which Jesus' message of the divine will stands in sharp contrast. The nature and spirit of the later Judaism of the Talmud have their origin here."

Gunther Bornkamm
Jesus of Nazareth
pp. 39-41

"When the Maccabeans (also called the Hasmonaeon House) turned corrupt with success, the Hasidim separated from the Hasmonaeons. As a result a new name is coined for them: they are the separatists, hence Pharisees. . . . It is estimated that at the time of Jesus there were approximately seven thousand members of this lay movement. They are intellectuals; they are socially concerned moderates. The aristocracy is Sadducee, and the angry and disillusioned are either the 'drop out' Essenes, who live in almost absolute separation at Qumran, or the fierce Zealots. . . . But what is most important for us to understand in trying to make sense of the Pharisees is that fundamental to these laymen is a much larger quest than their technical worries over Sabbath observance. These people are serious about knowing the will of God, and they really care about the truth, but they have become proud and self-righteous like anyone who develops a degree of expertise in such a quest. The result is that they are hypocritical and contemptuous toward ordinary people. It is clear, therefore, that the Pharisees are a complicated mixture of people, and it is important for interpreters of the New Testament accounts to keep this fact in mind."

Earl F. Palmer
The Intimate Gospel
pp. 43-44

"St. Paul, on the basis of his own experience as a Pharisee and as a Christian, gives an important statement of the nature of Christian perfection. He claims that as Pharisee he had achieved the kind of righteousness enshrined in the Jewish law, as understood by the Pharisee: he was, he says, 'blameless according to the righteousness which is in the law (Philippians 3:6). But as a Christian he has no further use for that kind of righteousness, for that kind of accomplishment.

"It is all too easy for us to treat the Pharisees as embodying all that is worst in humankind. But in fact they were probably the best men of their time, the most religious, the most devoted to the will of God, the most eager to express their loyalty to him in obedience to his every word, the most determined never to compromise with the world around them. But, as St. Paul came to see it in retrospect, they were exposed to a fatal flaw: the trouble with their outstanding righteousness was that, all too easily, it could be viewed as *their* righteousness. This meant that it could all too easily come adrift from its original inspiration in devotion to God and become self-sufficient, an end in itself. . . .

"The requirements of the Lutheran polemic (Ephesians 2:8-9) have, to some extent obscured the real objection that is being brought against the Pharisees. It is not that they are laying claim to some righteousness they have achieved *on their own*, in opposition to a righteousness conceded by the grace of God. So far as we can tell, the Pharisees were quite prepared to acknowledge their dependence on God's grace; there are some early Rabbinic texts which express such dependence in the most emphatic terms. Of course there is a risk that human beings will forget their dependence on God, and this is part of St. Paul's complaint; but the far more essential criticism is that the Pharisaic concept of righteousness is such that it allows a man to be self-consciously righteous, to treat it as something he can possess as his own, whether or not he thinks that he has achieved it on his own."

Simon Tugwell
The Beatitudes: Soundings in Christian Traditions
pp. 91-92

"Let us clearly understand who the Pharisees were. Their name has become so much a word of reproach among us that we are inclined to think they must have been very wicked people. Yet that is not the reputation they had among their contemporaries. They are very respectable and highly respected leaders of Israel, (Gamaliel and Saul of Tarsus).

. . . Their primary interest in life was to study God's law and to determine more accurately just what was required of them. . . . It is possible to define the requirements of ceremonial law down to the smallest detail. It is not possible to define the moral law, still less the law of love. Furthermore the elaboration of the ceremonial law frequently conflicted with the deeper obligations of justice, mercy, and charity. These were the serious faults of the Pharisaical position. Our Lord had to correct and rebuke them."

Ralph Milligan, ed.
All for the Love of God: A Holy Cross Omnibus
pp. 173-174

"The 'hypocrisy' for which Jesus renounced the Pharisees so trenchantly did not mean insincerity: the Pharisees were very sincere in their religion and in their moral conscientiousness. Rather was that hypocrisy the wearing of blinkers, the blinkers in which we can think we are serving Jesus without noticing some urgent aspect of our service of him — for instance, our attitudes and actions about race or poverty. . . . It is not being virtuous that makes a saint: the Pharisees were very virtuous, but they and their virtues needed conversion."

Margaret Duggan, ed.
Through the Year with Michael Ramsey
pp. 18, 38

"The Pharisees were those who stood for complete separation from all intercourse with the pagan world. Their religious life was throughout a protest against a prevalent tendency to obliterate the lines which marked off the religion of Israel from the heathenism of Rome."

G. D. Rosenthal
The Sins of the Saints
p. 70

New Illuminations:

On Jesus' Early Confrontation With the Pharisees

Matthew 9:1-14	Mark 2:5—3:6	Luke 5:21—6:11	John 5:9-21

"One remarkable fact that emerges from the Gospel records is the enmity of the religious. . . . It was not the publicans and sinners but those whose life-long purpose was to lead good lives, who by a strange paradox became the deadly enemies of God in human form. It is, I think a mistake to suppose that all the Pharisees were self-righteous humbugs whose hypocrisy Jesus mercilessly exposed. It would be truer to say that they were men ruled by principle, often with a great many conspicuous virtues, but they differed from Christ fundamentally in that the mainspring of their lives lay in observing the law and keeping their own souls unspotted from the world, while his lay in loving his Father with all of his being and his fellow men with the same love that he knew was eternally at the heart of his Father."

J. B. Phillips
Making Men Whole
p. 30

"Jesus by his actions and parables, detonated a mine field that had been carefully assembled by the religious genius of centuries — that men and women had somehow to qualify for God's love. He simply blew up one of man's noblest creations because he said it had come between God and his love for his children and nothing could come between it and them. God loves his enemies! . . . His love is not turned on by our supposed goodness nor turned off by our alleged wickedness. It was a message which reversed all the great spiritual systems of self-development and discipline by which men and women have sought to save themselves. . . .

"Those who had made a business or way of life out of controlling the passes to God's favor could not possibly look upon this teaching with anything but murderous disapproval, since it threatened the very ground of their existence. . . . They organized themselves against threats and challenges to their monopoly."

Richard Holloway
A New Heaven
pp. 23-24

"Jesus' attitude and message can in no way be interpreted as a reversal of all values (Luke 5:36-39), or a systematic revolution in the realm of moral and social standards. . . . Jesus' freedom displays itself not in an abstract criticism of accepted standards but in the way which he, as

a matter of course, makes himself accessible to those who need him, ignoring conventional limitations, and thus according outcasts proper recognition. This is the light which called forth the mocking and derisive words: 'This man receives sinners and eats with them.' "

Gunther Bornkamm
Jesus of Nazareth
p. 80

"Jesus disagreed with the religious leaders of his time, who also were expecting the coming of the kingdom of God. They said that the only way to bring the kingdom was to keep every detail of the Jewish law; and in the effort to keep it, they were co. .inually being frustrated by the necessity of compromising with the Romans and other heathen around them and still more by the members of their own nation who would not even try. These are the people called publicans and sinners. Sinners were people who would not keep the law, worked on the Sabbath Day, stayed away from the synagogue and ate forbidden foods, besides, no doubt, behaving in all sorts of other forbidden ways. The publicans were collaborators with the enemy, who contracted to collect the taxes for the Romans and made themselves rich in the process. The Pharisees, that is, the orthodox leaders, preached at them, despised them, blamed them, and tried to point out to them the error of their ways; but they could not love them and did not like to mix with them. They had very good reason for this. They had been taught that they had been trusted with the knowledge of the true God, and they knew that if they became at all slack or easy-going the whole thing might dissolve.

"It was this that brought them into conflict with Jesus. He showed himself entirely undiscriminating in his friendships. He went about announcing the coming of God's kingdom and invited the publicans and sinners to come in on the ground floor. It threatened a revolution; it threatened the death of Israel."

T. R. Milford
Foolishness To the Greeks
pp. 34-35

"Jesus sat at meat with publicans and sinners; he consorted with harlots. Did he do this to obtain their votes? Or did he think that perhaps he could convert them by such appeasement? Or was his humanity rich and deep enough to make contact, even in them, with that in human nature which is common to all men, indestructible and upon which the future has to be built.''

Dag Hammerskjold
Markings
p. 157

''To the religious people of his day, it was a scandalous thing that Jesus unlike the prophets of old made no denunciation of those who were called sinners. Perhaps I make this point clearer if, speaking for myself, I say that a high-pressure evangelist, whose technique depended on arousing and fostering a sense of guilt, would find himself woefully short of ammunition if he were only allowed to use as his text the recorded words of Christ. With the common run of ordinary sinners, Jesus appears to use the method of simple love. The sense of guilt, it would appear, might well take care of itself; so far as we can judge, he did not attempt to arouse it. Consequently, we find Matthew, loved and appreciated as a man perhaps for the first time for many years, giving up a profitable racket and following One who called him in love. We find Zacchaeus, whose keen business interests had shut him off from love and friendship, instantly melting into astonishing generosity when love touched his life.* . . .

''This method of making people whole by outflowing love was and is extremely risky, but it was a risk that Jesus was prepared to take. And we may infer that God is prepared to take this the chief risk among all the other risks that he has taken in giving man free will.''

J. B. Phillips
Making Men Whole
p. 29

''The real point of the narrative of the paralytic lies in the words: 'The Son of Man has authority on earth to forgive sins.' According to most Jewish thinking it is from sin and guilt that illness and demon possession arise. But the Jewish authorities had not read the signs of the times and they were deeply shocked by such a claim.** The forgiving of sins is for God alone and for anyone else to claim it is blasphemy. They are certainly right on the first point, and would be right on the second point in the case of any ordinary person such as they took Jesus to be. But it is just in taking Jesus as an ordinary person that their error lies. They fail to recognize that he is the Messianic agent of God and that, with his coming, the Kingdom of God is breaking in. That being so, the power that works in Jesus, of course,

---

*See also 97:2, Kane.
**See also 121:2, Krumm.

is the power of God himself;* and there is no blasphemy in his claim that it forgives sins. There being no way of checking the claim to forgive sin, to that extent the suspicion of the scribes is natural. . . . The evidential healing is a triumphal success, and, if in the face of all that, the scribes continue with their opposition, they are utterly without excuse. In fact they do continue, and it is of such stuff that the final charges against Jesus were composed.''

D. E. Nineham
Saint Mark
p. 90

''In the book of Genesis, we are told that God blessed the seventh day and hallowed it because that, in it, he rested from all his work that he had created and made. There is of course a very real sense in which God's activity never ceases at all, since his creative act perpetually upholds and energizes the universe; in our Lord's own words, 'My Father worketh hitherto, and I work.' Furthermore in his own inner being, God is not dead or static but is that unfathomable and inexhaustible energy of life and love which is the Holy Trinity. In him, rest and activity are reconciled. . . .

''In Judaism itself there is the expectation of the Great Sabbath of the Messianic age, in which God would complete his work and restore the world to its pristine integrity, a time when the blind would receive sight and the deaf would hear, and the dumb would speak and the lame would walk, and the dead would be restored to life. And we can hardly doubt that our Lord's miracles are not merely touching works of compassion but are also the signs that the great Messianic age has arrived. Thus it seems clear that in performing miracles on the Sabbath day, Christ was not simply flouting the stuffy conventions of his contemporaries and implying that one day was as good as another for the performance of corporal works of mercy. The Sabbath is not just a *legitimate* day for the working of miracles, it is the day *par excellence*, on which they should be worked, for they are the signs that the Great Sabbath has arrived, the day on which man is admitted once more to the rest of God. 'Ought not this woman, being a daughter of Abraham whom Satan hath bound, lo, these eighteen years, be loosed from this bond on the Sabbath day?' (Luke 13:16).''

E. L. Mascall
Grace and Glory
pp. 25, 29-30

''What had happened to the Sabbath is a very common reversal in man's religious systems. A tradition or custom is developed which was originally designed to assist Man's life, but it ends up by becoming a burden upon him. This happened to the Sabbath. It was a wise tradition designed

---

*See also 121:2, Hooke.

to protect man from the exploitation of his employers. It was meant to be good *for* man. It ended by being a burden *upon* man. Jesus reversed all this with the simple statement: 'The Sabbath was made for man and not man for the Sabbath.' By that saying and by his own actions on the Sabbath day, he took an axe to everything in the world that exploits and dehumanizes man in the name of an abstract principle. . . . In short he humanized the Sabbath, turned it to the service of man and not to his enslavement. And it was noted down and held against him by the religious establishment of his day.''

Richard Holloway
A New Heaven
p. 22

"Jesus was walking through the cornfields on the Sabbath, and as they went the disciples were plucking and nibbling some ears of corn. This was permitted by the Law (Deuteronomy 23:25), providing the corn was not cut with a sickle. The Pharisees had included 'reaping' as one of the thirty-nine activities forbidden on the Sabbath; and choosing to regard the action of the disciples as 'reaping,' they challenged Jesus with condoning Sabbath-breaking. Jesus might have argued that this was the Pharisees' interpretation of the Law, but not the Law itself. Instead he quoted with approval an Old Testament incident where King David technically broke the Law to satisfy the hunger of his followers. In Jesus' view, human need comes before slavish obedience to the letter of the Law. So in this case, satisfying the hunger of the disciples was more important than strict observance of the Sabbath. . . .

"Sabbatarianism, whether in Puritan or Victorian times, is rightly regarded not only as foreign to the spirit of Christ but also as an encouragement to busybodies and killjoys. When Sabbath or Sunday or Lord's day becomes a fetish or a synonym for gloom, depression and boredom, it serves neither the glory of God nor enrichment of the human spirit. . . .

"But the Bible would suggest one or two general principles. If we reject the interference of Sabbatarians for recreation and entertainment, we also have an obligation not to encroach on the freedom of others to spend Sunday as they wish by involving them in work beyond what is absolutely

necessary. For Christians, there is an overriding duty to keep the Lord's Day by taking part in the public worship of God.''

William Neil
The Difficult Sayings of Jesus
pp. 20-21

"Jesus did not try to bring people back to the good, old attitude of their ancestors. . . . For Jesus, fasting was not a general religious duty. His answer to the disciples of John leaves no doubt about this. On the other hand, he did not advise against it; but he wished his disciples to fast individually at the right time and in the right way. From his remark that his disciples would fast 'when the bridegroom would be taken away from them,' we understand that he considered fasting necessary for those who have to undergo crisis and suffering. . . . Fasting means facing reality when the crisis comes, staying sober without escaping into cheap consolations and delusions. By silence and withdrawal we confine our inner forces and cause them to flow, as it were, in the centripetal direction instead of being disseminated into the outer world.''

Fritz Kunkel
Creation Continues
pp. 113-115

"To fast can mean to strengthen our staying power. Whether it be the conquering of a bad habit or the establishing of a daily time of devotion, we need to concentrate on getting a firmer grip on our faith. . . . To fast means to hang on tighter. . . . It also can mean to accept certain needed disciplines so that bodily matters will not interfere with, nor dominate, the affairs of the soul. . . . In brief, to fast in this sense means to make more time for God and thus giving his Holy Spirit more of a chance to work in us.''

Mark A. Beaufoy
The Parables
pp. 67, 81

New Illuminations:

On the Adaptation of the New to the Old

| Matthew 9:14-17 | Mark 2:18-22 | Luke 5:33-39 |

"The Pioneer of the untrodden highway came to the natives of the side track, the prisoners in the *cul-de-sac*, first of all as one of themselves, but what he showed them was the perfection of human nature in its earthly state, and this was something entirely new that had never been seen before. And as such it was also the revelation to them of the character of God, no longer partial and fragmentary as it had been under the old dispensation, but complete. Mankind as a whole had been created to express God, to reflect him as the lake reflects the sky above it, but whereas each human person was only a single drop of water reflecting one small bit, Jesus was the whole lake. In him, the new Man, was revealed 'all the fulness of the Godhead bodily (Colossians 2:9).' And the poor sinful people among whom he lived were self-judged by their reaction to that supremely new revelation; like leather bottles into which new wine is poured, they had to stretch, God knows how wide, to hold it or else burst. The light shone in the darkness and the darkness could neither understand it nor put it out. It was not labeled as light, so everything depended on the individual's capacity for recognising the real thing when it was presented to him in the most unexpected forms and places. . . .

"The creative energy of Jesus in his own teaching appears first and most often as the kingdom of heaven or God, the mysterious kingdom that already is or is to be. This kingdom is contrasted with the old, already existing kingdom of the world, and *there is no other*. Men have got to belong to one or the other; indeed, since the one is already in possession and the other just beginning, the members of the new have to be won, rescued from the tyranny of the old."

Sister Penelope
The Wood
pp. 114, 116

"Jesus had the reputation of not fasting, although he had fasted at the time of his temptation in the wilderness. When the Pharisees questioned him about why he and his disciples did not fast, Jesus' answer shocked them. He said that the news of the dawn of God's kingdom made every day as joyful as a wedding day. Sorrow and fasting were out of the question at such a time. New traditions were being made which did not fit the traditions of the elders, any more than new wine could be held in old leather bags which would no longer stretch. This Jesus was a dangerous kind of teacher. He was undermining the ancient honored customs of the Jewish religion."

Edric Weld and William Sydnor
The Son of God
p. 28

" 'Realized eschatology' is also the meaning of Luke 5:35. To the question why his disciples do not fast, Jesus replies: 'Can the bridal guest mourn during the bridal celebrations?' In the symbolic language of the East, the wedding is the symbol of the day of salvation, as the language of the Apocalypse bears witness: 'The marriage of the Lamb is come' (19:7). The day is come. The wedding songs resound. Here is no place for mourning. This is the time for the bridal festivities; why then should my disciples fast?"

Joachim Jeremias
The Parables of Jesus
p. 117

"In 1892 Julius Wolff first noticed lines of stress in the cellular arrangement of the human skeleton. Caught up in his enthusiasm, Wolff declared that bones were in a state of great flux, adapting readily to changes in environment and function. Adaptations to stress are minor knobs and slight ridges along bones that have consistently maintained a definite length and shape.

"Behind each of the adaptations of divine law applied to a specific culture stands a basic principle. Respect for life must be cherished. The bone endures, the Body simply adapts to new stresses. . . . Jesus kept pointing to higher and more lofty demands, pointing to words like love and joy and fullness of life. When someone came to him for an explanation of an Old Testament rule, usually he pointed to the principle behind it. Jesus understood that rules and governing behavior were meant to free movement and promote growth."

Paul Brand and Philip Yancey
Fearfully and Wonderfully Made
pp. 101, 109

"Something had gone out of our dealings with one another as the mill and the smithy, the tailor and the little shops, had been taken from us. Crainies's ways had changed as every country community had changed. We belonged to a new generation that was everywhere bewildered by what had come upon the earth and might still be to come. But that was not the whole answer. How was it that, out of that generation, living in such close relationship, so 'God fearing' and mindful of the things that endure, another generation had come which did not hold in the same way to the faith of their fathers? Was it because of the new pressure of the world's doubts and uncertainties? Or could it be that the older generation, for all its steadfastness, had known less than it thought about the issues of life and had sent out its children unready for what was to come? . . . Did the kindliness of the community sometimes conceal from its folk that they had to reach out beyond kindliness?

"Perhaps it had reckoned too much with sins which disturbed its life and had left out of account the hidden sins, not looking into the darker depths. The children coming after that generation had been faithful to religious observance; but their lives had been ruled by the keeping of the commandments rather than by the Gospel of a grace by which men are saved; and the next generation, growing up now, had little with which to face a cynical world.

"They were paying the price, many of them, of inheriting a formal religion. Some were concerned only that the evils of the world should be held at bay while they had what they wanted out of life. Some had seen evils which must be fought and had crusaded against them; and many had been disillusioned when the victory did not bring what it had promised. Some had discovered, at the cost of despair and breakdown, that the evil they hated was in themselves. They had come unprepared into the fiery trial.

"I could not wish Crainie back in those days. In the contentment and security men had often been made blind to what the Lord was requiring of them, and their children had grown up without a hunger and thirst for righteousness, though they may not have known what they lacked. But how were we to find the hunger again? . . .

"The whole world is full of the living God. In their unbelief as well as in their belief, men bear witness to him.

Believers or unbelievers, the shape of their lives is determined by what they are towards God. . . .

"Unless the Church knows the full pressure of their unbelief by dwelling with them in it, it cannot be where God is; it is creating an unreal refuge of its own as a shelter from God and what he is doing in the world; and it cannot be the instrument of God's help. . . . Unbelieving men bear the marks of the God who girds them even when they do not know him, and believing men have to learn something of what they do not yet know of God from unbelievers — another hard discipline."

J. W. Stevenson
God in My Unbelief
pp. 107-108, 112-113

Analogues
[Editor]

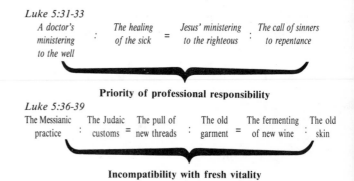

Luke 5:31-33

| A doctor's ministering to the well | : | The healing of the sick | = | Jesus' ministering to the righteous | : | The call of sinners to repentance |

Priority of professional responsibility

Luke 5:36-39

| The Messianic practice | : | The Judaic customs | = | The pull of new threads | : | The old garment | = | The fermenting of new wine | : | The old skin |

Incompatibility with fresh vitality

New Illuminations:

On Luke's Beatitudes and Woes

"Our Lord formulated the special character of the Kingdom of God in a discourse which Matthew and Luke have preserved in widely different versions. . . . In his Gospel, St. Matthew has made considerable additions to the original sermon, while St. Luke has omitted much of it. . . . This is perfectly in accordance with his method of adapting his Gospel for the Gentile readers. The lack of emphasis on opposition to traditional Judaism characterizes Luke's version of the sermon. We can see that the original sermon (of Jesus) defined Christianity in terms of perfect righteousness and in terms of a religion that is more interior and purer than that of official Judaism. The additions which St. Matthew makes from other discourses of our Lord serve to underline the practical consequences of this teaching. St. Luke is concerned, rather, to emphasize the essential trait of the message — charity (v. 36). It is around this theme of charity that the elements of the central section are grouped: the duty of loving one's enemies and the obligations of fraternal charity. It seems that St. Luke is far less interested in defining the spirit of Christianity than in pointing out the conduct which can give concrete expression to that spirit."

Wilfred Harrington
Explaining the Gospels
pp. 112-14

"Jesus' beatitudes are not wisdom sayings but, like the word of a prophet, they are a summons and a promise. Who are those that they address? The first beatitude names them and includes in itself all that follows: 'Blessed are you poor, for yours is the Kingdom of God.' . . . Since the days of prophets and psalms, 'poverty' and 'mourning' have had their place in the history of Jewish piety. One group after another claimed them for their own, to distinguish themselves from the impious and to make sure of God's good will towards themselves. . . . Yet there is nothing which permits us to look upon those to whom Jesus' beatitudes are addressed as to the members of religious groups or of a social stratum. . . . As Jesus uses the words, poverty and humility have their original meaning. The poor and they that mourn have nothing to expect from the world but have everything to expect from God. They look towards God and also cast themselves upon God; in their lives and in their attitudes, they are beggars before God. . . .

"The situation at the limit of human existence is not here glorified in itself. Misery and poverty mean distress and torture. But God waits beyond the limit, or rather, he no longer waits but comes to those who wait for him. Though his kingdom be in the future, yet it breaks even now like a ray of light upon the darkness of the oppressed with this oft repeated, 'Blessed are you.' Blessed are you does not mean you are entering heaven nor you are already in heaven; rather it means: God's kingdom comes to you."

Gunther Bornkamm
Jesus of Nazareth
pp. 75-77

"St. Matthew and St. Luke present the first beatitude in slightly different forms. St. Luke's is the cruder and perhaps the more basic: 'Blessed are you who are poor.' It is twinned with a corresponding woe: 'Woe to you who are rich.' There is a kind of material crudeness about this which should not be overlooked. It is only in the intertestimental period that Judaism begins to develop a sense that material prosperity does not necessarily go with piety, and that maybe it is even typical that the man who is devoted to God should be among the poor and down-trodden of the world. At first, no doubt, this was simply a factual observation. But in time it became a positive doctrine that the righteous man must not expect to prosper in this world, and this is probably to be connected with the growing sense that their present age is the age of the dominion of Satan. It is in the age to come, which is God's age, that his servants will be rewarded. Early Christian thought took over thc concept. There goes with it a sense of the real danger that prosperity in this world, as we know it, can be had only on the terms of the ruler of this world. . . . The essential thing is that we do not lose sight of the warning that we are unlikely to be allowed to eat at both tables (Luke 16:13). This a principle of very wide application as we can see from the way the Lord uses it in connection with people who made a great parade of their piety in order to impress the people around them. Our Lord's comment is simply, 'They have their reward' (Luke 6:2 and 5).

"Now from this point of view, it does not make very much difference what kind of short term objective we have. Once we have achieved our objective, 'we have our reward.' . . . If the Gospel is only telling us to wait patiently for the sun to shine in heaven, offering us pie in the sky in return for misery here below, it is at best a dingy kind of message. Maybe it was to clarify this that the beatitude was expanded to read, 'Blessed are the poor in spirit.' What is at stake is not just our relationship to material possessions,* it is a whole question of our attitude, our spirit. . . . We want to be able to draw the line between having and not having. The Pharisee in the Lord's parable (Luke 18:8-14) bolsters up

---

*See also 68:1, *University of Chicago Magazine*.

his own sense of what he has by contrasting himself with others who do not have what he has. . . . It is only the poor in Spirit who can actually have anything, because they are the ones who know how to receive gifts. For them everything is a gift.''

Simon Tugwell
The Beatitudes: Soundings in Christian Tradition
pp. 16-23

"We must remember that all we possess is a gift. The first beatitude is one of poverty, and only if we live according to this beatitude can we enter into the Kingdom of God. This beatitude has two aspects. First, there is a very clear fact that we possess nothing that we can keep. . . . We do not possess life in such a way that it is impossible for anyone to take it away from us. We have a body — it will die. We have a mind, yet it is enough for one minute vessel to burst in the brain for the greatest mind to be suddenly extinguished. We have a heart, sensitive and alive, and yet a moment comes . . . when there is nothing but a stone in our breast.

"So, in a way, we can say that we possess nothing because we are masters of nothing which is in our possession.* And this could lead us not to the sense of belonging to the Kingdom of God and rejoicing in it, but to despair — if we did not remember that, although none of these things are ours in such a way that they cannot be taken away from us, yet we *are* in possession of them.

"This is the second aspect of the beatitude. We are rich and everything we possess is a sign of the love of God and the love of men. . . . One of our theologians has said, 'All the food of this world is divine love made edible.' This is the Kingdom, the sense that we are free from possession, and this freedom establishes us in a relationship where everything is love — human love and divine love.''

Anthony Bloom
Beginning To Pray
pp. 14-15

"Blessed are those who know how poor and empty, apart from their Lord's indwelling, they truly are.** On the other hand, in union with Christ, men are 'God's work of art, created in Christ to live the good life as from the beginning he had meant us to live it' (Ephesians 2:10, Phillips). This work of art is the believer, one who in union with Christ has found his 'higher self' and consequently has a real 'I' or face with which to meet and commune, however humbly, with God. About this relationship Lewis exclaimed: 'To be loved by God, not merely pitied, but delighted in as an artist delights in his work or a father in his son — it seems

impossible, a weight or burden of glory which our thoughts can hardly sustain' (C. S. Lewis, *Weight of Glory*, p. 10).''

Leanne Payne
Real Presence: The Holy Spirit in the Works of C.S. Lewis
p. 58

"The confronting of man by the living God is not a ministry of comfort, but rather a ministry of high calling. It cannot be born by the proud, for it would take away the root and ground of religious pride which is the most deadly form of pride. But for those who come in poverty of spirit, knowing their need and being willing to be silent in order that God may speak, for them there is peace in God's acceptance as they are and a readiness to take the next step of the pilgrimage toward what they might become or do.''

Lewis J. Sherrill
Struggle of the Soul
p. 99

"Righteousness is the way to travel to where God wants us to be. We are blessed when we hunger and thirst for that goal now while on the way. Our knowing we are on the way now is because God never puts us in the position where we have made it.''

Robert Hewitt
Sermon Notes

"Righteousness is the operation of man's faith in God and the working out of God's grace in man.''

Harry Blamires
Where Do We Stand
p. 24

"Already in the Old Testament, the righteous one is the mature one who lives up to the will of God. To be discontented with our spiritual situation, to crave for something better with all the violence and recklessness of people who are starving to death, that is the inner situation of those who are blessed. . . . Nobody has this situation as a birthright. We have to deserve it by our own endeavor. We have to first understand that we do not have it. We are like landless peasants, like settlers without farms, hungry, thirsty, demoralized. Suddenly the message comes that there is land to be had. Everyone who is aware of his poverty joins the surging pioneers shouting for land. Jesus was well aware of this riotous feeling among his disciples: '. . . the kingdom of God is preached and everyone presseth into it.'*''

Fritz Kunkel
Creation Continues
p. 63

---

*See also 68:1, *University of Chicago Magazine*.
**See also 64:4, Kelsey.

---

*See also 82:1, Bornkamm.

"Although Paul had no doubt that man's salvation is all of God, equally he had no doubt that man has to strain every nerve to enter into the fullness of that salvation. What is ours by faith has to be equally striven for and appropriated. As was once said by Ignatius Loyola, the Christian has first to realize that he can do nothing by himself; he has to accept his utter helplessness and utter dependence upon God. But then, having reached this point, he has to act as if it all depended upon him himself. He resolutely sets his will (hungers and thirsts) to put into practice the implications of his discipleship. Not till long afterwards will he understand that the energies he has used in God's service were not his own but God's. He has been given the strength to persevere because God was within him, giving him the will and energy required."

Joost de Blank
Uncomfortable Words
pp. 108-109

" 'Blessed are you when men shall revile you and persecute you . . .' The proclamation of the Kingdom of heaven is a paradox. A step of development, an achievement of conscious growth, is proclaimed in appalling though simple terms. . . . The paradox says that to be persecuted and reviled is a blessing. . . . We are told to rejoice and be glad here on earth while we are persecuted. To laugh while we feel like weeping would be dishonest; Jesus does not teach us to wear a mask of joy while we suffer. The 'reward in heaven' must be realized immediately; loss must be felt as gain here and now not after death. The Kingdom must be an experience of growth and evolution before we die. It may continue after death, but it must begin on earth.*

"Matthew then adds: 'For righteousness' sake' and 'for my sake.' Those who hunger and thirst after righteousness are usually at odds with the majority of their contemporaries, and so were the Prophets of the Old Testament. The text does not say that those who persecute the followers of Jesus are bad or selfish or malicious. They are simply 'people' — neighbors, friends, relatives, everybody. . . .

"Do we correctly understand the final issue of this everlasting persecution? What is the Kingdom of Heaven? Matthew is not willing or not able to answer our question. He forces us to venture our own answer cautiously, tentatively, hypothetically. And we should be ready to change or develop our answer according to Jesus' teaching and our own experience."

Fritz Kunkel
Creation Continues
pp. 57-59

*See also 95:3, Ramsey.

"As long as we are going to get anything out of what we are doing, there comes a certain measure of self-seeking. But when in complete darkness, we chose love, when in complete happiness we choose what is right at the cost of happiness, we are somewhere near the Lord who for love of us endured darkness."*

Harry C. Griffith, ed.
*A Gift of Light: A Collection
of Thoughts from the Writings of Father Andrew*
p. 12

"There is a clear tradition in the New Testament that the Jews could be relied upon to persecute God's prophets. In Luke's beatitude (vv. 22-23) with its little appendix, it is surely intended to be significant that it is as prophets that Christians will incur opposition and hostility. Christians are not primarily persecuted for being righteous or for being followers of Christ, but from proclaiming righteousness, for declaring Christ's word of peace**. . . . And this possibly suggests that we come around full circle in this last beatitude, to echo the beatitude of the poor: theirs is the kingdom of heaven. . . .

"But it is not merely a matter of how people react to the proclamation of God's word of peace; the intentions and motives of the prophet himself are also concerned. In St. John's Gospel, the Jews are said to be incapable of believing because they receive glory from one another. There is apparently a radical incompatibility between human respect and belief in Christ. . . . If we are not concerned to impress our fellow men and women, then there is vaster reward in store for us, the reward of God's kingdom. . . .

"So even though it is not the primary business of the believer to please men, it is equally not his business to go out of his way to displease men either. . . . We do not become prophets simply because we go around being rude to and about everybody else. In fact those who just want to be disagreeable 'have their reward' simply in being disagreeable and in seeing their disagreeableness provoking people to annoyance and hostility. The reward that our Lord promises to those that are persecuted for his sake is not intrinsic to the situation of persecution itself. He promises the peace of his Father's kingdom. . . . This is why Christianity is an uncomfortable religion. It requires a head for heights and a taste for infinity."

Simon Tugwell
The Beatitudes: Soundings in Christian Tradition
pp. 123-124

" 'Woe to you that laugh.' The Gospel never mentions any laughter from Jesus. Vulgar, heavy, rousing, sarcastic

*See also 118:3, Father Andrew
**See also 103:1, Sheen.

laughter — how incompatible with the picture the Gospel paints of our Savior! Never 'laugh.' But he does tell them, 'Rejoice and be glad' (Matthew 5:12). This emotion which causes lively joy is of another emotion than laughter."

Monk of the Eastern Church
Jesus: A Dialogue With the Savior
p. 73

"The Christian ideal changed and reversed everything so that as the Gospel puts it, 'That which was exalted among men has become an abomination in the sight of God.' The ideal is no longer the greatness of Pharaoh or of a Roman emperor, not the beauty of a Greek nor the wealth of Phoenicia, but humility, purity, compassion, love. The hero is no longer Dives, but Lazarus* the beggar; not Mary Magdalene in the day of her beauty, but of her repentance; not those who acquire wealth, but those who have abandoned it; not those who dwell in palaces, but those who dwell in huts; not those who rule others, but those who acknowledge no authority but God's."

Leo Tolstoy
What is Art?

"To look upon the other worldly, uncompromising commandments of the Sermon on the Mount as a program of secular renovation is basically to misunderstand them. Jesus is not concerned with a social revolution or with a progressive advance towards some earthly realm of peace but with a transformation of man himself in order that he may have a share in the future kingdom of God. It would, of course, be a misunderstanding to regard the morality he is calling for merely as the ideal order of the future world, as the unrealized and unrealizable harmony of God's kingdom.   .   .   .
The demands of Jesus refer to conduct of the world here and now. They are directed to the heirs of the future kingdom and summon them to high purity of mind and determined action. And, to conclude, it would be also false to interpret this morality as affecting the brief period before the end, as a peculiar law in view of the future catastrophe. The intention of Jesus is not to release his disciples from the world and their surroundings, but from a worldly way of thought and life. Jesus is not asking how it may be realized practically in the circumstances of the world. But both Jesus and the early Church were convinced that it should be and, with God's assistance, could be so realized."

Rudolf Schnackenburg
God's Rule and Kingdom
pp. 108-09

*See also 84:1, Thielicke.

New Illuminations:

On Loving Our Enemies and Judging Others

Matthew 5:38-48; 7:1-5; 10:24-25   Mark 4:24   Luke 6:27-42

"Jesus crystalized his teaching on reconciliation, not retaliation, in the memorable words: 'Love your enemies.' Like the saying about turning the other cheek, he is still talking about personal relationships and not about nations at war or enemies of the state. More important, when he says 'love' he does not mean 'like.' How could we possibly like someone who is leading our children into bad habits? Yet Jesus tells us we should *love* such people. What does he mean? Surely he does not expect us to love those who do them an injury in the same way they love their wives and families, their parents and their best friends. He urges us, however, to take as our example God, who sends the blessing of rain and sunshine on all alike, good and bad, honest and dishonest. We must show a like good will in our own circle to all and sundry whether we like them or not, helping where our help is needed in the spirit of the Good Samaritan. Disregard of personal insults, forgiveness of wrongs done us, generosity of spirit to friends and enemies alike — these are the marks of Christian discipleship."

William Neil
The Difficult Sayings of Jesus
p. 5

"It is not easy to like certain people, but it is possible to love them. The difference is this: like is instinctive, emotional, organic, physiological, a sensible reaction over which we sometimes have as little control as over the grumbling of a stomach. Arguments are useless in convincing a boy that he ought to like spinach. . . .

"But loving is in the will not in the glands: it is in that part of our being which is subject to moral command and is not a bodily reaction, like a wink. Liking is reciprocal, but love is not necessarily reciprocal. The friends we say we like, like us. But a mother can love a wayward son even though he does not return the affection. God can love us even though we spurn his graces.

"The Divine Command was not 'Like thy neighbor' but 'Love thy neighbor' because it is hard to like certain kinds of people such as those who step on our toes. . . . When there is no spontaneous love, love begins only as a duty, but we learn to love only by loving. The 'I ought' passes after awhile to 'I love.'

"It is easy to like and love those who love us, but when it comes to loving those who are not very likeable, it takes the love of God to give the inspiration. . . . The Peace is in realizing that all human love is a spark from the flame which is God."

Fulton Sheen
Power of Love
p. 19-20

"The philosopher Hume told us that you can't argue any way from 'is' to 'ought.' You must either abandon the sense of 'oughtness' as irrational and unjustifiable or conclude that the mysterious demand you feel is imposed on you by some source of value beyond yourself. You can conclude that the sense of duty has a cause in the existence of an attractive power of Goodness beyond yourself which exerts a magnetic influence upon you. It calls a recognition forth from you the way beauty creates a response in you. We trust the sense we have that goodness is not just a matter of private taste or collective convenience but that it corresponds to what is Real. It imposes itself. Somehow it authenticates itself. How can we account for this except by positing some transcendent source of value which communicates to our nature, plants the intuition in our hearts."

Richard Holloway
Beyond Belief
p. 11

" 'But I say to you not to resist evil.' How scandalous and foolish is this statement in the eyes of men and especially of unbelievers. How do we interpret these precepts — about turning the left cheek to the one who struck the right, giving our cloak to the one who took our tunic, walking two miles with the one who forced us to go one, giving a blessing to him who curses us? Have we thoroughly explored the ways and means of loving our enemy — whether he be a personal or public one? 'You know not of what spirit you are' (Luke 9:55).

"It is a question of resisting the Gospel. The choice is not between fighting and not fighting, but between fighting and suffering — and by suffering, conquering. Fighting brings about only vain and illusory victories since Jesus is absolute reality. Suffering without resistance proclaims the absolute reality of Jesus. Understood in this light, suffering is then a real victory."

Monk of the Eastern Church
Jesus: A Dialogue with the Savior
p. 148

"The Authorised Version says, 'That ye resist not evil'; Moffat and Goodspeed have 'not to resist an injury,' and Weymouth 'not to resist a wicked man.' All these translations are correct. Psychologically the term 'evil' should be correct because then our passage becomes a profound lesson on the meaning and dynamics of evil.

"Jesus was not thinking of a new civil code without

police, where the bullies are allowed to exploit their victims. . . . Innocence must be defended. But Jesus here is speaking about something else. He teaches self-education. How can we exploit evil, injuries, and wicked men for our own spiritual growth? If our dignity is rooted in our creative relationship with God, a slap in the face cannot harm us. Jesus' own attitude when he was struck by the high priest's officer was bold and calm and of unshakable peacefulness. If we are aware of our power, feeling our contact with our Father in Heaven, we are not inclined to resist evil*. . . . However non-resistance must be a dynamic device, a way of development, or it remains a foolish idea in the stratosphere. If it is not the result of our spiritual wealth, it should become its cause.''

Fritz Kunkel
Creation Continues
p. 78

"In a pathetic passage in a prophetic Psalm, God's Servant says, 'I am a worm and no man' (Psalm 22:6). Those who have been in tropical lands tell us that there is a big difference between a snake and a worm, when you attempt to strike at them. The snake rears itself up and hisses and tries to strike back — a true picture of self. But a worm offers no resistance; it allows you to do what you like with it, kick it or squash it under your heel — a picture of true brokenness. And Jesus was willing to become just that for us — a worm and no man.** And he now calls us to take our rightful place as worms, for him and with him. The whole Sermon on the Mount with its teaching of non-retaliation, love for enemies and selfless giving assumes that is our position. But only the vision of the Love that was willing to be broken for us can constrain us to be willing for that. . . . Every humiliation, everyone who tries and vexes us is God's way of breaking us so that there is a yet deeper channel in us for the Life of Christ.''

Roy Hession
The Calvary Road
pp. 15-16

" 'Do not set yourself against the man who wrongs you' (NEB). A slap on the face is merely a picturesque way of describing a personal insult and, in this event, means refusing to return the insult but rather ignoring it.*** This saying therefore has nothing to do with arguments for or against pacifism, violence or non-violence. Jesus is dealing purely with personal relationships.

"And so often as in his teaching, he throws out a

challenge by startling his listeners with the unexpected. They have become accustomed to his way of making people think by saying something amusing — 'If someone gives you a clout on the side of the head' . . . (pause while they cudgel their brains as to what they were supposed to do, then comes the least likely answer) . . . 'let him clout you on the other side as well!' We can see from the next few verses that Jesus does not mean his hearers to take him literally, for he goes on to talk of a man being sued in a law court for the recovery of his shirt. If this happens, says Jesus, let him have your coat as well.

"The other two illustrations make it abundantly clear that Jesus' language is figurative.* The first is that of a Roman legionary picking on a passer by and ordering him to carry some heavy load for a mile along the road. If this happens to you, says Jesus, offer to carry it twice as far — the proverbial 'second Mile' — obviously the last thing a reluctant conscript would think of doing. But it is the principle of responding to harshness with kindness that Jesus is commending. So with Jesus' last example. 'Do not turn your back on the man who wants to borrow.' To obey this literally would encourage spongers and reward the shiftless and thriftless at the expense of those who work for their living. Jesus obviously is not commending indiscriminate charity, which is demoralizing, but rather urging us to cultivate the spirit of generosity. While this has strictly nothing to do with avoiding retaliation, it does show that the whole passage is not concerned with laying down laws for Christian behavior but with the attitude a Christian should adopt in dealing with people in general. Reconciliation and magnanimity must point the way.''

William Neil
The Difficult Sayings of Jesus
pp. 4-5

"The very act of reconciliation begins with a decision of the mind, not of the emotions. Reason is activated not feeling, when the words "I forgive you" are spoken. The intellect, independent of likes or dislikes, is where the decision to pardon the offense is made. Even when forgiveness is offered with full mental approval, it will not always wipe out the emotional annoyance. The pain of the affront can remain with us long after sincere forgiveness is complete. To be sure that we have forgotten in our mind although we still suffer in our emotions is not always easy. Only if we are able to pray for the one that hurt us, if we can promote his self esteem and not be critical of his mannerisms, can we know that we have truly pardoned him.

"Forgiveness is a sacrifice. When we excuse the offender, we show a willingness to forgo the satisfaction to even out the score. And more than that, we clearly demonstrate that we are ready to bear part of the burden of that offense. Although our emotions were upset, we prefer to suffer the

---
*See also 99:2, Webster.
**See also 111:1, Neil.
***See also 75:1, Bloom.

---
*See also 87:1, Neil.

hurt instead of responding with a similar deed. Such an act of reconciliation* arrests the spread of insulting emotions which would otherwise perpetuate the conflict. The graceful overture removes the barrier which would have separated us from God and from each other.

"When we forgive, we choose to love. By accepting the sacrifice of forgiving, we refuse the alternative of revenge and signal the unmistakable message that our love is still stronger than the deplorable episode. If, however, an offense damages love so deeply that it falters, love's sincerity should be questioned, not the value of forgiveness."

John Walchars
Voices on Fire
pp. 134-135

"I think that what one has to remember is that when people 'hurt' one another, in ninety-nine cases out of a hundred they intended to hurt much less, or not at all, and are often quite unconscious of the whole thing. I've learned this from the cases in which I was the hurter. When I've been really wicked and angry and meant to be nasty, the other party never cared, or even didn't notice. On the other hand, when I have found out afterwards that I have deeply hurt someone, it had nearly always been quite unconscious on my part. (I loathe 'sensitive' people who are 'easily hurt' by the way; don't you? They are a social pest. Vanity is usually the trouble.)"

W. H. Lewis, ed.
Letters of C. S. Lewis

" 'Be merciful, just as your Father is merciful.' Matthew reads 'be perfect!' In the Old Testament, mercy is attributed to God, rarely to men, while perfection is a goal to be sought by man."

T. W. Manson
The Sayings of Jesus
p. 55

"There always are a few little worms which do not reveal themselves until, like the worm which gnawed through Jonah's gourd, they have gnawed through our virtues. Such are self-love, self-esteem and censoriousness (even if only in small things) concerning our neighbors, lack of charity towards them and failure to love them as we love ourselves."**

St. Teresa of Avila
Interior Castle
p. 114

"Never allow yourself boldly to judge your neighbor; judge and condemn no one, rather have compassion and pity for him. But let his example be a lesson in humility to you. Realizing that you too are extremely weak and as easily moved to sin as dust on the road, say to yourself, 'He fell today but tomorrow I shall fall.'* Know that if you are quick to blame and despise others, God will mete out a painful punishment to you by letting you fall into the same sin for which you blame others. 'Judge not that you be not judged.' . . . Even if in his mercy God protects you from downfall, stop blaming others if you were blaming them. Do not trust your own steadfastness. . . . As soon as you think thus you will fall as easily as an autumn leaf from a tree."

Theophan
Unseen Warfare
p. 65

"The beam is the lack of love which expresses itself in censoriousness by searching for the mote. It is the critical spirit. Once the unkind, critical spirit is removed there will come the Christlike spirit that knows how with the delicate touch to take the mote away that the brother's visions too may be clear."

Selected

"Our Lord, soaked in the poetic tradition of his country, delighted to use parallelism. 'For with what judgment you judge you shall be judged; and with what measure you mete it shall be measured to you again' (Matthew 7:2). The second half of the verse makes no logical addition; it echoes with variation the first.' Ask and it shall be given you; seek and you shall find; knock and it shall be opened unto you' (Luke 11:9). The advice is given in the first phrase, then twice repeated with different images. We may, if we like, see in this an exclusively practical and didactic purpose; by giving to truths which are infinitely worth remembering this rhythmic and incantatory expression, he made them almost impossible to forget. I like to suspect more. It seems to me appropriate, almost inevitable, that when that great Imagination which in the beginning submitted to express itself in human speech, that speech should sometimes be poetry. For poetry too is a little incarnation giving body to what had been before invisible and inaudible."

C. S. Lewis
Reflections On the Psalms
p. 5

---

*See also 88:1, Thielicke.
**See also 58:1, Howe.

---

*See also 120:3, Williams.

"I will chide no breather in the world but myself, against whom I know most faults."*

William Shakespeare
As You Like It
3.2.295

"Try not to think much less to speak of someone else's sins. One's own are a much more profitable theme. And if on consideration, one can find no faults on one's own side, then cry for mercy, for this must be a most dangerous delusion."

C. S. Lewis
Selected

"True, the first emphasis about the beam and the mote seems to be a condemnation of censoriousness; but when the censoriousness is removed, the passage ends by saying, 'Then you shall see clearly to cast the mote out of your brother's eye' (Luke 6:42b). According to the New Testament, we are meant to care so much for the other man that we are willing to do all we can to remove from his eye the mote that is marring his vision and hindering his blessing. . . . The love of Jesus poured out in us will make us want to help our brother in this way. What blessing may come · to many others through our willingness humbly to challenge one another, as led by God."

Roy Hession
Calvary Road
p. 51

"We must familiarize ourselves with the greatest defects of good people and quietly leave them until the time when God shall indicate the moment that they may be cured of them; otherwise we may destroy the good grain with the chaff. . . . Those who correct others ought to watch the moment when God touches their heart; they must bear a fault with patience till they perceive God's spirit reproaching them within. Then they must follow his providence that gently reproaches them. . . . We wait for Providence to give the occasion and grace to open their hearts to receive it. If you would gather the fruit before its time you lose it entirely."

Thomas Kepler, ed.
Letters and Reflections of Francois de Fenelon
pp. 75, 77

*See also 88:2, Bro.

"Those things that a man cannot amend in himself or others, he ought to suffer patiently until God orders them otherwise. Think that it is better so for thy trial and patience, without which all good deeds are not much to be esteemed. . . . Endeavor to be patient in bearing with the defects and infirmities of others of what sort soever they may be; for thyself also hast many failings which must be borne by others. If thou canst not make thyself such a one as thou wouldst, how canst thou expect to have another in all things to thy liking."

St. Thomas a´ Kempis
The Imitation of Christ

"In a frank letter to an older man, Charles Simeon (Vicar of Holy Trinity, Cambridge England, 1782-1832) discloses as much of himself as he does of the one to whom he is writing:

I seem to feel that I can say anything to you without offense and without suspicion: without offense because of the ardent love I bear you and without suspicion because you well know that I am, and ever have been, as far from a timid temporizing character as ever a man could be. I have heard with deep concern that, whilst all unite in loving and honoring your general character, a great number of persons are grievously offended with the style of your preaching. . . . which I am told is unnecessarily harsh and offensive; and that on this being suggested to you by Mr. — you gave him notice to quit the curacy. Will you forgive me my dear friend, if I say that in both these respects you have erred. It is not by coarseness of expression or severity of manner that we are to win souls but by speaking the truth in love.

Simeon had always urged moderation on his zealous hearers. 'Young ministers,' he told one of his groups, 'should inquire, not what I can teach my people, but what they can receive. Jesus did not tell his disciples that which they could not bear, but spake to them as they 'were able to bear it.'. . . . These few excerpts from Simeon's many letters show him to have been a man of remarkable understanding and a very warm heart. Having been the butt of unkind criticism by so-called earnest Christians he was very well aware of how easily religious people can turn censorious. We can end this chapter by hearing him speak on how to cope with evil-speaking:

1st: To hear as little as possible what is to the prejudice of others.
2nd: To believe nothing of the kind until I am absolutely forced to.
3rd: Never to drink into the spirit of one who circulates an ill report.
4th: Always to moderate, as far as I can, the unkindness which is expressed by others.

As I should resist a man who should come to rob my house so would I a man who would weaken my regard for any human being. I consider too that persons are cast into different moulds: and that to ask myself what should I do in that person's situation is not a just mode of judging. I must not expect a man who is naturally cold and reserved to act as one who is naturally warm and affectionate. And I think it a great evil that people do not make more allowances for each other in this particular. I think religious people are too little attentive to these considerations.''

Hugh Evan Hopkins
Charles Simeon of Cambridge
pp. 133-34

''Love that has entered the soul is not free from fear of somehow hurting a fellow-being and, perhaps even more, of grieving the Holy Spirit by an impulse of the heart, a thought, or a word. Only through a more abundant measure of grace which manifests itself in love for enemies does the spirit become kin, as it were to God. Yet even with such love as this, we can still run into difficulties with people, since the very presence of divine action within us in a strange fashion provokes hostility in those who do not love God. . . . Those who are not reborn from above will never understand those who are. For a patient attitude to every ordeal makes the regenerated soul more able to apprehend the 'wisdom from above' (James 3:17).''

Archimandrite Sophrony
His Life Is Mine
p. 62

''Jesus uttered not one syllable of angry resentment nor murmuring complaint; no indignation for such perfect innocence so causelessly injured and abused; no wishes for revenge. . . . Never was such an instance of meek suffering, never so unwearied a love of enemies, never so kind an intercession for pardon, since the world began. Remember this thy soul, and when thou findest thyself apt to be out of temper for the affronts or wrongs thou sustainest, even when most unkind, even when most undeserved, compare (though in truth there be no comparison) thy sufferings with thy Lord's.''

Saint Anselm
Meditations

New Illuminations:

On the Potential Perfection of Man

Matthew 5:48   Luke 2:40, 52; 6:36

"Though on the creature man's first emergence, he was truly the crown of the created order and the highest created incorporation of God's likeness, he was then in a state of only potential perfection. Just as one may hold in one's hand a perfect acorn and say truly, 'This is a potential oak-tree,' so man as created was potentially perfect man, but with all his development before him.* The 'very goodness' of creation which culminated in him had yet to be actualized. And it could be so actualized only by man's reaching out beyond himself to God, whose likeness he was. . . .

"If you could plant an acorn today and then go out for a hundred years to look at it, the difference from day to day would be imperceptible. But at the end of time there would be no acorn but a forest tree; and there is a great deal of difference between a forest tree and the acorn from which it grew, though the tree existed potentially in the acorn from the first. By some gradual progress the human race ought to have gone steadily forward to its goal."

Sister Penelope
The Wood
pp. 25-26

"The New Life grows in secret. Nothing very startling happens. . . . The child grows as other children. The Lad works as other lads. I love to think that much in Christ's own destiny was mysterious to him. It was part of his perfect manhood that he shared our human situation in this too. . . . In a general way we too must go steadily on in pure faith and abandonment to God. When even the divine mind of Christ looks out from his earthly tabernacle, he seldom gets a clear view, so why should we demand a clear view? We can't break through the Cloud of Unknowing in which our lives are enfolded. Only the divine mind which has conceived each one of our destinies can lead us, but secretly. . . .

"All gardeners know the importance of good root development before you force leaves and flowers. God does not wish you to be one of those lanky plants that grows up too quickly and can't do without a stick. God wants you nice and bushy, rooted and grounded in him and growing all around, up to the sun, down to the hidden deeps, out to the world. We get notions sometimes that we ought to spring up quickly, we ought to show some startling sign of spiritual growth. But perhaps we are only asked to go on quietly, to be a child, a nice stocky seedling, not shooting up in a hurry but making root, being docile to the great slow

rhythm of life. When you don't see any startling marks of your own religious condition or your usefulness to God, think of the Baby in the stable and the little Boy in the streets of Nazareth. . . . Christ takes thirty years to grow and two and a half to act. The pause, hush, hiddenness between the Birth and the Ministry are all part of the Divine method. . . . Just so the light of the Spirit is to unfold gently and steadily within us, till at last our final stature, all God designed for us, is attained."

Evelyn Underhill
The Light of Christ
pp. 42-44

"Christ gave us baptism 'with the Holy Ghost and with fire.'* In the light of this knowledge we now see the path to eternal perfection. . . . In its eternal essence life is divine spirit and truth, therefore transcends all outward forms. . . . 'And Jesus increased in wisdom and stature, and in favor with God and man' (Luke 2:52). So we are charged with a like responsibility for growth. Man comes into this world to 'grow, wax strong in spirit, be filled with wisdom' (Luke 2:40): i.e. for human beings still far from perfect to grow morally, intellectually, and more importantly spiritually."**

Archimandrite Sophrony
His Life Is Mine
pp. 21-22

"Charles Simeon remembered David Brown (missionary to India) as having become a Christian while attending Holy Trinity, 'how his religious faith had not darted suddenly into his mind as the ray of heavenly light which overthrew an opposing Saul; but rather, as the least of all seeds, had grown with his growth and strengthened with his strength.' "

Hugh Hopkins
Charles Simeon of Cambridge
p. 143

*See also 67:4, Ramsey.
**See also 55:1, Dix.

*See also 92:2, Phillips.

"Living things need an appropriate climate in order to grow and bear fruit. If they are to develop to completion, they require an environment that allows their potential to be realized. Those who live near the desert know the miracle of a rainy year when suddenly a whole mountainside turns orange under a blanket of poppies, or a valley becomes a fairyland of color. The seeds have been there. The soil and the sun and the warmth have been there. Only one thing was lacking, and when that last climactic need was fulfilled, life was profuse beyond imagination. How seldom we wonder at the growth of the great redwood from a tiny seed dropped at random on the littered floor of a forest. From one seed is grown enough wood to frame several hundred houses. The human soul has seed potential like this if it has the right environment*. . . .

"What are the conditions for the soul which are equivalent to the sun and the rain, the soil and warmth for the seed? First, meditation is the attempt to provide the soul with the proper environment in which to grow and become. This is the reality of contact with a spiritual world. Then the soul must be prodded from within by human need, the moisture which makes the seed swell and burst its own limits and so start upon the growth process. Until we realize we need something beyond our own humanness, neither prayer nor meditation become a reality. And then there is the reality of love which seeks out and desires to touch us and bring us to itself. This unique understanding of God is the light of the sun which draws us forth.** Christians have been entrusted with the knowledge that God is like the loving caring Jesus of Nazareth who cared enough to die for any individual. This understanding means allowing oneself to be open to this almost incredible love. The final step is allowing ourselves to be expressions of that love in outer action that provides the warmth needed to encourage the seed to grow. . . . For both the seed and the soul, these things all take time. In both cases there is need for patience. Most of us know enough not to poke at the seed to see if it is sprouting, or try to hurry it along with too much water or fertilizer or cultivation. The same respect must be shown for the soul as its growth starts to take place. Growth can seldom be forced in nature. Whether it is producing a tree or human personality, nature unfolds its growth slowly, silently."

Morton Kelsey
The Other Side of Silence
pp. 31-32

"Patience with ourselves is a duty for Christians and the only real humility. For it means patience with a growing creature whom God has taken in hand and whose completion he will effect in his own time and in his own way. . . . It is God who gives the conditions. Our part is to accept them with humility and cultivate the quiet spirit of acceptance; to adjust our will to his great rhythm and not waste the strength he has given us fighting against the stream."

Evelyn Underhill
The Fruit of the Spirit
p. 25

"God has so ordered the life of man that each individual has certain definite courses mapped out for his soul's experience. Sooner or later, in this earthly life or in paradise, he must master each assignment.* Our Lord has told us that we are to proceed in the direction of perfection. These lessons are not a matter of intellectual obstacles but rather a series of standards of character based on wise spiritual understanding. Just as our Lord grew in stature and in favor with God and man, so are we charged with a like responsibility for growth. . . . The education of the soul is worked out by God on a fixed, though not legalistic, plan. Where you leave off on this earth, you begin in paradise without interruption. . . . Hence the Prayer Book directs us to pray: 'and we also bless thy Holy Name for all thy servants departed this life in thy faith and fear; beseeching thee to grant them continual growth in thy love and service. . . .' When life on this earth is understood as a school for the development and growth of the soul under the disciplined limitation of the physical body, it somewhat lessens our confusion because of the cruelties which crop out in almost every generation."

Austin Pardue
He Lives
pp. 39-40

"People who love themselves, as they love their neighbor, will endure their own failings as they do their neighbor's with charity. . . . They are not discouraged because they cannot be perfect in one day. They see the slightest imperfection in all its deformity; and they neglect nothing to cure themselves, but they are not fretful in the performance of this duty. . . . Useless murmurs only serve to discourage the soul, to weary, distract, exhaust it, and to prepare for it a sort of despair of being able to hold on its course. When we endure our imperfections, they will, like our trials, become sources of virtues."

Thomas Kepler, ed.
Letters and Reflections of Francois de Fenelon
p. 60

---

*See also 72:2, Thielicke.
**See also 62:1, Father Andrew.

---

*See also 55:1, Dix.

"Mystics tell us that spiritual progress requires moral progress. Indeed there is no point in proclaiming a higher love if ordinary love is lacking; there is no point in aspiring to see God if we persecute our neighbor; there is no point in preaching Christ with hatred or wrath in our hearts. As with so many things human, the lines between spiritual and moral, however, cannot be drawn clearly, and it is too much to expect that complete moral perfection precedes any degree at all of spiritual aspiration. None the less, as Rudolf Steiner says, one step forward spiritually ought to be prepared by three steps forward in the development of character. . . . Our approach to God is through charity, the virtue of self-giving love which finds expression also in a moral and patient encounter with ordinary things."

Patrick Grant
A Dazzling Darkness
p. 112

New Illuminations:

On Doers as Well as Hearers

Matthew 7:16-27; 12:33-35   Luke 6:43-49

" 'It is the man who shares my life and whose life I share who proves fruitful' (John 15:5 — Phillips paraphrase). The Old Testament tree, with its taproot drawing nourishment from the river, is a picture of a Christian, the taproot of whose soul is in contact with Jesus Christ and who is therefore sharing his life, drawing nourishment from him, and bearing his fruit. . . .

"To discover what fruit is, we need to examine the rings on the stump of a felled tree. These rings are called annual rings and reveal the tree's age. But the rings also reveal other information. The narrow rings were formed in years of drought. When the ring is larger, it indicates that the nourishment was ample that year. If only a small amount of nourishment is available, it is used to sustain the life already in the tree. When nourishment is available over and beyond this need, the tree grows in all directions. Hence we notice that some of the annual rings are larger than others. . . . The abundance of nourishment over and above that needed to sustain life and provide growth is transformed into fruit. Fruit is simply excess life. This is an important discovery to which there is a spiritual parallel. When we have partaken of the life of Christ in such abundance that our life sustaining and growth needs are met, the overflow of the love of Christ, the life of Christ, turns into fruit. . . .

"Adversity in our walk with God is part of our maturing process. He allows it to strengthen us and increase our fruit bearing. The experiences which God allows in our lives call for varying degrees of partaking in Christ's life, and we know he will water us every moment. Just as the tree draws additional nourishment in times of stress you can be a living illustration of the tree which spread out its roots by the river. Because it did, its leaf stayed green in heat and drought and it never ceased bearing fruit. This is the goal of every Christian — to be a fruit bearing disciple of Jesus Christ regardless of the adversities which may come his way. . . . Just as the tree draws nourishment to sustain life, so the taproot of the soul, which includes the mind, the affections, and the will, is God's provision for us to sustain our spiritual lives and to grow and to overflow into Christ-like fruit. . . . The first Psalm deals with this topic. 'He, (the fruitful believer) will be like a tree firmly planted by streams of water, which yields its fruit in its season, and its leaf does not wither; and in whatever he does, he prospers.' "

James Downing
Meditation: The Bible Tells You How
pp. 13-19

"Just as the streamlets that flow from the spring are as clear as the spring itself so the works of the soul in grace are pleasing to the eyes of both God and of men since they proceed from the spring of life in which the soul is as a tree planted. . . . When the soul on the other hand, through its own fault, leaves this spring and becomes rooted in a pool of pitch-black evil-smelling water, it produces nothing but misery and filth. It should be pointed out here that it is not the spring or the brilliant sun, which is in the center of the soul, which loses its splendor and beauty; for they are always within it and nothing can take away their beauty. If a thick black cloth be placed over a crystal in the sunshine, it is clear that, although the sun may be shining upon it, its brightness will have no effect upon the crystal. . . .

"I once heard a person I know say that one favor God had granted her was the ability to realize that any good thing that we do has its source not in ourselves but rather in the spring where this tree, which is the soul, is planted and in the sun which sheds its radiance on our work. She says that she saw this so clearly that whenever she did any good thing, she betook herself straightway to its source, realizing that without his help we are powerless. She then went on at once to praise God, and as a rule when she did any good action she never gave a thought to herself at all."

St. Teresa of Avila
Interior Castle
pp. 34-35

"The fruits of the spirit must and will more and more appear if we are unconditionally at the disposal of God. All must be subdued to a law of Charity coming from a spirit which pours itself out in love, first to God, then to all in common. All must be colored by the joy and peace of our spiritual inheritance and carried through with patience, faithfulness, and humble moderation. Saint Paul's list of the fruits of the Spirit (Galatians 5:22-23) represent a progressive series from one point and that one point is Love, the living eternal seed from which all grow. . . .

"The first fruit of his ingrowing presence, the first sign that we are on his side and he on ours, must be at least a tiny bud of this Charity breaking the hard and rigid outline of our life. If, adopting this starting point, we center all on the vivid presence of this growing plant of divine love in the soul, working in secret to transform us without our knowledge, and if we look at St. Paul's list of fruits which shall manifest that presence in our souls, then we see that those fruits fall into three groups. . . . The first result of that living love is joy and peace and therefore a deep delight in God. The second is a long-suffering gentleness, goodness in tranquil and complete acceptance and use of life, of our human relationships and environment. And third will be faithfulness, meekness and temperance — that is, quiet, creaturely acceptance of our own particular limitations and calling.''*

Evelyn Underhill
Fruits of the Spirit
pp. 7-8

"Our Lord tells us that life is a matter of the focus of the lenses of the heart and mind on the right thoughts and actions. Time and again he repeats this point in different ways. . . . And what we believe in our hearts we must have first concentrated upon with our minds, thoughts, and imaginations. This is a simple teaching, isn't it? Perhaps our difficulty is that it is almost too simple. We can't believe that most of the bad fruits that we produce with our lives are the direct results of the bad seeds we have consciously or unconsciously planted through thoughts and attitudes. It is difficult for people to see and believe this, for they insist on blaming their bad fruits on other people's faults or rotten breaks. Even the most scholarly will often fail to examine the seeds planted in their hearts to account for the tragedies that happen in their lives. This is why Jesus warned of the tragedy of spiritual blindness (John 9:41), for there is little hope for a man who refuses to look at his own life with honesty.''

Austin Pardue
The Single Eye
pp. 4-5

"We meet the case in which *one and the same* metaphor is combined with *different* partners: for example, the two kinds of tree and their fruit is linked at one time with weeds that cannot yield good fruit (Matthew 7:16-18), and another time about two kinds of treasure (Matthew 12:33-35); while the Gospel of Thomas combines the metaphor of treasure with the saying about the weeds. And finally, in Luke 6:43-45 all three metaphors are combined.''

Joachim Jeremias
The Parables of Jesus
pp. 91-92

"The passage about those who call on their 'Lord, Lord' in Luke 6:46 is uttered as a warning of Jesus to his contemporary audience. . . . It is not enough to invoke the name of Jesus. Moral behavior must accompany this. It is not

*See also 67:2, Drake.

sufficient to appeal to the Lord and the ones associated with him.''

Rudolf Schnackenburg
God's Rule and Kingdom
p. 236

"Everything depends on action. This is the message of the parable of the two houses. As the torrential autumn rains, accompanied by a storm, test the foundation of the houses, so will the sudden eruption of the Deluge put your lives to the test. The Sermon on the Mount closes with the Final Judgment! (Luke: '. . . and the ruin of that house was great.' Matthew: '. . . and it fell and great was its fall.') Who will survive it? The 'wise man,' i.e. the man who has recognized the eschatological situation.* The Scripture said that only the house built on the sure foundation-stone laid in Zion will abide the onset of the flood (Isaiah 28:15): 'He who believeth will not flee' (Isaiah 28:16). The contemporaries of Jesus taught that the man who knows the Torah and obeys it cannot be moved. Jesus takes them back to the Scripture, and he gives them a new answer to the question drawn from his own profound consciousness of authority: 'Whosoever hears my words and obeys them.' Merely hearing the word of Jesus may lead to perdition. Everything depends upon obedience.''

Joachim Jeremias
The Parables of Jesus
p. 194

"Both men built by a stream, for water is precious in Palestine. The house on the sand probably looked more attractive than the one on the rock, for what was saved on foundations could be spent on decoration. But it was the foundation that really mattered; and when the winter storms came, it was the house on rock that stood firm. . . . Other religions are founded on visions or opinion, but Christianity is based on the historical fact of Jesus Christ. Everything worthwhile has to be tested. In the winter storms of sorrow and failure, it is the life with the firm foundation that survives unharmed.** 'The foundations of God stand sure' (2 Timothy 2:19).''

Mark A. Beaufoy
The Parables
p. 83

*See also 68:1, Jeremias.
**See also 42:1, Kunkel.

"Now God has made a promise saying: 'Yet once more will I make the earth to tremble / Not the earth only — also the heaven' (Haggai 2:6). This means that in this final 'shaking,' all that is impermanent will be removed . . . and only the unshakeable things will remain. Since, then, we have been given a kingdom that is 'unshakeable,' let us serve God with thankfulness in the ways that please him, but always with reverence and holy fear'' (Hebrews 12:26-28).

The Holy Bible
Phillips Translation

"The voice of God shook the earth when the divine law was given on Mount Sinai — a divine law which reinterpreted by our Lord still stands and must be proclaimed. In the new covenant the voice of God shakes heaven as well as earth for the Incarnation at Bethlehem and the Resurrection from the tomb belong to both heaven and earth. . . . Today the earth is being shaken and many things are cracking, melting, disappearing; and it is for us who are Christians to distinguish the things which are shaken and to receive gratefully a kingdom which is not shaken — the kingdom of our crucified Lord. Within this kingdom, we offer to our Lord the worship he can accept. But as we do so, we are never in cozy security. We have an awe in our hearts for we are near to our God, and our God is a blazing fire."

Margaret Duggan, ed.
Through the Year with Michael Ramsey
p. 29

New Illuminations:

On the Heart of Man

Matthew 12:33-35; 15:15-20   Mark 7:17-23   Luke 6:45; 9:47; 12:34

"Jesus explained that just as the character of fruit depends on the character of the tree, so our actions are determined by our hearts. It is out of the heart that the mouth speaks. Similarly, it is not the spots which constitute the measles. The spots are only the symptoms of the disease which has invaded the system. Our sins are symptoms too. They reveal a spiritual disease, a disease which grips the very heart of man. 'The heart is deceitful above all things, and desperately corrupt. Who can understand it?' (Jeremiah 17:9). And Jesus said, 'From within out of the heart of man, come evil thoughts, . . . and they defile a man' (Mark 7:21-23). The Bible is full of references to this infection of human nature."

John Stott
Basic Christianity
p. 76

"God has provided us with a heart, a remarkable equipment that works with automatic precision according to our faith. . . . According to the Old and New Testaments and the liturgies of tradition you will see that it generally refers to that all-powerful organ of the psyche wherein reside the sum total of our attitudes toward life. Those attitudes, insofar as they remain constant in the heart, sooner or later seem to be fulfilled in the objective world. The heart is an impersonal agent that has great capacity for exerting power. It never ceases to assist us in achieving the goal given it by our will and conscious mentality.

". . . It must be remembered that beyond this great and powerful instrument of the heart there is an all-powerful transcendent grace that rules every aspect of life. True prayer approaches God with a heart that is in accord with the will of God as manifested in Jesus Christ."

Austin Pardue
The Single Eye
pp. 114-15

"The heart is taken generally to stand for the 'inner man,' and in particularly for the mind and the will. The Greek word used in the New Testament has a similar range. 'Blessed are the pure in heart' does not then refer to the heart as the seat of the emotions but to the whole interiority of the human conscience and activity. The heart is a symbol of what we are in ourselves, of the source of all our reactions and aspirations. 'Blessed are the pure in heart' will mean something like 'Blessed are those who have a pure source of life in them.' . . .

"Our Lord is very insistent that his kind of morality concerns the heart. He is not satisfied with any merely external morality. It does not impress him that we should just manage to behave ourselves properly. He is not prepared to get excited about any observance of external purity such as that of the Pharisees with all their washing of pots and hands and pans (Mark 7:31). For him the important thing is that it is from the heart that good and evil proceed. . . .

"A very important factor here is what we may call Christian spontaneity. It does not, perhaps, in the last analysis matter all that much what you do with forethought; what really matters, what is really revealing is what you do without thinking, what you do when you do not have time to work out how to respond. It is this that will reveal what kind of a person you are, and that is what is important. . . .

"The way the tree falls so will it lie (Ecclesiastes 11:3). The way it falls is certainly the result of a long process, but its actual falling is a crisis that comes suddenly. There is quite a lot we can do in advance to determine how we shall fall; but all of it is rehearsal for something we will have to do instinctively when the time comes. . . . We must unmuddy the very source of our reactions, so that our spontaneity itself is transformed. This can only come about through the Holy Spirit. . . . It is from within us, deep down within us, that the new life proceeds, and that means that anything which is not an expression of us will not be an expression of God either. But in some sense the converse of this is also true. What is not an expression of God will not be an expression of us. Man is made to express the image and likeness of God, and it is that image and likeness that is restored by grace, by the working of the Holy Spirit. Purity of heart is not just a matter of our own interiority. If we have a clean heart, it is because God has given us a clean heart. It is God dwelling in us that gives us a true interiority which is genuinely ours, but it is not simply our own. . . . God is the heart of our heart. . . . If we can unmuddy the source of life in us, if we can allow God to recreate us from deep within so that there is within us a Christ life as well as our own, then this must inevitably affect the way that we are and the way that we see. There is an interaction between seeing and being. The kind of person that you are affects the kind of world that you see. And conversely, what you see affects the kind of person that you are."

Simon Tugwell
The Beatitudes: Soundings in Christian Traditions
pp. 94-98

"There are at least three ways in which we see. St. Paul tells us that the 'eye has not seen nor the ear heard, neither hath entered into the heart of man, the things which God hath prepared for those that love him' (1 Corinthians 2:9). There we have pointed out three kinds of sight. There are physical vision . . . and mental sight. But there is still a third sight, as when the truth has 'entered into the heart of man'; ['occurred to the human mind' — Goodspeed; 'beyond our imagining' — NEB.] The heart has eyes too. Robert Burns saw in flowers thoughts too deep for tears. Not only did he see flowers with his physical eyes, not only did he understand the growth and culture of the flowers. Also he felt their message. Jesus looked at people and had 'compassion on them.' He saw them with his heart. A person sees God through the eyes of the heart. 'He that has seen me has seen the Father' (John 14:9). . . . Many scholars have studied his words without seeing him. Really to see God in Christ, one must experience him in the heart.* . . .

"One can have an indistinct and distorted picture of God. Sir Galahad and other knights set out in a quest for the Holy Grail. In the story, they found it, but each saw it through the mirror of his own soul. Sir Lancelot saw it but his heart was a sinful heart. He saw the Holy Grail covered with holy wrath and fire. Sir Galahad also saw the grail. He was the knight with the white soul. For him the vision was clear and radiant and glorious. How we see God depends on the condition of our hearts."

Charles L. Allen
God's Psychiatry
pp. 149-51

"Earth's crammed with heaven
And every common bush afire with God;
But only he who sees takes off his shoes —
The rest sit round it and pluck blackberries."*

Elizabeth Browning
"Aurora Leigh"
Book VII, Line 820

---

*See also 97:2, Brand and Yancey.

*See also 57:1, Mascall.

New Illuminations:

On the Healing of the Centurion's Slave

"The centurion was one of those pagans who could no longer be satisfied with polytheistic myths. The wisdom of the philosophers failed to still his religious yearnings, and so he adopted the monotheism of the Jews and the moral law which followed from it. He was numbered among those who feared God; he believed in the one true God and joined in Jewish worship; however, he had not gone over to Judaism completely. His faith, his love, and his veneration for the one true God found expression in his love for God's people and in the care he bestowed on the synagogue which he had built."

Selected

"In the tradition of Jesus' sayings, faith is always linked with power and miracle. As an example, this is very simply expressed in the words of the centurion of Capernium when Jesus agrees to come and help his servant: '. . . just say the word and my servant will be healed' (Luke 7:7).* He knows the power of the word in his military profession. Under the power of authority himself, he also exemplifies that power daily to his subordinates. The emperor in Rome issues an order, and the legions in the remotest parts of the empire move accordingly. And this applies also to the small area under the centurion's command. Thus he knows the power of the word but at the same time experiences its limitations at the sick bed of his servant. His faith is simply in Jesus' power to command. This is what surprises Jesus in this story."

Gunther Bornkamm
Jesus of Nazareth
p. 130

---

*See also 89:1, Monk.

"This centurion was probably in the service of Herod Antipas. As Jews were exempt from military service, he would be a Gentile, though there was no reason to infer that he was a proselyte. For a Jew to enter the house of a Gentile was pollution. Consequently some make Matthew 8:7 read as a question: 'Am I to come and heal him?' But it is much more in harmony with his character to take the words as a direct statement. It is interesting to observe that the only two miracles in which the healing occurs without Jesus seeing the patient are in the cases of two Gentiles — here and in the story of the Syrophoenecian woman (Matthew 15:21-28).

"According to Matthew the centurion comes himself. In Luke, the elders of the Jews act as envoys. Some think that this incident teaches symbolically that Jesus helped the heathen without entering into their world, and that the centurion is the first fruit of the gathering of the Gentiles into the Kingdom of God."

Abingdon Bible Commentary
p. 969

"The theme of the story is faith — the kind of faith that sets no conditions. The choice of a Gentile to illustrate this faith the first time the idea is raised in the Gospel is certainly deliberate. It sets a tone Matthew maintains in the rest of the book: The faith of the Gentiles gives them the title of the true Israel which the Jews have forfeited by unbelief in the Messiah."

John L. McKenzie
The Jerome Biblical Commentary
43:57

New Illuminations:

On Jewish Misconceptions of Messianic Prophecies

Matthew 11:2-19   Luke 7:18-35

"The Jews expected a coming from God of the 'Christ' or 'Messiah,' because their faith had for centuries been looking for this. When he came, he would bring in the Kingdom of God — the state of affairs in which men would acknowledge consistently and in practice that God is their absolute King and his holy will the binding law by which they always act in all things. But the Jews had come to identify the 'Kingdom of God' with their own triumph. They had come to expect that Christ would not only end the disbelief of the rest of the world in the revelation of God made to Israel in the Old Testament, but would save them from the evil of foreign rule, and make them in their turn supreme over their enemies."

Dom Gregory Dix
The Claim of Jesus Christ
pp. 19-20

"The prophets had foretold that he would be a son of David and that his kingdom would last forever. He would come like a king then, gloriously; and he would lead the Jews to victory over their enemies, over the hated Romans in the first place. He would set up his throne in Jerusalem. Palestine would be his kingdom, but as the center of a world empire; and all nations would serve the chosen people. Such were the grandiose expectations based on a too literal interpretation of the figurative language of the prophets, and fomented by the long years of subjection."

Wilfred J. Harrington
Explaining the Gospels
pp. 92-93

"Jesus entirely excluded the national and politico-religious elements from his *basilea* (rule) concept, and, in so doing, repudiated the wide-spread Jewish hope of a splendid Messianic kingdom of Israel. The Gospels clearly reflect the hard struggle Jesus had with these deeply rooted prejudices. Zealots and their admirers paid careful attention to the work of Jesus and made several attempts to enlist the 'prophet from Galilee,' and great wonder worker, in their cause.

"After he had multiplied the loaves, a handful of men conspired to proclaim him as a Messianic king (John 6:15), but he was aware of their intentions and withdrew into the mountains, 'himself alone.' It was no accident that these men were Galileans because Galilee was the home and

fruitful ground of the Zealots' movement. . . .

"Whether and to what extent the crowds accompanying Jesus on his entry into Jerusalem (again according to John 12:12, Galilean pilgrims) intended their welcome as a Messianic and political demonstration is disputed; but that it did arouse such hopes can scarcely be doubted from the acclamations, especially in Mark 11:10: 'Blessed be the kingdom of our father David that cometh.' It was impossible to eradicate this tragic misunderstanding even from the inner group of the apostles . . . both in the closer and wider circle of his disciples. He was frequently forced to distinguish his position from this current notion of the Messias, very fundamentally in his struggle with Satan shortly after his baptism in the Jordan and then repeatedly when dealing with men who seemed to have no other concept of the Messias. This misconception of the purely religious nature of the Messias (Servant of God) led to his estrangement from the masses and was perpetuated in his official indictment posted on the Cross."

Rudolf Schnackenburg
God's Rule and Kingdom
pp. 95-96

"In Luke 7:18-23,* we have an incident and a group of highly significant sayings which show what was passing in the mind of Jesus at the critical moment. The incident calls for the most careful consideration. During this first stage of Jesus' activity, John was lying in Herod's prison. . . . It is not an illegitimate use of the imagination to think of John as wondering why God had allowed him, the Forerunner — as he believed himself to be — to languish month after month in Machaerus, and nothing can be more probable than that he was waiting with burning anxiety for any sign of God's intervention. . . . It is not surprising that he should have sent messengers to Jesus asking whether he was the Coming One whom God had announced, or whether they must still wait. . . .

"As a result of Jesus' period of testing, he had committed himself to leaving it to God to make known to others who and what he himself was. We have spoken of what John must have been feeling, and it was unlikely that Jesus himself was not sharing to the fullest degree in those feelings; hence there must have been strong pressure upon his spirit to say the word that would lighten the burden of uncertainty for John, the 'I am' that he uttered before the high priest at the end (Luke 22:70). It was the return of the testing, but

---

*See also 10:1, Schnackenburg.

he was not to be moved from the path already chosen.* . . . Jesus, in effect, replies to John that the works of power and mercy of which the news has already reached him now in prison are those which the prophets had already declared to be the signs of the coming of the kingdom. But with regard to himself, all that he feels permitted to say is the deliberately veiled utterance, 'Blessed** is he who shall not find a cause of stumbling (or offence) in me,' (Luke 7:23). The implication of the saying is that he knows that there is in the manner of his presentation to Israel indeed a cause of offence, as he proceeds to point out later in the chapter in the contrast which he draws between John and himself. He knows that the carpenter's son from Nazareth in no way corresponds to the supernatural Messiah whom Israel is expecting. But until it pleases the Father to reveal him to those who are prepared to receive the revelation, he cannot give any other answer to John than the veiled intimation which we have here."

S. H. Hooke
The Kingdom of God
pp. 67-68

"Luke 7:22 was the reply Jesus gave to the question asked by the Baptist from his prison. But we are not intended to understand by it that these miracles were performed before the eyes of these messengers so that they might relate to their master what they themselves had just witnessed (v. 21). It is not the primary object of the passage to enumerate the miracles of Jesus. But Jesus here takes up the primeval prophetic images of the Messianic age. . . . The saying is simply a free quotation of Isaiah 35:5-6 combined with Isaiah 16:1 (The preaching of good tidings to the poor); the fact that the mention of the lepers and the dead goes beyond Isaiah 35:5 implies that the fulfilment exceeds all hopes, expectations and promises. It should be observed that Jesus omits the announcement of God's vengeance (Isaiah 35:4). It is his cry of exultation — 'the hour is come, . . . salvation is here, the curse is gone, paradise has come again, the end of the Age is upon us and manifests itself (as the spirit usually does) in a twofold way, by act and by word. This is my message to John, and if you tell him, add blessed is he who believes in spite of all disappointing appearances.' "

Joachim Jeremias
The Parables of Jesus
pp. 115-116

"I have been reading Acts 12. James was killed in prison; Peter was set free. God did not answer the prayers of those who loved James in the same way as he answered those who loved Peter. He could have done so, but he did not. 'And blessed is he whosoever shall not be offended in me.' The words seem to have been written across Acts 12. John must have wondered why the angel was not sent to James, or at least to have been tempted to wonder. Again and again, in Acts, the Lord seems to say those words under his breath, as it were. Let us turn all our puzzles, all our temptations to wonder why, into opportunities to receive the blessing of the unoffended."

Amy Carmichael
Thou Givest . . . They Gather
p. 76

"While the messengers are carrying back to John this answer from Jesus, the latter turns to those who are present and begins an impassioned utterance which reveals what was passing in his mind at this critical moment. . . . Jesus begins by giving his own estimate of John's place in the design of the Kingdom. He says that John is the greatest man born of woman and that with him the prophetic era has reached its close and a new era has begun. Here follow two obscure sayings, both of which have been misinterpreted. The first is usually translated 'but he that is least in the Kingdom of God is greater than he.' This has generally been understood to mean that John stood at the door of the Kingdom but could not enter it, and that the least important member of the church was in a more favored position than John.

"Now it is impossible to think that in the light of such a saying as that which we have in Luke 12:28, a saying which includes Abraham, Isaac, Jacob, and the prophets in the Kingdom of God, that Jesus could have excluded from the Kingdom one whom he has described as 'much more than a prophet.'* Hence it is necessary to seek another interpretation, and the suggestion is here offered that Jesus is speaking of himself in the same cryptic way as in the answer to the messengers of John. The whole tenor of this group of sayings is evidence that Jesus is intensely concerned with the relation between John the Baptist and himself, and that he was conscious of the popular comparison between them. In this saying (v. 28b), Jesus uses the word *mikroteros*, a comparative which our English versions translate by a superlative, 'least'; but if we translate it as a comparative, we may render the saying, 'the one who is less is greater in the Kingdom of God than he,' where 'one who is less' is Jesus' veiled way of referring to himself. . . . He knows that in the kingdom there is only one that is greater than John, and that is the one who is less than John in the popular scale of values, one who has willingly accepted the lowest place (Luke 22:25-27), but who is shortly to be revealed as the Son of Man in power."

S. H. Hooke
The Kingdom of God
pp. 68-70

---

*See also 13:2, Leslie.
**See also 13:1, Penelope.

---

*See also 31:1, Buber.

"John's unexampled moral grandeur is the greatest. But the reign of God belongs to another order of things, to be inaugurated by God's grace. Anyone who is permitted to enter this is placed above all that is earthly. This is to be understood as the divine reign of the future. There would be no question of John's exclusion since the first part refers to him in his earthly life. The second part would express the high value of the reign and kingdom. . . . In human effort and in his prophetic function, John is the greatest. But everyone who is allowed a share in God's kingdom (it is not stated, indeed it is improbable, that John is not of their number) experiences an elevation in grace through God (Luke 14:11) that cannot be achieved by even the mightiest human endeavor."

Rudolf Schnackenburg
God's Rule and Kingdom
p. 134

"Jesus relates his vocation with John the Baptist's quite frankly in verses 29-30: 'All the people that heard him (John), and the tax-collectors, justified God, having been baptised with the baptism of John; but the Pharisees and the lawyers rejected the purpose of God for themselves not having been baptised by John.' Jesus compares the people to children playing in the market place . . . who in their stubbornness and sulkiness cannot be made to do anything. . . . The Baptist was too gloomy for them, an eccentric ascetic, Jesus too worldly — not even giving due regard between the righteous and sinners — John and Jesus, extremes which are to be avoided. Of course the meaning of this parable is not to put a choice between the 'pessimistic' attitude of John and the 'optimistic' one of Jesus before the people, but to link each up with the other: John sent by God in the time of preparation for the end, and Jesus the bringer of the time of rejoicing. Task and destiny unite them both. And so the person and message of John have an important place in Jesus' preaching."

Gunther Bornkamm
Jesus of Nazareth
p. 50

"Vivid as is the description of this everyday street-scene, its application of the taunts which the people levelled at the Baptist and Jesus has never the less been the cause of much perplexity. . . . In my opinion, everything becomes clear if we listen to the suggestion of one who is familiar with Palestinian customs, that attention should be paid to the word 'sit in the market place.' From this it may be inferred that the children described by Jesus have cast themselves in the role of passive spectators and prefer the less strenuous guise of flute players and dirge singers leaving to their playmates the more strenuous exercises. But the latter will not comply and are consequently assailed with reproaches. Thus the dispute is not between the boys and girls sitting by the side of the street. They blame the other children for not falling in with their suggestions. 'And you,' says Jesus, 'are exactly like those domineering and disagreeable children who blame their companions for being spoilsports because they will not dance to their piping. God sends you his messengers, the last messengers to the last generation before the catastrophe, but all you do is to give orders and criticise. . . . You hate the preaching of repentance and you hate the proclamation of the Gospel. So you play your childish game with God's messengers while Rome burns. Can you not see that God is vindicated by his works, that is, that the signs that the decisive moment has arrived are God's vindication?* That the call to repentance and the preaching of the good news are God's very last and final warnings?' "

Joachim Jeremias
The Parables of Jesus
pp. 161-162

*See also 33:1, Bornkamm.

New Illuminations:

On Prophets

Matthew 11:7-11   Luke 7:24-28; 10:24; 16:16

"Inspiration is, as we mean it, any real communication of the Spirit of God Himself to the spirit of man; and the prophet is he through whom at first hand God speaks to us of Himself. The prophet is thus, first, in his own personality representative of man to Godward. . . . Above all else he is prophet, forerunner and preparer of Him who is more than prophet — not only the representative of man to Godward, but no less of God to manward."

William Du Bose
The Gospel According to Saint Paul
p 20

"Biblical leadership always means a process of being led. These men are leaders insofar as they allow themselves to be led, that is, insofar as they accept what is offered them, insofar as they take upon themselves the responsibility for that which is entrusted to them, insofar as they make real that which has been laid upon them from outside of themselves, make it real with the free will of their own being, in the autonomy of their person.*

"So long as we remember this, we can make the lives of these leaders clear. Almost always what we see is the taking of a man out of the community. God lifts the man out of the community, and cuts him off from his natural ties. . . . It is the same story whether it is a wandering over the earth like Abraham's, or a becoming utterly alone in the midst of the people like the prophets'. They are drawn out of their natural community. They fight with it, they experience in this community the inner contradiction of human existence. All this is intensified to the utmost precisely in the prophets. The great suffering of the prophets is the ultimate expression of this condition. . . .

"We must bear in mind that it was in verbal terms the young Jeremiah had received his summons as 'announcer to the nations.' It was there said to him, 'Thou shalt go; whatever I command thee thou shalt speak' (Isaiah 1:6). As the chosen *nabi*, the 'announcer' — that is, the one who utters the speech of heaven. . . .

"The time the prophetic voice calls us to take part in is the time of the actual decision; to this the prophet summons his hearers, not seldom at the risk of martyrdom to himself. . . . The prophet addresses persons who hear him, who should hear him. He knows himself sent to them in order to place before them the stern alternatives of the hour. It is always intended for particular men, to induce them, as directly as if they were hearers, to recognize their situation's demand for decision and to act accordingly. . . .

"The prophet speaks the word that it is his task to speak; he is borne by this task, proceeding from a divine purpose and pointing to a divine goal. The spirit moves him; not only his organs of speech, but the whole man is taken up into the service of the spirit."

Nahum Glatzer, ed.
Martin Buber: On the Bible
pp. 149-50, 175, 180

"You must understand this in the first place, that no prophecy in Scripture can be understood through one's own powers for no prophecy ever originated in the human will, but under the influence of the Holy Spirit men spoke for God" (1 Peter 2:20-21).

The Holy Bible
Phillips Translation

"A prophet is not merely a person who may tell the future or manifest knowledge of one's past or present. Such signs may authenticate the prophet's mission, but they do not constitute the mission itself. . . . We think immediately of such spectaculars when we hear the word prophet. But to see with the inner eye that a person is a prophet is to be aware that he really stands and speaks for God, that he is a unique mediator, that he dwells in the twilight between humanity and divinity. Out of this twilight, he speaks the message of God to mankind. . . .

"Jesus is *the* prophet, *the* mediator without peer. As prophet he is called to speak to the community of believers of all times. . . . The prophet Jesus, as the eternal word, reveals what the Father has willed for us from eternity as our unique life direction. He communicates to our deepest self how to follow him in our own way. The prophet, Jesus, mediates between God's eternal plan over our lives and our living out of this plan in time and space. . . . Listening to the prophet, Jesus, leads to transformation: a change of the person in the inmost being."*

Adrian Van Kamm
The Woman at the Well
pp. 76-77

*See also 30:2, Hooke.

*See also 11:1, Stott.

"In the Creation story in the first chapter of Genesis, we are told that God brought the world into being with his words: 'God said let there be. . . .' The created world is the expression of God's thoughts. So when the prophets of Israel gave God's message to God's people, they prefaced their utterances with the words: 'Thus saith the Lord.' God communicates his mind and purpose through words, and in this sense the whole Bible may be called the Word of God. When we say then that in Jesus God's Word was made flesh, we mean that Jesus is the self-expression of God in a human life, God expressed in human terms. God, who is ultimately incomprehensible, becomes comprehensible in the life and work of Jesus."

William Neil
The Difficult Sayings of Jesus
pp. 101-102

New Illuminations:

On Forgiveness I: Jesus Anointed at Simon's House

Luke 7:36-50

"Simon, like the Pharisees he represented, was a good man in his rigid keeping of the Law. Indeed, preoccupied in his attempts to avoid sinning himself, he had no sympathy for those who were not as strong as he. His unspoken but obvious condemnation of the woman who was a sinner betrayed a basic discontent in his own life, a discontent that grew out of a lack of relatedness with people. . . . This contact with the outside world is understood best in terms of personal responsibility. . . . It is because this 'ought' has an outward reference away from the self to the area of relationship that it is so important. . . . Man's life is to be understood not in terms of life under pressures of the 'I must' that push him in unconscious ways, or of the 'I can' which suggests self-actualization as a possible goal but rather in terms of the 'I ought' which relate man to the external world of value. It was the lack of a sense of personal obligation and responsibility to others that Jesus condemned so specifically not only in Simon, but in the Pharisees as a whole. . . .

"There is no better passage than the account of Simon's encounter with Jesus for seeing the typical method with which Jesus approached the Pharisees. The record in other places is quite clear that open denunciation was directed at the Pharisaical way of life. However, this encounter with Simon is more consistent with the general tenor of Jesus' ministry.* He used the current circumstance to point out the problem in Simon's life, kindly but firmly confronting Simon with the facts of his behavior. First allowing Simon to pass sentence upon himself, Jesus then drove home his point (Luke 7:7-47).

Robert Leslie
Jesus and Logotherapy
pp. 66-69, 72

"Luke 7:47, New English Bible: 'Her great love proves that her many sins have been forgiven; where little has been forgiven, little love is shown.' The 'love' in question is grateful love, or thankfulness, to God for his goodness as the Gospel passage plainly indicates. . . . Jesus' use of the word 'love' is odd in this context. We should have expected something like: Which of the two men will be most grateful? And indeed linguistic experts tell us that there is no word in Hebrew, Aramaic, or Syriac for 'thank' or 'thankfulness.' The word 'love' is used instead. What Jesus meant therefore was: Which of the two men will feel the deepest thankfulness? This makes more sense both of the parable and its

application in the case of the woman, for it indicates that throughout this passage, and especially the saying we are considering, it is not 'love' that Jesus is speaking about but 'gratitude.'

"Jesus in his sermon in the synagogue must have declared God's forgiveness for all penitent sinners. The woman had taken this to herself and had sought out Jesus, overwhelmed with thankfulness. Her deep gratitude as evidenced by her actions was proof that her sins had been forgiven. Simon, the virtuous Pharisee knew less of God's forgiving love than the poor prostitute, who was now closer to God than this righteous ecclesiastic. Her thankfulness was incomparably greater because the burden of her many sins had been lifted from her shoulders. The Pharisee, who thought that he had done little or nothing that needed God's forgiveness, had no sense of gratitude. He may have kept all the commandments, but if he was thankful to God, it may have been thankfulness that he was not like the rest of men.

"The climax of the incident is that Jesus gives the woman formal absolution, a confirmation that her past sins have been blotted out (Isaiah 43:25). . . . The whole passage shows us in a real-life situation the value our Lord placed on true gratitude to God for his gift of new life and, by contrast, his disapproval of rigidly moral behavior which leaves little room for the warmth of human feeling and compassion for the unfortunate.''

William Neil
The Difficult Sayings of Jesus
pp. 67-69

[There is a prophecy of Isaiah which is being fulfilled for them:] "You will hear and hear but never understand; you will look and look but never see. For this people has grown gross at heart; their ears are dull, and their eyes are closed [Simon]. Otherwise, their eyes might see, their ears hear, and their heart understand, and then might turn again and I would heal them [the sinful woman].''

The New English Bible
Matthew 13:14-15

"The woman's recognition of her failure to meet her own needs had opened her heart, made her available to God's mercy. 'The mercy of God is the tenderness which by the

---

*See also 97:2, Leslie.

infinitely mysterious power of pardon turns the darkness of our sins into the light of God's love' (Thomas Merton).''

Monica Furlong
Merton
p. 232

"Was much forgiven the sinful woman because she loved much? Or has she loved much because much has been forgiven her? The Greek text of Christ's statement admits of both interpretations. Both express a profound truth. The first makes pardon a reply to love. Even here love, which calls for a pardon, is already a grace which comes from the Savior's initiative. In the second interpretation, where pardon engenders love, the Savior's initiative remains equally sovereign; it provokes the first movement of repentance without which there can be no forgiveness, then forgiveness itself which ratifies this repentance, and finally love, which is the given soul's response.''

Monk of the Eastern Church
Jesus: A Dialogue with the Savior
p. 88

"Charity does not demand that we should not see the faults of others; we must, in that case, shut our eyes. But it commands us to avoid attending unnecessarily to them, and that we be not blind to the good while we are so clear sighted to the evil that exists. We must remember, too, God's continued kindness to the most worthless creature and think how many causes we have to think ill of ourselves; and finally we must consider that charity embraces the very lowest human being. It acknowledges that, in the sight of God, the contempt that we indulge for others has in its very nature a harshness and an arrogance opposed to the spirit of Jesus Christ. The true Christian is not insensible to what is contemptible, but he bears with it.''

Thomas Kepler, ed.
Letters and Reflections of Francois de Fenelon
p. 135

"The act of repentance facilitates forgiveness. Sorrow and regret lead the way to the triumph of reconciliation. How quickly we stretch out our hand when we sense the incident is thoroughly regretted by the offender. Can any of us remain unmoved when confronted by remorse? . . .

"In forgiving everyone, Christ remains our inspiration. As the redeemer of the world, he offered forgiveness to the apostles who failed him, the Pharisees who rejected him, the people who condemned him, and even to the Romans who nailed him to the tree. We, who are born into Christ, are bound with the same measure. If our forgiveness becomes selective, if we choose or attempt to exclude, we turn this divine mandate into a manipulated decision.

"Many are the ways in which we hurt each other, but there is no better way to heal the distress than by forgiveness. Divine forgiveness is God's contribution to make human weakness bearable. Human forgiveness is our contribution to make future goodness possible.''*

John Walchars
Voices on Fire
p. 138

———————
*See also 59:3, Underhill.

New Illuminations:

On the Kingdom of God I: His Rule and Gracious Action

Matthew 4:23; 13:33, 44-46	Mark 1:14-15; 4:26-29	Luke 8:1, 4-15; 13:18-21

"What is meant by the 'kingdom of God?' To Jesus' first hearers the word rule, or kingdom, of God was not as it is for most people today a vague or empty term. Yahweh's kingdom is praised in the Psalms. Every year the ancient Israelites celebrated in their worship Yahweh's enthronement, his ascending to be king of all nations, his victory over all his enemies. . . . The acknowledgment of Yahweh's reign is at the same time an expression of hope. . . . Upon this hope is the certainty that God is the Lord of this puzzling world, and will not always remain afar off but will reveal himself and vindicate his word. It is this certainty which makes the present lack of fulfilment the real difficulty for Jewish faith and invests the hope of the coming of God's kingdom with extreme tension.*

"Jesus' message lives by this same certainty. For him, too, God's kingdom means God's future and victory, overcoming the powers of the devil, a shift from this aeon to the next. . . . Blessed are you! means God's Kingdom comes to you. All the beatitudes are directed toward the coming Kingdom of God and are embraced in one idea — that God wills to be with us all, in as manifold and individual a way as our needs are manifold and individual. With special clarity, therefore, these very words show that the Kingdom of God cannot be described as an earthly thing or a distant wonderland for it is a happening, an event, the gracious action of God."

Gunther Bornkamm
Jesus of Nazareth
pp. 64-67, 77

"Jesus came among men announcing the Kingdom or Kingly Rule of God; that is the theme of one parable after another. . . . He is the Messiah of the reconstituted Israel in which the people of all nations are to find their home. In his teachings he set before the people and his disciples in the plainest terms the spiritual demands of the divine Kingdom. It meant not mere obedience to the precepts of the Law, as the scribes interpreted it, but an entire self-surrender to God. It meant renouncing not merely the sins of the flesh and other transgressions of the ten commandments but also self-righteousness which, in the last resort, is a worship of self and a refusal to worship God."

A. G. Hebert
Scripture and the Faith
p. 47

---
*See also 30:3, Jeremias.

"We can find the key to Jesus' whole ministry in his saying: 'The Kingdom of God is among you.' From his baptism onward, our Lord regarded himself as God's agent, not only proclaiming that the new age had come, but embodying it in his own words and actions. Jesus was himself the Kingdom of God, as Origen said, summoning men to accept the sovereignty of God over their lives, teaching them in the Sermon on the Mount, in his parables, and elsewhere the new way of life that God expected from those who would be citizens of his kingdom. . . . Jesus did not think of the kingdom of God as some utopian society that men would build by their own efforts with a little help from God. This would be in P. T. Forsyth's words: 'A kingdom of man with God to serve in it, rather than a kingdom of God with man to serve in it.' "

William Neil
The Difficult Sayings of Jesus
pp. 86-87

"The Kingdom of God in the teaching of Jesus is a spiritual conquest of men and women. It also has material benefits since the King's subjects are the Father's children, and his sovereignty and paternity alike guarantee freedom from anxiety over food and clothing and the necessities of life. The heathen nations go in search of these things, but God's children possess them already for they have entered his Kingdom. The heavenly Father, for the final coming of whose Kingdom we pray, can be trusted to supply our daily bread. Nevertheless the Kingdom is not 'from this world' (John 18:36). The phrase, writes William Temple in his *Readings in St. John*, 'represents both origin and character due to origin.' Its sphere is indeed this world, but its origin is divine and its character is the spread of the truth by which men are set free. It is not imperialistic. It has no territorial rights or ambitions. It works like leaven, conquering not by force from without but by grace from within (Matthew 13:33). It is something through and through spiritual. It is a personal relation between God and the individual human being. . . .

"Jesus clearly taught that the extension of the Kingdom depended upon the response which men and women make to its moral demands. The parables collected in the thirteenth chapter of Matthew's Gospel illustrate this growth from different aspects. If the mustard seed declares the extensive, the leaven declares the intensive development of the Gospel. But in the Parable of the Sower, the yield of the crop depends upon the condition of the soil. The birds, the sun, and the thorns can prevent the seed from bearing fruit. If the Parable of the Sower portrays some in whose lives the

Kingdom is never properly received, the Parables of the Treasure and the Pearl describe those who count everything else loss in comparison with the great gain of obtaining the Kingdom. The Kingdom is 'given' (Luke 12:32) — in order to be received or rejected.''

John Stott
Men With a Message
pp. 9, 19

"The parable of the seed developing with its inner vitality is a parable about God's reign, though the introductory formula is not explicit. At the conclusion, the harvest shows that the Kingdom of God is made manifest. Till then, it is emphasized, the seed is ripening 'of itself,' that is without the assistance of the farmer, 'whilst he knoweth not.' This negative aspect that no human co-operation is required and even that man has not the capacity to co-operate demands the positive sense that God is at work to bring about his perfect freedom. The power of growth in God's rule must be supernatural. What is brought out in the parable is precisely the supernatural character of the perfect reign of God which is approaching irresistibly.

". . . . The countryman waits quietly because he knows that the harvest certainly will come. Further, the individual phases of the development, blade, ear, full corn, are not stressed; they are merely descriptive details in the process by which the 'earth of itself' brings forth the fruit. This rules out the interpretation of God's reign as partly an earthly process. The language itself fixes our attention immediately upon the harvest. . . . The parable's main theme is the 'mystery of the reign of God' in itself, namely its concealed presence which by God's power will one day, gradually but inevitably, develop to its manifest glory.''*

Rudolf Schnackenburg
God's Rule and Kingdom
pp. 153-54

"Because the Messiah presides over the Messianic Kingdom, we shall only learn to understand it as we understand

---

*See also 91:2, Schnackenburg.

him. Just as he was misunderstood so the Kingdom has been misunderstood. St. Peter believed in the Messiah, but he found it very hard to believe in a suffering Christ. He had to learn the character of the King, and what a long, long time it has taken us to learn the character of the Kingdom! It is the representation in this world of the kingship of Christ, a kingship of wounds, not weapons; of love, not force; of peace, not strife.''

Harry C. Griffith, ed.
*A Gift of Light: A Collection
of Thoughts from the Writings of Father Andrew*
p. 67

"The Church and the Kingdom of God are not identical, but it is one of the functions of the Church to be the scene where man is confronted by the claims of the Kingdom of God, that is, by God himself and his moral demands as sovereign over human life.''

Lewis J. Sherrill
The Struggle of the Soul
p. 98

"The coming of the Kingdom* does not necessarily mean the triumph of this visible Church. . . . It means something far more deep, subtle, and costly: the reign of God, the all-demanding and all-loving in individual hearts, overruling all the adverse powers which dominate human life. . . . It means the reordering, the quieting, the perfecting of our turbulent interior life, the conquest of our rampant individualism by God's supernatural action, and that same supernatural action gradually making each human life what it is meant to be — a living part of the body of Christ.''**

Evelyn Underhill
Abba
pp. 34-35

---

*See also 59:2, Lewis.
**See also 75:2, Van Kamm.

New Illuminations:

On Parables

Matthew 13:34-36	Mark 4:34	Luke 8:9

"Rabbis relate parables in abundance, to clarify a point in their teaching and explain the sense in a written passage. . . . But great skill in interpretation was required by them and the contemporary scribes as practiced in their allegorical expositions, in order to recognise a deeper meaning behind every single expression and every letter. Often enough Jesus' parables, too, have been interpreted, since the earliest days of the church, as such deep allegories and thereby deprived of their real simple meaning. Originally they have nothing to do with allegories."

Gunther Bornkamm
Jesus of Nazareth
pp. 69-70

" 'Parable' is very difficult to define because the term is applied to many different kinds of literary pieces: a solemn sentence, counsel, short image, and stories. Perhaps it is best to conclude that a parable is a story illustrative of some teaching of Jesus. The parable is more than a 'mere analogy' because an 'inward affinity exists between the natural order and the spiritual order; . . . the Kingdom of God is intrinsically *like* the processes of nature and of the daily life of men' (C. H. Dodd, *The Parables of the Kingdom*, 10)."

Carroll Stuhlmueller
The Jerome Biblical Commentary
44:78

"The parables, like the miracles, were part of a vigorous assault made by God's dominion as it entered time. Some parables, like that of the Good Samaritan, were a blistering attack on the established religious policy. Others, like the Tenants in the Vineyard, were threats of imminent judgment on the Jewish authorities. Still others, like the Sower and the Mustard Seed, were an apologia for the slowness and insignificant results of Jesus' own ministry in Galilee. . . . Throughout the Gospel we hear the personal appeal of Jesus: 'He who has ears to hear, let him hear.' "*

David M. Stanley
The Jerome Biblical Commentary
78:138

"What we have to deal with is a conception which is essentially simple but involves far reaching consequences. It

is that the parables of Jesus are not — at any rate primarily — literary productions nor is it their object to lay down maxims (no one would crucify a teacher who told pleasant stories to enforce prudential morality), but each of them was uttered in an actual situation of the life of Jesus, at a particular and often unforeseen point. Moreover, as we shall see they were preponderantly concerned with a situation of conflict. They correct, reprove, attack. For the greater part, though not exclusively, the parables are weapons of warfare. Every one of them calls for an immediate response.

"The recognition of this fact indicates the nature of our task. Jesus spoke to flesh and blood; he addressed himself to the situation of the moment. Each of his parables has a definite historical setting. Hence to recover this is the task before us. . . . Similarly we will understand rightly each individual parable if we can reconstruct for ourselves the precise situation in which Jesus uttered it."

Joachim Jeremias
The Parables of Jesus
pp. 21-22

"If we think of such well known parables as those of the prodigal Son or the Good Samaritan, it seems pretty obvious that their purpose is to get across the particular point Jesus wished to make, by telling a simple story to illustrate it. . . . In the story of the Good Samaritan, Jesus is replying to the question, Who is my neighbor? by telling a simple tale which shows that our neighbor is anyone who needs our help. Instead of delivering a sermon on caring for our fellow men, Jesus chooses to make the lesson sink home by couching it in the form of a memorable illustration — an earthly story with a heavenly meaning. . . .

"The details of the parable of the Sower are familiar. Much of the seed was wasted. . . . Despite all of this some of the seed fell into good soil and when this happened, the yield far outweighed the losses and wasted effort. . . . It would be clear to the listeners on reflection that Jesus was talking about his own message, that the rule of God on earth had now begun. Despite opposition and much discouragement, he was calling on his hearers to have faith that from small beginnings God could bring a bumper harvest. Those who responded to God's call through Jesus to turn their backs on the past and embrace the new life were worth more than all the obdurate and indifferent who brushed it aside."

William Neil
The Difficult Sayings of Jesus
pp. 28-30

*See also 57:2, Jeremias.

"Jesus' parables are the preaching itself and not merely serving the purpose of a lesson which is quite independent of them. . . . Jesus' parables aim, as all parables do, at making things clear. They make use of all that goes on in the life and nature of man, his acts and his sufferings. . . . And yet all of this does not make the parables what they are. They become parable and preaching only by the fact that the kingdom of God, which is by no means familiar and commonplace, is related thereby to everyday life. . . .

"The mystery the parables contain is nothing but the hidden dawn of the kingdom of God itself amidst a world which to human eyes gives no sign of it. And this must surely be heard, believed and understood — not against a background of tradition or theory, but by the hearer in his actual world. This is what is spoken of in the two parables of the mustard seed and the leaven. The greatest of all, hidden in the least significant of all, is effective even in the smallest thing. What a contrast between the beginning and the end! More recent interpreters have rightly found the real point of these parables is this very aspect. . . . The hearer is directed to his daily experience, to the seed and the fruit, the sowing and the reaping, the fig tree and the vineyard, the farmer and the housewife. Of course he knows, when he so much as lifts his eyes, that the beginning and end, however incomprehensible the end may be, stand in a very definite relationship, one to another. . . . Thus our task is to understand the present in which the coming event always finds its beginning, the present in its apparent insignificance. For God's kingdom comes in concealment, even in spite of failure."

Gunther Bornkamm
Jesus of Nazareth
pp. 69-72

"Our Lord told stories that were so vivid that they became living pictures, not easily erased from the imagination of his listeners. Those who brooded over them were inspired with new visions, possibilities, and hopes. Their feelings and emotions were set on fire. . . . He said unto them, 'Hearken, behold.' He told them to look, see, visualize, imagine, and picture the story. Make it real, live it. Sense it, feel it, hear it, touch it. He knew that once they understood him by faith, he could trust them to approach him with reason. . . . He usually took men where they were in religion. Instead of beginning with sacrifices and crosses he introduced them to his Father with feedings and healings. . . . Had they come to him on a rationalistic basis first, love would have degenerated into a mere analytical critique. We knew that in religion a man must first seek the gift of faith, and once he has it, he can be trusted to use such intellectual powers as he might possess. Love and understanding are not to be approached with calculus and a slide rule. . . . 'Hearken; behold.' He did not say, 'Listen, I want you to think about God.' He says, 'Attention, look at this picture I am going to paint for you.' "

Austin Pardue
The Single Eye
pp. 56-59, 75

New Illuminations:

On the Inner and Outer Circles of Followers

Matthew 13:10-17   Mark 4:10-12, 33   Luke 8:9-10, 18   John 1:9-12

"It comes as a shock to seem to be told that Jesus' purpose in using parables was to confuse and mystify people. . . . Whatever else they were intended to do, parables were never, in Jesus' mind or in Old Testament times, intended to be misunderstood as Mark 4:12 seems to suggest. They were to make people think. . . . Jesus addresses the inner circle of those who had responded to the call — the Twelve and other committed followers. They had come to understand at least something of the message of God's love and forgiveness. . . . They had grasped the secret of the kingdom of God and were ready to receive further instruction in discipleship (Matthew 13:12a).

"For the rest, 'those who are outside,' the message must be presented in parables, in simple terms which they can understand, in the hope that they, too, in time might come to accept God's challenge. . . . If they were not spiritually deaf and blind and, moreover, dull witted, they would respond to God's word and receive his forgiveness (Mark 4:12b). So, far from trying to befog his hearers as this saying would seem to suggest, Jesus is putting his finger on a problem that still faces the church today."

William Neil
The Difficult Sayings of Jesus
pp. 28-30

"In the parables a mystery does lie hidden. The Gospels call it the 'mystery of the Kingdom of God,' which is given to the disciples to recognize but not to those 'outside.' Unquestionably the thought is here distorted by dogma (teaching and propaganda of the early church). For the saying maintains that Jesus spoke in parables to the people, in contrast to his way of speaking to his disciples, with the specific intention of not being understood by the people. But this interpretation of the parables as designed to alienate, breaks down in every parable of Jesus, and conflicts with Mark's own words at the end of his chapter of parables, a statement which alone fits the case: 'With many such parables he spoke the word to them (the people) as they were able to hear it' (Mark 4:33)."

Gunther Bornkamm
Jesus of Nazareth
p. 71

"Jesus distinguishes between people who hear the parables with understanding and those who hear them without understanding. He does not say that the parables represent the inferior method of teaching for inferior people, while the superior hearers, the disciples would be informed in a more abstract, intellectual way. The simple mind of the average hearer can receive the parable only as an interesting story; whether he will subsequently forget it or realize in later years its hidden meaning is not yet decided."

Fritz Kunkel
Creation Continues
pp. 189-90

"In Mark 4:11 (Luke 8:10) we find an antithesis between the disciples of Jesus ('to you') and those who are 'outside.' 'To you has God given the secret of the Kingdom of God.' This is surely nothing less than a cry of exultation! God's gift is for the disciples. Moreover 'the secret of the Kingdom of God' which constitutes God's gift must not be understood as implying general information about the Kingdom of God, but as the singular shows, a particular piece of the information, the recognition of its dawn in the present. This recognition is wholly the result of God's grace. . . .

"Mark 4:11b must be translated: 'But to those who are without, all things are imparted in riddles,' i.e., they remain obscure for them. In order to understand the 'in order that' clause of Mark 4:12 which follows, it is imperative that the words coming after it should be regarded as a free quotation from Isaiah 6:9f. Hence, 'in order that' is not expressing the purpose of Jesus but that of God: in the case of divine decisions, purpose and fulfillment are identical. . . . Hence we must translate Mark 4:11f: 'To you has God given the secret of the Kingdom of God; but to those who are without everything is obscure, in order that they (as it is written) may "see and yet not see, may hear and yet not understand, unless they turn and God will forgive them." ' Hence we conclude that the logion is not concerned with the parables of Jesus but with his preaching in general. The secret of the present Kingdom is disclosed to the disciples, but to the outsiders the words remain obscure because they do not recognize his mission nor repent. Thus for them the terrible oracle of Isaiah 6:9f is fulfilled. Yet a hope still remains: 'if they repent God will forgive them.' The last words afford a glimpse of God's forgiving mercy. . . .

"Mark, misled by the Greek catchword which he erroneously understood as 'parable,' inserted our logion into the parable-chapter. If however Mark 4:11f has no reference whatever to the parables of Jesus, then the passage affords no criterion for the interpretation of the parables, nor any warrant for seeking to find in them by means of an allegorical interpretation some secret meaning hidden from the outsiders. On the contrary it asserts that the parables too, like all the words of Jesus, announce no special 'secrets,' but only the one 'secret of the Kingdom of God,' to wit, the secret of its present dawning in the works and words of Jesus.''*

Joachim Jeremias
The Parables of Jesus
pp. 16-18

"I wonder if we have caught the sadness that hangs over the story of the sower. Jesus spoke this parable at a high point in his life and activity. The people were flocking to him in great numbers. Had Jesus been a man like others,

he would have pointed to the crowds and said to his companions, 'The dikes are bursting in these hearts. I came to kindle a fire and look how it is burning already!' But nothing like this happens. The very parable which seems to make eternity visible and near is for many others an iron curtain which leaves them groping blindly and helplessly at the gate of the eternal secret. . . . Is it so surprising that the Savior should be sad when he sees the fate of the word of God? 'The ones along the path are those that have heard, then the devil comes and takes away the word from their hearts that they may not believe and be saved.' ''**

Helmut Thielicke
The Waiting Father
pp. 52-53

---

*See also 47:1, Bornkamm.
**See also 14:1, Mascall.

New Illuminations:

On the Application of the Seed and the Soil

Luke 8:4-8, 11-15

"The consummation of all the cruelty and folly of waste was reached in the story of Jesus. He himself had noted how in the sowing of seed only perhaps a fourth part fell on good ground and brought forth fruit; the rest was virtually wasted. Whoever reads to the end of the Gospel narrative comes to realize with a shock that it is He Himself, the divine Word, Who is wasted, thrown away, trampled under foot, crushed, crucified. The supreme irony is that when God offers men His greatest Gift for their greatest good they simply waste Him and throw Him away.... We shall not understand the cross, but we dare not dismiss it, for it touches life at its basest and at its noblest points. Christ made of man's foulest crime the revelation of God's greatest glory."

Douglas Webster
In Debt to Christ
pp. 22, 25

"A person who never allows himself to be plowed and opened up and never waits for what God drops into his furrow, that person has already lost the game at the crucial point.... If we really want to understand what this picture of the birds means to say to us we must first get it straight that when the Word of God fails to take root in us this is because there are other forces in the field that destroy the divine seed and prevent it from germinating.

"... The devout of all times have been aware of these sources of domineering appeal and therefore mobilized *other* forces against them. Above all, they meditated upon Scriptures and prayed.... To meditate means to ponder the word of God in our hearts, contemplate it, think about it and constantly apply it to ourselves. Then and only then can these words become a power of thought which is able to do battle with the other forces.... This, precisely this, is what the birds are that fly in and keep pecking away. This is the devil which creates a false whirlpool within us. Martin Luther said: 'We can't stop the birds from flying over our heads, but we must take heed lest they build their nests in our hair.' Once they feel at home and

get a foothold in our heads or even in our hearts the seed is done for."

Helmut Thielicke
The Waiting Father
pp. 54-56

"The problem, of course, is not the understanding of the four groups of hearers; it is the understanding of our own inner situation. If our mind is a stony place, our only concern is to rid ourselves of the stones. The simple question, 'What are the stones in our soul?' may start a self-analysis which will occupy us for weeks and lead to extremely disagreeable though helpful discoveries....

"If we decide that thorns are in the way we will have to clear the soil, like pioneers who settle in a new land; and if our soul is like the wayside, we simply have to plow and build a new path skirting the field. In all three cases the soil can be prepared by human effort. The result of the parable, therefore, is a new impulse to religious self-education.... The very fact that the new impulse arises shows the dynamics of the seed-word, and the discovery that we are not able to 'hear the word' leads us to the discovery of the obstacles which prevented our hearing it; and this in turn will lead to the discovery of new means and ways to remove them. There is no end to the discoveries if the creative meditation has been started by the first vague hearing of the word."

Fritz Kunkel
Creation Continues
pp. 190-91

"The fact is that every individual has all four kinds of soil within him.... We dare not leave this rather grim hour of admonition without resolving to enter into judgment with ourselves and sternly asking ourselves: to what birds, what thorns, what superficiality am I exposing the

Word of God in my life; what are the threatening forces and the roots of peacelessness in my life?''*

[Thielicke shows how Luke has related the seed that falls on the traveled path to Jesus' claim that only "those who hear the word and do it are members of his family" (Luke 8:21).] "The good soil which yields a hundred fold are the people who not only 'hear' but also 'hold fast' to the Word. Hearing is easy. But to hold onto the word and budget one's life upon it, this is the great test. . . . Never will I get into the clear with God and never will

I have peace if I only hear and go on hearing, if I reflect and go on reflecting upon it. God must be obeyed if he is to be understood.* I must reckon with God — reckon with him and his promises in utter realism — if I want to bring him into my life."

Helmut Thielicke
The Waiting Father
pp. 58, 59

———————

*See also 57:2, Harton.

———————

*See also 39:1, Kunkel.

New Illuminations:

On the Disciples' Stewardship of the Light

Matthew 5:14-16   Mark 4:21-25   Luke 8:16-18

"The light was a metaphor used for Israel and for the Law. Now the Church is to be the 'light of the world' and 'the city set on the hill' (perhaps suggesting Jerusalem). God is lighting a lamp by means of the teaching Jesus is giving his disciples, and the purpose of this lamp is to give light to the whole world. . . . This light will be displayed to all when Jesus sends his disciples to all 'nations.' The light will be seen not so much in the words of the disciples as in doing 'the will of my Father who is in heaven.' "

D. E. Nineham
Saint Matthew
pp. 84-85

"St. Luke explains that without the light of faith, the signs of Jesus and his amazing wisdom will be wrapped in darkness. So in 8:16, he was speaking to the disciples about the spread of the Gospel."

Carroll Stuhlmueller
The Gospel of Saint Luke
p. 97

"Each of us has a particular possession of light that no one else can have, and if we refuse to take our possession, everyone else will suffer. In every saint's life there is a particular personal edition of the possession of light, and until that is partaken of with full-hearted confidence, all others suffer. The difficulty is that the round person wants to be in the square hole; this shows how we become deflected from the light that is in Christ. There is a possession of light that the Spirit distributes to each one according to the perfect wisdom of God. As we participate in the light and the Son of God is manifested in us in our particular setting, there will be marvelous blessing to all the people round about. The test for the apostles and teachers is not that they talk wonderful stuff, not that they are able to expound God's word, but that they edify the saints (Ephesians 4:11-12)."

Oswald Chambers
Our Brilliant Heritage
p. 42

"The coming of the light into darkness was of course no mere 'flash in the pan.' For wherever men accepted Christ as the very nature of God expressed in human terms, the same love, the same power of reconciliation and reconstruction became immediately active. Christ himself said of the man who believes in him that 'greater works . . . shall he do; because I go unto the Father.' There is, I think, no reason to visualize what we call the Incarnation as a sudden flash of light to be succeeded thereafter by nothing but inferior reflections. It is true that Jesus called himself the 'light of the world' (John 8:12), but using the identical words, he also called his followers 'the light of the world' (Matthew 5:14). And we must not through any false modesty deny the import of his promise when speaking of his faithful follower — 'the works that I do shall he do also' (John 14:12).

"Part of the astounding humility of the love of God lies not only in his human level of approach to coming down to where we are, but in his perfect readiness to use ordinary people like ourselves as channels and instruments in our day and generation in the vast sweep of his unchanging purpose. We may think it is a proper modesty on our part to assume that all work done in His Name must always be inferior in quality and effect to his own work done upon this earth. But I believe that by such thinking we are really belittling his amazing magnanimity and even cramping the operation of his Spirit because we have not properly grasped the generosity of his purpose. 'Beloved,' wrote St. John, '*now we are children of God*' (1 John 3:2). This is the kind of truth that we take as being only figuratively true, whereas I am quite certain it is nothing less than absolute fact, far more true indeed than any 'assured result' of scientific investigation. Such a high calling must simultaneously make us swell with pride and fall on our knees in humility."

J. B. Phillips
Making Men Whole
pp. 37-38

" 'Ye are the light of the world.' No personal pride, no individual superiority is meant. . . . 'Ye are the light' must not be repeated by his followers in the form of 'I am the light.' This latter statement is reserved for Jesus alone. . . . The fact remains, however, that one who burns cannot conceal the flame. He can extinguish it, for instance by pride, but as long as he is burning, he will set others afire. His influence will spread."

Fritz Kunkel
Creation Continues
p. 69

"Our Lord was teaching us one of the laws of his mind. If we disbelieve in the kingdom of God and doubt our power to conquer in the strength of Christ within us, we make ourselves weak; that 'have not' in our consciousness actually prevents our 'having' in our experience. If we only believe truly and triumphantly that the Kingdom of God is within us, we shall begin to find that it is coming about all around us*. . . . We cannot enjoy circumstances of peace if we have not peace within us; we cannot enjoy riches if we have not true riches within us; we cannot enjoy freedom if our spirit is not free."

Harry C. Griffith, ed.
A Gift of Light: A Collection
of Thoughts from the Writings of Father Andrew
p. 46

"The parable of the light is a parable of the preaching of the Gospel and our response to it. . . . Jesus is speaking of spiritual matters, not material things. We do not need our Lord to tell us that wealth begets wealth, by compound interest or shrewd investment. We can see this for ourselves. What we do need to be told is that we grow in our understanding of our faith and in God's promises only if we make the most of the insights we have received. It is in this sense that the man who has will be given more.* We have to deepen our knowledge of God and enrich our spiritual life, by using the means of grace that God provides. . . .

"But there is another terrifying side to the picture: '. . . the man who has not will forfeit even what he has.' Our knowledge of God will become a dead thing if through apathy or indifference we cease to listen to what he is saying to us. We inflict it upon ourselves. Jesus offers us a choice — the way of life or the way of death. It is not a choice that we have to make once for all. It is a choice that we have to make every day of our lives as we respond, or fail to respond, to the challenge of the Gospel."

William Neil
The Difficult Sayings of Jesus
pp. 32-33

---

*See also 91:2, Schnackenburg.

*See also 98:2, Neil; 55:2, Kunkel.

New Illuminations:

On the Stilling of the Tempest

Matthew 8:23-27   Mark 4:35-41   Luke 8:22-25

''The Lord Jesus was in the midst of that tempest, so he understands when we are beset by tempests. . . . 'But he was asleep.' The ship may be covered with waves, fears may cover one's heart, like waves washing over it and chilling all within it; but if *he* be there, and at rest in our midst, what does it matter? 'Why are ye fearful?' 'Where is your faith?' If he sees no reason for fear why should we? It helps us to remember that every test is a trust. Our Lord trusts us to stand the test and not give way. It helps too to remember that no test lasts forever. Hear what comfortable words our Father says to you about your soul which he has redeemed: 'I, the Lord, do keep it night and day' (Isaiah 27:3). . . .

'' 'In the hour of Job's deepest despondency, he wished to be as when the intimacy of God was over his tent.' He did not know that even then he was very near to a more wonderful intimacy than ever before. Is it not joyful to think that it may be so with us?''

> Amy Carmichael
> *Thou Givest . . . They Gather*
> pp. 77-80

''What can prevent you from praying is that you allow yourself to be in the storm, or you allow the storm to come inside you instead of raging around you. You may remember the story in the Gospel of the storm on the sea of Galilee: Christ asleep in the boat and the storm raging around. At first the apostles work hard and hopefully in order to survive. Then at a certain moment, they lose heart; and the storm that was outside comes inside — the storm is within them too. And then they turn to Christ and do what we very often do with God: we look at God in time of stress and tragedy, and we are indignant that he is so peaceful. . . . Instead of coming to God and saying, 'You are peace, you are the Lord. Say a word and things will come right,' they and we shake him out of his sleep and say, 'Don't you care that we are perishing?' . . . Christ reacts; he gets up and says, 'Men of little faith!' And brushing them aside he turns toward the storm; and projecting his inner stillness, his harmony and peace on the storm, he says, 'Be still, be quiet,' and everything is quiet again.*

''This we can do and we must be able to do it. Learn to be still, immobile in the present, face to face with the Lord. If you are silent, you can rest in the 'eye' of the cyclone or the hurricane, in the calm there, but leaving the storm around you to rage, while you are where God is, at the only point of total stability. But this is not a point where nothing happens. It is the point where all the conflicting tensions meet and are counterbalanced by one another and are held in the powerful hand of God.''

> Anthony Bloom
> *Beginning to Pray*
> pp. 57-58

''It was possible for Matthew to reinterpret the story about the calming of the storm as the example and the symbol of the following of Christ and of discipleship as such. He deliberately precedes the story by the two short scenes concerning discipleship and connects it to them by precisely the key word, 'Disciples.' He passes over details in the story which the text of Mark provides. On the other hand the cry of the disciples is a real prayer — no longer, as with the other Gospels just a call of help arising from fear and a feeling of helplessness — for now the prayer runs: 'Save, Lord, we are perishing.' Also in Matthew's story, the disciples incur the Master's reproach: 'Why are you afraid, O men of little faith?' even before Jesus rebukes the wind and waves. This reproach now forms the center and the miracle follows. Thus temptation, faith and little faith, but also the authority* of the Lord who can create the great calm amid the storm of fear and temptation, have become the core of the story in order to shame and comfort the believers.''

> Gunther Bornkamm
> *Jesus of Nazareth*
> pp. 150-51

'' 'Let us go over unto the other side.' Even when we go forth at Christ's command, we need not expect to escape storms; for these disciples were doing so, and yet they encountered the fiercest storms and were in great danger of being overwhelmed; so they cried out in their distress for Christ's assistance. Christ gave them a gentle rebuke, saying, 'Where is your faith?' Why did you not shout victory in the very face of the storm and say to the raging winds and rolling waves, 'You can do no harm, for Christ, the mighty Savior, is on board'?''

> Mrs. Charles Cowman
> *Streams in the Desert*
> p. 166

---

*See also John 14:1, 27.

*See also 18:1, Wright.

"The relation of Jesus to his fellow men can be summed up in two words: faith and love. Knowing them for what they are, he yet loves and believes in them as though they are already all that they are meant to be. And it is just that believing love of Jesus towards men that brings Peter out of Simon and the apostle of love out of the son of thunder. It acts like sunshine on the buried seed, generating in those who respond to it faith, love, and obedience toward himself *like that* which he himself renders to the Father. In his teaching, faith comes first, not a vague intellectual abstraction but confidence in a known person's complete dependability. 'You believe in God, believe also in me.' (Imagine hearing that from a local carpenter or garage hand!) 'Why are you afraid?' he asks wistfully as though he found it so hard to come by that which was for him the tissue of life."

Sister Penelope
The Wood
p. 115

New Illuminations:

On Jesus' Redemption of the Demon Possessed

Matthew 8:28-34	Mark 5:1-20	Luke 8:2, 26-39

"The Biblical term, 'demon possessed' is useful as a graphic description of the sense of helplessness that some know so well. The task to which Jesus addressed himself with the demoniac was the restoration of the man's sense of human dignity. The very essence of man is to be found in the characteristics which distinguish him from the animal. It is man with a conscience, man making free decisions, man accepting personal responsibility. . . .

"When the dignity of a human being has been injured, his sense of personal adequacy has been undermined, his freedom to be unique has been curtailed. Now his anger has not been turned outward toward his world but turned in against himself. Angry with himself, at war with himself, he feels only the conflict of the unresolved forces struggling within his makeup. The only name which seems to make sense to him is 'Legion: for we are many.' . . . So it must have been with the demoniac of the Garasenes whose wild ravings were completely subdued in the patient and understanding (and hence fearless) approach of Jesus. . . .

"It was important to him that Jesus was not afraid of him. Fearful of the impulses that raged unchecked within himself, he could not be helped by those who also feared him but only by one who stood outside of the fear, who could understand it but was not drawn into it. Sensing the unchecked anger that was driving the man, Jesus could confront him calmly with a direct approach: 'You are angry, but you don't have to be ruled by anger.' ('Come out of the man you unclean spirit.') . . .

"Whether the causal factors were ever really uncovered, the final scene, showing the 'demoniac' restored to normalcy, sitting and talking with Jesus, suggests the renewal of communication — the breakthrough from isolation to interpersonal relationships. . . . It is not strange that the man wanted to stay with Jesus. Having found someone who had helped him to accept himself and to see himself related in a more meaningful way to life, he wanted to hold on to this new interpreter of life, but Jesus would have none of it. The real test of life, he knew so well, was in the resumption of daily tasks at home among old friends. But even here the pattern of life was changed for now the man was no longer occupied with his own troubles but was commissioned to tell of the changes that God had made in his life. His orientation was no longer on himself but on his relationship with God. No wonder that men marvelled at the transformation."

Robert C. Leslie
Jesus and Logotherapy
pp. 102-110

"Beyond the lake there is a strange country called Gadara, a region of darkness and horror. This weird landscape exists within every human being. . . . Our vital roots reach down as deeply into the nether world as our spiritual functions strain up into the spiritual world of what we call divine. This split between the so-called 'lower life' and the higher life has to be overcome.* . . .

"The country of shadow exists within every individual and this dark power can and must be redeemed and changed into creativity. The two madmen (Matthew 8:28) represent complete madness, the madness of the split itself. As long as they are two, they will act without correlation, each one in his separate insane way; nobody can induce them to cooperate. They will destroy everything and finally themselves. That Jesus is able to cure the two madmen is a simple expression of the fact that the central light is able to redeem all darkness (John 1:9). When redemption takes place, the negative powers turn positive: '. . . and they found the man sitting down at the feet of Jesus.' The split is replaced by wholeness.

"Why then do the demons rush into the swine and the swine into the lake? If the redemptive process would reach ideal completion, such a thing would not happen; but nothing on earth is complete. Even Jesus could not convert the Pharisees. He had to leave them to the 'eternal fire' (Matthew 25:41)."

Fritz Kunkel
Creation Continues
pp. 149-52

"Paul had some very anxious despairing moments, 'being so utterly crushed that we despaired of life itself' (2 Corinthians 1:8). J. B. Phillips in discussing this matter, points out that as Christians 'we can be overcome by the most terrifying darkness and be reduced to a sense of inadequacy and reduced to near desperation.' "

Keith Miller
A Second Touch
p. 71

"Be sure there is something inside you which, unless it is altered, will put it out of God's power to prevent you from being eternally miserable. While that something remains,

*See also 36:2, Thielicke.

there can be no heaven for you, just as there can be no sweet smells for a man with a cold and no music for a man who is deaf. It is not a question of God sending us to Hell. In each of us there is something growing up which will of itself *be Hell* unless it is nipped in the bud.''

C. S. Lewis
''The Trouble With X''
Bristol Diocesan Gazette
August, 1948

''In Lewis' book, *Perelandra*, the anti-hero, Weston, not only cannot discern between good and evil powers but is actually possessed by an evil one. He has lost the good of reason and humanity. . . . When Weston refers to a force which pours up into him through the dark bases of his being, he describes very aptly the nature of the demonic as it works against the mind, annihilating the reason and volition, and finally taking over the passive organism that has yielded and opened up to his own Dark Will. It then floods up through the dark passions and instincts, and man is wholly brought into bondage wholly determined by a force that cannot create, but only destroy.''

Leanne Payne
Real Presence: The Holy Spirit in the Works of C.S. Lewis
pp. 122-23

New Illuminations:

On the Twelve and Seventy Sent to the Harvest

Matthew 9:35—10:16   Mark 6:7-13   Luke 9:1-6; 10:1-16

"One of the first things that Jesus did, according to the Synoptic Gospels, was to choose a small group of men to accompany him in his activities, to learn his methods, and to be the nucleus of the new community, the 'little flock,' to whom the Father intended to give the Kingdom (Luke 12:32). After a period of activity, the exact duration of which is difficult to determine, but which may have been seven or eight months, Jesus seems to have felt that the time was short, that the harvest was great and the labourers were few (Matthew 9:37). He, therefore, selected from the group which had gathered round him twelve whose names are given by each of the synoptists, and who are later known as the Apostles."

S. H. Hooke
The Kingdom of God
p. 65

"The last four verses of Matthew Chapter Nine, together with the first four verses of Chapter Ten, form a transition of great beauty. These eight verses can be understood as a unit in themselves, which, in its center, shows a gap of silence; that gap indicates the break-through of the eternal into our world of space and time. . . . The last verses of Chapter Nine describe Jesus' resolve to expand his one-man warfare by the commission of more or less independent helpers. The old system of religious leadership has failed. The people are like sheep without a shepherd. They still need guidance. Many laborers have to work before the harvest is secured. The old form of life has broken down; the new form is about to begin. The task of finding the laborers remains. . . .

"The disciples pray that the laborers may be sent — then the gap of silence. Then Jesus gives them the power over the evil spirits, urging them to preach the good news of the Kingdom. Their prayer has been answered. By praying, they themselves have become the laborers. They are apostles now, and they are ready to receive the instructions for the new task.''*

Fritz Kunkel
Creation Continues
pp. 163-164

"Jesus' gracious conversation with the woman at the well had been part of his ministry. Now the people of Sychar are approaching. Jesus witnesses to his disciples for the urgency of his ministry (John 4:35). . . . The fields had been planted in wheat and barley, covering the earth with a thrifty growth of green. . . . 'Look around you. Look at the field.' There on the path through the young grain the Samaritans are coming in their white garments, shining in the sun. They were the grain Jesus saw, white for the harvest, ready to be gathered into the divine grainery."

Adrian Van Kamm
The Woman At the Well
pp. 106-107

" 'And he sent them forth. . . .' To be cherished is to be sent. They are not separate but ultimately one reality. You see this in Gospel story after Gospel story. The disciples are called into fellowship with Jesus and become fishers of men. After the Resurrection, Jesus pours out his consoling, healing love on Mary Magdalene and then tells her, 'Go to my brothers.' . . . Indeed, this identity of "being cherished" with "being sent," which is a person's ultimate identity, finds its radiant symbol, its authoritative statement in Jesus, the beloved one, sent into the world. We saw this when we looked at the baptism of Jesus and his awareness of himself as the beloved of the Father sent in powerlessness for the others.** We are called to be in Jesus, sent for the Kingdom."

Thomas Kane
"Powerless and Weak"

"It is a peculiar task to 'inquire who is worthy' (Matthew 10:11) to give hospitality to the disciples. Jesus himself preferred sinners to the 'just' and ate with publicans as readily as with Pharisees. The word 'worthy' therefore cannot refer to good reputation or social standing. From a psychological point of view, it should mean 'close enough to a spiritual crisis,' so that the disciple during his visit can help the person to take a decisive step. The coming of the missionary, then, meant the beginning of a new development; but it also meant the beginning of much suffering, new decisions, sacrifice of old connections, and possibly disrepute and persecution. The inner peace of the household will be upset for a long time. It is important, therefore, to state that 'we come for the sake of peace!' in spite of all the turmoil that we bring***. . . .

*See also 68:2, Jeremias.
**See also 50:1, Webster.
***See also 70:2, Neil.

"Jesus sends his disciples as sheep in the midst of wolves. The more light we carry, the more darkness we shall provoke in our opponents. The purpose of this dangerous mission is twofold: on the one hand, under the influence of the sheep, some of the wolves might become sheep themselves. On the other hand, under the influence of the wolves, some of the sheep should grow 'wary and wise as serpents and be innocent — harmless, guileless, and without falsity — as doves.' ''

Fritz Kunkel
Creation Continues
p. 165

" 'And if the house be worthy, let your peace come upon it; but if it be not worthy, let your peace return to you' (Matthew 10:13). "True peace is the possession of the favor of God. This is found only in submission, faith, and obedience to his laws. It is the result of a pure and holy love for him. . . . Desire only the will of God; seek him alone and you will find peace; you shall enjoy it in spite of the world. Look upon everything as in the hands of God and as real blessings that he bestows upon his children, of which you receive your portion. Then the world may turn its face from you, but nothing will deprive you of peace."

Thomas Kepler, ed.
Letters and Reflections of Francois de Fenelon
p. 142

"In his significant tenth chapter, Luke has stressed more markedly than the other synoptics the apostles' activity in the service of the kingdom of God. The announcement, 'the reign of God is at hand' occurs twice in their missionary instruction (vv. 9, 11), on the first occasion, with the addition of 'to you' and in the second, as a warning to the places that reject the disciples. The reign of God thus comes with the disciples' preaching to men. . . . Luke also includes the assertion that the reign of God has reached mankind through the expulsion of devils by Jesus. And when the disciples on their return relate how evil spirits were subject to them in the name of Jesus (10:17), this dynamic entry of God's rule must have affected their activity. It is from this point that

the 'in your midst' of Luke 17:21 has to be judged. . . .

"It only remains to ask whether the context does not signify that the reign of God has already arrived. In Mark 1:15 we read, 'The time is accomplished.' This refers to an event that has actually happened. But it is the special eschatological consciousness of Jesus that the time has come when the prophecies of the final era are realized but not yet the fulfilment. His own advent and operation fulfil the time and are a certain guarantee that the perfect reign of God is immediately at hand. A glance at Isaiah 52:7 makes this even clearer. Jesus is the Messianic harbinger of joy who announces God's final kingship, but he is only the harbinger."

Rudolf Schnackenburg
God's Rule and Kingdom
pp. 139, 141

"The statements of Jesus, which externally do not differ from the prophets' gospel of repentance, must be interpreted in the sense that punishment and judgment refer to such as reject his offer of salvation from an inner hardening of mind and heart (Matthew 13:14-15). This is made explicit to the disciples prior to their mission. Only when men refuse to believe and reject their gospel of salvation are they to shake the dust from their feet as a sign and testimony (against them at the judgment) that they have parted from God's messengers and forfeited salvation. It is God's great offer of grace at the last hour. Anyone who in this critical moment refuses to hear God's voice behaves like the obdurate generation of Noah or the infatuated inhabitants of Sodom. . . .

"In other passages, Jesus declares that at the judgment, heathens would put to shame hard-hearted Israelites. The inhabitants of Nineveh and the queen of the South will then rise again at the judgment with 'this generation (the unbelieving contemporaries of Jesus) and, as witnesses, condemn them (Luke 11:31-32). Similarly Jesus introduces the heathen citizens of Tyre and Sidon, and even of Sodom, who would long ago have done penance in sackcloth and ashes had they witnessed miracles like those of Jesus in Chorazin, Bethsaida and Capernaum (Luke 10:13). This shows clearly that Jesus had no prejudices against the heathen."

Rudolf Schnackenburg
God's Rule and Kingdom
pp. 89-90, 102

New Illuminations:

On the Feeding of the Five Thousand and Walking on Water

Matthew 14:13-33; 15:32-39   Mark 6:30-52   Luke 9:12-17

"There are many stories in the Old Testament in which God fed his people. The children of Israel were fed in the wilderness with manna from heaven. Elisha fed one hundred men with the gift of one man, and food was left over. The great religious meal of the Old Testament people was a thanksgiving feast, the Feast of the Passover, held each year to celebrate the freeing of the Israelites from slavery in Egypt. . . . One reason the people expected a heavenly banquet when the Messiah came was because these stories were familiar to them.

"Jesus taught about God's kingdom. The crowds that followed him must have watched very closely for any signs that would mean the Kingdom of God was at hand. . . . No matter where Jesus went there were crowds, excitement, and rumors. People followed him into the country and slept in the open. But they had to eat and there was no place to buy food. The Roman soldiers and the Jewish leaders kept a close watch on everything, for they knew that crowds have great power. The rumors that spread about Jesus added to the excitement and expectation."

Edric Weld and William Sydnor
The Son of God
pp. 48, 45

"The feeding of the 5000 is parable as well as miracle — parable of the Lord's recreative mission to the starving world and of his intention to mediate his life by the hands of chosen men. The word Lord means 'bread-giver' by derivation; and, according to the Fourth Gospel, this miracle which took place on a Thursday was followed on the next Sabbath by the discourse in which he spoke of himself as the living bread come down from heaven for the life of the world — strange words that at that time alienated many friends."

Sister Penelope
The Wood
p. 118

"Matthew's version of the story shows that the early community continued to find new levels of symbolism in this miracle. The ritual gestures of Jesus (Matthew 14:19b), the focus on the bread (rather than the fish), and the careful collection of the fragments have strong Eucharistic overtones. And Matthew highlights the role of the disciples in the whole episode. They do not rudely oppose Jesus (as they

do in Mark 6:37) but are important mediaries who distribute the bread and gather the leftovers. The disciples share in Jesus' ministry. . . . The Gospel stresses the inclusion of the disciples in Jesus' power to feed and to heal."

Donald Senior
Invitation to Matthew
p. 148

"Miracles of fertility are the instances of miraculous feeding. They involve the multiplication of a little bread and a little fish. Once in the desert, Satan had tempted Jesus to make bread of stones; he refused the suggestion. 'The Son does nothing except what he sees the Father do'; perhaps one may, without boldness, surmise that the direct change from stone to bread appeared to the Son to be not quite in the hereditary style.* Little bread into much bread is quite a different matter. Every year God makes a little corn into much corn; the seed is sown and there is an increase. . . . That same day, he also multiplied fish. Look down into every bay and almost every river. This swarming undulating fecundity shows he is still at work 'thronging the seas with a spawn innumerable.' For it was he who at the beginning commanded all species 'to be fruitful and multiply and replenish the earth.' And now, that day, at the feeding of the thousands, incarnate God does the same: does close and small under his human hands, a workman's hands, what he has always been doing in the seas, the lakes and the little brooks."

C. S. Lewis
Miracles
p. 164

"Man's crude idea of God is that he is a sort of millionaire in worlds with the power to fling about miracles, who would do just what he liked, when he likes, and how he liked without any thought for economy or care for detail. But, if we look at our Lord's ways of acting, we find two characteristics about them — continuity and care. He takes what is and lifts it up to something higher, and he never wastes anything. When he was confronted by a hungry multitude, he did not say, 'I am God and I will send down manna to them.' He said to the Apostles, 'If you will give what you have wholly to me, we can feed the multitude.' He took what

---

*See also 13:2, Leslie.

they had and blessed and broke it and the multitude was fed.'

Harry C. Griffith
*A Gift of Light:
A Collection of Thoughts from Father Andrew*
p. 66

"The miracles are not just miracles; they are acted sermons. The feeding of the multitude was a demonstration of the kindliness of God towards those in need. Jesus, the compassionate Revelation of the love of God, demonstrated his caring for the weak, fumbling humanity. The important thing is to give our all to others with compassion. Do the best we can with what little we have is another lesson from the feeding of the thousands."

Selected

"Anxious for guidance by which to direct his steps, Jesus dismissed the crowd, sent the disciples across the lake in a boat, and then sought to be alone with God. He walked through the mountains, praying, talking, and thinking with his Father. He saw one great duty to the confused populace: to be right. If his reason and emotions were in alignment with the basic principles of God, he might at first be misunderstood, but the ultimate failure of his mission was impossible. Jesus knew that rightness could lead to a cross; he knew also that a cross endured for God's sake was an instrument of victory. . . . So, aware that the people had misunderstood him, Jesus talked with God for most of the night. And out of this communion came a deeper understanding and a renewed courage. . . . He was ready to go to calvary knowing that even though his followers deserted him, the right he stood for would eventually triumph. . . .

"The meaning of this episode is clear: when you give God the opportunity, he will set you right. You can walk above anything; you are a conqueror. . . . Don't let anyone tell you Jesus couldn't walk on the waters. As a matter of fact you can do things as great when, thanks to the grace of God, you are in the right."

Austin Pardue
The Single Eye
pp. 63-64, 66-67

"Peter walks on the water. As long as he looks at Jesus; as long as he goes towards him, he is able to walk on the lake. But when he looks about him, when he notices that the wind is strong, he is struck with fear. He begins to sink. Jesus has to stretch forth his hand to save him. If Peter had paid no attention to the waves and the wind, if he had concentrated his gaze on Jesus alone, he would not have found himself in danger. His faith would not have been shaken.

"In this, Lord, you have the cause of my falls. All my faults originate by a fading or disappearance of the Savior's image. . . . Such an image is not the work of one minute or one day. A hasty or superficial image of Jesus is as one drawn on water. It vanishes with the first breeze, with the first jolt. I have to form this image of Jesus slowly and deeply, or rather, I must develop and then preserve a certain docility so that Jesus might engrave his face on my heart."

Monk of the Eastern Church
Jesus: A Dialogue with the Savior
pp. 33-34

"In the walking on water we see the relations of spirit and nature so altered that nature can be made to do whatever spirit pleases. This new obedience of nature, of course, is not to be separated even in thought from the spirit's own obedience to the Father of Spirits.* . . . One thing at least we must observe. If we are in fact spirits, not nature's offspring, then there must be some point (probably the brain) at which created spirit even now can produce effects on matter not by manipulation or technics but simply by the wish to do so. If that is what you mean by Magic, then Magic is really manifested every time you move your hand or think a thought. And nature is not destroyed but rather perfected by her servitude."

C. S. Lewis
Miracles
p. 179

"Look at this picture. You see the stormy lake and the little boat with its low, free board and its shallow draught, just as used on the Lake of Galilee now, and the frightened faces of the fishermen. And standing above them is the solitary and tranquil figure of Christ ruling the storm; more than that, for in and through that storm, he is revealed to them as never before. We never realize that power in full until we too are caught and threatened by the hostility of events or the frightful storms of our own unstable natures. It is then that his mysterious action is felt within the circumstances of our lives. 'And he went up unto them into the ship and they were sore amazed' (Mark 6:51).

"Sometimes we are, as it were, in the middle of the lake, and the storm breaks, usually from a quarter we do not expect, and we are doubtful whether the little boat is going to stand it. We feel helpless, making no progress, and are inclined to say, 'I have gone to bits; I have no help, no support. *This* cannot be spiritual life.' We begin to lose our grip. It was like that when 'he went up unto them and the wind

*See also 19:2, Lewis.

ceased.' Then the situation was transformed by his presence. One way or another life brings every Christian soul this experience. God in Christ intervenes between us and the storm that threatens to overwhelm us. His power is brought into action just when our action fails. He comes to the rescue of those caught in the toils of circumstance. . . .

"Let us bring this element, this expression of the love of God, this passion for rescue, into relation of our life of prayer. . . . We are laboring at the oars, most of us, struggling against a head wind to keep our sense of direction. Natural surroundings and our own weaknesses are too much for us. They come down on us without warning and drive us off our course. . . . When that happens, all the calm beauty of our spiritual life seems a long way away. And it is just then, above all other times, that the miracle of prayer happens. We do not always recognize at first who or what that steadying, peaceful pressure is that enters the little boat of the soul, pitching and tossing on the waves. But somehow the wind does cease and the reassuring pressure does come. He enters the ship and overrules the hurly-burly and sends peace.''*

Evelyn Underhill
The Light of Christ
pp. 70-71, 77

_____

*See also 112:2, Harton.

_____

New Illuminations:

On Peter's Outburst of Faith

Matthew 16:13-19   Mark 8:27-30   Luke 9:18-22

"It is always rather difficult to realize that neither the preaching of the Baptist nor the course of the ministry itself had brought any widespread conviction of our Lord's Messiahship. With Peter's confession, he was expressing for the first time a faith that had cost the disciples hard travail of experience to bring forth — even at that time — and how much more later! Jesus was so different from the popular hero of expectation, so upsetting to their preconceived ideas and accepted standards, and in such ill odor with their religious leaders, that faith in his Messiahship, however limited its conception, was a real achievement."

Sister Penelope
The Wood
p. 118

"Peter was courageous enough to conceive and express the sacrilegious idea that a man, a carpenter, could actually be a 'Son of the living God.' . . . Mankind enters a new phase of evolution. The man Jesus achieves this 'sonship'; he becomes Christ, the spiritual man, the man of the future; and another man, Peter, is able to recognize this event. This experience is the boulder on which all Christianity is built. But each Christian, if he deserves the name, must find this boulder within himself. It is the rock on which the wise man builds his house."*

Fritz Kunkel
Creation Continues
p. 219

"The Christian Church does not offer men and women a route map to God. Instead it tells them by what means they might be found by him! The emphasis is always upon God's initiative. When Peter blurts out his confession of faith in Christ, Jesus, according to Matthew, tells him that 'flesh and blood has not revealed this to you but my Father which is in heaven.' The same point is made in John's Gospel when Jesus tells the Jews, 'No one can come to me unless my Father who has sent me draws him.' And most of the parables of Jesus emphasize the activity of God in his search for mankind."

Richard Holloway
A New Heaven
p. 71

"There are two contrasting energies at work, marring or making for wholeness in the lives of men: the big noisy passions of the world and the quiet, gentle, but immensely powerful work of the Good Shepherd. But there is something vital to add in terms of man's response. The Church began with the supernaturally inspired work of Peter who cried, 'Thou art the Christ, the Son of the Living God.' . . . At once our Lord seized upon the validity of real faith. . . . To Christ's matchless insight, here was the beginning of this world-wide fellowship of men and women of all races. Here was the tiny beginning of the society which would transcend all barriers. For Peter in a moment of true faith had seen who Christ really was.

"Until someone sees that God himself has penetrated into human life at man's own level, there can be no beginning to making men whole*. . . . But once this recognition has come to birth, the certainty is there, the guarantee is there, the power is there; the authority, the plan, the purpose are all there, and the building can begin. No wonder, Christ said of Peter's outburst of faith, 'upon this rock, I will build my church.' "

J. B. Phillips
Making Men Whole
pp. 20-21

"Jesus wishes to give Simon Peter 'the keys of the kingdom of heaven' (Matthew 16:19). Does this *basileia* refer to the present reign of God or the perfect reign of the future? Evidently the latter since this is confirmed by the metaphor of the keys which signify the handing over of full authority and in particular entry into the kingdom of God, participation in God's perfect reign. This is clear from Matthew 23:13, where Jesus accuses the scribes and Pharisees of shutting God's kingdom to men; they do not themselves enter nor do they permit those who want to enter to do so. . . .

"The key also denotes the authority as is shown in Revelation 3:7, which is referred to Christ. He possesses the Messianic power to open or shut God's house at the end of time. But in Matthew 16:19 Jesus transfers this authority in its earthly competence to Simon Peter. This earthly apostle is presented not as door-keeper of the Church (v. 18) or 'of heaven' (v. 19b) but as one with authority to determine who shall enter into the future kingdom. The purpose of this solemn declaration is then made clear**. . . . In contrast to

*See also 3:2, Van Kamm.
**See also 108:4, Schnackenburg.

*See also 27:2, Beaufoy.

the Scribes, Peter will have the capacity and power to lead men into God's kingdom. The purpose and mission of this community founded upon Peter as rock foundation is one day to enter as the perfect community of the redeemed into the kingdom of God.

"The authority promised in terms of the key is immediately specified as power to 'bind and loose.' Prescinding from the long discussion of this expression, it is sufficiently evident that it includes not merely an authority to teach but a power to guide and judge, functioning in the main though not exclusively in the forgiveness of sins. . . . This is the first eschatological act of Jesus, a sign of the salvation that has now dawned, a proof that God's rule is present and operative. Jesus transmits this authority to Peter and correspondingly to the apostles (Matthew 18:18, John 20:23) and enables the eschatological forces of salvation to develop more widely. The double formula, bind or loose, retain or forgive, makes it clear that we have here a power of decision, a juridical function."

Rudolf Schnackenburg
God's Rule and Kingdom
pp. 227-229

New Illuminations:

On the Suffering Servant Prophecies

Isaiah 42:1-4; 49:1-7; 50:4-7; 53:1-12   Psalm 22:6-18

"The poems of the Servant of the Lord in Second Isaiah show the servant of the Lord as enduring present suffering, but as vindicated by God at the last. It is that view of the matter which is shown to be right by the crucifixion and resurrection of our Lord. One psalmist sees that the real meaning of the sacrifice of the animal is that it is a symbol of the sacrifice of man himself*: 'The sacrifice of God is a troubled spirit, a broken and contrite heart . . . '(Psalm 51:17). And it is in that sense that the Second Isaiah says of the Servant of the Lord that his soul is made 'a sacrifice for our sin' (Isaiah). Thus the Old Testament, at the point of its very deepest insight, anticipates that sacrificial offering that the Son of God Himself made."**

A. G. Hebert
Scripture and the Faith
pp. 68-69

"In the Psalms in which Christ himself appears as the sufferer, a second meaning is most inevitable. If Christ 'tasted death for all men' — became the archetypal sufferer — then the expressions of all who ever suffered in the world are related to his. . . . In Psalm 22, the terrible poem which Christ quoted in his final torture, it is not 'they pierced my hands and my feet' (v. 16) that really matters most. It is the union of total privation with total adherence to God, to a God who makes no response, simply because of what God is: 'and thou continuest holy' (v. 3). All the sufferings of the righteous speak here, but in Psalm 40:12 all the sufferings of the guilty also speak — 'my sins have taken such hold upon me that I am not able to look up.' But this too is the voice of Christ, for we have been taught that he who was without sin became sin for our sakes, plumbed the depth of the worst suffering that comes to evil men who at last know their own evil."

C. S. Lewis
Reflections on the Psalms
pp. 126-27

" 'He saved others; himself he cannot save,' jeered some of the enemies at the Cross. But this is true of any great physician. He must share in imagination and, consequently, in vividness and reality the disorders he seeks to treat. The only point from which anyone can help save another man is *beside* him — not above or beyond him. The Great Physician must also be the Great Victim. The sins which are the special temptation of those who suffer — despair, self-pity, self-disgust — are met and overcome by the one who suffers too, but who uses suffering to identify with others and with God himself. The great altar piece at Eisenheim depicts a repulsive picture of Christ on the Cross. His body is covered with sores, his joints twisted and grotesque, his face contorted in agony. But what other picture of God could have brought hope and salvation from self-pity and alienation to the inhabitants of Eisenheim, victims of a leprous skin disease which was the scourge of Europe in the late Middle Ages."

John M. Krumm
The Art of Being a Sinner
pp. 95-96

"Whatever the precise origin of the idea of the Servant it is certain that it could not have arisen before the Exile, for in the Exile, the innocent had suffered with the guilty. To the problem of 'Why do the righteous suffer?' the suffering Servant is the answer. To the Jews he meant and still means the Chosen People suffering for and from the nations; and it is certain that in pre-Christian thought he never was identified with the Messiah. Yet in the last and the greatest of the Servant Songs, he is already an individual, for he is spoken of as being stricken 'for the transgressions of my people.' Thus the thought is contracted to him in whom the Chosen People at once fulfils its purpose of being the agent of redemption for the world, and is itself redeemed."

Sister Penelope
The Wood
p. 85

" 'For even the Son of Man came not to be ministered unto, but to minister, and to give his life as a ransom for many' (Mark 10:45). Where did this ideal come from? Was it a totally new conception brought into the world by Jesus, or was there foreshadowing of it in the ancient scriptures of his people? It was in Isaiah 53 that our Lord apparently found the pattern of his life. The passage is one of the poems composed in Babylon for the congregation of exiles. It is generally believed by scholars that the Second Isaiah was

*See also 116:1, Webster.
**See also 106:1, Newton.

thinking of Israel itself as the servant, or at least of the little inner core of the faithful, and of the shame and humiliation they had undergone. The prophet was sure their sufferings could not be punitive, and in a flash of spiritual insight he glimpsed the possibility that in some mysterious way God was making it possible for them to bear the sufferings of others. By suffering as they did, they were actually serving mankind and making the world a better place for other men to live in. The vision of the prophet was greater than he knew. . . . The ideal of human life which it embodies has never been realized anywhere but in the person of Jesus Christ. While he did not refuse the ancient title of king, he seems to have based his understanding of the function and dignity of kingship entirely upon the figure of the suffering servant of Isaiah 53.''

Robert C. Dentan
A First Reader in Biblical Theology
pp. 66-67

New Illuminations:

On Discipleship II: ". . . come after me, deny yourself . . ."

Matthew 16:24   Mark 8:34   Luke 9:23

"George Herbert wrote: 'Who goeth in the way that Christ hath gone / Is much more sure to meet with Him than one / That travelleth by-ways.' Are we going in a way that Christ has gone? A by-way is any other way, any easy way, any self-pleasing way. We shall not meet Christ if we travel in a by-way. Christ's way is the way that says 'no' to the 'I' that rises up so often and in many different guises."

Amy Carmichael
Thou Givest . . . They Gather
p. 173

"Our Lord is standing at the Crossroads saying, 'Beloved, what you have hoped for is not good enough. Come up higher; I have destroyed those hopes; I have let them become disappointments, not in order to rob you but to open to you a new thing, a better thing. Come up higher!'"

Selected

"If Jesus is to grow large, I must grow smaller and ever less important. Jesus can win the world only with people who want him and therefore want nothing for themselves. . . . Only the one who at the outset does not look outward at all, but is simply and solely intent on magnifying Jesus day by day in his own life quite automatically becomes a herald and conqueror in his own world. . . . God cannot be had cheaply. You come to God only if you allow yourself to be mobilized and if you march. This is not easy and it means saying goodbye to many things. But this is the only way to find peace."

Helmut Thielicke
The Waiting Father
pp. 60-68

"The trouble with a word like 'self-denial' is that we use it to refer to little pleasures and habits not really sinful in themselves but which we shall be better without. The call of Jesus is not to say 'no' to petty vanities and indulgences but to say 'no' to self-government of our lives and to hand the authority over to him. . . . And once is not enough. The life of self-negation has to be entered anew day after day until the end of time. . . .

"Self-denial, which is truly a denial of the self, lifts our

Christian faith and practice out of the realm of personal hobbies into the realm of divine power and redemption. It has nothing to do with a negative puritanism that decides quite arbitrarily what is, or is not, legitimate for a Christian to do. In fact, it is little short of tragedy that the average observer honestly believes that the churchman's self-denial is a deliberate attempt to evacuate life of all that gives pleasure and enjoyment. There is many a Christian who feels that his conscience is prompting him to renounce some harmless amusement but whose essential self-centeredness remains inviolate and unchallenged. . . .

"It took St. Augustine a long time to reach the point of conversion, and for him, the delay was due to the fact that though he prayed, 'O God, make me chaste,' he was honest enough to add the words — 'but not just yet.' "

Joost de Blank
Uncomfortable Words
pp. 7-8, 16

"Why are our pastors afraid to press upon us continually and urgently the basic condition of all Christian life: 'If any man will be My disciple, let him deny himself daily, take up his cross and follow Me.' No necessity could be plainer. And though we may go as far as desire impels in the personal choice of self-denial and be very resolute in self-discipline, it is life itself which provides the denying and the cross, and also the road of love, for nothing can be done apart from love. But this acceptance of life is not what self wants. Because of the twist in human nature, its desires are towards itself and its personal satisfactions so that it seeks what it selects as its good. . . . Explain it as you will, this is the mystery in which we are involved, this crookedness of being which prevents us from seeing where our true happiness lies and from pursuing it at all costs; though men seldom doubt that they are made for happiness. This belief is in fact confirmed by Christ, for He said that his kingdom is happiness, is leaping for joy.* He came to reveal and call me into this joy, with one declared condition for participation, namely the loosening of self in ever deepening degrees from all that seems to constitute what I think of myself and my claims. People and occasions, pursuits and pleasures, none bad in themselves, can any of them hinder not only my whole-hearted love of God by entangling me in themselves, but also my real love for man; therefore they call for my denial. I am split into a hundred selves as I run after this and that with insistence and clamor; God, however,

---

*See also 6:1, Underhill.

intends me as a unity. . . . To arrive at such a unity, I must be empty of all self-motivation, self-stirrings, self-absorption: what else is our Lord saying with his 'deny'? And as I find myself in him because he fills more and more of me, I shall receive back double, triple, a hundred fold of whatever I have given up for His sake (Luke 18:30)."*

Sibyl Harton
Doors of Eternity
pp. 86-88

"Letting ourselves be led by Jesus is a painful ascent. . . . The theme is still purity of heart. The pure heart is un-alloyed (one speaks of gold which is pure), an undivided heart, an unshared heart, its integrity preserved — or re-covered. . . . Only a heart which is given can grasp Jesus; but it must be given without turning back, complete without fault. . . .

"My child, you have sought your own happiness. Your whole life has made it clear to you that your road was closed to you outside the complete giving of yourself. Blessed are you to whom I have barred the roads which are not mine."

Monk of the Eastern Church •
Jesus: A Dialogue with the Savior
p. 12-13

"It is plain from the Gospels that Christ regarded the self-loving, self-regarding, self-seeking spirit as the direct antithesis of real living. 'If any man will come after me,' he said, 'let him deny himself (i.e., deny his tendency to love himself) and take up his cross (i.e., bear the painful cost of that denial) and follow me (i.e., live positively according to the principles that I teach and demonstrate).' Now the moment that a man does this, even temporarily and tenta-tively, he finds himself in touch with something more real than he has known before. There is a sense that he is touch-ing a deep and powerful stream that runs right through life. In other words, the moment he begins really to love, he finds himself in touch with the life of God. He now *knows* be-yond any doubting that this is real, happy, constructive liv-ing. . . . Of course he may relapse into his former way of self-loving. But all the time he was approximating to the liv-ing purpose of God, he *knew* that this was real life.

———————
*See also 95:3, Schnackenburg.

"Christ unquestionably claims to present accurately and authentically the Character of God. . . . But it would be a mistake to suppose that the eternal God is no 'bigger' than Jesus of Nazareth, limited as he was by time, and space, and circumstance. But the biggest, highest, and widest ideas of God that man can conceive arrange themselves without dissonance or incongruity around the character of Jesus revealed."

J. B. Phillips
Your God Is Too Small
pp. 91-93

"When humility delivers a man from attachment to his own works and his own reputation, he discovers that true joy is only possible when we have completely forgotten our-selves. And it is only when we pay no more attention to our own life and our own reputation and our own excellence that we are at last completely free to serve God in perfec-tion for his own sake alone. A man who is not stripped and poor and naked within his own soul will always do the works he has to do for his own sake rather than for the glory of God."

Thomas Merton
Seeds of Contemplation
p. 44

"The process of joining Christ's body may at first seem like a renunciation. I no longer have full independence. Iron-ically, however, renouncing my own value system and com-mitting myself to Christ, the Head, abruptly frees me. . . . I have found this process of renunciation and commitment to be healthy, relaxing, and wholly good. . . . We are called to self-denial, not for its own sake, but for compensation we can obtain in no other way. In actual fact, we are called to self-denial in order to open up a more abundant life. Crusty selfishness peels away to reveal the love of God ex-pressed through our own hands which, in turn, shapes us into his own image. 'To refuse to deny one's self,' said Henry Drummond, 'is just to be left with the self undenied.' "

Paul Brand and Philip Yancey
Fearfully and Wonderfully Made
pp. 48-53

———————————

New Illuminations:

On ". . . pick up your cross and follow me!"

Matthew 16:24   Mark 8:34   Luke 9:23; 14:27

"Some people when they say that a thing is meant metaphorically conclude from this point it is hardly meant at all. They rightly think that Christ spoke metaphorically when he told us to carry the cross: they wrongly conclude that carrying the cross is nothing more than living a respectable life and subscribing moderately to charities."

C. S. Lewis
Miracles
p. 95

"Our cross is not calamity, or experience of sorrow or loss. These are facts of life. It is not trying to live our own shortcomings nor keeping up obligations despite all. Jesus assigned us crosses that we might enter into a self-donating love: 'take up' love, grasp it, lay hands on it, pour it out without expecting a return."

William Pounds
Sermon Notes

"The cross has been taken out of Jesus' hands and smothered with flowers; it has become what he would have hated, a source of graceful ideas and agreeable emotions. When Jesus presented the cross to his disciples, he was certainly not thinking of a sentiment which can disturb no man's life nor redeem any man's soul, but of the unsightly beams which must be set up in the midst of a man's pleasure and the jagged nails which must pierce his soul. . . .

" 'If any man wants to go with me,' said Jesus, 'let him say "no" to himself and nail it to the cross day after day and follow me.' Nothing could be more demanding; and generally that demand will be focused on one habit, one practice or one attitude, the abandonment of which will mean an agonizing self-crucifixion. The road to fullness of life is concentrated on one narrow door through which it will be pain and grief to pass. But we declare ourselves willing, for otherwise we can no longer follow; and Jesus will go on without us. No sacrifice is too great if we may walk through life in step with him."

Joost de Blank
Uncomfortable Words
pp. 12, 16

"When we allow ourselves to be confronted by the Gospel's basic images and metaphors, we begin to discover the personal geography of our inner space, the country though which our Lord is leading us now. The land is sometimes a frightening landscape that looks different from the way we would like it to be. It is not a way traveled by our own wits but by the dark light of faith. For it is only Jesus, the Lord of the journey, who truly sees the way. Convinced of our own blindness and assured, in faith, that he calls us to go with him, we follow."

Thomas Kane
"Powerless and Weak"

"The Christian is told to take up his own cross not as a quick getaway into some mystic realm of sweet withdrawal but as a binding weight which will plunge him down into the squalid cel'ars of his own soul where psychiatrists can roam and rummage but only God can rehabilitate. The greatest English writer on the Cross, P. T. Forsyth, once wrote, 'Do not turn from the awful horror of the Cross, or you will lose the solemn power of it.'

". . . The Cross makes short work of all our illusions — and it begins with those illusions about ourselves, as Laurens van der Post says in his *Venture to the Interior*: 'We must shut our eyes and turn them inward, we must look far down to that split between night and day in ourselves, and then we must ask how can I bridge this gulf? How to cross from one side to the other?' If we then allow that question to become the desire for its own answer, and that desire to become a bridge across the chasm, then and only then, we shall see a cross. A gulf bridged makes a cross; a split defeated is a cross. A longing for wholeness presupposes a cross at the foundation of our being. . . .

"To be saved by Christ means at least willingness to suffer with Christ. Hence, 'If any man would come after me, let him take up his cross and follow me.' St. Peter, who on the occasion when those words were first spoken, had rebuked the Lord for speaking about his sufferings, had learned to think very differently as in later life he reflected upon the Cross. He then understood that Christians were called to suffering 'because Christ also suffered for you leaving you an example that you should follow his steps' (1 Peter 2:21)."

Douglas Webster
In Debt To Christ
pp. 25-26, 40

"It would of course be the height of impertinence for any man to suggest that he could bear the smallest part in Christ's strange work of reconciliation. That work was unique in that it could only be accomplished by God-become-Man. Yet it is true that in carrying out any work of Christ, there is an inescapable cost and pain to be borne, which is in a rather different sense the price of redemption. To follow Christ does indeed mean every man, taking up 'his cross daily.' And the carrying of that cross is a symbol, not merely of the denial of the selfish way of living but of a certain humble sharing of a price that must be paid in bringing wholeness to a world rebellious and awry. We are as God's 'ambassadors' cheerfully and humbly to bear the cost of that reconciliation. In all humility, we can say that, at any rate in the limited sense, God is in every Christian 'reconciling the world to himself.' "

J. B. Phillips
Making Men Whole
p. 42

saying and thinking, to what he was thinking about me and for me.

"This was where I had to begin to learn how to deny myself — by allowing him to speak, to correct, rebuke, change my mind. If not there where I was most myself, how was I likely to learn to deny myself out in the pressure of meeting with other men, where I thought I had to stand to my own defense and argue my rightness? This taking up of the cross would never be understood out there in the heat of the moment unless I was learning what it meant in the quiet where I could be shown what I was not yet willing to see. . . . It is our own self-love that must be crucified, we cannot blame others. It is there at the heart of us that we must learn to turn away from ourselves and the concern about what we feel and suffer, what we think and wish to do."

J. W. Stevenson
God In My Unbelief
p. 92

"I began to see how deep were the roots of the self that seeks its own good — this evil from which I must be delivered there, in the very core of my being. I began to see — or was shown. Just where it was the darkest, the light had to break, had to be turned upon me so that I could see myself. Was that where the battle had to be fought out? Was that where the cross had to be taken up? I had not been prepared to give God time for that there — time to turn the light on me, time to turn me from myself and all that I was

"When Jesus described the Christian life, often his invitation to it sounds more like a warning than a sale's pitch. He spoke of picking up a cross to follow him. While this attitude used to puzzle me greatly, I now believe that he was simply underscoring the need for loyalty, which in biological terms means the need for individual cells to offer up service for the whole body."

Paul Brand and Philip Yancey
Fearfully and Wonderfully Made
p. 53

New Illuminations:

On Dying in Order To Live

''Most of us would rather stay put than seek such an experience of growth. This process of allowing new life to open up is like death and resurrection for human beings. One gives up life to find a new way, like the seed that gives itself to nourish a living growing plant. While the seed seems to have no choice, the person must choose to experience dying in order to live, and this is painful. Few of us will knowingly expose ourselves to such an experience unless we are convinced that it leads to growth too valuable to avoid.''

Morton T. Kelsey
The Other Side of Silence
p. 42

''Throughout his life Jesus taught 'whosoever would save his life shall not lose it.' To save one's own life is to achieve nothing; to lose it in the right cause may be to achieve much. Canon Fison has written: 'Christ sacrificed his life to save its meaning. . . . There is no guarantee whatever in the Christian faith that the worst, as we understand it, will not happen. On the contrary, it is the Christian faith that the worst that could happen did happen and was turned into something better than if it had never happened. From the human standpoint that is the meaning of the crucifixion and resurrection of Jesus Christ.' ''*

Douglas Webster
In Debt to Christ
pp. 39-40

''I hesitate to take the step that would make me die to death and live to life. I was too accustomed to the worst in me and too unaccustomed to the better.''

Sherwood Wirt
Love Song: Augustine's Confessions
p. 116

''One day I felt the 'I' in me rising hotly, and quite clearly the word came to me, 'See in it a chance to die. . . . See in it a chance to die in every form. Accept it as just that — a chance to die.' . . . Of all plans for insuring success,

the most certain is Christ's own — becoming a corn of wheat, falling to the ground and dying.''

F. Houghton
Amy Carmichael
pp. 86, 183

'' 'In order to become myself, I must cease to be what I always thought I wanted to be; and in order to find myself, I must go out of myself; and in order to live, I have to die.' The 'going out' and the death of self is the action of life, and this can only come by God's grace. 'I who am without love cannot become love unless Love identifies with me Himself. But if he sends his own Love, Himself, to act and love in me and in all that I do then I shall be transformed. I shall discover who I am, and I shall possess my true identity by losing myself in Him.' ''

Monica Furlong
Merton
pp. 150-151

''It is only by remembering that 'Another lives in me' that we can die daily to that old, false, usurping self and that we continue to be drawn 'further in and higher up' into the life of God. . . . Our self-will, swollen with pride, is dreadfully diseased and blemished. It has dark spots in it. It requires a radical conversion. The conversion is painful, for it is the surrender of an inflamed self-will that has been, for years, a usurper; for it to surrender is a kind of death. 'This action, to be perfect, must be done from the pure will to obey, in the absence, or in the teeth, of inclination' (C. S. Lewis). Obedience even after a thorough conversion of the will is an ongoing thing. There is a necessity to die daily to the old self, for 'however often we think we have broken the rebellious self we shall still find it alive'.''

Leanne Payne
The Real Presence: The Holy Spirit in the Works of C.S. Lewis
pp. 76, 89

''The process of 'daily dying' (1 Corinthians 15:31) connoted by the technical word, 'mortification,' provides sufficient agony even to the most thoroughly disciplined. . . .

*See also 117:3, Father Andrew.

Its best pictorial representation is always the crucifix, which holds before our eyes a slow death on a lonely cross in a gathering darkness. . . . The overwhelming majority of us, however, are not called to this dread privilege. The best we can aspire to is the grace to undergo mortification fairly quietly because of our conviction that no human soul can ever be really alive to God without first being dead to this world. Conviction? The word is far too strong. Hypothesis is better. The willing spirit rejoices in Christ's ennobling assumption that some humans at least, really wanting to become their perfect selves, will aspire to this absolute heroism. 'Whosoever he be of you that he forsaketh not all that he hath, he cannot be my disciple' (Luke 14:33). His flesh, however is weak. . . . Thus is revealed, without any doubt, the uncomfortable truth that his mind does not really assent to the fundamental proposition that we must 'die in order to live.' ''

Gale D. Webbe
The Night and Nothing
pp. 15-16

"There is only one way for one of God's creatures to achieve its destiny* — contemplation of the life of Christ. Then we see that his teaching, healing, life-giving power may possess us, work through us; that we may lose our own lives and find his life, be conformed to the pattern shown in him, conformed to the cross.''

Evelyn Underhill
The Light of Christ
p. 46

"The New Testament sees the Cross as the first stage in the great stage of man's death and resurrection. He who hung on it two thousand years ago died not only the death of the body but died also and more importantly to the preoccupations with self-importance and self-justification. 'In that He died, He died unto sin once.' We are not to watch the spectacle simply in terror and pity but to believe that the only way to be saved from sin is to share His death to self. . . . The Man on the Cross represents the startling truth about human existence: that it realizes its greatest glory when it allows God to make whatever use He thinks best of all its achievements and undertakings. From the anxious Adam who snatched at life's possibilities in defiance and ruthlessness, we are asked to turn our hearts and minds toward another model of what it means to be a man: to the Second Adam, who trusts life and the God within it.''

John M. Krumm
The Art of Being a Sinner
p. 108

*See also 67:2, Drake.

"The fall is rightly called the counter-creation, for the fact that emerges is that there is in us all an inherited weakness of the faculty of free will which predisposes us to actual sin. And the result of the dethronement of the will, in the individual and in the world at large, is chaos in the place of cosmos. . . .

"There is, however, another side to this. As with a stream rising in the hills and subsequently polluted by contact with a lead mine, so the *source* of our life remains pure. The poison does not flow upstream; behind the original guilt there is still more original innocence. Free will also, though impaired, is still ours. God's loving purpose still holds, and the Restoration is even now in progress. Every butterfly that emerges is a pledge that, in spite of the fall and our ensuing bondage to death, 'it does not yet appear what we shall be.' ''

Sister Penelope
The Wood
pp. 35, 36

"The life of St. Francis is a joyful life, not a comfortable one. If Francis possesses the world, it is because he has stripped himself of everything. If he knows the fullness of joy, he has found it through the uttermost of pain and suffering. And it is evident that this pattern of life through death, which is at the heart of the Christian mystery, is the pattern which is to be found everywhere on the way to God. . . . The uniqueness of Christ's death and resurrection, of his conquest of death by death is evidently an inclusive not an exclusive thing.''

A. M. Allchin
The World Is a Wedding
p. 29

"If one lives for things which die, one dies with them. If one lives for those things which are eternal, one already has eternal life. One who has died already to the things that die need never die again, need never fear death.* Too occupied with the tasks to which God has set them here to yearn for death, they yet look forward expectantly and triumphantly to the fuller life that is beyond.''

James A. Pike
Beyond Anxiety
pp. 132-133

*See also 86:3, Gibbard.

"In coming to understand anything, we are rejecting the facts as they are for us, in favor of the facts as they are. The primary impulse of each is to maintain and aggrandize himself. The secondary impulse is to go out of the self, to correct its provincialism and heal its loneliness. In love, in virtue, in the pursuit of knowledge, and in the reception of the arts we are doing this. Obviously this process can be described as an enlargement or as a temporary annihilation of the self. But that is an old paradox; '. . . he that loseth his life shall save it.' ''*

C. S. Lewis
An Experiment in Criticism
Epilogue

"In our moral and emotional life, the first innocent and spontaneous desires have to submit to the death-like process of control or total denial; but from that there is a re-ascent to fully formed character in which the strength of the original material all operates but in a new way. Death and re-birth — go down to go up — it is a key principle. . . .

"Human death is the result of sin and the triumph of Satan. But it is also the means of redemption from sin; God's medicine for Man and his weapon against Satan. In a general way it is not difficult to understand how the same thing can be a masterstroke on the part of one combatant and also the very means whereby the superior combatant defeats him**. . . . And one can see how it might have happened. The Enemy persuades man to rebel against God; Man by doing so loses power to control that other rebellion which the Enemy now raises in Man's organism against Man's spirit. In that way Satan produced human Death. But when God created man, he created such a constitution that, if the highest part of him rebelled against Himself, it would be bound to lose control over the lower parts; i.e. in the long run to suffer Death. This provision may be regarded equally as a punitive sentence ('In the day that ye eat of that fruit, ye shall die'), and as a mercy. It is punishment because Death — that Death of which Martha says to Christ, 'But . . . Sir, . . . it'll smell' — is horror and ignominy. It is mercy because by willing and humble surrender to it, man undoes his act of rebellion. 'The readiness is all' — not, of course, the merely heroic readiness but that of humility and self-

*See also 77:3, Andrew.
**See also 61:2, Penelope.

renunciation. Our enemy*, so welcomed, becomes our servant; bodily Death, the monster, becomes spiritual Death to self, if the spirit so wills — or rather if it allows the Spirit of the willingly dying God so to will in it.''

C. S. Lewis
Miracles
pp. 155-156

"By the time Mark came to write his Gospel, large numbers of Christians were martyred by crucifixion and many died other horrible deaths. The words in Luke 9:24-26 are a challenge to Christians to be ready to face death, if need be as a proof of their loyalty to Christ, to be willing to forfeit life on earth in the assurance of gaining eternal life in the presence of God. To seek to escape a martyr's death by holding on to physical life in this world by denying Christ, is to lose true life in the hereafter. . . .

"The essence of martyrdom is self-sacrifice for Christ; and it would be an effrontery to claim that any small sacrifices that most of us are called upon to make should be bracketed with the supreme offering of life itself. . . . The pages of history of young churches overseas are studded with tales of heroic endurance of torture and death by Christians who have taken up their crosses and laid down their lives rather than deny their Lord. . . . Self-sacrifice, self-denial, and self-giving are the hallmarks of our true selves, the men and women that God means us to be. This is the abundant life to which Jesus calls us; compared with which worldly success, fame and fortune are tawdry baubles, which end with our bodies in the grave. But a life lived in the spirit of Christ will never die. It has a quality that is eternal.''

William Neil
Difficult Sayings of Jesus
pp. 38-39

"It is a solemn truth that some of us have to experience a death in some part of our spiritual life in order to be given a resurrection life of the Spirit. In this way we are permitted a tiny share in what may well have been our Lord's own experience.

"There are things which for Christ's sake we have to

*See also 122:2, Holloway.

allow to die — like a relationship which, though not harmful exactly, is not helpful. We all realize this and occasionally we have to 'screw our courage to the sticking place' and let the relationship die without hurting or hindering the other soul's progress. The rich young ruler left our Lord's life — he let the young man go. This death can be painful. I've experienced it, and to this day it can hurt. But I know that from the death came a life for each person rightly and deeply freer.

"The death is a dying to self, in whatever form it takes, whether it happens to you, whether in conscience you permit it to happen for love of him who gave himself to die.

It is a martyrdom of the self*, and we not only are vulnerable to it, we *need* it. We need literally to reach that point in life when we must die to live, since there is no other way left to live life. Lord, when thou wilt and as thou wilt, so that we may share Paul's discovery cry, 'Nevertheless I live — yet not I, but Christ liveth within me.' "

John Andrew
Nothing Cheap and Much That Is Cheerful
p. 29

---

*See also 120:2, Ramsey.

New Illuminations:

On the Kingdom of God II: Imminence and Realized Eschatology

Matthew 3:2; 10:7, 23; 16:28   Mark 1:15; 9:1   Luke 9:27; 10:9; 17:21

"At the time of Christ, the Messianic hope existed in two forms. There was the prophetic hope of the restoration of the House and Throne of David; and there was the apocalyptic hope of a sublimated king such as the Son of Man. In the Infancy stories, as we saw, our Lord is clearly the Davidic king of prophecy. But then he disappeared for thirty years, and when he begins his ministry, the emphasis is on the Kingdom, not the king. 'The Kingdom and Reign of God has come!' That is the Good News. Thereafter our Lord speaks parable after parable about the Kingdom of God; paradoxically he adduces his own miracles as proof that it *has* come and teaches his followers to pray that it *may* come, on earth as it is in heaven."

Sister Penelope
The Coming
p. 38

"There is a remarkable tension, it would seem, between such sayings of Jesus as speak of the kingdom of God as a future happening, and such as announce its arrival now, in the present*. . . . The attempts of the commentators to deal with this question are numerous. His prevailing mood, according to some, was of expectation of the coming of the kingdom, but in the elation of enthusiasm and joy he could, in bold anticipation of the fulfillment, consider the present as the dawn of the kingdom. . . . According to the others, this apparent contradiction is explained by the psyche of the prophet, who sees the future at one moment as present with us and at another as stretching far into the distant time. But such attempts at explanation bring to the text a point of view to which the text themselves, without exception, rebel. They tear asunder what ought to hang together. For quite obviously the problem lies not in the fact that these pronouncements appear side by side but that they are, paradoxical though it may seem to us, closely interwoven. . . . Just as we do not ascribe to Jesus merely the preaching of a 'realized eschatology' (C. H. Dodd), we should not make him an apocalypticist who merely renews the old expectations of late Jewish hopes in a more vivid form, and ascribe in either case the other point of view to the church."

Gunther Bornkamm
Jesus of Nazareth
pp. 90-91

"Israel experienced Yahweh's kingship in the historical action of its God. There is no 'kingdom' and no 'sphere of dominion' but a kingly leadership and domain which develops from Yahweh's absolute power and shows itself in the guidance of Israel. This original meaning, namely that Yahweh as king actively 'rules,' must be kept in mind through the whole growth of the *basileia* theme. God's kingship in the Bible is characterized not by latent authority but by the exercise of power, not by an office but a function; it is not a title but a deed. Israel was conscious that Yahweh was its king, king of the chosen people of the covenant.
. . .

"What Jesus is proclaiming is that the reign of God is at hand; it has even (through his driving out devils) already come. In all this the role of Jesus is not passive. His person has its significance for the advent of God's reign in the present. He announces it, but it can be announced only through his advent and actions. God uses him to make his rule effective for the salvation of men who are willing to be converted. His purpose is to confront men with a final decision and with complete assurance to proclaim his future kingship that will be openly manifested and which will bring with it the separation of the judgment and afterwards blessing and happiness for the elect and saved. . . .

"While Jesus is narrating the parable of the sower, the reign of God is already in a certain sense present. God's rule has made contact with men in the expulsion of devils by Jesus and surely also in the teachings of Jesus. . . . But on the other hand the inquiry into the actual historical circumstances is imperative. A large part of the people had already abandoned him or are about to do so. This is true of the final state of Galilean ministry and nothing prevents us from assigning this parable to this period. Jesus is declaring that a start has been made and the future kingdom draws inevitably near. Even under these conditions, God guides his work to its end.

"With this goes a stronger appeal for men to accept the Gospel of Jesus, that is, to be converted and believe: the sower does not stand in the forefront of the story, but Jesus can intend this as a discreet reference to himself, rising out of the situation. The mystery of God's reign (Luke 8:10a) that is operative and present through himself implies also the mystery of his Messiahship. And so in this parable, Jesus is teaching something of the reign of God which is actually taking place."

Rudolf Schnackenburg
God's Rule and Kingdom
pp. 13, 129, 150

---

*See also 35:2, Jeremias.

"If we consider Christ's own action as he moves, a man amongst men, declaring the Kingdom of God, we see that he sets about this in the most practical way: not merely inviting men to think of the Transcendent, but bringing down into the texture of their lives the redeeming action of the Transcendent. . . . He was acting as the link between the outpouring love and harmony of the Life of God, and the jangled and defective life of men. 'Tell John the blind can see, the lame walk, the lepers are cleansed.' . . . His injunctions to his agents follow the same lines. They are to heal disharmony and misery wherever they find it. . . . Christ announced the one and only purpose of his ministry to be the bringing in of the Kingdom of God by the quiet action of a flawless love giving back to our lost tormented planet its place in the orchestra of heaven.''

Evelyn Underhill
Abba
pp. 36-37

"Not unnaturally, Mark 9:1 (Luke 9:27 par.) has been the object of a great deal of discussion. C. H. Dodd proposes a different translation: 'until they have seen that the Kingdom of God has come with power,' and comments: 'The bystanders are not promised that they shall see the kingdom of God *coming*, but that they shall come to see that the kingdom of God *has already come* (i.e., in the words and works of Jesus) at some point before they became aware of it.' So interpreted the saying fits admirably with Professor Dodd's theory of 'realized eschatology.'* . . .

"The most natural explanation then is that, though in a very real sense the kingdom of God has already drawn near in the words and deeds of Jesus, its manifestation of its full and final form lies still in the future, though according to this verse in the very near future. . . . The difficulty that has been felt about this interpretation is that it makes our Lord foreshorten the perspective drastically and sets very definite bounds to the extent of his accurate foreknowledge in the day of his flesh. Nevertheless, especially in view of such a passage as Matthew 10:23, and of the expectations of the early Church (e.g., 1 Corinthians 7:29, 31), the interpretation is to be accepted, and numerous writers have shown that admission of such ignorance, and even error, on the part of our Lord is fully compatible with the belief in the Incarnation. . . .

"Others have supposed the prophecy referred to the fall of Jerusalem, the gift of the Spirit, or the spread of Christianity to the Roman empire. But though all of these are partial manifestations of the kingdom, none of them describe what Jesus had in mind in Mark 9:1 par.''

D. E. Nineham
Saint Mark
pp. 231-32

"A broad stream of tradition testifies that Jesus announced the coming of God's reign, and correspondingly of the son of man, for a near future but without further specification of the time, indeed with a specific refusal to provide more precise details. Against this only a few passages contain a reference to the generation then alive (Luke 9:27 par.). It was not possible to explain these passages. The attitude of the early Church may well point to the best method for ourselves: namely to nourish a living eschatological hope for the urgent prophetic teaching of Jesus without drawing false conclusions about that prophecy from individual passages. The early Church did not admit any mistake on the part of Jesus. Nor need we do so. . . .

"To approach these questions empirically, we shall have to abandon our empirical notions of time which envisage time in our Western thinking as a continuously moving line divisible into measurable sections ('spaces'). Biblical thought about salvation, on the other hand, asks what occurs in time and what 'fills' it, and inquires what action of God gives every time its character and significance*. . . . Now that Jesus has sown the seed, and since his ministry, God's reign is irrevocably present though as yet only in a provisional way; the harvest is there at the door and the Last Things draw near to us forcibly and insistently. . . . Jesus' call to conversion and belief was re-echoed by the early Church and must be repeated by every Christian preacher to his generation, and with the same insistent urgency of the eschatological hour which is always a 'today', till God sets an end to this 'penultimate' era of salvation.''

Rudolf Schnackenburg
God's Rule and Kingdom
pp. 212-14

"It has never ceased to be true that 'the Lord reigneth.' It is in this sense that Jesus could say that the 'Kingdom of God is among you,' a rendering which is to be preferred to 'the Kingdom of God is within you.' But he never confused the abiding reality of God's sovereignty with the vital problem of how that sovereignty was to be made effective in the world of men. So long as man was held captive by the power of evil, the Kingdom could not be said to have come. When Jesus announced that the Kingdom of Heaven was at hand and when he told his disciples to pray 'Thy Kingdom come,'** he had before him the vision, not of some amelioration of man's condition, but of the swift and final victory over Satan, and the establishment of God's Kingdom on earth. . . .

"We must begin now to examine the nature of the first great crisis through which Jesus passed, and it is here that we shall find Matthew's Gospel indispensable. Upon receiving the news of John the Baptist's imprisonment, which he took as God's sign to him to begin his work, he took up his

---

*See also 82:1, Schnackenburg.

*See also 53:2, Webster.
**See also 59:2, Lewis.

headquarters in Capernaum and immediately plunged into an intensive activity of preaching the Good News of the Kingdom, attacking the kingdom of Satan by the exercise of the power of the Spirit, and preparing for the imminent act of God which was, he believed, to bring in the Kingdom. . . .

"In Matthew 10, we have an account of the sending out of the twelve. . . . It is possible that some of the apocalyptic elements may rightly have a place here since there is reason to believe that Jesus thought the decisive act of God was very near. There is one saying in verse 23 which, taken at its face value, would seem to suggest that it would take place before the twelve had finished the mission on which he was sending them out: the latter half of this verse runs, 'for truly, I tell you, you will not have finished the cities of Israel until the Son of Man has come.' Jesus feels that the moment for God to act is very near and that the ground has been prepared by his work of the past months, but there is still need of labourers in the harvest; hence he sends out the chosen twelve with delegated powers, but warns them to expect the coming of the Son of Man before they have completed the task assigned to them. It is clear that he expected in the immediate future the decisive act of God which would consummate the victory over Satan, and would manifest Jesus himself as the Messiah come in glory."

S. H. Hooke
The Kingdom of God
pp. 56, 64-67

"Although our Lord looked forward to the final setting up of the Kingdom at the end of the age, he also thought of it in a sense as being present during his earthly life. For evidence that the Kingdom had been begun, he appealed to the fact that the demons were being cast out — that evil was being driven from the lives of men — through his agency and that of his disciples. That is, the dominant note of the Kingdom was redeeming power. The judgment which would accompany its final inauguration would then be redemptive in its effect, at any rate upon those in whom there was anything left to redeem."

Ralph Milligan, ed.
All for the Love of God: A Holy Cross Omnibus
p. 160

New Illuminations:

On Jesus Transfigured With Glory

Matthew 17:1-13	Mark 9:1-13	Luke 9:28-36

"Jesus declared that the Son of Man would come with the clouds (Mark 8:38). Meanwhile some of them would be granted a glimpse before death of the glory of his kingdom. This exceptional privilege of some as distinct from the common experience of all was granted to Peter, James, and John on the holy mount when they saw Jesus transfigured with glory. The evangelists by telling the story of the Transfiguration immediately show plainly that they understood Jesus' words to refer to this event. This is a common patristic interpretation of a difficult verse. The Transfiguration was a striking manifestation of the Son of Man in his Kingdom, and again the voice of acclamation was heard from heaven."

John Stott
Men with A Message
p. 15

"One probable reason for Elijah and Moses having been chosen for this sublime occasion might have been to attest to the dignity of the Lord Jesus. He was approaching the darkest hour of his career and it seemed as if heaven itself were astir to assure his friends and to convince the world of his intrinsic worth. . . . These two represented the two great departments of Jewish thought and Scripture: Moses the founder of the Law; Elijah the greatest of the prophets. . . .

"Another may be found in the peculiar circumstances under which they left the world. Moses died not by disease nor by natural decay. His spirit passed painlessly and mysteriously to glory. Elijah did not die. Disease and old age had nothing to do with taking down the fabric of his being. He did not sleep, but he was 'changed in a moment, in a twinkling of an eye.' We may not penetrate into the secrets of that mysterious borderland which these two passed and then repassed, attesting his dignity and then withdrawing that the interest might be turned at once and more intensely on the person of Jesus Christ."

F. B. Meyer
Elijah
pp. 147-50

"Spontaneous prayer is possible at the moments when the marvel of finding ourselves suddenly face to face with God prompts spontaneous prayer and it does not matter much what words we use. The words are merely a way of sustaining a mood, of speaking foolishly, madly, of our love.

You remember the passage concerning the Transfiguration in which Peter says to Christ, 'Shall we make three tents . . .' The Gospel says he was speaking nonsense because he was out of himself. He was faced with something so overwhelming that he said whatever came into his mind; he blundered out something that expressed his feelings."

Anthony Bloom
Beginning to Pray
p. 27

"Only in retrospect did the three understand the Transfiguration. How could it have been otherwise? For what they saw was that which none had ever seen, of which none had ever dreamt — the final fulfilled perfection of humanity. To that by act of will the Second Adam passed; from that, again by act of will, he returned to his earthly state. Why? As sinless man, death for him was no necessity. He could and did pass thus gently to his glory. But love overrides nature. The servant Christ willed to die that he might make his soul an offering for many.* Only by our road of death would he pass finally to the glory that was his right. We might well write beneath our Transfiguration pictures his own words:

For this reason the Father loves me, because I lay down my life that I may take it again. No one takes it from me, but I lay it down of my own accord. I have power to lay it down and I have power to take it again. This charge I have received from my Father' (John 10:17).**

"St. Luke adds a little bit to this story which the other evangelists have not got. He says that what Jesus and Moses and Elijah were talking about was 'the *exodus* which he was to accomplish in Jerusalem.' Thus the Transfiguration appears as the porch to the Passion, the actual entrance to the Great Deliverance. So from the mountain, when they came down, 'he set his face to go to Jerusalem.' "

Sister Penelope
The Wood
pp. 19-20

"The state of Jesus after his resurrection is represented by the transfiguration narrative which Mark links to the

---

*See also 123:3, Penelope.
**See also 118:1, Penelope.

passion predictions in a quite remarkable manner. The transfiguration narrative begins, 'And after six days. . . .' The only other place in the Gospel narrative where one finds anything like this is in the passion predictions with their uniform and remarkable 'after three days' with reference to the resurrection. It is impossible to resist the conclusion that these two references are related, that the 'after six days' of the transfiguration deliberately picks up the 'after three days' of the resurrection references, that the evangelist is deliberately linking the transfiguration narrative to the resurrection references in order to say something to his readers. This conclusion becomes even more certain when we notice Mark 9:9: 'And as they were coming down the mountain he charged them to tell no one what they had seen, until the Son of Man should have risen from the dead.' In other words, the transfiguration becomes important after the resurrection; it is symbolic of the post-resurrection situation.*

"The next step is to recognize that Mark and his readers both thought of Moses and Elijah as being already with God in the heavens. It was uniformly held that God had taken Moses to be with him in the heavens. That Elijah was already with God in the heavens was taught in 2 Kings 2:1-12, an account of Elijah being taken into heaven by a whirlwind. So when Jesus is seen in a transfigured state speaking to Moses and Elijah, he is seen proleptically in his post-resurrection state and situation: he is in heaven with Moses and Elijah waiting the moment of his return to earth as the Son of Man."

Norman Perrin
The Resurrection
pp. 24-25

"Coming down from the mountain of the transfiguration' the disciples see no one but 'Jesus only.' The obvious meaning of the phrase is that they no longer see Moses, Elijah and the divine glory. They join Jesus once again under his everyday appearance. Another meaning can be added

---

*See also 49:2, Bornkamm.

to this one: the soul which has been dazzled by the Savior's light sees this same light over all beings. Through men and things, it sees Jesus only. . . .

"I learn to look at Jesus in so far as I learn to be looked at by him. . . . The conditions of the vision are the same as those imposed on the three disciples whom he made witnesses of his transfiguration. Jesus 'took them with him'; 'he led them'; he led them up 'a high mountain where they were alone, apart.' Let us consider being alone with Jesus, letting ourselves be led by him. The ascent is painful, far above what is bad or mediocre in our lives. Ordinarily all these conditions remain necessary. (I say 'ordinarily' because there are exceptional cases: Saul on the road to Damascus.)"

Monk of the Eastern Church
Jesus: A Dialogue with the Savior
pp. 34, 12-13

"It is in the Christian tradition of the Byzantine Empire that we find an age which placed the mystery of our Lord's Transfiguration at the very center of its understanding of God, man's nature and the world. It is an age which affirmed that while God himself is wholly beyond the reach of our faculties, yet in his operations, the energies of his glory, he truly makes himself known even to our senses. Through the activity of the Holy Spirit in the lives of men and women, the heart and its perceptions are so cleansed that we may see with our bodily eyes 'the unseeable. / One glory of the everlasting world, / Perpetually at work though never seen' (Edwin Muir). . . . By the transformation of the heart, through the realization of God's presence at the center of man's being, it becomes possible to see that 'heaven and earth are full of God's glory.'* We discover our kinship with the material creatures; we see all things marked with the name of Jesus."

A. M. Allchin
The World Is a Wedding
p. 40

---

*See also 57:1, Mascall.

New Illuminations:

On the Messianic Secret

"The essence of the Old Testament faith in the Kingdom of God was that one day God would overcome the forces of evil and show on earth the forces of his power. . . . The common view was that he would send an individual to act as his representative and rule on his behalf. Since the greatest of Israel's kings had been David, it was natural for this future king to be thought of as one of his descendants. And since the kings of Israel were all anointed at their coronation, it was natural that he should be called the Anointed One (in Hebrew, 'The Messiah'; in Greek, 'The Christ')."

Robert Dentan
A First Reader in Biblical Theology
p. 62

"Jesus grew up knowing that he was by birth the heir of the House of David, the dynasty that had first made Israel great a thousand years before. About five centuries before Jesus, that royal family had been overthrown by foreign invaders. For most of the time since, Israel had been ruled by foreigners. Yet all through those 500 years God's people had dreamed that if ever they were to be free and great again, it would be through a Prince whom God would raise up of the House of David — the coming 'Christ' — who with the might of God himself would deliver Israel from all its oppressors. Prophets and psalmists and saints and patriots had kept that hope alive in their radiant certainty that God's promise *could* not fail. Yet the Babylonian conqueror followed the Assyrian, and the Persian followed the Babylonian, and the Greek followed the Persian, and the Roman followed the Greek, for five whole centuries, and still God's people were not free. But then the Baby was born in Bethlehem in the City of David, though almost in the gutters of it, and of the House of David, now reduced to utter obscurity.

"But still its heir was by right of blood and inheritance the true King of Israel — the heir of the gallant David and the gorgeous Solomon, the focus and center of all God's promises to his people. . . . There came a day when the turbulent peasants of Galilee would have taken him by force to make him a king to lead them against Rome (John 6:15). But he hid himself in the mountains alone. He could not trust even his disciples not to force his hand about this. But still men must have whispered that he was by rights the King. Even the blind beggars beside the road called to him as the 'Son of David.' This was a dangerous greeting; it implied a throne. All men must have wondered where and when he would make his bid for the throne which was his by right."

Dom Gregory Dix
The Claim of Jesus Christ
pp. 49-50

"Our Lord was indeed the Messiah, but he could not tell the people openly because of their false notion of the Messiah. He was indeed a king but his kingdom was not of this world. That is why he imposed silence: because of the idea of Messiahship as he conceived it — the spiritual Messiahship of a suffering Messiah — and because of the prevalent false notions on the subject. And that is why he called himself Son of Man. It was not a current Messianic title but it could, and in fact it did, designate the Messiah. . . .

"Jesus the Messiah is Son of God, Son of Man. Either title enshrouds the mystery of his person. But it was the second that he chose to use, and, in the circumstances, he could not have introduced himself in any clearer terms. While it is probable that in certain circles of Judaism a Messiah was awaited who was 'Son of Man,' it is certain that this conception of the Messiah was not wide spread, and the crowds were manifestly puzzled by the title. But the Jewish leaders realized that Jesus claimed to be more than the traditional Messiah, and that is the reason why he was accused of blasphemy. In likening himself to the 'Son of Man' in Daniel 7:13-14, he gave to the title 'Son of God' itself a meaning that was not metaphorical but proper and transcendent, one that was unacceptable to their strict monotheism."

Wilfred J. Harrington
Explaining the Gospels
pp. 93-94

"What astonishes us most is that Jesus does not directly make the claim of Messiahship but lets it be absorbed in his words and works without confirming the authority which the people are willing to acknowledge in him. As little as he fulfils the demands of his opponents for proof of his claim so little does he fulfil the expectations of his followers.

"In the Gospels, this very strange state of affairs has found expression in the paradoxical doctrine of the 'Messianic Secret' of Jesus. . . . Jesus' whole history leads up to Easter. Until then the fact that he is the Messiah remains concealed and is not to be revealed (Matthew 17:9). Again and again, however, it comes out in particular incidents and acts of Jesus. The evil spirits recognize him and know, fearfully, that the one that makes an end to their rule has come; the healed wish to make known his power; the disciples wish to confess and proclaim him the Messiah before his time. Jesus, however, repeatedly demands silence and will not permit this confession and message until he has died and risen again* (Matthew 17:9). . . . Because of the demands for silence which are often impossible to carry out, as well as the frequently repeated remarks about the disciples' lack of understanding (Mark 6:52; 7:18; 8:17-20), the oldest Gospel has been called paradoxically 'a book of secret epiphanies.' "

Gunther Bornkamm
Jesus of Nazareth
pp. 170-71

*See also 48:2, Perrin.

New Illuminations:

On the Misunderstanding of Passion Predictions

Matthew 16:21-23   Mark 9:31-32; 10:32-33   Luke 9:22, 44-45; 18:31-34

"What distinguishes sacrifice or martyrdom is that it is voluntary suffering. It is usually the result of a particular form of integrity or of a refusal to give up certain convictions and so lower one's standard of truth or conduct. We are all permanent debtors to the sacrifice of others who did something for us that we could not do or would not have done for ourselves. Human life has been immeasurably enriched because some have been prepared for sacrifice. . . . A way was chosen, a vocation accepted and a price paid. . . . Voluntary suffering is always highly developed in the Old Testament and supremely in the four Great Servant Songs of Isaiah. But this role of the suffering servant in the prophet's vision was perfectly fulfilled and worked out to the end. Jesus at his baptism deliberately chose to win his kingdom that way and no other. He would accept the Messiahship which was his destiny only in these terms."*

Douglas Webster
In Debt to Christ
pp. 23-24

"The stories of Jesus giving sight to a blind man at Bethsaida and blind Bartimaeus at Jericho are symbolic of the power of Jesus to give sight to the blind. They offset and highlight the central section of Mark's Gospel (8:27—10:45), in which Jesus attempts to give 'sight' to his disciples, that is, attempts to teach them the meaning of his impending passion. But in this he fails. The Jesus who could give sight to the physically blind could not give insight and understanding to the disciples. For Mark, this is one of the great motifs of the Gospel story; and as he tells the story, he is constantly reaching out beyond the disciples to his own readers, attempting to get them to understand what the disciples had so significantly failed to understand."

Norman Perrin
The Resurrection
pp. 19-20

"The disciples' failure to understand Jesus' perfectly straightforward words seems inexplicable except on St. Mark's theory of the supernatural blinding of their eyes; and in view of Mark 9:11-13, their fear of asking for an explanation seems equally hard to explain. It is difficult to deny the force of Bultman's words: 'The evangelist knew well the story of what took place at Jerusalem. When the events occurred, the disciples, taken apparently by surprise, fled. The detailed explanation of what was to come could only be reconciled with this result on the theory that the disciples did not understand what they were told.' "

D. E. Nineham
St. Mark
p. 248

"Peter's faith in Jesus' Messiahship was a foundation, and on it Jesus promptly built. 'The Son of Man must suffer . . . and be rejected . . . and be killed.* . . .' Peter did not listen to the last bit: 'and after three days rise again'; he was too much scandalized by the first. What could you do with a leader that spoke of his rejection and death the moment after you had called him the Christ? It was preposterous! 'This shall never happen to you!' How pitiful is Peter, foolish and ignorant; how pitiful too is the loneliness of Jesus breaking to his apostles the news of his Servant Christhood — that which was the very heart and center of the Good News and having it thus received! But he goes as ever, straightforward. Calling the crowds, he tells them not for himself only but for every human soul the way to the Cross is the way of life, *and there is no other*."

Sister Penelope
The Wood
pp. 118-19

"When for the first time, Jesus spoke the fateful words to his disciples disclosing his predestined death at Jerusalem, he added words which the disciples were utterly unable to understand, 'and the third day rise again.' They show that the faith of Jesus laid hold of the power of God and reached beyond the Cross; the Messiah's death was not only an end but a beginning."

S. H. Hooke
The Kingdom of God
p. 135

"Peter did not understand the divine *must*, for he rebuked our Lord for suggesting that he would suffer. It was at this point that our Lord called him Satan. Peter had done

*See also 40:1, Kane; 70:1, Hooke.

*See also 98:1, Thielicke.

exactly the same thing that Satan had done in the wilderness namely, tried to turn him away and make him a political Messiah who would give belly-bread instead of soul-bread. Our Lord implied that suggesting a merely human way out of a divine mission is merely a human way of being diabolical.* Then he told Peter that what he had said savored not of things of God but of things of men. . . . From now on he spoke openly of his death, never mentioning his Cross without his Resurrection; but they could not understand either clearly until Pentecost and the coming of the Spirit.''

Fulton J. Sheen
The Life of Christ
p. 88

"St. Luke says, 'They understood none of these things.' 'They understood not and were afraid to ask him.' There

---

*See also 13:1, Kunkel.

is something mysterious at the heart of man's life and becomes clear only, indeed can be endured only, with our surrender to God. Until then, we do not understand and are afraid to ask. . . .

"The Son of Man must suffer if he would fulfil all his possibilities. The crowning peace of the fully awakened fully Christian soul is always that demand. To the outer eye, the figure on the Cross may seem both lonely and idle — yet it is here as St. Bonaventure said, that 'great perfection is being taught to our souls.' . . . So here above all, by the crucifix and what it means to us, we test the quality of our discipleship. What we think about the Cross means ultimately what we think about life, for 'seek where you will,' says a Kempis, 'everywhere you will find the Cross.' And when you have found it what are you going to do about it? That is the question: look at it with horror or with adoration?''

Evelyn Underhill
Light of Christ
pp. 79-81

New Illuminations:

On the Dispute About Greatness

Matthew 10:40-41; 18:5   Mark 9:33-37   Luke 9:46-48; 22:24

"On one occasion when his disciples had been quarreling about which of them was the greatest, we are told that 'he took a child, set him in front of them and put his arm around him.' The little child in his simplicity and humility was to be an object lesson to those grown men who ought to have known better: that true greatness consists not in trying to be important, but in service of those who are of no importance as the world judges it."

William Neil
The Difficult Sayings of Jesus
p. 50

"We cannot know God if we do not understand the revelation of Christ. Why do we worship him? Because he would come down and be cradled in straw so that no little slum child might ever feel that his God wanted a better cradle than he. That is our God and that is what Christmas means, that the great God sank down to the dimensions of a child to reach children. . . . There is no enemy to prayer like pride, and spiritual pride is the death of spiritual prayer. God's mercy will always humble us while he leads us, for the ascent of the soul to the highest is conditioned by the descent of the self to the lowest. . . .

"When we can completely forget ourselves and think only how we can best serve other people, we pass from the evil atmosphere of selfishness to the peace and creative power of sacrifice."

Harry C. Griffith, ed.
*A Gift of Light: A Collection
of Thoughts from the Writings of Father Andrew*
pp. 36-37

"There is only one standard in God's service — not how much we can get but how much we can give. Those who think of their religion in terms of success and rewards have not begun to understand what Christianity is all about. The only measure that has validity in the Kingdom of God is that of love. To him or her who loves much, much is forgiven — and in the relationship of friendship and love, it

is all the recompense a sinner seeks. . . . The self-satisfied and envious disciples have not yet understood this utter self-abandonment."

Joost de Blank
Uncomfortable Words
p. 49

"Because heaven is a state of total, unselfish, perfect love, no selfish motive and no selfish action can get us one step nearer to heaven. And heaven isn't a selfish compensation for the frustrations of this world. Heaven is the glorious climax of the sacrificial love which ought to be seen manifested in this world. Think of the most heroic acts of sacrifice and love which can be counted in this world. Heaven is the consummation of that."

Margaret Duggan, ed.
Through the Year with Michael Ramsey
p. 43

"The introduction of the child in Mark 9:39 (par. Luke 9:47) would be more natural if he were used as in Matthew's parallel version (v. 18:3-4) as an example for the disciples to copy. . . . But in the Markan and Lukan version, the point lies not in the *child's* attitude but in the attitude of others *towards* him, the connection being that the true disciple achieves not by holding great offices but by doing service to individual people, such as a child. . . . What exactly is meant by 'receiving a child'— an expression as obscure in the Greek as it is in the English? St. Mark presumably meant it as meaning 'show kindness to.' But the fact seems to be that Jesus was in the habit of describing certain of his followers as 'little ones' or 'children,' and that, as a consequence, a certain amount of confusion arose between sayings of his about children and sayings about disciples.

"If the present saying referred originally to Jesus' disciples, 'receiving' them would be a perfectly natural expression especially as the Aramaic *gabbel* meant both 'to receive' and 'to hear' in the sense of 'obey' (cf. Matthew 10:14, Luke 10:8 and 10). It is noteworthy that both Matthew and Luke have versions of this saying as Jesus' charge to his disciples as he sent them out on missionary work — a setting which seems to be more likely to be the original. The sense would then be fully in line with the well attested principle of Jewish life that 'One who is sent (by the king) is as the one who sends him,' and it is probably a mistake to read a 'mystical' meaning into the idea of 'receiving' Jesus and the Father.''

D. E. Nineham
Saint Mark
pp. 252-53

New Illuminations:

On In the Name of Jesus Christ

| Matthew 18:5, 20 | Mark 9:37-41 | Luke 9:48-50; 10:17 | John 14:13-14 |

"If an ambassador speaks 'in the name of his government,' he indicates that his government or his nation with all its dignity and power is symbolically present. The prophet who preaches 'in the name of the Lord' means that God is present in his prophecy. The 'name,' in the ancient sense of the word, is not only the definition or the essence of the person — it is his presence."

Fritz Kunkel
Creation Continues
p. 95

"Once Moses saw a bush on fire which continued to burn without burning up. As Moses approached it, he heard a voice saying, 'Put off thy shoes from off thy feet for the place whereon thou standest is holy ground.' The meaning of this is that before God speaks to man, man must have proper respect and reverence."

Charles L. Allen
God's Psychiatry
p. 95

"(Mark 9:37), '. . . in my name' means simply 'for my sake' or 'on the ground of my name,' i.e., because of his connection with me. Some commentators take the meaning to be 'because my name has been invoked over him (in baptism).' . . . Verse 39 throws an interesting light on the contemporary outlook that Jesus is not represented as shocked or incredulous at the suggestion that his name could be used to effect cures in a semi-magical way unrelated to any personal knowledge or faith in him. In verse 41, 'because you bear the name of Christ' means literally 'in the name that you are Christ's — a phrase as odd in Greek as it is in English. 'Because you are Christ's is Pauline terminology."

D. E. Nineham
Saint Mark
p. 257

"Every right prayer is answered before the prayer itself is finished — before we have done speaking. This is because God has pledged his word to us that whatsoever we ask in Christ's name (that is in oneness with Christ and his will) and in faith shall be done."

Mrs. Charles Cowman
Streams in the Desert
p. 151

"None can be saved without knowing the name of Jesus, and none can be used effectively of God without knowing the authority of that name. To be sure it is the very self-same name of his humanity, but it is the name invested now with the title and authority given to it by God. . . . We must note in Scripture the recurring expression 'in the name' — that is to say the use to which the Apostles put that name. It is not only that he has such a name but that we are to use it (Luke 9:48). . . . One of the features of a work in his name is the question of the identification of my purpose with the eternal purpose of God. . . . God's name can never be a rubber stamp to authorize work that is ours in conception. . . . Even where God has initiated a work, if we are trying to accomplish it in our own power, God will never commit himself to it. To do so the object of all work must be to his glory. This means that we get nothing out of it for ourselves (Luke 10:20)."

Watchman Nee
Sit, Walk, and Stand
pp. 45-46, 51-55

"Jesus encourages his disciples to come simply and directly with the questions that are in their hearts. He promises that 'the Father will give it to you in my name' (John 16:23). Somehow in prayer we are given an authority — ask anything; yet at the same time the authority of Jesus Christ is preserved — 'in my name.' Jesus has posed a tension between our authority on one side, our privilege in asking, and on the other side his authority and reign over us."

Earl Palmer
The Intimate Gospel
p. 140

"Exorcism was commonly practiced in Jewish and Gentile circles in the time of Jesus. Often it was little more than black magic, when the exorcist exploited the credulity of superstitious people by calling on such powerful names as Abraham, Isaac, and Jacob. Later even pagan exorcists used the name of Jesus in this way. . . . On the occasion referred to by John, he and his fellow-disciples had tried to stop the exorcist who was using the name of Jesus — presumably having heard of our Lord's success in dealing with demon possession — on the grounds that he was not a follower of Jesus. 'He was not one of us,' said John. . . . And Jesus' reply is a condemnation of intolerance. Anyone who does Christ's work or acts in his name is not to be discouraged, even though he is 'not one of us' as John had objected. For he who is not against us is on our side.' . . .*

"The words of Jesus are timeless and we all stand accused. How ready we all are to build fences instead of bridges, how quick to point out in connection with someone who is undoubtedly doing Christ's work and serving the community in his spirit: 'But he is not one of us' not a member of our denomination, worse still, not even a Christian. Exclusivism and sectarianism have bedeviled the church throughout its history. . . . Over the whole range of Christian witness throughout the world, the truth is that what we have in common is far greater than what divides us; and we are coming to see that this holds true also for Jews and Christians.

"Jesus' words in our saying are all-embracing. Those who are not against us are on our side. . . . He asks us to be open-minded, to overcome our prejudices and to be ready to acknowledge the Spirit of Christ in those whose beliefs we may feel to be unorthodox, or who may not call themselves Christians at all. In this sense we can honor and respect those who are honestly seeking to promote the betterment of society, the relief of suffering, and a fairer deal for the underprivileged. What matters is not their labels but their care and compassion."

William Neil
The Difficult Sayings of Jesus
pp. 40-42

———————
*See also 61:1, Neil.

"Those acts we do on our own in an unregenerate state have a special purpose Lewis describes in a letter to his friend, Dom Bede Griffiths:

'The bad material tree cannot produce good fruit. But oddly it can produce fruits that by all *external* tests are indistinguishable from the good ones: the act done from one's own separate and unredeemed, though 'moral' will, *looks* exactly like the act done by Christ in us. And oddly enough it is the tree's real duty to go on producing these imitation fruits till it recognizes this futility and despairs and is made a new (spiritual) tree.'

"Although it is obvious that we must cease from our own works, we can't separate 'what exactly God does and what man does when God and man are working together.' . . .

"Yet Lewis considered himself as called merely to create a positive intellectual climate for the Christian faith. When asked if he thought the Spirit was at work in his own writing, Lewis replied, 'Who am I to say whether Grace works in my own stories? . . . If anything is well done, we must say *Non nobis* [not of myself].' "

Leanne Payne
Real Presence: The Holy Spirit in the Works of C.S. Lewis
pp. 100, 105

New Illuminations:

On Jesus' Sense of Urgency

| Matthew 16:21 | Mark 8:31 | Luke 9:22, 51-56; 13:31-33 |

"It is not certain at what period Jesus started to envisage his atoning death. It was only after Peter's confession at Caesarea Philippi that he began to initiate his disciples into the mystery of the sufferings of the Son of Man, but this does not mean that he then became conscious for the first time of his destined death. It would be better to assume that since his baptism and temptation he had seen his Messianic role in the light of the servant of God. All we can assert positively is this. Jesus desired to ('must') fulfil his Messianic task on earth humbly and in obedience as the servant of God and, conscious of the divine commission, he proclaimed the immediate dawn and future realization of God's reign, himself ready to do and endure everything which the Father had ordained for this service. But when the assurance of his death as vicarious atonement was communicated to him remains concealed in the mystery of his person."*

Rudolf Schnackenburg
God's Rule and Kingdom.
pp. 182-83

"When Jesus said *must* in Mark 8:51 (Luke 9:22) he meant this. He used the word in a sense in which it was often used in contemporary apocalyptic literature, as showing that certain future events were part of the firmly decreed will of God. Thus, to persuade Jesus to shrink from those events was to tempt him to disobey the will of God as Satan had done in the Wilderness."

D. E. Nineham
Saint Mark
p. 225

" 'The Son of Man must suffer many things.' All three synoptists use the word 'must' here, but Luke most frequently connects the pressing necessity with Jesus' passion."

Carroll Stuhlmueller
Jerome Bible Commentary
44:88

"In eternity grace was given to us in Christ Jesus and not apart from him. He is the one mediator between God and men. His mediation is seen preeminently in the cross,

but it did not begin at the cross. It began in eternity. 'He set his face to go to Jerusalem' is in context a record of the decisive act of the historic Jesus. It could well represent his eternal acceptance of his mission."

Ronald A. Ward
1 and 2 Timothy and Titus
p. 151

" 'Nevertheless I must go on my way today and tomorrow and the day following for it cannot be that a prophet should perish away from Jerusalem' (Luke 13:33). The real point of these words is obviously to reveal Jesus' true mission but also to show his readiness to seek the decision on his mission in the only place where it should be given, in Jerusalem.

"This decision to go to Jerusalem is undoubtedly the turning-point in Jesus' life. It must not however be too readily understood along the lines of the later tradition as though Jesus had sought only his death in Jerusalem. It appears that way according to the repeated prophecies of suffering and resurrection. . . .

"The reason why Jesus sets out with his disciples on his journey to Jerusalem cannot be doubted. It was to deliver the message of the coming kingdom of God in Jerusalem, 'the City of the Great King' (Psalm 48:2). That the road to Jerusalem had to lead to new and serious conflicts with the spiritual and temporal rulers, and that Jesus had to reckon with the possibility of his own violent end, we have no reason to doubt. The sources do not tell us clearly at what moment his readiness to accept death turned into the certainty of his imminent end. We may assume that first and foremost his journey to Jerusalem was undertaken in order to confront the people there, in the holy city, with the message of the kingdom of God and to summon them at the eleventh hour to make their decision. Luke says explicitly in several places that the disciples pinned to this journey their hope that the kingdom of God was about to appear (Luke 19:11). . . . It is beyond doubt that only on the journey with his followers to Jerusalem and the temple did Jesus seek the final decision."*

Gunther Bornkamm
Jesus of Nazareth
pp. 154-55

"In the Bible there are two Greek words for time. There is *chronos*, which means time in the sense of duration, that

---

*See also 53:1, Bornkamm.

*See also 53:1, Schnackenburg.

which can be measured on the clock or on the calendar, unrelated to anything we are doing, ticking on remorselessly. But the other word is *kairos*,* which means the right time, the opportune moment. Jesus thought of his own destiny in these terms. Throughout St. John's Gospel like a fugue we keep hearing the words 'Mine hour is not yet come.' He could not die until his hour came. This certainty of God holding all the strings of time kept Jesus calm amidst all threat (Luke 13:31-33). This is the doctrine of Providence, summed up in the Psalmist's affirmation: 'My times are in thy hand' (Psalm 31:15). And so it is with the transposition of the Cross into the Christian's life. If we respond to time as *kairos*, waiting for the right moment and then seizing the opportunity, we are using time creatively like God and are sharing Christ's mastery of time. . . .

"St. Paul also had a remarkable attitude to time. When he is warned by the elders of Ephesus of all the hardships that awaited him, he can say:

And now, behold, I am going to Jerusalem. . . . I do not account my life of any value nor as precious to myself, if only I may accomplish my course and the ministry which I received from the Lord Jesus, to testify to the Gospel of the grace of God (Acts 20:21-24).

Quite calmly and resolutely he accepted the limitations of the situation; the principle of the Cross was being transposed into his life. He, like his Master, would fulfil his destiny.

"The practical result of such an attitude to time will be a deliberate limitation of what we attempt, an assessment of our own priorities according to our own vocation and ministry and gifts, and a concentration on these priorities which will let nothing deflect us. Jesus set his face as a flint toward Jerusalem."

Douglas Webster
In Debt to Christ
pp. 117-19

*See also 47:2, Schnackenburg.

New Illuminations:

On Discipleship III: Its Demands

Matthew 8:19-22   Luke 9:57-62

"Discipleship means decision, Jesus' decision as regards certain individuals, but then it means no less their decision to follow him. It consists, in actual fact, in the determination to abandon everything and, in the first instance, to follow Jesus from place to place and to accept the fate of the wanderer with all its privations."

Gunther Bornkamm
Jesus of Nazareth
p. 146

"Jesus summons the first man with the words: 'Follow me.' The man asks permission to bury his father first but is peremptorily told: 'Leave the dead to bury their dead'; and he is further told that he must go and announce the Kingdom of God. . . . Jesus' words mean that there were plenty of others who were spiritually dead, i.e., who had not been seized by the importance and urgency of Jesus' mission. To them could be left the normal arrangements for burial. The man in question was being summoned to a task which must be ranked second to none and which brooked no delay. Jesus is simply forcefully asserting the primary duty of a committed disciple to put the service of God before any personal consideration and family loyalties*. . . .

"The second man seems to have been similarly told to join the band of Jesus' followers but asks permission to join his family first. This apparently harmless and natural request is dismissed with words to the effect that anyone setting out to plough a field and constantly looking back, instead of looking forward and concentrating on his job, is unfit to be Christ's follower.

"The Jesus of the Gospel is neither unsympathetic to human feelings nor unreasonable in his demands. We must therefore look for special grounds for what seems to be a more callous attitude on the part of Jesus. And indeed, if we see this incident in the context of Jesus' whole ministry and plan of campaign, much becomes plain. Jesus was approaching the close of his Galilean ministry. He had hoped that his message would gradually win men's hearts and minds and make them ready to commit their lives to the service of God. This had not happened. . . . The time left to him to create this new Israel was all too short. Consequently nothing but absolute renunciation of all natural and material ties would qualify a man to belong to this chosen band. . . .

"Jesus was therefore involved at this time in a process of sifting out a small group who would be totally and unconditionally committed to this missionary task. . . . This demand of Jesus was designed to meet a particular situation — the creation of a tightly knit band of men who could be trusted to carry on the Lord's work after his death. Have we merely succeeded in making a hard saying easy by limiting its challenge to the men of Christ's own time? This is far from true. These words of Jesus would say to all of us that Christian discipleship involves self-discipline and self-denial and means constant examination of our motives. Christ's service is not something to be entered upon lightheartedly. We have to count the cost."

William Neil
The Difficult Sayings of Jesus
pp. 70-72

"Our Lord says nothing of *turning* back. He says *looking* back. I believe that there is an eternal truth contained in his choice of that verb. If the plower, even while his feet are still following the plough, looks anywhere but straight forward, his furrow goes crooked.

"The devil is continually trying to persuade us to look back. He delights to engage our thoughts with ourselves, our sins, our worthlessness, our failures. This is a backward pull which greatly hinders our plowing, and Paul was thinking of it when he wrote about 'forgetting those things which are behind and reaching forth to those things which are before.' . . . May God give us the heart which is fixed, and keep us with our eyes on the track, not looking to the right or left or backward, but plowing a straight furrow.'"*

Amy Carmichael
Thou Givest . . . They Gather
pp. 139-40

"Jesus assumes on the part of his followers a readiness to make a complete surrender.** This is the implication of the ploughman who must look straight ahead of him. The very light Palestinian plough is guided with one hand. This one hand, generally the left, must at the same time keep the plough upright, regulate its depth by pressure and lift it over the rocks and stones in its path. The ploughman uses the other hand to guide the unruly oxen with a goad about two yards long fitted with an iron spike. At the same time he must continually look behind the hindquarters of the oxen,

*See also 76:2, Thielicke.

*See also 62:1, Pardue.
**See also 74:1, Nee.

keeping the furrow in sight. If the ploughman looks around the new furrow becomes crooked. Thus whoever wishes to follow Jesus must be resolved to break every link with the past and fix his eye only on the coming Kingdom of God."

Joachim Jeremias
The Parables of Jesus
p. 195

"Ever since Lot's wife turned to have a look at the old hometown, she has been the universal symbol of the futility of living in the past. It is one thing to have a good and proper reverence for great tradition and to weave the living present with a dependable thread; but it is quite another thing to stand stockstill, transfixed by yesterday. . . . We can stand, looking back, coveting yesterday's joy and yesterday's grief and die. Or we can bring these things into the present where God transforms them and us with new life."

Robert G. Hewitt
Grace Tidings

"Jesus does not make this demand on all. Some he leaves within their own circle without taking them from their home, their work, their family. He does not blame them for any lack of determination or half-heartedness nor exclude them from the kingdom of God. Nowhere in this respect is an exclusive line drawn between them and the disciples. It is precisely against such tendencies that these words seem to warn: 'For he that is not against us is for us.' On the other hand the Gospels nowhere show the intention to include then and there those who have experienced Jesus' healing powers among his intimate disciples, although they too, in their own spheres, are witnesses to Jesus, and he visits their homes."

Gunther Bornkamm
Jesus of Nazareth
p. 147

"To follow Christ, the disciples have to leave much behind, much that is good. But because of the call, all will be transformed. In a real sense what they are will remain, for they will stay fishermen; but now they become fishers for the mysterious kingdom that they have glimpsed for a moment. What that will look like, or what it will cost they do not know. But Jesus will do it. . . . That call echoes now in my heart and in yours, calling us to follow this One, to leave behind old ways. This is the beginning of a Journey."

Thomas Kane
"Inhabiting the Gospel"

" 'He who wants a future must not inquire into the past' goes a saying of Stalin's which reminds us immediately of a saying of Jesus: 'No one who puts his hand to the plow and looks back is fit for the kingdom of God.' This similarity is not a coincidence but originates in the fact that Jesus' word and Bolshevism today are both concerned with the future, that future which transcends all our history. Both wish to open up our future, a future which is not somewhere in heaven but which shall become real on earth. Nevertheless, the difference is fundamental; and these revolutionaries, when they wanted to claim Jesus as an ally in the struggle for a new world or social order, have had to learn again and again that they could not rely on this ally, and that the kingdom of God which he proclaimed would not square long with their expectations. It is therefore not surprising today that this completely secularized Marxist doctrine of salvation has replaced that of Jesus. . . . The modern analogy is given merely to indicate the contemporary relevance of the first thrust of Jesus' preaching mentioned above."

Gunther Bornkamm
Jesus of Nazareth
p. 102

New Illuminations:

"When a man is converted or enters consciously into his inherited Christian faith, he remains the same person that his previous choices and actions have already made him. The good points and the weaknesses in his character remain the same, acting and combining all the time to make him the particular individual that he is. That is always the material that the grace of God (the personal action of God in his soul) has to work on. Even if a man surrenders his soul to the action of grace as completely as he knows how, grace will never destroy either his individuality or his freedom.* A Christian is not meant to become just another specimen of a machine-made pattern of sanctity, identical in all its examples. A man by grace ought to become more himself, more individual. By the grace of God the *consequences* of his defects of character should be prevented from working out as faults. But these traits will remain in his character. God's grace works with man's freedom to heighten and deepen the things in his character which make him *that* man, unlike everybody else. As he goes on in the life of grace, he should become *that* man perfected.** Belief in the Atonement of Jesus Christ does not alter the person that lives his 'real life.' It alters the *center* of his life and so the whole quality of it."

Dom Gregory Dix
The Claim of Jesus Christ
p. 66

"Be sure that the ins and outs of your individuality are no mystery to God; and one day they will no longer be a mystery to you. The mould in which a key is made would be a strange thing if you had never seen a key: and the key itself a strange thing if you had never seen a lock. Your soul is a curious shape because it is a key to unlock one of the doors in the house with many mansions. For it is not humanity in the abstract which is to be saved, but you — you the individual reader, John Stubbs or Janet Smith. Blessed and fortunate creature your eyes shall behold him and not another's. Your place in heaven will seem to be made for you and you alone,

---

*See also 26:2, Pardue.
**See also 26:1, Sophrony.

because you were made for it — made for it stitch by stitch as a glove is made for a hand."

C. S. Lewis
The Problem of Pain
p. 147

"The graces of our Lord are not mere adornments of our deepest self or spirit. They transform that self, render it new and radiant, set it on the road to divine fulfilment. . . . We change substantially in the melting fire of grace without knowing it. We are not the same as we were before. . . . Yet this gradual metamorphosis is done with infinite respect for what we already are in God's plan by birth and background.

"The mighty water of a river bends and twists itself in adaptation to the fundamental form of the canyon it streams through. Yet it polishes and streamlines the walls of the canyon it touches daily. Similarly the living water of grace welling up inside us adapts itself to the fundamental form God gave to our deepest self. Yet it gently washes away the dirty spots, the rough edges, the dark shadows that mar the original beauty God intended from eternity for this unique self."

Adrian Van Kaam
The Woman at the Well
p. 56

"Individualism can appear in two opposite forms. The negative form is egocentricity. It destroys society as well as the individual himself. The positive form is individuation: each member of the group is responsible for himself and for the group also. Individual freedom and collective responsibility coincide. Its religious goal is stated in St. Paul's description of the 'mystical body of Christ' (1 Corinthians 12:12-31). . . .

"The servants in the parable of the talents, as well as the vine-growers in Luke 20:9-10, behave as if they were or could become independent proprietors, though they know they are and always will be part of a larger 'household.' However they are actually free to do as they choose. Their Lord wants them to act independently, and he will give them more power and more responsibility if they are faithful and wise.* Individualism is their temptation. If they claim sovereignty, they are caught in egocentricity and perish. If they find their way into individuation, they will grow into greater freedom."

Fritz Kunkel
Creation Continues
pp. 62, 276

*See also 37:2, Neil; 98:2, Neil.

New Illuminations:

On Jesus' Thanksgiving Prayer and Great Invitation

Matthew 11:25-30   Luke 10:17-22

"Jesus had sent out the disciples in the belief that they were on the very verge of divine intervention, and he was expecting that before the completion of the mission the Son of Man would have come (Matthew 10:23b). We do not know how long an interval elapsed between the sending out of the disciples and their return, but it was an interval fraught with extreme tension for Jesus. . . . Then they returned, delighted that they had been able to cast out demons; but that act of God, the decisive intervention which Jesus was expecting, had not taken place, and the words which Luke attributes to Jesus at this juncture should be understood as expressing the contrast between his sense of disappointment and the pleasure of the disciples at what was far from being that final victory over the power of Satan which he was expecting. There is evidence in the usage of the Greek in common speech that the word which the authorized version renders inaccurately 'I beheld,' and Monsignor Knox more correctly translates 'I watched,' may imply expectation; further it is an imperfect and it may be suggested that the true meaning is 'I was watching for Satan falling like lightning from heaven.' That is, Jesus says that the success of the disciples is only, so to speak, a preliminary skirmish and not the final victory for which he had been watching. It is indeed a matter for joy that their place in the Kingdom is assured, but the time to raise the song of triumph is not yet. . . .

"The closing passage in Matthew 11:23-30, which follows immediately upon the recognition by Jesus that his works of power had failed to produce repentance in the Galilean cities, reveals in the most moving fashion the way in which Jesus accepted the situation. . . . Matthew rightly does not describe the feelings of Jesus at this critical moment; he simply says, 'at that time Jesus answered and said, "I thank Thee, O Father, Lord of heaven and earth because thou hast hid these things from the wise and prudent and hast revealed them unto babes; even so, Father, for so it has seemed good in thy sight." ' This is not exultation but quiet submission; he accepts the situation with the appearance of failure as the Father's will. He accepts as the Father's ordering that the sole result of his activity hitherto should be the small group of simple men who had seen in him what was hidden from the religious leaders of Israel; and for this result, he thanks the Father. . . .

"The passage that follows (Luke 10:22; Matthew 11:27) brings out still more clearly the way Jesus met the situation. It has commonly been interpreted in the light of the Johannine sayings, such as John 3:35 *et.al.*, 'The Father loves the Son and has given all things into his hand'; but it needs to be understood in the light of the situation. . . . Jesus is saying, in the light of his experience, that the Father-Son relationship and all its implications can only be known by those

that are in the circle of that relationship. He was in the relationship consciously and was seeking to bring others to share it. The essential characteristic of the relationship as he knew it was joyful obedience, the obedience of a son, delighting in the Father's will, whatever it might bring. Hence he speaks of this as *his* yoke, the yoke he carried; he calls it *chrestos*, inadequately rendered by 'easy,' since that yoke, the yoke of the Kingdom, is often far from easy; the word means rather 'good,' 'fit for use.' Jesus was using a metaphor from his own craft; he knew how to make a yoke that fitted the neck of a patient ox, and how hard an ill-fitting yoke might be; elsewhere he spoke of the other yoke, heavy and grievous to be borne, which the teachers of the Law sought to bind on the shoulders of their people. . . . Jesus stands and offers the way of the yoke, the yoke of the Kingdom, the way of rest for the soul."

S. H. Hooke
The Kingdom of God
pp. 76-78

"Jesus distinguished between those to whom the mystery of God's reign is unveiled and those who did not believe or understand. In his prayer of praise Jesus thanked the Father that he had concealed this from the wise and prudent and revealed it to the little ones (Luke 10:21, par.). The contrast is drawn slightly differently from that in Luke 8:10 where the wise must be the scribes opposed to Jesus and the little ones are simple believers. These are, in the first place, the disciples of Jesus whose eyes see what the prophets desired to see and did not see. . . . Knowledge that salvation is present in the person of Jesus is confined to the close circle of the disciples. Thus the prayer of praise must be applied first of all to the disciples. It introduces only the two extreme groups, but it does not confirm that the revelation is limited only to a narrow circle."

Rudolf Schnackenburg
God's Rule and Kingdom
p. 188

"The unique paragraph (Matthew 11:25-30), which reveals Jesus in an unusually exalted mood, is built up of two sections. The first, Matthew 25-27, occurs in Luke also. The second is found here alone. Some conclude from this that they belong to separate occasions. However that may be, it shows unique insight and understanding on the part of

Matthew that he should have welded them together; for the worth and glory of the invitation in verses 28-30 depend on the person and character of the person who gives it. . . .

"The chief element in this revelation is the unique relationship of Jesus to God. He is his Son and in consequence his Gospel is a Gospel of God. To unveil before men the ineffable glory of the divine Fatherhood is the glad and holy privilege entrusted to Jesus. The content of his message and the truth he declared are all from God."

Abingdon Bible Commentary
p. 974

"Jesus' human life in regard to his heavenly Father is like that of one of those modern ships that are guided from the shore by a beam of light; it has no independent steering-gear; it just goes straight forward as the beam directs. His life is utterly simple because for him only one thing matters, and that is the will of God which he is always doing. His faith and his love and his obedience never falter under all the hard conditions imposed by the fallenness of this world. His prayer is his life, and he alone in this dislocated scene is completely single-minded and at rest."

Sister Penelope
The Wood
p. 115

"If among the Savior's words, I had to choose one of them, only one, which could sum up for all believers all the good news, I would choose without hesitation these words: 'Come to me all who are burdened and I will refresh you.'* Would you call this merely humanism? No, because it is a question of who dares to speak in such a way.

"This text really says everything. It is a call to all the suffering in this world, to all those whom evil weighs down. This is the proclamation of himself — Christ — that he is himself the remedy for men's suffering. Would a man who is only a man say these things? . . . My Savior, I see the vast suffering mass of people crushed to the ground; I see this mass stretching forth its arms to you, crawl along, get up, try to go on towards you, groping, tottering. You are drawing them without their knowing you."

Monk of the Eastern Church
Jesus: A Dialogue With the Savior
p. 66

"It was the purpose of Jesus to lift people above their state of necessity, to strengthen them, so in turn they could strengthen others. He said, 'Come unto me all who travail

and are heavy laden, and I will refresh you.' As a matter of fact, he was delighted when people asked for help because he then knew that they were humble enough to know that of themselves they did not have the strength to save themselves."

Thomas Kepler, ed.
Letters and Reflections of Francois de Fenelon
pp. 134, 170

" 'He that has entered into his rest' he also has ceased from his own works. . . . Let us labor therefore to enter into that rest' (Hebrews 4:10-11). And labor here means 'Make haste.' Is the word used to remind us that we shall not drift into rest? There must be the will to enter in, and perhaps the thing demanding the most will is the resolution to cease from our own works — the busy traffic of our thoughts — and stay our minds on our God. . . . Let us not lose one hour in needless, ineffective distress. Let us hasten by an act of the will, by God's enabling, to enter into his rest, to come to him for rest, to rest again."

Amy Carmichael
Thou Givest . . . They Gather
pp. 54-55

"Just as the man who carries a load places the yoke upon his neck and shoulders so that the load may be taken by the chains or cords at each end of the yoke, so should Jesus' disciples take their master's yoke upon their shoulders to lighten the load. Jesus' burden is lighter than that which formerly lay upon their shoulders."

Joachim Jeremias
The Parables of Jesus
p. 194

"It is not a yoke that Jesus imposes, but it is the yoke that he himself carried, and a yoke by the very nature of it includes two. He says then — standing beneath a yoke — 'Come and share my yoke with me and we will pull the plow together through the long furrow of life.' . . . Christ's yoke was his Father's will. Christ voluntarily emptied himself and was content to live a life of perpetual dependence upon God. . . .

"Take the yoke now by your own will. You know that when you are driving a horse, if that horse frets and kicks, it simply gets itself into a lather; but it has to go your way after all. Much better for the young horse if it would only take the collar and the bit right away. You will never get it right in that way. Quietly take what God permits and understand that, in that, there is the secret of rest; and a new

*See also 102:3, Thielicke.

131

tranquility will come. You will say, 'Yes, Father, for it was well pleasing in thy sight.' ''

F. B. Meyer
The Christ Life for Your Life
pp. 117-18, 123

"All you asked was that I cease to want what I willed, and begin to want what you willed. But where had my free will been hiding all those years? From what secret cranny did you summon it at a moment's notice so I might bend my neck to your easy yoke and my shoulders to your light burden, Christ Jesus, my strength and my redeemer? How good it felt to be done with the delectable trifles of life! Those things I had been afraid to let go, it now became a joy to dispense with. You drove them away from me; you are the true and highest joy. . . . My mind was free at last from the corroding anxiety of running around trying to get somewhere."

Sherwood Wirt
Love Song: Augustine's Confessions for Modern Man
p. 119

―――――――――――――――

New Illuminations:

On Eyes That See and Ears That Hear

Matthew 11:15; 13:16-17   Mark 4:9, 23, 8:17-18   Luke 8:8; 10:23-24; 14:35

"The great grace of the presence of Jesus is evident from the greeting of Jesus to his disciples, Luke 10:23 = Matthew 13:16: 'Blessed are the eyes that see what you see (Matthew: because they see, and your ears because they hear). For I say to you many prophets and kings have desired to see the things that you see and have not seen them, and to hear the things that you hear and have not heard them.' The priority accorded to the apostles over the prophets and kings of the Old Covenant can only consist in their actual experience of the era of salvation and precisely in the preaching and operation of Jesus."

Rudolf Schnackenburg
God's Rule and Kingdom
p. 122

"Blessedness is above all else an energy or activity of our own souls; however, it is also true that it is any energy or activity of God in our souls. We conclude, therefore, that the Gospel is as much still our own obedience to the law as it is, over and above that, the grace or power of God to attain that obedience. . . . The fact remains that the highest act of God in us is also the highest activity of ourselves; and, that which is nought without God in us, is equally nought if it is not ourselves in God."

William P. Du Bose
The Gospel According to Saint Paul
pp. 54, 33

"The end of man, we are told, is the vision of God; and our Lord's promise to the pure of heart is that they shall see God. . . . 'Blessed are the eyes that see the things that you see,' said our Lord to his disciples. And of these things that are revealed to us in Christ, none is more wonderful than the fact that God is no simple undifferentiated monad, but is that eternal and infinite ocean of self-giving and self-receiving love, the Ever-blessed and Glorious Trinity. . . .

"For the world before Christ to see God was to die. But we know that, for the man restored in Christ, to see God is to live. But we walk by faith and not by sight, we see in a mirror darkly and not face to face. Grace is indeed a beginning, but it is only a beginning. For 'God, who commanded the light to shine out of darkness, hath shined in our hearts to give the light of the knowledge of the glory of God in the face of Jesus Christ' (2 Corinthians 4:6).* . . .

"It will be useful to consider a little more fully the nature of the virtue of faith, by which we know God on earth and which is so sharply contrasted with the sight which we shall have of God in heaven. . . . St. John of the Cross who writes about it at length in the Second Book of *The Ascent of Mount Carmel*, insists that faith purifies and perfects the understanding. It gives us absolute certainty of the reality of God, but it does not do this by making him visible to us. On the contrary, it is precisely when God cannot be *seen* in any sense of the word that faith does its greatest work for us."*

E. L. Mascall
Grace and Glory
pp. 33-36, 39-41

" 'Blessed are we, O Israel; for what pleases God is known to us' (Baruch 4:4, NAB.). And if we consider how much more we Christians are endowed by the Lord than were the prophets and righteous men of the Old Testament, we, too, must lift up our voices and cry in grateful triumph: 'Blessed are we, hallowed Christians, for the Lord has desired to be so united with us that His life has become ours.' . . .

"The Lord himself bore witness to this when he told his disciples: 'Blessed are your eyes, for they see: and your ears, for they hear. . . .' (Matthew 13:16-17). And St. Peter declared that great were the good tidings 'which things the angels desire to look into' (1 Peter 1:12b). St. Paul, also, in the epistle to the Ephesians 3, wrote that 'knowledge in the mystery of Christ which in other ages was not made known to the sons of men . . . was now revealed unto his holy apostles and prophets by the Spirit,' and went on to tell them that to him had been given the grace to 'make all men see what is the fellowship of the mystery, which from the beginning of the world hath been hid in God.' "

Archimandrite Sophrony
His Life Is Mine
p. 58

"The evidence suggests not indeed that Jesus invested himself with Messianic claims and titles in a formal way, but that he so preached the Kingdom of God as to show that its inauguration was happening by his presence and his coming death. Thus the disciples are blessed because they

*See also 48:2, Allchin.

*See also 28:2, Browning.

can see and hear what kings and prophets had longed in vain to see and hear.''

Michael Ramsey
Jesus and the Living Past
p. 37

''The word of the Lord came to me, saying, Son of man you dwell in the midst of the house of the rebellious, who have eyes to see and see not, who have ears to hear and hear not; for they are a rebellious house'' (Ezekiel 12:1-2).

''Having eyes do you not see (with them), and having ears do you not hear and perceive and understand the sense of what is said? And do you not remember?'' (Mark 8:18).

''And some seed fell into good soil, and grew up and yielded a crop a hundred times (as great). As he said these things, he called out, 'He who has ears to hear let him be listening and consider and understand by hearing!' (Luke 8:8).''

The Amplified Bible

''The latter phrase corresponds in Matthew's style and probably in Jesus' own style also, to the 'selah' of the Psalms. We should stop to listen to the inner voice. . . . Go ahead! Your own experience will convince you. Your deafness and blindness will disappear. You will feel like a dead man who has come to life.''

Fritz Kunkel
Creation Continues
p. 176

''The warning-cry, 'He that hath ears to hear let him hear,' forms a special class of parable-endings: Matthew 11:15, 13:9, 43b; Mark 4:9, 23; Luke 8:8, 14:35. The Gospel of Thomas gives the warning-cry at the conclusion of no less than five parables, doubtless as an appeal to the Gnostics to give careful heed to the secret meaning of the parables.* This survey shows that the warning-cry is in most cases secondary.''

Joachim Jeremias
The Parables of Jesus
p. 109

---

*See also 34:1, *D. M. Stanley Jerome Bible Commentary*.

''A boy born and reared in an old back street of a great industrial city may be so clever that he studies his way through school, through university, to a science doctorate: yet he is unaware of the sublime picture of the night sky, he cannot see its declaration, for he is unable to see it when circumstances at last provide the opportunity. He may, when invited, lift his glance to the silent sailing moon, he may look, but there is no accompanying opening of the interior eyes which will enable him to take hold of, to apprehend in even a small degree, that upon which he looks. He that has eyes has ears; let him see, let him hear, for the life of the eye and the ear is within. It is more likely that for such a person the heavens will be found in some artifact of modern man. . . . For anything anywhere any time may suddenly become a channel of light. . . . The showing that comes to us may illuminate our knowledge of the natural world, it may enlighten the mind in regard to truth in any sphere we are searching, or it may uncover treasures of the heavenly realities which outdistance dialectics. . . . But we require the soul's interior faculties to perceive what is beyond the light of natural knowledge. The more directly the acknowledged presence of deity manifests his glory, the more interior and elevated must be the soul's powers of reception. . . .

''Communication between God and his people is a fact and reality, for his voice declares his intentions, his desires and requirements: and this voice must be obeyed. In the Old Testament, 'to hear' and 'to obey' translate the same Hebrew word; and obedience is the foundation of the relationship between the children of Israel and their God. 'If you obey my voice, I will be your God and you will be my people.' Too often, reiterate the lamenting and reproachful prophets, men refuse to listen to the Almighty's voice, to accept his counsels. Our Lady Saint Mary expressed her entire conformity with God's design for her: 'Be it unto me according to thy word.' . . .

''Saint Mary's blessed Son went on from there. He begins with the phraseology and concepts of the Old Testament: 'Blessed are they who hear the word of God and keep it,' and to the tempter he says that man lives by every word which comes from the mouth of God.''*

Sibyl Harton
Doors of Eternity
pp. 13-15, 62-63

---

*See also 36:2, Thielicke.

New Illuminations:

On the Unlimited Nature of the Duty of Love

| Matthew 22:37-40 | Mark 12:28-34 | Luke 10:25-42 |

"The ten commandments, although a series of negative prohibitions, set forth our duty to God and to others. This is even more clear in the positive summary of the law which Jesus made by joining a verse from Leviticus (19:18) to a verse from Deuteronomy (6:5). It is important to observe that the first commandment concerns our duty to God and not our duty to our neighbor (Matthew 22:37-40, par.). We are to love God first; and then we are to love our neighbor as ourselves. Sin is the reversal of this order. We put ourselves first, our neighbor next, and God somewhere in the background."

John Stott
Basic Christianity
p. 78

"Here, the Lord asks only two things of us: love for His Majesty and love for our neighbor. . . . The surest sign that we are keeping these two commandments is, I think, that we should really be loving our neighbor; for we cannot be sure that we are loving God, although we may have good reason for believing that we are; but we can know quite well if we are loving our neighbor. And be certain that the further advanced you find you are in this, the greater the love you will have for God. For so dearly does His Majesty love us that he will reward our love for our neighbor by increasing the love which we bear to himself, and that in a thousand ways: this I cannot doubt. It is most important that we should proceed in this matter very carefully. Our nature being so evil, I do not believe we could ever attain perfect love for our neighbor unless it had its roots in the love of God."

St. Teresa of Avila
Interior Castle
pp. 114-115

"Christianity exists to reveal love to the world in all its overwhelming and almost outrageous fulness. Only by the contemplation of the love which is God can we have any love for our neighbors, just as a mirror has brilliance — power to reflect light — only when turned toward the sun so that it receives the image of the sun within itself. . . .
"Love in the divine sense is the giving of one's whole being to another; and when we say that God is love, we mean that he gives his entire Self to every single object of his love, to every creature that he has made. Whoever fails to respond to it is simply self-condemned by contrast. Of course the gift is received in varying degrees by different creatures as the light of the sun shed with equal brilliance upon all parts of the earth is reflected more perfectly by a mirror than by a brick."

Alan W. Watts
Behold the Spirit
pp. 90-91

"It is understandable that theology has stressed again and again the radical contrast between *eros* and *agape*. Christian thought as a rule cannot do enough to bring out the different implications of this antithesis: *eros* the love which demands; *agape*, the love which is generous. One seeks what is in its own interest, the other what is in the interest of the other person. In spite of the incontestable truth which must be asserted by this antithesis, we must beware of a mere formal exhibition of the antithetic structure of the two conceptions. In practice this has meant a temptation to rob *agape* of its human aspects and to condemn *eros*. But Jesus' commandment of love calls man as he really is in the light of God's love into new being and into new activity."

Gunther Bornkamm
Jesus of Nazareth
pp. 116-117

"A child needs to be loved in order that he may love himself, and loving himself be able to love others who also need love. Love of self here has the meaning of the Lord's commandment — 'Thou shalt love thy neighbor as thyself' — and is distinguished from egocentric self-love.* Only those who have been loved and who love others are free and able to love others. The ability to love is always the result of having been loved. This is true of our relation to God. We read in the Epistle of St. John: 'Herein is love, not that we loved God, but that he loved us' (v. 4:10). Love is always a response to being loved."

Reuel L. Howe
Man's Need and God's Action
pp. 81-82

---

*See also 25:3, St. Teresa of Avila.

"When we do to our neighbor all that God does to us, a new, vivifying, re-creative atmosphere comes into our life. For one thing is sure and that is that every human being wants to love and be loved. . . . For loving and being loved is a natural process like inhaling and exhaling. When a man ceases to love, his own inner being ceases to breathe and he suffocates. Therefore, through my loving, I must provide the initial spark. Often a single word breaks the dismal spell.

"Vincent Van Gogh once wrote to his brother Theo: 'Many a man has a great fire in his soul and nobody comes to warm himself at it, and often the passers-by see only a bit of it above the chimney and they go their way hence.'

"Don't I see that my neighbor, this enigmatic fellow that is such a stranger to me, also has this fire in him and he wants someone to be warmed by his love? But his inner man is like a stove that has been shut tight. The fire grows smaller and smaller and emits nothing but acrid, biting smoke which torments his fellows. He is no longer able to open the drafts by himself. Should I not help him to get a fresh breath of air? Am I really determined, as Van Gogh says, to go my way hence? Then I would be denying him who died for this unfortunate man with the fire locked up within him. I would be 'just,' true enough. Nobody would blame me. But could I face the man who would then have died for this man in vain?"

Helmut Thielicke
The Waiting Father
p. 113

"That a learned theologian should ask a layman about the way to eternal life was just as unusual then as it would be today. The probable explanation is that the man had been disturbed in conscience by Jesus' preaching. Jesus surprisingly tells him that action is the way to life: the enquirer's theological knowledge is to no avail if his life is not governed by love to God and his 'friend.' The counter-question as to what the scripture meant by 'friend' is justifiable. . . . Jesus was not being asked for a definition of the word 'friend' but for an indication as to where, within the community, the limits of the duty of loving were to be drawn. How far does my responsibility extend? That is the meaning of the question. . . .

"In the good Samaritan story embodying the answer, the audience, after the priest and the Levite, would now have expected a third character, an Israelite layman. It would have been completely unexpected and disconcerting for them to hear that the third character who fulfilled the duty of love was a Samaritan. . . . It is clear that Jesus had chosen an extreme example; by comparing the failure of the ministers of God with the unselfishness of the hated Samaritan, his hearers should be able to measure the absolute and unlimited nature of the duty of love.

". . . A much debated question is the form which Jesus' question took — 'Which of these three do you think proved to be a neighbor to the man who fell among the robbers?' While the lawyer's question concerned the object of the love (Whom must I treat as a friend?), Jesus, in verse 36, asks about the subject of love (Who acted as a friend?). The lawyer is thinking of himself when he asks: what is the limit of my responsibility? Jesus says to him: Think of the sufferer; put yourself in his place; consider, Who needs help from me? . . . Jesus illuminates the suggestion with a practical example. . . .

"In this parable Jesus tells his questioner that the example of the despised half-breed was intended to teach him that no human being was beyond the range of his charity. The law of love called him to be ready at any time to give his life for another's need."

Joachim Jeremias
The Parables of Jesus
pp. 202-205

"Our Lord loved to teach people by painting word pictures, and in the parable of the good Samaritan he paints a picture of the love of God.

"Humanity is as a man who has fallen among thieves and been robbed and left there incapable of saving himself. We feel that we have been foolish, that we have been robbed, that we cannot save ourselves. We have been robbed by our own stupidity. This man ought not to have been traveling alone. The first person who comes along is the priest who may stand for formal religion. Formal religion passes by and leaves humanity where it is. Then comes a type we know very well, the good-natured person who comes and looks at the man and goes away and leaves him. Many people do that. They discuss the troubles of life and look at the slums, and go away and leave them.

"Then the Samaritan passes by and comes where the man is. In that sentence is told all the deep mystery of our Lord's incarnation. He came down to be in the poverty of the poor. He did not pass by. He did not come down and look at it and then go back to heaven. He did not come to tempted men and say, 'You ought not to have that temptation,' but he came to where the tempted man was. He came into the place of suffering and willed that his own coronal should be a crown of thorns. The story of the good Samaritan is the story of the Incarnation. It is a picture of the love of God."

Harry C. Griffith, ed.
A Gift of Light: A Collection
of Thoughts from the Writings of Father Andrew
pp. 21-22

"The differing approach to hospitality shown by Mary and Martha gives considerable insight into the effectiveness of the ministry of Jesus. Paul Tillich helps us to recognize the significance of these few verses when he writes that 'the words he speaks to Martha belong to the most famous of the words in the Bible.' A part of the appeal for this incident comes from the sympathy commonly felt for Martha. . . . From her perspective, her complaint was entirely in order, and she must have expected that Jesus would support her. But Jesus didn't. On the contrary he used Martha's demands as an opportunity to try to help her to understand herself better. . . . It was as if he were saying: 'Instead of being critical of Mary's behavior, look more carefully into your own.'

"As Jesus well understood, work can become feverish activity to cover over a meaningless life. . . . Indeed it is significant that the Mary-Martha incident follows the parable of the good Samaritan, as if to say that service itself does not tell the whole story of life. . . . Jesus' gentle rebuke to Martha is not because she is wrong in her activity, but because she is less right than Mary is. . . . To the credit of Martha, it should be said that creative values are essential to life. The rebuke then is important not because her service as hostess is unimportant but because it can be a block to relationships at a deeper level. . . . It is unlikely that Martha changed her role under the instruction of Jesus. But at least she must have sensed that Mary was performing a service too.

"Even more important than experiencing something is encountering someone. The 'good portion' which Mary chose was the 'one thing needful' — a personal encounter. As Mary sat at the feet of Jesus and listened to his teachings, we can sense how important this must have been for him. The incident takes place shortly after the record indicates that 'he set his face to go to Jerusalem,' facing the inevitable crisis which would lead to his death. Mary found meaning for her own life as she made Jesus' concerns her concern. . . . She has put the priority where it rightly belongs. She sees encounters as more important than achievements. She values people more than things. . . . There is no emphasis in Jesus' ministry more basic than the priority of personal relationships. The criticism that Jesus leveled most often against the Pharisees was that their keeping of the law had become a barrier to a relationship of justice and mercy to other people. So the support that Jesus gave to Mary was in order."

Robert Leslie
Jesus and Logotherapy
pp. 84-91

"Contrary to the normal view which takes Mary to be the type of the more advanced, contemplative soul over against the harassed and distracted Martha, Eckhart's fascinating re-interpretation of the story takes Martha as the type of the mature Christian. And she is worrying about her sister, afraid that she is just wallowing in sentimental devotion instead of getting up and maturing in the tussles of real life. Christ reassures her that Mary is all right; she too has chosen the best part, but she is not yet very far advanced in it."

Simon Tugwell
The Beatitudes; Soundings in Christian Traditions
p. 104

"There are two ways of life in the Holy Church. One is the active, the other is the contemplative life.* Active is the lower, contemplative the higher. The active life has two parts, a higher and a lower; and likewise the contemplative has two parts, a lower and a higher. These two ways of life are linked, and though they are different, each is dependent on the other. For what we call the higher part of the active life is the same as the lower part of the contemplative. A man cannot be fully active unless he be partly contemplative, not fully contemplative (at least on earth) without being partly active.** Active life is begun and ended in this life; not so contemplative. It begins in this life and goes on eternally. 'The part that Mary chose shall not be taken away.' Active life is 'careful and troubled about many things'; contemplative sits peacefully with one.

"The lower part of active life consists of good, straightforward acts of mercy and charity. The higher part (which is the lower part of contemplative living) is made up of various things for example, spiritual meditation, an awareness of one's own sorrow and contrition, a sympathetic understanding of Christ's passion and that of his servants, a gratitude which praises God for his wonderful gifts, his kindness and works in all parts of his creation. But the higher part of contemplation — at least as we know it in this life — is wholly caught up in darkness, and in this cloud of unknowing, with an outreaching love and blind groping for the naked being of God, himself and him only."

Clifton Wolters, trans.
The Cloud of Unknowing
pp. 71-72

---

*See also 95:4, Milford.
**See also 77:1, Webbe.

New Illuminations:

On Teach Us To Pray

"They stood one day on the deck of a ship in the midst of a raging sea. They heard him say quietly but with authority, 'Peace, be still,' and they were amazed as the winds and the waves obeyed his voice. He would speak to one paralyzed for many years, and they watched the man get up and walk. . . . They heard him speak as no man ever spoke. They felt the magnetism of his own life. . . . Could it be true that such power could be theirs? He said so (John 14:12), thus it was so. But how? One day the answer burst upon them. There was one golden key to the power-house of God. Eagerly they said 'Lord, teach us to pray.' Learning to pray was the one, the only secret, they need to know. . . . Today there are millions of people who can say that prayer, but very few ever learn to pray it. The power comes not in the saying but in the praying of the prayer. The power of the Lord's prayer is not in the words but rather in the pattern of thinking in which our minds are formed. The Bible tells us, 'Be ye transformed by the renewal of your mind' (Romans 12:2). When our thoughts begin to flow in the channels of the Lord's Prayer, our minds do become new and we are transformed. We remember how the king in Shakespeare's 'Hamlet' miserably fails in prayer. In explanation, he says:

'My words fly up, my thoughts remain below;
Words without thoughts never to heaven go.'

That's it. We too fail when our 'words are without thoughts.' "

Charles L. Allen
God's Psychiatry
pp. 87-88

"I think of the Lord's Prayer as not just a set of words. If there is anything tragic about the way we currently pray liturgically in our church, it is the way we rattle off the set words without giving any thought to what they mean. . . . What is certain is that it was more than just a prayer. It's sort of a framework, the skeleton, the pattern for a life of prayer. You can pray the Lord's Prayer in thirty seconds or pray it all night or over the weekend or for a month's retreat. You can pray with that pattern. It's not just a prayer. It's prayer itself."

William Frey
Praying and Living the Lord's Prayer
Taped Retreat Discourses

"For Christ, man was able to lay hold on the Eternal and experience another level of life. How different such a doctrine and practice were from those of his own or any other time is shown by the demand of the disciples who had witnessed his nights of solitary prayer in the hills: 'Teach us *how* to pray.' Those who asked this were good and pious Jews who already accepted the worship of the Name and practice of daily prayer as a normal part of life. But now they realized how far beyond these orderly acts of worship and petition was that living intercourse with the living Father, which conditioned every moment of Christ's life and was the source of his power in the world to which he was sent. Here for the first time they saw prayer not as an ordered action, or religious duty, not even an experience; but as a vital relation between man in his wholeness and the being of God. Here was one who knew in the full and deep sense how to pray; and in the light of his practice they perceived the poverty and unreality of their own. . . .

"We easily assume that we have long ago exhausted the inexhaustible significance of the Lord's Prayer. The result of this persistent error has been to limit our understanding of the great linked truths which are here given to us. . . . But when we 'center down' as Quakers say, from the surface of human life to its deeps, and rouse those sleeping truths and take them with us, and ask what they look like there — in the secret place where the soul knows its need of God — then all looks different. . . . The Paternoster reminds us how rich and various, how deeply rooted in the Supernatural, the Christian life is or should be: how utterly it depends on God, yet how searching is the demand it makes on man. This scheme of prayer covers all the realities of our situation, at once beset by nature and cherished by grace. . . . Man's state of sin, his sufferings, helplessness and need do not stand in the foreground; but the splendor and beauty of God, demanding a self-oblivion so complete that it transforms suffering and blots out even the memory of sin. We begin with a sublime yet intimate invocation of Reality. The Infinite God is the Father of my soul. We end by the abject confession of our dependence and need of guidance: of a rescue and need of support coming to our help right down in the jungle of life. Following the path of the Word Incarnate this prayer begins on the summits of spiritual experience and comes steadily down from the Infinite to the finite, from the Spaceless to the little space on which we stand. Here we find all the strange mixed experience of man, over-ruled by the unchanging glory and charity of God."

Evelyn Underhill
Abba
pp. 3, 7-9

"If a person does not think of Whom he is addressing, and what he is asking for, and who it is that is asking and of Whom he is asking it, I do not consider that he is praying at all. . . . True it is sometimes possible to pray without thinking of these things, but that is only because they have been thought about previously."

St. Teresa of Avila
Interior Castle
p. 32

"Tonight we came into the Divine Presence with just the word 'Father'; now that's unusual because many of us are liturgically programmed to do it a little bit more formally. Nothing wrong with that and yet to some extent, at least, that's a liturgical way to keep God at arm's length. Our music and our worship tonight have reflected a certain degree of comfort in approaching the 'Almighty and everlasting God Who alone inhabits eternity' with a sense of intimacy — 'Father.'* Some are scandalized because they think wrongly, I hope, that we are trying to sort of put ourselves by our own act on a sort of chummy relationship with God and thereby miss the grandeur and the glory. I hope they are wrong about that because I don't want to miss the grandeur and the glory. And there are things about God that we have not begun to imagine — depths that you and I will never begin to plumb. And we don't want to forget that."

William Frey
Praying and Living the Lord's Prayer
Taped Retreat Discourse

"Jesus meant not only 'pray in these words' but pray with this sequence of thought and desire. God first, the Father, the heavenly Father, 'hallowed be thy name.' His name is his character to be dwelt upon, honored, loved, our hearts and minds to be soaked in it. And *then* we ask that his reign may come and his will be done on Earth as it is in Heaven . . . The goal of relationship between you and God and God and you is 'Heaven.' I want to suggest that you do not think about heaven as much and as often as you ought to. Heaven is simply the coming perfection of that fellowship between you and a God who made you, a God who loves you infinitely. Beautifully does St. Augustine describe the goal of Heaven. 'We shall rest' — cease from our self-important busy-ness, acknowledging that what God does is infinitely significant, and that what we do signifies so little. 'And we shall see' leads on to 'we shall love,' for seeing him how shall we fail to love him with the fullness of affection and love? And love not only him but all the fellow creatures destined to share heaven with him and us — a perfection of the love and service of man for man in the

sight and eyes of the Creator. We shall know that all flows from God and so finally 'we shall praise.' . . . Our existence on Earth is but a brief prelude to Heaven and our thinking about it will make all the difference to what we are doing this day and this hour in this world."

Margaret Duggan, ed.
Through the Year with Michael Ramsey
pp. 26-28

"For me words are the movements of the conductor's baton: not the music. It does not matter very much who first put them together. If they are our own words they will soon, by unavoidable repetition, harden into a formula. If they are someone else's, we shall continually pour into them our own meaning. At present, for one's practice changes, I find it best to make 'my own words' the staple but introduce a modicum of the ready-made. . . . Perhaps I shan't find it so easy to persuade you that the ready-made modicum has its use; for me, I mean — I'm not suggesting rules for anyone else in the world. First, it keeps me in touch with 'sound doctrine.' Left to one's self, one could easily slide away from 'the faith once given' into a phantom called 'my religion.' Secondly, it reminds me 'what things I ought to ask' (perhaps especially when I'm praying for other people). The crisis of the present moment, like the nearest telephone post, will always loom largest. Isn't there a danger that our great, permanent, objective necessities — often more important — may get crowded out? Finally, they provide an element of the ceremonial.

"*Festooning Ready-Made Prayers*: I call the private overtone I give to certain petitions 'festoons' because they don't obliterate the plain, public sense of the petition but are merely hung on it. . . . *Thy kingdom come.** That is, may your reign be realized here as it is realized there. But I tend to take *there* on three levels. First, beyond the horrors of animal and human life; in the behavior of stars and trees and water, in sunrise and wind. May there be *here* in my heart the beginning of like beauty. Secondly, as in the best human lives I have known: in all the people who really bear the burdens and ring true, and in the quiet, busy, ordered life of all good families and really good religious houses. May that be true *here*. And finally, of course in the usual sense: as in Heaven,** as among the blessed dead. And *here* can be taken not only as 'in my heart,' but as 'in this college' — in England — in the world in general. But prayer is not the time for pressing our own favorite political or social panacea. Even Queen Victoria didn't like 'being talked to as if she were a public meeting.'

"*Thy will be done.* My festoons on this have been added gradually. At first I took it exclusively as an act of submission, attempting to do with it what Our Lord did in Gethsemane. I thought of God's will purely as something that would come upon me, something of which I should be

*See also 78:3, Kelsey.

*See also 47:2, Hooke; 33:2, Underhill.
**See also 125:1 Penelope.

the patient. And I also thought of it as a will which would be embodied in pains and disappointments. Not, to be sure, that I supposed God's will for me to consist entirely of disagreeables. But I thought it was only the disagreeables that called for this preliminary submission — the agreeables could look after themselves for the present. When they turned up, one could give thanks. This interpretation is, I expect, the commonest. And so it must be. And such are the miseries of human life that it must often fill our whole mind. But at other times other meanings can be added. So I added one more.

" 'Thy will *be done*.' But a great deal of it is to be done by God's creatures; including me. The petition, then, is not that I may suffer God's will but also that I may vigorously do it.* I must be an agent as well as a patient. I am asking to be given 'the same mind that was also in Christ' (Philippians 2:5). Taken this way I find the words have a more regular daily application. . . . 'Thy will *be done* — by me — now' brings one back to brass tacks."**

C. S. Lewis
Letters to Malcolm
pp. 11-12, 24-26

"We are to ask God for what we need without any false embarrassment. He is our Father and he expects to provide for us. At the same time it's bread he provides mostly, not caviar."

Trueman Dicken
Living With God
p. 2

"The only measure of forgiveness as between the members of the Kingdom is the forgiveness with which they have been forgiven, and that is limitless; it is the ground on which all the members of the Kingdom stand (Matthew 18:32-33). But the man who abuses the forgiveness of the Kingdom places himself by his own act outside the sphere of its operation. For such a one, nothing remains but the consciousness of a self-imposed separation from God."

S. H. Hooke
The Kingdom of God
p. 115

"Power to change comes when the Emmaus disciples meet the unconditional forgiveness of Christ that helps them work through anger and guilt. In walking at their pace, Jesus accepts the disciples' angry feelings toward the chief priests and leaders for putting the Messiah to death and toward the prophets for apparently misleading the disciples. . . . After Jesus explains the Scriptures to them, they need not be depressed by their foolishness because it puts them in touch with a forgiving Christ. As they feel Jesus accept them, they have forgiving hearts that burn within them. The disciples return at once to Jerusalem to be with people who put Christ to death and to extend to them the unconditional love that Christ extended on the Emmaus road."*

Dennis and Matthew Linn
Healing Life's Hurts
p. 29

" 'Forgive us our trespasses.' A whole type of prayer, a special and intimate relation with the Unseen, brought into existence by the very fact of our mixed half-animal nature, the ceaseless tension between the pull of earth and the demand of heaven is summed up in these four words. . . . Our souls are sick and helpless, for sin has sapped their energy; we need a new dower of vitality from a power beyond ourselves. Forgive! Here in the constant exercise of the divine economy of penitence and pardon, is one of the strongest links which binds the soul to God. But this is not all. . . . God's forgiveness means the compassionate recognition of the weakness and instability of man. And this requires of us the constant compassionate recognition of our fellow creatures' instability and weakness, of the fact that they too cannot help it. If the Christian penitent dares to ask that his many departures from the Christian norm are indeed to be set aside, because — in spite of all — he longs for God and eternal life, then he too must set aside and forgive all that others have caused him to endure.**. . . . We may not put off the effort. It is to be made now. Forgive us, as we forgive, or as another reading has it, 'Forgive and we will forgive.' Show us, O Lord, your indulgent charity and we will try to show it in our turn. 'Having already said Thy will be done,' says St. Teresa 'it follows that we cannot harbor any kind of grudge.' . . . There is nothing more purifying, more redeeming than the penitent love which is awakened by the generous forgiveness of another love. It opens a door in the brick wall which self-esteem has built between itself and God."***

Evelyn Underhill
Abba
pp. 61-67

---

*See also 69:2, St. Teresa of Avila.
**See also 112:2, Harton.

*See also 100:1, Jeremias; 100:1, Underhill.
**See also 100:1, Payne; 32:2, Walchars.
***See also 100:2, Ramsey.

"In C. C. Torrey's explanation of the 'temptation' clause in the Lord's Prayer, he says that there is a verb in Aramaic (as there is in Hebrew) that means 'to enter' or 'go in' and also 'to succumb' or 'fail.' Whoever first translated the Lord's Prayer into Greek knew only the first meaning; and so he rendered that petition 'Lead us not — that is, suffer us not to enter — into temptation.' But what Our Lord said was, 'Let us not fail in temptation.' In the same way in Gethsemane, he said to the three apostles, 'Awake and pray that you will not fail in temptation.' We have got to enter into temptation for there is no other way of coming to the full grown Man. But thanks be to the Second Adam we have *not* got to fail.''*

Sister Penelope
The Coming
p. 110

———————

*See also 109:2, Blamires; 111:2, Penelope; 13:1, Kunkel.

————————————————

New Illuminations:

On Christ's Instruction About Prayer

"Many of the parables of Jesus begin with the disturbing question, a question which grips one right away without any preliminaries: 'Which of you . . .?' ['Suppose one of you . . .' 'Can you imagine that . . .?'] It is always a question aimed straight at the hearer himself. . . . He is challenged in the very secular reality of his life here in this world. He is arrested in the place where he actually is and compelled to answer the question. Thus the strangest appeal is made to his understanding."

Gunther Bornkamm
Jesus of Nazareth
p. 70

"Verses 5-7 in Luke 11 should be regarded as one continuous rhetorical question: 'Can you imagine that if one of you had a friend who came to you at midnight and said to you, "My friend, lend me three loaves because a friend has come to me on a journey and I have nothing to set before him," that you would call out, "Don't disturb me . . ."'? Can you imagine such a thing?' The answer would be — 'Unthinkable!' Under no circumstances would he leave his friend's request unanswered. Hence it is only if we understand verse 7 not as describing a refusal of the request, but rather the utter impossibility of such a refusal, that the parable's real point becomes clear. . . . Verse 8 is seen to be no longer concerned with the neighbor's reiterated request but solely with the motive that actuates the friend to whom he is applying for help: if he will not grant the request for friendship's sake, he will at least do it so as not to appear disobliging. The parable is not concerned with the importunity of the petitioner but with the certainty that the petition will be granted. . . . If the friend roused from his sleep in the middle of the night hastens to fulfill the request of a neighbor in distress, how much more will God. He is a God who hearkens to the needy and comes to their help. He does more than they ask."

Joachim Jeremias
The Parables of Jesus
pp. 158-59

"Jesus considers that the children of God have a right to the prayer of petition. . . . Just as man is given the freedom to pray, so Jesus gives him the definite promise of his prayers being heard. 'Ask and it will be given to you; seek and you will find; knock and it will be opened to you. For everyone who asks receives, and he who seeks finds, and to him who knocks it will be opened.'* It is worth noting how the same words of command and promise are repeated here, and hence the command and encouragement to pray become one. In this sense it could almost be said, with a rather bold use of the importunate friend, that God himself in Jesus' story appears, as it were, in the role of the importunate and will not allow himself to be refused by man who wants to be left in peace behind shut doors. Thus the imperatives 'beat' and 'knock' against a door which ought to open."

Gunther Bornkamm
Jesus of Nazareth
p. 134

"All doors open from within, and it is the dweller in the house that has the key. If anyone wants to come in, he must knock. There is the door of the vision of God, and we must wait his will to open that door for us. God lives behind the door of his own mystery. He says to us, " 'Knock at my door,' and that is all we can do. We can but knock; we must wait for him to open. The revelation of God can only come from God. . . . Only God can give the spark of life to a nation, a group, or an individual soul. What may seem perfect, seen superficially, unless God is working in it has no real life or growth."

Harry C. Griffith, ed.
*A Gift of Light: A Collection
of Thoughts from the Writings of Father Andrew*
p. 67

"We must knock at a door. At this point certain problems become very acute. If the door were that of some church, it would be very simple; we could come and knock. But the trouble is that we usually do not know where to knock. How often people want to pray and ask themselves 'Where shall I turn my gaze and my heart?' . . . The moment you try to focus on an imaginary God, or a God you can imagine, you are in great danger of placing an idol between yourself and the real God. . . . Only if we stand completely open before the unknown, can the unknown reveal itself, Himself, as he chooses to reveal himself as we are to-day. So, with this open-heartedness and open-mindedness,

---

*See also 78:3, Thielicke; 85:3, Lewis.

we must stand before God without trying to give him a shape or imprison him in concepts and images, and we must knock at a door.

"Where? The Gospel tells us that the kingdom of God is within us first of all. If we cannot find the kingdom of God within us, if we cannot meet God within, in the very depth of ourselves, the chances of meeting him outside ourselves are very remote. When Gagarin came back from space and made his remarkable statement that he never saw God in Heaven, one of our priests in Moscow remarked, 'If you have not seen him on earth, you will never see him in heaven.' . . . St. John Chrysostom said, 'Find the door of your heart; you will discover it is the door of the kingdom of God.' So it is inward that we must turn and not outward — but inward in a very special way. I am not saying that we must become introspective. It is not a journey into my *own* inwardness. It is a journey *through* my own self, in order to emerge from the deepest level of self into the place where he is, the point at which God and I meet."

Anthony Bloom
Beginning to Pray
pp. 18-20

"Without a power from outside, the teaching of Christ remains a beautiful ideal, tantalizing but unattainable. Ideals fail for very spiritual poverty. But the fact of Christ's coming is itself a shattering denial of the closed system idea, (you can't change human nature), which dominates our thinking.

And what else is Christ's continuing advice to 'have faith in God' but a call to refuse, in spite of all appearance, to be taken in by the closed system type of thinking? 'Ask and you shall receive; seek and you shall find; knock and it shall be opened unto you.' What are these famous words but an invitation to reach out to the Permanent and Real? If we want to cooperate, the Spirit is immediately available. 'If you then for all your evil know how to give good gifts unto your children, how much more shall your heavenly Father give the Holy Spirit to them that ask him?' "

J. B. Phillips
Your God Is Too Small
p. 135

"St. Matthew's version says 'your heavenly Father will give good things to them who ask him.' But St. Luke says, 'give the Holy Spirit.' Yes, that is it, the best gift of all, himself in you — the Holy Spirit of heroic love. . . . And so for this too, for this most of all, we pray, 'Lord teach us to pray. Teach us to want the one thing needful. Help us to ask that we may receive the Holy Spirit. Help us to seek that we may find thee. Help us so to knock, that thou mayest open to us the gates of everlasting life.' "

T. R. Milford
Foolishness to the Greeks
p. 94

New Illuminations:

On Jesus' Response to Pharisaic Unbelief and Blasphemy

Matthew 12:22-32, 43-45; 16:4   Mark 3:22-27; 8:11-12   Luke 9:49-50; 11:14-32

"The Pharisees were faced with a situation which they had to explain. Jesus had been performing many miracles. Most impressive of all, he had cast out demons. Obviously, he had supernatural power. They could not deny that. Whence did this power come? If it came from God, Christ was unquestionably a highly endowed agent of Jehovah. His claim to be the Messiah would have to be taken seriously. This the Pharisees were not willing to admit. They were students and interpreters of the Old Testament Law. . . .

"If the Pharisees had admitted that Christ's power came from God, they would have had to admit the divine origin of his attack on their position. They would have had to admit that they had been misinterpreting God's laws. This they flatly refused to do. Since they could not deny Christ's supernatural power, since they would not admit it was from God, they took refuge in the only alternative. They said Christ's supernatural power came from the devil: 'It is by Beelzebub, prince of devils, that he drives the devils out.'

"Here is the blasphemy against the Holy Ghost which our Lord warned is, if persisted in, the unforgivable sin. In issuing this warning, he made it clear that it was not unforgivable because it was an attack on him. Our Lord recognized fully that it was hard for men to realize that he was God made man, the long expected Messiah. Even the Apostles found it difficult. That men might be slow of heart to understand the Gospel was quite forgivable. But to assert that his good acts, done solely from the good motive of helping others and so clearly the work of the Holy Spirit, were the work of the devil was to call good evil. It betrayed a complete reversal of values. It called the Holy Ghost the devil. That was the unforgivable sin."*

Ralph Milligan, ed.
All For the Love of God: A Holy Cross Omnibus
pp. 169-70

"Jesus had just healed a dumb man and enabled him to speak. In the thought of the times, the man had been possessed of a demon or devil, and Jesus' exorcism of this evil spirit had restored the man's speech. There were some present, however, who attributed the man's cure not to the power of God working through Jesus but to the power of Satan. In his reply Jesus totally refutes this charge. . . .

"It is obvious from this that Jesus is not thinking of the Kingdom of God as being in any way inside people. J. B. Phillips recognizes this in his translation of Luke 11:20: 'If it is by the finger of God that I am expelling evil spirits,

then the Kingdom of God has swept over you here and now.' . . . The rule of Satan is crumbling and is being replaced by the kingdom or rule of God, ushered in by God's appointed Messiah. . . .

" 'He who is not with me is against me' (Luke 11:23, Matthew 12:30). 'He who is not against us is on our side' (Luke 9:50, Mark 9:40). Surely both of these sayings cannot be attributed to the same teacher! But in fact, they can for both are true; and they illustrate the importance of never taking isolated sayings out of their context but always interpreting them in their total setting. In the case of the saying quoted by Matthew and Luke, Jesus is being accused by the Pharisees of healing the sick by diabolical powers and not by the power of God. The meaning of Jesus' words in this case is that anyone who does not refute this charge and prefers to stay silent is as good as agreeing that the Pharisees are right. Jesus is asking his followers, therefore, to stand up and be counted.

"The saying in Luke's and Mark's Gospels, on the other hand, has quite a different setting and a different purpose. Jesus on this occasion is engaged in a private conversation with his twelve disciples. John tells Jesus of an incident which presumably happened on their mission of teaching and healing. They had come across a strange exorcist — not a Christian — making what John considered an improper use of the name of Jesus in driving out evil spirits. . . . Jesus' reply here is a condemnation of intolerance."*

William Neil
The Difficult Sayings of Jesus
pp. 86-87, 40

"The idea of God as Inhabitant, Indweller in mankind** underlies the little parable of the Strong Man and the Stronger. Our Lord gave utterance to it when he, in whom dwelt all the fullness of the Godhead bodily, had been accused of casting out the devils by the power of their prince. The Strong Man, fully armed is in full possession of the house *until* the Stronger comes, takes from him all the weapons on which he counted for maintaining it, and divides the spoils. . . . Here the Strong is in possession of a *house* and is turned out of it. Our Lord had just been casting devils out of people. It is man created for divine indwelling who is enemy-occupied; and the Son of David, the Stronger than the Strong, has come to arrest from the

*See also 52:2, Neil.
**See also 3:1, Payne.

*See also 66:1, Payne.

144

usurping foe his trusted weapons of suffering and death, and restore the house to its owner."*

Sister Penelope
The Coming
p. 25

"An analogy used frequently in recent theological discussion about the atoning work of Christ is that of military engagement. Bishop Gustav Aulen has sought to revivify the ancient symbolism of Christ by his Cross putting to flight the demonic forces and breaking their power. In the years after Aulen's book was published, a new aspect of military aggression became the daily experience of many Europeans: living under the power of an occupying army. Here is a further illustration and symbol of sin — its pervasive and controlling influence. breaking morale and crushing hope. But to the occupying country, there comes a flash of incredible good news — a liberating army has landed, has engaged the occupying forces in a crucial battle which fairly tested the strength of both sides, and has emerged clearly and splendidly victorious. The power of the occupying force is, of course, still very much of a daily reality, but this crucial piece of good news has broken that power in the hearts and minds of the country's people."

John M. Krumm
The Art of Being a Sinner
pp. 87-88

"Just as in the Old Testament the Songs of the Suffering Servant stand almost alone as showing *how* redemption is to be effected, so there is one little bit of the Lord's teaching which explains *how* the old kingdom is to be destroyed and the new set up. First the Strong Man comes swaggering on to the stage. He is armed to the teeth and he lives in a fortified palace full of goods. These 'Goods' include all the wretched groaning captives whom the Lord of the house has taken, and he keeps them there by means of his weapons. 'Goods' is a good name for them for it is all they are, poor stunted personalities living in constant fear of those death-dealing spears and swords and with no chance of escape or development. The Strong Man struts about the stage for a bit, so that you may take him well in; and then another character walks quietly on stage, unarmed and all alone. You shrink in horror. What chance has the other against the tyrant? But the Newcomer goes straight up to the Strong Man and wrenches from him his sword, his spear, and all his weapons on which he depended; and with them he defeats and binds him, and all the prisoners are loosed. There is a new Lord of the house of humanity, the same who by his human birth at Bethlehem had already dedicated it to God in his own person.*

"The lesson here is the same as in the Suffering Servant, seen from another angle. The 'weapons' of the evil one are all the consequences of sin which culminate in physical death. With them he keeps the human race in subjection and prevents it from developing according to God's plan.** The Servant and the Stronger than Strong are One; but whereas the Songs show you the reality and terribleness of the sufferings by which he saves, the Gospel shows you the reality of his joy in doing it. . . . The drama of the Strong and the Stronger than he, like the story of David and Goliath, is gloriously and divinely humorous. The Strong One is beaten with his own weapons. Evil is made to be the instrument of its own overthrow. This is the secret of redemption and of life. Who but Love himself, eternal and infinite, could have thought of that?"***

Sister Penelope
The Wood
pp. 116-17

"The time when we must be especially cautious concerning the forces of evil is when we think that we are most righteous, holy, and intellectually self sufficient. No situation conditions the devil's activity as spiritual and mental pride do. . . . Our Lord warned us of the brilliant tactics of the evil one, who watches for the time when we become penitent and cast out our besetting sins through the power of the Holy Ghost, and then, inwardly swept and garnished, overconfidently ignore the still existing dangers the devil subtly puts before us. Jesus said it is then we must beware. If we have not replaced with some positive substitute the negative power which was eliminated, far worse evils will usurp the vacancy (Luke 11:24-26). Listen to this splendid description in Ephesians 6:10-11: 'Be strong in the Lord and in the power of his might. Put on the whole armor of God that you may be able to stand against the wiles of the devil.' "

Austin Pardue
He Lives
pp. 75-77

"St. Gregory, the theologian, explains what the Lord said of the unclean spirit which goes out of a man, and then returns again rendering that man's last estate worse than the first. . . . 'The unclean spirit, banished by baptism, and not caring to be homeless, seeks rest, walking here and there; finding no home, he returns to the house from which he came out, for he is shameless. If he finds that Christ is held by the attention and love of the baptised man and is established and dwells in the place from which he had been cast

---

*See also 110:2, Jeremias.

*See also 122:2, Holloway.
**See also 14:2, Lewis.
***See also 46:3, Lewis.

out, that is in the heart, he fails to enter and again turns away. But if he finds his former place empty, occupied by no one, through absence of attention towards God and memory of him, he enters hastily with greater malice than before. And the last state of that man is worse than the first.' I have purposely spoken at length about this to urge you to remain ceaselessly in your heart with the memory of our Lord and Savior and with prayer to him if you wish to be victorious in troubles caused by thoughts which assail the heart.''

Theophan the Recluse
Unseen Warfare
p. 98

'' 'Sign' is a symbolization, a sensory presentation of a manifested truth, a percepted reality which, no matter whether it is more or less 'wondrous', always reminds people once again of that truth. In the same sense, after Moses says (Exodus 3:11) 'Who am I that I should go to Pharaoh and that I should lead the children of Israel out of Egypt?', YHVH provides the assurance. 'Indeed I shall be present with you,' and he promises Moses a 'sign' — that the people would come to this same mountain where they would engage in the service of their God. This is what must serve Moses as a sign that it is this same God that sent him. We have to understand this as meaning: what is now existent in words will then take on real existence. Then Moses will experience the mission of this God as an expression of his being; not as a spiritual mission, as now, but as a reality apparent to the senses. Unlike this, the word 'sign' in the supplement (Exodus 4:8f) appears as a proof of reliability produced by way of supernatural arts.''

Nahum Glatzer, ed.
Martin Buber: On the Bible
p. 53

''He who will not submit to the word of God will not be converted by a miracle. The demand for a sign is an evasion and a sign of impenitence. Hence the sentence is pronounced: 'God will never give a sign to this generation' (Mark 8:11). . . . The parabolic saying about the 'sign of Jonah' is interpreted by Luke (11:30) as God's legitimation of his messenger through the deliverance from death. In Matthew 12:40 this interpretation is expanded and its emphasis shifted. The point of comparison is now the period of three days and three nights (Jonah 2:1). . . . The meaning of the sign of Jonah in Luke is the older form, according to which the return of God's messenger from the dead is the subject of comparison. The *Parousia* is the only sign that God will give, too late, however for repentance; he gives no other sign.''

Joachim Jeremias
The Parables of Jesus
pp. 108, 187

''Jesus' ministry is a sign of the reign of God which is already dawning. He is the only sign which is given to this 'adulterous and sinful generation' as once Jonah was a sign to the Ninevites. Forgiveness and salvation take place through his word for the sick and the sinners, who came to him or were brought to him *in faith*. In Jesus himself, the dawn of the Kingdom of God becomes a reality.''

Gunther Bornkamm
Jesus of Nazareth
p. 170

''At the outset of his ministry, the exercise of the power of the kingdom was foremost in the mind of Jesus. He saw God in him violently breaking into the realm of Satan and challenging the power of evil to the last conflict. . . . Here is no question of miracles, of signs to compel men's belief. It is a matter of the conscious use of the power entrusted to him for a sharply defined purpose. . . . It is worthwhile to notice that Luke attaches to the end of this controversy the Pharisees' request for a sign. The answer to this request is given in its Marcan form (8:12): 'And he groaned in his spirit and said, ''Why does this generation seek a sign? Truly, I tell you, no sign shall be given to this generation''.' This attitude of Jesus with regard to the use of power needs to be borne in mind constantly.''

S. H. Hooke
The Kingdom of God
p. 50

New Illuminations:

On the Light

| Matthew 6:22-23 | Luke 11:33-36 | John 8:12 |

"Jesus teaches about the true fulfillment of the ancient Old Testament yearning for light. . . . The Feast of the Tabernacles uses the symbol of light to recall the great pillar of fire that had faithfully led the children of Israel during the wanderings in the wilderness. . . . Light in the Exodus sense is the pillar by which people find their way."

Earl F. Palmer
The Intimate Gospel
p. 88

"Unfortunately we do not know what meaning Jesus gave to the simile of the lamp whose place is on the lampstand. According to the context, Mark and Thomas relate it to the Gospel, Matthew to the disciples, Luke to the inner light. From the exegesis, a conjecture may be hazarded as to what was the original meaning. What is the meaning of 'neither do they place a lamp under a bushel'? If a bushel measure were placed over the small clay lamp, it would extinguish it. In the little, one-roomed peasants' houses which have no chimney, this might well have been the customary method of putting out the lamp. . . . A free rendering then would be: 'They do not light a lamp in order to put it out again immediately.' No! Its place is on the lamp-stand, so that it may give light to all the inmates. The sharp contrast between kindling and extinguishing would be most intelligible if the saying had been uttered by Jesus in reference to his mission, possibly in circumstances in which he had been warned of danger and urged to protect himself (cf. Luke 13:31). But it was not for him to protect himself. The lamp has been lit, the light is shining, but not in order to be put out again! No, but in order to give light! . . .

"The simile of the eye as the lamp of the body in Matthew is addressed to the disciples; in Luke it is a rebuke to the crowd. If it is not a warning against covetousness (cf. Matthew 6:19ff) but against inner blindness, then Luke is right in recording the saying as addressed to the crowd and with reference to Jesus' opponents (cf. John 9:39-41). To be blind means to be hardened. You are hardened. What a fearful darkness! If bodily blindness is terrible, what, then, must inner blindness be? (Concerning the idea of the 'inner light' which shines from within a man, cf. Gospel of Thomas 24: 'Within a man of light there is light and it [or he] lights the whole world')."

Joachim Jeremias
The Parables of Jesus
pp. 120-21, 162-63

"Jesus said, 'The light of the body is the eye: if therefore thine eye be single, thy whole body shall be full of light. . . . If therefore the light that is in thee be darkness, how great is that darkness!' The text has a real message for me and I hope it has for you. There is an enormous secret hidden inside it. I know only a small part of it, but believe me it can change your whole life. . . .

"Most of us do one of three things as we focus our energies upon life. First, we may be so fickle and scatterbrained that we never concentrate long enough on any one point to get a clear and constructive result. . . . Secondly, we may focus on the wrong things. . . . Thirdly, we may focus on that which is right, good, and constructive. The result is that we then create good pictures of life which turn into joy, courage, sacrifice, health, and strength.

"Christ is direct and clear-cut in telling us that the mind's eye is the all-important criterion of a man's future. Our Lord deals specifically with this subject. A revealing Greek word as used. It is *haplous*, which means the giving of one's attention to an object or singleness of vision — or keeping your eye on the ball.* The principle that Christ teaches time and again is that the thing we believe in our hearts — the thing we focus upon — will come true in our lives."

Austin Pardue
The Single Eye
pp. 3-5

"In seven words, our Lord sums up his mission: 'I am the light of the world.' In his sacred heart was the ineffable longing that those to whom he came should come out of the unrealities of their twilight to the realities of his light, and being set free from their sins, they might enter into the light and glory of the knowledge of God. As he came that we might have life more abundantly, so he came that we might have light more abundantly, and the light eternal is one with life eternal. It is the knowledge of the Father whom he came to reveal."**

Harry C. Griffith, ed.
The Gift of Light: A Collection of Thoughts from the Writings of Father Andrew
p. 66

"There is much more in the notion of 'light of light' than of 'living light' or 'life's light.' Life's light is to say that light

---

*See also 54:1, Carmichael.
**See also 26:2, Kelsey; 3:2, Van Kamm.

is a quality belonging to life. The light of life (John 8:12) says that the quality can be communicated. The light of life is a radiation that engenders life.''

Monk of the Eastern Church
Jesus: A Dialogue With the Savior
p. 125

"We feel very tiny as we stand on a vast Cathedral floor and see the great pillars rising all around us to the dim vault; and the windows with their pictures of a perfect holiness and love are all the more daunting because they show that holiness and love within the arena of our own lives, so far beyond us and yet so divinely near. . . .

"But as we get used to the cathedral light, we feel something comes through the windows that is strangely akin to us, that streams down into our souls and there awakes a first response — the light of the world to show us Reality, the *Lumen Christi*. . . . And it is in fostering, strengthening, steadying the response to that Light that we fulfil our true meaning, become more real in the sight of God and make our tiny contribution to the Triumph of Life. For in the deepest sense, even that response is not truly our own. It is God Incarnate, God in his deep humanity, the Spirit proceeding from the Father and the Son, indwelling his little creatures, who stirs in us and initiates our new life towards him — a life, as Bruner says, which 'puts an end to our falsehood and our solitude.' Think of these words. They reach to the root of our unrest.''

Evelyn Underhill
The Light of Christ
pp. 96-97

"At the birth of the Son of God, there was brightness at midnight; at the death of the Son of God, there was darkness at noon. The context of the cry — 'My God, My God, why hast thou forsaken me?' — was the great darkness which stretched over the whole land and lasted for three hours. In the human mind and in the imagination as well as in the Biblical symbolism there is a close link between darkness and evil. 'If thine eye be evil, thy whole body shall be full of darkness.' 'The people that walked in darkness have seen a great light: they that dwell in the land of the shadow of death, upon them hath the light shined' (Isaiah 9:2). Men whose works are evil love the darkness rather than the light, as St. John observed (John 3:19).''

Douglas Webster
In Debt to Christ
p. 47

"What Jesus condemned was the half measure. Man cannot serve God and mammon (Matthew 6:24); he cannot attach his heart at once to the heavenly and earthly treasures. Possibly the intervening picture of 'light in thee,' at least as Matthew understands it, is to be taken in the same sense. God's light in us, his companionship and nearness, tolerates no shadows.''

Rudolf Schnackenburg
God's Rule and Kingdom
pp. 109-10

New Illuminations:

On Woes to the Pharisees for Their Hypocrisy

Matthew 23:1-36   Mark 7:1-13   Luke 11:37-52; 12:54-59

"Jesus did not reject the Old Testament nor supersede it. What he rejected was the travesty of the Law and Prophets which Judaism had become. It was the elaboration of ceremonial, the paraphernalia of the temple, the dead weight of moral obligations, the spiritual arrogance, the racial exclusiveness, all of which Jerusalem encouraged as being the proper witness of the people of God that drew forth Jesus' wrath and incurred his sternest condemnation.

"The God whom Jesus knew and loved was the God of Jeremiah, Amos, Isaiah, and Micah. The morality that Jesus commended was the morality of the Mosaic Law. The community that he founded was continuous with Abraham and the fathers, with Elijah and the seven thousand who did not bend the knee to Baal. It was new, but it was a new Israel. It was the reconstituted people of God, reformed and cleansed and given its proper direction."

William Neil
The Message of the Bible
pp. 122-23

"Jesus is seen as Religious Man. It is his custom to be in the synagogue on the Sabbath. He joins in the religious rites of the Jewish church and nation. He prays often, apart and alone. And when he prays, he draws upon the words of Scripture and Psalm. Yet he also appears as the Man against Religion. He assails the religion of his contemporaries, a religion so encased in departmental professionalism that in the very midst of the things of God, it was forgetting mercy and judgment and blinding men's eyes to the activity of God outside the religious camp. Religion in its turn resents Christ and assails him, and it is by religion that he is done to death outside the gate of the city."

Michael Ramsey
Sacred and Secular
p. 54

"Nothing is more remarkable in our Lord's dealing with men than his gentleness and forbearance. He was always kindly and generous in his judgments. He was always tolerant of failure and imperfection. His faith in the inherent goodness of human nature must have been sorely tried at times, but it never broke down. In him, Isaiah's prophecy of him found its fulfillment: 'A bruised reed shall he not break, and the smoking flax shall he not quench.' . . .

"There is one exception to this which stands out in striking contrast to his habitual attitude: it is his treatment of the Pharisees. To other sinners, even to the most degraded, he never says a single word which would lead them to despise themselves, still less that would encourage others to despise them. But to the Pharisees he does. 'Woe unto you, Scribes and Pharisees, hypocrites.' 'Ye fools and blind, ye serpents, ye generation of vipers, how can you escape the damnation of hell?' 'Verily I say unto you that the publicans and harlots will go into the Kingdom of God before you.' So too he says to his disciples: 'Except your righteousness shall exceed the righteousness of the Scribes and Pharisees, ye shall in no case enter the Kingdom of Heaven.' Such language, which coming from his lips, sounds so strange and startling to us must have sounded much more strange to those who heard it. . . .

"If we can imagine the startling effect which would be produced by an itinerant preacher addressing the House of Bishops in language which our Lord used in renouncing the Pharisees, we shall be able to form some idea of the amazement with which his words were received.

"Why is it that Christ condemned the Pharisees? What was the fatal flaw in their character and their religion which placed them in his judgment on a lower level than all the publicans and harlots? It was the sin of self-satisfaction. . . . Towards the sins that we are most ready to condemn, sins of the flesh, our Lord showed a peculiar tenderness. . . . The sins against which he was most severe were the sins that are 'admired of many,' the cold, inhuman, respectable sins of the Pharisees, the hard, sour, religious complacency of men who trusted in themselves that they were righteous and despised others. There is truth in the saying that the sin that in its malignancy slew the Lord of Life was the sin of Churchgoers, of religious people, of the pillars of the Temple who, when Supreme Goodness stood before them, would not see it, would not allow themselves to see it, but in spite and hate, in sheer intolerance struck it down and stampeded on it."

G. D. Rosenthal
The Sins of the Saints
pp. 68-72

"At first Jesus had to deal only with local authorities. Now the government sends its experts from Jerusalem. At first they raise a minor point about washing hands, probing his position. He could easily divert their attack into one of endless debates, but he immediately hits back with his strongest weapon: 'Why do you yourselves transgress the commandment of God for the sake of your tradition?' This is a declaration of war. He has lost all common ground with his opponents."

Fritz Kunkel
Creation Continues
p. 207

"It is not because Jesus seeks human glory that he criticises his listeners for their unbelief. Rather it is that their unbelief demonstrates that they have no true love of God. They prefer their own will to God's. . . . Thus having rejected the glory of God in favor of the glory that comes from men (Matthew 23:5-7), they have made it impossible for themselves to believe. It will therefore be unnecessary for Christ, to whom judgment has been given, to appear before God to denounce them; they stand self-denounced by their obduracy. Moses, here taken as the author of the Old Testament revelation, will himself denounce them, since the Old Testament itself has pointed the way to Christ (John 5:41-47)."

Bruce Vawter
The Jerome Biblical Commentary
63:87

"Those who pay attention only to external practices of virtues leave their hearts to be moved by their own volitions and the volitions of the devil. . . . As a rule they always wish to be preferred to others. They are blind to everything related to themselves but are very clear-sighted and officious in examining the words and works of others. If anyone interferes with them in their pious occupations and works, they immediately become indignant. . . . Thus it is clear that they are in great danger. Their inner eye, that is their mind, being darkened, they see themselves with it and see wrongly. Thinking of their external pious works and deeming them good, they imagine that they have already reached perfection and, puffing themselves up, begin to judge others. . . .

"Thinking very highly of oneself closes the door of one's mind or spirit, through which alone divine grace can enter. It gives this grace no way to come and dwell in a man who thinks of himself that he is something great, that he himself knows everything and needs no outside help. God severely reprimands those who are stricken with this passion of vainglory and self-esteem, saying through the prophet: 'Woe unto them that are wise in their own eyes and prudent in their own sight' (Isaiah 5:12). And the Apostle tells us: 'Be not wise in your own conceits' (Romans 12:16)."

Theophan
Unseen Warfare
pp. 22-23, 26

"The worst of all sins are not the so-called sins of the flesh. The devil played a trick on the church by beguiling it into concentrating on the blue laws. . . . But there is no statutory regulation against the most terrible of all sins; yet if it is taken care of first, all lesser sins are attacked at the same time. It is the sin of pride. By pride I don't refer to the perfectly legitimate thrill coming from a reasonable degree of personal independence. I don't refer to the satisfaction which comes from the power to stand on one's own feet. In other words, I don't refer to a wholesome self-respect, which is a virtue. In speaking of pride, I refer to a disease which causes a swelling of the ego, an expansion of self-love, an inflammation of self-importance, and a constant diminishing of the sense of duty to God and man. This is the basic sin that Jesus came to destroy and it has many manifestations.

"Intellectually, the sin of pride shows itself in unteachability — an unwillingness to take criticism however constructive it may be. . . . The Bible refers to this as hardness of heart. Emotionally, the sin of pride fills us with the sin of revengefulness and hatred whenever anyone blocks our way or puts blame upon us. . . . Socially, the sin of pride drives us to 'play to the gallery' and thus become immune to truth. We become enslaved by our own illusions. Spiritually, the sin of pride makes us put a fondness for our religious hobbies in the place of dedication to Christ. We confuse means and methods with ends. . . . The sin of pride is what turns lay people into Pharisees, making them thankful they are not as other people and giving them a sense of being an authority on all religious matters. . . . Morally, pride is the basic problem of mankind. If we could solve this problem, the tensions of the world would melt away, for it is pride that is the great barrier, the bulwark against God's will being done on earth as it is in heaven."

Austin Pardue
The Single Eye
pp. 39-40

"Alms to the poor (Luke 11:41) would cleanse the Pharisee of his sins, providing it reduced him to the status of the lowly who desperately needed salvation. The Pharisees were defeating the purpose of the law by their innumerable legal interpretations. At the same time they destroyed justice (the fulfillment of God's plan of salvation) and charity (salvation freely given and humbly shared) because they attributed salvation to this human work of keeping the law.

"These men felt no need of redemption, as they sat in a semi-circle around the Ark (where the sacred scrolls were preserved) confidently facing the congregation. To come near to the Pharisees was to contaminate oneself with the touch of the spiritually dead! The people mingled freely with the Pharisees thinking them to be good men, and all the while they were being infected with their vices (Luke 11:44).* In Matthew's Gospel, Jesus calls them 'whitewashed sepulchres.' "

Carroll Stuhlmueller
The Gospel of St. Luke
pp. 98-99

"When our Lord rebuked the Pharisees' over emphasis of the ceremonial Law, he was careful to distinguish between their misinterpretations and the sanctity of the Law itself. Thus on one occasion, he said the Pharisee was so faithful to give one-tenth of all he possessed that he even tithed the herbs that he grew in the kitchen garden but 'omitted the weightier matters of the Law — justice, mercy and faith'

---

*See also 65:1, Hooke.

(Luke 11:42). Thus he rebuked the Pharisees' exaggeration of the ceremonial Law at the expense of the moral. These (weightier matters) you ought to have done — and not to leave the other undone. Yes, the ceremonial Law was still in force, and it was to be observed with care. . . . Our Lord came not to destroy but to fulfill the Law. 'Love is the fulfilling of the Law' (Romans 13:10). But love has its own Law which must be obeyed.''

Ralph Milligan, ed.
All For the Love of God: Holy Cross Omnibus
pp. 174-75

"The seventh woe (Matthew 23:29f, par. Luke 11:47f) is the longest; and it no doubt reflects the execution of Jesus, the Messiah, and the ultimate fulfillment of prophecy, and the attacks of Jewish authorities against the Apostles and missionaries of the early Christian community. Hostility to the prophets is traced back in an unbroken chain to the origins of the nation. . . . The argument by which the present generation is linked to its ancestors in the killing of the prophets is somewhat involved and rabbinical in character. By building the tombs of the prophets and disclaiming the actions of the ancestors, the Jews confess that they are sons of the prophet killers; and by the peculiar conception of sonship, the designation which they themselves accept, shows that they have the disposition of their fathers. . . . The benevolent purpose of divine revelation is frustrated by the unbelief of men, and the effect of the revelation is to harden the hearts of those who refuse to receive it. . . . The collective guilt of the murder of all the innocent from Abel to Zechariah is indeed a terrible load to bear.

"It is here especially that the passage is to be understood in the light of the great catastrophe of A.D. 70, in which Jerusalem and the Temple were destroyed and thousands of Jews perished. To those who were accustomed to think Biblically, this event was a manifest judgment of God; and the horror of the disaster shows that it was a judgment for no ordinary crime but suitable to a vast burden of guilt. Abel is the first victim of murder in the Bible and Zechariah is the last victim in the Hebrew Bible.''

John L. McKenzie
The Jerome Biblical Commentary
43:162

"In Luke 11:52, (par. Matthew 23:13), Jesus accuses the Scribes and Pharisees of shutting God's kingdom to men; they do not themselves enter nor do they permit those who want to enter to do so. . . . Judaism thought that salvation culminated in a share in the 'future aeon.' This was secured through a faithful observance of God's Law, and the Scribes had the official responsibility of showing men the way, yet Jesus charges them with blocking this way through their perverted legalistic interpretation and their behavior. Luke speaks of the 'key of knowledge' — key to the kingdom of God, one that consists in knowledge. This must have had reference to the teaching of the Law. In point of fact, it is not merely knowledge since the legal decisions made by the Scribes also affected salvation.''

Rudolf Schnackenburg
God's Rule and Kingdom
p. 227

"Archbishop William Temple's definition of original sin perfectly describes the sin of self-satisfaction: 'I am the center of the world I see, where the horizon depends on where I stand. . . . Education may make my self-centeredness less disastrous by widening my horizon of interest. So far it's like climbing a tower, which widens the horizon for physical vision, while leaving me the center and standard of reference.' Now our self-centeredness does not only manifest itself against God. It also reveals itself against our fellows (v. 11:52). We seldom have what St. Paul called a sober judgment of ourselves.''

John Stott
Basic Christianity
p. 79

" 'How blind you are. You can read the signs of the weather but cannot realize the signs of the times.' No, you are blind. You are hardened. You cannot see that the call to repentance and the preaching of the good news are God's very last and final warnings. In Luke, the parable concerning going before the judge severely rebukes the populace for its failure to grasp the gravity of the present moment. The whole stress lies on the threatening situation of the defendant. It says to him, 'You are shortly to appear before the judge, in danger of condemnation and imprisonment. At any moment you may be arrested. Act at once while you are still at liberty, and settle the matter while it is still possible.' There can be no doubt that Luke is right: the parable is an eschatological one, a parable of crisis.* The crisis is imminent, the final crisis of history. The opportunity must be seized before it is too late. . . . Jesus lives in expectation of the great catastrophe, the last crisis of history which his death will introduce.''

Joachim Jeremias
The Parables of Jesus
pp. 162, 43-44

---

*See also 105:1, Montague.

New Illuminations:

On Sin I: Man's Offense Against God

"Sin is not a convenient convention of parsons to keep them in their job; it is a universal fact. The Biblical writers are quite clear about this. 'There is no man who does not sin,' says Solomon (1 Kings 8:46). 'Surely there is not a righteous man on earth who does good and never sins' adds the Preacher in the *Book of Ecclesiastes* (7:20). Several of the Psalms lament the universality of human sin. 'If thou, O Lord, shouldst mark iniquities, who could stand?' (Psalm 130:3). The prophets are as insistent as the psalmists on the fact that all men are sinners. 'All we like sheep have gone astray; we have turned every one in his own way' (Isaiah 53:6).

"Nor is this a fancy of Old Testament writers. . . . St. Paul describes in vivid terms the degraded morals of the pagan world and adds, in his Epistle to the Romans, that the Jew is no better, since, possessing God's holy law himself and teaching it to others, he is yet guilty of breaking it. . . . St. John is even more explicit when he declares that 'If we say we have no sin, we deceive ourselves,' and 'If we say we have not sinned we make him a liar' (1 John 1:8, 10). The universal extent of human sin is, however, not a truth that can be known only by revelation. It is a fact of our own everyday experience. . . .

"But what is sin? What is its nature? Several words are used in the Bible to describe it. They group themselves into two categories, according to whether wrongdoing is regarded negatively or positively. . . . All imply the existence of a moral standard. It is either an ideal which we fail to reach, or a law which we break. 'Whoever knows what is right to do and fails to do it, for him it is sin' (James 4:7). That is the negative aspect. 'Everyone who commits sin is guilty of lawlessness; sin is lawlessness' (1 John 3:4). That is the positive aspect. [We have left undone those things which we ought to have done, and we have done those things which we ought not to have done.'] . . .

" 'Original sin is the fault and corruption of the Nature of every man. . . . And this infection of Nature doth remain.' It is a tendency, or bias, towards sin and self-centeredness, which we inherit, which is rooted deeply in our human personality, and which manifests itself in a thousand ugly ways.

"It is because sin is an inward corruption of human nature that we are in bondage. It is not so much certain acts or habits which enslave us, but the evil infection from which these spring. . . . We know this only too well. We have high ideals, but weak wills. We want to live a good life, but we are chained and imprisoned. We are not free, we are slaves. . . . We need a Saviour. It is not the education of the mind only which can help, it is a change of heart. Man needs spiritual power, power to set him free from himself, power to control himself."

John R. W. Stott
Basic Christianity
pp. 62-63, 76-78

"Adam, unfallen, had no identity problem. He was a creature in communion with the Law-Giver. As a single flower opens broadfaced to receive its life from the sun, so Adam lifted his face and received Joy, power, his very being from God. In his disobedience and resulting Fall, Adam's relationship to God was broken. . . .

"In ceasing to direct her every action and thought to her creator, Eve displayed this self-will which, as Lewis says, is the only sin conceivable as the Fall. Her self-will was, in effect, a denial of her creaturehood. The created finite would contend with the Infinite. 'From the moment that a creature becomes aware of God as God and of itself as self, the terrible alternative of choosing God or self for the center is opened to it. This sin is committed daily by young children and ignorant peasants as well as by sophisticated persons, by solitaries no less than by those who live in society: it is the fall in every individual life, the basic sin behind all particular sins: at this very moment we are either committing it, or about to commit it, or repeating it' (C. S. Lewis, *Weight of Glory*)."

Leanne Payne
Real Presence: The Holy Spirit in the Works of C.S. Lewis
pp. 57, 59

"It is sin which opposes reconciliation, and repels the love of God, for sin cannot exist in him. At the root of all sin is always the exalting self-assertion, the incessant return upon self, to the exclusion of God. There is no room for God there. 'His own received him not.' . . .

"Man is free and man chose and chooses the return upon self, the sterility of self-assertion. That is the anatomy of sin. . . .

"We all know how we tend all the time to think of 'myself' as the center of all existence. We entrench ourselves, so to speak in the center of the circle of existence, and from there look out on everything and everybody else as the circumference. . . . We know, of course, that we did not create ourselves, but we take it for granted that about the most important thing God has done is to create 'me,' and that everything and everybody else revolves around that 'me.' Push that unconscious principle just a little further — into action in 'real life' — and all the pride and greed and hatred and lust and cruelty and sloth in human life is the result. That is the result of self-regardingness, self-centeredness, and return upon self to the exclusion of God. That is the root of sin.''

Dom Gregory Dix
The Claim of Jesus Christ
pp. 42-43, 67-68

''Sin, as a noun, describes either an act of sinning, which brings us back to the verb; or a habit of sinning — and that brings us back to the verb again. If we understand the verb 'to sin', we shall understand both the act and the habit. What is it then to sin? It is to do the wrong thing in relation to some person. . . . When we are said to sin against God or man, it is understood that we are in some measure responsible for the collision. It will be in a very weakened sense, if at all, that a man will be held to sin in violating divine claims of which he is simply unaware.''

Austin Farrer
Saving Belief
pp. 88-89

''We do not understand that by sin man 'casts out grace, deadens his own ear until God's voice sounds fainter, and comes more seldom and at last there follows the stillness of death. It is heard no more. God leaves the soul and it is dead.' These words of E. B. Pusey should be a warning to all, but especially to those that argue that because their conscience does not trouble them they are free from sin. We should remember what Albert Schweitzer has said: 'The good conscience is an invention of the devil.' ''

Manasses
Go In Peace
p. 16

''The false sense of proportion leads us to think lightly of little sins. They do not seem to be important because our standards of measurement are distorted. We fail to realize that infidelity to conscience in small things is infinitely connected to like infidelity in larger ones; for example, little lies are seeds of greater ones; little treacheries are like holes in a piece of cloth, the beginning of larger ones. The little sins which we commit every day, the trivial acts of selfishness, the passing gusts of temper, the slight habits of self-

indulgence, may seem to have comparatively insignificant consequences on the outward life. But they are of incalculable influence on the interior life. They weaken the will, lower the moral tone, limit its range, destroy the sensibility, and help to put out the light of conscience. . . .

''Take an illustration of the same truth. You can destroy a mirror by a single blow of a hammer, shivering it at once into a thousand fragments. You can also destroy it quite effectively in a different way: go behind it with a needle and with a delicate touch make the smallest line through the silver coating at the back. Continue this day after day and six months will not have passed before the mirror will be so scratched as to be worthless. Similarly it is not necessary to commit grave and notorious sins in order to destroy the moral sense. Constant little daily faults, venial sins as we call them, if we commit them often enough, can take the silver off from the back of conscience.''

G. D. Rosenthal
Sins of the Saints
pp. 150-151

''One day a diver in a pearler's fleet found an oyster with a pearl as large as a pigeon's egg in it; but when the delighted owner of the fleet began to clean the outside of the shell before chipping out the pearl, he found that a marine worm had bored a hole from the outside through the shell and into the heart of the pearl; and so it was not worth anything at all. A ruined pearl is worthless. The ruin was wrought by a single tiny worm. The story will speak to every one of us if we give it time. It needs no explanation. It explains itself. May God give it to us to fear sin and save us from saying, 'It is only a little sin.'

''The oyster could not prevent the worm from boring a little hole in its shell. We can. The moment we feel a worm crawling on our shell, we can get rid of it. We cannot prevent it from choosing our shell as a nice place to crawl upon, but we can be sure that it will be swept off the moment we know it is there. . . . If we keep ourselves in the Love of God — and we can if we will — then that mighty stream of Love, driven by the breath of the Lord will so flow over us that no worm shall have a chance to burrow in and spoil our pearl.''

Amy Carmichael
Thou Givest . . . They Gather
pp. 97-98

''Jesus came to save sinners whose sins are scarlet and whose encounter with him turns despair into hope and opens the way into a new life. Those of us whose sins are grey, all grey, have the same need for repentance and forgiveness and for cleansing from the dust of the way — the daily failures, the daily judgments, the selfish impulses. As

P. T. Forsyth wisely said: 'It is not the sins that damn but the sin into which sins settle down.' "

William Neil
The Difficult Sayings of Jesus
p. 78

"There are forces within us that work against community in spite of our hunger for community. This is just another way of saying that we are sinners. Sin has been defined as our assertion that we do not need relationship with God or man. It is our resistance to God's plan. This is why sin always leads to the most acute loneliness. We feel rejected and discarded. We develop hostility toward ourselves, toward others, even toward God. We are in Hell.

"The good news of God is that he loves us in spite of our brokenness. 'God shows his love for us in that while we were yet sinners, Christ died for us' (Romans 5:8). He accepts us in the midst of our unworthiness. We are loved in order that we may become lovable. We are forgiven and we are so grateful that we strive to become worthy of our forgiveness."

Everett H. Jones
His Witnessing Community
pp. 25-26

"From the point of view of strict justice, all sin ought to be unforgivable. For what is sin? It is the revolt of the creature against his creator. . . . It is a flouting of God's Law, a spurning of his love. If the insult to God were not so horrible and the consequences to us so tragic, sin would almost be funny. We who depend on God for everything seek to be independent. . . . Sin is an infinite offense against God. We commit it deliberately of our own free will. It is true that we are tempted, but God never permits us to be tempted above that which we are able to resist. He always gives us sufficient grace to overcome our temptation. Again and again we reject that grace."

Ralph Milligan, ed.
All For the Love of God: A Holy Cross Omnibus
pp. 164-165

"Virtue (which, after all, means strength) grows strong through exercise; and in what do we get so much exercise as in, by God's grace, conquering our chief sin or weakness? If, therefore, my underlying fault has always been cowardice — both physical and moral — and if I keep on fighting to be courageous, why, God will be forming within me the virtue of impregnable bravery. So with all our faults. It is, as it were, in their teeth that we build up the opposite virtue. The man or woman who has never known

the temptation of jealousy, or meanness, or discouragement, has little chance to build up simplicity or generosity or hope.

"It is a great comfort to me, and I am sure it is to you, to realize that we shall be strongest at that very point where we have been most weak; just as a broken arm, when once it is well again is strongest at the place where it was fractured."

Alan G. Whittemore
Joy in Holiness
pp. 31-32

"Sin is both a mark of man's high dignity and a proof of his weakness. Sin is a possibility only because man has been given the responsibility of deciding for himself what it means to be a man. . . . Men need food and they need clothing and shelter and relaxation and some expression of their sexuality. So their sin is often an anxious attempt to provide for these needs with a preoccupation that thinks too much of self and not enough of others and their responsibilities toward them. We are led along unthinkingly, seeking one satisfaction of the body after another, transferring more things from the luxury list to the necessity list, all of it defensible except that it leads to an indefensible concentration upon self and self-satisfaction in a world crying out for sacrifice and renunciation as the prerequisite of meeting its needs. So some of man's sins are sins of the flesh, though the needs of his body are innocent enough in themselves. . . .

"If sin were only weakness, it would be unfortunate; but because man compounds the felony by attempts of self-justification, it is calamitous. So a weakness that might easily be overcome entrenches itself by posing as virtue. It is very difficult for man to denounce what Albert Camus called 'the satisfaction of being right, the joy of self-esteem.' So genuine, full-hearted repentance is one of the rarest things in the world. Even when the evidence of one's failures becomes almost unavoidable, resistance grows stronger. . . .

"Man as a sinner is perversely displaying the grandeur of his calling to be a child of God. He can not just sin in his weakness and let it go at that. If he sins, he must pretend somehow that it is a virtue. Hypocrisy is a sign that man is not totally depraved in his sin. His weakness might be cured, or at least its destructive possibilities mitigated, if he would admit it and keep himself sensitive to the evidences of it but the worst part of his sin is that it will not let him confess it. So his grandeur is in part the cause of his misery. He not only goes astray like a lost sheep, but he insulates himself more and more within the walls of his self-esteem and impeccable reputation. And when God cannot reach him or touch him, his condition is desperate indeed. This is the tragedy of his sin.

". . . No one believes that he has lived up to his best all of the time, but most men would not go so far as to say they are altogether bad — which is what the Bible and the Christian tradition sometimes seems to be saying in the General Confession: 'And there is no health in us.' I make mistakes; I fall short of my best; I have little lapses — but I am not bad through and through. To put it briefly, most men would admit they commit sins once in a while, but they would not want to be classified permanently under the heading of 'sinners.'

"We must not exaggerate, however, what the Christian tradition means when it talks about sin as our natural condition. It cannot mean that there is nothing good about us at all. If one means by 'total depravity' that there is not a scrap of goodness in man at all, then it is a logical contradiction. If men really were totally depraved, they would be so bad they would not even be aware they were bad. . . .

"Christianity means by total depravity that sin creeps in everywhere and infects every part of the personality and leaves its mark on every operation and function of the self."

John Krumm
The Art of Being a Sinner
pp. 42, 46-47, 53-57

"The problem of evil does exist. No one who has any experience of life or who thinks at all about it can deny that things are wrong. We cannot explain the origin of evil, but we do notice that there is no problem of evil without good. Unless we knew good, we could not know that there is evil. . . . It is the opposite of what love would will or sense would think. . . . evil is parasitic on good. It is absence of good where good ought to be; and that may be a positive fact. Absence of ground is nothing; but a hole in the road is absence of ground where ground ought to be and when you fall into it, you fall.

"God does not will evil, but it is here. We have suggested that in taking the risk of eliciting freedom, God took the risk of admitting evil. This is not a complete explanation, and if we ask further questions about where things began to go wrong, we are led back and back to a region where nothing can be known, some say, before creation.

"We apprehend evil as pain, error, and bad will; these are the symptoms of radical sickness. . . . Good will, that is creative love, fights pain and ugliness and error. Bad will increases pain, loves ugliness, and propagates error, besides producing more bad will. In the end it destroys everything else, and itself as well; wages of sin is death."

T. R. Milford
Foolishness to the Greeks
pp. 44-45

"We need to be delivered from the source of our inhumanity, Jesus taught, and he told us first of all to pray. 'Deliver us from the evil one.' Then in various ways, he showed that the task is to look within and to know what is causing the trouble and whether we are nursing anger or harmful desires in our hearts. Christians are to recognize the source of evil within themselves so that they can seek help in order to stand outwardly against it.

"One way is to reflect on the need and suffering in the world. If one looks honestly at the things that happened, for instance, in the Communist and Nazi concentration camps, as Jung suggested, only someone with a warped sense of humor could honestly claim that the death ovens of Dachau represented only an 'accidental lack of perfection' or an absence of good. In our own times we have seen a cruelty overtake otherwise normal and civilized persons which one might call bestial except that this maligns the instincts of the animal world. . . .

"The idea that we have outgrown our need to turn to God for help in dealing with evil, or the idea, in fact, that there is no such thing as cosmic evil would be funny if it did not show such a tragic lack of understanding. This force has to be faced and dealt with or it will keep turning our homes and our world into a battlefield. We sometimes find it hard to understand why Jesus said that the poor in spirit, the meek and sorrowing are blessed, but perhaps it was because they are the ones that know they can't manage their lives by themselves.* Once a person realizes that there is a spiritual world as well as a physical one, that person learns that there are forces of evil more destructive than the simple human ones and that these spiritual forces of evil are ones that the individual cannot deal with on his own. . . . Failure to comprehend evil as an autonomous force with a power to affect human life is a kind of unconsciousness that can lead to disaster. . . .

"When we do awaken and realize our own helplessness, then the door is opened to the inward way. The realization of our spiritual poverty and our need for help beyond ourselves is the moisture that breaks open the seed. Once the depth of your soul has been penetrated, you have little choice; either you follow the religious way like a search for rare treasure, or else you must turn back to the ordinary world with resolute detachment and probably despair. At times one wishes that one could back up and start over, but consciousness was apparently designed without a reverse gear."

Morton T. Kelsey
The Other Side of Silence
pp. 51-53

"At times we say piously, 'God is testing my patience, my faith and my humility.' We find all sorts of ways of turning God's judgment on us into a new way of praising ourselves. We are so patient that we can put up even with God!

"Is this not true? When I was a young priest, I preached a sermon and a young girl came up to me and said, 'Father Anthony, you must be appallingly evil.' I said, 'I am certainly evil, but how do you know that?' She said, 'Because you have described our sins so well that you must have

---

*See also 24:2, Payne.

committed them all yourself!' Of course the shocking description of evil thoughts and evil attitudes which I am giving you now are probably mine and not yours, but perhaps they are yours too however little.

"What we must start with if we wish to pray is the certainty that we are sinners in need of salvation, that we are cut off from God and that we cannot live without him and that all we can offer God is our desperate longing to be made such that God will receive us, receive us in repentance, receive us with mercy and with love."

Anthony Bloom
Beginning to Pray
p. 7

"I would say that every man who desires salvation will learn how to conquer his invisible foes, in order to acquire the treasure of true and divine virtues and to be rewarded with a true and incorruptible crown and a token of eternity — union with God, both in this life and in the future. Arm yourselves so as to strike down your inner and invisible foes which are the soul-destroying passions and their originators and instigators — the demons. Remember how at Holy Baptism you vowed to renounce Satan and all his works, all service of him and all his pride, i.e., love of lust, glory, love of money, and other passions. So strive with all your might to turn him back and to overcome him. And what of the rewards that await you in this victory? Hear of them from the Lord himself: 'He that overcometh shall inherit all things, and I will be his God and he will be my son' (Revelation 21:7)."

Theophan the Recluse
Unseen Warfare
p. 17

New Illuminations:

On Jesus' Warnings and Reassurances I

Matthew 10:16-33   Mark 4:22; 8:38   Luke 9:26; 12:1-9

"In early Hebrew ritual regulations still followed by the orthodox Jews, all leaven had to be removed from the dwellings before the celebration of the Passover, nor might leaven form any part of the sacrifices. In a significant passage in 1 Corinthians 5:6-8, Paul says, 'Know you not that a little leaven leavens the whole lump? Purge out therefore the old leaven that you may be a new lump, even as you are unleavened.' Paul is using the symbol of leaven in a wholly bad sense. . . . We have to ask then, what was Jesus warning the people against when he told them to beware of the leaven of the Pharisees.

"Jesus was concerned with something fundamentally wrong in the direction of their teaching — something that made him describe them as 'blind guides.' He found them guilty of giving them a false and unreal idea of what God was like and of what he required of men. It was this idea of unreality and falseness that was on his mind when he used the word which the Gospel writers have rendered as 'hypocrisy.'* The insidious infection of unreality, so often a result of a religion that has become merely conventional, was the danger of which he wanted the disciples to be aware. Where it was present and allowed to work unchecked, the end could only be corruption."

S. H. Hooke
The Kingdom of God
p. 91

"All decent human society requires some standard of human goodness. This constitutes the moral light of society. The rebels against this are the men who love the darkness first of all because it enables them to escape detection. . . . The works of darkness are disreputable actions. But a man may be living a perfectly respectable life and still be living in 'the darkness' and doing the 'works of darkness.' . . . Like the Pharisees, men may make the commandment of God of no effect by their traditions. Thus Christ came to penetrate all hypocrisy, conscious or unconscious, and all conventional morality with the searchlight of perfect goodness. He is the light of the world and the light condemns the darkness of conventional respectability as well as the darkness of disreputable sins."

Charles Gore
The Epistles of John
pp. 67-68

"The logion in Luke 12:2 has been very differently interpreted by the Evangelists. By Mark (4:22) it is seen as a statement about the preaching of Jesus (the secret of the kingdom will become manifest to all); by Luke it is regarded either as a warning against the hypocrisy of the Pharisees (their hypocrisy will avail them nothing since what is secret will become manifest), or as a promise relating to the preaching of the disciples (cf. 12:3, also 8:17); in Matthew (10:26) it is the basis for an exhortation to fearlessness (no hostility will be able to frustrate the preaching). Hence the Evangelists no longer knew the original meaning. . . . It may be assumed that for Jesus it had an eschatological meaning; the future tense and the antithetical form of the saying support this view. Above all it is clear from Matthew 6:4, 6, 18 that Jesus also declared elsewhere that on the Last Day what was hidden would be revealed. Hence, whatever was the particular application, the logion speaks of the eschatological reversal of the situation."

Joachim Jeremias
The Parables of Jesus
p. 221

"The advent of the perfect, fulfilled Kingdom will one day come, and unexpectedly, but in a form visible to all men, according to God's sovereign will and only through his all powerful action. This will occur when the Son of Man, accompanied by the hosts of heaven, comes 'with power.' This Son of Man is no other than Jesus himself.* For the present, in the form of humiliation and to a certain degree in concealment, he is fulfilling his Messianic tasks on earth. But then he will manifest himself to all the world possessed of kingly dignity and divine power to establish in God's name."

Rudolf Schnackenburg
God's Rule and Kingdom
p. 177

"Remember that God wants to lift us up and poise us in the light that he is in so that everything that is dark now will one day be as clear as it is to him. Think of all the things that are dark just now. Jesus said, 'There is nothing covered that shall not be revealed.' Things are dark and obscure to us because we are not in the right condition to understand them. Thank God for all that we have understood, for every

*See also 63:2, Stuhlmueller.

*See also 105:2, Penelope.

bit of truth that is so full of light and liberty and wonder that it fills us with joy as we walk in that light and allow the Son of God to meet every circumstance by his virtues, by his powers and by his presence, we will understand more and more with a 'knowledge which passes understanding.' "

Oswald Chambers
Our Brilliant Heritage
p. 47

"St. John says 'perfected love' has no place for servile fear of punishment which the Day of the Lord will bring with it. But he does not say that perfect love is not based upon and cannot grow out of a very imperfect sort of love which must consist with a large element of fear. Our generation is extraordinarily without the fear of God, but its fearlessness seems a foolish fearlessness due only to its failure to consider the awefulness of the divine presence and judgment our Lord himself bids us fear — 'fear him who is able to destroy both soul and body in hell.' And it is only too possible to be premature in claiming the fearlessness which belongs to love, only when it is perfected."

Charles Gore
The Epistles of John
p. 187

"Be sure there is something inside you which, unless it is altered, will put you out of God's power to prevent your being eternally miserable. While that something remains, there can be no heaven for you, just as there can be no sweet smells for a man with a cold in the nose and no music for a man who is deaf. It's not a question of God's sending us to hell. In each of us there is something growing up which will be hell unless it is nipped in the bud."

C. S. Lewis
"The Trouble with X"
Bristol Diocesan Gazette
August 1948

"God's consciousness penetrates all that exists. 'Are not two sparrows sold for a farthing? And yet not one of them is forgotten in God's sight; but the very hairs of your head are all numbered.' Every moment of our life, our very heart beat is in his hands. He is in truth the 'Light in which is no darkness at all' (1 John 1:5). And there is no one and nothing that can escape his all-seeing eye."

Archimandrite Sophrony
His Life is Mine
p. 26

"Each of us is created in God's own image, and it means that though we are creatures and full of sins and defects, there is a deep down likeness between us and God, and our destiny is to be with him. When we say that God loves us, we mean that he cares for each single one of us as if there were no one else for him to care for. He cares for you in all the unique individuality that is yours. He wants *you* to be with him forever, to share with you all that he has to share. That is heaven. It is the perfection of the God-and-man-relationship."

Margaret Duggan, ed.
Through the Year with Michael Ramsey
p. 38

"How can visible human beings express the image of God? We certainly cannot look like him sharing characteristic features of eyebrow or earlobe, for God is invisible spirit. Philosophers and theologians have long speculated on all that could be contained within the mystery of that single phrase. . . . What else could that image be but our capacity for relationship with other people and with God*. . . . Among all God's creatures, only humanity receives the image of God, and that quality separates us from all else. We possess what no other animal does; we are linked in our essence to God."

Dr. Paul Brand and Philip Yancey
In His Image
p. 20

"One well-authenticated passage deriving from two sources is of great importance because it compares the attitude of men to Jesus with that of the men of the time when the Son of Man is to come. Mark 8:38 (see Luke 9:26) reads: 'He that shall be ashamed of me and my words ("in this adulterous and sinful generation" — only in Mark), the Son of Man also will be ashamed of him when he shall come in the glory of his Father with the holy angels (Luke: "in his majesty and that of the Father and the holy angels").' An even older version is found in the tradition preserved in Matthew and Luke, and the most ancient of all in Luke 12:8-9: 'Whoever shall confess me before men, him shall the Son of Man also confess before the angels of God (Matthew: "my Father who is in heaven"). But he that shall deny me before men shall be denied before the angels of God.' In Matthew 10:32, 'Son of Man' is replaced by the first personal pronoun. The identification of Jesus and the Son of Man is taken for granted. The expression, from the Matthew-Luke tradition portrays the Son of Man not as a judge but as a witness before God. The logion in Mark 8:38

*See also 67:2, Drake.

conforms to the picture of the Son of Man in Daniel. The positive aspect is omitted because the statement is taken as a warning.''

Rudolf Schnackenburg
God's Rule and Kingdom
p. 168

''Jesus made his disciples share in his authority. The promise that Jesus gives his disciples is contained in Luke 12:8-9. Faithfulness and unfaithfulness toward their Master here on earth will receive their confirmation and answer on the Day of Judgment.* The community they have entered

*See also 86:1, Penelope.

by becoming the disciples of Jesus is thus full of promise and full of danger. . . .

''The use of the term 'Son of man' refers, quite in accordance with apocalyptic expectation, to the Son of man as he comes on the clouds of heaven (Daniel 7:13). . . . It is worth noting that Jesus does not here call himself the Son of man, but speaks of himself in the third person, and puts the decisions that are made concerning himself in the closest connection with the future decisions of the judge of the world.''

Gunther Bornkamm
Jesus of Nazareth
pp. 149, 176

New Illuminations:

On Blasphemy Against the Holy Spirit

Matthew 12:31-32   Mark 3:28-29   Luke 12:10

"Blasphemy refers to irreverence toward or defiance of God. The scribes saw men who were out of their minds restored to sanity, but instead of giving God the glory and acknowledging Jesus as his agent, they chose instead to accuse our Lord of being an agent of Satan. They had been guilty of the one sin that is beyond forgiveness. They refused to admit that actions that were prompted by motives of mercy and compassion were in fact good in themselves, because they disapproved of the person that was responsible for them. This indicates a state of moral blindness and perversity which in the long run could make us incapable of repentance and therefore put us beyond forgiveness. When we are prepared to call good evil, we are on the way to damnation, which means ultimately separating ourselves from God. . . .

"We call good evil and sin against the Holy Spirit when we attribute unworthy motives to some social reformer trying to better race relations, or to campaigners for improving the environment and securing a better deal for the underprivileged because we want a bigger slice of the national cake for ourselves. The lesson of Jesus' words is therefore that we must constantly keep a watch on ourselves, scrutinizing our judgments and analyzing our motives; otherwise our minds could become so distorted that we are no longer able to tell good from evil and become permanently the victims of our own fears and prejudices."

William Neil
The Difficult Sayings of Jesus
pp. 23-24

"All sins are forgivable. There is no act of sin, however wicked, however despicable, however devastating, that has not been atoned for by the all-suffering sacrifice of Christ. Each and every sin is forgivable if the sinner will accept forgiveness. There is the one, the necessary condition. There is the clue to the unforgivable sin. . . . Our repentance is the work of the Holy Spirit in our souls. He enables us to distinguish right and wrong. When we have done what is wrong, he prompts us to sorrow for our sin. He bids us face it, admit it without evasion, without excuse. He encourages us to turn from our sin and throw ourselves humbly on the undeserved mercy of God. He gives us the hope with which to expect the divine pardon and the humility with which to accept it. Thus the Holy Spirit makes us receptive to God's forgiveness.*

---

*See also 71:1, Manassas.

"But we can reject the work of the Spirit in our souls. We stifle the voice of conscience until it is no longer heard. . . . We can set out to build for ourselves the Kingdom of Heaven according to our own blueprints and relying on our own strength. We can become so intoxicated with our self-esteem that we assume God must be well pleased with us. It never occurs to us that we need his help, much less his forgiveness. This is the sin against the Holy Ghost. . . . The great danger of this is that by its very nature we are unaware of its sinfulness when we commit it. By definition it is a state of unawareness of sin. It must be embraced deliberately, of course, otherwise it would not be sin. But little by little we can become complacent about the state of our souls. Thus we can slip deliberately, yet imperceptibly into the sin against the Holy Ghost. . . . Those that seriously believe that good is evil, and conversely that evil is good, are incapable of repenting their evil acts, and therefore incapable of asking and receiving forgiveness."

Ralph Milligan, ed.
All For the Love of God: A Holy Cross Omnibus
pp. 166-68, 170

"It is blasphemous to attribute the darkness in Satan, of that arising in any creature, to any Person of the Blessed Trinity. Christ solemnly declared 'That any sin of man can be forgiven, even blasphemy against me but the blasphemy against the Holy Spirit can never be forgiven. It is an eternal sin' (Mark 3:28-29). Where good and evil are reconciled, the character of the Holy Spirit is presented as at once divine and demonic, and he who was sent as Comforter, as Stirrer of men's hearts toward God, becomes an ambiguous and fearful figure. This is even as Jung himself acknowledges, blasphemy. . . .

"God's love in us, or we might say, his Holy Spirit within us, is the divine energy which overcomes the evil or darkness in each individual life. Lewis has said, 'The union between the Father and Son is such a live concrete thing that this union itself is also a Person.' To blaspheme the Holy Spirit is to blaspheme Love,* and God's way of saving man. God is Love, and this Love has been from all eternity, a Love going on between the Father and Son. To fear and thereby to shun the Holy Spirit is to fear Love and thereby to step back into separateness."

Leanne Payne
The Real Presence:
The Holy Spirit in the Works of C.S. Lewis
pp. 181-182

---

*See also 61:1, Milligan.

"Now what are the respective ways in which we specially sin against the Holy Spirit? These will include all that diminishes joy and peace which ought to spread from Christian souls: all deliberate restlessness, fuss, anxiety, bitterness, all excursions into gardens to eat either religious or political worms, those meditations into our own unworthiness and unfortunate temperaments, and so on which we sometimes mistake for humility.* All these are sins against the Spirit of joy and peace."

Evelyn Underhill
The Fruits of the Spirit
p. 17

"I do not want now to discuss the ideology of Germany, nor yet that of Russia which, in a rather different way, is also a repudiation of Christendom. Nor do I want to talk about our own war aims and peace aims, and how far we are single-minded about them. All I want to say on this point is that, however deeply we have sinned — and God knows we have done plenty of evil in our time — we have not gone so far as to have altogether lost all claim to stand for Christendom. There is a great difference between believing a thing to be right and not doing it on the one hand and, on the other, energetically practicing evil in the firm conviction that it is good. In theological language, the one is a mortal sin which is bad enough; the other is the sin against the Holy Spirit which is without forgiveness simply and solely because the sinner has not the remotest idea that he is sinning at all. So long as we are aware that we are wicked, we are not corrupt beyond all hope. Our present dissatisfaction with ourselves is a good sign. We have only to be careful that we do not get too disheartened and abashed to do anything about it all."

Dorothy Sayers
Creed or Chaos
p. 27

*See also 92:1, Milligan.

New Illuminations:

On the Holy Spirit

Matthew 3:11, 16   Mark 1:8, 10   Luke 2:26-27; 3:22; 4:1, 14; 10:21; 11:13; 12:12   Acts 1:8

" 'I believe in the Holy Ghost.' Perhaps the best way to begin to make clear what is the Christian faith concerning the Holy Ghost or Holy Spirit is to look again at the word 'spirit' and inquire more closely about its origin. We find that it has come into the English from the Latin word *spiritus* which can mean spirit but also stands both for 'wind' and 'breath.' We can go further and ask what was the situation in Greek. There we discover that the word *pneuma* can likewise stand for 'spirit' or 'wind' or 'breath.' Strangely enough exactly the same is true in the Hebrew language, the action of spirit is akin both to that of the wind which operates in our external world and to that of breath which operates in the inner framework of our bodies.

"Now let us turn to the Old Testament and see how men used this kind of language when they were speaking of God's activities in human life. Sometimes when the wind came sweeping down the mountain gorges and stirring everything to new life, they said, 'That is God's breath.' Or yet again when there came some new impulse to go forward along the paths of righteousness and peace, some said, 'That is God's breath.' . . . Breath and wind were the most vivid images that they could find to describe the altogether powerful and yet altogether beneficent activities of the God whom they worshiped and served.

"Generally speaking, then, we may say that the Bible uses the term 'The Spirit of the Lord,' to represent God in action in human life. . . . The Spirit who moved upon waters at creation was the same Spirit who descended upon Jesus in the waters of baptism: the Spirit who empowered Gideon and Saul to become deliverers of their people was the same Spirit who empowered Peter and Paul to be heralds of redemption through Christ. The Divine activity comes gradually to be seen more clearly and understood more fully, but all the Biblical writers are concerned to bear witness to the one living God who works in the midst of human life by his Spirit."

Frederick W. Dillistone
The Holy Spirit
pp. 3-5

"In the Gospel of Luke there is an enormous emphasis upon the Spirit of God, the Holy Spirit. This can be seen in the Lukan account of the Baptism of Jesus. The Baptism has been relegated to one of three antecedent clauses — all the people baptised, Jesus baptised, Jesus praying — which serve to set the stage for the action of the main verbs — the heavens are opened, the Spirit descends. If we did not read Luke in the light of Mark (1:9-11), we would not call the pericope 'the Baptism of Jesus'; we would call it 'the descent of the Spirit upon Jesus.'* This emphasis upon the Spirit continues throughout the Gospel of Luke. I call attention to the synagogue scene at Nazareth, the frontispiece of the account of the ministry of Jesus, where part of the prophecy that is fulfilled is 'The Spirit of the Lord is upon me,' and to the Lukan account of the Crucifixion wherein Jesus formally returns the Spirit to the Father (23:46).

"The same emphasis is found in the Acts of the Apostles. The descent of the Spirit upon the apostles is interpreted as a baptism in Acts 1:5: 'before many days you shall be baptised with the Holy Spirit.' As the gospel begins with the baptism/descent of the Spirit, so also does the Acts of the Apostles, and the parallelism continues with reference to the work of the Spirit, as frequent and as important as they are in the gospel. Clearly Luke sees Jesus and the apostles as inspired by the same Spirit."

Norman Perrin
The Resurrection
pp. 70-71

"The self-offering or self-giving seen in Christ's obedience unto death is given to us by the indwelling of the Holy Spirit so that we make it our own, are filled with it and cleansed by it. Again, there is the Johannine imagery of the glory of Christ being given to the disciples, 'the glory which thou hast given me I have given to them' (John 17:22). What does this mean except that the self-giving love in the passion of our Lord is by the Holy Spirit brought within our lives to oust and replace our sinful self-centeredness?"

Michael Ramsey
Jesus and the Living Past
p. 75

" 'The spirit of glory and of God resteth upon you.' (1 Peter 4:14) God Almighty is the creator, lover and keeper of the soul of man. Perhaps it is in this last work of guardianship and protection and consecration that the Holy Ghost shows himself peculiarly the Spirit of Glory. As the Spirit of Glory, the Holy Ghost is not only himself, glorious, but he is the giver of the glory. . . . We should try to understand what is meant by glory. Glory is ultimate and absolute

---

*See also 12:1, Penelope.

perfection. The glory of a person is the achievement of his true destiny, the crown of his life's endeavor. The glory of a thing is the exact fulfillment of the purpose for which it was made.* The glory of a watch would consist not in the beauty of its case, however rich and costly, but in the perfection of time keeping. It is the work of the Holy Ghost to lead man to the complete achievement of God's eternal purpose. . . .

"It was God's purpose according to the terms of man's creation that his destined fellowship with God should come by the gift of the Holy Spirit, and that it should be the Spirit's part to insure that conformity to the image of God which is man's characteristic glory.** God could only look upon human life as complete in the consecrating and fulfilling power of the indwelling Spirit. So we can understand how for the fullness of his human perfection Jesus availed himself of the endowment of the Holy Spirit. As we watch the growth of Jesus, we see him fulfilling the ideal of human childhood: 'The child grew and waxed strong' in the power of the Holy Spirit. All through the silences of the thirty years of retreat it was the Holy Ghost who equipped him for the tasks of the carpenter's shop and sustained his human soul in communion with the Father. When his 'hour' was come and the toils of his public ministry began it was 'in the power of the Spirit' (Luke 4:14) that he taught and 'with the finger of God' that his miracles were performed (Luke 11:20), and at length it was 'through the eternal Spirit' that he 'offered himself without spot to God' (Hebrews 9:14). So the glory of that perfect human life in all its manifold experiences of suffering, agony, and grief was achieved in the power of the Holy Spirit. . . .

"The Holy Spirit alone creates in us the life of Jesus. St. Paul expresses the different attributes of the character of Christ which the Spirit forms in us as the 'fruit of the Spirit' — love, joy, peace, long-suffering, gentleness, goodness, faith, meekness, temperance (Galatians 5:22-25). It is impossible not to set the phrase 'fruit of the Spirit' side by side with the words of our Lord, 'I am the vine, you are the branches. . . . The branch cannot bear fruit of itself, except it abide in the vine; no more can ye, except ye abide in me.' This fruit is the result of our unbroken union with Christ, which the Spirit assures. The blessed Spirit is the sap of strength and vital energy which carries the life of Christ through all the branches, the safeguard of unity, and the source of fruitfulness. 'Without me ye can do nothing' (John 15:4-5).''***

F. W. Drake
The Spirit of Glory
pp. 4-6, 8-10, 22

---

*See also 105:2, Penelope; 46:2, Underhill.
**See also 65:2, Brand and Yancey.
***See also 27:2, Underhill.

"I have before me a remarkable document, a letter from a former Rabbi.

'Why did I, a former Rabbi, become a Christian?' he writes. 'Did I of myself become a Christian, following a plan, a purpose, after due consideration? No, the grace of God made me Christian. My conversion is a mystery to me before which I bow my head in awe. It was the Holy Spirit; he alone transfigured me. When I accepted Christ, the Laws of Deuteronomy ceased to be a means of drawing near to God. . . . As for religious ethics, they are much the same in Judaism as in Christianity: the commandments concerning ethics are often expressed in identical terms. In practice, however, they differ vitally. The Christian ethic is given from on high by the Holy Spirit, Who came to us only after Christ's resurrection. It is the same Spirit that pious Jews dream of to this day: they feel Him, see Him, but only *from afar*. But the true Christian lives in the Holy Spirit through faith in Jesus Christ. And so it was not I of myself who became Christian — it was God who sent down the grace of the Holy Spirit and made me so. This is the process: faith attracts the Holy Spirit, while the Holy Spirit strengthens faith, cares for you, sustains you, encourages your ardent desire for the Kingdom of God.' . . .

I have quoted this triumphant cry of a soul who found the Christ-God because, though many have had a similar experience, few find words to express the well-nigh inexpressible.

"The Holy Spirit comes when we are receptive. He does not compel. He approaches so meekly that we may not even notice. If we would know the Holy Spirit, we need to examine ourselves in the light of the gospel teaching, to protect any other presence which may prevent the Holy Spirit from entering into our souls.

". . . When we turn away from the path indicated by Christ — that is, from the deification of man by the power of the Holy Spirit — the whole point of Man's coming into the world disappears.''

Archimandrite Sophrony
His Life Is Mine
pp. 47-49, 70

"Christ commanded and empowered his followers to heal because he knew that all men, in their exterior relationships and within themselves, are broken and separated. . . . The key to the healing of all these relationships has to do with incarnational reality — with being filled with God's Spirit and with seeking to dwell in His Presence.* It has to

---

*See also 2:2, Lewis; 3:1, Payne.

do with man's choosing union and communion with God rather than with his own separateness which is, in effect, the 'practice of the presence' of the old Adamic fallen self. To be filled with the Spirit is to choose the heaven of the integrated and emancipated self rather than the hell of the disintegrated self in separation. To be filled with the Spirit is to choose the same love that has bound together the Father and the Son throughout all eternity.''

Leanne Payne
Real Presence: The Holy Spirit in the Works of C. S. Lewis
pp. 57-58

"The Christian affirmation is that the Trinitarian structure which can be shown to exist in the mind of man and in all his works, is in fact, the integral structure of the universe, corresponding with the nature of God in whom all that is exists. I shall try to demonstrate that the statements made in the Creeds about the Mind of the Divine Maker, so far as I am able to check them by my experience, represent true statements about the mind of the human maker. . . .

"Augustine of Hippo, in his great treatise, says in effect: 'a Trinitarian structure of being is not a thing incomprehensible or unfamiliar to you. There is a trinity of sight, for example: the form seen, the act of vision, and the mental attention which correlates the two. These three, though separable in theory, are inseparably present whenever you use your sight.' . . .

"For the purpose of examining the three-fold structure of creative activity, I shall use the mind of the creative writer because I am more familiar with its working than with those of other creative artists. But what is true of the writer is also true of the painter, the musician and all workers of creative imagination in whatever form. . . . For every work (or act) of creation is three-fold, an earthly trinity to match the heavenly.

"First, (*not in time but merely in order of enumeration*) there is the Creative Idea, passionless, timeless, beholding the whole work complete at once, the end in the beginning: and this is the image of the Father.

"Second, there is the Creative Energy (*or Activity*) begotten of that idea, working in time from the beginning to the end, with sweat and passion, being incarnate in the bonds of matter: and this is the image of the Word.

"Third, there is the Creative Power, the meaning of the work and its response in the lively soul, and this is the image of the indwelling Spirit. . . .

"By our response to the act of creation we are caught up into the stream of the author's Power which proceeds from his Energy revealing his Idea to us and to himself. . . .

"When the writer's Idea is revealed or incarnate by his Energy, then, and only then, can his Power work on the world. More briefly and obviously, a book has no influence until somebody can read it. Before the Energy was revealed or incarnate it was already present in Power within the creator's mind, but now that Power is released for communication to other men, and returns from their minds to his with a new response. It dwells in them and works upon them with creative energy, producing in them fresh manifestations of Power.''

Dorothy Sayers
The Mind of the Maker
pp. 15, 46-47, 111

"Do you remember how in St. Patrick's *Confession*, he tells how one night he *saw* Christ, praying in him and above him; and he was overwhelmed with awe considering who prayed within him, and a voice said, 'I am the Spirit who prays in thee?' So it has always been with the saints, channels of the Spirit, and so it may be with us. . . . Christ's Spirit, if I let it, can act through mine — praying in me and above me as St. Patrick said. And I was given to him in baptism and gave myself to Him of my own free will *for* this purpose, to be one more transmitter of God's power and love.''

Evelyn Underhill
Light of Christ
pp. 94-95

"Think of yourself on a cold dark night. You slip into a room. No lights are on. It seems dark and cold. But presently just a little light, just a little warmth reaches you. You move closer. A fire is burning.

"You begin to see. In the brightness of the fire you notice in the room shapes, forms, outlines. If there is someone else in the room, you see his face reflecting the fire. Thus the Holy Spirit enables you to see, and to see like a Christian — perceiving things as they really are in the eyes or mind of Jesus; perceiving people as they really are with the light of Jesus upon them; perceiving meanings and purposes instead of shapeless confusion; perceiving what a Christian ought to be doing. Remember the words in the *Veni Creator*:

'Enable with perpetual light
The dullness of our blinded sight.'

Remember too the words in the Whit Sunday Collect where we pray that the Holy Spirit may give us 'right judgment in all things.' The Holy Spirit keeps the light of Jesus glowing in us. That is how we see as Christians should see.

"The fire as you approach it gives you warmth. Warm itself, it makes you warm. So the warmth of the love of God within you can warm your heart to love him in response. This is not a matter of sentiment only. The very love of God can penetrate you and warm your faculties to love him. So we say:

'Thy blessed unction from above
Is comfort, light and fire of love.'

and an old Christian writer speaks of *incendium amoris* (love's kindling). . . .

FLAMES OF FIRE AND BURNING, TOO: Light, warmth — and burning, too. The Holy Spirit will burn us.* If we are to have vision and if we are to have warmth of love, we must be exposed to the pains of burning. All that is unloving, selfish, hard, must be burnt out of our existence, burnt to destruction, burnt to ashes. The Spirit will burn his way into the core of our being in the ever painful process of disclosure, of penitence, and of divine forgiveness. Only by such burning can our heart be fully exposed to the warmth and our mind be fully exposed to the light. There is no seeing and no warming without that burning. It is thus that we realise the saying of Jesus Christ found in one of the apocryphal documents: 'He that is near me is near the fire.' "

Margaret Duggan, ed.
Through the Year with Michael Ramsey
pp.103-105

"The life in the abiding Spirit is not literally carefree, but it is the life that has the capacity for dealing adequately with those inescapable cares which do as a matter of fact confront us. Persisting in the way in which God's Spirit guides us, we find that faithless fears and worldly anxieties are scaled down to realistic and manageable size. For, as we make our deliberations with genuine faith in the direction promised us through the Holy Spirit, we find that the promise works out to be abundantly true beyond any previous hopes we might have had for it. While the gift of the Spirit, given permanently and without reservation, serves as no infallible guarantee of right decision on our part, he does nevertheless operate within us, in all the power for right that God possesses. . . . This is precisely why much of the 'other benefits' can properly be taken summarily as a gift of the sense of direction and accomplishment."

Ralph Milligan, ed.
All For the Love of God: A Holy Cross Omnibus
p. 56

*See also 26:1, Sophrony.

"The former warden of the College of Preachers, Canon Ted Wedel, didn't have much confidence in what most people thought of the Holy Spirit. In his inimitable way he said that 'most Episcopalians think that the Holy Spirit is some sort of ecclesiastical gas floating around.' That was said a generation ago; since then extraordinary interest in the Holy Spirit has been expressed throughout the Church. But I would wager that for many Christians 'Holy Spirit' remains a vague term, definitely less tangible than speaking of God as Creator or Redeemer. . . .

"To speak of the Holy Spirit is to raise the issue of the unholy spirit, the spirit of fanaticism. Whenever religious people want to justify their own claims of infallibility ('I have the Spirit, you don't'), inevitably they appeal directly to the Holy Spirit. How can we tell that it is the Holy Spirit acting through them, and not some unholy spirit?

"Here the Roman Catholic theologian, Hans Kung, comes to our aid. In his book, *On Being a Christian*, he writes that 'the Holy Spirit is sharply distinguished from the unholy spirit of man and his world. . . . The Spirit is no other than God himself: God close to man and the world. . . . He is not a third party, not a thing between God and men, but God's personal closeness to men.' He adds the key thought that our understanding of the Holy Spirit is to be tested in the light of Jesus Christ.

"For the Christian to understand the Holy Spirit separate or cut off from Jesus Christ is impossible. Religious fanaticism does exactly that. In its zeal and power, supposedly instilled by the Holy Spirit, the Spirit of Christ is absent. It is after all in the power of the Holy Spirit that we are called to stand for what Christ stood for. It is to appeal to the Spirit of freedom: freedom to love, to be merciful, to do justice; freedom to combat guilt, sin, and death. That we may not substitute the unholy spirit for the Holy Spirit (in the words of a beloved hymn), 'Come Holy Spirit our souls inspire!' "

Mellick Belshaw
"Spirit Holy or Unholy"
Anglican Digest
Pentecost, '83, pp. 3-4

New Illuminations:

On Warnings Against Anxiousness for Material Security

Matthew 6:19-21, 25-33   Luke 12:13-34

"The situation which Luke 12:13-15 depicts is necessary for the understanding of the parable of the rich farmer. The younger of the two brothers complains that the elder refuses to give him his share of the inheritance. Jesus does not base his refusal to give a decision merely on the fact that he has no authority to do so, but primarily on the ground that possession of property is irrelevant to the life of the Age to come. The parable explains why Jesus regards earthly wealth as wholly negligible. . . .

"This rich farmer who thinks that he need not fear bad harvests for many a year (v. 19) is a fool (v. 20), that is according to the Biblical meaning of the term, a man who in practice denies the existence of God (Psalm 14:1). He does not take God into account and fails to see the threat of death hanging over his head. Here it is necessary to avoid a too obvious conclusion. We are not to think that Jesus intended to impress upon his audience the ancient maxim, "Death comes suddenly upon man." Rather do all the appeals and parables of warning taken together show that Jesus is not thinking of the inevitable death of the individual as the impending danger, but of the approaching eschatological catastrophe, and the coming Judgment.* Jesus expected his hearers to apply this parable's conclusion to their own situation: we are just as foolish as the rich fool under the threat of death if we heap up property and possessions when the Deluge is threatening."

Joachim Jeremias
The Parables of Jesus
pp. 164-65

"In a story that Jesus told, our Lord ridiculed a man who built himself enormous barns to hoard his crops in. That very night he was visited by death. . . . Our Lord makes a very down to earth observation about earthly property. 'Do not store up for yourselves treasures on earth,' he says to us; and in addition to the moral factor involved, he reminds us that in any case we cannot very successfully store up treasures for ourselves. It simply doesn't work. Even if we managed to preserve our goods from the inroads of moths and rust and burglars, we cannot preserve them very long for ourselves, simply because we cannot preserve ourselves to enjoy them."

Simon Tugwell
The Beatitudes: Soundings in Christian Tradition
p. 20

"Terminal materialism is the sense critics use when they apply the term to Americans. What they mean is that we not only use material resources as instruments to make life more manageable but we reduce our ultimate goals to the possession of things.* It means that the object is valued only because it indicates an end in itself — a possession, a status symbol. There is no sense of reciprocal reaction between the object and the end."

"Reflections on Materialism"
University of Chicago Magazine
Volume 70, Number 3

"Listen, man, about the anguish. There are things you can intelligently do about it. Not easy, no hopeful slogans, no crap. Angst is a big mess, can't help being horrible. It is the result of truth and life getting fouled. So what burns you is good, but it is working against you in such a way that it is against you instead of for you. First big thing is not to get so damned attached to the angst that all that you are able to do is tread the mill and keep it going round and round. Get off the treadmill if you can. . . .

"God is in you, crucified in you. This ought to be enough for anybody; your troubles are his more than yours; you should worry. But O.K., you worry. It is possible to worry less. He is God. You got enough good sense to tell the true from the false. Wheat and cockle growing together. . . . God will take care of the cockle, and meanwhile get some angel to lift the stone out of the way so you can be a little more easy."

Monica Furlong, ed.
Merton
p. 294

"Anybody who has taken everything in hand must then keep on moving that hand. He can no longer be still. . . . Hence, we never get away from constant care and concern. That's why we go about worrying about how we will pass tomorrow's examination, what will happen to our children, and what will happen when the market turns. We are literally beset by threatening possibilities. We have forgotten how to rely on the fact that it is God who clothes the lilies and feeds the birds of the air, that he provides our daily

---

*See also 27:2, Jeremias.

*See also 24:1, Tugwell, Bloom; 81:2, Milligan.

ration of food, and that his kingdom comes no matter what happens. . . . The *Titanic*, our world, is unsinkable and our navigation is perfect. What can be made has been made and we can dispense with this 'Christian navigation.' We don't need the Man who walks the waves. 'Nearer, my God, to thee'! No nearer to the statue of liberty! We and our children are winning history's blue ribbon — what glorious things we have accomplished!

"But why is it then that the captain keeps pacing the bridge so anxiously? Why does he worry? Because now there is nobody there upon whom he can cast his cares. Why is he active and overwatchful? Because he no longer sees the eyes that watch him. Why can't he sleep? Because he no longer lets himself go. Not for one moment can he live like a lark or a lily."

Helmut Thielicke
The Waiting Father
pp. 84-85

"Again, one of the evils in human life is fear, and fear springing from lack of trust is the soil in which so much self-concern and protective selfishness grows. But live near to God, rejoicing in God's providential care, and you won't worry, you won't fear, you will be every hour and every minute in the presence of God who cares for the lilies and clothes the grass, and cares infinitely for you."

Margaret Duggan, ed.
Through the Year with Michael Ramsey
p. 214

"Faith is self-committal to God. It is the awakening of the mind to the full conviction that God *is*, our Creator and our Father and our Redeemer. Hope is the corollary to faith: for hope is the setting of the heart upon God and the things of God; the focusing of all intention and aspiration upon what God is and what he has purposed. By faith we ground ourselves in God's loving omnipotence; by hope we direct our gaze and our purposes upon God's abundant riches and mercies. In faith we make God our starting point; in hope we make God our goal. . . .

"There must be trust and confidence in God. That is the only *must*. Of course the expectations which common sense encourages are not to be all sceptically rejected. If the doctor says you are to go out next week after a month of illness, it is certainly proper to look forward to the event. But we do so only trusting to God's good providence to order things to our benefit and never assuming to ourselves the right to prejudge what form that ordering of things will take — still less what form it *ought* to take. . . . As Christian hope takes root in our hearts, our tight fingers relax their grip, our hands open, and the future drops from our grasp like a basket. We cease to carry about this burden of mingling sorrows and joys all equally unreal. This dragging

weight of potential delights and potential sorrows, this cumbersome accumulation of dreamed-up triumphs and dreaded tragedies. We let the thing go. For our feverish grip upon it has been the sure and certain sign of our self-centeredness. The future is wholly in the hands of God; and if we try to snatch it into our own we blaspheme."

Harry Blamires
The Kirkbride Conversations
pp. 122-23

"A characteristic of the little flock, which is most strongly emphasized in Jesus' metaphors, is the absolute security of his disciples in God's hands. . . . The Father's care is depicted by Jesus in the incomparable images of the Birds of Heaven and the Flowers of the Field. The full measure of the security of which these images speak can only be estimated by realizing their context. Jesus forbids anxiety. (v. 22) The word means: (1) to take anxious thought, (2) to put forth an effort. Only the second meaning is intended in Matthew 6:27 and Luke 12:25 where the meaning to take anxious thought does not make sense. Most of all it is proved unequivocally by our two metaphors, which do not speak of anxiety but of effort. Jesus thus forbids his disciples to spend their effort in pursuit of food and clothing. How can a prohibition of work be possible? The words with which Jesus forbids his disciples to work find their parallel in Mark 6:8 where they form part of his charge when he sends them out on a mission. . . . They must allow nothing to hinder them, not even an exchange of greetings, much less the expenditure of effort for food and clothing. God will give them what they need.* Hence what Jesus deprecates is not work, but its duplication. But that surely involves the possibility of having no food, nothing to wear, of starving and freezing! Such anxieties find their answers in the two similes of the Birds and Flowers touched by Jesus with a gleam of humor. . . . The Father knows what you need; he will not let you starve."

Joachim Jeremias
The Parables of Jesus
pp. 214-15

"Our growing awareness of God as our loving Father can be expressed in more living terms by saying that a person has really begun to be religious who knows at all times that God has given him what is best for him. In addition to this, he has begun to see that the worldly definition of success has a bad habit of missing the point entirely. This is partly because it judges between person and person as if they had the same needs and responded equally to the same situations (which they don't) but mainly because prominence, prestige, position, and a sound bank balance are not

*See also 40:1, Kunkel.

the ultimate sources of security. As he perseveres on this course, he will approach the time when he is not bothered by insecurity at all because, in desiring solely the will of God, he is finding the only security there is."

Gale Webbe
The Night and Nothing
p. 37

"Much of our trouble is due to our faithlessness. We do not really believe the promise our Lord attaches to this Uncomfortable Word: 'Seek ye first the Kingdom of God and his righteousness, and all these things (i.e., the necessary material requirements of life) will be added unto you.' We are so used to giving most of our time to material pursuits that we dare not neglect them for a moment. It need hardly be said that our Lord's words do not invite either idleness or laziness but rather that, when we have our priorities right, our occupations fall into proper order. And further, the necessary material requirements are not ignored, but, instead of their drawing us away from God, they are now sacramental [the outward and visible signs] of citizenship in God's Kingdom. The Gospel of the Incarnation is not a denial of the material. On the contrary, it recognizes the importance of the material when it is seen as the means whereby we can live triumphantly in God's Kingdom, and when it is used to hasten that Kingdom which in Christ has already come."

Joost de Blank
Uncomfortable Words
pp. 113-114

" 'Seek ye first the Kingdom of God, and all these things — a happy conscience, a kingly carefreeness, a liberation from the anxiety of life, a new appreciation of people and the beauty of the earth — will be yours as well.' Then we shall see with new eyes the birds of the air, the clouds in the sky, and the winds in their courses. And even the people who give us trouble will be ennobled by the dignity which Jesus gave them when he died for them. When Christ is king, everything is changed. Eyes see differently, the heart no longer beats the same, and in every hard and difficult place, the comforting voice is there; and the hand that will not let us go upholds us."

Helmut Thielicke
The Waiting Father
p. 157

"Christianity is a two-way religion because it is incarnational: it concerns both our relation with God (to be sought and adored) and with the human world (to be served and loved). . . . Culture, prosperity, love, and peace are true and proper concerns, but they are by-products of grace and prayer; and a by-product, by definition, is absolutely dependent on its primary process. If we forget how to extract gas from coal, we are not going to get much coke. 'Seek ye first the Kingdom of God, and all these things will be added unto you.' Christianity is a search, a disciplined routine investigation and not a game of hide and seek."

Martin Thorton
Christian Proficiency
p. X

"We turn to St. Augustine. In him we find the transitoriness of earthly things, but in him it is combined with the assurance of the things which do not pass away. In his writings the world's heartbreak is expressed with no less poignancy, but with this there is a confidence and peace in the assurance that, when the things that are shaken are removed, the things that cannot be shaken will remain. . . . For the Christian, all those partial, broken, and fleeting perfections which he glimpses in the world around him, which wither in his grasp and are snatched from him while they wither are found again perfect, complete, and lasting in the absolute beauty of God, with whom is no variableness, neither shadow of turning. . . .

"What is our attitude of the world to be? Treat it as if it were all that there is and as if all that you need is to be found in it, and it will dangle its gifts before your eyes, decoy you, tantalize you, and finally mock and desert you, leaving you emptyhanded and with ashes in your mouth. But treat it as the creation of God, as truly good because it is God's handiwork and yet not the highest good because it is not God himself; live in this world as one who knows that the world is God's and yet as one who knows that his true home is not here but in eternity, and the world itself will yield up to you joys and splendors of whose very existence the mere worldling is utterly ignorant. Then you will see the world's transience and fragility, its finitude and its powerlessness to satisfy, not as signs that life is a bad joke with man as a helpless victim, but as pale and splintered reflections of the splendor and beauty of the eternal God — that beauty ever old and ever new — in whom alone man can find lasting peace and joy."

E. L. Mascall
Grace and Glory
pp. 82-83

New Illuminations

On Watchfulness and Faithfulness

Matthew 24:42-51   Mark 13:33-37   Luke 12:35-48

"He who understands the hour as he waits God's future is he who holds himself in readiness, as the servants watch and wait for their master. For the servant who waits in wisdom and faithfulness takes, one might say, no time for himself; and, in contrast to the world he is the very man who has time. It is characteristic of those who do not hear God's call from the time of the flood to the last judgment, that they have no time. 'They ate, they drank, they bought, they sold, they planted, they built . . . marrying and given in marriage' (Luke 17:28). . . .

"Before God, however, the wise and faithful servant is at the same time the one who has no time, who is faithful to his task, faithful to the management and increase of the estate entrusted to him and faithful in his love toward the least of Jesus' brethren, constantly ready for action, with his torch alight (Luke 12:35). His waiting is not for the nothingness of the unknown, nor for the silence of death, but for the Lord who has met and will meet his disciples."

Gunther Bornkamm
Jesus of Nazareth
p. 89.

"The recognition of the fact that the primitive Church related the parables on the delay of the Parousia to its own concrete situation is of fundamental importance for the understanding of the little parable of the nocturnal burglar. . . . In itself, the meaning of the parable is clear. Jesus draws the parable from an actual happening, some recently effected burglary, about which the whole village is talking; he uses the alarming occurrence as a warning of the imminent calamity which he sees approaching. Guard yourselves, says he, that you may not be caught unawares like this householder who had just had his house broken into. But the application of the parable to the return of the Son of Man is strange (Luke 12:40). For if the subject of discourse is nocturnal burglary, it refers to a disastrous and alarming event; whereas the Parousia, at least for the disciples of Jesus, is the great day of joy. . . . If we disregard the reference to the Son of Man, the nearest parallels are to be found in the parable of the Flood and the destruction of Sodom (Luke 17:26ff.). Here too, events, although of extreme antiquity, which overwhelmed men unprepared, are used by Jesus as a warning of terrors to come. He sees the approaching fate, the disaster at the door; with his coming, it has indeed already broken in. But those around him are as heedless as that householder living in the shadow of doom like those before the Flood and the Reign of Fire, as though there were no danger. Jesus wishes to arouse them to open their eyes to the peril of their position. Terror draws near, as unexpected as the housebreaker, as fearful as the deluge. Prepare yourselves! Soon it will be too late. Thus would Jesus' hearers have understood the parable of the housebreaker: as a rousing cry to the crowd in view of the oncoming eschatological catastrophe. The primitive Church applied the parable to its members.

"Further on Luke expressly emphasizes the fact that it only concerns the apostles, the responsible leaders of the community; since to the appended question of Peter, 'Are you speaking this parable only to us, or also to all?' The answer is given in the former sense by the parable of the steward who is put to the test by the delay of his Lord's return: It is spoken to you, upon whom a special responsibility rests. Thus the parable becomes a summons to the leaders of the Church, in view of the delayed Parousia, not to sleep; and the burglar, by means of Christological allegorizing becomes a figure of the Son of Man."

Joachim Jeremias
The Parables of Jesus
pp. 48-50.

" 'Who then will be the faithful, thoughtful manager, whom his master will put in charge of his household, to give the members of it their supplies at the proper time? Blessed is that slave if his master when he returns finds him doing it' (Luke 12:42)."

The Holy Bible
Edgar J. Goodspeed, trans.
Luke 12:42-43

"While the parable in Luke 12:41-48 was not told primarily to teach the lesson of God's concern for justice (it was rather a warning to be prepared for the Lord's coming), it does reveal incidentally the profound sympathy Jesus had for the underprivileged and his profound dislike for those who exploited them. . . . The ideal servant — 'the faithful and wise' — is the one who deals out fairly his 'portion of the meat in due season.' The Lord when he comes will deal justly and — as justice requires — will deal more severely with those who have been honored by great responsibilities than those who have but few."

Robert C. Dentan
First Reader in Biblical Theology
p. 237

"There is a terribly sad word in one of the old translations of Luke 12:46; it is 'untrustworthy.' The Lord's great desire is to say to each one of us at the end of the day, 'Enter thou into the joy of thy Lord.' It must be grief beyond our imagination to conceive, when he has to say of one whom he died to redeem, 'Place him with those who are untrustworthy.' Am I trustworthy — one who is worthy to be trusted with any service? Am I one who is worthy to be trusted with anything of any sort, without any preparation or any explanation? The Lord make us all *trustworthies*!"

Amy Carmichael
Thou Givest . . . They Gather
p. 124.

"If we wish to ascertain the original meaning of the parable of the servant entrusted with authority, we must ask how the picture of the servant, distinguished by a position of special responsibility, suddenly tested by the unexpected return of the master would have affected Jesus' audience. From the Old Testament, they were familiar with the designation of leaders, rulers, prophets, and sacred persons as servants of God. For them the scribes were overseers appointed by God, to whom the keys to the Kingdom of Heaven had been entrusted. Hence they would have seen in the responsible servant of the parable the religious leaders of their time. When this is recognized, the parable falls into close relationship with the situation of the life of Jesus. It is seen to be one of his many stern words of warning to the leaders of the people, above all to the scribes, that the day of reckoning was at hand when God would reveal whether they had been faithful to the trust committed to them or had abused it. . . .

"In Luke 12:47-48a, the conclusion is made up of two independent logia. These logia, which are missing in Matthew, ill consort with the content of the parable, since the latter is not concerned with the knowledge or the ignorance of the Lord's will but with the use or abuse of entrusted authority. The description of the punishment of the unfaithful servant has attracted to itself the logion dealing with the varying degrees of punishment."

Joachim Jeremias
The Parables of Jesus
pp. 57, 104

"Let us place ourselves in his hands so that his will may be done in us; if we cling firmly to this maxim and our wills are resolute, we cannot possibly go astray.* And you must note that you will merit no more glory for having received many favors. On the contrary, the fact that you are receiving more imposes on you greater obligations to serve. The Lord does not deprive us of anything which adds to our merit, for this remains in our own power. . . .

"Each occasion when the Lord grants favors, brings with it trials; and thus the soul does not think about receiving more but only about how to put those it receives to good use. It is true that to have these favors must be the greatest help towards attaining a high degree of perfection in the virtues. But anyone who has attained the virtues at the cost of his own toil has earned much more merit (Luke 12:44, 48b)."

St. Teresa of Avila
Interior Castle
p. 192

*See also 59:3, Lewis.

New Illuminations:

On "A Baptism To Be Baptized With"

Matthew 10:34-36; 20:20-23   Mark 10:35-40   Luke 12:49-50

"There is a significant saying in Luke, 'I have a baptism to be baptized with, and how I am straightened until it be accomplished.'* His mind traveled back to that act of obedience at Jordan, when he was consecrated to the task of bringing forgiveness (redemption) to his people, and forward to a more awful baptism when he should surrender himself finally to the accomplishment of that task.** Until then he was straightened, that is, he was conscious that the power of the kingdom in him was cabined and confined. Even the acts of healing are fewer and are done with greater difficulty in this last stage. The two different healings recorded in Mark 7:31-7 and 8:22-26 belong to this period and are omitted by Matthew and Luke. It is noteworthy that all he can offer to James and John, seeking places of honor in the kingdom is participation in his baptism."

S. H. Hooke
The Kingdom of God
p. 112

"Only after the scene at Caesarea Philippi, when the Passion was revealed to his disciples, do we come across several texts in which the atoning death of Jesus is associated with the realization of the perfect kingdom. This occurs clearly enough in his answer to the sons of Zebedee (Mark 10:35-40). To the petition of these apostles, among the first he had summoned, that they might have the first places in his kingdom he immediately replies, 'You know not what you ask.' He then speaks in a double simile of the fate that awaits him and which they also will share. In the context this can only mean that this mysterious event ordained by God ('drink the chalice' and 'be baptized with a baptism') is the pre-condition for Jesus' rule, and correspondingly for his disciples' share in that rule. This is a precise application of the teaching developed after Caesarea Philippi that the Son of man must suffer severely and be rejected (Luke 9:22 par.) and that the disciples must be resolved to go the same way as their master. . . .

"This double simile bears the stamp of genuine authenticity in its figurative form and in the two-fold form used by Mark. (Matthew has only the simile of the chalice. The baptism simile is a similar expression peculiar to Luke.) But in whatever way the two be interpreted, and both have an identical meaning, it is a scarcely-veiled prophecy of his Passion. But death is associated in his mind with the coming kingdom, for Jesus repudiates the false notions of his

disciples about his Messianic kingdom, answers them from his knowledge of the *basileia* and looks towards this kingdom which is wholly subject to the Father's disposition.''

Rudolf Schnackenburg
God's Rule and Kingdom
pp. 190-192

"We saw how the first movement of Christ's soul was self-donation to the purpose of the Father, already stirring in his childish heart. 'I must be about my Father's business' — the one role of his life. It seems the most lovely of vocations at that point. The last movement of his soul was the utter self-giving of the Cross. . . . It is the end that tests to the utmost *our* courage and love. 'Can you drink of my cup and be baptized with my baptism?' Not unless we care more about him than we care about our own souls."

Evelyn Underhill
Light of Christ
pp. 81-82

"Our Lord reveals his intensity of faith in his unbounded confidence in his Father's power, his unhesitating assumption of his infallibility and authority which depended for its sole source on the Father's will. It was this trust and confidence which urged him forward to the obedience of sacrifice which his ardent love burned to offer. 'I have a baptism to be baptized with: how intensely I long for its accomplishment, its consummation.' So must it be with us. From our faith in God's will springs our confidence that we shall have grace to fulfill it, a confidence which helps us to overcome the hardships and humiliations, often so unfathomable and surprising, which life presents."

Sibyl Harton
Doors of Eternity
pp. 82-83

"The servant is not greater than his Lord. The Christ had stood in the waters of Jordan making himself one with the company of sinful men;* and he had said, 'Ye shall indeed be baptized with the baptism that I am baptized with.'

*See also 12:1, Krumm.
**See also 117:4, Underhill; 50:1, Webster.

*See also 12:1, Penelope.

"That should be one of the compelling signs of his church — that we are standing with him where he stands in baptism; ourselves sinful men saved by the sinless one, but baptised into the saving of others; standing with men in their sinfulness, yet facing God for them like him.*

"One night, on my way to a visit from which everything in me recoiled, I knew suddenly that this new impulse was upon me. I was going to be with a man who had sinned greatly, to put my sinfulness beside his, and, by the strange miracle, at the same time to be there with Christ in his saving power; to stand in common need and be the means of its answering. And I was going for love of him. It was the motive assumed in every minister; it was implied in the vows of ordination which I had taken; but it was only now being born in me; or perhaps it was being reborn.

". . . Not so very far from us in Crainie there was a minister, a familiar figure in the back streets of his parish in an industrial town, looking for the men and women to whom Christ would lead him because they were broken and in despair. . . . By going where he had no need to be, but where he was sure Christ was, he found what no one else had found. And as he went with his shuffling steps along the pavements and up the dingy stairs, men and women knew it was no ordinary love that was seeking them.

"Was it this love that was being born in me? Was I being baptized with Christ into the saving of others? . . . A ministry was being given back to me now which was not my own; a love and a joy and a thankfulness for the miracle that he who has so little to give can be serving the Lord of heaven and earth."

J. W. Stevenson
God in My Unbelief
pp. 141-143

"The function of religion in the Jewish-Christian stream is not merely to bring peace and comfort; its function, just as truly, is to disturb us repeatedly within the very peace and comfort which we enjoy. If religion's function were *only* to bring peace and comfort, it would basically be a denial of life, for life does not so serve us. But rather and contrary to much that is commonly assumed, Christianity embodies the profoundest acceptance of life, in a sense that it discloses a way to deal with the peace-disturbing aspects of existence and transmit them into good.** Thus we have the paradox that the soul can be made perfect only through suffering. . . .

"The classic expression concerning this role of the Christian religion is the saying of Jesus: 'Think not that I am come to send peace on the earth. I came not to send peace but a sword' (Matthew 10:34). For it is precisely when man is *in* peace, comfort, security, satisfaction, complacency that God confronts him in crisis and judgment."

Lewis J. Sherrill
The Struggle of the Soul
p. 21

"Jesus appears to be saying that his mission was almost as if he were proclaiming a holy war. If, however, we look at the words that follow Matthew 10:34, Jesus' meaning becomes clear. . . . Jesus is not speaking of war at all, either of war between nations or of civil war within the same nation, but of conflict within the same family. Luke 12:51 confirms this: 'Do you suppose I came to establish peace on earth? No indeed, I have come to bring division.'*

"We can see this happening within the story of the early church when within ordinary families one or two members would become converts to Christianity. Other members of the family would continue in their old faith — whether Jewish or pagan — and argument, discord, and bitterness would ensue. The harmony of the family was destroyed. But we do not need to look at the ancient world. Any missionary today can tell story after story of the breaking up of families in India, Africa, and elsewhere when some have responded to the Christian Gospel and others have continued in their old ways. The result is a divided house. It must require superhuman courage for a member of a Hindu or Moslem family to break with the traditions of centuries and face the contempt — indeed hatred — of relatives who see conversion to Christianity as a betrayal and unforgivable sin.

"There is however a wider sense in which Jesus' words in Matthew 10:34 may be taken. Having lived through two major wars in a half a century and with the ever-present shadow of possible annihilation darkening our future, most of us think of peace as the absence of armed conflict and in some moods can wish nothing better for our children than that they should grow up in a world from which war and fear of war has been banished forever. But as Studdert Kennedy said, 'War is kinder than a Godless peace.' There are some kinds of peace that are not worth having — peace at any price, peace that perpetuates injustice, peace that exists under tyranny. . . .

"Christ certainly came to bring peace as every page of the New Testament confirms. But he stood for real peace and not a bogus peace. His peace must be fought for, and that involves conflict and division (Luke 12:51). As followers of Christ, we are committed to fight against the evil in ourselves and in our society in the light of the guidance we have been given. The Gospel is a Gospel of peace through strife, not peace through apathy or evasion of responsibility. Of course this will mean disagreement and discord,

---

*See also 88:1, Augsburger.
**See also 70:3, Leslie.

*See also 40:1, Kunkel.

opposition and open bitterness. But the peace that Christ came to bring can only be realized by striving to reconcile our differences in charity but with honesty, or, as St. Paul puts it, by speaking the truth in love (Ephesians 4:15).''

William Neil
The Difficult Sayings of Jesus
pp. 6-8

''It is indeed the supreme paradox of our condition, that an Almighty power respects our free will; but his respecting of it does not mean that he sits back and watches it. He works upon free creatures through all the infinite operations of his providence.

''When Scripture speaks of a state of war, a mutual hostility between God and man, it is giving expression to this fact. . . . Between God and sinners there is a real battle of wills. The fighting is let up from time to time on the human side, for sinners have to sleep. It is never let up on the divine side, for God neither sleeps nor slumbers. The divine antagonist may fight like a strong, compassionate man struggling to master an armed lunatic; he fights all the same until we surrender. . . . The battle of the divine will with ours is a battle against our enmity; and when it breaks our opposition, it secures our reconciliation.''

Austin Farrer
Saving Belief
pp. 97-98

''Peace of mind does not come by searching for it; like happiness, it comes 'on-account-of' something else. It is a by-product of meaningful activity rather than a legitimate goal in itself. Indeed the most complete sense of peace of mind is generally experienced only after the successful completion of a task, a task which oriented the worker away from himself and on to something greater than himself. Real peace of mind comes not from a tensionless situation but rather from the completion of a tension-creating task.* Contrary to much popular thought, the tensionless state of ease and pleasure leads more often to the frustration of an existential vacuum than it does to any real peace of mind.''

Robert C. Leslie
Jesus and Logotherapy
pp. 65-66

''Christ said, 'I came not to send peace but a sword' (Matthew 10:34) and 'division' (Luke 12:51). Christ summoned us to war on the plane of the Spirit, and our weapon is 'the sword of the Spirit, which is the word of God' (Ephesians 6:17). Our battle is waged in extraordinarily unequal conditions. We are tied hand and foot. We dare not strike with fire or sword: our sole armament is love, even for enemies. This unique war in which we are engaged is indeed a holy war. We wrestle with the last and only enemy of mankind — death (1 Corinthians 15:26). Our fight is the fight for universal-resurrection.''

Archimandrite Sophrony
His Life is Mine
p. 68

*See also 70:2, Sherrill.

New Illuminations:

On Repentance II

"The turning of the being of man and the divine response are often designated by the same verb, a verb that can signify to turn back as well as to turn away, but also to return and to turn toward someone; And this fullness of meaning was taken advantage of in the Old Testament. Already in one of the earliest of the Biblical prophets, in Hosea, we hear God speak first of all, 'Return, Israel, unto the Lord,' and once again, 'Return.' Then it says, 'I shall heal your turnings away'; but now follows, 'I shall love them freely, for my wrath is turned away from them' (Hosea 14:2, 5). This correspondence, expressed through the repetition of the verb, between the action of man and the action of God, is not at all a casual but a purely dialogical connection between the two. . . . The king of the Ninevites calls to his people, to whom the exact data of their destruction have just been announced, 'Every one shall turn back from his evil way,' and then adds, 'Who knows, God may return; he may be sorry and may turn back from the flaming of his wrath and we shall not perish' (Jonah 3:8f).

"The mystery of the dialogical intercourse between God and man is that of man's creation as a being with the power of actually choosing between the ways, who ever again and even now has the power to choose between them. Only such a being is suited to God's partner in the dialogue of history. The future is not fixed for God wants man to come to him with full freedom, to return to him even out of a plight of extreme hopelessness and then to be really with him. This is the prophetic *theologem*, never expressed as such but firmly embedded in the foundations of Hebrew prophecy. . . .

"The prophetic faith involves the faith in the *factual* character of the human experience, as existence which factually meets transcendence. Because and so long as man exists, factual change of direction can take place toward salvation as well as toward disaster, starting from the world in each hour, no matter how late. This message has been proclaimed by the prophets to all future generations, to each generation in its own language."

> Nahum Glatzer, ed.
> *Martin Buber: On the Bible*
> pp. 176-78

" 'Why do you not know how to interpret the present time?' Jesus asks his hearers. To interpret the present time means: to lay hold on the hour of salvation. But it also means to recognize the last hour, before the catastrophe of God's judgment breaks forth. The people come to Jesus with stirring news. . . . The question which Jesus is asked is the ancient one about the correlation between fate and guilt.

The question looks back and tries to fathom God's justice. But Jesus replies: 'Do you think that these Galileans were worse sinners than all the other Galileans because they suffered thus? I tell you, No; but unless you repent, you will likewise perish.' Thus he puts an end to the question of God's justice in relation to this catastrophe and that, and turns it into a new question to his questioners, facing them with themselves and the future of God. It is not a miracle that these have been struck down but that you have escaped.

"What does this miracle mean? This is immediately followed by the parable of the unfruitful fig tree which year after year has borne no fruit and well deserves to be cut down now. But the gardener, ready once more to take all possible trouble with it, begs the master of the vineyard for one last chance: 'Let it alone, sir, this year also.' The miracle is therefore God's undeserved patience, passing all comprehension."

> Gunther Bornkamm
> *Jesus of Nazareth*
> p. 87

"Repentance and the acceptance of God's forgiveness* is a definite act, a healing transaction between man and God. The need for this act never lessens. . . . This interaction with God, with our fellow men, and with those things within ourselves is not to be replaced by a daily, lifelong scrutiny and horror of the self. Such would constitute the practice of the presence of the 'old man' and fail to comprehend the presence of the new man or the higher self."

> Leanne Payne
> *The Real Presence:*
> *The Holy Spirit in the Works of C.S. Lewis*
> p. 72

When conscience begins to accuse, there starts the process called repentance. It is a long, a life-long process. If we think of repentance as the work of the conscience, we may be inclined to accept the common view that it is like starting a motor: turn on the ignition key, press the starter, let the engine run and then turn off the key until it is time to begin the journey. But repentance is the work of the Holy Spirit.** It is he that will convince the world of sin (John 16:8), and he does not cease to work. He cannot be turned

---

*See also 100:2, Hooke.
**See also 66:1, Milligan.

off and on with a key, and once he has begun his work in us, he will not cease until we are truly a dwelling place of God through the Spirit. In that long process, we can trace what we might call stages which overlap. We cannot cut them apart and stop the process and determine to go no further. We can indeed go no further, but then we find that we have slipped back and have not repented at all. . . . The first stage is largely emotional; despair, shame, horror sweep over us in varying degrees. . . . Of these four emotions, only one has any value, and that is horror because it is objective. It is concerned with the thing we did and not with the person who did it. Our feeling of horror is the particular work of the Holy Spirit. If horror grows, we will pass on to true repentance; but if horror is drowned in a flood of emotion, we have not repented at all. Horror leads us to the knowledge that sin is an offense against God and will lead us like the Prodigal Son to arise and go to our Father. It will cause us to take action instead of just wallowing in sentiment.''

Manassas
Go In Peace
pp. 17-18

''. . . O Savior, as thou hangst upon the tree,
I turn my back to thee but only to receive
Corrections, till thy mercies bid thee leave.
Oh think me worth thine anger, punish me,
Burn off my rusts and my deformity;
Restore thine image so much by thy grace,
That thou mayst know me — and I'll turn my face.''

John Donne
''Good Friday Riding Westward''

''God is known only when the chips are down. You can think, you can celebrate about God only on your knees. Anybody who shies away from repentance, from bowing down, from dying, is slamming the door upon God. For him the 'last station' may be yearning or despair or stubborn defiance, but it can never be peace.''

Helmut Thielicke
The Waiting Father
p. 59

''God does not offer men the forgiveness of the Cross after they have come to him in contrition and remorse; he holds out to them the forgiveness of the Cross as an initial

gesture in the hope that it may lead to a recognition of the depth of their sin and make the path of repentance not a crushing humiliation but a self-forgetful opening of the heart to divine love.''*

John Krumm
The Art of Being a Sinner
p. 100

''How tactfully Jesus readies the simple woman at the well for full encounter with his love. With what mildness does he remind her of the painful past so that she might see how futile her life has been so far. There is no reproach, no threat, no sign of repulsion or rejection, only a quiet remembrance of the facts of her life, leaving it up to her to come to a final conclusion. . . . In the wake of this new awareness, he begins to instill in her the softening attitudes of repentance and humility. They will plow the frozen ground of her hidden self, help dig the open furrows in which the seeds of grace may fall. Soon she will taste the sweetness of repentance. How can repentance be sweet? Repentance is the awareness of forgiveness in the midst of sorrow.''

Adrian Van Kamm
The Woman At the Well
pp. 68-69

''Repentance frees us from our claim of self-righteousness, treating sin as something we have to atone for. It causes us to treat sin for what it is. We have to repent, turn around, and redirect our lives. We can then be free for service and witness — the consequence of God's taking our hard hearts, melting them and making witnesses of them.''

William Pounds
Sermon Notes

''Who will make it so you will come into my heart and captivate it, so I can forget my rottenness and take hold of you, the one good thing in my life? . . . Perhaps you had better tell me straight out, Oh Lord my God, Just what you are to me. Say to my soul, 'I am your salvation.' Speak so I can hear you. I will come running after that voice and lay hold on you; the house of my soul lies in ruins, you will have to rebuild it. There are things in it I know and confess that are offensive to your sight. But who will clean it up? To whom else beside you can I cry out, 'Clear me from my hidden faults? Keep back thy servant also from presumptuous sins.' . . .

_____
*See also 120:2, Harton.

175

"I have no intention of putting myself in a false position by letting my sins trip me up. That is why I refuse to contend in judgment with you because, if you were to mark iniquity, Lord, who could stand?"

S. E. Wirt
Love Song: Augustine's Confessions for Modern Man
p. 4

"Batter my heart, three person'd God; for you
As yet knocke, breathe shine, and seek to mend;
That I may rise and shine, o'erthrow me, and bend
Your force to break, blow, burn, and make me new.
I, like a usurp'd town, to another due,
Labor to admit you, But Oh, to no end.
Reason, your viceroy in me, should defend,
But is captive and proves weak or untrue.
Yet dearly I love you and would be loved faine,
But am betrothed unto your enemy;
Divorce me, untie or break that knot again,
Take me to you, imprison me, for I
Except you enthrall me, never shall be free,
Never chaste, except you ravish me."

John Donne
"Sonnet #10"

"Jesus' sternest warning of disaster was addressed to the Messianic community, among whom also the final separation was to be effected. . . . It is not the purpose of the parable of the fig-tree to propound a moral precept, but to shock into realization of its danger a nation rushing upon its own destruction, and more especially its leaders, the theologians and priests. But above all it is a call to repentance.

It is the last hour. The axe lies at the root of the unfruitful fig-tree. But God, marvelously suspending the fulfillment of his holy will, has allowed yet one more respite for repentance. . . .

The first three years of a fig-tree's growth were allowed to elapse before its fruit became clean (Leviticus 19:23), hence six years had already passed since it was planted. It is thus hopelessly barren. A fig-tree absorbs a specially large amount of nourishment and hence deprives the surrounding vines of their needed sustenance. Manuring a vineyard is not mentioned in any passage of the Old Testament; moreover the undemanding fig-tree does not need such care. Hence the gardener proposes to do something unusual, to take the last possible measure. . . . The request is not refused but granted; an announcement of judgment becomes a call to repentance. God's mercy goes so far as to grant a reprieve from the sentence already pronounced. . . . But the stay of execution granted by mercy is the irrevocable final limit (vv. 3, 5). When the limit granted by God is run out, no human power can prevent it."

Joachim Jeremias
The Parables of Jesus
pp. 170-71

"Jesus, you are present at my sin. When I sin you are still within me, silent. Your very presence condemns what I do. But at the same time, you understand me and understand my sin more profoundly than I understand myself or my sin. . . . Your presence and pity are felt during the very act of that sin which I do not have the courage to interrupt. This same presence and pity make it possible for me to utter a cry of disgust, anguish and horror and to appeal to you, to your name: Jesus!"

Monk of the Eastern Church
Jesus: A Dialogue with the Savior
p. 105

"It is humiliating, of course, to have to admit that we are just like Peter, Paul, the Corinthians, Pontius Pilate and the rest. It is humiliating to have to give up once and forever the attempt to justify ourselves. . . . But what a relief it is to realize that you have not got to justify yourself at all. You have not got to keep up appearances before the neighbors, or appear infallible to your children, or make out that the right is always on your side. What a freedom comes when you are ready to be put in the wrong. After all, you knew that you were there already, and your hope is that still you are forgiven. Once you have given up the claim to expect anything from God by right, you find innumerable unexpected mercies; and the greatest is this, that when you are wrong, whether you know it or not, there is one more proof that you are one of those for whom Jesus died. . . .

"What will you dare say to Jesus if you come to the foot of the Cross? Will you say to yourself, 'Down to your knees; never mind if it makes you look a fool, you are a fool, repent before it is too late'? Will you say to him, 'Lord, save me, fool that I was'? If you will do this, philosopher, Greek or Hindu, or university professor, you will know that the foolishness of God is wiser than men, and the weakness of God is stronger than men.'"*

T. R. Milford
Foolishness to the Greeks
pp. 57-59

*See also 119:2, Krumm.

On the Smallest of Seeds and the Leaven

Matthew 13:31-32	Mark 4:30-32	Luke 13:18-21

''The parables of the mustard seed and the leaven are so closely connected by their content that it seems necessary to discuss them together. The purpose of the parables is to compare the Kingdom of God with the final stage of the process there described — with the tall shrub affording shelter to the birds and with the mass of dough wholly permeated by the leaven. The tree which shelters the birds is a common metaphor for a mighty kingdom which protects its vassals, and the dough in Romans 11:16 is a metaphor for the people of God. The eschatological character for the metaphor of the tree or the shrub is established by the fact that the Greek word for 'branches' is actually an eschatological technical term for the incorporation of the Gentiles into the people of God.

''The features of the parables which transcend the bounds of actuality (mustard is not a tree; no housewife would bake so vast a quantity of meal) are meant to tell us that we have to do with divine realities. Thus we are shown the mustard seed, the very smallest thing the human eye can perceive — every word emphasizes its smallness — and when it is grown, it is 'the greatest of all herbs and puts forth great branches' — every word depicts the size of the shrub. . . . Again we are shown a tiny morsel of leaven, absurdly small in comparison with the great mass of more than a bushel of meal. It is not the purpose of either parable merely to describe a process. . . .

''The modern man, passing through the ploughed field, thinks of what is going on beneath the soil and envisages a biological development. The people of the Bible passing through the same plough-land look up and see miracle upon miracle, nothing less than resurrection from the dead. Thus did Jesus' audiences understand the parables of the mustard seed and the leaven as parables of contrast. Their meaning is that out of the most insignificant of beginnings, invisible to the human eye, God creates his mighty kingdom which embraces all the peoples of the world.

''If this is right, the occasion of the utterance of the two parables may be taken to be some expression of doubt concerning the mission of Jesus. How differently the beginnings of the Messianic Age appeared from what was commonly expected! Could this wretched band comprising so many disreputable characters be the wedding guests of God's redeemed community? 'Yes,' says Jesus, 'it is. With this same compelling certainty will God's miraculous power cause my small band to swell into the mighty host of the people of the Messianic Age, embracing the Gentiles.' Not knowing the power of God, ye do greatly err' (Mark 12:25, 27).

''In order to understand the impact of this statement, attention must be drawn to the final fact. Jesus' audience knew the symbol of the high tree (Ezekiel 31), where it symbolizes the world power; and the tiny piece of leaven was familiar to them from the Passover as a symbol of malice and wickedness. Jesus is bold enough to employ both symbols in the opposite sense. They apply not to the powers of evil but to God's royal majesty.''

Joachim Jeremias
The Parables of Jesus
pp. 146-49

''The divine power, God's rule, can permit a glorious finale to crown an insignificant beginning. He provides the promise and guarantee that his kingdom will come. Again this supposes that God's reign is present in the word and work of Jesus and that here is continuity between its commencement and its future realization, a continuity like that between the sowing season and the harvest time. Manifestation on a cosmic scale is certain because God's rule is even now present and its power and reality can be sensed. The double parable does not contain an allusion to the person of Jesus; but from the circumstances of his ministry, we may conclude that its beginning is found in his activity.''

Rudolf Schnackenburg
God's Rule and Kingdom
p. 156

''We can no longer determine with certainty a parable's setting in the life of Jesus in every case. But we can accept a very real probability that the parables of the seed and the leaven are an answer to the headshaking and questions that have been posed hundreds of times right from the first day: An unknown rabbi of Nazareth in a remote corner of Palestine? A handful of disciples who, when it came to a showdown left him in the lurch? A doubtful mob following him — publicans, loose women, sinners and a few women and children and folk who got help from him? On the Cross, the sport of passers-by? Is this the Kingdom of God? The shift in the Ages? . . . Questions and protests such as these are behind the demands for signs that are made by Jesus' opponents. . . . These parables give the conclusive answer which sums up Jesus' way and works.''

Gunther Bornkamm
Jesus of Nazareth
pp. 72-73

"Count von Moltke when he was an old man was asked what he was going to do in the quiet closing phase of his life. His reply was 'I want to see a tree grow.' Would he have been able to say such a thing if during the years of his great responsibility he had not already had time to see that Another and Higher being was carrying out His plans and guiding events to His goals without us (or through us and in spite of us). The man who does not know how to let go is a stranger to this quiet, confident joy in Him who makes the trees grow and the rainbow shine. . . . Can the reason that many aging people are melancholy be that for decades they have never been able to 'let go and let God' and now can no longer see a tree growing and therefore are nothing but run-down merry-go-rounds?

"The art of living or mental hygiene are only the by-products of the very thing our parable of the seed growing secretly means (Mark 4:26-29). When it says that God lets his seeds sprout in this namelessly quiet way, that this miracle occurs without any aid whatsoever from man and without any agricultural intervention — in that way in which God carries forward his work despite all human efforts. . . .

"What an unspeakable comfort it is to know that in the midst of man's mischief, his activism and his failures, there is still another stream of events flowing silently on, that God is letting his seeds grow and achieving his ends."*

Helmut Thielicke
The Waiting Father
pp. 86-87

---

*See also 26:2, Kelsey.

New Illuminations:

On the Narrow Door and the Straightened Way

Matthew 7:13-14, 21   Luke 11:52; 13:23-24

''Merely hearing the word of Jesus may lead to perdition (Luke 6:49); everything depends upon obedience. But the obedience required must be complete. The door of the festal chamber which is to be the scene of the banquet of salvation is a narrow one; he who is to gain admittance must strive for it while there is still time; many will seek to enter it but will not put forth the necessary effort. . . . In this logion (Luke 13:24; Matthew 7:13-14), Matthew lays the emphasis on the point that if the disciples wish to be saved they must cut themselves off from the mass of their people and tread the *via dolorosa* of the little flock. Luke has preserved the setting of the logion. Some nameless person asked the question: 'Lord, are there only a few who will be saved?' Jesus replied with the exhortation to strive earnestly, because many will lack perseverance. It is a summons to become a follower, where the emphasis is laid solely on the high stake demanded.''

Joachim Jeremias
The Parables of Jesus
pp. 194-95

''The Kingdom of God is entered by the straight gate, by self denial, and humiliation. The broad gate through which we see the multitude pass, and which is ever open, leads to perdition; let us beware of entering it. We must seek the path worn by penitents who have climbed the precipice and gained a sure footing upon the heights by the sweat of their brows, and even then, and at the very last step, it may require a violent effort to enter in at the straight gate of eternity. . . . let us live and let us die, then, with Him who came to show us the true way to heaven. We must take up the cross if we would follow Him. We suffer in the narrow way, but we hope.''

Thomas Kepler, ed.
Letters and Reflections of Francois De Fenelon
p. 124

''The wonderful Door opened at the Cross is *a low Door*, that is, we have to bow our heads low in repentance if we are to enter by it. Scripture mentions again and again the disease of the 'stiff neck.' It is a figurative way of speaking of man's self-will and stubbornness. When our necks are like that and our wills unbroken to acknowledge our sin, we can never enter by that Door. . . .

Then we must understand that this Door is *a narrow Door*. At first, the road to the cross seems broad, and we can all go together. But as we get nearer to that place of repentance the path gets narrower. There is not room for us all abreast. At last when we come to the One who is the Door Himself, there is not room even for two. If you are going to enter, you will have to stand there utterly alone. . . . If in any way we are not finding Jesus a real Savior who brings us fully out of darkness and defeat into light and liberty, it is because at one point or another we are not willing to be broken and see ourselves as sinners.''

Roy and Revel Hession
We Would See Jesus
pp. 49-50

''The Christian Way, and Christ warned us that it was narrow and little traveled upon, yet is the royal road to God. I want to use the four-fold pattern of Christian sacrifice as the broad outline of a program of spiritual formation of discipline in order that God might find us and give us what we crave but are unable to achieve by ourselves. . . .

''Christians have found that their Way to the Father lies through Christ. What is that Way? It is the Way of sacrifice and its symbol for Christians is the Eucharist. Here is St. Augustine: 'You are to be taken, consecrated, broken, and distributed that you may be the means of grace and the vehicles of the Eternal Charity.' Behind this is the experience of the Christian Eucharist in which we take, bless, break, and distribute the Holy Bread . . . And we are to be taken into that Way because it is the eternal rhythm of the soul's movement to God: it is to be taken and consecrated, broken and distributed if it is to find God and rest in his will. If we would really be found by God, therefore, we must let ourselves be taken, we must allow ourselves to be consecrated; we must prepare ourselves to be broken, and we must suffer ourselves to be given away.''

Richard Holloway
A New Heaven
pp. 78-79

''In the saying in Luke 18:17, it is not so much the simplicity or humility of little children that our Lord is commending, but their total dependence. This is the attitude that God wants in those who wish *to enter* his kingdom. But what do these rather puzzling words mean? The word translated 'kingdom' really means 'sovereignty' or 'kingly rule,' and to enter the kingdom of God means to accept the sovereignty of God over our lives, and that is something we can begin to do here and now. . . .

"We must not be confused by terminology. The Gospels speak of *entering* the kingdom. But sometimes, particularly in the Fourth Gospel, they speak of entering 'life' or 'eternal life.' Both expressions mean the same thing. Jesus said, 'I have come that men may have life, and may have it in its fulness' (John 10:10). He might equally well have said: I have come that men *may enter* the kingdom of God. *But* they must accept life — the kingdom, the new relationship with God — as a free gift of his grace, and trust him as completely as a little child trusts his parents."*

William Neil
The Difficult Sayings of Jesus
p. 51

"Jesus lays down the *conditions of entry* into the Kingdom. For Jesus there was a difference between entering the Kingdom and the coming of the Kingdom. . . . The publicans and harlots who had believed the message of John were entering the Kingdom already (Matthew 21:31). But when Jesus speaks of the coming of the Kingdom, which he associates with the coming of the Son of Man, he is referring to his conviction that the moment is close at hand when the Kingdom will be established in power and he himself manifested as Messiah."

S. H. Hooke
The Kingdom of God
pp. 112-113

*See also 94:1, Jeremias.

"All that life holds is presented to us and we accept, we affirm, we use, we enjoy; then responding to divine pressure and to spiritual light, we refuse, deny, leave aside, learning to live by grace as well as, even more than, by nature; and so that finally we may be free, unfettered, whole, and able therefore to possess all because we are possessed by God in love. This is what Christ called the narrow way which leads to life, in which he who perseveres to the end shall be saved."

Sibyl Harton
Doors of Eternity
pp. 29-30

"We find repeatedly sayings about 'entry' or 'admission,' characteristic of Jesus and employed only by him, and which formulate a share in the perfect reign of God as the urgent goal of all moral endeavor. . . . The large collection of sayings that are dominated by the idea of entering into or failing to enter the kingdom of heaven is one of the most fundamental motives in the proclamation of the kingdom both by Jesus and the Christian community. In this Jesus was adopting thoughts deeply rooted in the Old Testament, such as entry into the Promised Land and into the Temple."

Rudolf Schnackenburg
God's Rule and Kingdom
pp. 108, 163

New Illuminations:

On Exclusion from the Kingdom

Matthew 7:22f; 8:11-13; 13:41-42; 25:1-13   Mark 12:9   Luke 13:22-30

"The process by which a new parable has arisen out of the fusion of the conclusion of a parable with certain similes is to be found in Luke 15:24-30, a passage which is intended to be taken as a unity. Jesus is urging men to enter by the narrow door before the master of the house rises and shuts it. He rejects the late comers since he will have nothing to do with the wicked. Shut out, they must wail and gnash their teeth as they behold the patriarchs and prophets seated at the feast of salvation and the gentiles seated at the table with them. The interpretative conclusion is furnished by the saying about the last who become first, and the first who become last. From a glance at the Matthew parallels, it appears that we have to do it from a mosaic: through the fusion of one parable (Matthew 25:10-13) with three similes (Matthew 7:13f, 22f; 8:llf) which are related to it in illustrative content, a new parable has come into existence: the parable of the Closed Door."

Joachim Jeremias
The Parables of Jesus
p. 95

"All ten virgins had oil in their lamps. What distinguished the foolish was that they had no reserve in their vessels. Theirs is not a persistent testimony for they live a hand to mouth existence. . . . It is not a question of the initial reception of Jesus Christ; it is a question of the extra oil in the vessel — of the light being sustained by the miraculous supply of the Spirit within (for whereas in the parable, there is both a lamp and a vessel, in reality we are the lamp and the vessel). . . . And so the Lord is taking steps to bring us to the knowledge of fullness now. . . . It is not a question of spiritual gifts and manifestations outwardly but of the personal presence and activity of the Holy Spirit within our spirits, guaranteeing that the light in the vessel will burn long after midnight if need be.

". . . Some are troubled by the Lord's words: 'I know you not.'* But we must recognize the whole point of the teaching which is surely that there is some privilege of serving him in the future which his children may miss by being unprepared. They said, 'Lord, Lord, open to us.' What door? Certainly not the door of salvation. If you are lost you cannot come to the door of heaven and knock. When therefore, the Lord says, 'I know you not', he surely uses these words in some such sense as the following illustration. The son of a police court magistrate was taken up for careless driving. He was brought to court and found his father

sitting on the bench. The boy was asked, 'What is your name? What is your address? What is your occupation?' Astonished, he turned to his father and said, 'Father, do you mean that you do not know me?' Rapping on the desk, the father said sternly, 'Young man, I do not know you.' He did not, of course, mean by this that he did not know him at all. But *in that place and at that time*, he did not know him. Though still his father's son the boy must go right through the court procedure and pay his fine.

". . . Get clear about the will of God. If God is an unchanging God, he will be wise. . . . wisdom is connected with time. Those who are wise redeem the time. By cooperating with the Lord, the wise provide God with what he wants — handy instruments immediately available to him."*

Watchman Nee
Sit, Walk, and Stand
pp. 31-35

["Out of my sight, all of you, you and your wicked ways.' (Luke 13:7, NEB).] Men have lost happiness because they have forgotten how to experience their spiritual selves, and therefore cannot be whole or free. The Jesuit John Higgins wrote: 'It is this estrangement from himself, from society, and from God that has resulted in modern man's incapacity for any kind of spiritual experience.' And to be unknown to God is altogether too much privacy. My false and private self is the one that wants to exist outside the reach of God's will and God's love — outside of reality and outside of life. . . . Merton's fear at this stage of his life was not of any kind of wicked 'them' who persecuted the defenseless — he had become too aware of the guilt of the ordinary bystander — but rather was a fear of the dehumanized man ('worker' of iniquity) who did what he did for good logical reasons or simply obeyed orders. . . .

"Auschwitz and Hiroshima fuse into a common proof of the dehumanization of man, which he saw as the critical challenge that this generation must face. The problem for all was to gain some lost perspective before it was gone for good, a perspective that would make it impossible to project so much evil onto an enemy or a racial minority that any outrage might be committed. For Merton, the problem was the loss of some sense of 'measure.' Without some such measure, the sense of the unimportance of the ego in comparison to the true center on which it would rightly be focused, there was a total disharmony between individuals and society, a loss of all true happiness, and a corresponding

---

*See also 76:1, Bornkamm.

*See also 54:1, Jeremias.

attempt to fill the void in ways that were destructive and suicidal."

Monica Furlong
Merton
pp. 264-268

" 'O Jesus, the mystery of Judas, or rather the mystery of all sinners who die without turning to you depresses me. I know what you said about the separation of the sheep from the goats and of the fire which dieth and cannot be erased from the book. I know that the possibility of certain of his creatures saying "no" to God is a terrible but necessary consequence of the liberty which has been given to us. I also know that we have no certainty that any man has ever been rejected forever. And yet why did your Father create that kind of man whom he foresaw would not adhere to him?'

. . .

" 'My child, I could simply tell you: this question is beyond you; wait with confidence for the day when you will know and you will see. However, I shall remind you of what you already know. I have helped you to believe and understand a little that the mystery of choice takes place in me. It is in me that those who love me are accepted. What I should like to convince you of now is that it is also in me that the mystery of rejection receives its solution and light.

. . .

" 'Just as there is a link between every chosen one and the justice which I have acquired for him on the cross, so also there is a link between every non-repentant sinner and myself in so far as, in his place, I assumed on the cross his sin and his condemnation. Because I took the place of the sinner, even though the sinner spurned the exchange, there was a certain exchange between him and me. . . . listen to me carefully. I did not say that on the cross I saved those who did not want to assimilate throughout their life the salvation which I offered. I mean only one thing *at this very moment*: a real contact has been established between myself and the non-repentant sinner.

" '. . . I wish only to show you the horizon without giving you the possibility of measuring it. Believe with all your heart every word of my gospel concerning the sinner who does not repent. Do not indulge in speculations and discussions on the number of these sinners, on the duration and form of their rejection. Be well aware, my child, that you do not yet know the depths of my heart. Stand in fear of being rejected. Do not trust those who attach little importance to their personal salvation. But never forget that the good shepherd leaves all his faithful sheep to look for and to bring back on his shoulders the fugitive lost sheep.

. . .

" 'Some day you will see my justice and my sanctity shining forth. My mercy and my love will not be less resplendent. Justice will blaze forth through mercy and mercy through justice. It will then be capable of being as much a joyful mystery as a glorious one. The very mystery of the non-repentant sinner will reveal my love for men but without evil obtaining any impunity or complacency.' "

Monk of the Eastern Church
Jesus: A Dialogue with the Savior
pp. 107-11

"Lord, grant that I may live
To fish another day
And when it comes to my last cast,
I then most humbly pray:
When I'm in the Lord's safe landing net,
That in his mercy, I be judged
Big enough to keep."

Anonymous

"Luke 13:30 is a saying which circulated unattached in the early church. In this context it is presumably to be understood as an encouragement to the disciples (i.e., the rich and prosperous who are *first* in this world shall in many cases be *last* in the world to come, and vice versa) or as a warning to them (i.e., they who have been called first must not count on being first in the kingdom)."

D. E. Nineham
St. Mark
p. 276

New Illuminations:

On Humility

"The word 'humility' comes from the Latin word *humis* which means fertile ground. To me, humility is not what we often make of it: the sheepish way of trying to imagine that we are the worst of all and trying to convince others that our artificial ways of behaving show that we are aware of that. Humility is the situation of the earth. The earth is always there, always taken for granted, never remembered, always trodden on by everyone, somewhere we cast and pour out all the refuse, all we don't need. It's there, silent and accepting everything and in a miraculous way making out of all the refuse new richness in spite of corruption, transforming corruption itself into a power of life and a new possibility of creativeness. . . .

"God has never said that when you walk into a situation in his own Name, He will be crucified and you will be the risen one. You must be prepared to walk into situations, one after the other, in God's name, to walk as the Son of God has done: in humiliation and humility, in truth and ready to be persecuted and so forth. When, for instance, someone hits us on one cheek, we turn the other one, although we don't expect to be hit at all; but we expect to hear the other person say, 'What, such humility!' It does not work that way.* You must pay the cost and very often you get hit hard. What matters is that you are prepared for that. So if you accept that this day was blessed of God, then every person you meet is a gift of God, every circumstance you will meet is a gift of God, whether it is bitter or sweet, whether you like or dislike it. It is God's own gift to you; and if you take it that way, then you can face any situation. But then you must face it with the readiness that anything may happen, whether you enjoy it or not. This is the weakness in which God can manifest his power, and this is the situation in which the absence of God can become the presence of God. We cannot capture God. But whenever we stand outside the realm of 'right,' only in the realm of mercy, we can meet God."

Anthony Bloom
Beginning to Pray
pp. 11, 47

"So long as we are on this earth, nothing matters more to us than humility. . . . As I see it we shall never succeed in knowing ourselves unless we seek to know God, let us think of His greatness and then come back to our own baseness; by looking at His purity, we shall see our foulness; by meditating on Jesus' humility, we shall see how far we are from being humble."

St. Teresa of Avila
Interior Castle
p. 38

"When St. Augustine was asked — What is the first important thing in the Christian religion? his reply was — 'Humility.' What is the second?' 'Humility.' And what is the third?' — the reply was — 'Humility.' And if this be true, we need not wonder that Jesus should have been so earnest in teaching this lesson; or that he should have urged so strongly on his disciples to learn it. . . .

"And when he gave us his command to learn this lesson of humility, he gave us at the same time his example to show us *how* to do it.

"He was illustrating this command by his example when he washed his disciples' feet. When he chose to be born of poor parents, he was giving us an example of humility. When he said, 'The Son of Man came not to be ministered unto, but to minister': and when he borrowed an ass to make his triumphant entry into Jerusalem, though he could say in truth, 'Every beast in the forest is mine, and the cattle upon a thousand hills,' he was setting an example of humility. When he allowed himself to be taken prisoner, though he knew that had he asked his Father in heaven, he would at once have sent 'more than twelve legions of angels' to deliver him, he was giving an example of humility. When he allowed the Roman soldiers to scourge him with rods and put him to the most shameful of all deaths, he was giving the most wonderful example of humility that ever was heard of: Jesus the Lord of glory hanging on the shameful cross! — O, this was a type of humility that must have filled the angels of heaven with surprise and wonder! And when we think of all that Jesus did and suffered to set us an example of humility, it should make us ashamed of being proud."

Richard Newton
The Life of Jesus Christ
Vol. 3, pp. 164-67

---

*See also 25:2, Neil.

"To become ready for grace, we need a growing awareness that our search for fulfillment outside of God has been in vain, that it has wounded us. This awareness may give rise to humility and repentance, two sure means to clean up our inner garden, to ready it for the seeds of grace and for their fruitful sprouting in our lives.

"Humbleness must pervade our wounded self as a fine fragrance, making us attractive to God. An atmosphere of repentance must create and gently maintain a movement of inner distancing of self-created idols and the frenzied agitation they evoke. These 'little beyonds' we create as substitutes for the Eternal are weeds that suffocate the tender shoots of grace in our garden. No matter what we do to get rid of them, such weeds seem to show up persistently. That is why we need to tear them out over and over again in patient love. Then the weeds may diminish enough to allow the seeds of grace to sprout forth freely and flourish. The gardeners of our spiritual life — awareness of idle pursuits, unmasking of idols, humbleness and repentance — are needed."*

Adrian Van Kamm
The Woman at the Well
pp. 65-66

"One of the finest fruits of mortification is the great virtue of humility. . . . Technically considered, humility is the recognition of creatureliness — the cheerful acknowledgment that we are dependent upon our Creator for all things, including that very dependence. Obviously this God-centeredness leaves no room for any annoying human pettiness like self-importance, fanaticism, edginess, anger, boasting. Above all, when it is revealed in human life, humility shows itself as a complete unpretentiousness. The humble person adopts no postures. . . .

"It is noteworthy that even the shallowest people often find it quite refreshing and restful to be in the presence of humility. They sense an extra dimension — the dimension of true human greatness as opposed to mere ability. The strong aura of humility has reached out to them, persuading them to forgo for a while the exhausting effort of their own pretendings. This well-known, if too rare, experience indicates that there is nothing weak in humility. . . .

"Despite these realizations, even despite our own desire for humility as we become more sick and tired of play-acting, it is the hardest of all virtues to acquire. One reason for this adheres in the fact that it is directly opposed to the essential unreality that besets us — pride. In the subtle possessiveness of this pride we perversely feel that humility threatens our being instead of constituting its fulfillment. When we stifle this feeling and get down to actual practice, the difficulty becomes supreme. The sensitive nerve of pride, which began to quiver when merely looked at, comes into its own when violent hands are laid upon it. Another way of indicating the difficulty of making this basic virtue ours is by pointing out the 'circular' nature of humility: to be humble, or honest, or really ourselves is in one sense the end result of successful life, while in another sense it is the successful beginning of all progress. Humility, the ending of selfish desires, is only the beginning of desire for what God wants — and when and how.

". . . There are two worlds in which we may freely choose to live — the supernatural world of God's grace or the natural world of man's dis-grace. Unfortunately it often happens that the virtues of one world are not especially valuable in the other. Humility is a classic illustration of this. . . .

"An unfailing flow of opportunity to grow in humility is found in humiliation itself. An ample inner supply of this is always available in our sins and (perhaps not so often for we are clever in our concealment) in the humiliation of being discovered in them. Incidentally an unfailing test of growing humility is found in our reaction to criticism. If our first impulse is to feel that our critic is probably right, we have come a long way. . . .

"Enormous raw material is ready at hand in our temptations. In these experiences, a spiritual person relearns the depth of his own incapacities for good. He uses the constant proof of his own sinfulness to lead him into deepening dependence upon God. . . . Every life has its critical moments when we know with special clarity that we dare not trust our own strength. There are times when the whole human and cosmic affair is too big for us. We are adrift on a tiny raft in the middle of a boundless ocean. In this situation when a person is really thrown out upon really basic resources, he can easily be reckless or despairing in a hundred different ways. On the other hand, profiting from the experience, he can learn a deeper degree of his dependence on the strength of God. These three factors — humiliation, temptation, crisis — that come our way in the providence of God or the maliciousness of events provide the most excellent material for growth in humility.

"Our own cooperating life of prayer as we grope toward the virtue is the final factor that will be mentioned here. It has already been hinted that humility does not originate in our squashing ourselves down. Such self-abasement is born of pride. True humility, on the contrary, comes through magnifying God. (Indeed everything that can be said on our subject is in commentary on the Magnificat.) It is born and flourishes as a by-product of the cultivated habit of looking up and away from oneself."

Gale D. Webbe
The Night and Nothing
pp. 29-31, 34-35

"It is impossible to overestimate the value of true humility and its power in the spiritual life. For the beginning of humility is the beginning of blessedness and the consummation of humility is the perfection of all joy. Humility contains in itself the answer to all the great problems of the life of the soul. It is the only key to faith, with which the spiritual

---

*See also 33:2, Underhill.

184

life begins: for faith and humility are inseparable. . . . If we were incapable of humility, we would be incapable of joy because humility alone can destroy the self-centeredness that makes joy impossible. . . .

"A humble man is not disturbed by praise. Since he is no longer concerned with himself, and since he knows where the good that is in him comes from, he does not refuse praise because it belongs to the God he loves. In receiving it he keeps nothing for himself but gives it all, with great joy, to his God. . . . The humble man receives praise the way a clean window takes the light of the sun. The truer and more intense the light is, the less you see of the glass. . . .

"True humility excludes self-consciousness, but false humility intensifies our awareness of ourselves. . . . A humble man is not afraid of failure. In fact he is not afraid of anything, even of himself, since perfect humility implies perfect confidence in the power of God, before whom no other power has any meaning and for whom there is no such thing as an obstacle. Humility is the surest sign of strength."

Thomas Merton
Seeds of Contemplation
pp. 108-09, 111-13

"My Dear Wormwood, I see only one thing to do at the moment. Your patient has become humble. Are you sure you have drawn his attention to the fact? All virtues are less formidable to us once the man is aware that he has them, but this is especially true of humility. Catch him at the moment when he is really poor in spirit and smuggle into his mind the gratifying reflection, 'By jove! I'm really being humble,' and almost immediately pride — pride at his own humility — will appear. If he awakes to the danger and tries to smother this new form of pride, make him proud of his attempt — and so on through as many stages as you please.

"But there are other profitable ways of fixing his attention on the virtue of humility. By this virtue, as by all the others, our enemy wants to turn the man's attention away from self to Him and to the man's neighbors. Unless they attain this end, they do us little harm; and they may even do us good if they keep the man concerned with himself. . . .

"You must, therefore, conceal from the patient the true end of Humility. Let him think of it, not as self-forgetfulness, but as a certain kind of opinion (namely, a low opinion) of his own talents and character. Some talents, I gather, he really has. Fix in his mind the idea that humility consists in trying to believe those talents to be less valuable than he believes them to be. . . . To anticipate the enemy's strategy, we must consider His aims. The enemy wants to bring the man to a state of mind in which he could design the best cathedral in the world, and know it to be the best, and rejoice in the fact, without being any more (or less) or otherwise glad at having done it than he would be if it had been done by another. The enemy wants him in the end to

be so free from any bias in his own favour that he can rejoice in his own talents as frankly and gratefully as his neighbor's talents — or in a surprise, an elephant, or a waterfall."

C. S. Lewis
The Screwtape Letters
pp. 44-46

"Self-humiliation for Charles Simeon consisted not of belittling the gifts that God had given him or pretending that he was a man of no account, or of exaggerating the sins of which he was very conscious. He went about it by consciously bringing himself into the presence of God, dwelling thoughtfully on his majesty and glory, magnifying the mercy of his forgiveness and wonder of his love. These were the things that humbled him — not so much his own sinfulness but God's incredible love."

Hugh Hopkins
Charles Simeon of Cambridge
p. 156

"The practice of the presence of God does not much fatigue the body; yet it is proper to deprive it sometimes, even often, of many little pleasures which are innocent and lawful. For God will not permit that a soul which desires to be devoted entirely to him should take other pleasures than with him: that is more than reasonable.

"I do not say that therefore we must put any violent constraint upon ourselves. No, we must serve God in a holy freedom; we must do our business faithfully, without trouble or disquiet, recalling our mind to God meekly and with tranquility, as often as we find it wandering from him."

Brother Lawrence
Letters and Conversations
"Letter IV"

"Within the stream of religious experience, there have been men and women whom it has been natural to describe as saints. Their characteristic has been a rare humility. The saint's virtues don't inflate him because he is humble before God, who is their source and he is ever conscious that he falls far short of the perfection which is his goal. But while his sins may be bitter, they do not cast him down, as the divine forgiveness both humbles and restores."

Michael Ramsey
Jesus and the Living Past
p. 52

"With his doubts wearing his mind into ruts, Kenneth found something happening to him which no doubts could reach. But when he came to me it was to cry with Paul 'Who will deliver me? I've been trained to be sure of myself. It's my business to be sure and to let people see that I'm sure. Now I've to throw all that kind of confidence out the window — and let people see that I've thrown it out. I've to be ready to admit I'm the kind of man who can get things wrong. But how can I when I've built up an opposite way ever since I was at school. Every day in the office adds to it. But then the Gospel says, Repent and be changed. But how can I want to be changed?

"It was no new dilemma; it was only the shape of it and the sharpness that was new. No one has ever been able to want it enough. We have become men who do not have it in them to want it. This is why we need a Saviour. I had to say the old word: 'It isn't your repentance that's going to get you through — it's Christ's repentance for you, Christ's repenting for you before you are able to repent for yourself, paying the price before you are willing to give anything. You've got to humble yourself to take it.'

"This is not a new or strange position for men to be in, but they do not know it because their eyes are blinded by the world, and they will not ask and will not accept. This is where we stop having our own ambitions for ourselves. . . . But we must know God's humility towards us before we can become humble in the presence of arrogant men. As the scholars would say, the Christian life cannot be an ethic until it has been a worship. There is no fellowship, no community, no church, without this."

J. W. Stevenson
God in My Unbelief
pp. 118-21

New Illuminations:

On the Heavenly Banquet

Matthew 22:1-14   Luke 14:12-24

"Nearly every page of the Synoptics presents an incontestable loyalty and adherence to the word of Jesus, and at the same time an astonishing degree of freedom as to the original wording. In fact, one can go on to say this: the tradition is not really the repetition and transmission of the word he spoke once upon a time, but rather it *is* his word today.

". . . For the clarification of the contemporary nature of Jesus, let us here refer to a single obvious example. When one compares the different versions of Jesus' parable of the Great Supper, one sees that Luke tells it differently from Matthew. A rich man invites his friends to the feast, but the guests refuse the invitation with plausible though fatuous excuses. The account in Luke remains in the quite natural setting of a parable. In Matthew the story is strengthened by lurid features. The man of means has become a king. The meal has become the marriage feast for his son. The servants (no longer only one) are maltreated and killed. We read further in Matthew that the infuriated king sends out his armies against the thankless and murderous guests and burns down their city. One sees at once that this is no longer a simple parable. Each separate feature demands interpretation and understanding. The king is a standard picture of God. The king's son is the Messiah. The marriage is a picture of the joy of the Messianic age. In the fate of the servants we recognize the martyrdom of God's messengers. In the military campaign we recognize the Jewish war, and in the destruction of the city we recognize the catastrophe of A.D. 70. The old people of God, having become rebellious, will be rejected and a new people will be called. But the new people is still a mixture of good and bad on the way to judgment and the final separation of the unworthy.* (Only in Matthew does the parable end with the rejection of the man who came to the wedding without a wedding garment.) In Matthew's version, we find clearly worked into the parable of Jesus' own story, a picture of Israel and a picture of the early Church. The word of Jesus long ago has become today's word.

"Luke, at least at first, has better preserved the original character of the simple parable, but he also reveals the tendency of the word of Jesus to become contemporary. He makes the servant of the nobleman go out not only twice but three times. After the first refusal he is sent to the poor, lame and crippled *in* the town, and after that once again to those in 'the highways and hedges' *outside* the town. There can be no doubt that the evangelist intended to represent thereby the advance of the mission from Israel to the heathen world."*

> Gunther Bornkamm
> *Jesus of Nazareth*
> pp.17-19

"Luke's parable is not fully understood until attention is paid to the note of joy which rings through the summons: 'everything is ready.' (v. 17) 'Behold, now is the accepted time; behold, now is the day of salvation.' (2 Corinthians 6:2) God fulfils his promises and finally comes out of concealment. But if the 'children of the kingdom,' the theologians and the pious circles, pay no heed to his call, the despised and ungodly will take their place; the others will receive nothing but a 'Too late' from behind the closed door of the banquet hall."

> Joachim Jeremias
> *The Parables of Jesus*
> p. 180

"Here an invitation is being refused. Have we ever known what it is like to try to do something for somebody and be given the cold shoulder? It is just this kind of hurt that was inflicted when these people brusquely dismissed the messengers of the king and made light of the invitation. *Why* did they react so strangely?

"In the Lukan parallel it says that they 'began to make excuses.' In other words these people are putting the everyday concerns of their life *before* the call from eternity, before the great Joy that is being offered to them. . . .

"But is all this really so utterly incomprehensible as it may seem at first glance? . . . They did not understand. . . . They had no idea that what they considered a state of renunciation is actually peace, is actually the abundant life.

". . . In any case, the better people refuse. They have more important things to do than to jump up forthwith and to forsake their business to go chasing some hypothetical bird in the bush. After all every one of us has certain areas in his life which he will not give up and hand over. . . . At some *other* point in my life I am willing to let him in, but not *here*, not at *this* point. . . . Presumably this is just what the invited guests in our parable said. 'Some other time we

---

*See also 74:1, Nee.

---

*See also 5:2, Stott.

will be glad to accept your invitation; but not right *now*. I have no use for you in what I plan to do *today*; here you simply cannot butt in and get in my way.'

"But here too the rule applies: if they do not open the door to him *today*, at the point where it is hardest for them to do so, God turns away and goes elsewhere. True enough it is perhaps much simpler to become religious after the 'second heart attack.' But the point is that God wants me now, when I am on the rise or at the high point of life, and where my work and my struggles and my passions will clash with much that God commands and demands of me.* I have no promise that God will come to me again if I make an appointment to meet him later in the pleasant pastures of retirement; and who knows whether they will be so pleasant after all? . . .

"But when the better people failed and rejected the invitation, the messengers of the king were sent out again. This time they went to the people in the highways and the hedges.

". . . So his banquet did not fall through. When the bearers of the Christian tradition, the Church Christians, walk out and descend into dogmatic hairsplitting or church politics, he turns to the neo-pagans and rejoices in the freshness of their new-found Christianity. For God has no prejudices. A man can come as he is, even as an utterly poor, utterly sinful, and utterly unlovable person who cannot understand what God can see in him. The fact is that he cannot see anything in him, but he makes something of him; he makes him his beloved child."

Helmut Thielicke
The Waiting Father
pp. 186-89

"The conclusion of Matthew's version has long troubled the expositors as they found themselves confronted by the puzzling question why a man called in from the streets should be expected to have a wedding garment. . . . Why did Matthew (or his source) insert the second parable? Clearly care is needed to be taken to avoid a misunderstanding which might arise from the indiscriminate invitation of the uninvited, to wit, that the conduct of the men that are called was of no significance. Jesus was not afraid of this misunderstanding, as is shown by the other parables about the good news, for instance, the parable about the Prodigal Son (Luke 5:22). . . .

"What exactly did Jesus mean by the clean garment which was the necessary condition for admission to the wedding feast? . . . It may be remembered that Jesus spoke of the Messianic Age as a new garment (Luke 5:36) and that he compared forgiveness with the best robe with which the father clothed the Prodigal Son (Luke 15:22, Revelations 6:11). Hence we cannot doubt that it is this comparison that underlies Matthew 22:11-13. God offers you the clean garment of forgiveness and imputed righteousness. Put it on,

*See also 54:1, Neil.

one day before the flood arrives, one day before the inspection of the wedding guests — today!'"*

Joachim Jeremias
The Parables of Jesus
pp. 65, 188-89

"It is very important, then, to see what this unhoped-for invitation really means. In the first place we must see that it is a real 'invitation' and by no means an order to report for service. The message does not come as a 'thou shalt,' a categorical imperative. It does not come to us as a duty and a law. Rather, God addresses us as a friend and host. He comes to us as a royal donor, the giver of every good gift and joy. For this is an invitation to a wedding feast. . . . True, God demands of us obedience. We must even turn our whole life around, and we must pay for our Christianity with all that we are. But first he gives us something, first he simply invites us to come.

". . . So there they were, all seated around the table. *And then the king appeared.* This is the main thing — to be able to see him and to speak to him. This is the real end and aim of the invitation — to be with him. . . .

"Then at its close Matthew's parable takes a dramatic turn. One of the guests got into the worst kind of trouble because he wasn't wearing a wedding garment and was thrown out of the banquet hall. What is the meaning of this wedding garment?

"To be sure, we can accept the call to come into the Father's house just as we are. We need not be ashamed of the highways and hedges from which we have come. But this by no means implies that we can *enter* the Father's house as we are. And this is precisely what the parable means by this metaphor of the wedding garment. We seat ourselves at the banquet table without a wedding garment when we allow our sins to be forgiven but still want to hang on to them. . . .

"And right here is where God's warning comes in. The person that comes without the wedding garment, the person that permits the fact that he can come as he is to make him shameless instead of humble, who, instead of being concerned with sanctification and discipline, allows himself to play a frivolous game with the grace of God, that person is just as badly off as the people who refuse *altogether*, who, indeed, kill the messengers of the king. This is why there is such great sense in the custom of making confession and setting various things to rights before going to Holy Communion. This is comparable to putting on the wedding garment.

"But even with the grievous thought of being cast into outer darkness, which we cannot contemplate without anxiety, the message of joy still breaks through. And this is the last point which we shall consider. For joy remains the real theme of our parable, despite all its dark and somber

*See also 78:2, Thielicke.

features. How, then, can even the analogy of the wedding garment constitute a message of joy? When Jesus speaks here in these figurative terms of sanctifying and preparing oneself, he is by no means thinking of somber penitential exercises and agonizing starvation cures. On the contrary the very imagery he uses for all of this is the festive image of the wedding garment, the image of joy*. . . .

"How, then, do you go about becoming a Christian in order to enter that lighted, festive hall, into this fulfilment of life? My answer would be this. We answer it only if we start out by simply allowing someone to tell us that there is One who rules the world with a father's heart, that he is interested in me and that I am not too paltry or too vile for him to love; and that he wants to love me out of the terrible loneliness and alienness and guilt of my life and bring me to the Father's house."

Helmut Thielicke
The Waiting Father
pp. 184, 189-191

"Jesus closes the parable (Matthew 22:14) with the significant words: 'Many are called but few are chosen.' God calls out to everyone, but only those who are conscious of their sin and who experience his forgiveness respond, and in responding choose and receive the wonders of his grace."

Joost de Blank
Uncomfortable Words
p. 48

---

*See also 103:2, Holloway.

New Illuminations:

On Discipleship IV: The Cost

Matthew 5:13, 10:34-37	Mark 9:50	Luke 12:51-53; 14:26-35

"The Messianic element in Jesus is contained in his preaching and activity, but for himself he claimed no Messianic title. But if this were so, how could we give a positive explanation to his statements? How could we do justice to his summons to follow him and his demand that men shall attach themselves to him? The sentence of Luke 14:26, 'If any man comes to me and hates not his father and mother and wife and children and brethren and sisters yea and his own life also, he cannot be my disciple' is properly understood by Matthew as meaning, 'He that loveth father more than me is not worthy of me' (10:37). We have here a unique claim, an invitation to a religious following directed to the person who gave it and with definite religious objectives. Further, it is not merely an individual following but a corporate movement, the movement towards a community, the Messianic community of salvation."

Rudolf Schnackenburg
God's Rule and Kingdom
p. 118

"We must sketch out the application of mortification to people — that forsaking of father and mother about which our Lord has spoken. From dependence on people setting people above higher loyalties, we must disentangle. No one would argue that statement in theory. In actual practice, the parting involves sweet sorrow, particularly in a society inclined to believe wholly the half-truth that real life is based on meeting, reciprocity, and acceptance. Especially if we are influenced by the present fashion in opinions, we will find it exceedingly painful to grow into the likeness of the true servant of God. . . .

"Yet all this external detachment, this building of defenses against the encroachments of the present temporary abode that presses upon us is only a beginning. . . . The very mention of 'cross' introduces the highest form of God's activity leading us to our death from the merely natural. This is the murky subject of pain and suffering. Pain is surgery sent or permitted by God in order to detach us from ourselves and from the world. . . . The soul that is really beginning to be dead to natural values and united to supernatural ones* is discerning that all the pains as well as the pleasures of life are from the hand of God or in the hand of God. . . . Mortification, having produced detachment, has begun to allow room for Attachment."

Gale D. Webbe
The Night and Nothing
pp. 26, 28

---

*See also 58:3, Wolters.

" 'If any man come to me and hate not his father. . . .' At first reading we are shocked by these words. Can it be possible that our Lord who was gentleness itself really uttered so shattering a statement? Why — we have always thought of Christianity as the main bulwark of family life. . . . But it is precisely the value that our religion sets on family ties that compels our attention to these words. . . . Nobody would dare to drive a wedge into the family to separate its members from one another unless there were a higher loyalty to which even family ties must take second place. This higher loyalty Jesus recognized. Man's first allegiance must be to God. There is a higher loyalty that demands man's primary obedience even at the cost of family unity and solidarity. . . .

"The truly happy home is a family all of whose members are bound together in a common loyalty to God and to one another. Such a home is made up of people who seek God's will together. Jesus left us in no doubt that there might be times when we should have to choose between family and God, but if the whole family is united in a passionate desire to do God's will, such a choice need but seldom be made. In such devoted homes there should never be the pain and anguish of misunderstanding, though the pain and anguish of separation and sacrifice are an inescapable part of the life of discipleship. . . .

"We are to *hate* father or mother, child or parent, yes — life itself, lest any of these should deflect us by one hair's breadth from our total commitment to God. We are shocked by the use of the word *hate*, but our Lord is determined to leave us in no doubt that anything or anyone that comes between the disciple and his obedience to God deserves our hatred. The strength of the language is an indication of the importance of putting first things first whatever the cost or the consequences. . . .

"Our being instructed to *hate* our dear ones is a matter of the will and not a matter of feeling or emotion. We know that our Lord understood the importance of family love. But so far as the direction of our wills is concerned, nothing and no one may impede our instant obedience to every whisper of the divine will. Only so can we be his disciples."

Joost de Blank
Uncomfortable Words
pp. 18-19, 22-26

"Ordinarily, Jesus calls 'Come unto me!' — and here instead of pleading, he repels and actually warns us against himself. Instead of saying, 'I give you eternal life,' he says, 'Count what it will cost you in this life and consider whether you are equal to my discipleship.' Instead of inflaming, he pours on cold water. How can we reconcile all of this? . . .

"So now we shall consider the enigma that lies behind this parable of the building of a tower, behind these words that warn instead of invite, that separate instead of linking us closer together. Jesus had set out to win the world back to God and bring back to his Father the multitude of the lost and broken, of those who had become unfaithful and therefore unhappy. And setting out to do this, he had something like success. The people crowded about him in shoals. He impressed them and a gleam of new hope was kindled in the despairing eyes and care-marred faces of thousands. If these masses could be committed to this man, the blaze that would be kindled would spread like a prairie fire among them all and beyond them to many others. But strangely enough, Jesus renounced every kind of mass influence of the kind that suggests itself so readily to our own time. Rather he challenged men to cast up a balance and make a sober estimate of the cost.

"Why did he do this? Or perhaps we should ask another question first: What are the crowds of people looking for in Jesus? . . . Jesus sees all these people gathered around him. You and I; we are among them too. And he sees that these people are unhappy and peaceless. Why are they so? Simply because their hearts are so divided. They want a little bit of God, and this little bit of God is just enough to bother their conscience and deprive them of their unconcern. Anybody who wants to be partly devout and partly a worldling is sure to be unhappy. . . .

"Now perhaps we understand what Jesus' intention was in demanding of us such a radical decision. At first sight this seems harsh and implacable, but it is only the sternness of a physician who tells a man: 'Only a radical operation will help you.' So Jesus' intention was to free us from this confounded dividedness. He says to us, 'If you want to follow me and if you set any real value on what this discipleship means to you, then you must also make a radical change in your life. Then you must say good-by to many things to which you cling. He wants to bring us onto the straight road to the Father (Luke 3:5-6) in order that we may get back to his heart. When Jesus is as stern as this saying shows him to be, this is really his mercy. When he takes something from us, he does so only because he wants to give us more, nay, everything (Luke 18:29-30). . . .

"There is one more question which must be touched upon in closing. How shall we go about counting the cost? Are we actually to make estimates of what Christianity will cost us, as a man who builds a tower must do, or as a king must do before he declares war? The first thing we must say is that anybody who is facing the question whether he is to be in earnest with Jesus, whether he is to venture his life with Jesus, should for once in his life put aside all calculation. After all to make an estimate of cost, one must know beforehand the important items that enter into it. But here a man does not know the important items beforehand. After all Jesus is not a huckster who ballyhoos his wares beforehand. What he has to offer we receive and experience only if we are willing to take a chance with him. And

the longer we are with him the more deeply do we grow into his riches. . . . Yes, we should all like to have the gifts that Jesus gives. Naturally, we too will not be able to dodge the counting of the cost. We cannot have these gifts and these riches without the Cross. We must commit many things to death. We must say good-by to many things, even though we shall get back a hundredfold what we offer up for him. But at the beginning we must be ready to sacrifice."

Helmut Thielicke
The Waiting Father
pp. 148-51, 156

"Now Jesus, in Luke 14:34, goes on to say, 'Salt is good; but if salt has lost its taste, how shall its saltness be restored? It is fit neither for the land nor the dunghill; men throw it away.' In the Middle East, salt is scarce; and the Arabs would give anything for a pinch of salt because with salt they preserved their meat and their fish. Because it was scarce, however, there were substitutes on the market — good to the taste, all right for immediate consumption — but the moment they tried to preserve their food with these substitutes it went putrid and bad. It was not even fit for the dunghill! As in the case of substitute salt, there is a form of activity which is all right for immediate consumption. It is self-activity. But the work of God is that you believe and maintain, unrelentingly, total dependence upon the One whom God has sent to fill you with himself. He is the true salt through whom you are made the salt of the earth."

Ian Thomas
The Saving Life of Christ
p. 31

"When Christ declared, 'You are the salt of the earth,' he is not paying us a compliment. He is laying down a challenge. He is putting us on our mettle. . . . What Jesus is talking about in the parable is your attitude toward self preservation. You will remember that he goes on to say in his Sermon on the Mount: 'You are salt to the world. And if salt becomes tasteless, how is its saltness to be restored? It is now good for nothing but to be thrown away and be trodden under foot' (Matthew 5:13). He is saying that unless you are prepared to be used up like salt, absorbed like salt, to become nothing, like salt in the process of purifying, cleansing, preserving, bringing flavor back into a world that has lost its holy taste; if you sit there knowing that this is what you are meant for and refuse to allow yourself to be used by him, then the reason for your existence in his ministry to the world ceases: you take your place as road material, the useless dust for the unheeding traffic of history's purposeless meanderings. So it is that the truth of Christ's saying comes to light and life: that he who seeks to save his own life shall lose it*. . . .

"There has to be commitment. There has to be conversion to the Lord who is here in the world to make it and all things new. This is why our faith and our love for him is crucial, and I use the term advisedly, for its roots are in the Cross itself. For was not Christ himself God's salt among us? Did he not restore to newness the divine flavor in us?

Did he not cleanse us, bringing humankind back to what it is destined to be and enjoy, namely the likeness and the eternal companionship of the heavenly Father? To do this, he gave himself totally and poured himself out as the redemptive process he performed secures us for time and for eternity. We are to be the salt of the earth because he is first that salt for us."

John Andrew
Nothing Cheap and Much that is Cheerful
pp. 120-22

*See also 46:3 Lewis

New Illuminations:

On the Merciful Father

"There is the difficulty that 'sinner' is too broad a word to designate a class. It has been suggested, therefore, that it is the evangelists' way of referring to the 'people of the land,' those Jews who had not the opportunity nor the inclination to study the law and carry it out in detail as the Pharisees did. The Pharisees always shunned the company of such people. 'The multitude that does not know the law is accursed' (John 7:19)."

D. E. Nineham
Saint Mark
p. 100

"In Luke 15:2 we are told that Jesus received publicans and sinners and ate with them. The term 'sinners' means: (1) People who led an immoral life (e.g., adulterers, swindlers). (2) People who followed a dishonorable calling (i.e., an occupation which notoriously involved immorality or dishonesty), and who were on that account deprived of civil rights, such as holding office or bearing witness in legal proceedings. Examples of the use of the term are tax-collectors, shepherds, donkey-drivers, peddlers and tanners. When the Pharisees and scribes asked why Jesus accepted such people as table companions, they were not expressing surprise but disapproval; they were implying that he was an irreligious man, and warning his followers not to associate with him."

Joachim Jeremias
The Parables of Jesus
p. 132

"While to the Jewish way of thinking, repentance precedes the condition which affords the sinner the hope of grace, it is now the case that repentance comes by means of grace. The tax collectors and sinners with whom Jesus sits at meal are not asked first about the state of their moral improvement any more than is the prodigal when he returns home. The extent to which all talk of the conditions which man must fulfill before grace is accorded him is here silenced. This is shown by the parables of the lost sheep and the lost coin, which tell of the finding of what was lost and in this very manner describes the joy in heaven over one sinner who repents. So little is repentance a human action

preparing the way for grace, that it can be placed on the same level as being found."

Gunther Bornkamm
Jesus of Nazareth
pp. 83-84

"According to Luke 15:2, the 'Parable of the Lost Sheep' was occasioned by the Pharisees' indignant question. It was with the object of justifying the Gospel against its critics by means of a parable that just as a shepherd, gathering his flocks into the fold, rejoices over the lost sheep he has found, so God rejoices over the repentant sinner. He rejoices because he can forgive. 'That,' says Jesus, 'is why I receive sinners.'

"The parable has an entirely different audience in Matthew. . . . When it is brought into the context of the admonition not to despise one of the least (18:10), and of the instruction concerning the discipline of an erring brother (18:15-17), the concluding sentence clearly means: it is God's will that you should go after your apostate brother as persistently as the shepherd of the parable seeks the lost sheep. Thus in Matthew the emphasis does not lie in the joy of the shepherd but in the persistence of his search. . . . Hence the Matthean context does not help us to determine the original situation in the life of Jesus which produced the Parable of the Lost Sheep. There can be no doubt that Luke has preserved the original situation. As in so many instances, we have Jesus vindicating the good news against its critics and declaring God's character, God's delight in forgiveness as the reason why he himself received sinners. . . .

"Finding creates boundless joy as the shepherd rejoices over the lamb brought home, and the poor woman over her recovered drachma, so will God rejoice. The future tense in Luke 15:7 is to be understood in an eschatological sense: at the final judgment, God will rejoice when among the many righteous he finds a despised sinner upon whom he may pronounce absolution, nay more, it will give him even greater joy. Such is the character of God: it is his good pleasure that the lost should be redeemed, because they are his. Their wanderings have caused him pain and he rejoices over their return home. It is the 'redemptive joy' of God of which Jesus speaks, the joy in forgiving. This is Jesus' defense of the Gospel: 'Since God's mercy is so infinite that his supreme joy is in forgiving, my mission as Savior is to wrest his prey from Satan and to bring home the lost.' ''*

Joachim Jeremias
The Parables of Jesus
pp. 39-40, 135-36

"In an absolutely proper sense, no man can, by searching, find God. He is at the point of faith when he realizes the collapse of his own proud efforts. What he once failed to achieve by will, he might now receive by grace; for it is the fundamental insight of the Gospel that we do not find God, he finds us in our lostness. . . . He comes after us like a shepherd searching for his lost sheep; like a woman searching for her lost coin; like the waiting Father who sees his lost son while he is yet a great way off and runs towards him to embrace him and bring him back home. The Christian doctrine of the incarnation gathers this theme into one arresting proclamation which asserts that God himself has come after us by submitting to our nature and its limitations in the person of Jesus."

Richard Holloway
A New Heaven
p. 71

"Mercy has behind it all the wealth of the Old Testament *hesed*. It is a word associated with the covenant, and it may be described as God's persistent and loyal love. This steadfast love is everlasting and unshakeable and is not to be thwarted. The Greek word means pity or compassion. . . . There is no deficiency in God's mercy. It is dependent on his will and not on any emotion which he is supposed to have (Romans 9:15, 18). Mercy is thus God's settled purpose. It can anticipate the covenant relationship and thus, paradoxically, 'loyal love' can be shown in advance, when we hardly could have expected the word 'loyal.' . . . Regeneration is in virtue of mercy."

Ronald Ward
Timothy and Titus
p. 24

"Mercy is the tenderness which by the mysterious power of pardon turns the darkness of our sins into the light of God's love."

Monica Furlong, ed.
Merton
p. 232

---

*See also 6:2, Webster.

"I, even I, am the one who wipes out your transgressions for my own sake; and I will not remember your sins."

Isaiah 43:25
New American Standard Bible

" 'You are right,' Jesus says, 'you are lost if you look only to yourselves. You are right when you give yourself up as lost. But look, now something has happened that has nothing to do with your attitudes at all, something that is simply given to you. Now the kingdom of God is among you; now the Father's house is wide open. And I — I am the door, I am the way, I am the life, I am the hand of the Father. He who sees me sees the Father. . . . You see that God so loved the world that he delivered me, his son, to these depths, that it cost him something to help you, that it cost the very agony of God, that God had to do something very contrary to his own being to deal with your sin, to recognize the chasm between you and himself and yet bridge it over.* All this, see when you look at me!'

"So Jesus who is telling the parable is pointing to himself between the lines and back of every word. If this were just anyone telling us this story of the good and kindly Father, we could only laugh. We could only say, 'How do you know there is a God who seeks me, who takes any interest in my lostness, who indeed suffers because of me? Why do you tell such nursery tales?' Or another says, 'What are you saying? God intervene with forgiveness and a new beginning?'

"But this is not just 'anybody.' This is Jesus Christ himself speaking, and he is not merely telling us about this Father; the Father himself is in him. Does he not seek out the lost? Is he not the very voice of the Father's heart that overtakes us in the far country and tells us that incredibly joyful news, 'You can come home. Come home!'?

"The ultimate theme of this story, therefore, is not the prodigal son, but the Father who finds us. The ultimate theme is not the faithfulness of me but the faithfulness of God. And this is also the reason why the joyful sound of festivity rings out from the story. Wherever forgiveness is proclaimed there is joy and festal garments**. . . . The ultimate secret of this story is this: there is homecoming for us all because there is a home."

Helmut Thielicke
The Waiting Father
pp. 28-29

"It is not likely that any of us will find out that there is a loving and forgiving Father waiting to be met until we turn to him. . . . It is like finding a vein of gold. Not many

---

*See also 117:1, Penelope.
**See also 76:2, Jeremias.

194

people strike it rich until they believe that there is gold to be found deep in the mountains and that it is valuable. The same thing is true of finding God. . . . It is the Good News of Christianity; it asserts that God is like Jesus, that at the heart and core of reality is the same loving, forgiving concern expressed in the life and teaching of Jesus and in his story of the prodigal. . . .

"Jesus of Nazareth tells us to approach God by addressing him as 'Abba.' This is one of his unique contributions to religious thought and practice. Christians are told to turn to the force that moves the sun and other stars and speak like small children who need their father and call out 'Daddy!'* knowing that they will be answered. In other religions and even among many 'Christians' there is a very different idea of God.

"Most of the world pictures the ruler of the universe like an Oriental potentate who must be approached almost crawling on one's belly. His justice is not questioned. He is feared because he is infinitely distant, infinitely just, and he administers the justice with a heavy hand. Often he appears very much like an almighty steamroller whose majestic will and wrath and judgment must be accepted with resignation and without hope. There are even people to whom God appears to be an unreasonable tyrant who strikes out angrily one moment and heals the next. No wonder people have little desire to relate to such a God and prefer to leave prayer to the professionals. Those who hold such ideas of God within themselves cannot help but pray very differently from Christians who find the love of a father at the heart of their most central experiences."

Morton Kelsey
The Other Side of Silence
pp. 58-59

---

*See also 59:2, Frey.

"God is no piker; and he has said that he who comes to him will not be cast out. But you must come to him. You must beseech and besiege him and find out if you meet with any resistance. . . . What is at stake is the joy of homecoming. And it is not at all as if only you were always waiting and longing. There is another who is always waiting for you; and he is already standing at the door, ready to come to meet you.**

"The deepest mystery of the world is that God is waiting for us all. The person who understands this and takes it in is near to the blessedness of the royal wedding feast. Already there shines about him the flooding light of the festal hall even though he still walks in the midst of the valley of the shadow."

Helmut Thielicke
The Waiting Father
p. 192

"The recognition that Luke 15:11-32 is primarily an apologetic parable, in which Jesus vindicates his table companionship with sinners against his critics, carries with it a very important consequence. He vindicates his revolutionary conduct by claiming in the parable, 'God's love to the returning sinner knows no bounds. What I do represents God's nature and will.' Jesus thus claims that in his (Jesus') actions the love of God is made effectual. Thus the parable, without making any kind of Christological statement, reveals itself as a veiled assertion of authority: Jesus makes the claim for himself that he is acting in God's stead, that he is God's representative."

Joachim Jeremias
The Parables of Jesus
p. 132

---

*See also 60:1, Bornkamm.

New Illuminations:

On The Two Sons

Luke 15:11-32

"The parable is not an allegory but a story drawn from life: 'Father, I have sinned against heaven (i.e. God) and against thee.' Thus the father is not God, but an earthly father; yet some of the expressions used are meant to reveal that in his love he is the image of God. . . .

"The son was forced to be in contact with unclean animals and could not have observed the Sabbath: hence he must have been reduced to the lowest depths of degradation and practically forced to renounce the regular practice of his religion. 'And no one gave him anything to eat.' Hence he must have stolen any food he got. 'He came to himself', 'he came into himself' is in Hebrew and Aramaic an expression of repentance. 'I will go at once.' After the legal settlement he has no further claim, not even to food and clothing. He asks to be allowed to earn both."

Joachim Jeremias
The Parables of Jesus
pp. 128-130

" 'I wanted to be free' says the prodigal son to himself — perhaps he cries it aloud, 'I wanted to become myself: and I thought I would get all this by cutting myself off from my father and my roots, fool that I am! I have found nothing but chains,' and bitter laughter goes up from the pigsty. . . . To separate ourselves from the Father is at bottom not merely 'unbelief' at all, but simply the most monstrous kind of silliness. Does not mankind often present the spectacle of a Mardi Gras parade, reeling about like a man who has lost his balance and his bearings? And now this is the point to which the prodigal son has come. Now comes the great crisis in his life. Now he is in a fever to get home. Now he is ready to turn around and look at himself. . . . The repentance of the lost son is therefore not something merely negative. It is not just turning away from something, but turning back home. Whenever the New Testament speaks of repentance, always the great joy is in the background. It does not say, 'Repent or Hell will swallow you up,' but 'Repent, the Kingdom of Heaven is at hand.' When the son thinks he has come to the end of his road, then God really begins with his way. This end, from Man's point of view, and this beginning from God's point of view — this is repentance. Disgust with himself could never help him. It might perhaps make a nihilist of him, but in no case would it have shown him the way back home. No it was the other way round. It was because the father and the father's house loomed up before his soul that he became disgusted with himself. It became a disgust that brought him home. It was the father's influence from afar, a by-product of sudden realization of where he really belonged. It suddenly made him realize what estrangement and lostness is. And now the lost son arises and goes home."

Helmut Thielicke
The Waiting Father
pp. 26-27

"When the prodigal son 'came to himself,' he recognized error in his life orientation and set out to correct it in a responsible way. It is clear that such a change involves one's whole life. . . .

"The Christian faith has always been more than a system of belief. It is a way of life, a responsible and committed way of action. The real secret of the personal ministry of Jesus can never be understood apart from his personal closeness to God. He found freedom for his life as he first of all accepted personal responsibility in the search for meaning. And he found meaning as he exercised his freedom, under God, in service."

Robert Leslie
Jesus and Logotherapy
pp. 116, 123

"Repentance is not a woebegone renunciation of things that mean a lot to me; it is a joyful homecoming to the place where certain things no longer have any importance to me because I know for whom I am doing all this and because the joy of heaven over one sinner who repents simply communicates itself infectiously and makes this act of repentance itself a thing of joy. After all the prodigal son did not moan over the fact that now he would have to leave this interesting, fascinating far country, the great adventure of his life. On the contrary he saw the lighted windows of his father's house, where a fervent welcome awaited him, and suddenly the far country became a gloomy dream that dissolved behind him.

Helmut Thielicke
The Waiting Father
p. 191

"The drama of man's losing or finding God happens at an appointed place, ordained by God. He comes in search of us. He has been drawing us to himself from all eternity. . . . Yet all the time we are searching for him. God in search of man. Man in search of God. How is the connection made? . . . We only know real happiness when we keep that appointment. If we miss it as we so often do, we experience a mysterious sense of loss. Make no mistake, behind the brave fronts and cheerful faces that many people put on, there often lies a great deal of heartbreak and dissatisfaction. But most people are hardly able to identify the unease that afflicts them. Their lives have not turned out quite the way they wanted them to. . . . If your face is at all worn by time and your heart battered by chance, then you will admit that there is a strange, aching gap between what you are and what you once longed to be. . . .

"Our hearts are never at rest, says Augustine, not because what we long for does not exist, but because we once knew it and have wandered far from it and have forgotten how to return. Mankind is in the far country of exile from the Father. He is born remembering yet cannot find by searching. In his *Confessions* Augustine draws a helpful analogy from the activity of thinking and remembering. The very word re-member suggests bringing back together of broken and forgotten fragments into their original unity, and this is the very activity we call thinking. It is an activity of collecting together and making unities of fragmented and partial truths, rather like the piecing of a jigsaw together. This is why we are able to recognize and approve when a 'new' idea is put to us. We say, 'That's right! Why didn't I think of that before?' . . .

"I believe most men and women have God-hunger, which is often deeply repressed but which shows itself in a prevailing sense of personal dissatisfaction. . . . The Christian Gospel recognizes all of this, but it begins with the recognition that no effort on humanity's part will resolve the fundamental problem: we are without God in the world, yet we have a deep and ineffaceable natural longing for him. The Gospel, however, witnesses to the fact that God himself has come in search of us! He finds us in our need and makes himself known. This is the meaning of Jesus Christ who was the presence of God yesterday and is still that presence today and will be that presence forever."

Richard Holloway
A New Heaven
pp. 65-68, 72

"There are two types of sons in our Lord's parable, the repentant and the elder brother. There are only two kinds of men; sinners who know themselves sinners and sinners who think themselves righteous.

"Yet let it not be forgotten that God loves the elder brother also. If we are members of the Church, we are his children, and God in his mercy is very gentle in all his dealings with us. If we recognize in ourselves the self-righteousness of the older brother, we have at least begun to be penitent. Let us never forget God's mercy. To labor too much over the depth of our repentance is but another expression of self-centeredness. Action is the cure — to arise and go to our Father and say that we have sinned."

Manasses
Go in Peace
p. 28

"Again and again in the Gospels the deep gloom which hangs over the righteousness of the 'good' becomes apparent: in the grumbling of the Pharisees and the scribes over Jesus' eating with sinners; in the indignation with which they hear the words of forgiveness that he speaks to the sick of the palsy; in the anger they show when they call him a drunkard and a glutton. It is heard in the parable of the prodigal son, in the words addressed to the father by the elder son, when he remains outside and refuses to take part in the feast: 'You never gave me a kid that I might make merry with my friends.' But this is the very thing which decides who will finally be lost, who in the end are the first and who are the last. 'Or do you begrudge my generosity?' is the Lord's last words to the grumblers in the parable of the laborers. 'It was fitting to make merry for this your brother was dead and is alive; he was lost and is found' were the last words of the father to the elder brother. The joy is the joy of deliverance from death. It is a matter of nothing less than this. For this reason, the last words of both parables, far from sounding a note of reproach and fault-finding, have a note of questioning and of urgent persuasion. What becomes of the younger son, we know. But what will become of the elder brother?"

Gunther Bornkamm
Jesus of Nazareth
p. 85

"The elder son was also lost from his father and his brother because he had been living a life of self-righteous resentment and had made no effort to recognize it. In a burst of irreconcilable contempt and wrath he rejected his father's effort towards reconciliation."

Selected

"Obedience, that great theme in Lewis, is the key to joy and harmony with God for all who have been empowered by the Spirit. Man's *will* chooses either to be indwelt by the real presence of God's Spirit, dying to self-will and self-love; or it chooses to be its own 'god.' If we reject God, we reject the union that completes us, that brings us into personhood, and that grants access to all true creativity. . . . To be filled with the Spirit is to enter the Great Dance of healthy relationship with the self, others, God, and his creation. . . . In rejecting God, we step outside of the Great Dance and into the Bent Will which is the ruler of the *in*-coherent planet.''

Leanne Payne
Real Presence:
The Holy Spirit in the Works of C. S. Lewis
pp. 90-91, 58

''Whenever real love and relationship develop between human beings, they face the demanding task of coming to terms with the less pleasant elements of themselves. God offers us a far more accepting love than any human relationship, and we actually shy away from it because of the deepening honesty and growth it requires, both of which involves shedding one's skin time after time. This is difficult and demanding.''

Morton Kelsey
The Other Side of Silence
p. 58

''The parable of the Prodigal Son not only vindicates Jesus' kindly regard for sinners, but the refrain 'dead come to life' makes us think of Jesus' passion and resurrection. Jesus by his union with human nature becomes the wayward son.''

Carroll Stuhlmueller
The Jerome Biblical Commentary
44:119

''It is the heart and core of 'the Gospel' that something drastic has to be done about goodness and sin, and that what I cannot do God has done. It is the heart and core of the Gospel that in the life, death, and resurrection of Jesus of Nazareth, God acted about sin and its contradiction of goodness: 'Christ died for our sins and rose again for our justification' — to become goodness in us. That was the original point of the Gospel. Any religion that does not center on that has 'missed the point' of the *Christian* religion, whatever else it may say. . . . The Atonement, the fact that God and men have been reconciled in Christ is like a ray of light on the tangled question of 'seeking God' with sin in my own heart. . . . The first simple, untheologically-minded Christians of the first years had seized on this truth as the fundamental point. 'Repent and be baptized every one of you in the name of Jesus Christ for the remission of sins.' . . . It was sin and goodness wherever they were found that God had acted upon.''

Dom Gregory Dix
The Claim of Jesus Christ
pp. 12-14, 20

''One of the most beautiful symbols employed in the New Testament for describing the experience of a Christian's entrance into the new relationship with God 'through Christ' is that of a death and a resurrection. 'You who were dead in trespasses, God made alive with him, having forgiven us all our trespasses' (Colossians 2:13). The sacrament of baptism dramatizes this surrender of self and this rebirth into a new life. Man must learn to say to God: 'Thy will be done' not mine. Death to self comes hard to all of us. The somber symbol of dying is not too violent to designate this act. Only the good news of resurrection on the other side of death will induce the necessary courage. A repentant sinner, acknowledging his nothingness before the holy God, knows what dying to self means. But he also finds the resurrected life on the other side in the gift of forgiveness.''

Theodore Wedel
The Christianity of Main Street
p. 104

New Illuminations:

"My Savior, your presence at my sin is a great grace. Your hand is stretched out to draw me from the abyss. But if by committing the sin, I reject the final grace, what will become of me? You do not pass any formal sentence. Your very person, Master is the sentence which condemns me, but it is also a proclamation and a pardon. There would be no talk of pardon if there had been no talk of judgment. My guilty past or present belong to the order of grace in so far as all human destiny is linked to the plan of grace willed by God. My personal discords still remain parts of the universal symphony of grace. Yet this consideration cannot justify the discord because it is opposed to grace — and that is death. Discord and sin, the opposition to grace, are still potentially in the order of grace as long as my sorrow and your forgiveness can still intervene. For that, O Savior, be blessed."

Monk of the Eastern Church
Jesus, A Dialogue With the Savior
pp. 105-06

"Grace is one of the great New Testament words. The original is Greek (*charis*). . . . Grace moves from the superior to the inferior, from the greater in character and power to the lesser; from God to man and not from man to God. It is entirely undeserved. Grace is free (*gratis*). The term itself is abstract, though convenient for use. It means that we are concerned with a gracious God who acts personally with men. We must not make grace a thing-in-itself, working impersonally. Grace means God himself working for and in men; and he thus works in Christ. In fact grace is alive in Christ who embodies it. . . . God's *purpose* has not been abstract or arbitrary but was inspired by his grace, . . . the grace *which he gave us in Christ Jesus ages ago*. This is a startling thought. We did not then exist. Perhaps we can glimpse a dim picture by thinking of those wealthy men who set up a trust and settle large sums of money on their grandchildren, perhaps even on grandchildren yet unborn. We did not exist; but God did and Christ did. If we wonder why God gave to men as yet unborn with no guarantee that they would accept the gift, we reply that the gift was in the eternal purpose of God and that he took steps to see that it would be accepted. . . . When we speak of it we should think of Christ crucified and risen. Grace is thus a particular case of love. It is love loving the unlovable and pardoning the unpardonable. It is utter purity cleansing the defiled. It is the perfectly clean touching the leper. It is the exalted

coming down to lift up the fallen. There is love between the Father and Son but never grace. How could there be?"

Ronald A. Ward
1 and 2 Timothy and Titus
pp. 23-24, 151

"All our forgiveness is antedated. This is the meaning of divine grace. God has not only forseen. He has also foreacted. Christ died for our sins before we even lived to commit them. God's grace precedes our faith. God's pardon precedes our sinning. . . . The initiative never rests on human penitence but on divine love. . . . Divine forgiveness was not bought by the Cross; it is not the result of the Cross but rather its cause. . . . As P. T. Forsythe put it in his characteristic way: 'The atonement did not procure grace; it flowed from grace.' "

Douglas Webster
In Debt to Christ
pp. 31, 36

"God's Grace of Spirit is not a sort of plastic substance which is inserted into the soul and acts henceforth like a homing device in a glider. God's Grace is dynamic and personal; it is God himself loving us and willing us on, cheering and supporting us. Like the will which we constantly give over to God, God's Grace is constantly poured out upon us in exact correspondence to our activity of self-surrender. . . . The Grace of God is poised over us, ready to penetrate and forgive at the very instant our need expresses itself. This was the knowledge which Christ labored to make known: the infinite and unremitting accessibility of Grace. The prodigal son is met by his father while he is a great way off. The penitent thief is promised the gateway to life on the basis of a single, honest, and kindly insight*. . . . God's Grace responds instantly to every tremor of longing that we feel. He wants to take us so that he can consecrate us. . . .

"The challenge of temptation to sin is matched by the grace to overcome the temptation; the challenge to witness for God is matched by the power of God within us, if necessary the very words we need. Every challenge that the suffering and confusion of the world places before us draws from

---

*See also 117:2, Dix.

us, by the power of the Spirit, an appropriate response. Yet the paradox holds. God does not switch us on to a sort of automatic pilot which he then controls. We are still in control; our will must be given over to God moment by moment, and his Grace corresponds to that activity. Nay his Grace *prompts* that activity of self-offering so that we can feel the full power of Paul's classic paradox which states the central psychological experience of Christian life: 'I live; yet no longer I; Christ liveth in me' (Galatians 2:20)."

Richard Holloway
A New Heaven
pp. 102-03, 105

"Suppose one accepts this staggering claim that Jesus of Nazareth was and is the power and wisdom of God in action seeking and reconciling the sinful world to himself — what comes of it? The claim is true — you are reconciled with God if you accept it. What happens? Because you have been 'reconciled,' because sin in you has been as it were cancelled out by the At-one-ment in Jesus Christ, the Love and power of God can now work freely in you to produce that 'goodness' which is the likeness of God. And you on your side are able freely to cooperate with God in this, without sin in you always repelling the goodness of God. The New Testament calls this free working of God in your soul 'grace': '. . . when he came to himself . . .' (Luke 15:17). That is the effect of reconciliation that God can regard you differently, work with you and in your soul freely; and you can *accept* that new relation to him freely and cooperate with him. . . .

"You know that all the time you *depend* for the *rightness* of your own being on God, on something God did and does, something that you cannot conceivably do for yourself. You are continually aware that left to yourself, your own being is not right in itself. God did not start you off so to speak and then leave you to your own importance. Not only your existence, but the rightness of that existence, is dependent all the time on the grace and love and mercy of God given in Jesus Christ."

Dom Gregory Dix
The Claim of Jesus Christ
pp. 58-59, 68-69

"On the individual level, there is no forgiveness without a creative development. The turning point where the negative energy of regret changes into the positive energy of the new life is the mysterious point which is described by the word 'Grace.' Something is given to you not only to compensate for the debt you have incurred; a new capital is added, and together with the new urge to try again and to avoid

the old mistake, you now have the chance to do better than ever before."

Fritz Kunkel
Creation Continues
p. 109

"St. Augustine does not argue that, if you remove 'righteousness' (a matter of faith and grace), you will be left with an unChristian civilization, a pagan polity. No, he argues that if you remove 'righteousness' (a matter of faith in God and the working out of his grace), you will be left with 'bands of brigands' in place of an ordered society."

Harry Blamires
Where Do We Stand?
p. 23

"There are passages in the New Testament which seem to describe some characteristics of Christian spirituality. One of these is in the fifth chapter of the Epistle to the Romans, verses 1 and 2: 'Therefore since we are justified by faith, we have peace with God through our Lord Jesus Christ. Through him we have access to this grace in which we stand. . . .' Here indeed is a picture of what the Christians were experiencing: a new access to God. . . . In the Apostolic age there are present themes concerning the Christian life which are rooted in the history and are so characteristically Christian that their recurrence through the subsequent centuries is not surprising. . . . In every case there is emphasis upon the priority of God's Grace to the human response to that grace. It may, therefore, be asked whether the priority of God's grace and the subsequent response to it may not be realized many times in the Christian centuries without a necessary recourse to the original history. Here it must be said that what the grace of God in the events of the Gospel does is not only to initiate a series of acts of grace in subsequent centuries, but also to create the redeemed society, the Holy Catholic Church, within which successive generations of Christians grow together in the life in Christ."

Michael Ramsey
Jesus and the Living Past
pp. 57, 59-60

"In 1 Corinthians 15:10, Paul speaks about the Grace of God three times. First, he says that because God expressed an attitude toward him that was nothing more than Grace, he took him from what he was and made him what he became: 'I am what I am by the Grace of God. . . .' It is the most exhilarating thing imaginable. The Grace of God takes us from where we were and gives us a chance to be where we were not. When his grace becomes operative, he has really chosen to take those who are moral failures, regenerate them, reconcile them, recycle them and make them his children and take them to eternity. . . . Here's the second thing Paul then discovers that the Grace of God has become — a dynamic stimulus, '. . . not a barren gift. I have worked harder than any of the others. . . .' The point is, has the Grace of God become operative to such an extent that we have been stimulated to fulfill God's revealed will to us and to be obedient out of sheer gratitude? This leads us to the third thing: God in his Grace gives us the Holy Spirit. So the Grace of God is the daily enabling: '. . . the Grace of God with me.' How do we get around to being obedient? We exercise the gifts of the Spirit in the power of the Spirit. So it starts with the Grace of God which is the divine attitude, moves into the dynamic stimulus which is the Grace of God, and resolves itself in the gifts of the Spirit which is the daily enabling of the Grace of God.''

Stuart Briscoe
Sermon Notes

"God cast us as free men with minds and wills and brains. To help us when we had fallen into trouble, he sent his Son to show us how to live according to his will. Even more, he provided a means whereby we might make up for our mistakes even though our troubles seem insurmountable. In theological terms, these provisions are called Grace and Forgiveness. No man can live without both. If you are having trouble, that is probably the cause — a lack of these two necessities.''

Austin Pardue
The Single Eye
p. 77

"Through the centuries there has been the phenomenon known as the Christian experience or Christian spirituality. It has been marked by a dependence upon God's gracious activity and by a relationship to the person of Jesus. . . . There is the realization of divine grace as the power to implant ideals of conduct, to enable a striving beyond natural powers, and to resist the onslaught of temptation. There is a liberation of the person from fear and hesitancy into joyful trust and courage, compassion and hope. . . . The fruit of such experience is not autonomous, self-sufficient virtue but a realization of creativity mingled with a humble and child-like dependence.''*

Michael Ramsey
Jesus and the Living Past
pp. 51-52

———————

*See also 94:1, Kane.

New Illuminations:

On the Right Use of Money

"Jesus tells the story of 'The Dishonest Steward' or 'The Clever Rascal' to a mixed gathering of disciples and Pharisees. It is about a rich man who employed a steward to manage his estates. . . . He was robbing his employer; but, what was of more concern to him, he was creating a number of accomplices who, if his falsifying of the books were not discovered, would be in his power and maintain their benefactor in reasonable comfort. We must assume that the plan miscarried and that the owner made sure that his money was safe, for the story ends with the owner of the estate commending his steward for his astuteness. He was a rascal, but his master applauds him for being a clever rascal. There is no question of our Lord's condoning the steward's unscrupulous behavior. . . .

"John Calvin went right to the heart of this parable when he wrote: 'How stupid it is to want to interpret it in every detail! Christ simply meant that the children of this world are more diligent in their concern for their own fleeting interests than the sons of light for their eternal well being.' The steward is not being held up to us as a paragon of virtue — quite the contrary. He is recognized by his master and by Jesus as a crafty knave. But he is no fool. He is resourceful and refuses to accept defeat. These are good qualities in any man although in this case they are put to wrong use. . . .

"We have all known of business tycoons that have sacrificed everything that most ordinary people value in order to build up a fortune. Jesus' comment would mean that the church could do with more of this spirit, but directed into the channel of service for others and not for selfish ends. We are often told that as Christians we show up badly in zeal and enthusiasm compared with the energy and self-denial that communists display in promoting their godless cause. . . . Jesus summons us from the pursuit of self-interest and self-enrichment to follow him along the way which he has marked out for us, and which he tells us is the way to life in all its fullness."

William Neil
The Difficult Sayings of Jesus
pp. 79-81

"This story is well known for its difficulty of interpretation. Most commentators suggest that the follower of Christ should be as shrewd about his spiritual future as the rascally steward was about his own immediate security. Personally I do not feel satisfied with this view as it introduces a note of careful calculation for the future which is quite at variance with Christ's teaching elsewhere. . . .

"I am myself quite attracted by the suggestion of Professor C. C. Torrey who in his own translation makes the two difficult remarks in verses 8 and 9 into questions. If this interpretation is true then the parable is one of faithfulness, illustrating the fact that since even in worldly matters men can not 'get away with it' — how much more essential is faithfulness in spiritual matters. My translation then would read: 'Now, did the employer praise this rascally agent because he had been so careful for his own future? For the children of this world are considerably more shrewd in dealing with the people they live with than the children of light. And do you think I am recommending you to use the false means of money to make friends for yourselves, so that when it fails you, they could welcome you to houses fit for eternity? No, the man faithful in little things will be faithful in big things, and the man who cheats in little things will cheat in big things too. . . . You cannot serve God and the power of money at the same time.'

"But to be fair to the Greek that we possess, one cannot translate the statements by questions; and I have therefore tried to make the best of it by suggesting that our Lord says, in effect, that the Christian must 'outsmart' the 'smart' by turning money which has so many potentialities for evil into a spiritual opportunity. But this still leaves the following verse about faithfulness rather in the air."

J. B. Phillips
The Gospels
Appendix, p. 242

"In all the parables of Jesus, one must find the salient point, and they must by no means be interpreted as moral example-stories. This would certainly lead one up a blind alley.

"Sometimes when we read the parables of Jesus it may appear as if Christ has even concealed the salient point somewhat, as one must carefully search for it. Perhaps the Lord did this intentionally in order to make us really reflect upon the parables carefully and ponder them in our hearts and pray over them before we think we have understood them. . . . So we shall not linger too long over the portrait of the unjust steward; and above all we shall not see in him a model, but rather ask ourselves what in this story is the 'salient point' or the 'hidden figure.'

"For the man himself really does not occupy the center of the story at all. The real theme of the story is *money*, the leading role is played by 'unrighteous mammon.' What does this thing mean or, better, what does this power mean in the life of the person who wants to be obedient to God?

. . . The first thing we should note is that we should use money and possessions in order to make friends. What this means we shall see. The main thing at this point is to accept the statement that we should use this mammon. . . . Jesus tells us to take this dirty money right into our hand; he tells us to do something with it. Hence we positively should not flee from the world and become unrealistic in the name of our faith. In other words, the rightness of our conduct is determined not by *whether* we deal with unrighteous mammon but the *purpose* for which we use it. And this is precisely what is made clear for us in this parable of the steward. The steward with all his corruptness and cunning is intended to show us by means of a negative image what money is really for. . . .

"The point is that this man used money and possessions *for* something, they were not an end in themselves. If a purely materialistic child of the world like the dishonest steward can manage on *his* level to compel money to serve his ends and thus give it its relative importance, how much more — and at the same time how differently — should the children of light do this on *their* level! . . .

"Strange as this dishonest steward may be, one must still grant that he does not hang on to money; he does something with it. He has only a few days left. Soon he must separate from all the money he has in his charge. . . . And in this brief respite the dishonest steward lets the money fly. He bestows it upon people who need it, but by so doing he performs a work of mercy and makes friends. In any case he is above the money and is not a slave to it. He compels the money to perform a service. The money will one day forsake him, but those whom he has helped with it will remain faithful to him and take him in. This is what Jesus means by the words: 'Make friends for yourselves by means of unrighteous mammon; so that when it fails, they may receive you into the eternal habitations.' . . .

"What does this mean? Here again we must hear the words 'how much more' which appear so often in the parables of Jesus: How much more is this so for the children of light! How much more does this use of money for service, which the man in the parable practiced so dubiously, apply to you who should be using your money for service in the sight of God!* In other words it is being made perfectly clear to us that the day will come when we shall be stripped of all things in which we put our confidence here below. We shall stand before the throne of God in utter poverty. . . . And in that place, God will ask: 'Who can testify for you?' And then perhaps someone of the company of the redeemed will step forward, perhaps there may even be some who will cry out from the nethermost pit of hell and say: 'He once gave me his last penny. He once shared with me his last cigarette in prison. He once put me on my feet again when I was a refugee, even though it was hard on his meager resources' (cf. Luke 21:1-4).

"And then perhaps the devil, if he should still be there and be allowed to speak his piece, will angrily interrupt and say: 'Hear! Hear! It looks as if you could do business with this accursed mammon even in heaven. . . . Do you think you will get by with this before the master of heaven?' So says the devil.

"But then God will brush aside the accuser and say: 'I have heard what these have said in your behalf. I have heard that they want you to be with them in their eternal habitations. Blessed are you, my faithful child. You have made the unrighteous mammon righteous because you used it to feed the poor and hungry and to clothe the naked.* Enter into the joy of your master!'

"That's the way it is with the unrighteous mammon. . . . Doesn't the money in the offering plate and in the hat serve an altogether different master? And doesn't this hallow it and wash away the dirt that may have clung to it as it passed from the mint through all kinds of shady and honest transactions to the offering plate and finally to the eternal habitations? Is there not something like an 'alien righteousness' — a righteousness not its own? Let us, therefore, hallow the unrighteous mammon by the use we make of it. Let us not make of it a god or an idol but a servant."

Helmut Thielicke
The Waiting Father
pp. 94-96, 101-02

"Christian materialism,** which has been characteristic of this country, is actually closer to the position of the Pharisees that our Lord rebuked than is blatant atheistic materialism. For the Pharisees believed in God. They simply identified their own selfish interests with the service of God. They were trying to serve God and mammon at the same time. Our Lord pointed out that they had to choose between them. They refused to admit the necessity of that choice."

Ralph Milligan, ed.
All For the Love of God: A Holy Cross Omnibus
p. 172

"To give God second place would mean to give him no place. I am tempted to serve two lords and even to compromise God's position in my life with some one or something else. This is enough to deny him.*** Idols are not a phenomenon of the past era."

Peter Von Bremen
As Bread That Is Broken
p. 24

"Of all sins, that of denying God's covenant and throwing off one's allegiance to it is the most disastrous. And it

---

*See also 95:2, McKenzie.

*See also 84:1, Tugwell.
**See also 68:1, *University of Chicago Magazine*.
***See also 95:2, Neil.

is precisely this that is likely to result from worldly possessions because they are always liable to provoke a conflict of loyalties. . . . It is a very real question for all of us, how far we can expect to achieve worldly success of any kind at all without compromising our fidelity to God. There is a very fine and difficult decision between using the mammon of unrighteousness to win friends for ourselves who can usher us into eternal life and attempting to serve God and mammon.

"There is no room here for puritanism or fastidiousness. As Barnabas reminded us, it is not possible for us in this world to have completely 'clean hands.' The 'talent' we have to trade with is always going to be, to some extent, tainted; there is no currency other than the mammon of unrighteousness. . . . We must accept that there is a question mark hanging over all our undertakings in this world. In whatever way we are inserted into society, we are going to run the risk of serving mammon. Whatever we are trying to do in this world, to some extent we shall unavoidably find ourselves influenced by the prescriptions of the world.

Simon Tugwell
The Beatitudes: Soundings in Christian Traditions
pp. 18-19

"Mortification applies to created things the searching, if not the simple, test of whether they administer to or detract from our eternal purpose. Hence in detachment, the fruit of mortification, we own but we are not owned. We enjoy this passing world but without any possessiveness towards it. . . . Our Lord's own words on this whole matter are that, since we cannot possibly serve both God and mammon for any extended length of time (one will ultimately crowd the other out, for each has a growing edge, or contagious quality), it is wisdom to hold God in direct vision and mammon in peripheral vision rather than the other way around."*

Gale D. Webbe
The Night and Nothing
p. 22

---

*See also 95:2, Neil.

New Illuminations:

On the Storming of the Kingdom of God

"It is Matthew 11:12 which expresses in the clearest terms how Jesus understood John and his own mission, that strangely dark saying which has puzzled many up to the present time: 'From the days of John the Baptist until now the kingdom of heaven suffered violence and men of violence take it by force.'* Since the days of John the Baptist, therefore the kingdom of God is on the way, although it is still being held up and opposed. But its hour has struck, although in affliction and concealment. John is herewith raised above all the prophets before him. He is no longer the herald of the future only, but already belongs himself to the time in which the promise is *being* fulfilled. This constitutes his greatness, and yet at the same time through this he is overshadowed by Jesus himself in whose words and work the kingdom of God, hidden therein, has begun. Here lies, according to Jesus himself, the reason for the Christian tradition which gives to John only the role of the forerunner. From then on he signifies for the Christian Church, in terms of later Jewish apocalypticism, the returned Elijah who was to prepare the people of God for the coming Messiah. . . . The way to Christ and the kingdom of God did not merely at one time lead through John the Baptist, but it leads once and for all along that path of repentance shown by him. Faith in Jesus Christ is only there where the believer, for himself and within himself, lets the shift in the aeons take place in his own life."

Gunther Bornkamm
Jesus of Nazareth
p. 51

"The general tenor of the passage (Matthew 11:10-15) makes it clear that Jesus regarded the advent of John as the end of an epoch and the beginning of another. For him the long period of prophetic activity closed with John and from then something new was happening. The precise meaning of Matthew 11:12 is doubtful, and many interpretations have been suggested; the main difficulty is to find an exact Aramaic equivalent for the Greek words 'suffereth violence.' The Greek verb may be taken as a middle instead of a passive; in this case the meaning may be '. . . the Kingdom of Heaven exercises effective action,' the intention of the saying being to make a contrast between the prophetic period of announcement and the period of decisive action which had been ushered in by John the Baptist."

S. H. Hooke
The Kingdom of God
p. 21

"One of the most difficult of disputed passages is the so-called 'violence' sentence in Matthew 11:12 (Luke 16:16). . . . The meaning in Matthew depends upon the way in which we understand the sequence of the two parts. Is the second portion intended to explain the first (synonymous parallelism) or does it make a new assertion (synthetic parallelism)? Many exegetes accept the first view and interpret the second part in a bad sense, to wit, that since the days of John, attempts have been made to do violence to the kingdom of God; in other words violent men tried to rob men of it. . . . Linguistically, the sentence could be applied to men of good will, hungry for salvation: men who believe the gospel and harness all their energies seek the kingdom of God and nothing else since the days of John the Baptist. . . . The first portion would then refer not to *their* violence (the kingdom of heaven is taken by storm) but to the power within God's rule itself (it forces its way in). We would then have not a repetition of the same idea but a meaningful union of two statements belonging to the proclamation of the reign of God: God's rule makes its way with great force and keen enthusiasts lay hold on it, that is, want to share it. Jesus means that God's eschatological act has unloosed a storm for the man who hungers and thirsts for salvation. It is thus a cry of joy which recognizes that the period of waiting and hope (the era of the 'Law and the prophets') came to an end with John the Baptist. If this interpretation is accepted, Luke did not misunderstand the passage but intensified the note of joy. Every man strives to force his way into God's kingdom. This interpretation is definitely preferable. In either case the royal rule of God in this passage is a present, dynamic reality*. . . . It forces its way in with power and makes it possible for the violent to lay hold on it for their salvation. And the somewhat ambiguous addition 'since the days of John' (is this inclusive or exclusive?) fixes a starting point for this process and leaves no doubt that since then the rule of God presses forward and manifests its power 'until now.' And so the passage fits in with the statement of Jesus that the reign of God is at hand with himself but is not yet perfect and does not yet show itself in its glory."

Rudolf Schnackenburg
God's Rule and Kingdom
pp. 129-132

"The Baptist was stirred and so are we by 'what the Christ was doing' (Matthew 11:2 Goodspeed). The expression must have been significant for Matthew's first readers.

---

*See also 47:2, Nineham.

---

*See also 34:2, Kunkle.

Jesus was gone but there was this miraculous power which cured the sick and enabled the people to die for Christianity. . . . A new phase of evolution has begun. 'They are pressing into the realm of heaven: these eager souls are storming it!' (11:12 Moffat).''

Fritz Kunkel
Creation Continues
pp. 175-176

'' 'There was a large concourse of his disciples and great numbers of people from Jerusalem and Judea and the seaboard of Tyre and Sidon, who had come to listen to him and to be cured of their diseases. Those who were troubled with unclean spirits were cured; and everyone in the crowd was trying to touch him, because power went out from him and cured them all' (Luke 6:17-19).''

The Holy Bible
New English Translation

'' 'Amazement fell on them all and they said to one another: ''What is there in this man's words? He gives orders to the unclean spirits with authority and power, and out they go.'' So the news spread and he was the talk of the whole district' (Luke 4:36-37).''

The Holy Bible
New English Translation

''In God's pre-eternal Providence for man, we are meant to participate in his being, to be like unto him in all things. And we as Christians must never renounce our goal less we lose the inspiration to storm the kingdom of heaven.''

Archimandrite Sophrony
His Life is Mine
p. 21

New Illuminations

On Jesus' Fulfilling of the Law

Matthew 5:17-20   Luke 16:17

"Leaving the tribes encamped at the foot of the mountain Moses went up to receive for them a revelation, and he returned with what we call the Ten Commandments. He told these to the tribes, and they replied, 'All the words that Yahweh has spoken we will do.' In this way Abraham's seed entered into covenant with Abraham's God. The old thought of fellowship effected by sacrifice is here enriched by a new element: the fellowship of Yahweh with his people is conditional upon their keeping his law. It dealt not only with the relations of man to God, but also with those of man to man. . . .

"The giving of the primitive Law made evil appear primarily as *sin*, that is, as man's deliberate disobedience to a known command of God. And this at once puts the emphasis in human life on to the right use of free will. Long afterwards St. Paul discerned that the function of the Law was that 'sin might be shown to be sin.' He saw it as acting rather like a fomentation, drawing the all pervading sinfulness of human nature up to the surface where it could be recognized and dealt with. When sinful man had learnt by bitter experience his inability to keep the Law even when he would, then the time was ripe for God to act again.* In this way the Law was our schoolmaster to bring us to Christ (Galatians 3:24); and of that Law, ever increasing like a rolling snowball through the centuries, the Ten Words given to Moses were the nucleus. It was the possession of this unique moral Law, this connection of worship with conduct, that from Sinai onwards marked out the seed of Abraham as a people apart, slow as they were to recognize their separateness. . . .

"In so far as the Chosen People were faithful to the Ten Words, they had a right to Yahweh's care and protection, a claim upon him, founded in some sense on their own merit, which other peoples had not. . . . But as Ezekiel was beginning to see that, as Jeremiah had already suggested, the Mosaic covenant could never in itself bring in the glorious future. Somehow or other it had got to be superseded, and Yahweh must himself effect the redemption from sin which his people could not accomplish for themselves. The Law was beginning to fulfill its office of pedagogue to lead men to Christ."

Sister Penelope
The Wood
pp. 55-56, 80

"When we are facing the worst things and wrestling with the most secret bondages in our lives, the real menace by

---

*See also 117:1, Penelope.

no means lies only in the fact that our will is too weak to achieve our goal but rather that we cannot even *will* to do it with our whole heart. This is undoubtedly what Luther meant when he said that the Law may well point the way, but that it is far from being the strength in one's legs. Therefore the Law only makes us more miserable."

Helmut Thielicke
The Waiting Father
p. 184

"God began his work of personal rescue in the Man who was God in human form — God focused and scaled down to meet our human need. The work of making men whole was begun.

"Although the coming of the integrating principle into a dark and infected world began, so to speak, on the ground level, can we not begin to see that this is, without qualification, the only way in which God could restore wholeness to mankind? Every effort to impose wholeness by regulation from above must fail, partly because it is forever external to human nature itself; partly because it neither excites the love nor provides the power to overcome spiritual human poverty. St. Paul was right when he said the law 'was weak' (Romans 8:3). When it attempted to change human nature, it was not weak in one sense, in that it represented the eternal principles of human conduct. But it was completely powerless in practice because of its utter incapacity to change man's nature from within. . . .

"In Ephesians 2, St. Paul speaks with confidence, having observed the result of God's method through Christ. Into human life and at the human level, so to speak, he inserts his own life with its immeasurable potentialities for converting, redeeming, reconciling and bringing into harmony. . . .

"The religion of the Hebrews was a kind of contract, a *quid pro quo* performance, while Jesus' was the spontaneous outliving of unadulterated love. It must often have looked to them as though he was ready to drive a coach and six through the law and the prophets. But in fact he went far above and beyond any righteousness that the law could produce. When directly challenged, he declared that the whole of the prophet's message and the law's morality depended upon the two most important commandments, namely to love God with the whole of the personality and to love one's neighbor as oneself (Matthew 22:37-40). St. Paul, seeing the same truth in a slightly different way — and not, I think, ever quite able, despite his protestations to shake himself completely free from the law in which he was nurtured — declared, 'Love therefore is the fulfillment of the law' (Romans 13:10).''

J. B. Phillips
Making Men Whole
pp. 19, 30-31

"Jesus demanded an obedience to the law far more radical than its official teachers understood: an obedience going to the roots of motive as well as to outward action, and involving positive acts of goodness as well as the negative avoidance of certain evils.

"This meant that Jesus was bringing men and women into touch not just with the law, but with the God whose law it is, the God whose holiness requires total obedience to him, and whose compassion requires total compassion to others on any day of the week.

"It was a message about God and God's sovereignty. It, therefore, cut at the heart of the idea that just to keep the law is the way to spiritual security. It is idle for the rich young ruler to say, 'All this I have observed from my youth up.'* It is idle for the Pharisee in the parable to count upon fasting twice in the week and giving tithes of all he possessed, for righteousness is about God and about humility.

"The law cannot save. God, whose law it is, can save and does.''

Margaret Duggan, ed.
Through the Year with Michael Ramsey
p. 68

"Notice that in the picture in Romans 7:1-4 by which Paul illustrates our deliverance from the Law there is only one woman, while there are two husbands. . . . This picture is not drawn by me but by the apostle Paul. The first husband is the Law; the second husband is Christ; and you are the woman. . . . The Law makes demands and leaves us helpless to fulfil them; Christ makes demands, but he himself fulfils in us the very demands he makes. Little wonder that

*See also 95:1, Leslie.

the woman desires to be freed from the first husband that she may marry that other Man! But her only hope for release is through the death of her first husband, and he holds on to life most tenaciously. 'Till heaven and earth pass away, one jot and one tittle shall in no wise pass away from the law until all things be accomplished.' (Matthew 5:18)

"The Law is going to continue for all eternity. If the Law will never pass away, then how can I be united to Christ? There is one way out. If he will not die, I can die, and if I die, the marriage relationship is dissolved. . . . Now the vital question arises: 'How do I die?' And the preciousness of our Lord's work comes in just here: 'Ye also were made dead to the law through the body of Christ' (Romans 7:4). . . .

"Being united to him in death, I am united to him in resurrection also, and in the power of resurrection life, I bring fruit unto God. The risen life of the Lord in me empowers me for all the demands God's holiness makes upon me. The Law of God is not annulled; it is perfectly fulfilled, for the risen Lord now lives out his life in me, and his life is always pleasing to the Father.''

Watchman Nee
The Normal Christian Life
pp. 149-153

"If there could have been a Law which gave men spiritual life, then that Law would have produced righteousness. . . . But as things are, the Scripture has all men 'imprisoned,' because they are found guilty by the Law, that to men in such condition the Promise might come to release all who believe in Jesus Christ.

"Before the coming of faith, we were all imprisoned under the power of the Law, with our only hope of deliverance the faith that was to be shown to us. Or, to change the metaphor, the Law was like a strict governess in charge of us until we went to the school of Christ and learned to be justified by faith in him. Once we had that faith we were completely free from the governess's authority. For now that you have faith in Christ you are all Sons of God.''

J. B. Phillips
The New Testament
Galatians 3:21b-26

New Illuminations:

On the Rich Man and Lazarus

Luke 16:19-31

"In this story everything depends upon finding the key that unlocks it. And this key is none other than the speech of Abraham in which he says that a man must hear Moses and the prophets if he is to come to terms with his eternal destiny. It all depends upon one's identifying oneself with one of the five brothers and taking the right attitude toward the Word of God. This is the point of the story. . . .

" 'There was a rich man. . . . Just imagine that here is a case where nothing can be said except that he feasted sumptuously every day and that he possessed a magnificent wardrobe. . . . He cannot look at Lazarus' sores, otherwise his own well-bathed and perfumed body would begin to itch in his purple and fine linen. Therefore, keep Lazarus at the back door so that he won't be seen. . . . And there is still another thing that he evades and that is God. He has every reason to believe that he has lost his own soul, so he evades him to whom he is answerable for his soul (Luke 12:5). And the man who reminds him of this responsibility, Lazarus, his neighbor, he relegates to the back door. . . . The rich man dies. And when he thus quite literally 'comes to an end' he sees that he is absolutely separated from God.* Now it becomes apparent how dreadfully different are the standards by which God measures our life. How foolish was our own assessment of ourselves and how foolishly we allowed ourselves to be assessed by others. . . .

"Then we come to the poor man. His name is Lazarus which means 'God is my helper.' Externally this is about all that can be said about him. It was not riches that brought the rich man to hell nor was it poverty that brought the poor man to heaven. . . . Lazarus had this one thing in life, that he could count on the mercy of God. But this one thing accompanied him across the chasm and it never forsook him. He now rests in the eternal fellowship of his God. . . . Lazarus once waited for the crumb of bread from the rich man's table; now the rich man waits for the drop at the end of Lazarus' finger. . . . And here in the extremity of his need the rich man feels, for the first time something like love. He is thinking of his five brothers and with horror he sees them going on living their lives, in innocence, stumbling along without the slightest notion that in this life, nothing less than our eternal destiny is at stake.

"We have only the Word, the Word made flesh and crucified, which came to us in one who was as poor and despised as his brother Lazarus.** For he really wanted to be his brother. That's why he renounced all royal pomp and show. That's why he had to risk the effect of ambiguity and forgo the demonstration of his power. He wanted to be the brother of the poorest and in this way show them his love. And therefore, like his brother Lazarus, Jesus too lay at the world's back door when he was born in a stable in Bethlehem.* No one would have believed his love and brotherliness if he had come in the splendor with which human imagination is accustomed to clothe the image of God. . . . Accordingly there remains to us, the five brothers, nothing but 'Moses and the prophets' and all that they have to say about this Jesus. He who does not hear *these* and is not saved *here* cannot be helped by the messengers from the dead (2 Timothy 3:16)."

Helmut Thielicke
The Waiting Father
pp. 42-50

"Timothy's spiritual roots were deep in '. . . the sacred writings which are able to instruct you for salvation' (2 Timothy 3:15). *The sacred writings* here mean the Old Testament, the Bible of the early church. Timothy may have read it first with purely Jewish eyes; but after conversion, he must have found in due course 'Christ in all the scriptures.'

" 'Instruct for salvation' contains a dual idea. The Scriptures will instruct a man with a view to his salvation. The thought here is to salvation accepted, or conversion. But the Scriptures will also continue to instruct him. They show a seeker what he must do in order to be saved. They show him further how he is to enjoy salvation here and now, how he is to behave in accordance with his salvation and what he is to expect in heaven."

Ronald A. Ward
1 and 2 Timothy and Titus
pp. 198-199

"There has always been room for wealthy and successful believers in the church. But they need to heed the warning that their very salvation depends upon their generosity to the genuinely poor. Our salvation depends on our being in effective fraternity with society's rejects, however such fraternity is expressed.**

"At the same time, however important it is not to spiritualize this principle out of existence, it is equally important not just to turn it into merely this — world concern to identify ourselves with any particular social, economic, or

---

*See also 85:2, St. Teresa of Avila.
**See also 24:4, Tolstoy.

*See also 5:3, Father Andrew
**See also 81:2, Thielicke.

political group. The division into 'rich' and 'poor' from the point of view of God's kingdom cannot be that simply translated into mundane categories. All of us are to some extent worldly successes, and all of us to some extent are worldly rejects, if only because the world has no universally agreed criteria of acceptance or rejection."

Simon Tugwell
The Beatitudes: Soundings in Christian Traditions
pp. 19-20

"Reading, thinking, and praying are so interwoven that thinking may not be had unless reading or hearing comes first. It is the same for all: clergy read books and the man in the street 'reads' the clergy when he hears them preach the word of God. Beginners, and proficients, cannot pray unless they think first.

"Prove it: God's word, written or spoken, can be likened to a mirror. . . . Just as you cannot see or know that there is a dirty mark on your actual face without the aid of a mirror, or somebody telling you, so spiritually, it is impossible for a soul blinded by his frequent sins to see the dirty mark in his conscience, without reading or hearing God's word.

It follows that if a man sees where the dirty mark is on his face — true spiritually as well as literally — then, and not till then, he runs off to the well to wash himself. If the dirty mark is deliberate sin, the 'well' is the Holy Church, and the 'water' confession, and all that goes with it. If it is sin deeply rooted and productive of evil impulses, then the 'well' is all-merciful God, and the 'water' prayer, and all that involves. Thus we see that beginners and proficients cannot think unless they read or hear first, and they cannot pray without prior thinking."

Clifton Wolters, trans.
The Cloud of Unknowing
pp. 102-103

New Illuminations:

On Hell

"Across the appalling distance the rich man sees the transfiguration of Lazarus. To see this is really what hell is. For to be in hell simply means to be utterly separated from God, to be forced to see the glory of God and have no access to it. The opposite of the peace of God, and thus the fulfillment of life, is not the silence of extinction, but the voice from the depths: 'I am the door forever locked, the road that leads nowhere, the everlasting dark. . . .' And when this parable talks about heaven and hell it is not concerned with the geography of the hereafter. What would that matter to us? Why should we be concerned about the molten core of the earth where some have thought they could locate the inferno."

Helmut Thielicke
The Waiting Father
pp. 48, 49

"It seems quite clear that in most parts of the Old Testament there is little or no belief in a future life, certainly no belief that is of any religious importance. The word translated 'hell' means simply 'the land of the dead,' the state of all the dead, good and bad alike, *Sheol.* . . . behind this one can discern a conception not specifically Jewish but common to many ancient religions. The Greek Hades is the most familiar example to modern people. Hades is neither Heaven nor Hell; it is almost nothing. I am speaking of the popular beliefs; of course philosophers like Plato have a vivid and positive doctrine of immortality. . . . But in real Pagan belief, Hades was hardly worth talking about; a world of shadows, of decay. How the Greeks felt about it in Homer's time is startlingly shown at the beginning of the Iliad where he says of men killed in battle that 'their souls' went to Hades but 'the men themselves' were devoured by dogs and carrion birds. It is the body, even the dead body which is the man himself, the ghost is only a sort of reflection or echo. . . .

"Such a conception, vague and marginal even in Paganism, becomes more so in Judaism. Sheol is even dimmer, further in the background, than Hades. It is a thousand miles away from the center of Jewish religion; especially in the Psalms. They speak of Sheol (or 'hell' or 'the pit') very much as a man speaks of 'death' or 'the grave,' who has no belief in any future state whatsoever — a man to whom the dead are simply dead, nothing, and there's no more to be said (Psalms 89:46; 39:6; 49:10, 19; and 30:10). . . . Elsewhere, of course, it sounds as if the poet were praying for the 'salvation of his soul' in the Christian sense. Almost certainly he is not. 'Thou hast brought my soul out of hell'

means 'you have saved me from death.' '. . . the pains of hell gat hold upon me' means as we should say, 'I was at death's door.' . . .

"As we all know from our New Testaments, Judaism had greatly changed in this respect by our Lord's time. The Sadducees held to the old view. The Pharisees and many more believed in the life to come. . . . It is surely, therefore, very possible that when God began to reveal himself to men, to show them that he and nothing else is their true goal and the satisfaction of their needs, it may have been absolutely necessary that this revelation should not begin with any hint of future Beatitude or Perdition. These are not the right points to begin at. An effective belief in them coming too soon may even render almost impossible the development of the appetite for God; personal hopes and fears, too obviously exciting, have got in first. Later when men have learned to desire and adore God, it is another matter and it is by that door that a truly religious hope of Heaven and fear of Hell can enter as corollaries to a faith already centered upon God, not as things of an independent or intrinsic weight. It is even arguable that the moment 'Heaven' ceases to mean union with God and 'Hell' to mean separation from him, the belief in either is a mischievous superstition. . . . As for Hell I have often been struck, in reading the 'hell-fire sermons' of our older divines, at the desperate effort they make to render these horrors vivid to their hearers, at their astonishment that men, with such horrors hanging over them, can live as carelessly as they do. But perhaps it is not really astonishing. Perhaps the divines are appealing on the level of self-centered prudence and self-centered terror, to a belief which, on that level, cannot really exist as a permanent influence on conduct."

C. S. Lewis
Reflections on the Psalms
pp. 36-42

"In the examples of the erring hand or foot (Mark 9:43-47), Jesus is obviously not talking about self-mutilation but about the need for self discipline, nor is he speaking of occasional lapses. He is speaking of the corruption of mind or will into which we inevitably drift unless we take steps to check our besetting sins, whatever they may be. He tells us in forthright terms that our choice is between self-discipline, which fits us for eternal life, or going to 'hell and the unquenchable fire.' These are words that cannot be shrugged aside although they certainly do not imply the eternal torments of the damned which figured prominently in Christian literature and art in past times, or in the fire and brimstone preaching of Victorian evangelists. . . .

"There are two Greek words which are usually translated as hell in English. . . . Here it is Gehenna, which literally means the Valley of Hinnom just outside Jerusalem. In Old Testament times this had been the scene of the abhorrent practice of child sacrifice under some of Israel's godless kings. Gehenna was thus regarded with loathing and was used eventually as the dumping ground for the sewage and refuse of the city. It was, therefore, a place of crawling worms and maggots, and fires burned continually to destroy the garbage. So the name Gehenna came to be used as a symbol of punishment. Isaiah (66:24) had already spoken of the 'undying worm and the unquenchable fire' as a metaphor for the destruction of rebels against God. It is in this sense and not in the sense of physical torment that Jesus uses these words in Mark 9:43 and 48. . . .

"But let us beware of thinking that we have taken the sting out of this saying by describing it in terms of metaphor and hyperbole. Jesus is in deadly earnest. He is talking of nothing less than the danger of being ultimately separated from God."

William Neil
The Difficult Sayings of Jesus
pp. 44-45

"When it comes to a discussion of hell, we know very little. It may be that there is such a place, or a state of complete disintegration, for those who deliberately defy our Lord if they know better within their hearts. Generally, hell is that state or condition whereby we are separated from God and all that is good. Most of us have had moments of such an experience here upon earth. It should not be hard to compare some of our awful hours of remorse, disgrace, and pangs of conscience, resultant from unrepentant and unforgiven sin, with the possibilities of hell. A real state of hell undoubtedly exists, although it must be far from the old naive pictures of pitchforks, furnaces, and physical tortures. Suffering will be nonetheless real but of a different nature."

Austin Pardue
He Lives
p. 36

"We must picture Hell as a state where everyone is perpetually concerned about his own dignity and advancement, where everyone has a grievance and where everyone lives the deadly serious passions of envy, self-importance, and resentment. . . . The greatest evil is not now done in those sordid 'dens of crime' that Dickens loved to paint. It is not done even in labor camps and concentration camps. In those we see its final result. But it is conceived and ordered (moved, seconded, carried, and minuted) in clean, carpeted, warmed and well-lighted offices, by quiet men with white collars and cut fingernails and smooth-shaven cheeks who do not need to raise their voices. Hence, naturally enough, my symbol for Hell is something like the bureaucracy of a police state or the offices of a thoroughly nasty business concern."

C. S. Lewis
Screwtape Letters
pp. xxiv-xxv

"And now, sisters, let us consider the condition of those who are in hell. They are not resigned, as this soul is, nor have they this contentment and delight which God gives it. They cannot see that their suffering is doing them any good, yet they keep suffering more and more. . . . These unhappy souls know that they will have to suffer this way forever and ever: what then will become of them? . . . I assure you it is impossible to explain to anyone who has not experienced it what a grievous thing is the soul's suffering and how different it is from the suffering of the body.* The Lord will have us understand this so that we will be more conscious of how much we owe him for bringing us to a state in which by his mercy we may hope that he will set us free and forgive us our sins."

St. Teresa of Avila
Interior Castle
p. 200

"You have told me, O God, to believe in hell. But you have forbidden me to hold with absolute certainty that any single man has been damned. I shall, therefore, make no attempt to consider the damned here nor even to discover — by whatsoever means — whether there are any. I shall accept the existence of hell on your word, as a structural element in the universe, and I shall pray and meditate until that awe-inspiring thing appears to me as a strengthening and even blessed complement to the vision of your omnipresence which you have opened out to me. . . .

"The existence of hell, then does not destroy anything nor does not spoil anything in the divine *milieu* whose progress all around me I have followed with delight. I can even feel, moreover, that it effects something great and new there. It adds an accent, a gravity, a contrast, a depth which would not exist without it. The peak can only be measured from the abyss which it crowns. . . .

"O Jesus, closing my eyes to what my human weakness can not as yet understand and therefore cannot bear — that is to say to the reality of the damned — I desire to at least make the ever present threat of damnation a part of my habitual and practical vision of the world, not in order to fear you, but in order to be more intensely yours."

Teilhard de Chardin
The Divine Milieu
pp. 147-149

*See also 84:1, Thielicke.

"It is the deliberate choosing to remain in illusion and to see God and the universe as hostile to one's ego that is of the very essence of Hell. The dreadful moods when we hug our hatred and misery and are too proud to let them go are foretastes in time of what Hell eternally is. So long as we are in time and space, we can still, by God's grace and our own wills assenting, repent of Hell and come out of it. But if we carry that determination and that choice through the gates of death into the state in which there is literally no time, what then? Death, which was the bitter penalty of man's knowledge of evil, is also man's privilege and opportunity. . . . In knowing evil, man had to know death as a crisis — the sharp sundering of mortal and immortal and in that crisis he sees his choice between reality and illusion.

"But if, seeing God, the soul rejects him in hatred and horror, then there is nothing more that God can do for it. God, who has toiled to win it for himself, and borne for its sake to know death, and suffer the shame of sin, and set his feet in Hell will nevertheless, if it insists, give it what it desires. The people who think that if God were truly nice and kind he would let us have everything we fancy, are really demanding that he should give us freehold of Hell. And if that is our deliberate and final choice, if with our whole selves we are determined to have nothing but self, he will, in the end, say, 'Take it.' "

> Rosamond Sprague, ed.
> *A Matter of Eternity:*
> *Selections from the Writings of Dorothy Sayers*
> pp. 84-85

"It would be hard to stress too much the unique place of Man's will for it stands as Lewis says at the very frontier, that place where man meets God:

There are only two kinds of people in the end: those who say to God, "Thy will be done," and those to whom God says, the end, "Thy will be done." All that are in Hell, choose it. Without that self-choice there could be no Hell. No soul that seriously and constantly desires joy will ever miss it. Those who seek find. To those who knock it is opened (Luke 11:9).'* The Great Divorce, pp. 72-3.

Lewis says of the damned soul that there is always something it prefers to joy, and that it wills to choose it, though it gain all the illusions of Hell and lose the utter reality of Heaven."

> Leanne Payne
> *Real Presence:*
> *The Holy Spirit in the Works of C. S. Lewis*
> pp. 89-90

---

*See also 60:1, Bornkamm.

New Illuminations:

213

On the Particular Judgment

"The life of even the most godless man is different from hell in two important respects. First, here on earth the godless man is able to hide from himself his true condition. . . . What is here no more than a slight ticking sound in our conscience suddenly becomes the trumpet tone of judgment which can no longer be ignored. Lazarus is permitted to see what he believed, but the rich man is compelled to see what he did not believe. Second, inevitably comes the time when all the decisions have been made. Here God is calling us and we are the ones to speak. But one day God will open the books and he will be the one to speak. . . .

"The mercy of God is boundless, yes; but it is not offered indefinitely. Here we are still living by the grace of God and the merit of Christ. We still have a reprieve, a season of grace. We still have time to live and turn back home. But one day comes — finality, period. . . . The hour of the waiting, expectant mercy of God has run out. The 'acceptable time' is past. Now there is only the yawning chasm that none can pass over. . . . It means that this hour of my life is not determined by the fact that it contains sixty minutes but by the fact that it is charged and loaded by all the gravity of eternity, and that sometime it will run out. . . .

"So the fact is that high and awful gravity hovers over this story, which at first one may read as only a colorful tale. Here the question is the ultimate limits of our life and the ultimate limits of the patience of God."

Helmut Thielicke
The Waiting Father
pp. 48-49, 51

"Of course, the summons to penance is part of the teaching of Jesus, and his warnings of judgment and woes are connected with it. But in the first place he brings out the divine mercy and to all without exception. . . . God's mercy comes first, unparalleled in generosity and forgiveness. His wrath and judgment enter into force only when the grace received has been despised. . . . With Jesus, weal and woe are more than they are with the prophets. He proclaims salvation as already present and operative though not yet fully and perfectly realized. It could be said that the present is the hour of salvation because the gospel is proclaimed and divine mercy draws near to men through the action of Jesus."

Rudolf Schnackenburg
God's Rule and Kingdom
pp. 88-90

"Christian artists have let their imaginations run riot in depicting a last judgment at the end of time with rewards and punishments handed out in accordance with our achievements or failures. The Fourth Gospel points us to a deeper interpretation of the mind of Jesus. Those who heed the teaching of Jesus and put their trust in God are judging themselves now by their response to Christ's words (John 5:24). They do not, therefore, come up for the last Judgment at the end of time or even when they die. We have a choice here and now between following a way of life, or the way of death. If we choose the way of life, the way of obedience to Christ, the way of faith in God, we have already died to our past failures and are now alive in Christ, which is life eternal. . . . God has not destined us to the terrors of judgment, but to the full attainment of salvation through our Lord Jesus Christ."

William Neil
The Difficult Sayings of Jesus
p. 96

"It is the plain teaching of history that the Resurrection of man will precede the judgment — 'At whose (that is, Christ's) Coming all men shall rise again with their bodies and shall give account for their works.' They will be judged in their final body for what they have made of themselves, or let God make of them, in the earthly one. Thus the four things, the Second Coming, the Resurrection, the Judgment,* and the Everlasting Life, all hang together; you cannot have one without the other three. . . .

"The language about the Resurrection of believers is paradoxical. Those who are in Christ already share his risen life, yet look to be raised hereafter. But here again there is no real confusion; the paradox of the mystical and the literal Resurrection is only that of the potential consummation and the actual. And whatever else may be obscure, it is quite clear that the Resurrection will be general. Man will rise, Man as an entity, the human *genea* will be brought by Christ at his Second Coming to its final form; and in — perhaps we might say *by* — that form it will be judged. . . . 'For this is the will of my Father that *every one* that beholdeth the Son and believeth in him should have eternal life, and I shall raise *him* up at the Last Day' (John 6:40).

"After the Resurrection, Judgment. Here the same paradox obtains; for the Judgment, like the Kingdom of God and the Resurrection of believers appears in the New Testament as present as well as future. But the relation of the

---

*See also 65:3, Bornkamm.

two is clear. The final Judgment will reveal the results of the process of Judgment, of sifting and sorting, which Christ initiated when he came into the world, and will conclude it. What do the Scriptures tell us of that august, supreme event?

". . . The Judgment of Man will be the judgment of individual men; and the criterion will be each man's personal reaction to and treatment of the Person of the Judge. Our Lord's own teaching puts this in two ways. There is the conscious, direct encounter, as in the passage quoted above; beholding him challenges men to faith in him, which surely is to love him. There is also the indirect encounter with the Christ in other men, as set forth in the tremendous picture of the separation of the sheep and the goats. Both come to the same thing. It is love that matters; and on love and by love's Self, who bears our nature and has travelled by our road, will Man and men, be judged in the revealing light of the Last Day."

Sister Penelope
The Coming
pp. 46-48

"As the soul passes out of the flesh, it sees God and sees its own sin. The crisis and confrontation are technically known as the Particular Judgment. If in the very moment of that crisis the true self is still alive, however feeble; if deep down beneath all perversities of self-will, the absolute will is still toward God's reality, and the soul can find it within itself, even at the last moment to accept Judgment — to fling away the whole miserable illusion and fling itself upon truth — then it is safe. . . . There is no power in this world nor the next which can keep a soul from God, if God is what it really desires. . . . It is of the essence of heaven, and hell, that one must abide forever with what one has chosen."

Rosamond Sprague, ed.
A Matter of Eternity:
Selections from the Writings of Dorothy Sayers
pp. 84-85

"This judgment of death is final, compelling and inescapable. It contains some of those elements of our Lord's teaching of the Kingdom which have not found fulfilment in the present judgment of the Holy Spirit (John 16:8-10). But there are further factors which are still without expression. When all is said and done this particular judgment is, so to speak, a private affair. The individual stands before God and is judged and judges himself (1 Corinthians 3:10-15). The present continuing judgment of the Holy Spirit demands and points ahead to the particular judgment of death when the soul will stand alone before its Maker, delivered from perplexity, freed from circumstance, ready for the cleansing and redemption of the undeflected blazing light

of the moral judgment of God, holy, righteous and loving. But unless we keep in mind the present judgment of the Spirit, the particular judgment of death, if we think of it at all, will be seen not as the eventually gracious completion of our present experience of judgment, but as a tyrannical punishment of our human weakness, our inevitable failures in the face of tremendous odds, of, in short, our humanity itself."

Ralph Milligan, ed.
All For the Love of God: A Holy Cross Omnibus
pp. 161-163

" 'Any man who builds on the Foundation using as his material gold, silver, precious stones, wood, hay, or stubble, must know that each man's work will one day be shown for what it is. The Day will show it plainly enough, for the Day will arise in a blaze of fire, and that fire will prove the nature of each man's work. If the work that a man has built upon the Foundation will stand this test, he will be rewarded. But if a man's work be destroyed under the test, he loses it all. He personally will be safe, though rather like a man rescued from a fire'."*

The Holy Bible
Phillips Translation
1 Corinthians 3:12-15

"Paul describes his ministry and the responsibility of all who follow him as they build upon Christ, the unique foundation. Succeeding preachers and disciples must take care how they build on this foundation. When Christ returns as victorious judge, it is to test the quality of various building materials. Fire is the customary Biblical metaphor describing the might and majesty of divine judgment. The fire tests the work, destroying what is of poor quality and perishable. A wage will be paid only for good, durable work. The man whose work will not endure the searching test of judgment will suffer a loss. Like one escaping from a burning house, he will be saved, but his work and his reward will be lost. . . . The metaphor suggests an expiatory punishment — which is not damnation — for faults that, although not excluding salvation, merit punishment."

Richard Kugelman
Jerome Biblical Commentary
51:23

"A fundamental motif which expresses the idea of a reward is the expectation of the divine judgment

---

*See also 16:1, Underhill.

(1 Corinthians 3:14). With all his decisions, his thoughts and deeds, man moves toward the everlasting decision of God. The things which for us are the past, and which we consider finished are before God eternally present — even the most humble deed, a cup of water given even to the smallest (Matthew 10:42). This expectation gives to all we have done and left undone its importance for life and for death. The verdict of the coming God alone decides concerning our life and actions — how can we then speak of any value that may be attached to the deed itself? This is the fundamental reality attached toward which man moves whether he knows it or not, whether he believes it or not. How pompous and lamentable is the earthly life of the rich man at whose door Lazarus lay when seen in the light of eternity; and how temporary and light was the tribulation which Lazarus had to bear. . . . Thus the idea of a reward is an inalienable part of the last judgment. It places man as an individual before the heavenly judge, an expression of the abiding relevance of his temporary earthly life to the eternal decision of God.''

Gunther Bornkamm
Jesus of Nazareth
pp. 139-140

''The history of the Kingdom of God is, directly, one of a reunion. The total divine *milieu* is one of incorporation of every elected spirit in Jesus Christ. But to say elect is to imply a choice or selection. It is precisely because Jesus is the one who unites that he is also the one who separates and judges. The Gospel speaks of the good seed, the sheep, the right hand of the Son of Man, the wedding feast and the fire that kindles joy. But, there are also the tares, the goats, the left hand of the judge, the closed door and the outer darkness. And at the antipodes of the fire that unites in love, there is the fire that destroys in isolation.* The whole process out of which the New Earth is gradually born is an aggregation underlaid by a segregation.''

Teilhard de Chardin
The Divine Milieu
p. 146

''Is heaven for all? We must not bypass this rather difficult question. Can we be sure that everyone is going to rejoice in the life to come? . . . I cannot find in the New Testament any clear statement that the life to come is a kind of second chance, though our growth in sincerity of love may well be in that life both a purification and enrichment. This life, it appears, is our chance, and that is why *this* life is so important, why justice, here and now, and love and

concern are so important. God will estimate us according to our opportunities (Luke 12:48; Mark 4:24-25). Some of those who have had smaller opportunities may be far ahead of us — a Moslem, if he is true to the light he has received. The same may be applied to an atheist if he is open and truly seeking for reality. It is, of course, through Christ that all such people are being brought to final joy because, although they may not recognize him, it is Christ who seeks to enlighten and guide every man. Jesus tells us that some dishonest tax collectors and prostitutes will be received into the Kingdom of Heaven before many religious people. . . .

''Judgment is much nearer than we think. In fact it has begun. We do not have to wait for death or for some judgment after death because we are judging ourselves now (John 3:18)*. . . . What comes in the future will only disclose what we have already become. The New Testament makes that quite clear.''

Mark Gibbard
Apprentices in Love
pp. 82-83

''The penitent thief behaves entirely differently from the thankless thief. The astonishing Third Man on the middle Cross has touched something deep and uncorrupt just by being there. He does not make a claim. He simply asks to be remembered. What an answer he got! 'Today thou shalt be with me in Paradise.' . . . . And that is the promise of the Crucified to all that die penitently even at the end of a shipwrecked life.**

''. . . This incident coupled with our Lord's promise is the charter for death-bed conversions. The problem is not God's willingness to forgive a man who repents in his last hour but man's capacity for turning to God in his last hour when the whole bent of his life has been turning away from God in every other hour. Eternal salvation does not depend on having lived the good life. Even the good cannot earn it or deserve it (Luke 17:10). Like the penitent thief, they too can only put in their request for mercy and remembrance. . . . In his death Jesus 'opened the Kingdom of Heaven to all believers.' He loved the impenitent thief as much as the other. He did not condemn him, but the impenitent thief could not respond to his love. The act of God in Christ's Cross is the act of love too. In one of his meditations, Saint John of the Cross heard these words from the lips of Jesus: 'When I was hanging on the Cross I thought of you and shed one drop of blood for you.' ''

Douglas Webster
In Debt to Christ
pp. 41-42

---

*See also 11:1, Bornkamm.

*See also 46:2, Pike.
**See also 117:2, Dix.

"The subject of judgment is one that our age does not say much about. We live in an era of wide-spread sin where judgment is hardly a welcome idea. Much of the philosophy of today suggests that you can 'get away' with much if you are clever and, therefore, the thought of a day of reckoning is distasteful. The Creeds teach that our Lord himself is to be the one who judges us. From him 'no secrets are hid.' He sees right through us at all times. We must learn that we cannot break the rules of the universe and evade the cost. The doctrine of judgment is the only rational approach to the universe and to life. . . . The important thing to remember about the judgment is that it will be based on the loving kindness and mercy of our Lord. Certainly no one can look at the spirit of his life and believe he insists upon such distasteful doctrines as eternal damnation for unbaptized babies."

Austin Pardue
He Lives
pp. 34-35

New Illuminations:

On Stumbling-Block or Stepping-Stone

Matthew 5:29-30; 18:6-9   Mark 9:42-47   Luke 17:1-2

"It is inevitable that temptations to sin, (stumbling blocks) should come, but woe to him through whom they come."

New American Standard Bible
Luke 17:1

"Let us never put a block in the path of a brother to trip him up. . . . It is not right to do anything that makes your brother fall. (Romans 14:13b, 21b)"

Frank Laubach
The Inspired Letters
p. 39

" 'To each is given a bag of tools,
An hour-glass and a book of rules;
And each must build ere his work be done,
A stumbling-block or a stepping-stone'

Our bag of tools, — our body with all its various powers; the hour glass — time; the book of rules — our Bible; the stumbling-block — that which will hinder others; the stepping-stone — that which will help them nearer heaven. We cannot build both stumbling-block and stepping-stone. We must choose which we will build. . . . Every true, loving, faithful thought or word or deed helps to build the stepping-stone (cf. Matthew 25:34-40). Every untrue, unloving, unfaithful thought, word or deed helps to build the stumbling-block over which others will fall (Matthew 25:41-46). God help us all to be stepping-stones."

Amy Carmichael
Thou Givest . . . They Gather
pp. 120-121

"What is more important is not that we are sorting ourselves out, but that we are influencing the people we meet, even if we meet them only for a short time. We are part of their environment. Each person we meet, we move, even if only a millimeter. We either encourage them to come nearer to fullness of life, or else we repel them from it. That is why if we are hard and unimaginative, lacking in real listening and understanding, we are pushing people away, instead of drawing them nearer, to reality, to love, and to God.

"We ought to be like windows flung wide open, with the sunshine pouring into other people. But in fact we easily become closed; shut in on ourselves. The windows are not only closed; they are often coated over by some long standing insensitivity within us or else by the equivalent of an all pervasive industrial smut: a daily accumulation of little inhumanities, a lack of love in action. We know ourselves sufficiently to realize we cannot clean ourselves up. We cannot really open ourselves. Only love can unloose locked-up love. God's love came and comes to us, in Jesus, to do just that for us. Are we ready to be loved? Facing that question is a bit demanding."

Mark Gibbard
Apprentices in Love
pp. 83-84

"It is in connection with the sin of the unforgiving spirit that Jesus' teaching about 'offenses' should be mentioned. The offending hand, foot, or eye which are to be cut off and plucked out if they hinder entry into the Kingdom, are probably offending practices which cannot be retained if Kingdom membership is desired."

John Stott
Men with a Message
p. 20

"Jesus was a master of hyperbole, and that by overstatement and exaggeration he tried to startle his hearers and make them think*. . . . First of all Jesus is not talking about self-mutilation at all, but about the need for self-discipline. Our hand can be our undoing if it leads us to rifle a till or forge a check. Obviously the hand is merely the outward agent, prompted by a dishonest intention. It is this that must be checked. Similarly our feet can be our undoing if they take us into places where we have no business to be. But again our feet merely do what we want them to do. . . . Here Jesus is speaking as the Surgeon, calling on us to cut out any evil tendencies that threaten our lives. This means rigorous self-discipline and constant vigilance over our wayward thoughts. Self-discipline is not a fashionable idea in our day. . . . We badly need a recovery of self-discipline

---

*See also 25:2, Neil.

218

among our teenagers, but we cannot expect our pleas to fall on responsive ears unless we show clearly that we are serious about disciplining ourselves.''

William Neil
The Difficult Sayings of Jesus
pp. 43-44

''Fine flour is flour which has been milled to the uttermost. The natural man abominates the mill. Our holy Saviour was fine flour from the beginning, and yet in an awful sense, he 'went through the mill' of hard human experience: he suffered, being tempted; he was crushed. I have been reading about friction. The microscope shows the surface of, for example, wood, even planed wood, to be covered with what looks like prickies. Two surfaces meet; there is friction. Friction is caused by the presence of prickles. To each Christian soul, there comes the choice: will you at all costs be made into fine flour, or are you content to be covered with prickles to the end? It is self in one form or another that makes us prickly. We come up against difficult things or people and there is friction of the spirit. It was not so with our dear Lord. The meekness and gentleness of Christ, the yieldingness, the self-forgetfulness show the fine flour in a very lovely way. So let us never try to slip out from between the millstones. Let us trust and not be afraid. As we think of how very unlike fine flour we are, these words come as strong consolation: 'The Lord will perfect that which concerns me' (Psalm 138:8).''

Amy Carmichael
Thou Givest . . . They Gather
pp. 106-107

New Illuminations:

On Forgiveness II: Seventy Times Seven

Matthew 18:12-15, 21-22   Mark 11:25   Luke 17:3-4

"The parable of the lost sheep as found in Matthew 18:12f is concerned with the theme of the discourse — that nothing belonging to the Kingdom, however insignificant must be lost. This leads up to the saying about how to deal with a breach in the relationship between two members of the Kingdom, the object of such dealing being to see that the Kingdom does not suffer loss — 'thou hast gained thy brother' (Matthew 18:15). It is the work of the principle of forgiveness which is in question. . . . Peter takes the occasion to raise the question of the limit of forgiveness. He wishes to reduce the business of forgiveness to a matter of bookkeeping, to obtain from Jesus a ruling as to how far forgiveness must go. . . . Jesus' reply to Peter's suggestion that seven times would seem to be a suitable and even generous limit to assign to the operation of forgiveness must have been startling to the disciples, as it was intended to be. He says, 'I say not unto thee seven times, but until seventy times seven.' There is no legal bookkeeping here; long before such a paradoxical limit could be reached the fulfillment of a duty would have become the instinctive outflow of nature."

S. H. Hooke
The Kingdom of God
pp. 113-114

"We should not be concerned primarily to be 'just' to our neighbor, but rather to love and support him. And this we can do only if we are ready to forgive. And I can be ready to forgive only if I have learned that Jesus Christ has forgiven *my* sins and given me another chance.

"The business of forgiveness is by no means a simple thing. It is hard because in our mania to be just we proceed to divide the burden of forgiveness among both partners. We say, 'Very well, if the other fellow is sorry and begs my pardon, I will forgive him; then I'll give in.' We make of forgiveness a law of reciprocity. And this never works. . . .

"Forgiveness — and this is the secret of it — is never merely following suit when the other person has led with his regret; forgiveness is always taking the initiative.* It is initiative or it is nothing. Life generally follows the law of retaliation. . . . But forgiving means breaking through this natural law. And this happens only when somebody takes the initiative, when one person makes a new beginning and does not merely keep on repeating the old muddled beginnings. . . . The Gospel means that God has broken the inexorable law of sin and retribution, has cut straight through

_____
*See also 25:3, Walchars.

the world's tragic entanglement, and made a new beginning with us."

Helmut Thielicke
The Waiting Father
p. 112

"There is no forgiveness in the cheap little game of looking the other way when a wrong is done. Forgiveness never overlooks or winks at sin. It does not make light of a wrong. . . . Nor is it just forgetting. You will forget when you truly forgive. . . . Forgetting is the result of complete forgiveness; it is never the means. It is the final step, not the first. Never say forget it; it is nothing! To avoid or overlook evil is basically dishonest. . . .

"When God forgave us, he did not wink at our sin or overlook it. He took our lostness in sin so seriously that it took him all the way to Calvary to substitute himself for us, to die in our place, to pay the price of forgiving such a vast debt. The Cross shows how hard it was for God to forgive*. . . . Either the sinner bears his own guilt — that's cold justice. Or the one sinned against, the first party, may absorb what the second party did — that's forgiveness! . . .

"Forgiving is self-giving with no self-seeking. It gives freedom where the enemy deserves punishment. . . . It gives back to the other person his freedom and his future. . . . Christ gives you the strength to forgive. To give forgiveness and acceptance to others no matter what may come. Or how often. The whole seventy times seven."

David Augsburger
The Freedom of Forgiveness
pp. 19, 23, 39-40

"When we take the wrong done us into the presence of God, we can usually be somewhat fair minded. 'He trespassed against me but I understand why and I forgive him, God, the way I want you to forgive me.' . . . But carrying forgiveness into action is a whale of a job. . . . Sure, we maintain a forgiving frame of mind but we are unable to forget the rankling incident. Now this is an experience we all have and probably have repeatedly. What to do when our mind is made up and our will is able to hold our actions in line but our emotions hold out on participating in the forgiveness! We can act but not react our forgiveness.

_____
*See also 70:2, Stevenson.

In such a situation we need the very help of God. First off, it helps to hunt some blame to take on ourself. In accepting as large guilt as is reasonable, we lessen the degree of fault we have to forgive in the other person. Second, we can go out of our way to put our forgiveness into action seek out our debtor and actually do him a good turn. . . . But the third step in forgiveness is the really difficult one: not to allow our mind to dwell an instant on the debt we have forgiven. . . . When a wound is once clean, no good can come of opening it: indeed there is a danger of making it septic again. Only a mind uncluttered by yesterday's trespasses against us — or for that matter, by yesterday's triumphs or forgiveness — can present it itself empty of self before God so that he can give us himself. . . .

"Keeping one's eyes on one's own imperfections* as contrasted with the consummate goodness of God is the quickest way to feel kinship with the worst sinner we know. The measure of our forgiveness is the amount of love we can pour out upon the ones who wronged us. Love manifests in a kind of spiritual energy which takes time daily to hold the trespasser in the light of God's love until his well being can be freely and unreservedly committed into God's hands.''

Marguerite Harmon Bro
More Than We Are
pp. 80-83

"What is forgiveness? It is more than letting off. It is more than non-resentment. It is the whole reaction of injured love, which is not satisfied until it has healed the wound and achieved reconciliation. It is fairly easy if you have not been hurt too much to say, 'Of course I forgive him, but I don't want to have anything else to do with him.' In fact, forgiving in this way is rather pleasant, and gives one a nice feeling of moral superiority; and the other person may find it positively infuriating. 'Who is she to forgive me? If there is any forgiving to be done it ought to be the other way around.' When injury goes deep, forgiveness is costly. . . . If it is a mortal injury, the cost of forgiveness is something that feels like death. It always means a death of pride, a readiness to appear to be in the wrong, to let the other fellow get away with it. But you have got to get closer to him than that. . . . You can forgive an injury done to yourself only if you are willing to pay the price of bearing the result without resentment.''

T. R. Milford
Foolishness to the Greeks
pp. 55-56

---

*See also 25:4, Shakespeare.

" 'Forgiveness is the one way in which the power of sin in the world can be absorbed, neutralized and brought to nothing.' It is 'a power of spiritual alchemy whereby men can literally transform sin's evil product into the means of increasing the world's output of goodness and love.' This was the goodness Jesus exercised and bequeathed on his Cross.' '' (L. Hodgson, *The Doctrine of Atonement*, p. 64)

Douglas Webster
In Debt to Christ
p. 35

"Forgiveness is the fragrance of the flower on the heel that crushed it.''

Anonymous

"No tie binds men more closely together than the tie of the common sense of sin. In Christopher Fry's play *The Dark Is Light Enough*, the Countess Rosmarin has taken pity on a rather disreputable, irresponsible, and undependable deserter from the army, taking him into her house and into the circle of her friends. As they settle down in her drawing room for their after-dinner coffee, she senses the resentment, the suspicion, and the animosity:

. . . . Let us say
That we are all confused, incomprehensible, corrupt;
And in that condition pass the evening
Thankfully and well. In our plain defects,
We already know the brotherhood of man.

When men know enough about their sin to be sorry for it, they are ready to accept one another on a deeper level than ever before. The realistic equality is an equality in the need of forgiveness and in the gratitude and love which the assurance of such forgiveness can create. Here in the society of the forgiven is the most hopeful thing about our confession of sin. . . . Resting on the mercy of the ever-loving God we can undertake to minister at large the grace of reconciliation.''

John M. Krumm
The Art of Being a Sinner
pp. 77-78

New Illuminations:

On Faith

"On only two occasions does the Gospel tell us that Jesus was surprised at something. In both cases it is a question of faith. . . . Jesus is amazed at the incredulity of Nazareth, and he is amazed at the centurion's faith. Nazareth's orthodoxy is not the living faith, the saving faith. If such a faith had animated them, the men of Nazareth would have opened their hearts to Jesus. They abide by a precise and fruitless religion. Their hearts remain closed. We don't know exactly what the centurion's faith may have been, but he opened his heart to Jesus. He suspects in him a Savior and a Lord. His faith is based on confidence and obedience — not on sentimentality. It is an impulse of his whole being. He has no doubt that Jesus can and will cure his servant. In some way he stakes his life on Jesus' word. 'Only say the word . . .': a humble and fervent expectation."*

Monk of the Eastern Church
Jesus: A Dialogue with the Savior
pp. 39-40

"While it is true that God forces his way into no man's personality, yet he is always ready where the right conditions are fulfilled, to enter and redeem and transform. The chief of the right conditions is what the New Testament calls faith; the willingness to use the faculty which can touch God and which can, as it were, provide an opening through which the ever-present loving purpose can enter and operate."

J. B. Phillips
Making Men Whole
p. 33

"Moving mountains and planting trees on the bed of the ocean are things which are obviously impossible. . . . By describing things that are impossible in this way, Jesus arrested the attention of the Palestinian audience and made them think of the essential meaning behind his exaggeration and overstatement. [Hyperbole is not used for deception but for emphasis as a device of exaggeration. — Ed.] So in this saying it would be quite clear to the listeners that Jesus was not really talking about mountains or, for that matter, about mustard seeds, which are proverbially the smallest of all seeds. He was talking about *faith* and impressing upon the audience that even the tiniest particle of faith could achieve results that are comparable to shifting mountains. . . .

*See also 29:1, Bornkamm.

"But, says Jesus, men with faith can do things which look just as absurd and impossible. But what is faith? Someone complained once that the word 'faith' is a marvelous out for preachers. When there is something or other in Christian teaching which is difficult to understand, he tends to say, 'This is a matter of having faith,' as if faith were a magic ingredient which we throw into a mixture of reason, experience, tradition, and Scripture in order to make sense out of life. But this is not at all what the author of the letter to the Hebrews says about faith in chapter eleven. He says faith means trusting in God despite all opposition and discouragement, venturing forward into the unknown future believing that God has a purpose for us and for the world, which in the long run he will accomplish despite all the power of evil does to thwart it."

William Neil
The Difficult Sayings of Jesus
pp. 10-11

"Here are some of the wrong notions of what faith is. First of all, it is not an emotion, not a feeling. It is not a bland subconscious urge towards something vaguely supernatural. It is not a feeling of God's existence. It is not something that bubbles up out of the recesses of your soul and fills you with an indefinable 'sense' that everything is all right. It is not something so purely yours that its content is incommunicable. . . . But also it is not an opinion. It is not a conviction based on rational analysis. It is not the fruit of scientific evidence. You can only believe what you do not know. As soon as you know it, you can no longer believe it, at least not in the same way as you know it.

"Faith* is first of all an intellectual assent. It perfects the mind, it does not destroy it. It puts the intellect in possession of Truth which reason can not grasp by itself. It gives us certitude concerning God as He is in Himself; faith is the way to a vital contact with a God who is alive, and not to an abstract First Principle worked out by syllogisms from the evidence of created things. But the assent of faith is not based on the intrinsic evidence of a visible object. The statements which demand the assent of faith are simply neutral to reason. We have no natural evidence why they should be true or why they should be false. We accept their truth as revealed, and the motive of our assent is the authority of God who reveals them. . . .

"Faith is not expected to give complete satisfaction to the intellect. Yet it does not frustrate the intellect, or deny

*See also 19:2, Bornkamm.

it, or destroy it. It pacifies it with a conviction which it knows it can accept quite rationally under the guidance of love. For the act of faith is an act in which the intellect is content to know God by *loving* Him and accepting His statements about Himself on His own terms. . . .

"Faith reaches the intellect not through the senses but in a light directly infused by God. . . . And if you make the simple assent of faith, submitting through love to the authority of God revealing Himself, you will receive this interior light. . . . and faith turns into understanding."

Thomas Merton
Seeds of Contemplation
pp. 79-81

"Jesus came telling us that all the great spiritual systems of self-development and discipline cannot save us, but that he would. Unless you grasp this you have failed to understand the central scandal of the Christian faith: Christ saves us from religion and law; we are no longer justified by them, saved by them, but only by his grace. The basis for real holiness is now no longer a neurotic, moralistic craving for a sterilized perfection but a relaxed and unself-conscious following of God's will in joy. And this affects our belief too. Faith, like holiness, grows out of the experience of being justified and accepted. Faith grows from the experience of the love of God. . . .

"The event which we call the crucifixion of Christ was the action and direct intention of God. In it, according to the Christian faith, God acted decisively on behalf of mankind. . . . And this cannot be known except by that strange knowledge we call faith, and there can be no arguing about or into faith. The contemplation of this event, which is more than event, speaks decisively to our hearts and we answer from within. We recognize what it means and we make our response. . . . As an old hymn puts it: 'Faith our outward sense befriending, makes the inward vision clear.' "

Richard Holloway
A New Heaven
pp. 23, 33-34

"On the lower level faith simply means the acceptance of Christian doctrines as true; and for a long while Lewis could not understand why this should be regarded as a virtue. After all one believes the Christian doctrines are true or one does not believe. . . . Later Lewis understood that this level of belief involved virtue to the extent that it 'is the art of holding on to things that your reason has once accepted, in spite of your changing moods.' It turns out that our emotions and our imaginations, our wishes and our desires often 'carry out a blitz' on our belief, that is, our conscious, reasoning acceptance; and we must, therefore, train the habit of faith. Once the human mind has accepted a thing as true, it does not necessarily or automatically go on regarding it as true."

Leanne Payne
The Real Presence:
The Holy Spirit in the Works of C. S. Lewis
pp. 101-02

"The journey of the soul through life is strangely like the progress of the child Alice through Looking Glass Land. For both, the plot has an active, visible and obvious side, and a quiet, deeply hidden, mysterious side. Alice, that small representative of the spirit of man, finds herself wandering through a strange unfamiliar world of circumstance, and undergoing many bewildering experiences which seem, as the experiences of our life often do, chaotic and unmeaningful. She travels through a country which is divided like a chessboard into light and dark patches. She has no map and little sense of direction. . . . But if we turn back to the first page of the bewildering story, we find what Alice wanted but could never discover, a plan of the chessboard as the Player sees it with each piece in the right place in relation to the whole. Then we see that everything which happened to Alice, however unmeaningful, disconcerting, or apparently hostile to her interests, was a real move in her game. All these changes and chances, these pains and frustrations, were queer but deliberate devices for getting the child, who began as a pawn, to the eighth square where she must end as a Queen.* The help and correction that she received from the creatures that she encountered and the imperceptible pressure of events never varied in intention. However great the obstacles, the apparent confusion and absurdities, the goal was always the eighth square. The best advice was often that which seemed the most foolish as when the rose told Alice to walk away from the Red Queen if she wanted to meet her. The really important moves were not recognized till long after they were made. It is true that Alice went through one of the earlier squares by train; but she was actually passing through another, almost at the end of her journey, when she thought herself hopelessly lost in the dark forest with nothing to help her but the muddling statements of the White Knight. Once she was called right off the path to befriend the silly and untidy White Queen. Yet it was in running after the queen's lost shawl and jumping the little brook over which it had floated that Alice made her next move and reached the fifth square. Here we easily recognize our own experience and so too that puzzling phase when life seemed to Alice to be a shop full of possessions and sometimes to be a river on which she had to row. . . . Yet in spite of her bewilderment, the child caught in the web of circumstance was never really lost; each baffling experience contributed something to the whole. The hand of the Player was hovering over the pawn. . . .

"This seems a childish allegory to use as the veil of so great a mystery — the mystery of faith. But its inner meaning gives new significance to the jumble of incidents, the griefs, and joys, the errors and recoveries, frustrations and

---

*See also 11:2, Pardue.

compulsions, which seem to make up most of our life. 'That Thou being our ruler and guide we may so pass through things temporal' — the light and dark patches, field and forest, and sudden changes that lead to a new square — 'that we lose not the things that be eternal.' . . .

"The pawn does not know what will be required of it nor what may be before it; but its relation with the Player is always direct and stable, and the object of the Player is always the good of the pawn."

Evelyn Underhill
Abba
pp. 73-75, 78

"Faith is a gift from God. We must seek it, pray for its growth and exercise it. But always realize that it is a quality of spiritual power given by God and not a thing or a specific kind of information. Faith is a power added to the mind as a telescope is added to the eye. It enables you to see truths which cannot be understood with the human reason or brain. Thus, with the aid of faith, a simple peasant can see truths that a brilliant professor cannot see without faith.

"It is important that you desire faith, but of yourself you cannot create faith. You already have its rudiments. As St. Paul says in 2 Timothy 1:6, you are told to 'stir up the gift of God, which is in thee by the putting on of my hands.' In other words, to those who have sought the gift of faith, it has been given.

"How are you to stir up and develop the gift of faith? By four general processes. First, by seeing the necessity of faith and by using your own will to want or desire faith. Secondly, by praying for the gift to grow and develop within you. Thirdly, by seeking help, by going to the Holy Communion and receiving God's grace as often as you can. And, fourthly, by exercising or acting upon the faith that you already have. . . . Start to seek the increase of the gift of faith that is already in you. Touch Christ with faith and see what happens."

Austin Pardue
The Single Eye
pp. 52-53, 55

"We may, in our preliminary thinking about 'whether there is a God,' or in our moments of doubt and depression, derive some limited help from those arguments to which thoughtful Christians have given weight in centuries past. But no one will expect true, personal faith to depend on such arguments. This has other sources. What are they?

"St. Paul said that faith is not 'of ourselves' — we cannot stir it up or create it — 'it is the gift of God.' This chimes in with what the great saints have said and thought, and with the experience we have always shared. 'Thou wouldest not be seeking me if thou hadst not already found me' was the word Pascal heard from God, and to have found God in this sense means to have been found by him. St. Augustine, and endless other saints of God, have testified to their belief that God was seeking them long before they were seeking him. . . .

"In any case, the Christian who says 'I believe in God' — meaning by that not 'I consent to the probable existence of a personal God,' but 'I throw myself in trust upon a personal creator' — does so in response to initiatives outside himself.

". . . Always we must distinguish between knowing about God and knowing him. Christian faith is not holding right views about God: it is living in a certain relationship with him. If we would know him better, we must trust him more fully and obey him more completely. There is no other way. We must catch (from our Lord himself, or from our contemporaries whom he can use) the confidence that he *is* there, that he *is* here, that he can be trusted and that if we try to obey him he will help our weaknesses and reward our faith. 'He that cometh to God must believe that *he is*, and that he is the rewarder of those that diligently seek him' (Hebrews 11:6).

"Faith stands in contrast to unbelief, to credulity, and to 'sight.' There will always be an element of *venture* in it. 'Hope that is seen is not hope.' If we could see and prove all, there would be no place left for faith. But if we desire faith, if we long for God, if we want to obey him, 'we shall know of the doctrine.' We can always say, 'Lord, I believe; help thou my unbelief.' "

R. R. Williams
I Believe and Why
pp. 14-16

New Illuminations:

On Discipleship V: Total Dedication as Servants

Luke 17:7-10

"Luke does not give us a Gospel that is easy. The conditions of discipleship are strict and uncompromising. If anything he shows us the sterner side of Jesus. . . . The Jesus of Luke's gospel who so remarkably strikes us as the great hearted friend of the outcast is also the Jesus who tells his disciples: 'Even . . . when ye shall have done all the things that are commanded you, say, We are unprofitable servants: we have done that which is our duty to do.' This mingling of the compassion and severity of Christ is one of the most valuable angles the third gospel gives us on Jesus' nature.''

William Neil
The Message of the Bible
p. 94

"In the Old Testament, two sorts of servants are mentioned. There are the *hired servants*, who have wages paid to them and who have certain rights. Then there are the *bond-servants*, or slaves, who have no rights, receive no wages and have no appeal. When we come to the New Testament the word in Greek for servant of the Lord Jesus Christ is not 'hired servant' but 'bond-servant,' by which is meant to be shown that our position is one where we have no rights and no appeal. . . . 'We have done that which was our duty to do.'

"I see here five marks of the bond-servant. First he must be willing to have one thing on top of another put upon him, without any consideration being given him. . . . How quickly there are murmurings and bitterness in our hearts when that sort of thing is expected of us. But the moment we start murmuring, we are acting as if we had rights, and a bond-servant hasn't any! . . . Secondly, in doing this he must be willing not to be thanked for it. . . . And thirdly, having done all this, he must not charge the other with selfishness. . . . But there is a fourth step to which we must go. Having done all that, there is no ground for pride or self congratulation, but we must confess that we are unprofitable servants. . . . The bottom of self is quite knocked out by the fifth and last step — the admission that, doing and bearing what we have in the way of meekness and humility, we have not done one stitch more than it was our duty to do. Man's sin has simply consisted in his refusal to be God's bond-servant. A man, then, has not not done anything specially meritorious when he has consented to take that position, for he was created and redeemed for that very thing.''

Roy Hession
The Calvary Road
pp. 56-59

"Jesus in the words of our saying, draws a parallel between the relationship of the farmer and his slave and the relationship between God and the Christian disciple. When you have obeyed all the commandments of God, he says, you deserve no credit. You have only done what is your duty. This picture of God as the all-demanding Taskmaster is much less attractive than the picture of God as the Father in the Prodigal Son. Yet it is a useful corrective to much slushy sentimentalism, which tends to overlook the rigorous demands of God altogether. 'Our picture of God,' says Charles Coulson, 'must resemble more the violence of a sunset painting by Turner than, as one of my friends once put it, a watery wash by a maiden aunt.' . . .

"If we take our Christian faith seriously, we have to recognize that the relationship between God and ourselves, between the Creator and his creatures, is one of God's absolute authority and our absolute dependence. God owes us nothing: we owe God everything. Like the slave in the parable, we can take no credit for any good we do, for it is God who gives us the power to do it. We have only done our duty and earned our keep. We deserve no thanks from God. If the farmer in the story can expect as his right the total commitment of his slave to his service, how much more right has God to expect the service of his creatures. . . .

"This hard saying of Jesus is a salutary corrective in our moods of self-pity. We feel that we are doing more than our share, in our jobs, in our home, in the work of the church. This point never comes, says Jesus, for you have only done your duty. It is also a cure for our pride, our feeling that in a variety of ways we are better Christians than our neighbors, more charitable, more sympathetic, more active in good causes. Not so, says Jesus, whatever you have done you have only done your duty. Yet if we take these apparently harsh words to heart, and live by them, we find that by the strange alchemy of God's providence his service turns out to be our perfect freedom.''

William Neil
The Difficult Sayings of Jesus
pp. 83-84

"Even on earth a king may have many vassals, and they do not all get so far as to enter his chamber. Enter then, enter within yourselves, my daughters, and get right away from your own trifling good works; for these you are bound, as Christians, to perform, and indeed, many more. It will be enough for you that you are vassals of God; do not try to get so much that you achieve nothing. Look at the saints who have entered the King's chamber, and you will see the difference between them and ourselves. Do not ask for what you have not deserved. For we have offended God, and, however faithfully we serve him, it should never enter our heads that we can deserve anything.''

St. Teresa of Avila
Interior Castle
p. 60

"Beneath the vast sweep of the divine plan, we who are followers of Jesus Christ see ourselves as both humble and uplifted. We are humbled because at the very most we can only play a tiny part in the great scheme of salvation, and, as our Lord once pointed out (with a smile, I imagine), when we have done all that has been commanded we can still only reflect that we are 'unprofitable servants.' At the same time, we are uplifted because through the incredible generosity of God we are called in our day and generation to take part in this tremendous purpose. . . .

"And for ourselves, we must be sure that we are taking our full part — whatever the vocation to which we are called — in working together with God. . . . We have thought already of the immensity of God outside us, of what is known technically as the transcendence of God, but what is so often lacking in present-day Christians is an adequate sense of God within us, that is, what is known technically as the immanence of God. . . . Certainly Christians admit that they need the help of God in the tasks to which they are called, and certainly they seek it. But I have an uneasy feeling that men do not really believe that God Himself actually operates within their personalities. . . . In the experience of St. Paul and his followers, the revolutionary thought — 'the mystery that has been hid from all ages' (Colossians 1:26) — is that God is no longer the external power and authority, but One who lives *in* them, transforming their thinking and feeling, renewing their minds, inspiring their hearts, and effectually preventing them from being conformed to this fleeting world.''

J. B. Phillips
Making Men Whole
pp. 50-51

"And we humbly beseech thee, O heavenly Father, so to assist us with thy grace, that we may continue in that [thy Son's] holy fellowship, and do all such good works as thou hast prepared for us to walk in.''

The Book of Common Prayer
Post-Communion Thanksgiving

New Illuminations:

On the Kingdom of God III: Its Unknowable Timetable

Matthew 24:23-26	Mark 13:3-7, 28-37	Luke 12:40; 17:20-21

"As announced by Jesus, the reign of God is not an awareness of God's sovereign power over the universe or of God's kingship over Israel, long established and still enduring, though both these concepts are presupposed. It is the announcement of God's kingship in its full realization, fully active, eschatologically irrevocable. . . .

"In the preaching of the prophets, warnings and words of comfort are found side by side. In later Judaism, the awareness of sin becomes stronger, prayers of penance multiply, men petition earnestly for God's mercy. A mood of melancholy descends upon devout people without of course stifling their hope. But for all that the apocalyptic literature is a flight into the realm of visions and dreams, a flight away from a steady faith, because men were calling for portents and calculating when the hour would come. They wanted, so to speak, to take a peek at the cards in God's hands. . . .

"The Jews at the time were in the grip of Messianic excitement and an intense eschatological expectancy. When Jesus with his apostles approached Jerusalem, they imagined that God's reign would be manifested 'on the spot' (Luke 19:11). Flavius Josephus speaks continually of popular pretenders whose Messianic promises found a ready ear among the people. The Qumran community shows us a contemporary group of Jews living in a sensitive atmosphere of eschatological expectancy and in a state of serious legal, liturgical, and moral preparation for the time of 'God's visitation.' This concentration on eschatology was quite common among the Jews. The expectancy varied only in kind, but the Gospel of the reign of God preached by Jesus stands out as unique and incomparable.

". . . Jesus remained aloof from any apocalyptical calculation of the end, the point in time when the reign of God would manifest itself. For him the future kingdom of God is a reality, subject only to God himself and over which God has sovereign control; it is wholly beyond the range of human curiosity and speculation."

Rudolf Schnackenburg
God's Rule and Kingdom
pp. 82-83, 86-87, 99

"What generally happens is that we tend to be content with a vague idea of what the Kingdom of God means, but in the saying of Jesus in Luke 17:21, we need to have more than just a vague idea. It really means the sovereignty or kingly rule of God. The phrase is not found in these actual words in the Old Testament; but the idea was there from early times that the power of evil in the world would not

last forever, and that one day God would confound his enemies, vindicate his chosen people Israel, and inaugurate a new age of peace and righteousness. By the time of Jesus, religiously minded people had come to the conclusion that the world had become so corrupt that nothing short of a cataclysmic end to the old order and the creation by God of a new heaven and a new earth would make it possible for the kingly rule or Kingdom of God to begin. This was the point of the Pharisees' question in Luke 17:20. They ask Jesus: 'When will the Kingdom of God come?' His reply is in effect that they are asking the wrong kind of question, and he adds the difficult words of our saying: 'In fact the Kingdom of God is among you.' "

William Neil
The Difficult Sayings of Jesus
pp. 85-86

"There is a much debated passage in Luke 17:20-21: 'And being asked by the Pharisees when the kingdom (reign) of God should come, he answered them and said, The kingdom of God cometh not with observation. Neither shall they say, Behold here or behold there. For lo! The kingdom (reign) of God is within you.' One point is evident. Jesus is proposing an opinion opposite to that held by his questioners; it stops them in their tracks and makes them think. Their question is rooted in their nationalist and apocalyptic hope of a kingdom that looked and longed for as immediate a realization as possible. To this Jesus gives a negative answer in two sentences. . . . He is saying that men cannot calculate the temporal advent of the reign of God any more than they can determine it in space and place. Jesus is well aware of the tendency (especially in circles influenced by the apocalypses) to calculate the when by means of portents. To this Jesus replies first that it is not a matter of observation and then that, even if it does come, men cannot look for it or establish its presence in this or the other place. His audience, in other words, has a completely false idea of the reign of God. . . .

"To substantiate his double negative ('not, neither') Jesus now emphasises his contrary position (for lo!). The reign of God is 'within you.'* The major controversy centers around this last expression. Usually the Greek word means 'within, inwardly' but it may occasionally signify 'in the midst of, amid.' Luke 17:21 could be read as follows: You need not go here or there, the reign of God is within your own range. . . .

"The old and spiritual interpretation that prevailed with the Fathers and throughout the Middle Ages referred it to an inner realm of grace within the heart; this was maintained by Luther among others and has been held to our own times. Its main weakness is that it does not fit in with the normal view of Jesus about the reign of God. For this reason, most exegetes today accept very properly the version 'among you.' ''

Rudolf Schnackenburg
God's Rule and Kingdom
pp. 134-36

"It is difficult to refrain from giving a critical judgment on the obvious tendency to set up, as it were, a 'calendar' of the final events, in view of Jesus' own words which forbid such apocalyptic speculation. The quite varying history of the identification of this 'apocalypse' (Luke 21:15-36 par.) with ever new historical figures and events shows how questionable these assertions are. . . . Hence the enlightened assertion that such explanations are typical products of an excited apocalyptic fancy obsessed with the idea of the end of the world seems to be very near the mark. One cannot dispute the relative validity of such a view, when one considers all the fanatical attempts to give historical names to the stages which must be gone through as the world moves towards its end. But it is all too clear that even that enlightened standpoint proves itself, in the light of the message of Jesus, somewhat audacious. . . .

"Thus we are brought back again to the 'Take heed, watch!' which noticeably pervades even this 'apocalypse' of the Gospels. Jesus' message demands that we reckon with the future, lay hold on the hour, do not calculate the times. Those who wait in the right way are therefore called to fulfil the will of God with all their might."

Gunther Bornkamm
Jesus of Nazareth
pp. 94-95

"The radical moral demands made by Jesus that form part of the most unchallengeable tradition are based primarily on eschatological motives: in Luke, entry into the Kingdom of God (13:24), a share in the divine banquet (13:29), reign with God (22:30) etc. . . . .

"The eschatological character of the divine rule he was proclaiming assumes a special form we must now examine. It is exclusively the 'seed and deed of God.' . . . Men can pray for this to come, implore God both day and night, strive and struggle to enter into it; men are to look for it, prepare themselves for it, hold themselves in readiness; but with their own resources, they can do absolutely nothing to bring it into existence or to hasten it or on the other hand to delay or hinder it. The seed grows of itself and so the

kingdom of God comes from divine power and grace.*

"This supernatural character of the rule is discernible in Luke's expressions such as God 'gives' it (12:32) or 'disposes' it (22:29 seq.). To certain individuals it is attached by Jesus as a 'promise,' as admission or exclusion, reclining at table, and also eating bread, drinking of the fruit of the vine. These images portray the rule as a saving benefit in the future, of which God alone can dispose. . . .

"From Luke's passage in 17:20, one thing is certain, Jesus was not and had no desire to be an apocalyptist. He kept deliberately clear of apocalyptic questions, including that of prophetic calculation. This assertion may seem to contradict the presence of portents in the eschatological discourse. But the events there described are not intended to provide tangible data; their purpose is a practical one. Sufferings, persecutions, and temptations to disbelief are to come upon the disciples and they must be prepared to confront them. It is only the additional simile of the fig-tree, with its practical application to the disciples that seems to present the events described as genuine 'portents.' Yet is this an original meaning? Perhaps it referred to signs already evident in the operation of Jesus that could reveal the nearness of the reign of God to all who could see**. . . .

"If we are thus compelled to bring out the prophetic quality in the preaching of Jesus, it is just as necessary to absolve him from all typical apocalyptic tendencies. We have a proof of this in the saying in Mark 13:32: But of that day or hour no man knoweth neither the angels in heaven nor the Son of the Father.''

Rudolf Schnackenburg
God's Rule and Kingdom
pp. 84-85, 209-10

"Let us go on to the last paragraph of the discourse (Mark 13:28-37 par.). It is an exhortation to watch, to expect the End foretold, which to its immediate hearers applied to both Ends, but for us, as for all since A.D. 71, refers only to the End of Man. In it Christ uses two analogies. The first is that of the fig-tree whose bursting leaf buds herald the approaching summer. The second is that of a man who, sojourning in another country, gives each of the servants in his *house* — notice the word — a task, but especially charges the porter to watch for his return, lest coming suddenly he find them sleeping.*** Thus the End appears paradoxically as both forewarned and sudden; the servants know their Lord is coming, but do not know exactly when. In this paragraph, verse 30, occurs the statement, 'Verily, I say unto you, This generation shall not pass away until all these things be fulfilled.'

" 'Verily,' is the word with which our Lord was want to preface his weightiest assertions. 'I am telling you the truth,' says the Truth. But, because of its apparent lack of

---

*See also 37:2, Father Andrew.

---

*See also 33:2, Schnackenburg.
**See also 104:1, Hooke.
***See also 111:2, Harton.

truth, this statement has led many in the past to doubt the authenticity of the entire discourse. But wait a minute. As we have said our Lord is dealing with two things, two Ends. . . . The key word in Mark 13:30 has double meaning in Aramaic and Greek. Greek *genea* means 'race' or 'stock,' as well as generation; and Hebrew-Aramaic *dor* means generation, period or age, and habitation. 'Generation' meets the case for the first End, for the Temple was destroyed within the lifetime of our Lord's contemporaries. 'Race,' 'age,' and 'habitation' meet the second case, the End of Man. The human race, this Beth-El which is Man, shall not pass away till all these things be accomplished, nor shall this present Messianic Age.''

Sister Penelope
The Coming
pp. 37-39

New Illuminations:

On the Pharisee and the Publican

Luke 18:9-14

"Most of the Pharisees refused to be led. In the parable of the Pharisee in the temple, our Lord told them why. Look at the Pharisee as he prays. He walks boldly up to the throne of God, head erect in confident assurance. He does not have to make any apologies to God. He has not committed any bad sins. He has kept the Law better than is necessary. He has not come to ask God for anything — only to demand his right. The Pharisee has fulfilled his part of the bargain with God. Now let God keep his promise and prosper the Pharisee in this world and the next.

"The Pharisee is not as other men are. His sin is far worse than theirs. It is the root sin — pride, spiritual pride. He thinks that he can save himself, indeed that he has. He need not ask God's forgiveness. All that he asks is God's approval. Of course he will not let the Holy Spirit show him how he has misinterpreted God's Law. It is only because he has narrowed the Law down to external requirements that he can believe that he has been keeping it perfectly. He will not let the Holy Spirit guide him into a broader more demanding concept of it. Such a concept would undermine his self-righteousness, would make him bow his head and confess his need for God's mercy and help. This he will not do. He commits the sin that asks no pardon. Therefore it is unpardonable.*

"Like the Pharisees we are the devout Church people. It may be that, like them, we have misinterpreted and unduly narrowed the concept of Christian duty. . . . If, like the Pharisees, we have reduced the service of God to manageable proportions, so that we can accomplish it without too great effort of sacrifice, we have much to learn, much to repent. . . . The question is can we repent? Do we consider our respectability a sufficient guarantee that we stand in right with God? In spite of our conventional protests that we are miserable sinners, do we really believe, deep in our hearts that God ought to be pleased with us? . . . Do we thank God that we are not as other men are? Ours is such a sensible, dignified, comfortable religion. Are we in danger of going down to our house unjustified because we need no repentance?

"The publican went home justified. He had faced and admitted his sin. He bowed his head, beat on his breast and said, 'God be merciful to me a sinner.' He is the sinner who has committed his particular sins. He does not compare himself to others. He simply throws himself on God's mercy. He knows he has nothing of which to boast. He knows he can do nothing to save himself. He knows he does not deserve pardon. He accepts his status as sinner and turns to God. He becomes a forgiven sinner. . . . Forgiven sinners depend both for their salvation and their sanctity on the undeserved mercy of God. With joy and thankfulness in their hearts they call themselves sinners. This abiding penitence is the foundation for the Christian life. On no other foundation can it be built. The building up of the positive side of the spiritual life is a long, hard process. But it cannot even begin until we have escaped from spiritual pride into a humble and lasting penitence."

Ralph Milligan, ed.
All For the Love of God: A Holy Cross Omnibus
pp. 175-177

"I would like to remind you of the parable of the Pharisee and the Publican. The Publican comes and stands at the rear of the church. He knows that he stands condemned; he knows that in terms of justice there is no hope for him because he is an outsider to the kingdom of God. But in the cruel, violent, ugly life he leads, he has learned something of which the righteous Pharisee has no idea. He has learned that in the world of competition, the only hope one can have is in an act of mercy, an act of compassion, a completely unexpected act which is neither rooted in duty, nor in natural relationships, which will suspend the action of the cruel, violent, heartless world in which we live: All he knows, for instance, from being himself an extortioner, a moneylender, a thief and so forth, is that there are moments when for no reason, because it is not part of the world's outlook, he will forgive a debt because suddenly his heart has become mild and vulnerable: that on another occasion he may not get some one put into prison because a face may have reminded him of something or a voice has gone straight to his heart. There is no logic in this. It is not part of the world's outlook nor is it a way in which he normally behaves. It is something that breaks through, which is completely nonsensical, which he cannot resist. He knows also, probably, how often he himself was saved from final catastrophe by this intrusion of the unexpected and the impossible — mercy, compassion, and forgiveness. So he stands at the rear of the church knowing that all the realm inside of the church is a realm of righteousness and divine love to which he does not belong and into which he cannot enter. But he knows from experience also that the impossible does occur and that is why he says, 'Have mercy, break the laws of righteousness, break the laws of religion, come down in mercy to us who have no right to be forgiven, to be allowed in.' And I think this is where we should start continuously all over again. . . .

"From the outset prayer is really our humble ascent toward God, a moment when we turn Godward, shy of

*See also 66:2, Sayers.

coming near, knowing that if we meet him too soon, before his grace has had time to help us to be capable of meeting him, it will be judgment. And all we can do is to turn to him with all the reverence, the worshipful adoration, the fear of God of which we are capable, with all the attention and earnestness which we possess, and ask him to do something with us that will make us capable of meeting him face to face, not for judgment nor for condemnation, but for eternal life.''

Anthony Bloom
Beginning To Pray
pp. 8-9, 7

"A great deal of sentimental (i.e., unreal) stuff has been spoken and written about the matter of sin and forgiveness, and we must therefore clear our minds a little more before we see the significance of what Christ had to say about this very important subject. Let us start then by making these observations.

"We are not concerned with artificial guilt or sin. Conscience can make a man feel guilty simply because certain standards and taboos have been established in his mind, and he has failed to 'toe the line.' All religions, Christianity unfortunately not excepted, tend to excite in certain people an artificial sense of guilt which may have little or no connection with a man's actual standing before God. Probably Pharisaism, which Christ attacked with bitter scorn, represents this tendency at its highest; but it is a mistake to think that Pharisaism disappeared after the death of Christ. The danger of such a system is that its values are artificial. The proud and correct feel 'right with God' just when they are not, and the sensitive, humble man feels hopeless and overburdened *for the wrong reasons*. (Christ's iittle cameo of the Pharisee and the tax-collector is an unforgettable commentary on this point.)

"We are not concerned with mere comparison with perfection. . . . A great deal of the sense of sin and shame and guilt induced in certain types of people is simply due to their (imaginary) comparison of their human standards with what they conceive to be the Divine Standards. Of course they feel failures. You have only to raise the standard, and go on raising it, to make anyone feel a hopeless, blundering idiot. But to put it at its crudest, it would be an extraordinary ungentlemanly thing for God merely to keep raising the standard! After all it is a foregone conclusion that no man can compete with his creator, and there is neither sense nor justice in thinking that the Creator intends his creatures to feel permanently inferior and humiliated compared with himself.''*

J. B. Phillips
Your God Is Too Small
pp. 107-08

---

*See also 26:1, Penelope.

New Illuminations:

On Self-Righteousness and Censoriousness

Matthew 23:1-7, 26-28   Mark 12:38-40   Luke 11:39-43; 16:15; 18:9; 20:45-47

"Why is it that our Lord condemns self-satisfaction so mercilessly? He gives us the reason in the closing words of the parable of the Pharisee and the publican: 'Everyone that exalteth himself shall be abased; and he that humbleth himself shall be exalted.' We read in St. John that when Jesus had healed a blind man, some of the Pharisees who were standing by asked scornfully: 'Then we are blind also?' To which Jesus answered solemnly: 'If you were blind you would be guilty of no sin, but as it is you say, "We can see"; so your sin continues.' . . . In every department of life the law holds good that self-satisfaction is the enemy of progress. In the arts and in business, the man who is content with what he has done has shot his bolt; his day of good work is over. . . . In the life of the soul this law holds even more strikingly, because here self-satisfaction is more absurd, more false, and more dangerous than in secular affairs. . . . What is the cause of self-satisfaction? How does it come about that in spite of our Lord's stern warnings on the subject we can still tamper with conscience and extract its sting? One cause is our common tendency to be content with a low standard. . . . What we all have to realize is that God will judge us not by the standard of public opinion, but by the standard of the Man whom he has ordained, the Lord Jesus Christ (Luke 16:15). When we look at our lives in the light of his teaching and his example, no room is left in us for Pharisaic complacency. We stand far off, echoing the publican's prayer, 'Lord be merciful to me, the sinner.' . . . Another cause of self-satisfaction is the neglect of self-examination. 'Know thyself' is a precept of psychology no less than religion. . . . St. Luke tells us that our Lord addresses this parable to certain who 'were confident of their own uprightness, and thought nothing of others. . . .' Self-satisfaction always breeds intolerance."

G. D. Rosenthal
Sins of the Saints
pp. 74-79

"When a proud man thinks he is humble, his case is hopeless. Here is a man who has done many things that were hard for his flesh to accept. He has come through difficult trials and done a lot of work, and by God's grace he has come to possess a habit of fortitude and self-sacrifice in which, at last, labor and suffering become easy. It is reasonable that his conscience should be at peace. But before he realized it, the clean peace of a will united to God becomes the complacency of a will that loves its own excellency. . . .

"As soon as you begin to take yourself seriously and im-

agine that your virtues are important because they are yours, you become the prisoner of your own vanity and even your best works will blind and deceive you. Then in order to defend yourself, you will begin to see sins and faults everywhere in the actions of other men. And the more unreasonable importance you attach to yourself and your own works, the more you will tend to build up your own idea of yourself by condemning other people. Some of the most virtuous men in the world are also the bitterest and most unhappy, because they have unconsciously come to believe that their happiness depends on their being more virtuous than other men."

Thomas Merton
Seeds of Contemplation
pp. 40, 43-44

"There is one vice of which no man in the world is free; which every one in the world loathes when he sees it in someone else; and of which hardly any people, except Christians, ever imagine that they are guilty themselves. . . . The essential vice, the utmost evil, is pride. Unchastity, greed, drunkenness, and all that are mere flea bites in comparison: it was through pride that the devil became the devil. Pride leads to every other vice. It is the complete anti-God state of mind. . . . As long as you are proud you cannot know God. A proud man is always looking down on things and people; and, of course as long as you are looking down you cannot see things that are above you. . . . The real test of being in the presence of God is that you either forget about yourself altogether or see yourself as a small dirty object. It is better to forget about yourself altogether."

C. S. Lewis
Mere Christianity
pp. 108-111

"We must not be discouraged at the imperfections of our fellow creatures. The only security from disappointment is to receive from them what they are able to give us, as from trees the fruit they bear. God bears with imperfect beings and even when they resist his goodness. We ought to imitate this merciful patience and endurance. It is only imperfection that complains of what is imperfect. The more perfect we are, the more gentle and quiet we become toward the defects of others. . . . Charity does not demand of us that we should not see the faults of others; we must in that case shut our eyes. But it commands us to avoid attending unnecessarily to them, and that we be not blind to the good while we are so clearsighted to the evil that exists. We must remember too God's continual kindness to the most worthless creatures and think how many causes we have to think ill of ourselves. . . . We who complain so much of what others make us suffer, do we think that we cause others no pain? We who are so annoyed at our neighbor's defects, are we perfect? God, who knows all and has seen all our faults, demands of us that we exercise toward our brother a little of the mercy which he who is our Master bestows so abundantly upon us.''

Thomas Kepler, ed.
Letters and Reflections of Francois de Fenelon
pp. 98, 135

"We will have others severely corrected and will not be corrected ourselves. The large liberty of others displeases us and yet we will not have our own desires denied us. And thus it appears how seldom we weigh our neighbor in the same balance with ourselves. If all men were perfect what should we have to suffer from our neighbor for the sake of God? Now God has ordered it that we should bear one another's burdens (Galatians 6:2) for no man is without fault; no man but has his burden. No man is sufficient of himself; no man is wise enough of himself; but we ought to bear with one another, comfort one another, help, instruct, and admonish one another.''

St. Thomas á Kempis
The Imitation of Christ

"Let us look at this saying of Jesus: 'Pass no judgment and you will not be judged' (Luke 6:37). At verse 39 there is this curious saying: 'Can one blind man be guide to another? Will they not both fall into the ditch?' It is not clear what the connection between these two passages is until we look at the corresponding passage in Matthew 15:12-14. There it is made plain that the 'blind guides' Jesus refers to are the Pharisees. It is the outlook and mind of the Pharisee that Jesus has in mind when he tells his disciples to pass no judgment, for the Pharisees were notorious for finding fault with those they considered to be less godly than themselves. . . . Luke reminds us (16:14-15) that 'the Lord does not see as man sees; men judge by appearances but the Lord judges by the heart.' We cannot tell why other people behave as they do. We know little or nothing of their problems. Jesus urges us to look into our own hearts before we judge our neighbor (Matthew 7:2-5), remembering that we all stand under the judgment of God. We cannot

expect God to be merciful to us unless we are merciful in our judgment of others.''

William Neil
Difficult Sayings of Jesus
pp. 65-66

"Another of our human weaknesses is to expect our own experience of God to be reproduced in identical terms in the experience of another. Worse than this we sometimes tend to think that if another's experience is not the same as ours, it must be either spurious or incomplete. Now here we must be very firm with ourselves and use our common sense as well as our charity. People themselves differ greatly in their capacities and gifts, and also in their particular inward needs. We all tend to overlook the beam in our own eye to which we are so accustomed, and to magnify the mote which is in our brother's eye. Only God knows the relative size and importance of the assorted beams and motes that exist between us, and much the most sensible thing to do is to leave God to deal with each individual Christian with the infinite variety and delicacy of his own love and wisdom. If we feel we must do something about the spiritual life of another Christian, the most constructive thing we can do is to keep our hands off and our tongues quiet, and to pray.''

J. B. Phillips
Making Men Whole
p. 65

"If one that is once or twice warned will not give over, contend not with him but commit all to God, that His will may be done and His name honored in all His servants, for He well knoweth how to turn evil into good.''

St. Thomas á Kempis
The Imitation of Christ

"Forgiveness is not only a religious obligation, it is also a psychological injunction. How pretentious of us to presume that we are able to judge what really goes on in the mind of another human being! There is only the visible appearance of the action for us to rely on to use as a criterion of judgment. The inner motives completely escape our scrutiny. How easy to say an acquaintance is antisocial, and how hard to pinpoint the *why*!

"If someone is upset by personal feelings of inferiority, isn't it natural for him to shy away from companionship in order to be alone with his lack of self-esteem? In his self-pity, his behavior may appear rude and offensive, but if we consider his reasoning, we should be able to understand and forgive his manner. His exterior roughness may be just another way of saying: 'Pay attention to me! Speak to me! Love me!' Many are the charades we use to convey our messages of need! Why are we so slow to hear when others appeal for love? Shocking as the words may sound, a cry of 'I hate you' can make sense. Often hate is nothing more than the absence of love. . . . When we are not able to hear the real feeling behind such a cry, we only add to the anguish.''

John Walchars
Voices on Fire
pp. 135-36

New Illuminations:

On Faith and Childlikeness

Matthew 18:2-4; 19:13-15   Mark 10:13-16   Luke 18:15-17

"Probably it was mothers that 'brought children for him to touch' — for a blessing from the famous Teacher and Healer. The disciples that 'rebuked' them were not necessarily stern and rude. They were probably merely trying to shield Jesus from a clamoring crowd and doing their best to give him some peace.

"Jesus, however, was less concerned about not being disturbed than that the children should have his blessing. He was indignant with his disciples for trying to stop them from approaching him. Only Mark records that 'he put his arms around them, laid his hands upon them and blessed them.' This moving conclusion can hardly have come from anyone but an eyewitness of the scene. We shall not be far from the truth in considering this one of many indications that Mark owed much to the reminiscences of Saint Peter who had been with Jesus, had seen and had remembered."

William Neil
The Difficult Sayings of Jesus
p. 49-50

"The nature of the act of faith was revealed by our Lord's attitude toward the unbelieving Pharisees. They had seen miracles work and prophecies fulfilled. They were not lacking for motives in belief, but they still refused. Our Lord took a little child in his midst and said '. . . whoever shall not receive the Kingdom of God as a little child shall not enter it.' By this he meant that the act of faith has more in common with trusting belief of a child in his mother than with the assent of a critic. The child believes what the mother tells him because she said it. His belief is a trusting homage of love to his mother."

Fulton J. Sheen
Go to Heaven
p. 77

"The point here is not that Jesus liked little children. It is, rather, another of Jesus' paradoxes. Jesus' consistent call is an invitation to adult decision, to take responsibility for one's life. The child cannot do that. He cannot take control of his own life but must depend on others. Written into this simple story is the invitation to recognize that ultimately we cannot save ourselves, and, freed by the Father's love

for us, to accept that and choose to put our trust in him as our Father, to choose to be his children.* This is the paradox: that someone who really has a sense of his own worth, who can deal with other people, cope with life, who in a multiplicity of ways is strong and successful, who is an adult, should freely choose to rely on the Father's love. This is the way into the Kingdom."

Thomas Kane
"Powerless and Weak"

"Jesus spoke to his heavenly Father in as childlike, trustful and intimate a way as a little child to its father. Here we probably have the key to Matthew 18:3 — children can say *Abba*. 'If you do not learn to say Abba, you cannot enter the Kingdom of God.' In favor of this interpretation 'to become again like a child' are its simplicity and the fact that it is rooted in the heart of the gospel. Thus the first step in conversion and the new life is learning how to call God *Abba* with childlike confidence, safe under his protection, and conscious of his boundless love."**

Joachim Jeremias
The Parables of Jesus
p. 191

" 'Except,' said Christ, 'ye become as little children' — and the words are sometimes quoted to justify the flight into infantilism. Now children differ in many ways, but they have one thing in common. Peter Pan is a case for the pathologist. All normal children (however much we discourage them) look forward to growing up. Except you can wake on your fiftieth birthday with the same forward-looking excitement and interest in life that you enjoyed when you were five, 'ye cannot see the Kingdom of God.' One must not only die daily, but every day one must be born again."

Dorothy Sayers
Creed Or Chaos
p. 15

*See also 80:3, Ramsey.
**See also 73:2, Neil.

"It is with concern surely to disqualify complacency that our Lord tells us that, when we have done everything that we ought to have done, not to pat ourselves on the back but to say, 'We are useless servants' (Luke 17:10).

"And this is at least part of the saying that we must become as little children if we want to enter the kingdom of God. In all three synoptic gospels there is what is surely meant to be a significant contrast implicit in the juxtaposition of the scene with the little children and the story of the rich man who wants to know what he should do to inherit eternal life. . . . The Lord loves him as soon as he sees him. But he sends him away with a flea in his ear: 'How hard it is for those with money to enter the kingdom of God.' The disciples are dumbfounded. . . .

"The rich man wanted to discover something he could do to inherit eternal life. There is nothing any of us can do. We must simply receive the kingdom of God like little children. And little children are precisely those who have not done anything. The ancient world was not sentimental about children and had few illusions about any pretended innate goodness in them. The Lord is not suggesting that heaven is a great playground for Arcadian infants. The children are our model because they have no claim on heaven. If they are close to God, it is because they are incompetent, not because they are innocent.

". . . When our Lord tells us to become as little children, he is bidding us to forget what lies behind. Children have no past, be it good or evil, great or small, it is, strictly speaking, irrelevant in our stance before God. It is only *now* that we are in the presence of God. . . . In the naked 'now' there is no room for any picture of ourselves. And that is where God is."

Simon Tugwell
The Beatitudes: Soundings in Christian Traditions
pp. 6-7

"You probably remember passages from St. Paul where he says, 'My power is manifest in weakness' (2 Corinthians 12:9).* Weakness is not the kind of weakness we show by sinning and forgetting God, but the kind of weakness we show by being completely supple, completely transparent, completely abandoned in the hands of God. We usually try to be strong and we prevent God from manifesting his power.

"You remember how you were taught to write when you were small? Your mother put a pencil in your hand, took your hand in hers and began to move it. Since you did not know all that you were meant to do, you left your hand

---

*See also 121:2, Hooke.

completely free in hers. This is what I mean by the power of God being completely manifest in weakness. You could think of that also in terms of a sail. A sail can catch the wind and be used to maneuver a boat only because it is so frail. If instead of a sail you put a solid board, it would not work: it is the weakness of the sail that makes it sensitive to the wind. The same is true of the gauntlet and the surgical glove; how fragile is the glove, and yet in intelligent hands it can work miracles because it is so frail. So one of the things which God continues to try and teach us is to replace the imaginary and minute amount of disturbing strength we have by this frailty of surrender, of abandonment in the hands of God."

Anthony Bloom
Beginning to Pray
p. 10

"Father John Main preferred 'empathy more than surrender. Empathy is perfect reciprocity — our dear and courteous Lord invites us to this. Surrender suggests a power of struggle but the essence is pure gift — God gives himself to us and we enter into the fullness of gift — this is empathy. It puts ourselves in a much truer light than surrender — surrender seems to lessen the marvel of his courtesy. . . .

" 'Oh yes, there must be no desire for God — rest in him — do not want to possess him. Be still. Desire is not in itself desirable. . . . Realize do not desire.' "

Neil McKenty
In the Stillness Dancing: The Life of John Main
pp. 129-30

"The utmost man can achieve on his own capitulates before the unspeakable simplicity of the manger — the methods of God. After all, the shepherds got there before the Magi, and even so the animals were already in position when the shepherds arrived. . . . There never was a less highbrow religion. 'Whosoever shall humble himself as this little child, the same shall be greatest in the Kingdom of heaven.' There is no use in being too clever in life. Only so far as we find God in it do we find any meaning in it. Without him it is a tissue of fugitive and untrustworthy pleasures, conflicts, and ambitions."

Evelyn Underhill
Light of Christ
pp. 38-39

New Illuminations:

On the Quest for Eternal Life

| Matthew 19:16-29 | Mark 10:17-31 | Luke 10:25; 18:18-30 |

"The rich man's salute of Jesus as 'good' is not a meaningless compliment, nor is it a recognition of the perfect teaching capacity of Jesus or of his moral perfection. The Greek word translated 'good' on the lips of this suppliant is used more in the sense of gracious, benevolent, kindly disposed. . . . The answer of Jesus is nevertheless a mark of his profound humility and in harmony with such statements as in John 14:28, 'My Father is greater than I.' The source of all benevolence is in God himself*. . . . The enquirer is a Jew, in whose heart riches are slowly dethroning God, and the words of Jesus may have been perfectly spoken to bring him to think of his relations to God."

The Abingdon Bible Commentary
p. 984

"Each evangelist adds certain touches to complete the portrait of the rich nobleman. Luke links him with the wealthy aristocracy in order to emphasize Jesus' teaching about riches. Matthew calls him a 'young man'; and Mark verifies this by saying he impulsively threw himself at Jesus' feet. With genuine affection, he goes on to call Jesus 'Good Master.' Never in the entire Talmud is any rabbi addressed that way. In reply, Jesus delicately directed the ruler's attention to God, the one source of goodness. His question about eternal life must not be directed to our ideas of sanctifying grace and immortality. Palestinian Jews could not envisage the future life unless it be with a resurrected and glorified body. To obtain this happiness, Jesus pointed out that one was expected to keep the commandments in the spirit of faith. The ruler was disappointed. He wanted to do more. He had experienced the failure of the Law alone to satisfy; i.e., to attain 'eternal life.' "

Carroll Stuhlmueller
The Gospel of St. Luke
pp. 120-121

"The rich young ruler in the Gospel record personifies the contemporary junior executive. Like many men in young maturity in our culture, he had arrived at position and status, had acquired wealth and prestige. But there was something lacking; he found no real pleasure in his life, sensed no real meaning in his existence. He had no clear sense of any personal life task.

". . . The search for a way of life so meaningful that it is worth living eternally is not limited to any one group but is typically characteristic of young maturity. Here is a young man who recognized his own need and had pushed through the initial resistance and asked for help. Not only did the young man take the initiative, but there is a sense of urgency expressed in impulsive eagerness; how else can one interpret the running up to Jesus and kneeling before him (Mark). . . .

"The key to the handling of this man's problem is found in the first words spoken by Jesus. He lifts the whole encounter into another dimension. Whereas the young man sought an answer in terms of acts he would perform, or in terms of doing good and avoiding evil, Jesus implies a much more basic God-centered orientation in which every aspect of life is open to spiritual values.

". . . To be sure Jesus did refer to a specific code. His reference, however, was first to God, to a God-centered life, to a life oriented around supreme values. The commandments become, then, an expression of a relationship to God rather than simply the rules for personal conduct, rules which the young man had so scrupulously followed. He knew the rules, but . . . he needed to put the words of the commandment into the broader harmony of a meaning-centered life.* To make such a change, however, was more than this young man could manage. . . . If any change were to be made, Jesus adopted the one pathway likely to effect it. 'Jesus, looking upon him, loved him' (Mark 10:21). The key is found here not only to the personal ministry of Jesus, indeed, to any effective ministry. Here is represented what Sullivan speaks of as the 'quiet miracle of developing the capacity of love.' It is only in the atmosphere of loving acceptance that barriers to relationships can be lowered. First the assurance in the look of love, and then the challenge. Note however, that the challenge is there. There is little that is non-directive in the ministry of Jesus. The imperative could hardly be more direct: 'Go! Sell! Come! Follow!'

"He offers his own constant support by proposing that the young man throw in his lot with the disciples. Presenting a task that would arouse obvious tensions, Jesus offers personal support to help in the struggle. . . . A fellowship of accepting people is also needed, a fellowship that will stand by as hesitant and stumbling attempts are made to break away from meaningless routine and to explore more meaningful patterns of relationship. It is the very nature of man that he is free to say 'no,' just as he is free to say 'yes.' But Jesus does not despair, for even as the speaker turns away sorrowfully, he has been exposed once again to the

---

*See also 96:2, Hooke.

*See also 83:2, Ramsey.

worthwhileness of life and to the possibility of involvement in it in a very personal way.''

Robert Leslie
Jesus and Logotherapy
pp. 36-45

"When Jesus told the young man that he must sell everything he possessed and give to the poor, Jesus had put his finger on the man's problem. His money had obviously come between him and God*. . . . The man was not condemned by Jesus because he was wealthy. He was self condemned because his wealth was his chief concern. On another occasion, Jesus said, 'You cannot serve both God and mammon.' But Jesus' last word on the subject makes his meaning plain. Wealth makes it difficult for man to be in the right relationship with God, but not impossible. The grace of God can move a man to use his wealth for the good of others.''

William Neil
The Difficult Sayings of Jesus
pp. 53-54

"I believe that through the Lord's goodness there are many souls in the world most desirous not to offend His Majesty. This is certainly a desirable state and there seems no reason why they should be denied entrance to the very last of the Mansions. . . . We all say that we desire it, but if the Lord is to take complete possession of the soul, more than that is necessary. Words are not enough any more than they were for the young man when the Lord told him what to do if he wished to be perfect. I have had that young man in mind for we are exactly like him. . . . For if, when the Lord tells us what to do, we turn our backs upon him and go away sorrowfully, what do you expect His Majesty to do? For the reward which he is to give us must, of necessity be proportionate with the love which we bear him. . . . Yet do not suppose that the Lord has any need of our works; what he needs is the resoluteness of our will.''

St. Teresa of Avila
Interior Castle
pp. 59-61

"Jesus reduces to concrete practice God's absolute claim on the man who is to have a share in his kingdom. . . . The following of Jesus signifies adopting his life and living in close company with him (cf. Luke 9:57-62). But other demands are linked with this. . . . It is not always easy to know whether a sentence of Jesus is asked for a particular sacrifice

from one man (for example, the rich man) or is directed to all men. Jesus did not demand from everyone the abandonment of home and family, profession and property, as he did from the twelve apostles. Yet his words against riches have a very sharp ring, and he makes absolute demands upon each disciple. On the other hand one should not say that Jesus regarded the possession of riches as incompatible with a share in God's kingdom; but rather that he called for a renunciation of earthly goods when these became an obstacle to entry into the kingdom.''

Rudolf Schnackenburg
God's Rule and Kingdom
pp. 110-11

" 'It will be hard for a rich man to enter the Kingdom of God.' The dialogue with the youth is followed by a saying of Jesus about riches and reign; 'reign' here suggests the idea of kingdom. . . . 'Who can be saved?' In popular Jewish belief wealth was one of the rewards God conferred upon righteousness; and the saying of Jesus was more paradoxical than modern readers perceive. The paradox is not softened by the saying that what is impossible with men is possible to God, and this does not mean that it is possible for the rich to retain their wealth and still be saved. It means that God makes possible what man finds impossible — the renunciation of riches.''*

John L. McKenzie
The Jerome Biblical Commentary
43:135

"Strange are the ways of the Lord. Man by himself cannot discover them. God by his appearance revealed to us the peculiar path to eternal salvation. He gave us an example in all things. He taught us how the Holy Spirit acts in us. He filled us with imperishable light away from which there is no true knowledge anywhere, no salvation for anyone. From him we learned of the unlimited possibilities for those who were created in his image.''

Archimandrite Sophrony
His Life Is Mine
p. 63

"The irrepressible Peter could keep silence no longer. He was proudly conscious that he had forsaken his boats and his nets to follow Jesus. The rich young man had failed to pass the test whereas he and his fellow disciples had passed with flying colors. And so, brimful of self-satisfaction, he

---

*See also 81:2, Van Breemen; 81:3, Webbe.

*See also 81:2, Thielicke.

asked: 'Behold, we have forsaken all and followed thee. What shall we get therefore?' What an unbelievable question! Here is a man setting up a profit and loss account with God. Here is a man who, conscious of the special sacrifices he has made, thinks that in consequence he should be specially rewarded. Jesus in fairness has to honor the justice of his plea (Luke 18:29-30).''

Joost de Blank
Uncomfortable Words
p. 44

"There is a strain of world renunciation in the teaching of Jesus. There must be not only an indifference to the world's riches, but, to some to whom Jesus spoke an abandonment of them. There must be a disregard for security in this world, a readiness to accept injury and injustice, and to forsake parents, wife and family. These precepts are not principles on which a new and better order of society will be founded, rather will their literal application disrupt society. But the renunciation ('for my sake') points forward to a reward hereafter.* But the reward will not be quantitative nor hedonistic. It will be, as the parable of the laborers in the vineyard shows us, the same for the man who has worked one hour and the man who has borne the burden of the heat of the day. It will be entry into the reign of God. It will be an existence God-centered and God-ruled. It will be admission into the presence of Jesus. It will be a vision of God which the pure in heart will be allowed to see.''**

Michael Ramsey
Sacred and Secular
pp. 116-117

"In the Apostles' Creed, we declare our belief in 'the life everlasting.' Some people find the thought of life going on and on as unattractive. Most modern translations tend to use the word 'eternal' instead, which is less open to misunderstanding. Jesus said, 'I have come that men may have life and have it in all its fullness' (John 10:10). A full life, a life which is rich in the experience of God, life lived on a higher plane, is a kind of life that everyone would surely wish to continue forever. It is this, then, which Jesus promises, not a life that begins after death but a new kind of life that can begin here and now. Some words of Baron von Hugel are worth reflecting on: 'Only an eternal life already begun and truly known in part here, though fully to be achieved and completely to be understood hereafter, corresponds to the deepest longing of man's spirit as touched by the prevenient Spirit, God.' Jesus lays down two conditions for knowing the beginning of eternal life in this

imperfect world — obedience to his teaching and trust in God (John 5:24).''

William Neil
The Difficult Sayings of Jesus
p. 94

"In the great picture of the judgment, the Son of Man addresses the 'blessed of the Father' as follows: 'Possess the kingdom prepared for you from the foundation of the world.' Synonymous expressions occur in other passages: 'enter into life,' 'receive life everlasting.' The hundred-fold reward to be received by those who abandon everything for his sake consists in eternal life.* But this is identical with a share in the future reign of God.''

Rudolf Schnackenburg
God's Rule and Kingdom
p. 93

"No sacrifice of our natural powers and freedom of action is too great if it promotes a better relationship with God and prevents a guilty conscience. If we put ourselves under God's discipline, we are no longer free to do as we like. We have to keep ourselves in check, restrain our impulses, exercise self-control. We may feel that in the process we are destroying part of ourselves, depriving ourselves of things that less scrupulous people enjoy. But Jesus tells us that what seems to be a loss now is in fact a gain, for we have to think in terms not of this present life but of our life in eternity.''

William Neil
The Difficult Sayings of Jesus
p. 44

"Those who call concern for eternity 'escapism' simply have not troubled themselves to understand it. If reality is not whole without God and his part in personal life, if the meaning of this life can only be seen in the light of eternal life which interpenetrates this world as well as being a continuation of it, then entering into eternal life is an escape indeed. It is an escape from earthboundness, from the futility, cynicism, and despair which are bound to come from a candid meditation on the conception of human life which ends with the grave, with no over-arching meaning, with no permanence — in personal terms — for the gains that are made in spiritual depth and interpersonal width. The ignoring of eternal life is escapism indeed. It is an escape *from* truth, an escape *from* the claims of the ground of our

---

*See also 103:1, Phillips.
**See also 24:3, Kunkel.

*See also 44:2, Harton.

existence, an ostrich-like reaction to the real meaning of the universe.''

James Pike
Beyond Anxiety
p. 133

"This is the eternal life which was manifested to us in Jesus Christ, and our purpose of being here on earth is that we should have it and exercise its powers and so carry on the redemption of the world. That is what Christians are for.

"A Christian is a two-edged being, rooted at the bottom in daily life, which of itself has nothing of eternity, and reaching at the other into God, whose life is eternal. The Christian is the connecting link between the two*. . . . He is like the trolley-car, which must be in contact with the conductor and also earthed, otherwise the power will not flow. As the old lady said to the policeman, 'Is it dangerous to tread on this rail?' 'No, Ma'am,' he answered, 'not unless your other foot is on that wire overhead.' ''

T. R. Milford
Foolishness to the Greeks
pp. 78-79

*See also 58:3, Wolters.

New Illuminations:

On the Laborers in the Vineyard

Matthew 19:30; 20:1-16	Mark 10:31	Luke 13:30

"Leaving entirely out of account allegorical interpretations, the parable of the laborers in the vineyard does not bear the meaning of the summons to the divine vineyard. Such an interpretation misses the point of the conclusion to the parable which shows that the emphasis does not lie on a call to the vineyard, but on the distribution of the wages at the end of the day. . . .

"The evangelist Matthew has inserted into a Marcan context the parable about the 'first' and the 'last' in order to illustrate the saying in Mark 10:31, 'But many who are first shall be last and the last first,' with which Mark ends the previous address to Peter. Transposing the 'first' and 'last,' Matthew has used the saying as the conclusion to the parable; and doubly by the words 'for' (20:1) and 'so' (20:16), he has expressly brought it into relation with 19:30. In its Marcan context, what this saying asserts is that in the age to come, all gradations of rank will be reversed; and it is uncertain whether it is meant to confirm the promises which Jesus has just made to the disciples or as a warning to them against presumption.

"For Matthew, Jesus' parable represented the reversal of rank which would take place on the last day. He will have drawn this conclusion from the instruction given to the steward (v. 8b): '. . . Pay them all their wages beginning with the last group to the first.' But that is clearly an unimportant detail in the course of the parable. . . . In fact, no complaint is made later on about the order of the payment which, taken in its context, should merely emphasize the equality of the last with the first. It may be simpler to take verse 8 as meaning rather — 'Pay them all their wages including the last.' In any case, Jesus' use of the parable, certainly conveys no lesson about the reversal of rank at the end since all receive exactly the same wage.

"We must go behind Matthew and study the parable without reference to its context. It is possible the concluding evidence in verse 16 may bear an entirely different meaning from that which its present Matthean setting demands. The seer of IV Ezra is perplexed by the question whether the preceding generation will be at a disadvantage in comparison with those who survive to the end. He receives the answer — 'He said to me: I will make my judgment like a round dance; the last therein shall not be behind, nor the first in front' (IV Ezra 5:42). First and last, last and first — there is no difference, all are equal. This interpretation of the parable is generally accepted today, namely that it is intended to teach the equality of reward in the Kingdom of God (20:1).

"Light begins to break if we disregard verse 16. This verse was originally an independent logion which has been added to our parable as a generalizing conclusion, but does not tally with its meaning. If the parable originally ended with verse 15, without offering any explanation, its shocking character was forced upon the attention. Here is a story of bare-faced injustice. . . . Why does the master allow the last to receive a full day's pay for only an hour's work? Is this a piece of purely arbitrary injustice? a caprice? a generous whim? Far from it! There is no question here of limitless generosity since all receive only an amount to sustain life, a bare subsistence wage. No one receives more. . . . The master sees that they will have practically nothing to take home; the pay for an hour's work will not keep a family. It is because of his pity for their poverty that the owner allows them to be paid a full day's wages. In this case the parable does not depict an arbitrary action, but the behavior of a large-hearted man who is compassionate and full of sympathy for the poor. This, says Jesus, is how God deals with men. This is what God is like, merciful. Even to tax-collectors and sinners he grants an unmerited place in his kingdom, such is the measure of his goodness. The whole emphasis lies on the final words: 'Must you be jealous because I am generous?'

"Why did Jesus tell the parable? Was it his object to extol God's mercy to the poor? If that were so, he might have omitted the second part of the parable (vv. 11ff.). But it is precisely on the second part that the stress lies for our parable describes two episodes: (1) the hiring of the laborers and the instructions about their payment (vv. 1-8), (2) the indignation of the injured recipients (vv. 9-15). Now, in all the double-edged parables, the emphasis lies on the second point. What then is the purpose of the second part? . . . The parable is clearly addressed to those who resembled the murmurers, those who criticised and opposed the good news, Pharisees for example. Jesus was mindful to show them how unjustified, hateful, loveless, and unmerciful was their criticism. Such, said he is God's goodness, and since God is so good, so too am I. He vindicates the Gospel against his critics. . . . Over and over again we hear the charge brought against Jesus that he is a companion to the despised and outcast, and we are told of men to whom the Gospel is an offense. So here this is what he is saying, 'This is what God is like, so good, so full of compassion for the poor; how dare you revile him?' "

Joachim Jeremias
The Parables of Jesus
pp. 34-38

"In Exodus 3:12, God promises to be present with those chosen by him, to remain present with them, to assist them. . . . This is reminiscent of a later statement of God to Moses:

'I shall be merciful to whom I shall be merciful' (Exodus 33:19). But in it, the future character is more strongly stressed. . . . He who promises his steady presence, his steady assistance, refuses to restrict himself to a definite form of manifestation. How could the people even venture to limit him?''

Nahum Glatzer, ed.
Martin Buber: On the Bible
p. 59

"Just because of the exalted position we give to justice, we are in danger of so isolating justice as to make it not only impersonal, but inhuman. The most perfect judicial system can never disregard the personal element. . . . Cold justice is not enough. It has to be tempered by that acknowledgment of personal considerations which we call mercy.

"In the story of the laborers, most of us are inclined to think that the grumblers had a very good case. . . . If you look at the story solely in terms of rights, they had done more work and were therefore entitled to more pay. But there is more to life than demanding our rights. . . . We have to realize that there is no room for envy in our lives. The laborers were not complaining that they were underpaid nor that their employer had not kept his side of the bargain. No their only complaint was that those that had worked shorter hours should be equally rewarded. . . . The kind of recognition other people receive must not weaken our resolve or devotion one iota. All that matters is that our lives, our whole aim and ambition, should be pleasing to our Lord. If we think we are going to be fairly treated as the world counts fairness, we are far away from divine reality, and we shall be disgruntled by the success of others. Jealousy can have no place in the Christian life.''

Joost de Blank
Uncomfortable Words
pp. 40-45

"The train of thought that had started with the rich young man's inquiry about the 'good' and Jesus' reply that there was only one place where that good might be found, ends with the revelation of the goodness in the heart of the one with whom Peter and all of us must have to do*. . . . The young man had asked how he could get eternal life, and nearly a century later the greatest of New Testament thinkers wrote, 'This is life eternal that they might know thee, the only true God, and Jesus Christ whom thou hast sent' (John 17:3).

"Nowhere else, perhaps, is the inward character of the Kingdom as Jesus saw it more clearly displayed than in the parable of the laborers in the vineyard. It is important to observe that while Jesus continues to speak in what seem to be conventional terms about the establishment or coming of the Kingdom in power and his own manifestation as Son of Man and Messiah, yet his mind is occupied with grace. And when Peter seeks assurance about the rewards of the Kingdom, Jesus directs their minds to the essential and inward character of the Kingdom as he has come to apprehend it, to the only reward worth having — the knowledge of the grace of which they were the objects.''

S. H. Hooke
The Kingdom of God
pp.119-20

---

*See also 95:1, *Abingdon Bible Commentary*.

New Illuminations:

On The Direct and Personal Ministry of Jesus

| Matthew 20:29-34 | Mark 10:46-52 | Luke 18:35—19:10 |

"A blind beggar on the streets of Jericho learns that the Son of David is passing by. From the thronged roadside he calls, 'Jesus, thou Son of David, have mercy on me' (Luke 18:39). Those around him endeavor to quiet him. They feel he may be disturbing important matters in the Master's ministry. But Jesus catches that plaintive cry above the confusion, and he asks that the blind man be brought to him. . . . Others may not be sensitive to the call of the suffering, Jesus always is. There is not one instance in all the Gospel record where anyone came to Jesus with an anxiety or illness but that the Master ministered to him and healed him. His arms always reach out to human need."

Robert B. Munger
What Jesus Says
p. 60

"There are important differences between the healing of the blind man in Bethesda and this healing. Here the blind man hears Jesus is coming, and, painfully aware of his blindness, he begins to cry out. The paradox is that he sees how desperate his situation really is; and that grounds his resolve. He pushes aside what others think. He cuts through the opposition of the fickle crowd. Nothing else counts but to get to Jesus who alone can heal him. . . . This brings out something new. Having begun to sense our own blindness, when we enter into this story, we very quickly take Bartimaeus' words as our own. With a deep sense of our own desperate state we cry out 'Jesus, Son of David, have mercy on me!' Then we hear the Lord say, 'What do you want me to do for you?' Here again it is crucial to have entered so deeply into the story that we become him. Then the words are addressed to us personally. 'What do you want me to do for you?' The response that comes welling up out of our depths is 'Master.' This is not merely politeness. It shows that Jesus is becoming the Master of our lives and the Master of our journey. And although we cannot see very well, yet we have been learning to follow him, to trust him. Here the request is 'Heal me of this blindness,' though at this point we know that this will, indeed it already has, entailed a stripping. There is another shift in this story. The blind man is freed to follow Jesus along the way, to join in his journey even to Jerusalem. As we, in prayer, inhabit this story, we know the Lord is there healing us, bringing us with him on his journey."

Thomas Kane
"Inhabiting the Gospel"

"When Zacchaeus is seen as a man excluded from relationships, driven into the position of the enemy because of rebuffs in an attempt to find a position for himself within the community, we then begin to sense what that Gospel incident is really all about. To be sure, Zacchaeus is reported to be small in stature, and his climbing a tree is apparently to compensate for his lack of height. But in a far deeper sense he was 'up a tree.' He could not meet people on the level, in a face to face relationship. . . . There was a good reason for his behavior.

"Each person develops his own 'security operation,' his own ways of defending his sense of self-esteem and feelings of personal significance. . . . Because the security operation once served a useful purpose, it tends to reinforce itself as a habitual pattern of behavior and resists evidence that demonstrates its ineffectiveness. To risk a change is to expose the self, to make one vulnerable to personal hurt. . . .

"So Zacchaeus, trying to protect a tottering self-esteem deserted his own people and threw in his lot with the conquerors. But he wasn't happy. . . . Unable to risk seeking out Jesus about whom his curiosity had been aroused, he could only try to see him from a distance. It is not by happenstance that the colloquial expression 'up a tree' has crept into common usage; to be 'up a tree' is to be caught in an awkward and embarrassing and somewhat helpless situation. Zacchaeus, however, did not stay up the tree. . . . Even Zacchaeus could change. Caught up as he was as a 'Quisling,' a traitor to his own community, he could nevertheless change. But change never comes easily. We have already noted that like most people Zacchaeus could not seek help openly. No change would take place unless an atmosphere conducive to change was created. The key to change belongs clearly in the quality of a relationship with another person. . . . Jesus risks himself in such a genuine way that Zacchaeus finds the courage to take the risk of change himself. . . . Braving the criticism of the assembled people, Jesus puts himself in the intimate relationship of a guest in the home of Zacchaeus. In this simple act he tosses aside any prerogative of authority and becomes the one who trusts Zacchaeus to take care of His human need for refreshment and His spiritual need for companionship. Totally ignoring the crowd, he demonstrates in this active and specific way his acceptance of the outsider. . . . This was acceptance not predicated on change, but acceptance that anticipated change. Acceptance in Christian standards is always of this nature, an acceptance that takes a person where he is but does not leave him there. Seeing a person at his best makes possible his becoming his best. Goethe's maxim states it very clearly 'If we take people as they are, we make them worse. If we treat them as if they were what they ought to be, we help them to become what they are capable of becoming.'

. . . The completeness of the change is implied in the final words of Jesus: 'For the Son of Man has come to seek and to save that which was lost' (Luke 19:10).''

Robert Leslie
Jesus and Logotherapy
pp. 27-29, 32-35

"He drew a circle that shut me out —
Heretic, rebel, a thing to flout.
But Love and I had the wit to win:
We drew a circle that took him in."
Edwin Markham, "Outwitted"

"For a week or ten days I go back to the same story again and again. Gradually it works deeply into me. I don't just understand Zacchaeus; I become him. I have his fears, his illusions, 'I'm desperate but he can't be interested in me; I'm a sinner.' Then Jesus calls out 'It really is you I want.' I'm not just dealing with ideas. I'm confronted by the Lord. I can hear the unexpected, the unheard of, that he wants me. And my world crumbles. In the revelation of the Lord's love for me, I am freed from some of my illusions. My self-righteous world crumbles; and I sit there stunned. . . . Jesus only shatters us so that beyond the ruins of our world he can invite us into the world he is creating for us. To live within these stories is to begin to move more deeply into the world of his Father's love."*

Thomas Kane
"Inhabiting the Gospel"

" 'I am in the midst of you as he that serveth' (Luke 22:27). I shall not attain Jesus if I seek him reigning in the place of honor. I have to look for him and find him in that place where he is hiding, in his suffering and humiliated members. It is because they are not looking for him there that so many men cannot believe in him or have only a nominal faith in him. Zacchaeus has to join Jesus in the crowd."

Monk of the Eastern Church
Jesus: A Dialogue with the Savior
p. 64

"Malcolm Muggeridge, who wrote a book on Mother Teresa admits she does not accomplish much by rescuing a few stragglers from a cesspool of human need. Then he concludes with the statement, 'But then Christianity is not a statistical view of life.' Indeed it is not, not when a statistical view of life.' Indeed it is not, not when a shepherd barely shuts the gate on his ninety-nine before rushing out heartbroken, and short of breath, to find the one that's missing. Not when a laborer, hired for one hour, receives the same wage as an all-day worker. Not when one rascally sinner decides to repent, and ninety-nine upstanding citizens are ignored as all heaven erupts in a great party (Luke 14:4-7). Christian love, agape, giving love, is not statistical either. Perception by the skin is more basic than perception through an eye or an ear. It senses a need and responds instinctively, personally*. . . .

"An old Chinese proverb says: 'Nothing can atone for the insult of a gift except the love of the person who gives it.' If I go up to a person who looks poor, press a ten-dollar bill in his hand, and walk away, I am really insulting that person. My action says, 'You can't take care of yourself. Here is a gift for you.' But if I involve myself in his life, recognize his need, and stand alongside him, sharing what resources I have with him, he is not offended."

Dr. Paul Brand and Philip Yancey
Fearfully and Wonderfully Made
pp. 144-45, 147

"It is quite clear that Jesus gave primary attention to correcting a wrong view of life. Whether dealing with the rich young ruler, or with the Samaritan woman, or with Martha, or with Simon the Pharisee, or with the disciples, the record is very clear; his major concern was to help them to see life from another perspective.** Moreover in those incidents where no extended conversation is indicated, it is clear that a conversation must have taken place (i.e., with Zacchaeus and the paralyzed youth and the Bethesda invalid). And in each instance Jesus was never satisfied with minor changes but always pointed to the most fundamental sort of reorientation. So he challenged the rich young ruler to cut loose from his dependence on things and the Samaritan woman to seek meaning on a more primary level than sex. Wherever people were moving down dead-end roads, he pointed out their error and helped them to find a new pathway. . . .

"Basic as the relationship to God was, Jesus nevertheless began his contacts with people on a direct, more personal plane. . . . Over and over again in the midst of a crowd he singled out individuals and related to them. His awareness of the one woman who touched him even while the crowd is pressing in on him (Mark 5:25-34) is typical of his sensitivity to individuals. In the midst of the Jericho crowd he singled out Zacchaeus and called him by name. Among the throng at the Pool at Bethesda, a single sufferer was ministered to. In the crowded courtyard of the high priest it was only Peter that was called to account and at the same time ministered to by the look of love . . . He counted on

---

*See also 22:2, Phillips.

*See also 28:2, Allen.
**See also 32:1, Leslie.

no technique but rather on a personal relationship. His approach was the very opposite of any studied objectivity. He gave himself fully to each relationship, improvising from the circumstances in which he found himself and with what resources he had available. It is easy to imagine that his choicest parables were prompted by current scenes: a farmer sowing, a house built on a rock cliff, a Pharisee praying; and that his teaching was in response to specific situations of need. The importance of the individual, of course, was the cornerstone of Jesus' teachings.''

Robert Leslie
Jesus and Logotherapy
pp. 113-14, 121

New Illuminations:

On the Parable of the Pounds

Matthew 25:12-30   Mark 4:25   Luke 19:11-27

"To provide a setting for Luke's version of the parable an introductory saying has been prefixed (Luke 19:11). It states that the parable was related in order to refute false expectations that the Kingdom was to appear immediately. Hence we see how Luke interpreted the parable: Jesus, perceiving the existence of an eager expectation of the *Parousia*, announces the delay of that event; and for that reason he instructs his disciples that the intervening period is to be a time of testing for them."*

> Joachim Jeremias
> *The Parables of Jesus*
> p. 59

"The disciples were saying to themselves: Now the time has come. They had traveled up and down across the country with this amazing Man from Nazareth. They had experienced unheard-of things, things undreamed of in their philosophy. They could not forget the grateful eyes of those whose fetters this master had broken, of those from whose poor blind eyes he had banished the night, of those upon whom he had bestowed new life. So they had gained the definite impression that wherever this man had appeared he had made deep inroads in the front of the realm of death and that now he was able to roll up this whole front. In a mighty crescendo, his redemptive powers would overrun the old aeon and then within a short time the new world of God would be erected on the ruins of the old. . . .

"Deep sorrow must have pierced the heart of Jesus as he watched his disciples cherishing their dreams and their pious utopias. He knew that his departure from Jerusalem was not the beginning of a dream kingdom of peace, but rather the signal of a new night, the deep darkness on Calvary about the sixth hour. He knew that he must suffer many things before he entered into glory, and that all would forsake him. In agonizing loneliness, Jesus knew that this present world would not simply collapse, as the disciples thought, but would, humanly speaking, triumph over him and spew him out as it would a poisonous, malignant substance, and that then death, suffering and sin would continue to mar the face of this unhappy earth until the last day**. . . . The disciples would either have to understand the mystery of the Passion or else be shipwrecked upon it.

"So Jesus must now prepare them for this kind of an end to the world, for the catastrophe on Calvary. How does

he do this? Does he perhaps let them down easy by telling them the truth gently? No, Jesus proceeds quite differently. He puts his disciples to work. While he is away and the dreadful silence prevails, he gives us clear tasks to perform. 'Make use of your opportunities; trade with your pounds,' he says (Luke 19:13). Why, do you suppose, did he choose this way? Well, when I work for someone, then I share responsibility for his work; then I also think about him. This follows automatically. When Jesus puts me to the work of faith, then I also have daily contact with him. When he sets me at the task of loving my neighbor, he is actually confronting me with his image every day. For it is none other than himself who meets me in my brother and my sister.

"So in this parable we are summoned before the Lord to receive our assignment of work. We all have our work here, including you, and Luther, and the Apostle Paul. For everybody receives exactly the same amount when the orders are given out. Each receives the same operating capital for his Christian life and each receives the same command, to trade with it (Luke 19:13). . . . In other words, when it comes to the things that matter, God treats all his children alike. At the very point on which every thing depends, the great people have no advantage over us. The little girl who says her bed-time prayer and commits her doll to God's protection has just as much as Luther had when he said his prayer at Worms.

"Well, what is this pound that is the same for every servant? . . . All of us have a name, and God calls us by name. We are known. . . . We are not nameless little people; we are children who are known and loved. And this name, the name we bear as children of God, *this* is the pound. . . .

"And there is something further connected with this. Anybody who has once learned and experienced the fact that he possesses this noble name and is thus valued by God also knows that it was of all those who live in loneliness and in the shadow that Jesus was thinking when he cried out, 'It is finished!' They too bear a royal name. Must I not look at my neighbor with completely new eyes when I realize this? Will not the scales suddenly fall from my eyes, and will I not see him in a completely new light?

"This is the pound I am to trade with. Here I face task after task laid upon me by my Lord during his absence. A great multitude of people troop past me during the course of my life. . . . They all have claims, hidden or plain to be seen. They are all crying for redemption; and in every one of them, there suddenly appears the Savior, hungry, cold, imprisoned, naked. He is not ashamed to be their Brother.

"Is not this knowledge I have concerning my fellow man a tremendous endowment? . . . This then is the pound the Lord has given us to trade with and invest. This is what we

---

*See also 104:1, Hooke.
**See also 50:1, Penelope.

are to take and then go right out into the thick of the world and let this thing that has been entrusted to us do the work.''

Helmut Thielicke
The Waiting Father
pp. 137-141

''In the parable of the talents (Matthew) and of the pounds (Luke), the theme is about making money, but as in all parables there is a deeper meaning. Most of us recognize that the talents or, as in the New English Bible, the 'bags of gold,' which the man in the story entrusts to his servants, stand for the gifts with which God endows each of us in varying quantities (Matthew), and what Jesus is saying is that what matters is not the gifts we possess but the use we make of them. We also recognize that the man who buried his talent in the napkin is the man who made nothing of his gift, who did not make use of the capabilities and skills which he had been given. So in the story, his 'bag of gold' had been taken from him and given to the servant who had made the best use of the money that had been entrusted to him.''*

William Neil
The Difficult Sayings of Jesus
p. 32

''The Lord told a parable about a man who goes away, leaving a certain amount of money to his servants. One of the servants very prudently wraps the money up and buries it. He wants to be sure he does not lose it. He is typical of fallen man. He wants to take no risks; but precisely because of this, he loses the talent which had been entrusted to him. The master wanted his servants to take risks. He wanted them to gamble with his money.

''The Lord calls us to the poverty of being always ready to relinquish everything that has been given us so that it can be given back to us enhanced and multiplied. Unless we are prepared to play the game of time like this, and risk losing everything, even what we thought we had will be taken away from us sooner or later. To try to 'possess' in that way is in fact to possess nothing.''

Simon Tugwell
The Beatitudes: Soundings in Christian Traditions
p. 23

''The third servant, if he were living today, would probably say, 'I personally cannot have anything to do with the Lord, but there is no doubt that the Christian enterprise must continue. . . . I can wrap religion in my handkerchief and conserve it.'

''It is worth noting that Jesus not only radically rejects this position but also the arguments by which he does so. He says, 'I will condemn you out of your own mouth, you rascal of a servant.' This obviously means: I am now assuming your position and meeting you on your own level. You say that you feared the Lord, and therefore you took him seriously. But this is just what you did not do. . . . If you had taken me seriously you would have flung your pound away. You said 'no' to me and yet you were not willing to burn your bridges. You went only half way. You were only lukewarm; you see that is why you did not take me seriously at all. There are really only two ways to take a thing seriously. Either you renounce it or you risk everything for it. Either you fling away your pound, or you use it and trade with it. There is no third choice. Throw your Christianity on the trash heap, or else let God be the Lord of your life. . . . But don't wrap him up in your handkerchief.''

Helmut Thielicke
The Waiting Father
pp. 144-145

''How would Jesus' audience have understood the parable? What in particular would they have thought about the servant who buried his talent? Would they have applied the figure to the Jewish people to whom so much had been entrusted, but who had not made use of their trust? Would they have thought of the Pharisees, who thought to secure their personal salvation by a scrupulous observance of the law, but who by their selfish exclusiveness rendered their religion impotent? Jesus' hearers would have thought in the first place of their religious leaders, especially of the scribes. Since Jesus in Luke 11:52 had reproached them for withholding from their fellow-men a due share in God's gift, we may assume that Jesus originally addressed the parable of the talents to the scribes.

''God had entrusted the scribes with much, the spiritual leadership of the nation, the knowledge of his will, the key of the Kingdom of God. Now the judgment of God is about to be revealed; now it will be decided whether the theologians have justified or abused God's great trust: whether they have made good use of God's gift or have turned it to their own advantage and to the imposition of burdens upon their fellow-men; whether they have opened the door of the Kingdom of God or closed it. Their judgment will be specially severe.''

Joachim Jeremias
The Parables of Jesus
pp. 61-62, 166

---

*See also 37:2 Neil; 55:2 Kunkel.

"God obviously has no need of the products of your busy activity since he could give himself everything without you. The only thing that concerns him, the only thing that he desires intensely, is your faithful use of your freedom and the preference you accord him over the things around you.

"Try to grasp this: the things that are given to you on earth are given to you purely as an exercise, a 'blank sheet' on which you make your own mind and heart. You are on a testing ground where God can judge whether you are capable of being translated to heaven and into his presence. You are on trial so that it matters very little what becomes of the fruits of the earth, or what they are worth. The whole question is whether you have learned how to obey and to love. . . .

"The divinization of our endeavor by the value of intention put into it pours a priceless soul into all our actions. . . . It is certainly a very great thing to think that, if we love God, something of our inner activity will never be lost. But will not our achievements, what we bring into being, our *opus* — will not this too in some sense be 'eternalized' and saved? . . . 'Indeed, Lord, it will be. It requires no less than what men call the Absolute, no less than you yourself to set in motion the frail liberty which you have given us. And that being so, everything which diminishes my explicit faith in the heavenly value of the results of my endeavor, diminishes irremediably my power to act.' "

Pierre Teilhard de Chardin
The Divine Milieu
pp. 54-56

New Illuminations:

On Christ's Day of Triumphal Entry Into Jerusalem

Matthew 21:1-22; 24:1-2   Mark 11:1-25   Luke 19:29-46

"In Judah every anointed king (Messiah) was looked on as a savior sent by God to his people. The salvation here does not go beyond the political salvation to be achieved by the king. . . . Psalm 72 may be taken as the clearest expression of the king-savior. He is the savior of his people from external danger. Nowhere is the king presented as a future eschatological deliverer. . . . The fact that the Davidic line no longer ruled after the Exile meant that there could be no ideal king until the indefinite future. These expectations came to center on one supreme king who would represent Yahweh's definitive intervention to save his people. . . . While this king-savior would be a political savior, he would be a savior in virtue of the charisma and power of Yahweh, and so his saving acts would never be merely political."

John L. McKenzie
The Jerome Biblical Commentary
77:155-63

"Kingship is demanded under Samuel and it is granted by God; for by the anointing of the king a man is transformed into the bearer of a charge laid upon him. . . . The leader himself who fails, who cannot stand the test of the charge, who does not make the anointing come true in his own person is a crucial problem in religious history. . . . How do human beings stand the test of what is here called the anointing?

"The history of the kings is the history of the failure of him who has been anointed to realize the promise of his anointing. The rise of Messianism, the belief in the anointed king who realizes the promise of the anointed is to be realized only in this context. . . .

"When the Bible then tries to look beyond these manifestations of leadership to one who no longer stands amidst disintegration and failure, then the idea of the Messianic leader is conceived. It means nothing else by it than at the last the answer shall be given: from out of mankind itself, the Word shall come. . . . This is what the Messianic belief means, the belief in the real leader — [the one who will grant salvation, 'Hosanna.' -Ed.]."

Nahum Glatzer, ed.
Martin Buber: On the Bible
pp. 147-148

"The Transfiguration appears as the porch to the Passion, the actual entrance on the Great Deliverance. So from the mountain, when they came down, he 'set his face to go to Jerusalem' (Luke 9:51). Nor were he and his the only travellers on the road. The crowds were assembling for the Passover, preparing to commemorate once more Israel's deliverance from Egypt by the blood of the lamb and by the Act of God. It was the Passover crowds which, in a sudden burst of enthusiasm, cried to Jesus as he entered the Holy City, 'Hosanna to the Son of David!' Hosanna means *Save now*.

"This was exactly what he was going to do."

Sister Penelope
The Wood
p. 120

"The signs of the Kingdom were not to be blazoned abroad. The teaching of the Kingdom was private. This is the famous 'Messianic secret.' . . . But the Kingdom's character was made as plain as could be by a public fulfilment of Zechariah's prophecy as Jesus rode into the capital not on a prancing war charger as a military conqueror but on a docile donkey as the Prince of Peace (Zechariah 9:9)."

John Stott
Men with a Message
pp. 8-9

"In the end, Jesus himself forces on the crisis. On Palm Sunday, he rides into Jerusalem in deliberate and pointed fulfilment of the prophecy — 'Tell ye the daughter of Zion, behold thy King cometh unto thee . . .' (Isaiah 62:11). And the crowds endorse the silent claim and go wild with enthusiasm. All the romantic loyalties of the lost cause that comes again, all the aching patriotism outraged for so long, all the vague but tremendous hopes that quivered for every Jew behind the word 'Messiah' — these things flame up in a moment. But their cry as St. Mark reports it — 'Blessed be the Kingdom of our father David which cometh' — is a political, not a religious cry. The whole city takes it up, and Jesus of Nazareth, the King of the Jews, rides in triumph to the temple gates. . . .

"Will he launch them [the Jewish people] now to the attack? He has only to wave one arm, shout one word. . . . The Son of David always had a taking way with him, a way that would have made simple men glad enough to die for him and his claims. The great classical historians are agreed that there were sullen surgings of discontent against Roman rule over the Near East at that time. If the right leader had come forward at that time, he might have swept the Roman eagles right out of Asia and even beyond. Perhaps it is all there in the cool spring sunshine of Palm Sunday afternoon — 'the kingdoms of this world and the glory of them' (Matthew 4:8). At least the chance of them was there for the taking — if he will only give one signal. 'When he had looked around about upon them all, he went out of the city into Bethany with the twelve' (Mark 11:11). You can almost *feel* the anticlimax!

"The next day the temperature rises again. He cleanses the temple in defiance of all the authorities. They can do nothing. The people are behind him. He is still the Master of the City."

Dom Gregory Dix
The Claim of Jesus Christ
pp. 51-52

"There is so much that is obvious about Palm Sunday, our Lord's deliberate and literal fulfilment of Zechariah's prophecy about the peaceful king, the bitter contrast between the triumph and the Passion following, that other things no less significant often get overlooked. For instance, a procession with branches and Psalm 118 was a feature of the feast of tabernacles which was also the feast of New Year and full of the thought of God's Kingship. Also the goal of that procession was the Temple altar, the place of sacrifice. So that impromptu procession of Passover pilgrims on the first Palm Sunday combined the themes and types of both these two great feasts. But over and above all that, the festal coming of Christ was a symbol of his final, finished coming to his Father of the Son of Man. That, at least, is how St. Bernard sees it. The liturgical Palm procession, he says, which reenacts that entry, represents the glory of our heavenly fatherland. As we walk in it, we should think what joy will be ours when we are caught up to meet Christ in the air;* and we should long with our whole heart to see when Christ the Lord, the Head with all his members, shall be received into the heavenly Jerusalem bearing the palm of victory and with all the Angelic powers and the peoples of both testaments crying on every side, 'Blessed is he who comes in the name of the Lord!' That is your goal he says."

Sister Penelope
The Coming
p. 29

"Jesus always looked at attacks impersonally, with sadness for the people involved; for think, just think what his mission could have done for them. They had admired his miracles, they wanted to imitate them but feared his mysterious, personal power that reached out and touched a force about which they knew nothing. In fear they knew not what they were doing nor why."

Austin Pardue
The Single Eye
p. 74

"Jesus wept tears of disappointment over the Holy City. This is what man in his pride and his folly had actually done — to God. The love that Jesus gave so lavishly was unrequited love. The efforts that Jesus made to bring the nation to repentance and to save it from destruction failed. Most of them did not repent and in the next generation Jerusalem was destroyed. The Cross did not avert this anymore than it averted Belsen or Hiroshima. History must take its course and it will. God can endure disappointment and he does. For that reason the Cross is planted firmly in the midst of our disappointments. It is true to type. And beside the disappointment and sorrow of God, all our grumblings dwindle into insignificance. . . .

"The great problem of waste naturally disturbs those with a sense of responsibility. Waste is the central impression of all tragedy. Is this not the final impression that we received at the end of all the great tragedies of Shakespeare? Why should human life, so precious itself, be wasted because of human ambition or jealousy or greed or revenge?"*

Douglas Webster
In Debt to Christ
p. 21

"Plainer than any parable to proclaim the theme of the strong man and the stronger were Jesus' symbolic actions. Twice, if we take the Gospels as they stand, he ejected from the new and lovely temple at Jerusalem those who were using it for alien purposes. The first occasion, recorded in John 2:13-22, was at Passover soon after he began his ministry. The disciples were reminded by that fierce, effective anger of the words of Psalm 69:9: 'The zeal of thine house shall eat me up.' And when the Jews asked him what sign he showed that he acted thus, he answered, 'Destroy this temple and in three days I will raise it up.' His words were received with derision, but, says the Evangelist, looking back on the scene in the light of the Resurrection, 'He spoke of the temple of his body.' Jesus was never forgiven for that temple saying; the Synoptists, who do not record its origin, tell how he was reproached with it, of course in twisted form, while the destruction of the temple of his body was in process on the Cross (Matthew 27:40). It is the Synoptists also who gave the story of the second cleansing, again at Passover, within a few days of his death. It appears as a climax of his triumphal entry into Jerusalem. On this occasion, Jesus

---

*See also 105:2, Penelope.

---

*See also 25:2, Kunkel.

250

conflates two sayings from the prophets to support his action. 'Is it not written, my house shall be called a house of prayer for all nations? But ye have made it a den of robbers.' "

Sister Penelope
The Coming
pp. 25-26

"Our Lord met positively the second temptation of Satan by entering the temple and driving out the buyers and sellers.* Gradually the vendors of articles of sacrifice had pushed themselves closer to the temple choking the avenues that led to it until finally some of them gained entrance to Solomon's porch, there selling doves and cattle and changing money. Every visitor to the feast was obliged to pay half a shekel to help defray the expenses of the temple and, since no foreign money could be exchanged, the sons of Annas trafficked in the barter of coins. There were men with great wicker cages filled with doves while dealers brought into the temple whole flocks of oxen and goats and sheep and lambs. The cries of animals mixing with the noise of crowds suffocated prayer and worship.

". . . The Savior now moved to his high mission of purifying the temple by making war on mummeries and hypocrisies and shams. . . . Taking ropes from the necks of the cattle, he made cords which served as a scourge as he drove out the traitors with their sheep and their oxen. Then with a majestic gesture he overthrew the tables of the money-changers."

Fulton J. Sheen
The Life of Christ
pp. 49-50

"The disciples were conscious that the entry into Jerusalem was no ordinary Passover visit. They, too, knew that something was going to happen. . . . They may well have observed with concern the 'straitening' of which Jesus had spoken (Luke 12:15), and were keenly on the watch for any indication that his power was impaired. Moreover the incidents of the day, the unequivocal assertion of authority by Jesus in the act of cleansing the Temple, forcing the priestly officials to decide on a course of action which was to result in his death, must have raised the expectations of the disciples.

"It is against this background that we must view the apparently trivial incident of the fig tree. We have seen from Mark that the words of Jesus when he found the fig tree barren were observed by the disciples, but according to Mark nothing happened at the time to attract their attention. Something, however, did happen but in the mind of Jesus. The Synoptic Gospels have recorded what Jesus felt. He wept over Jerusalem and uttered words of fateful import (Luke 19:41). This sense of doom, of rejection, lay heavy on his heart; and when he came looking for some poor sustenance from the fig tree and found nothing there, it became a symbol of the rejecting city, the unbelieving nation. . . . The words Jesus uttered were addressed not to the fig tree but to barren Israel. All of this was hidden from the disciples; yet from behind the apparently trivial words, 'and his disciples were listening,' lies a hint of the tension in their minds too, the eagerness with which they were watching for any favorable sign. More than ever, after what had happened in the Temple, were they on the watch for the same thing the priests demanded, a sign that there was power behind the authority that cleared the Temple of the defilement. So on the next morning, Peter seized on the withered fig tree as a welcome sign that their leader's power was unimpaired (Mark 11:20-21). If Jesus could put a curse of such efficacy on a tree as to cause it to wither, then they had nothing to fear from the issue of conflict which they saw to be impending. . . . Once more, as at Caesarea Philippi, Peter was not thinking about God's things but about man's things.

"There are several important points to note in Jesus' answer to Peter, an answer intended for all the disciples and for all time. Again the tree, this time not only barren but withered, was a sign and symbol to Jesus of what was destined to happen to his unhappy people, a destiny in which he was fatefully involved with them by the purpose of God. That is why his first words were, 'Have God's faith.' In Hebrew there is a fundamental link between 'faith' and 'faithfulness'; God's faithfulness to his word calls forth man's response of faith, and Jesus is here occupied primarily with God's faithfulness rather than man's faith. So that while man's faith is the natural concomitant to God's faithfulness, I do not think that Jesus was thinking here about man's faith in God, and the words should not be so rendered. His next words show, as against Mark's form of the saying, that he was not occupied at all by what had happened to the fig tree, but with the apparently insuperable obstacles which confronted him, just as the mountain mass of Olives lay between him and the city. The fig tree was a sign to Jesus that he had not mistaken the direction of God's purpose, and, laying hold of that faithfulness, he believed that even the obstructing mountain of unbelief and hostility could be removed by God's power."

S. H. Hooke
The Kingdom of God
pp. 124-26

---

*See also 13:3, Rosenthal.

New Illuminations:

On Forgiveness III: Forgivingness, Unreadiness, and Abuse

Matthew 6:14-15; 18:21-35	Mark 4:12; 11:25	Luke 5:20-25; 19:44; 22:34

"The deepest secret of the love which characterizes realized discipleship is that they have learned how to forgive. They extend to others the divine forgiveness which they have experienced, a forgiveness which passes all understanding. The parable of the unmerciful servant is concerned with this. . . . It combines an exhortation with a warning: God has extended to you in the Gospel, through the offer of forgiveness, a merciful gift beyond conceiving. But God will revoke the forgiveness of sin if you do not whole heartedly share the forgiveness you have experienced, but harden your heart against your brother.* Everything is here at stake. Woe unto to you if you try to stand on your rights. God will then stand on his and see that his sentence is executed rigorously. Jesus makes use of the two measures, but he completely transforms Jewish apocalyptic which taught that God rules the world by two measures — of mercy and of judgment; but at the Last Judgment he only makes use of judgment. . . . On the other hand Jesus taught that the measure of mercy is in force at the Last Judgment also. The decisive pleasure is: When does God at the Last Judgment use the measure of mercy and when the measure of judgment? Jesus answers, 'Where God's forgiveness produces a readiness to forgive, there God's mercy grants forgiveness of debts again at the Last Judgment; But he who abuses God's gift faces the full severity of judgment, as if he had never received forgiveness.''

Joachim Jeremias
The Parables of Jesus
pp. 210, 213-14

"The man who abuses the forgiveness of the Kingdom places himself, by his own act, outside the sphere of its operation: 'His Lord delivered him to the tormentors' (Matthew 18:24). For such a one nothing remains but the torment of a heart that has seen the divine forgiveness and refused it. The torment of Hell consists in a self-imposed separation from God."

S. H. Hooke
The Kingdom of God
p. 115

"The lord of the unmerciful bond-slave forgave him a debt beyond repayment. That too is the soul's situation,

entrusted with the seed of sanctifying grace to cherish, the talent of holiness to increase; incorporated in the Mystical Body of the Incarnate, fed with his abundant life. It has received the unpriced gifts of the spirit that it may bring forth the fruits of the spirit; not in the interest of any personal beatitude, but because they are demanded by the eternal purposes of God. Love, joy, peace, long-suffering; these are a part of man's debt, and here he can hardly say in his own strength, 'Have patience with me and I will pay you all.' Here then he cannot dare to say, 'Pay what thou owest!' to other men. . . .

"There are two perennial situations in which the human creature, individually or as a group, has to exercise that self-oblivious charity which is the essence of forgiveness. First the case in which it considers that its established rights have been infringed — trespasses. Secondly, the cases in which it considers that its own just demands on affection, deference, consideration, possessions or status have not been met — debts. Either by attack or neglect, the creature's self-love, its fundamental pride, is injured; and its anger aroused. At once the walls close in; it is inevitably cut off from the society of the sons of God, and is alone with its own wrath, its own rights. But those in whom the life of prayer is operative are required to abandon the standpoint of self interest, whether personal or corporate; quietly and humbly to forgive the trespass, freely remit the debt, if they want to know the living peace of God.''*

Evelyn Underhill
Abba
pp. 68-69

"In his *Letters to Malcolm*, C. S. Lewis seems to be referring to one major healing in his own life. He writes about forgiving 'someone I have been trying to forgive for over thirty years,' and of his discovery that 'forgiving (that man's cruelty) and being forgiven (my resentment) were the very same thing.' . . . 'Mere time does nothing to the fact or to the guilt of a sin. Guilt is washed out not by sin but by the blood of Christ.' For years Lewis had not been able to forgive himself for his failure to love his father; nor had he been able to appropriate God's forgiveness for this sin.** But when finally enabled, he was most incredulous of the peace and ease he experienced. This is the peace promised

---

*See also 59:3, Linn.

---

*See also 59:3, Linn.
**See also 59:3, Underhill.

by Jesus Christ; and when it is received, it floods the finite soul — the dweller in chaotic time.''

Leanne Payne
Real Presence:
The Holy Spirit in the Works of C. S. Lewis
pp. 73-76

"Naturally to those that think that Jesus cursed the fig tree (Mark 11:21), the subject of forgiveness would seem strangely irrelevant. But for Jesus it was wholly and immediately relevant as he now faced the final issue of what was to be done at Jerusalem: God's forgiveness and God's power were inseparably connected (Luke 5:20-26). . . . If no one but God could forgive sins, then it was indeed no easy thing and its difficulty lay not with God but with man. God was ready to forgive, but man was not ready to be forgiven.*

"With the shadow of death upon him, Jesus knew and told his disciples that power was there and that faith could set it in motion, but the ultimate condition for its working was forgiveness. For all that men were going to do to him, forgiveness would be required from him. Here was the actual challenge of how it was to be done. . . . He himself had to establish the condition in his own experience in order that power might be liberated to do the hardest thing of all, to remove the mountain that lay between man and God. Here he had to learn in his own experience both how God forgives and what it is to need forgiveness. Since what men were going to do to him would be done to God, would be man's final act of hostility and rejection, in his forgiveness God's forgiveness was involved. It had to pass through him as its channel.** Through him God must pass over to the other side and bridge the gap. So the Omnipotence willed to work and to suffer.''

S. H. Hooke
The Kingdom of God
pp. 127-28

"The Lord always makes generous allowances for excusable ignorance. The soldiers at the Cross were only the paid hands to put into effect the evil plans of other men's minds, and they were under orders. Their unhappy position arose from each of them being a *potential* Christian. Suppose that one of them later actually became a Christian and recalled that he had actually driven the nails into the Son of God, he would never be able to forgive himself. Jesus anticipates this. He would forgive him in advance. All of

our forgiveness is antedated.* Christ died for our sins before we even lived to commit them. God's grace precedes our faith; God's pardon precedes our sinning. The initiative never rests on human penitence but on divine love.''

Douglas Webster
In Debt to Christ
pp. 30-31

"With the memory of his abysmal failure on that calamitous night in the court-yard of the high priest's palace torturing and assailing his conscience, Peter hears the Lord's astounding commission, 'Feed my sheep.' Forgiveness is never just a matter between two persons — the aggrieved one and the offending one. Who can forgive sins but God only? Only he who is ultimately responsible for the maintenance of life's meaning. So the sinner who needs forgiveness — and that will mean most of us most of the time — will persist in the question, 'Who shall deliver me?' (Romans 7:24). He will understand that the very anguish of his sense of failure argues that somewhere there is a reality that maintains his pressure upon him. Only such a reality can deal with his problem.''

John M. Krumm
The Art of Being a Sinner
pp. 76, 82

"To have been forgiven oneself is the greatest possible impulse toward forgiving others, and the will to forgive others is the test of having effectively received God's forgiveness.** The true Christian is essentially the 'forgiven person.' It is this characteristic that helps him to be humble towards God, and to serve his fellows without becoming self-assertive or aggressive while he does so.''

Margaret Duggan, ed.
Through the Year with Michael Ramsey
p. 136

"The life which Christ gives is redeemed and always being redeemed. The very life-blood is being forgiven; it is continually incorporating into itself things which are in themselves wrong. . . . The past which is in itself wrong and irretrievable is retrieved by Christ; the forgiven sin in the present becomes a new evidence of his love and a new ground for gratitude. This life is also redeeming. Wherever a

---

*See also 71:1, Payne.
**See also 117:3, Pike.

*See also 59:3, Underhill.
**See also 59:3, Underhill.

Christian is, there offences are forgiven, misunderstandings carried, and the wrong put right. This is clean contrary to the natural order of things, in which the result of evil is to propagate itself, so that one hatred leads on to another without end. The Christian is always being converted, turned around, and is always converting evil into good."

T. R. Milford
Foolishness to the Greeks
p. 78

New Illuminations:

On Jesus' New Confrontation with Official Jewry

Matthew 21:23—22:46   Mark 11:27—12:44   Luke 11:53-54; 19:47—21:4

"The leaders of the nation felt that it was altogether intolerable that Jesus should criticize the respectable religion of good-living people, and call the righteous Pharisees hypocrites. They dared not face up to it; they said in their hearts, 'We will not have this man to reign over us' (Luke 19:14). They were indeed looking for the advent of their Messiah; but they wanted a Messiah who would render a proper respect to their well-intentioned religion. Very many would follow one who would claim temporal power and organize a Holy War against the Roman government but not a Messiah who brought the reign of God's rule so uncomfortably near. When, by claiming authority over the temple and expelling the traders, he forced them to say 'yes' or 'no' to the one question that mattered, the chief priests finally made up their minds that there must be an end to it: that man was not God's Messiah, but a cursed pretender.

"There was and is only one question at issue between the Lord Jesus and all who believe in him on the one hand, and the Jews and the world at large on the other. . . . It is the question whether he really was the promised Christ; whether in him, the Lord God of Israel has visited and redeemed his people; whether he is the Son of God and the Savior of the world. . . . And every man must say for himself whether he accepts also the spiritual demand which that involves on himself, or is content that Jesus should be crucified."

A. G. Hebert
Scripture and the Faith
pp. 48-49

"What the Gospels report on numerous occasions about Jesus' attitude to and influence on the different people he encounters is important. Every one of the scenes described in the Gospel reveals Jesus' astounding sovereignty in dealing with the situation according to the kind of people he encounters. This is apparent in the numerous teaching and conflict messages in which he sees through his opponents, disarms their objections, answers their questions, or forces them to answer for themselves. He can make his opponent open his mouth, or he can put him to silence. . . . In his encounters with others we see time and again that he knows men and uncovers their thoughts with insight into the character of his interlocutors. . . .

"Jesus acknowledged John the Baptist and relates his own vocation with that of John. Thus when questioned by the high priests, scribes and elders as to his own authority,

he answers with this surprising question in return, 'Was the Baptism of John from Heaven or from men?' And his opponents do not dare answer lest they jeopardise their position. Their silence is answered with silence. Unmistakeably this is his 'Yes' which he pronounces on John and his Baptism, and the meaning of this 'Yes' is: the decision concerning John and his Baptism of repentance is also the decision concerning Jesus and his mission."*

Gunther Bornkamm
Jesus of Nazareth
pp. 58-59

"The episode of challenging Jesus' authority, Matthew appends the short parable of the two sons, which is explained by Jesus in the saying, 'Truly I tell you that the tax-gatherers and the harlots are going before you into the Kingdom of God. For John came to you to show you the way of righteousness and you did not believe him, but they did believe him; and when you saw this, you did not afterward repent and believe him' (Matthew 21:32)."

S. H. Hooke
The Kingdom of God
p. 23

"In the teaching of Jesus, conversion and belief are two sides of the same basic attitude. Only the convert can believe that the time of salvation is already there and that God's full reign is at the door. Belief, in its turn, is a conversion because it includes a recognition of guilt before God and the need for salvation and also the readiness to fulfill God's will in the radical form in which Jesus presents it. This closely-knit union of conversion and belief is well expressed in the parable of the dissimilar sons (Matthew 21:28-31). It is clearly directed toward the devout Pharisees whose reaction to the teaching of John the Baptizer and to that of Jesus was one of superiority and stiffness. . . .

"A want of belief that 'the hour is at hand' leads to a neglect of God's will. This is brought out in the parable of the sons. All these zealots proclaim their loyalty to God's commandment, and yet, at the decisive moment, they are disobedient. Sinners who till now defied God's will begin

---

*See also 10:2, Krumm.

to reflect because they believed the Baptizer's preaching and they now accept Jesus' gospel of salvation. They have become God's obedient sons and have gained an entry into the kingdom.''

Rudolf Schnackenburg
God's Rule and Kingdom
pp. 106-107

"Hostility toward Jesus on the part of the Jewish religious leaders was reaching its climax, and they only waited for a suitable opportunity to arrest him without provoking a riot among the people. Meantime, they attempted to incriminate him by imposing trick questions, in the hope that his answers would condemn him out of his own mouth. On this occasion the *agents provocateurs* consist of members of the Pharisaic party and the entourage of Herod Antipas, who was in Jerusalem for the Passover. This unholy alliance prefaced their question with a flattering and completely insincere tribute to Jesus. The question itself was crafty and dangerous in the extreme. Judea at that time was under direct control of the Roman Emperor through his local representative, the procurator Pontius Pilate. As a symbol of their subjection and as a contribution toward the cost of government, a head tax of one silver denarius, about twelve cents, was levied on the population. . . . The question, 'Shall we pay taxes or not?' was therefore loaded. If Jesus said 'No,' he would have been arrested and charged with treason. If he said 'Yes,' he would at once lose the sympathy of his supporters. . . . It was a real dilemma for Jesus. He asked for a denarius to be brought to him. This would entail getting one from outside the Temple since the idolatrous Roman coin was not allowed within the sacred courts. . . .

"Jesus' answer was not at all an evasive one. It said several things: first, that Jesus himself was no revolutionary. Second, it acknowledged Caesar's right to the tax. The coin was his. Let him have it! But third, far more important than what is owed to Caesar is what is owed to God — obedience, loyalty, service, the offering of ourselves in thanksgiving for all that God has done for us. It is little wonder that Jesus' reply was received with astonishment. He had turned what had intended to be a political trap into a powerful assertion of the paramount authority of God.''

William Neil
The Difficult Sayings of Jesus
pp. 55-56

"Jesus did not produce the stock revolutionary answers to stock questions. They tried to trap him with the question which sorted out a man's politics: whether or not it was right to pay taxes to Caesar. He neatly avoided the one-way street they tried to drive him up by affirming that Caesar had a legitimacy, but that it was far from ultimate.

"The real answer to the revolutionary accusation was that Jesus was not against any man or group, but for them all. He wept over Jerusalem; he did not plan to blow it up. And his anger at his opponents was the tragic side of his love for them, since they were so blind to their own real needs. He made every thing on this earth relative and provisional, unable to bear any ultimate loyalty: only God must have that. . . .

"Christ passes through the midst and makes his own way whenever we try to enroll for Right or Left or Center. What could be more unpopular than that? Where *did* he stand, this Will o' the Wisp who would not genuflect to anyone's pet theory. . . . Who was he to march to the beat of a different drummer from anyone else? Just who did he think he was? Soon these revolutionary hosannas turned into 'Crucify, crucify,' and yet again Jesus went his own way. It is ironic to note that they released a noted revolutionary, a paid up party member called Barabbas, on the crowd's demand. But Jesus they delivered up to be crucified.''

Richard Holloway
A New Heaven
pp. 30-31

"In its willingness to render unto Caesar the things that are Caesar's, the Church has sometimes been dangerously near to rendering to Caesar the things that are God's. . . . Be that as it may, it has rarely been a deliberate betrayal; and generally the Church has called a halt to any further accommodation when its fundamental obedience to God has been called into question. . . . As soon as the Church in Germany raised the standard of revolt against Hitler's neo-paganism, hostilities broke out; and in the conflict the state could claim the imminent extinction of the Church as other tyrants had done in days gone by.

". . . The German Church, predominantly Lutheran, did its best to avoid interfering in the affairs of the State. But the moment came when it had to withstand the dreadful machinations of the Nazis, and its persecution followed. Germany is an obvious example of the conflict that can arise between this world and God's world, and it will be with us until the end of time. . . . We feel like honoring the man who pledges his allegiance in such terms as 'my country, right or wrong.' But this is to confuse loyalty with identification. Loyalty does not mean an agreement based on an absence of principles or standards. Nevertheless, as a Christian, man's primary standards must be to God. If his temporal conflicts with his spiritual loyalty, the latter must come first. For this reason there were good men, both good Christians and patriotic Germans, who in the last war could only hope and pray for the defeat of their fatherland. They could see no other means of bringing their own beloved country to its senses.''

Joost de Blank
Uncomfortable Words
pp. 30-34

"The Hebrews in Old Testament times thought of life after death as a shadowy existence in the underworld, more or less like the Greek or Roman Hades. Gradually, however, by New Testament times, this was replaced by the idea of resurrection. Unlike the Greek philosophers who taught that the body died but the soul was immortal, the Hebrews believed that the body and soul were inseparable; therefore, any life after death must be in terms of a bodily resurrection. This was the belief of most of the Jews in Jesus' day. Only the conservative Sadducees, who claimed the idea of a bodily resurrection was a 'modern' view and had not the authority of Moses behind it, refused to accept it. In controversy with the Pharisees and, in the case of Jesus' saying in Mark 12:25, in controversy with our Lord, they thought to show that the whole idea of resurrection was fantastic (Luke 27:27-40). Jesus is accosted by some Sadducees who tell an unlikely story about seven brothers. . . .

"Jesus, in his reply, made two points accusing his questioners of knowing neither the Scripture nor the power of God. He meant that God can create new orders of life where the conditions are far different from those we know here. In the life beyond death, where death no longer exists, the physical side of marriage (as distinct from companionship) and, consequently birth, finds no place. Like food and drink, these belong to the earthly sphere. Life after death, says Jesus, is like that of the angels in heaven, a higher order of being where there is perfect communion with God. He then goes on to challenge the Sadducees' skepticism about a future life by reminding them that the early ancestors of Israel were long since dead. Their bodies moldered in their tombs, but God was still God. They were alive with him in his presence, for God is not the God of the dead but the God of the living."

William Neil
The Difficult Sayings of Jesus
pp. 58-59

"On Tuesday comes the 'day of questions' — the attempts of his Jewish opponents to make him declare himself openly. If he claims outright to be the Messiah, the Roman government with its troops will have to deal with him. If he denies it, the disappointed people will probably lynch him and probably desert him. . . . At the end comes his devastating counter-attack. 'What think ye of the Christ? Whose son is he?' They say unto him (what else could they say?) — 'David's.' All the world knows who that is now. His enemies have publicly admitted — been trapped into admitting that *he is the Christ!* How men must have held their breath at that moment! Now will he make his claim — the claim the people are longing to rise up for and if need be die for? And instantly he raises the whole question to another level. 'If David called Christ his (Divine) Lord, how then be he David's son?' No wonder St. Luke says that after that 'no man durst ask him any more questions.' It was too dangerous! He might have precipitated the whole

explosion with that one alarming thrust — but he knew exactly what he was doing.

"He cannot truthfully deny that he is the Messiah, and Son of David. In sheer fact, he is these things. . . . Yet he knows that the deliverance that the Christ must bring to man from God is something far deeper and more piercing than the deliverance from any other outward force at all. For it is something that goes down to the very ground of their being — deliverance from sin, from their overpowering claims of their own selves upon them against the claim of the love of God. All through the week, the terrible cross purposes go on. By extraordinarily skillful fencing he insists all the time on being *rejected on his own terms*. And all the week the people are cooling from him. He is missing his chances, time and time again — just balking at making the one claim they are longing to hear, waiting to rise for. A day or two and in this disappointment, they will howl for his blood. The moment it is safe, his enemies make sure of him by a secret night arrest."

Dom Gregory Dix
The Claim of Jesus Christ
pp. 53-54

"There is little doubt that Luke understood Psalm 110 as Messianic in that it reflects the outlook of David's dynasty. 'David himself calls him "Lord"'; how then can he be David's son?' The question Jesus poses is simple in itself. . . . Of possible interpretations, only one is convincing in the long run. Jesus is in effect insinuating that the Messiah is really something more than a son of David, having a more exalted, transcendent origin than David himself. This would be another step in the self-revelation of Jesus. Jesus' question, rather than a denial that the Messiah is David's son, is a statement that he is more than that. While humanly descended from David, the Messiah had a character transcending mere blood ties with David; so the latter could rightly refer to him by the name otherwise reserved for Yahweh."

Edward Mally
The Jerome Biblical Commentary
42:74

"This Psalm is purely Messianic and was always considered to be so. When Jesus quoted it in his conversation with the rulers, it is perfectly evident that they looked upon it in that light. It is equally certain that he made use of it in that sense. While we believe the authorship of many of these psalms to be uncertain, we claim that the words of Jesus put the question of authorship in this case beyond dispute. Then the beauty of the song is seen in all its fullness. David, the king, sings of another as Lord, and therefore superior to himself."

G. Campbell Morgan
Notes on the Psalms
p. 213

"David, great man that he was, never ascended to heaven. For he himself both died and is buried and his tomb is with us to this very day. But he said, 'The Lord said to my Lord: Sit thou at my right hand till I make thine enemies thy footstool.' What is the meaning of this mysterious sentence? What 'Lord' is David referring to, whom the Lord God is commanding to sit at his own right hand until his enemies were made his footstool? Surely he is prophesying of the Holy One, the Christ, the one who should not see corruption, even though he were put to death. Can you not see that David with the insight of a prophet was foreseeing his own Lord and ours, this very Man Jesus, the Christ of God, whom God would not permit death to hold, and whom God has now raised to the highest place of power? My brothers, the whole household of Israel must know beyond a shadow of doubt that this Jesus, whom you crucified, God has made both 'Lord' and 'Christ' (Free translation of Acts 2:34-36)."

J. B. Phillips
The Young Church in Action
p. 86

"The point of the story is that the Pharisees could not solve a simple exegetical problem. Jesus thus demonstrates that they are not competent religious teachers; even their vaunted skill of religious interpretation breaks down. They cannot be judges of the identity of the Messiah if they cannot deal with a Messianic text. Whether they accept Jesus as the Messiah is meaningless because they do not understand the Scripture in which the Messiah is revealed. (Hence verse 46, 'Beware of the scribes.' —Ed.)"

John L. McKenzie
Jerome Biblical Commentary
43:153

"The present setting of the story of the widow's gift may be due simply to the catch word *widow* (Luke 20:47), but a more apt position for it could hardly be imagined. Not only does it form a fitting contrast to the previous section ('in contrast to the bad scribes, who "eat" widow's property, we have now the tale of the good widow and her sacrifice' — Montefiore); but with its teaching that the true gift is to give 'everything we have' (Mark 12:44), it sums up what has gone before in the Gospel and makes a superb transition to the story of how Jesus 'gave everything' for men."

D. E. Nineham
Saint Mark
pp. 334-35

"Some people might look at a picture and think it good or bad and the opinion might not matter. The thing that would matter would be the opinion of an artist. . . . The opinion that really does matter is the opinion of our Lord, Jesus Christ. The value of an act is the spiritual quality that he sees in it. He sat at the door of the Temple and saw people giving their alms, and he was not the least impressed with the clattering offerings that fell from the hands of the rich, but he was moved to speak immortal words about one poor woman who gave a farthing."

Harry C. Griffith, ed.
A Gift of Light: A Collection of Thoughts from the Writings of Father Andrew
p. 72

New Illuminations:

On the Parable of the Wicked Vineyard Tenants

Matthew 21:33-46   Mark 12:12   Luke 20:9-18

"The God of the Bible is often portrayed as a disappointed God. The Old Testament reveals his disappointment with Israel. Nowhere is this put more poignantly than in Isaiah's parable of the vineyard:

'My well loved had a vineyard in a very beautiful hill: and he made a trench about it and gathered out the stones thereof, and planted it with the choicest vine, and built a tower in the midst of it, and also hewed out a winepress therein. And he looked that it should bring forth grapes, and it brought forth wild grapes. And now, O inhabitants of Jerusalem and men of Judah, judge, I pray you, betwixt me and my vineyard, said the Lord. What could have been done in my vineyard that I have not done in it? Wherefore when I looked that it should bring forth grapes, brought it forth wild grapes?'

"The divine problem is brought before human minds in two solemn questions. 'What could have been done more to my vineyard that I have not done in it?' God has withheld nothing. He has been utterly generous, giving all that we could take. In our Lord's remodeling of this parable, he even sends his beloved Son into the vineyard. . . . We like the Psalmists are always bursting out with our questionings to God, why? why? This is God's Why to man, to us."

Douglas Webster
In Debt to Christ
pp. 19-20

"The prophet is the man who has been set up against his own natural instincts that bind him to the community, and who likewise sets himself up against the will of the people to live on as they always have lived which, for the people is identical with the will to live. It goes without saying that not only the rulers but also the people treat the prophet as their enemy in the way in which, as a matter of history, it falls to the lot of such men to be treated. These experiences of suffering which thus come upon the prophet join together to form that image of the servant of the Lord, of his suffering and dying for the sake of God's purpose."

Nahum Glatzer, ed.
Martin Buber: On the Bible
pp. 148

"An interesting reference to Jesus' act of ransom was a parable that is almost biographical, namely the parable of the dishonest tenants. The rulers had just been questioning our Lord as to the authority by which he acted. . . . Our Lord answers them in a parable showing them the kind of guardians and guides they were. God had enclosed his people with his own hands, and prepared them to be a fruitful vine. The letting out of the vineyard to those who tended it meant the commitment to his own people of responsibility. . . .

"The next scene is one in which the owner of the vineyard claims the returns, namely, fidelity and love of God (Luke 20:10). Our Lord describes that the messengers, who are the prophets, were subjected to cruel treatment and often murder. . . . Then Jesus draws his last arrow from the quiver of the parable. He sets himself apart from the servants or the prophets and tells his auditors that he comes from the owner of the vineyard — God himself. Christ here presents himself as God's last appeal to the sinful world, a supreme gift of infinite love. The Father hopes that his Son will be counted as standing for himself, and that the gratitude and affection and reverence which is due to him will be shown to his Son. 'But they took him and killed him and cast him out of the vineyard.'

"Our Blessed Lord, under this symbol, reminds his hearers of the melancholy fact that he will receive but little reverence from mankind. Rebuffs and injuries and insults would be the greeting extended to the Beloved Son of the Heavenly Father."

Fulton Sheen
The Life of Christ
pp. 94-95

"The evangelists tell us that the parable of the wicked husbandmen was addressed to the members of the Sanhedrin (Luke 20:1 par.). This must be correct. In the Song of the Vineyard to which Jesus refers, the people of God are compared to the vineyard, since then the vineyard had been the usual symbol of Israel. But it may be assumed that since Jesus is not speaking about the vineyard, but about its tenants, he is not talking of the people as a whole but of their leaders. Moreover it is very possible that the parable was spoken in connection with the cleansing of the temple, as the present context says. In that case it would be the temple authorities, especially the priestly members of the Sanhedrin to whom the parable's terrible threat refers (Luke

20:16-18). God, who has waited with such inconceivable patience is now about to demand his dues, and the last generation must expiate the accumulated guilt.''

Joachim Jeremias
The Parables of Jesus
pp. 166-67

''In the much discussed parable of the evil vinedressers, we are concerned only with the question whether and in what way the early church applied it to the Gentiles. That it did so is evident from one verse (21:43) of Matthew who was universal in outlook in spite of his Jewish Christian readers. 'Therefore, I say to you the kingdom (reign) of God shall be taken away from you and shall be given to a nation yielding the fruits thereof.' The meaning is clear. God's ancient people will be rejected because it repudiated God's messengers and also his Son and a new 'people' enters, the New Israel, to which the Gentiles too belong. What is surprising is the way that this is formulated and the idea of the 'reign of God' that underlies it.

'' 'To take away the kingdom (reign) of God' is a curious expression in the New Testament, and it compels us to understand the kingdom of God as a reality already present in the history of Israel. We are familiar with the Rabbinical notion that in the past the 'kingship' was with Israel, but that it was taken from them when they sinned and 'given to the peoples' in their stead. But they were not referring to God's reign, though Israel's political reign was closely connected with God's action. The verse in question would seem to be influenced by views and expressions of this kind, now transferred to God's reign. . . . Strictly speaking the kingdom (reign) of God should not be identified with the vineyard for this represents Israel (the evil vinedressers are its leaders); but such lack of precision is apt to occur in 'applied' interpretations. The idea expressed in Matthew 21:43 cannot be dissociated from Jesus. In Matthew 8:11-12, the people stream in and receive a share in God's kingdom while the 'sons of the kingdom' (Luke 13:28, 'you'), the unbelieving Jews, are excluded.''

Rudolf Schnackenburg
God's Rule and Kingdom
pp. 240-41

''The final question not only expresses a Messianic tradition of great antiquity in the Bible — the cornerstone on which rests the Kingdom of God — but it also explains Jesus' rejection by official Judaism. Luke's special contribution is verse 20:18, a clear reference to the Passion. Jesus' death will fall like a rock on all men breaking his enemies to pieces and grinding his followers to his own lowly state. The con-

clusion is best understood to read: 'They (the leaders) feared because the people knew that Jesus had aimed this parable at them,' i.e., at the leaders.''

Carroll Stuhlmueller
The Gospel of Saint Luke
p. 130

''Christ spoke of himself as the stone which will break all who fall on it and will grind to powder all on whom it falls. What then? Is it we who have fallen on this great and wondrous stone, or has the stone fallen on us? We do not know, but however that may be, we are precipitated into a world of realities whose existence we did not suspect before. In the old days when life for the majority flowed in broad channels of established tradition, the word of Christ did not disturb. But now with the whole earth fraught with man's despair, with the protest of consciences outraged, with violence threatening to wipe out all life, we must need to make our voices heard. All of us today are in vital need of a firm faith in Christ's eternal victory that we, too, may become spiritually invincible. A very great deal depends on ourselves. . . .

''It is usual for a Christian to be aware concurrently of the presence of the never-fading celestial glory and of the brooding cloud of death hanging over the whole world. Though the feeling of death torments the soul, it cannot extinguish the fire of faith. . . . The age-old experience of life in the church has proved irrefutably that for prayer — that is, for God — no sickness of spirit is incurable. We may be born into the most unfavorable circumstances. We may grow up in ignorant, rough, even criminal surroundings, and be attracted by the general example. All that is unfortunate in the contemporary world may make its mark on us, possess us, even; but from the moment we turn to God, resolved to follow his commandments, a process of basic healing begins.''

Archimandrite Sophrony
His Life Is Mine
pp. 50-51

''The Gospel is nothing else but the message of the divine initiative. The master of the vineyard did not descend like a thunderbolt on the vinedressers when they maltreated the first and second deputation of servants. He ventured a new beginning. . . . When Paul speaks to me of the righteousness of God, he no longer means that God reacts to me like a judge, that he gives to me what is coming to me. It means rather that God wants to be just to me as his *child*. We live by virtue of this miracle, this initiative of God. . . . If we do not make use of what Christ has done for us, if we do not seize the chance to be bearers of new beginnings, then Christianity becomes a burden and a judgment. And it is upon this note of judgment that the parable closes.

"What is this burden which Christianity can become? Can I muster up the strength to take the initiative? Can I really believe in all this dogmatic, supernatural business? How can I simply brush aside all my intellectual difficulties? It is as if we were facing a stone wall. But after all, we must start somewhere, and this means starting at *one* point. . . .

"Perhaps for once we should begin with forgiveness, with what we have called the initiative. . . . If we never take the risk, never risk it in the name of him who first took the initiative and moved towards us, then being a Christian will only be a burden because we let grace go to waste.* 'What

is not used becomes a heavy burden' we read in *Faust*. Is it any wonder then that people dodge becoming a Christian and avoid the zones where such decisions are made? 'Who among us can dwell with everlasting burnings?' says Isaiah (33:14). 'The everlasting burnings' — this is what we face: if they devour a man he avoids them; if they warm him he seeks them. The vinedressers made their decision. They simply wanted to be master of their own lives, and therefore, they had to stamp out the everlasting fire."

Helmut Thielicke
The Waiting Father
pp. 112-114

---

*See also 56:2, Monk.

New Illuminations:

On Jesus' Warnings and Reassurances II

| Matthew 24:9-14, 37-44 | Mark 13:9-13, 32-37 | Luke 21:12-19 |

"Once upon a time there was a rich man named Job, who was not only rich but upright. . . . Satan did not like to see a son of God making good. He taunted God that Job was faithful only because he was rich. 'Just give me a chance,' Satan said to God, 'and I will show up Job.' And God, who looketh on the heart, had faith in Job that he could lose his things without losing his way. He said as much to Satan, so Satan want to work to show God. . . . 'and in all his calamities, Job sinned not nor charged God foolishly.'

"Three friends came to visit Job arguing with him, telling him how foolish he was to trust a God who would let these calamities happen. But Job said, 'When God has tried me, I shall come forth as gold. . . . His way have I kept.' Job was not bragging. He was just clinging to his deepest hunch, born of experience and thought, that God would sustain his suffering and use it to free his soul of dross. Moreover, Job prayed to God to forgive his friends; he knew that they could not see as far as he because they had not suffered as far.

"Satan gave up and then the story says that God blessed Job. No doubt Job was pleased with his prosperity. But the chances are that the thousands of cattle did not seem very important because he now owned something far more satisfactory. He owned his soul. 'By your perseverance you will win your souls' (Luke 21:19)."

Marguerite Harmon Bro
Every Day A Prayer
pp. 236-237

"We find Christ accepting pain and disease, injustice and evil, which many people advance as the greatest hindrance to religious faith, as part of the stuff of life. He did not pretend that they do not exist. . . . He made no promise that those who follow him would enjoy special immunity from pain and sorrow — nor did he himself experience such immunity. He did, however, promise enough joy and courage, even enough love and confidence in God to enable those who went his way to do more than survive because they would be in harmony with the very life and spirit of God.* They would be able to defeat evil. They would be able to take the initiative and destroy evil with good."

J. B. Phillips
Your God is Too Small
pp. 103-04

"Nothing is more beautiful in Jesus' character than the way that he prepared his apostles for that unpalatable lesson

of seeming defeat as the condition of victory. How slow they were to understand the story of why he *must* suffer, but with what infinite patience he instructed them. . . . He began by telling them that they would suffer themselves. He warned them that as a result of their companionship with him, they too would have to suffer. 'The servant is not above the master.' He even tells them they are to consider themselves 'blessed' when 'men shall hate you and cast out your name as evil.' This was a strange forecast to give disciples, namely because they followed him, they would have missiles cast at them. Before him and since, many have preached that if you are good, you will be prosperous:* Jesus tells them that, if they are good, they will be persecuted: 'You will be hated by everyone because you bear my name' (Luke 21:17, Goodspeed). . . . The conclusion was inevitable. He was bidding them to a life of sacrifice because he would be sacrificed. He did not yet say he would offer himself for the sinners of the world; rather, he said that because his sacrifice was a divine 'must' laid upon him by love, they must be prepared for the same maltreatment because they were his servants."

Fulton J. Sheen
The Life of Christ
pp. 81-83

"The most important feature of bone is its hardness. That one feature separates it from all other tissues in the body, and without hardness, bone is virtually useless. An analogous body as advanced and active as Christ's followers also needs a framework to give it shape, and I see the church's doctrine as being just such a skeleton.

"Do I hear a groan? Our age smiles kindly on musings about unity and diversity and about contributions of individual cells. But the drive that stirred church councils and framers of the Constitution has stalled. Bones are dusty, crumbling, dead, belonging to a musty museum display case. The skeleton is relegated to Hallowe'en, a spooky remnant of the past, leeringly inhuman.

"Today one can easily muster up sympathy and support for Jesus' ethics governing human behavior, but squeezed in between uncompromising statements about our duties and responsibilities, are scores of harsh and uncompromising statements about our duties and responsibilities, and about heaven and hell."

Dr. Paul Brand and Phillip Yancey
Fearfully and Wonderfully Made
pp. 75-76

---

*See also 95:3, Ramsey.

*See also 24:3, Tugwell.

" 'And you shall be hated by everyone because you bear my name. Yet not a hair of your head will perish! It is by your endurance that you will win your souls' (Luke 21:17-19, Goodspeed). The soul loses command of itself when it is impatient. Whereas when it submits without a murmur, it possesses itself in peace, and God is with it. To be impatient is to desire what we have not, and not to desire what we have. An impatient soul is a prey to passions unrestrained either by reason or faith. What weakness, what delusion! . . . We may preserve peace in the midst of the bitterest pain if our will remains firm and submissive. Peace in this life springs from acquiescence even in disagreeable things, not in an exemption from suffering. . . . We must trust to God for whatever depends upon him and only think of being faithful ourselves in the performance of our duties. This unceasing dependence and acquiescing of the soul in whatever may happen is the true, silent martyrdom of the self.''

Thomas Kepler, ed.
Letters and Reflections of Francois de Fenelon
pp.128-29, 62

"Individual moments of weakness and failure will come. We can expect them and need not regard them too highly. This is possible and we know it but so is the grace of God which rises to meet the dangers at every point. . . . The Christian faith is a religion of victory, a religion of enabling power, of grace, of blessing. All those acts of denial and self surrender are the necessary concomitants of the reception of God's amazing gift of grace. Like the beggar in all those fairy stories which are about you and me, we must strip off our rags (and possibly take a bath) only because we are being clothed upon with the garments of joy and gladness.* We are offered the very spirit of God as our anointing. We are to take up a heroic vocation to be sure, but we are also offered the power to fulfill it.

". . . God has given us the power and the freedom to make a difference in the world. We are used to this in the realm of the natural universe. Our actions make a difference for good or ill in the natural universe. But we can never know the exact effect of our prayers in the way we can know the effect of our physical action; however, they do make a difference. . . . We cannot tell the battles that are waged between God and the mystery of evil which seeks constantly to frustrate his will, but we do know that in the end all will be well. Our prayers are weapons of the spirit in this great conflict, but they are under the command of God who alone knows how to dispose them effectively.

"If it is asked why God cannot bring all this to pass without our assistance, then the answer is that, doubtless, he could if he wanted to, but he has chosen to give us a role. He has made us free. It could be argued that he could easily organize things in a way that would not involve us in any free act at all. But he has made us free spirits, not little robots. He allows us to make a difference because he wants

*See also 76:3, Thielicke.

us to cooperate with him in his work of love. Something else follows from this. We lose power if we don't use it. . . . We can allow our spiritual powers to lose their effectiveness, to atrophy. This is particularly true of the power of prayer. This is obvious in the physical realm. If we never walk, we soon lose the power of our legs. If we want to be powerful intercessors, then we must exercise the intercessory power we have, frequently and systematically. There really is as little point in asking someone to pray for you if they rarely pray, as there is to ask someone who has spent the last five years in bed to join you in climbing Ben Nevis.''

Richard Holloway
A New Heaven
pp. 104-105, 98-99

"God would not weaken a will by making things clear and easy for it; he would not bribe a will by some glittering promise of a reward. He would not frighten a will by some threat. He would win a will by the revelation of his love, love that was tested by hatred and stayed true, love that was tested by faithlessness and stayed faithful. . . .

"Gold is tested by being put in a crucible and letting the fire prove it to be gold. God willed that we should test him on Calvary, and the fire of hate and sin wrapped round the body of God as he hung there on the Cross, but nothing came forth from him but love. Let us seek so to prepare our souls that the Lord entering in may find a place prepared for him (Luke 21:19, 36). It is not strange that even when he was in prison and chained to the soldier who kept him, St. Paul was able, while his mind held such thoughts, to write a letter to faulty people filled with thankfulness.

"It is not the will of God that, because of bad drains, typhoid fever should become prevalent, but it is his will that doctor or priest should love patient or parishioner better than life, and so, if in going where love calls him a man meets death, he need not think that it was God's will that he should die, but he may be sure that it was God's will that he should love and can know that death cannot matter very much (Luke 21:12-13). Humility arises from one's knowledge of the truth about oneself and charity from one's knowledge of the truth about God.''

Harry C. Griffith, ed.
A Gift of Light: A Collection of Thoughts from the Writings of Father Andrew
pp. 17-20

" 'This shall be your chance to witness for me' (Luke 21:13). Life is a steep climb, and it does the heart good to have somebody 'call back' and cheerfully beckon us on up the hill. We are all climbers together, and we must help one another. The mountain climbing is serious business, but glorious. It takes strength and steady steps to find the summits. The outlook widens with the altitude. If anyone among us has found anything worthwhile, we ought to 'call back.' "

Mrs. Charles E. Cowman
Streams In the Desert
p. 362

"As an inner intelligence, patience perceives the erratic moods of daily living and adjusts ingeniously to the motion of survival. If we become agitated, we will rarely be at our best since we lose command of the strength at our disposal. . . . The calm provided by patience marshalls our powers in a most proficient manner. 'Your endurance will win your lives' (Luke 21:19).

"Patience, God's waiting room on earth, reminds us that whatever happens to us — either the sublime or the ridiculous — is of only passing importance. Difficulties great or small, doubts nagging or temporary are of momentary anguish. How easily we forget our Lord's warning that we have many sufferings to endure in the world. . . . Whenever the shifting wings of fortune call for an adjustment, patience — the least glamorous of virtues — can be our most reliable asset.

"Kindred to courage, endurance appeals to those of us who are determined to cope successfully with the peculiarities of our human existence. . . . We strive to learn when to be gentle, when to be harsh, when to be aggressive and when to yield, all the while realizing that this lesson might be the most important one we are ever asked to master. . . . Just as the impulsive and quick-tempered come up with an impressive reserve of temper, so also is the patient voice capable of beckoning thunder and lightning from the heavens."

John Walchars
Voices on Fire
pp. 103-104

New Illuminations:

On the Tribulations To Come

Matthew 24:1-8, 15-28   Mark 13:1-8, 14-23   Luke 17:20-37; 21:5-17, 20-24

''We have in Mark xiii, with parallels in Matthew and Luke, a discourse on the manner in which the coming of the Kingdom may be expected; it has been called the Little Apocalypse and reproduces the main lines of the apocalyptic expectation found in the contemporary apocalyptic literature. The signs which herald the coming of the Kingdom are wars, famines, earthquakes, and general disorder; the elect will suffer persecutions, and false Messiahs will make their appearance; but those who endure to the end will be saved. Then comes the sign given in the Book of Daniel, the erection of an idolatrous symbol in the Holy Place (Mark 13:14), which is the culmination of the tribulation and the signal for flight; lastly come signs in heaven, the sun and the moon darkened, and the falling of the stars,* and then 'they shall see the Son of Man coming in the clouds with power and great glory.' We can see from Paul's letters that with certain important modifications, this remained the general pattern of early apostolic preaching about the manner of the coming of the Kingdom, but it would not be wise to assume that the discourse in Mark xiii represents the actual utterances of Jesus just before his death**. . . .

''Matthew follows Mark very closely, but expands the Marcan discourse by the inclusion of a considerable amount of material which is placed by Luke in other contexts. . . . Luke evidently has the Marcan discourse before him, but treats it very freely. His most important departure from Mark is that he makes the destruction of Jerusalem in A.D. 70 the fulfilment of the apocalyptic woes, suggesting that towards the end of the first century of the Christian era the delay in the fulfilment of the apocalyptic expectations was causing questions, and that attempts were being made to explain it, or to find a fulfilment in the contemporary events.

''Thus the rather confused state of the Synoptic tradition with regard to the apocalyptic material which all three Synoptists give at the end of their Gospels makes it doubtful whether this detailed picture of the last things really represents the eschatological expectation of Jesus. On the other hand, it is hard to believe that such an expectation could have been so firmly rooted in the teaching of the early Church unless it had to some extent been based on the utterances of Jesus.''

S. H. Hooke
The Kingdom of God
pp. 62, 131

''The parable of the Unjust Judge is very far from being a lesson on how to pray, on which interpretation the widow is the central figure in the parable. But Jesus' interpretation (Luke 18:6-8b) shows that he intended to direct attention to the figure of the judge. Why did Jesus tell the story? He gives the answer himself in verses 7-8a: he expected his hearers to draw the conclusion from the judge to God. If this inconsiderate man, who had refused to hear the widow's case, finally gives heed to her distress, and that after long delay, only to rid himself of the incessant pestering of the plaintiff, how much more will God! . . . If the parable, as v. 8b assumes, is addressed to the disciples, it was clearly called forth by the grief and anxiety of the disciples in view of the time of tribulation which Jesus had depicted for them with unmitigated clarity (Luke 17:26-36): persecutions, injuries, denunciations, trials, martyrdoms, a final failure of faith at the revelation of Satan. Who can endure to the end? Have no anxiety in the face of persecution, says Jesus. You are God's elect. He will hear your cry. By the intervention of his holy will he will even shorten the time of tribulation (Mark 13:20). Let their be no doubting his power, goodness and help. That is the final certainty. Your concern should be with a different matter: when the Son of Man comes will he find faith on earth?''

Joachim Jeremias
The Parables of Jesus
pp. 156-157

''The Son's return to earth to fetch the lost sheep home is something of importance to the universe. How should it not be heralded by signs? 'When shall these things be?' We have to ask the question, though we cannot answer it. There are no cosmic signs, as yet. So we can hardly echo Donne's 'What if this present were the world's last night?' But the pattern of tribulation that precedes the End does seem to be intensified in our own day. Wars there have always been; but not two world-wide wars in one generation, nor wars so ghastly in their weapons and effects. Famines have always been; but the threat of universal famine, because the earth's supplying power has been so exploited that it no longer meets the needs of its inhabitants, is new. False teaching, persecutions, antichrists also seem increasing. 'When the Son of Man comes, will he find faith on earth?' It looks as though the tempo of the pangs is quickening.''

Sister Penelope
The Coming
pp. 43-44

---

*See also 98:1, Jeremias.
**See also 91:2, Schnackenburg.

New Illuminations:

On the Day of the Lord

| Matthew 24:29-36 | Mark 13:24-33 | Luke 21:25-36 |

"The day of the Lord is a Christian and Pauline use of the Hebrew *yom yahweh* which appears in the prophetic literature as early as Amos (eighth century B.C.), where it means the visitation of God's judgment on the nations, particularly on Israel, implying the vindication of God's rights accompanied by cosmic catastrophes. It is a day of punishment for sinners. . . . During the exile, the expression 'day of the Lord' came to mean the time when God would vindicate his own people against their oppressors and restore them. In Malachi the meaning is extended to that of the final judgment of the world, when the wicked will be punished and the good rewarded. A day of doom and darkness for the wicked, the 'day of the Lord' will be a day of light for the just. 'For you who fear my name, there will arise the sun of justice with its healing rays . . .' (Malachi 3:20).

"Paul keeps all of the Old Testament elements, transferring to the glorified Christ the title Lord in the 'day of the Lord.' The day of his appearance will be a day of punishment for the wicked, but one of salvation, reward, and glorification for the saints. Christian life is a preparation in love and holiness for that day*. . . .

"The day that surprises those in the darkness of blindness within, of infidelity to God, is not the natural dawn that follows night, but the 'day of the Lord' that bursts suddenly on the unprepared. It is for these that, according to the Prophets, the day of the Lord brings darkness rather than light. . . . When Paul tells his readers that they are all sons of the light, sons of the day (1 Thessalonians 5:5), he means that they already share in the eschatological salvation. The Christian is already part of that new world to be made at the 'day of the Lord.' He welcomes the Parousia as something for which he was made, much as a fish seeks water or a trapped miner air and light. . . .

"Why should Christians be alert? Lest they be surprised, caught by Christ's sudden return? No. We might have expected that, for the synoptic tradition does stress the unexpectedness of the return as a motive for 'watching.' For Paul, however, we must watch not because we know not the day nor the hour (Matthew 25:13) but because 'we are of the day.' That is, the Parousia for us is not an ambush but a consummation. Made for the day and eagerly awaiting it, let us show it by staying awake and working. . . . The reason for living in constant alert is paradoxical: because God has not destined us for his wrath but to attain salvation. A moralizing preacher might more easily have said we must act because salvation is up to us. Instead Paul says it is up to God who has already determined to save us. However, instead of engendering the complacency based on a mere emotional conviction that 'I'm saved,' he considers

the destiny as one demanding constant diligence, the best of one's efforts. The image is not one of partnership but of total subordination (though free and active) of man's action to God's."

George Montague
The Living Thought of St. Paul
pp. 21-25

" 'And lo, I am with you always, to the close of the age' (Matthew 28:20). I am developing the thesis that whereas Mark sees the resurrection of Jesus only as a necessary prelude to his parousia, Matthew sees it as the occasion for the commission of the disciples as the Christian church, and hence as the inauguration of a distinctive new age, the age of the Christian church. But there is a definite limit set to this age. Matthew sets this limit, the limit of the 'close of the age.' This is particularly interesting in that it equates the close of the age with the parousia. *Parousia* is a technical term in the New Testament for the coming of Jesus as the Son of Man, and Matthew uses it this way in 24:3: 'What will be the sign of your coming (Greek: *Parousia*) and of the close of the age?' This is the introduction to the apocalyptic discourse, and Matthew continues to use the term in this way throughout the discourse. So we can see that Matthew is concerned to make and to maintain the point that the age inaugurated by the resurrection of Jesus, the age within which the church is commissioned to work, is an age to which a definite limit will be set by 'the close of the age' by the parousia of Jesus."

Norman Perrin
The Resurrection
pp.53-54

"He 'came down from heaven' and 'ascended into heaven' in the past. 'He sits at the right hand of the Father' now. Thence, at the end of these Last Days, 'he shall come again with glory. . . .' This is the faith which we Christians are pledged to hold and to hand on in its integrity. Why is it that we hear and read so little about the future part?

"The trouble starts from the fact that the promise of our Lord's return was given nearly two thousand years ago, and still he has not come. Delay (as it appears) has generated doubt. Because some, at any rate, of the first generation of Christians looked for him to come in their own life time, the idea has grown up that perhaps the Church herself was

---

*See also 63:3, Jeremias.

mistaken in expecting his Return at all. Such a notion, if it were valid, would make inspiration meaningless. If you believe in the Holy Spirit, you must accept the future Second Coming of our Lord as just as integral a part of the faith once delivered to the saints as is the First. Then our Lord said to Caiaphas, 'You shall see the Son of Man sitting at the right hand of power and coming on the clouds of heaven,' he was referring not to his coming to *earth* but to his coming to *heaven*. . . . But this 'realised eschatology' is only half the truth, half of the paradox of the Sixth Word — 'It is finished.' The Ascension from the Mount of Olives was an incident prefiguring the final consummation, not the End itself. Like the Sixth Word, Christ's words to Caiaphas show how, in his Passion, he was expecting that final End, his ultimate and perfect coming to the Father as the Head to the Body, the Bridegroom with the Bride.*

"Jesus' fullest expectation to that blessed End is in the thirteenth chapter of St. Mark, verses 1 to 4 (par. Luke 21:5-7; Matthew 24:1-3). Observe the setting, both in time and place. It is Tuesday evening in Holy Week. As Jesus and his disciples pass the Temple on their way back to Bethany, one of them points to it. Our Lord replies that it is going to be entirely destroyed. . . . *The Temple*, that only yesterday Jesus had so significantly cleansed is the matter in hand as well as the object in view; *and the Temple is a type of Man, created for God's indwelling.* . . . The Prophet of prophets is speaking, to whom the Spirit was not given by measure; he sees two things and keeps the two entirely distinct. Both things are Ends — the End of the Temple first, that is of the type; and then the End of Man, whom the Temple typifies.

"And let us be quite certain what we mean by End. . . . The end of a thing is the purpose for which it exists. When a smith says 'it is finished,' he means that it is ready to be used.' Only when it has served its purpose and has no longer any *raison d'etre*, does an end of a thing mean its ceasing to exist. The End of the Temple was the destruction of the Temple, because the type was no longer needed when the thing typified, the New Humanity had come. But when Man comes to his End, he will be finished in the sense of being ready, at last, for the purpose for which he was made**. . . .

"In Mark 13:24, (par. Matthew 24:29; Luke 21:24b), our Lord passes from the type to the thing typified. The transition is marked first by the adversative conjunction 'but,' implying that these two prophecies are not to be confused; then by a note of time, 'In those days, after that tribulation.' That is to say, the second End will happen after the first, but in the same Last Days; there is no indication of the length of the interval, one way or the other. And that is all the answer Jesus gives to the disciples' question, 'When shall these things be?' But he answers their second question, 'What shall be the sign when these things are about to be fulfilled?' explicitly. The signs of the End of the Temple were to be terrestrial — false teaching, famines, wars. But the signs of the End of Man will be celestial — cosmic. 'The sun shall be darkened and the moon shall not give her light, and the stars shall be falling from heaven, and the powers that are in heaven shall be shaken. And then they shall see the Son of Man coming in the clouds with power and great glory.'* God will use the sky as his blackboard at the End, as he did at the first; and, when we see his writing there, we shall know that the End of earthly human history is near**. . . .

"Our Lord has laid on us the command to watch for his Coming. Expectation is a Christian duty, never more urgent than at the present day and never more neglected. For this is a dark hour, even if not yet that darkest that must come before the Dawn; and if we are to keep our faith and sanity, we must face it for what it is, the filling up of the Passion of Christ in his mystical Body, that must precede his final Resurrection, as travail precedes birth. It may be that our lack of faith delays the Consummation, as Israel's lack of faith delayed her coming home to Canaan. . . .

"The humble Coming of the past is on our level and can be visualised; the glorious future one defeats imagination. . . . We must go on to see our Lord's two Comings in relation to each other and to that single coming to the Father which they serve; we must prepare to meet him not only at the altar, but when he comes again. That Second Coming is not foretold in the New Testament alone. Some of the Old Testament prophecies look forward to the consummation too. The vision in Isaiah 52 is one of these; and we look for another sudden Coming of the Lord whom we seek to his Temple, in the figurative sense, besides the lowly literal one that Simeon saw. . . .

"It is always good for us to look away from ourselves and the present and our earth in general to where the sign of the Son of Man shall one day herald his Coming, and one particular constellation seems a sort of picture of the subject of this book. There is One Coming of Christ, the One Man, to the Father in heaven; and in the process of that Coming, there are three great moments of From, Into, and Thence, the last of which will lead to the Consummation. That is the way in which God fulfills the purpose of Creation and puts right the wrong, by making evil minister its own defeat. Cassiopeia is like a W, the first limb down, the second up, the third one down again. The fourth and last also goes up, and there it stays."

Sister Penelope
The Coming
pp. 34-37, 51-54

"In 1 Thessalonians 4:13-18, Paul breaks into a new topic, the Second Coming of Christ, the Parousia. His concern as not, however, with the Parousia in general but rather with the hitherto unexplained point which is troubling the community. The death of some of their members raised the problem of how these would profit by Christ's glorious

---

*See also 125:2, Penelope.
**See also 67:2, Drake.

---

*See also 99:2, Penelope.
**See also 65:1, Schnackenburg.

return, and, as a solution, Paul would have introduced them to the doctrine of the resurrection of the Christian dead. . . .

"What Paul now says, he says with the authority of the Lord — literally, 'in the word of the Lord.' The Gospels do not reveal any express equivalent of the apocalyptic description that follows; Paul must therefore be appealing to some unwritten statement of Jesus handed down in oral tradition, or to a private revelation made to him by Christ, or perhaps merely to an inspired commentary on the apocalyptic discourse of Jesus (Mark 13 and par.). At any rate the certitude of it is as great as the facts of the death and resurrection of Jesus. . . .

"Paul shows his dependence on Jewish and Christian apocalyptic, and reflects the cosmology of the times. It would be wrong to imagine this scenario as a blow by blow description of the events; it is not always possible, in the apocalyptic genre, to distinguish figure and reality. Paul's description is sober and restrained and goes swiftly to the point, which is that the resurrection of the dead is in the first scene of the drama, not in the finale. . . .

"In the Old Testament the trumpet seems to be a necessary accompaniment for great manifestations of God's majesty and power or the assembling of his people. The prophets use it as one of the sound effects of the Day of the Lord (Joel 2:1, 15) or the inbreaking of the Messianic victory (Zechaniah 9:14) or the restoration of Israel (Isaiah 24:13). We find it in the apocalyptic description of Matthew 24:31, there called a great trumpet.

"Christ, in heaven since his ascension, descends, but he does not reach the earth. The faithful got to meet him. But before they do, the dead in Christ will rise first (1 Thessalonians 4:16). Here the Christian deceased are not 'those who sleep' but the 'dead in Christ' — they died in union with him and even in death this union has never been severed. In Romans 8:11 Paul will give the profound basis for this union and its consequences: 'If the Spirit of him who raised Jesus from the dead dwells in you, then he who raised Jesus from the dead will also bring to life your mortal bodies because of his Spirit who dwells in you.' And then all together the risen and the dead will be taken on the clouds to meet the Lord in the air. . . . As Christ comes on clouds so Christians at that moment will have the same accoutrements as he. The cloud image has a theological content. In the Old Testament the clouds are God's chariot but also his dwelling place or cloak, or his footstool. The cloud was a symbol of his presence over the meeting tent in the desert and of his guidance and protection of the Israelites in the desert.

"It is worth noting that the living and the resurrected do not await Christ's arrival on earth but go out to meet him. . . . St. John Chrysostom uses the image of the imperial reception to explain the 'going out to meet the Lord': 'When a city receives the emperor, the high dignitaries and those that are in his favor go out from town to meet him, while the criminals are kept within the walls under guard to await the emperor's sentence upon them. Likewise, when the Lord comes, those who are in his grace will go to meet him in the air, while sinners and those whose consciences are darkened by many evil deeds, will remain on earth to meet their judge.' "

George Montague
The Living Thought of St. Paul
pp. 13-19

New Illuminations:

On the Preparation for the Passover

Matthew 26:17-19	Mark 14:12-16	Luke 22:7-13

"The last and most wonderful work that God did through Moses took place on what is called the night of the Passover. The Israelites had been told to kill a lamb for every family. The blood of this lamb was sprinkled on the posts of the doors. Then, as the night went on, the people were holding a feast. It was called the 'feast of the Passover.' . . . God said to them, 'Ye shall observe this thing for an ordinance to thee and thy sons forever' (Exodus 12:24). . . .

"There were two reasons why God commanded the Israelites to keep this 'feast of the Passover' every year. One of these reasons had to do with the *past*. It was to help them in keeping alive in their hearts a grateful memory of God's wonderful mercy in delivering them from Egypt. It would remind them of the state of bondage in which their forefathers had been held. . . . Another reason had to do with the *future*. There was a sort of prophecy in this feast and the solemn sacrifice connected with it.* It was all intended to point to Christ. The lamb that was slain at this feast pointed to Christ, the spotless, perfect Lamb of God that was to be slain on Calvary. The protection which the Israelites had on that night from the death of their first born, by means of the blood sprinkled on their doors, pointed to that deliverance from everlasting death which all the people of Christ have through faith in the blood which he shed for them on the Cross. . . .

"Jesus met his disciples on the night on which he was betrayed to celebrate for the last time the Jewish Passover. The feast was kept in the usual way. And when it was ended, Jesus established another solemn service, which was to take the place of the Jewish Passover, and to be observed by his followers until the end of the world."

Richard Newton
The Life of Jesus Christ
Vol. I, pp. 136-138

"Exodus 12 and the ensuing chapters tell the monumental story of the national liberation of the children of Israel from Egypt, marked by the terrible night of the tenth plague. God assigns Passover its date. . . . The meaning of Passover is surely the feast of salvation. On this day, because of the blood of the lamb ('without blemish, a male . . .' Exodus 12:5) the Hebrew nation was delivered from bondage. Clearly, in both Testaments, the blood of the Lamb delivers from slavery — the Jew from Egypt, the Christian from sin.

"It is no mere coincidence that our Lord Himself was sacrificed on Passover. At the meal he stated plainly, 'This is my blood of the New Covenant shed for many for the remission of sin' (Matthew 26:27 par.). John the Baptizer clearly marked the person of Jesus Christ as a blood sacrifice when he stated, 'Behold the Lamb of God which taketh away the sin of the world' (John 1:29). The Christian celebrates Passover, in effect, by participating in the sacrifice of the Lord. Back in Egypt, the Jew marked his house with the blood of the lamb. Today the Christian marks his house — his body, 'the house of the spirit' — with the blood of Christ. The Angel of Death will pass over each Christian as surely as he passed over each Israelite in Egypt. We are already living our eternal life. . . . Passover then represents our salvation. We do not keep the feast in memory of the exodus from Egypt, since that was the mere shadow of the greater redemption to come."

Zola Levitt
The Seven Feasts of Israel
pp. 2-4

"Carrying water jars is simply not a thing that men do, and yet we had not gone far into the city when we saw a tall young man carrying a jar still wet from being dipped into the well. We were amazed. . . . This master of ours had strange powers. Now and then there was something about him that frightened us — an unearthly, holy power. Yet instead of making him less human, it seemed to bring us closer to him. It made us love him more and enabled us to feel his love for us. I wish I could explain it.

"Everything happened exactly as he said it would. The man carrying the jar went into a large house. We did not dare to speak to him until he was greeted at the door by an older man, the owner of the house. Then my companion spoke the words Jesus had told him. The teacher asks: Where is my room where my disciples and I are to eat the Passover supper? The owner smiled as my companion stumbled out the words. His reply showed how gracious he was. 'I am so glad that Jesus will come and use my place. I have a large room upstairs where you can be quite private and secluded. Come and see it.'

"As the sun was setting the twelve began to gather. We found the room perfect and there was an air of expectancy among us. We sensed that something was about to happen. Of course, we thought that Jesus might be ready to bring his kingdom into being. We gathered in knots of three or four talking about what we would be doing when the kingdom became a reality. We thought with relish of the power we might have, what part of the world we might rule, how the Romans would have to serve us. Jesus came in. We

*See also 43:1, Hebert.

greeted him with warmth. Wondering what he would do, we gathered around the table and took our places.''

Morton Kelsey
The Other Side of Silence
pp. 251-52

"Jesus puts this question to the master of the house: 'Where is my guest room where I may eat the pasch . . .?' This question takes on a much richer meaning if we refer to the Greek text of St. Mark: 'my dwelling, my reception room.' In this question there is a blending of humility and command. Jesus asks where 'his' room is. He demands this with assurance, with the authority of ownership. This room is his, he has engaged it. But he was obliged to borrow it from a man. Jesus begs for my soul, in order that he may celebrate his paschal meal there. For my soul belongs to him. He is willing to come as my guest; he demands my hospitality.

" 'The Master saith, my time is near at hand. With thee I make my pasch with my disciples.' 'With my disciples . . .' because the master's pasch is always social. It is never only individual. . . . If I am with Jesus, I have to be with all those who either in past centuries or today have been or are the Savior's disciples. I cannot isolate myself from his brethren without separating myself from him. I must commune with them in the same faith, with the same affection.''

Monk of the Eastern Church
Jesus: A Dialogue with the Savior
pp. 119-120

"Jesus celebrates the Supper with his disciples in the expectation of the approaching kingdom of God and of his parting from them. . . . His words place Jesus' death in the light of the coming kingdom of God. They distinguish Jesus and his destiny from that of the disciples — 'I shall not drink again . . .' — but the saying welds the disciples who are left behind together and gives them the promise of a new oneness with him in the kingdom of his Father (Luke 22:28-30). The antecedent words of the institution of the Sacrament, given in the tradition, express the meaning of its fellowship and its basis.''

Gunther Bornkamm
Jesus of Nazareth
pp. 160-61

New Illuminations:

C. S. Lewis knew and experienced Christianity in its sacramental context. The sacraments of Baptism and Holy Communion were for him not mere symbols of union, but means by which the Real Presence and the very life of Christ are channeled to believing man. . . . The sacramental view of reality affirms that Spirit can be and is encountered through material forms. God who is Spirit became man! . . . Christ's Incarnation, though perhaps the most amazing expression of God's loving descent into his own 'matter,' did not end when he ascended to the Father. Christ is risen, but is also, by virtue of what began at Pentecost, risen *in us*. . . .

"Though uniquely Christian in its fullness, this view is rooted in Judaism. Very simply, *sacramental reality has to do with the means by which the Presence of God is mediated to fallen man*: and as principle, it was in effect before Christ descended into the flesh. Moses, we recall, descended from the mountain radiant with the glory of God.

"Before the Fall man experienced God's Presence continually. Our first parents fell and the first thing they did was to hide themselves from the Presence. That is what the Fall was and is — separation from the Presence. Man fell from God-consciousness into the hell of self, and of self-consciousness. The history of fallen man can be summed up as a flight from the reality of the Presence and the Face of God. Even then, after the Fall, there was a provision made for men to meet with a 'mediated Presence.' They brought their blood sacrifices to the altar where they worshiped and met with God. . . .

"The Old Testament Tabernacle had a Holy of Holies within which rested the Ark of the Covenant. Inside the Ark dwelt the Uncreated, the Divine Presence, so powerfully that only the High Priest could enter the inner sanctuary and live. To understand the special Presence in the Tabernacle and in the Ark is to understand, at least partially, sacramental reality. Israel knew that Yahweh was in His heaven, but they also knew that He was with them in a unique, if barely approachable, way in the Holy of Holies. After Christ, we are to know the Presence of God indwelling us. Individually and corporately, we are the *Body*, the 'Ark' or the 'Temple' of the Presence — an idea almost staggering if we could really comprehend it. We are the indwelt — the fellowship of the Holy Spirit. . . .

"Oddly enough we have made objects out of vital acts and experiences. One almost hesitates in the face of the vitality of the New Testament accounts of Baptism to label this event by the word 'sacrament.' Perhaps we hesitate because the word's connotation is that of a 'thing' or a doctrine rather than an experience of the Holy Spirit full of mystery and awe. . . . Who is great enough to completely understand these mysteries? It is therefore, as Lewis might say 'mad idolatry' that would replace the Presence with a definition of how it works. Nevertheless definitions are necessary, if not always adequate, and so it is with caution that we approach the meaning of the word 'sacrament.'

"A sacrament is most usually defined as a outward and visible sign of an inward and spiritual grace, a rite which Christ ordained and through which we receive him, his grace and his gifts. As we have seen, the mediating word of the Holy Spirit is the vital agent in effecting this inward and spiritual grace. It is possible to come to Baptism or the Lord's Supper and to perceive nothing but the symbol. One's spirit must be open to the Holy Spirit's work to effectively appropriate the grace which the visible sign represents. . . .

"Finally, Lewis was convinced that no definition, no explanation of the sacraments could remove their essential mystery and he himself refused to attempt any technical definition:

'I do not know and cannot imagine what the disciples understood our Lord to mean when, his body still unbroken and his blood unshed, he handed them the bread and wine saying *they* were his body and blood. . . . I get on no better with those who tell me that the elements are mere bread and wine, used symbolically to remind me of the death of Christ. . . . If they are, if the whole act is simply memorial, I cannot see why *this* particular reminder should be so uniquely important as all Christendom (and my own heart) unhesitatingly declare.' (*Letters to Malcolm*)

That Christ is the mystery to be received, and that his Presence comes to touch and to heal the believing one through the sacraments is as far as Lewis is willing to go toward an explanation."

Leanne Payne
Real Presence:
The Holy Spirit in the Works of C. S. Lewis
pp. 29-38

"Let me make it quite clear that when Christians say the Christ-life is in them, they do not mean something mental or moral. When they speak of being 'in Christ' or of Christ being 'in them,' this is not simply a way of saying that they are thinking about Christ or copying him.* They mean that Christ is actually operating through them; that the whole mass of Christians are the physical organism through which Christ acts — that we are his fingers and muscles, the cells of his body. And perhaps that explains one or two things.

*See also 3:1, Kunkel.

It explains why this new life is spread not only by purely mental acts like belief, but by bodily acts like baptism and Holy Communion. It is not merely the spreading of an idea; it is more like a biological or super-biological fact. There is no good in trying to be more spiritual than God. God never meant man to be a purely spiritual creature. That is why he uses material things like bread and wine to put the new life into us. We may think this rather crude and unspiritual. God does not: he invented eating. He likes matter; he invented it.''

C. S. Lewis
Mere Christianity
p. 65

''We must be careful not to divide the Holy Trinity and think of the Crucifixion as something done by our Lord without the consent, so to speak, of the Father or of the Holy Spirit. It was the Father who sent the Son, and he in all of his life and in his death was guided by the Holy Spirit; the Crucifixion was an act of the Holy and undivided Trinity; the Son died upon the Cross by the will of the Father and by the inspiration of the Holy Ghost. Here we see revealed to us in a moment of time and in a particular place the breadth, length, depth, and height of God's love for men. . . . So that the Crucifixion is a sign, an outward and visible sign, of God's love; it is a sacrament; indeed it is *the* sacrament from which all other sacraments take their meaning. Once we understand that the Crucifixion is a sacrament of the eternal truth that God loves us now and at all times, then we shall truly turn to him and beg for pardon; for we cannot but love him who loves us so much. . . .

''At the institution of the Holy Eucharist our Lord's words were, 'This is my blood of the New Covenant.' The blood (the blood is the life) of him who has conquered the world, the flesh, and the devil is made available to us so that we are enabled to enter into the new relationship with God.''

Manassas
Go in Peace
pp. 29-30, 36

New Illuminations:

On Jesus' Institution of the Eucharist

Matthew 26:26-29	Mark 14:22-25	Luke 22:14-20, 28-30

"The thought of animal sacrifice is distasteful to modern minds, and we tend to regard it as merely barbarous and revolting. Men of an earlier age, however, less refined in their physical sense than we, but possibly more discerning of fundamentals, were filled with awe at the sight of shed blood because, as a matter of experience, *the life was in it.* . . .

"The sacrificial value of a death depended upon the intention with which the victim was killed. A sacrificial killing was done, not with the intention of destroying life, but with the two-fold intention of releasing life as a gift to God and of promoting life to those who made the oblation. The intention of sacrifice was expressed in certain ritual acts: these and these alone invested the death with sacrificial significance. The blood of the victim was sprinkled on the worshipers (Exodus 3:8). Part of its body, consumed by fire, signified both the etherialization for God's use and his acceptance of the whole. Where a portion only was so consumed, the rest of the victim's body remained as food for the worshipers. Animal sacrifice was followed on most occasions by this sacrificial meal. The flesh of the victim, having been given to God by man and by him accepted and given back to them, was regarded in some sense as his own flesh, the vehicle of his life, thus it became the effective instrument of fellowship between them. It is through these primitive ideas of sacrifice, purified and enlarged through the succeeding centuries that we are able to understand what was done on Calvary.''*

Sister Penelope
The Wood
pp. 48, 50

"The thanksgiving in Luke 22:17 and 19 was a great deal more than merely saying grace over the bread and wine. Just as other people's minds were occupied at that time with the historic Exodus then being commemorated, so our Lord's was all on the divine Exodus which he was even then accomplishing. To thank God for anything is to recognize that it comes from him and so to unlock its resources as a channel of blessing. And what Jesus gave thanks for in the same night he was betrayed was his *Passion*, involving all his armory of weapons that he was wresting from the hands of Satan. In the crucible of love they are transmuted; by his willing, thankful receiving of them from his Father's hand, he makes *himself* the supreme channel of blessing from God to man.**

---
*See also 118:1, Ramsey.
**See also 112:2, Harton.

"That he was a victim, the manner and context of his gift plainly declared. The apostles were expecting, either then or on the following evening to eat the flesh of the sacrificial lamb which united them to God and to each other. It must have been obvious to them, even at the time, that the Lord was in some sense *substituting himself* for the expected food. But it is hard to realize the shock to Jewish ears when he said of the cup, 'This is my blood of the New Covenant; *drink* ye of it.' . . . The Jews were emphatically forbidden to drink blood or to eat meat containing blood because the life was in it. Exactly so. Peter and Andrew, James and John, and all the rest of you so painfully mystified, be not unbelieving. . . . What you are now bidden to drink is the blood of the incarnate Word, which by anticipation he is already pouring out in sacrifice for the sins of the whole world. Through earthly flesh and blood, you, like the rest of us, have received the earthly nature of the first Adam; by the same agency in its final and fulfilled perfection, the Second Adam gives you now his life. . . . And they did receive it. Then and there the new Covenant was inaugurated, the new humanity, hitherto embodied in the sole person of Jesus was extended to them.''

Sister Penelope
The Wood
pp. 123-24

"To a Greek of the old faith, an icon is a window into eternity. They believed that it is a true vision of the eternal captured out of an instant of time. The picture and story I present here opens a similar window for me. It may awaken the same picture in your imagination; perhaps it will stir enough imagination in you to open such a window of your own:

"Jesus took a fresh round loaf of bread, he said a prayer of thanks, broke the bread and gave it to us. As we each took a piece of the bread he said, 'Take, eat; this is my body.' My mind reeled at this. Did I hear correctly? He was giving us his body to eat. What is this strange paganism, I wonder? And then came something even more startling. He took the cup of wine, the cup of blessing in his hands. He gave thanks to God, and then he handed this cup to us. And our Master said to us, 'This is my blood which is poured out for many, my blood which seals God's contract with men.' Do you have any idea what these words did to me and to the rest of us other loyal Jews? . . . Blood was the very life of any living thing. One could not eat it. It was unthinkable to eat it purposely. But human blood, our Master's blood. . . . I wondered if he had gone mad, or had he perhaps used this image to drive it home so that we would never forget? Reflecting later, I am sure it was the latter reason. He wanted us to remember, wanted us to have a way of knowing that he shared his very life with us . . . the reality of his being, his body and his blood.

"As I took the cup, I was closer to him than I had ever been before. I was part of him and he was part of me. I can't explain it. It had just happened. He had shared himself as never before and he had done it not only in words and actions, but with his very being. . . . Every time we share the mysteries, I see that night again. It is burned into my heart; and when we pass the cup and share the bread, I can sense his presence. Jesus is there. It is the only thing that has kept me going as the way has gotten rougher. The followers of the way are persecuted more and more often. People seem to be afraid of love, but when we gather early in the morning and share the cup and break the bread, the reality of the whole message comes back. He is there. His body and blood give me an infusion of new life. There is nothing like it."

Morton T. Kelsey
The Other Side of Silence
pp. 239, 253-54

"The Holy Communion means, of course 'the Holy Fellowship' — not 'a' but 'the,' that fellowship which above all others is holy, the end of which is to make all who participate in it holy. It is fellowship with the Father in Christ not merely with Christ. Nor is it an ordinary fellowship. Ordinary fellowship allows two lives to intertwine; but here so close is the relationship that 'Christ *with* us,' 'we *with* Christ' is inadequate to describe the intimacy. . . . In Christ is the whole parable of the vine and the branches in two syllables."

Bishop Brent
Things That Matter
pp. 93-94

"Consider a vitally important abiding, that precious interabiding, promised in John 6:56. 'Whosoever eateth my flesh and drinketh my blood abides in me, and I in him.' By lifting up the human and earthly as oblations — our souls, our bodies, bread and wine provided by the labor of many hands — by lifting these up to God, God and man are reconciled.

"The Prayer of Humble Access puts these facts more clearly: 'Grant us, therefore, gracious Lord, so to eat the flesh of thy dear Son Jesus Christ, and to drink his blood that we may evermore dwell in him and he in us.' Ourselves, souls and bodies, these are what we offer for his redemptive purposes.

"The Holy Spirit sanctifies the bread and wine, making them the vehicles of the transformation of our nature by the union of it with the Divine. At Holy Communion, we receive back what we have given: We make our divine exchanges! The Holy Food that we break refreshes us, that henceforth we may be able to live our lives to God's glory.

"No one can follow the Christian liturgy without realizing that it re-presents, re-enacts the sacrifices on Calvary. We do not come to Holy Communion with the sole idea of seeking help, but rather of offering ourselves, our souls, and bodies, our loved ones here had gone, and the deepest desires of our hearts. Truly, then, the word that was made flesh *dwells* among us."

Richardson Wright
A Sower Went Forth
pp. 23-24

"Jesus went to his death in the faith that through him, God was redeeming Israel, his people. God's hour had come in which the divine Reign foretold by the prophets was being established, in which the New Covenant announced by Jeremiah (31:31) was being inaugurated. Because of the sin of man, above all of self-righteousness, it could happen only through sacrifice, through the martyrdom of the Servant of the Lord who should 'bear the sins of many' and his soul be made 'a sacrifice for sin' (Isaiah 53:12, 10). . . .

"The fact that the Old Testament promises are fulfilled in Christ (Luke 22:37) makes it necessary that the Old Testament imagery should thus receive a mystical or spiritual interpretation. Such an interpretation follows straight from Jesus' action at the Last Supper when he interpreted his death as the sacrifice for sin. . . . 'This is my body of the covenant' (Mark 14:24) refers directly to the words of Moses at the ratification of the Old Covenant at Sinai: 'Behold the blood of the covenant which the Lord has made with you' (Exodus 24:8). Here, then, we have a principle of 'spiritual interpretation' which depends on the necessary connection of the New Testament fulfillment with the Old Testament type. . . . For at the Last Supper, Jesus added to the familiar ritual of the supper-meal some words in which he designated the broken bread as his body and the cup of wine at the end of the meal as 'the New Covenant in my blood' (Luke 22:20). 'My blood' meant 'my sacrifice': by that sacrifice the New Covenant was being ratified, the New Covenant was written in men's hearts bringing them to true knowledge of God and forgiveness of sin (Jeremiah 31:33b-34)."

A. G. Hebert
Scripture and the Faith
pp. 49, 52-53

"The sufferings of Jesus begin in the upper room where he has spent the evening. There he has just given to the embryo church its own peculiar rite, that astounding confluence of spirit and matter, of heavenly and earthly, of eternity and time. . . . Christ's vision of the rite of the Last Supper, his creation and establishment of this supreme religious operation, would heighten his every faculty, stretch every sensitive nerve, demand all spiritual energy, and while exalting would also drain the Lord's system of natural vitality. Any artist knows the condition of weariness and emptiness when strength and power have been drained away by a prolonged activity of high creation. . . . Far beyond the disciples' immediate comprehension are the mysteries and half light of the symbolic acts and veiled words of this last family-meal, but they surely stir and deepen the obscure fears and deepening apprehension which fill the disciples. Dark dread envelops them all. For how long had the Master known that one of his chosen band was plotting his betrayal with his avowed antagonists? One who could read men's hearts perhaps had carried the precognition that this *denouement* was inevitable even from the moment of selection. The warning had been given to the company when Christ had told them the parable of the wheat and tares growing together until the end of time. Though to know in advance would eliminate surprise, it would not diminish his grief for the apostasy and his pain at such travesty of love.''

Sibyl Harton
Doors of Eternity
pp. 55-56

"A pasch is an intimate meal with Jesus in which we are united to the divine life which is given for the salvation of the world, a union with the broken body and the shed blood. This special union distinguishes the pasch from union with Christ in a general sense. The whole paschal mystery, the Cross and the Resurrection, is in the Lord's Supper. The mystery of the Last Supper is not limited to the visible participation in the Eucharistic gifts, in the assembly of the faithful. An internal, invisible, purely spiritual Last Supper can take place in my soul at every moment and everywhere. 'If any man opens the door to me, I will come in and sup with him' (Revelation 3:20). The invisible Last Supper is no less real than the visible one but is of another order and to distinguish between these two orders we must have a deep respect.''

Monk of the Eastern Church
Jesus: A Dialogue with the Savior
pp. 118-19

"St. Paul taught that Christians form a mystical union better than we do today, perhaps because they experienced more fully the work of the Holy Spirit in their lives. . . . The rite of Baptism and the Lord's Supper were understood as special means by which God's grace was revealed and received, by which his Spirit and the real presence of Jesus

and his Spirit were revealed to man in the sense of an *anamnesis*, that is, the bringing forward of an event out of the past, not simply an act of psychological remembrance.''

Leanne Payne
The Real Presence:
The Holy Spirit in the Works of C. S. Lewis
pp. 30, 186

"In the first historical witness in the New Testament to the institution of the Eucharist (1 Corinthians 11:23-26), Paul already affirms that it is a well-anchored tradition, even in the details, one of which was that it was on the night on which Jesus was betrayed — a point which should immediately alert the Corinthians to the sobriety and gravity of the occasion:

'For even if one be a very stone, yet when he considers that night, how he was with his disciples, "very heavy," how he was betrayed, how he was bound, how he was led away, how he was judged, how he suffered all the rest in order, one becomes softer than wax and is withdrawn from earth and all the pomp of this world. Therefore Paul leads us to recall all these things' (Chrysostom).

"Paul's version of the words of the institution are more than Mark's and Matthew's which lack 'for your sake' and less than Luke's which has 'given for your sake.' The words taken alone could mean that the Body is given for the benefit of the disciples, although this would seem a belaboring of the obvious in a text where every word counts. The parallelism with the blood of the covenant demands, however, taking 'for your sake' as an affirmation of the sacrificial nature of this body which brings salvation to his disciples. . . . Here then the body is identified with the body immolated on the Cross (so likewise, John 6:51).

"In a still more important way, Paul's version differs from that of the synoptics. The words, 'Do this in memory of me,' do not appear in Mark and Matthew and appear only once in Luke (22:19), whereas Paul has them twice. Obviously the Apostle is concerned with the iteration of the rite — that the Eucharist meal of Christians by the Lord's own will is identical with the Lord's sacrificial meal the night on which he was betrayed. The memorial (*anamnesis*) is not the faculty of memory, but the act of bringing to mind, of observing a memorial service. Paul's insistence on the recalling and repetition reflects his conception of the Eucharist as the Christian fulfillment of the Passover feast of the Jews, in which the recollection and repetition of the original Passover meal was minutely prescribed. . . . What in the Passover Haggadah was 'remembrance of the day you came forth from Egypt' is now 'in remembrance of me.' . . .

"Finally, the Eucharist belongs to the sacramental order, the time between the Lord's Resurrection and the final reunion with him ('until he comes'). It is through the Eucharist, the Passover meal of the New Covenant, that the deliverance by the Savior is made contemporary reality and the covenant renewed until his final coming.''

George T. Montague
The Living Thought of St. Paul
pp. 116-19

''After the failure of his preaching to the Jews, Jesus regards his Passion as a necessary precondition for the coming of the perfect kingdom. He is certain that his table companionship with the disciples will be realized in God's future kingdom in a new and perfect way (Luke 22:16, 18, 30b). How this will be possible, in spite of and because of his death, is shown in his words over the Eucharistic cup. This represents the 'new covenant' to be established through the blood of Jesus which acquires an atoning power. . . . The covenant of Jesus is the fulfillment, elevation and perfection of the old covenant which God once bestowed on the people of Israel. The word 'new' is not used in Matthew and Mark, but it is a new and eschatological institution. The words of Jesus then reveal that this promised covenant is to be realized through his bloody death and is to be made effective for those who partake of this meal. He will not unfold his full glory until the disciples share in God's full reign in the perfect kingdom; and Jesus assures them of this full share in God's reign because of this institution of the covenant in the Upper Room (cp. Luke 22:29 with 20)*. . . . If Jesus sees this new covenant established in his blood and at the same time awaits God's perfect kingdom, the only explanation is that his saving death guarantees the advent of the eschatological kingdom. . . .

''This naturally presupposes that the Last Supper with its sacred acts was more than a farewell feast for the loyal disciples of Jesus, that it was in fact a genuine institution for the future when he would be separated from them. Such an intention on Jesus' part is to be seen not merely in the injunction that they are to repeat this. Luke 22:16-18 makes it clear that the disciples, in contrast to Jesus, go on celebrating the 'Pasch,' naturally a 'transformed' Christian Pasch. . . .

''Mark 14:25 (= Matthew 26:29) includes one of his sentences at this parting meal which lifted their gaze to the kingdom of glory: 'Amen I say to you that I will drink no more of the fruit of the vine from henceforth until that day when I shall drink it new with you in the kingdom of God.' The sentence is found in Mark and Matthew at the conclusion of the Eucharist account. In Luke on the other hand (in somewhat altered form and duplicated), it is found before it, namely in the account of the Passover meal (Luke 22:16, 18). . . .

''There can be no doubt that Jesus is giving an image of the future kingdom in which he would be reunited with his disciples. The saying of Jesus presupposes a parting from the disciples and contains, notably in the two-fold form in Luke, a mysterious prophecy of death. . . . Jesus will no longer sit at table with his disciples on earth but at a new meal in the coming kingdom of God. For this, the death he is awaiting is a necessary condition, since the disciples can partake of the eschatological banquet only in the strength of the atoning blood of Jesus. The parallel texts make it evident that the saving power of the blood of Jesus applied to the disciples is not restricted to their number but has a universal efficacy ('for many,' that is for humanity, for all). Thus in his last hour, Jesus expresses his firm confidence that God will inaugurate the kingdom he has proclaimed so rich in grace for all those who gain a share in the new covenant, established by Jesus.''

Rudolf Schnackenburg
God's Rule and Kingdom
pp. 250-55, 192-94

---

*See also 42:1, Schnackenburg.

New Illuminations:

On True Greatness

Matthew 20:25-28	Mark 10:42-45	Luke 22:24-27

"Some of our Lord's uncomfortable words are hard to understand. But there is nothing difficult about his meaning of greatness, although there is nothing more difficult than its application. We cannot get around it nor evade its challenge because placarded before our very eyes is the Son of Man's own life of service. . . . He lived the truth of his own words that he had not come to be ministered unto but to minister, to serve others but not to be served. . . . 'You call me "Master" and "Lord" and rightly so, for that is what I am. Then, if I your Lord have washed your feet, you also ought to wash one another's feet' (John 13:12-14). . . .

"How much more might the contamination by the world's idea of rank and greatness been avoided had the church been as sedulous in the practice of washing one another's feet. This then is to be the pattern of our lives: greatness is to be measured in terms of service, and the greatest of all is the servant of all. But such a reversal of the world's standards will never be easy. As a citizen of heaven greatness is measured solely by humble service — and the two do not go easily together. . . .

"Yes, the greatest of all is everybody's slave. The house slave in the time of our Lord was in the same plight. He had absolutely no rights. The slightest wish of the least member of the master's household was law for him — not to obey was quite unthinkable. This is perhaps the hardest of all lessons to learn — that the Christian is never off duty. . . . We who would be true to our Lord and Master and would obey his commandment to love one another have to learn to put others' needs before our own. The only measure of our service is that we should love others as Christ loved us. He was actively engaged in redeeming the world, but he had time to look after the needs of those around him, the crowds in the desert who had grown hungry, the disciples who were overtired, his mother in her sorrow as he hung there dying before her eyes. And there can be no limit to our self-forgetfulness in the service of others. It is along this road that true greatness is to be found.

". . . George Morrison in one of his volumes of sermons tells the story of a distinguished Scottish minister who dreamed that he had gone to heaven. There was St. Peter standing at the gate, and the minister said to him: 'You know, I am the minister who preached to those large congregations Sunday by Sunday.' St. Peter said sadly, 'We've never heard of you.' But then he added, 'Are you, by any chance, the man who used to go into his garden every morning to feed the sparrows?' And when he replied that he was indeed that man, St. Peter said with a smile, 'Come in, the Master of the sparrows wants to thank you.' "

Joost de Blank
Uncomfortable Words
pp. 50-61

"In Christ's supreme act of love, God has told us that love knows no equal rights; that love's incentive makes possible a transfer of identity in which we become servants to one another, deferring to one another's needs, giving priority to one another's interests, willing to pluck out our eyes that others may see, to be the grain of wheat which dies redemptively. . . .

"Christ's example teaches us also that authentic submission is not grudging nor is it the result of imposed authority. It is rather a chosen, deliberate, voluntary love initiated response to another's need. It as an act of worship to a God whom we serve in serving others (Matthew 25:40). It is appropriate to the purpose for which we were created, since in serving his creatures, we are serving and worshiping our creator, and it acknowledges the dignity of our humanity because it is service freely rendered from a will surrendered to the loving purpose of God."

Elaine Stedman
A Woman's Worth
pp. 56-57

" 'I am not come to be ministered unto, but to minister.' This is what everyone should say who has any authority over others. It is a ministry. We must truly serve those whom we appear to command. We must bear with their imperfections, correct them with gentleness and patience, and lead them in the way to heaven. . . . We must never be discouraged and pray God to give us that change of heart that we cannot produce by our own efforts. Let us examine ourselves in relation to those who are committed to our care, and for whom we are accountable to God."

Thomas Kepler, ed.
Letters and Reflections of Francois de Fenelon
pp. 164-65

"Jesus is not judging the Gentile's use of power; he is condemning it. He simply describes existing institutions. But absolute power is not to be used by leaders in the Church. . . . Leaders in the Church are to be 'servants' and 'slaves.' The latter represents the lowest social stage, the class of persons who are unable to impose their will on any one but must suffer the imposition of the will of others. Jesus adds that this is his own position. He has become the servant of all, and the service that is imposed upon him is the supreme sacrifice of life. It should be noticed that the term 'ransom' follows the context of service. The ransom, the price paid, means that Jesus describes himself as reduced to the level of a means by which a purpose is achieved for others. . . . The value of his life is not determined by self-assertion nor by self-aggrandizement, but simply in terms of its value for other reasons. This carries out the figure of the slave who could have no personal ends to achieve."

John L. McKenzie
The Jerome Biblical Commentary
43:140

"The general character of the sayings collected in Mark 10:41-45 makes them an appropriate enough appendix to vv. 35-40. . . . The Evangelists introduced them in whole or in part, wherever they seemed the most appropriate. The demand they contain for humility and self-giving is clinched in the last verse by a reference to Jesus' own life and particularly to his death; so the message ends as commentary on the meaning of Jesus' approaching Passion. Whether the reference to the Passion is original here or is the work of the Evangelist is a question which has been almost endlessly discussed. The most that can be done is to list some of the other considerations which have been advanced for and against the originality of Mark 10:45b and Matthew 20:28. Against — and probably the majority of scholars are against — are:

1. The Lukan version of the sayings (22:27b), which appears to be derived from sources independent of Mark has no reference to the Passion, ending instead with the words: 'But I am in the midst of you as a servant.' These words in their complete simplicity and congruity with the thought of the preceding verses seem more likely to be original. . . .

2. Though Jesus may have included his death in his work of love and service for men, there is little or no evidence in the Gospels that he thought of it in terms of sacrifice or ransom. . . . On the other side, it is urged that the link between service and vicarious suffering would be a natural one to make if he was influenced by the conception of the servant in Deutero-Isaiah, whose service consisted precisely in such vicarious suffering."

D. E. Nineham
Saint Mark
pp. 280-81

"To enter into a loving, obedient relationship with God is not only to find oneself a child of God; it is also to find oneself, even as the incarnate Lord, a servant to all. Servanthood does not come easily to the proud, that is to the fallen. . . . On the other hand, even the best Christian, that

one who most consistently chooses to serve others, is 'not a man who never goes wrong, but a man who is able to repent and pick himself up and begin over again after each stumble — because the Christ life is inside him repairing him all the time.' " (C. S. Lewis, *Mere Christianity*)

Leanne Payne
*The Real Presence:
The Holy Spirit in the Works of C. S. Lewis*
p. 90

"God wills that we should fit into his design consciously and freely. It follows that he wishes us to experience, in full awareness the joy of his service. . . .

"It may be that our striving, which we understood for the benefit of others has been used by God primarily as a spiritual discipline for ourselves in which failure plays a part. . . . It may be that God has used the experience to teach us that we are not indispensable, or that he used it to show us that when we were acting altruistically, we were really serving our own wills in consciously 'virtuous' self-expression. Or it may be that failure of some plan is quite simply and directly a corrective. . . . In so far as we start out to do God's will, we acted to God's satisfaction. But man is free and it may be that the circumstances of our up-bringing and education have given us the wrong picture of how to act in God's service. When our scheme fails, if we pray sincerely and submissively, we shall understand what was erroneous in our conception and service. Corrected we try another, better way of service. The pattern of failure and correction will be repeated until we learn a better way. . . .

"If prayer is successful, there is no problem. If the venture is richly blessed in its outcome, I have reason to believe that God's purpose has been served. God loves us too much to shower upon us the very circumstances that will most readily feed our pride, vanity, and self-dependence. Do we not, if we pray at all, pray daily to be delivered from temptation? This prayer God answers in abundance when he denies continued successes to those who are only beginning to learn to serve him*. . . . Once more, however, this does not mean that every failure you experience is a direct expression of God's will. . . . On the contrary, it introduces into every situation, joyous or tragic, an element of purposefulness. . . . That was God's way during his incarnate life. The defection and treachery of Judas did not defeat him; nor did the judgment of Pilate nor the hatred of the Jews."

Harry Blamires
The Will and the Way: A God Who Acts
pp. 44-46

---

*See also 59:4, Penelope.

New Illuminations:

On Judas' Betrayal and Peter's Denial

Matthew 26:14-75; 27:3-10	Mark 14:10-45, 66-72	Luke 22:3-6, 21-23, 31-62

"Judas, one of Jesus' own disciples enters into a plot with certain leaders of Jerusalem to do away with Jesus. . . . In narrating the story of the betrayal, Luke brings the history of Jesus around full circle. Satan had left Jesus at the beginning of the public ministry (Luke 4:13) but only 'for a while.' Satan now reappears and Luke transforms the Passion narrative into a struggle against him: 'Satan entered into Judas.' These words are very close to John 13:2 and 27. . . . Luke attributes Judas' action to diabolical possession. The Christian must also carry his cross after Jesus and engage in active battle with Satan; for this reason, Jesus leaves him the food of the Eucharist so that he might 'continue with me in my trials.' "

Carroll Stuhlmueller
Jerome Biblical Commentary
44:151

" 'What will you give me if I deliver him unto you?' . . . Jesus announces to his Apostles that one of them will betray him. They do not doubt the Master's word. They do not cry out: 'Master it is impossible!' But they become sad and say one after the other: 'Is it I?' The experience of my own falls should make me very humble. I can never exclude the possibility of a new offense. I should ask, 'Am I going to betray again?' . . .

"Jesus knows that Judas is going to betray him. At the Last Supper he gives him, before the others, 'bread dipped.' The episode is disturbing. Is there in it a sign of condemnation or a last appeal of grace? 'And after the morsel, Satan entered into Judas (John 13:26-27). Perhaps we are allowed to think that the external mark of predilection which Judas receives shows again mercy on the part of the Savior. He is offered one last chance. If we consider carefully the circumstances in which we fall into sin and especially the immediate prelude to our falls, we see that to the last minute the Master multiplies his veiled interventions, his discreet appeals, the descending movements of grace, the touches of secret affection, in order to sustain our weakening will. The history of each of our sins is also the history of a manifestation *in extremis*, as it were, of divine piety. If only we knew we could read the signs!' "

Monk of the Eastern Church
Jesus: A Dialogue with the Savior
pp. 103, 122

"Being sorry for one's sin, of course is not a healthy or constructive thing. There is a kind of sorrow that may become just as self-destructive as indifference or complacency. We see this kind of sorrow in Judas who was as heartbroken as Peter, but whose sorrow led to very different consequences. 'He went out and hanged himself.' The difference between Judas and Peter was not the fact that one had done better than the other in following and supporting and understanding his Master. They both had failed him — Peter's failure was one of weakness; Judas' failure was the more determined and cold-blooded one of actual conspiracy — but both had to face the stark reality of their terrible inadequacy. . . . Even if the authorities had taken back the money, it would not have undone the betrayal or satisfied Judas' conscience. Nobody can annul the consequences of his mistakes. They are part of the stuff of history and go on doing their fearful work forever. But when even his pathetic little gesture was refused, Judas had only one thing left to do — the desperate deed of self-destruction. So there was nothing hopeful about the kind of sorrow that Judas experienced. It did nothing to open his heart to the forgiveness and mercy of God. It only turned him in upon himself. . . . If he cannot satisfy his own life by his own efforts, at least he can terminate it. The other face of pride is despair. . . .

"The only real choice any of us have is to go the way of Judas or the way of Peter. . . . Peter let his remorse and grief lead him to a new level of faith and trust in life and in the God who works graciously and redemptively within it. Judas let his remorse and grief lead to self-destruction, just as many modern people seek escape in alcohol or in a mental breakdown, or in a more decisive act of suicide. What made the difference in their answers? We are bound to give an old-fashioned answer to the question about Judas and Peter, and it has to do with a trust in a gracious and loving and forgiving and powerful God. One of the 'death of God' theologians insists that 'it is to the world and not God that we repair for our needs and problems.' But where in the world that Judas saw around him on that dreadful morning was Judas to look for a resolution to his dreadful sin? The world's reply to his plea for help was summarized in the scornful dismissal of the priests and elders, 'What is that to us? See thou to that' (Matthew 27:4)."

John M. Krumm
The Art of Being a Sinner
pp. 79-81

"The disciples have, Jesus says, a Father who cares for them, and, moreover, they have a Master who prays for them. The great crisis is imminent, to be ushered in by the Passion of Jesus. . . . Even Jesus' disciples will not be spared. Satan, the accuser and destroyer of God's people, has asked permission from God to sift them in the tempest of tribulation (Job 1:6-12; 2:1-6), as a man separates the chaff from the wheat. And God has allowed it. It is his will. But Jesus has prayed for Peter that his faith will hold fast, and that, in the eschatological time of sifting that is at hand he may again strengthen his brethren. Peter is the leader. In praying for him Jesus has prayed for them all. His intercession will bring them through since Christ is stronger than Satan."*

Joachim Jeremias
The Parables of Jesus
pp. 215-16

"The story of the look that pierced Peter was only told, only *could* be told, *after* the raising of Jesus. Peter told the story of his own betrayal after an event which changed everything and yet changed nothing. . . . Peter, to the very end of his life, betrayed Jesus. Nothing changed in Peter, and yet everything changed because he had seen something through his own tears which enabled him to go on through betrayal after betrayal, right up to the end. Peter discovered that there need be no permanent failure in his life because nothing that he did was able to overcome the love of Christ. Every time he fell, Christ picked him up. The reconstitution of Peter was never a single event. It was the constant renewal of the love of Christ which fought with his own weakness. Shortly after the death of Christ, according to the twenty-first chapter of John's Gospel, Peter's three-fold denial was overlaid by a three-fold confession of love.

". . . And Peter followed Christ as well as he could. Almost as poignant as the scene in the courtyard is that scene outside Rome, where an old and stumbling Peter is fleeing from the first political persecution of the Church. According to the legend, Peter meets Christ traveling the other way, going on to Rome. 'Quo vadis, Domine? — Where are you going, Lord?' Peter asks. 'I'm going to Rome to die for you again.' No word of reproach. Just the Wayfarer, endlessly going up to Jerusalem to die. And Peter turned and went back to his own passion, and the tradition tells us, and it breaks the heart to think of it, that the old Jewish fisherman insisted upon being crucified upside down because he was not worthy to die as his Lord had."

Richard Holloway
A New Heaven
pp. 51-52

"We have to recognize quite clearly that sin is sin, but we may learn many things through our falls. . . . We can understand how the fact that he had denied our Lord helped Peter, the prince of penitents, to maintain lowliness of heart. The first lesson a sinner may learn from sin is the grace of humility. Our Lord said to Peter, 'I have prayed for you that your faith fail not, and when you are converted strengthen thy brethren.' The gracious words teach us two other lessons that may be learned from sin: dependence on God and sympathy with sinners. The sinner who comes to the Friend of sinners can find not only forgiveness but humility, dependence upon God in faith, and sympathy with other sinners and the power to heal them."

Harry C. Griffith, ed.
A Gift of Light: A Collection of Thoughts from the Writings of Father Andrew
p. 36

"Christ seems to have been deeply aware of the fragility of human nature: the folly of heroics, the danger of demanding or attempting too much. Watch and pray that you enter not into temptation. . . . Our idea of our own power of resistance usually exceeds what we shall really manage when the pinch comes. 'If all shall be offended in thee, I shall never be offended!' said St. Peter. We know what happened to the one who said that. All that we dare to ask is that God will reinforce our will by the energy of his grace and bring us safely through these normal temptations which none escape. . . . To watch and pray means an acceptance of weakness and limitation, a meek willingness to learn the way of prudence which is taught by the wisdom of God. It means putting aside all ambition to find out how much we can endure."

Evelyn Underhill
Abba
pp. 79-80

"Unless we are ready to ask for forgiveness of sins by God, the examination of conscience may be only a vain form of introspection, which can make a soul worse if it ends in remorse instead of sorrow. Judas 'repented unto himself,' as Scripture tells us; Peter unto the Lord. A moral evil results from the failure of the soul to adjust itself to God. Despair is such a failure. Judas despaired but Peter hoped.* Despair comes from unrelatedness, from the refusal of the soul to turn to God. . . . The final stage of this sadness resulting from unrelatedness to God is a desire to die, combined with a fear of death — 'for conscience doth make cowards of us all.' "

Fulton Sheen
Peace of Soul
pp. 200-201

*See also 61:2, Penelope.

*See also 110:3, Sayers.

280

"It was characteristic of Jesus that the emotional support that he gave so freely was always honest in its appraisal and candid in its frankness. He never felt impelled to soften the facts in the interest of supporting a sagging self-esteem. Knowing Peter's temperament, he called attention to how easy it was to make assertions of loyalty, when carrying them out would be quite a different matter. Indeed it was this very quality of candor which helped his words of challenge, when they were uttered, to carry weight. His typical relationship was not clouded over with well meaning but untrue assurance. People knew where they stood with him. . . .

"Not only was it important for Jesus to speak openly to Peter of too easy professions of loyalty, it was also desirable for their relationship to be free enough for obvious displeasure to be expressed. When Jesus was critical of the sleepy Peter who obviously could not stay awake during his personal crisis in the Garden of Gethsemane, he spoke about it freely. . . . The really supportive aspect of Jesus' relation to Peter was the acceptance present regardless of how Peter acted. The look that passed between the two in the courtyard of the high priest would be hard to describe, but it was certainly a look of understanding acceptance and not one of rejection. Indeed the record seems to indicate that it was out of understanding acceptance of Jesus that Peter was able to measure up to the challenge of leadership; first the acceptance and then the change. . . . The basic change that took place in Peter's life turned him from reliance upon personal resources to a reliance upon powers far greater than his own. Personal failure counted not at all; the success of the mission to which he had been called became all-important. . . . Accepted as he was, he risked change to become the man he was capable of becoming."

Robert Leslie
Jesus and Logotherapy
pp. 80-83

"Peter wavered between regression and progress. His egocentricity broke down; but his guilt, the outer manifestation of inner darkness, was balanced by the experience that Jesus had forgiven him this weakness many times. Once more Peter found himself on the side of darkness, weeping bitterly and craving desperately for the light. He was not strong enough to reach the light, but his strength was just strong enough to endure the darkness."

Fritz Kunkel
Creation Continues
p. 293

"The Church asserts that there is a Mind that made the universe. In him we shall discover a Mind that loved his own creation so completely that he became part of it, suffered with it and for it, and made it a sharer in his own glory and a fellow worker with himself in the working out of his own design for it. . . . Accepting the postulate then, and looking at Christ, what do we find God 'doing about' this business of sin and evil? And what is he expecting us to do about it? Here the Church is clear enough. We find God continually at work turning evil into good. He takes our sins and errors and turns them into victories, as he made the crime of the Crucifixion to be the salvation of the world. . . . 'O felix culpa!'* exclaimed St. Augustine contemplating the accomplished work. . . .

"There is a good result of evil. . . . When Judas sinned, Jesus paid; he brought good out of evil, he led out triumph from the gates of hell and brought out all mankind with him. But the suffering of Jesus and the sin of Judas remain a reality. God did not abolish the fact of evil; he transformed it. He did not stop the Crucifixion; he rose from the dead. . . . Judas despaired of God and himself and never waited to see the Resurrection. . . . In this world, at any rate, he never saw the triumph of Christ fulfilled upon him, and through him, and despite him. . . . St. Peter, who had a minor betrayal of his own to weep for, made his act of contrition and waited to see what came next.** What came next for Peter and the other disciples was the assurance of what God was and with it the answer to all the riddles. If Christ could take evil and suffering and do that sort of thing with them then, of course, it was all worth while; and the triumph of Easter linked up with that strange, triumphant prayer in the Upper Room (John 17), which Good Friday's events seemed to make so puzzling. As for their own parts in the drama, nothing could now alter the facts that they had been stupid, cowardly, faithless, and in many ways singularly unhelpful; but they did not allow any morbid and egotistical remorse to inhibit their joyful activities in the future.

"Now indeed they could go out and 'do something' about the problem of sin and suffering. They had seen the strong hands of God twist the crown of thorns into a crown of glory, and in hands as strong as that they knew themselves safe. They had misunderstood practically everything Christ had ever said to them, but no matter: the thing made sense at last, and the meaning was far beyond anything they had dreamed. . . . It had been said to them of old time, 'No man shall look upon my face and live'; but for them a means had been found. They had seen the face of the living God turned upon them, and it was the face of a suffering and rejoicing man."

Dorothy Sayers
Creed or Chaos
pp. 10-13

*See also 119:2, Krumm.
**See also 110:2, Sheen.

New Illuminations:

On Jesus in Gethsemane

Matthew 26:30-32, 36-46	Mark 14:26-28, 32-42	Luke 22:35-46

"Jesus said, 'It is enough,' when his disciples presented him with two swords. The disciples had not understood the meaning of Christ's statement: 'He that has not (a purse) let him sell his coat and buy a sword.' What Jesus meant was that there are times when we must sacrifice the most ordinary thing in order to concentrate our attention on the assaults of the evil one. But defense and attack are both spiritual."

Monk of the Eastern Church
Jesus: A Dialogue with the Savior
p. 149

"When the disciples went out on their earlier missionary tours, they did not need to provide for or defend themselves; every door was open to them because they were his. Now every door would be shut in their faces precisely for the same reason: Jesus is now 'numbered with outcasts' (Isaiah 53:12; Luke 22:37). This whole passage may be taken in one of two ways: (1) It may be taken literally. Jesus is telling his disciples that they must be ready to defend *themselves* if necessary, though not to defend him (cf. Matthew 26:52). They were not ready for martyrdom yet, and had not done their work. (2) The other explanation is profounder. If they decide to defend themselves by force, the time will come when they will have to sell the very clothes off their backs to buy weapons. They do not understand him — how could they? — and think he is appealing to them for protection. 'Lord, here are two swords,' they say; and he replies, 'Let it go at that.' The second explanation is more convincing."

Abingdon Bible Commentary
p. 1055

"Jesus in his passion 'began to grow sorrowful and be sad' (Matthew 26:37). His human nature knows from experience all the attacks, all the agitations to which our nature is liable. His divine nature, however, remains in perfect peace — the divine peace of a soul humanly 'sorrowful even unto death' (v. 38). . . . It is this doctrine of the two natures of Christ which warrants our belief that in Jesus both the divine and human remain wholly integral, and yet they are united with each other. The storm may strike the foot of the mountain, but the summit is in full sunlight."

Monk of the Eastern Church
Jesus: A Dialogue with the Savior
pp. 157-58

"Jesus' Last Supper with his disciples is followed by his night of solitary struggle with prayer in the garden of Gethsemane. The story should not be read simply as a historical record. The very fact that no human being witnessed Jesus' struggle is evidence of this. Yet this story is a historical document in a higher sense: it presents Jesus alone at the fiercest point of his temptation, separated from his disciples not as 'divine being,' but in his complete humanity."

Gunther Bornkamm
Jesus of Nazareth
p. 162

"Surely it is out of character and foreign to the whole spirit of his ministry if Jesus is simply asking to be spared physical suffering and death. The agony in the garden was caused by more than apprehension of torture and the horror of a cross. Many martyrs have gone to the stake confidently and calmly, their faith sustaining them. If this were all that Jesus was concerned about, it could hardly bring about the 'horror and dismay' Mark speaks of or explain Jesus' own words, 'My heart is ready to break with grief'* (Mark 14:34). His agony was much more the horror of complete innocence and perfect sinlessness being confronted by the awfulness of the human situation, the malevolence of the priesthood, the indifference of the masses, the disloyalty of his closest followers, the total ugliness of evil."

William Neil
The Difficult Sayings of Jesus
pp. 61-62

"Lewis' keen sense of the humanity as well as the divinity of Christ is illustrated quite forcefully in a letter in which he speaks of Christ's human will and feelings:

'God could, had he been pleased, have been incarnate in a man of iron nerves. Of his great humility he chose to be incarnate in a man of delicate sensibilities who wept at the grave of Lazarus and sweated blood in Gethsemane. Otherwise we should have missed the great lesson that it is by his *will* alone that man is good or bad, and that *feelings* are not, in themselves, of any importance' (*Letters of C. S. Lewis, The Made Collection,* p. 210).

So it is that we see both his manliness and his perfect obedience and see more clearly the cost involved in the

---

*See also 25:2, Hession.

Gethsemane prayer: 'Nevertheless, not as I will but as you will.' A root meaning of the word 'obey' is 'listen.' To obey is to listen. And Christ listened always to the Father. . . . It was the Father's will that he, by being obedient unto death, should taste death for all mankind, thereby bringing many sons into glory. By willing always to do the Father's will, Christ became our brother.''

Leanne Payne
The Real Presence:
The Holy Spirit in the Works of C. S. Lewis
pp. 86-87

'' 'Behold, there he stands
behind our wall
gazing in at the windows
looking through the lattice.'
(Song of Songs 2:9)

"For St. Bernard the wall is the flesh that hides our Lord from us, yet it is 'our' wall because God shares it with us; and the apertures are the human senses through which he gained experience of our needs and learned obedience by the things he suffered.* There is a lot to think about there, but Origen has more. Where St. Bernard's Latin version gave him 'lattices or windows,' Origen who used the Greek, read 'nets.' And he equates these nets with the 'snares of the fowler' (Psalm 91:3), the temptations that the devil lays across our paths to trip us up (Luke 22:40, 46). But through these same temptations our dear Lord looks out at us and, finding him in them, we advance beyond them by their means.''

Sister Penelope
The Coming
p. 111

"If Jesus' pains were not simply his concern once upon a time but are of actual use to us now, we must be sure that we know them. . . . No episode of the Passion has a greater mobilization of agony than the hour in the garden of Gethsemane, yet none is so readily accessible to our understanding and actual experience, for the more we analyze it the more it displays all the modes and categories of our own sufferings. Despite our undoubted spiritual insufficiency and blindness, we will, with whatever humility and reverence we can summon, try with all meekness to think, feel, and pray with Jesus in that garden, approaching him interiorly as we watch him externally. . . .

"It is in sadness and obscurity that Jesus and his few friends walk out of the city to the quiet garden, well known to them as a place for their talk and prayer. Nightfall with its growing silence underlines gravity. Surely there must have been a sense of finality communicated from the Lord to his

disciples? The perfect Son must have already said farewell to his mother. Each would have been aware of the other when impending separation was near. Jesus adds to his own pain the inclusion of his mother's and he gives his to her. Yet in her perfection she would accept what her Son wished her to accept and thus give to him her energy of strengthening compassion. His mother, yes; but how will the disciples react? He knows they will all, all, forsake him, run away, forswear. Sick with foreboding they already are, for what depresses and gnaws at courage more than prescience that catastrophe is approaching when there is ignorance of its details? Those heavy hearted men must feel with their Lord that they are all trapped in danger.

"Why does Jesus want his friends to be with him now, the men who have, he said, been with him through all his temptation . . . For accomplishment of his mission each one is necessary, even Judas to whom the Lord is so courteous (John 13:26). Between the Man Jesus and his brethren there is a separating gulf, the deep gulf of the inner silence where he dwelt with the Father. Not that he was self-sufficient, but, rather, he was God-sufficient. Yet now in this hour of anguish, Jesus underlines his human nature — our nature — by wanting the presence of his most familiar friends. Where is he to find refuge, a covering from the avalanche of evil which his spirit recognizes as advancing upon him? Where if not in their love? Jesus wants the solace of his friends and they are with him. But he departs from the group to go on into the olive grove with the chosen three who had seen his transfiguration in glory on Mount Tabor, for, remembering that, surely they would now support his transfiguration in torment. I cannot bear this terrible aloneness, I cannot face what is coming to me, be with me now in my agony. He actually tells them he is filled with dread and woe as never before (Mark 14:34), and he begs for the sympathy of their company. . . . So will they now watch with him in that stillness of night when senses and susceptibilities are refined to a special degree of knowledge? Watch:* in its original Greek this word carries this sense of being awake in the night, the night which is the normal time for repose and recreation in sleep; but he begs that they shall be vigilant and stay awake. . . . Yet when in the unbearable restlessness of anguish, Christ rises from his knees to come to them for support, even his three are asleep (worn out by grief, says St. Luke). Why can you not keep awake for one hour? Small wonder though that they shrank from seeing Jesus in this unusual condition of apparent defeat and exhaustion, he who had always been in complete command of every situation, who had never failed in control. Now he is gripped in some imminent crisis and is failing them. Oblivion is their refuge. Once before he had begged his Father to save him from this hour; yet, then, hardly were the words out of his mouth than he had instantly asserted that for that very hour he had come. Now it has come, the hour has struck and can it be eliminated? God is almighty; He could even now alter the pattern of salvation and spare the beloved Son the unspeakable sufferings which are advancing fast as an engulfing tidal wave, 'Father, let this hour pass.'

---
*See also 59:4, Penelope.

---
*See also 91:2, Penelope.

Yet not for one instant does Christ cease to struggle. His ultimate will must unify his whole being into the choice of not his own but his Father's will. Christ has come to the moment offered to him and he, with total energy, accepts it.

"So intense are the tug, the strain, the conflict that the soul and body are almost rent apart and the blood which maintains his life begins to ooze through the pores of his skin. He must have help and once more Jesus comes for it to his three closest friends. They are asleep. Peter it is who stirs at his beloved master's approach and hears the sad exclamation, 'What, can you not watch for even one hour?' Apparently not! . . . The state of division, darkness, and disintegration of body and soul which man brought upon himself by his initial act of self-enthronement, by his disobedience of the law of his created being, denying his essentially dependent nature is now to be experienced by perfect Man who freely and of his own choice takes upon himself the full horror and fearfulness of sin. . . .

"When is the final sweating of man? At his death of which it is frequently the sign. . . . Jesus breaks into the great sweat of blood, not a mild, gentle perspiration but an exudation of great drops which colors the ground and stains his clothes: or how would the apostles have known? . . . This fearful flow of blood will drain away the Royal Lamb's life now, and as there is no possible human help, once again a celestial creature shall succor him. And what is the purpose of this supernatural strengthening? To maintain Jesus in life so that he may suffer yet further, and display publicly, in the face of all space and time, the whole sea of his passion. . . . But it is here in Gethsemane that we are aware that in some degree the battle with all the forces against him is already over, because there in the garden it has already been won. With the will of his whole nature unmovably enclosed within that of the Father, Jesus now moves forward in the triumph of serenity and power to whatever sequence of suffering is ahead. He is again the master of circumstances. . . . This is the Jesus they know, the perfection of being, this is a glory. It is a perfection and power which is the result of obedience to suffering."

Sibyl Harton
Doors of Eternity
pp. 54-61

New Illuminations:

"Since we are human, suffering has to come in as a warning. I must suffer in my body when it is burned or I would be continually burning my body. I must suffer in my soul when I do something wrong, or I might go on doing wrong. I can give that answer to the world's great 'Why?' Did anyone ever cry out into the dark that saddest of sad words with greater pathos and pain than Jesus, who has given the one answer to the riddle of life? He, hanging there, seemingly deserted by God, in the unutterable darkness trusted God; and he, hanging there, looking down on the mocking faces of men, still loved them. . . . As Catherine of Siena said, 'Nails had never held him to the cross if love had not held him there.'

. . . Never judge God by suffering, but judge suffering by the Cross. . . . The way of pain is the way of sympathy. I should find it very hard indeed to pray to a God if I thought that I could suffer something that he had never suffered. I should find it very hard to worship a God if I felt that I could plumb a deeper depth of suffering than he could know. But I know I cannot. Whatever I may suffer I cannot suffer a tenth of what he suffered. And I know very well that I can only have true sympathy with suffering people if I myself can feel pain. So this inexplicable mystery of suffering may be to us the way of sincerity, may give to us the chance of proving to others that we are true, of proving to ourselves and God that we are worthy of the name of the children of God. It may also be the way of sympathy linking us all together."

Harry C. Griffith, ed.
*A Gift of Light: A Collection
of Thoughts from the Writings of Father Andrew*
pp. 17, 64, 76

"The doctrine of providence does not claim that every misfortune (even every natural disaster) is divinely purposed; only that it is divinely purposeful. There is a great difference here. We have no right to claim of any given misfortune (especially another's misfortune) that it is directly expressive of God's will: only that it can be made an instrument for the expression of God's will. . . . It is necessary for us to take pain and disappointment into the centre of our experience precisely because they are in the centre of God's experience. Suffering does not lie on the fringe of God's experience but at the core. . . . He is not a God whose realization of suffering is occasional and fitful: for suffering is eternally a chosen mode of his love for man. The thorns are a familiar crown and the sword pierces his heart. This follows: if God's incarnate course was in character,

that God embraces suffering and makes it his own. . . . Do we pray to that truly incomprehensible God who chooses for his sinless Son the way of suffering and grants to his sinful sons the realization of all their cherished earthly dreams? The Christian God chooses the action of suffering. And when a rebellious voice within us cries out, 'Ah, but he is a God of Love!' the Church, if she is faithful, has only one answer: 'Are you sure that you know the nature of Love?'"

Harry Blamires
The Will and the Way: A God Who Acts
pp. 42, 49-50

"While we must not refuse to think about evil, our primary task is to fight against evil. We have to admit that we have an unsolved dilemma on our hands. . . . In the end we are faced by the choice, either to believe in God and accept this problem of evil, or to reject any belief in God and somehow find an adequate explanation for the goodness in the world. Of these alternatives, I find the former far less difficult because of another, for me, very significant factor. It is the following: There are times, I grant, when life is like a sky covered over with the black clouds of evil, suffering, cruelty, injustice, disasters to say nothing of personal difficulties and frustrations. Yet I am sure that at least one ray of light pierces those clouds. That is enough to assure me that beyond the evil there is love. That ray is the person and life of Jesus Christ who, I am convinced, discloses to us that which is at the heart of reality — God and his love."

Mark Gibbard
Apprentices in Love
pp. 36-37

"Our own willingness to face our inner cloud of loneliness is like cloud seeding — like dropping little bits of chemical into the clouds so that drops of moisture begin to form . . . and then a rain comes and perhaps the whole cloud system dissolves into rain showers so that the sun can begin to shine through. So it is with us when we turn into our own darkness. . . . Strange that sometimes it is only the pain of being alone that can precipitate the fog around us and cause it to drop. How strange it is that running from the darkness can only make it darker, whereas entering into it can cause it to dissolve, and then we can see. . . . And then there is a ray of light . . . and the person standing quietly there at the edge of the room, waiting for us to speak: 'Lord, have you been there all the time and I didn't know?' 'Yes, I have been here waiting for you to pass through yourself and find that I was here. I have been here all the time, but I force myself on no one. . . . But those who look deep within themselves and find the darkness and emptiness and loneliness, they are the ones that really need me and find me.' "

Morton Kelsey
The Other Side of Silence
p. 286

"The blessed gift of faith is ours by virtue of baptism, the foundation of all our life in Christ. It is no cool act of intellect, no easy shrug of assent, no thoughtless or superficial impulse. . . . Faith it is which enables me to accept and use any type of trouble, with both hands if I can, as my immediate way of union with God; for if suffering is indeed part of the answer to the lock of life, then faith is the first key to use. There is no arrogance or self-sufficiency in holy confidence; it is stayed upon humility. In my own power and strength, I do nothing of value, but I can do and bear the impossible through Christ and his grace. The more I can see and acknowledge my dependence upon him for grace and for my pliability in circumstances, the deeper is my rest upon God. It was the Lord's way: '. . . nothing of myself, but as the Father taught me.' Yet I may have no consciousness of trust as I carry my heavy burden; all my energies, both internal and external, may be absorbed in accepting it uncomplainingly and willingly as were Christ's in the garden. But if faith is authentic and vital it is accompanied by the activity of confidence without any feeling of it, as certainly as wetness accompanies water. So I am held in inner calm and spiritual strength, a calm which can astonish me when it is maintained in the face of tempests*. . . .

"Though the trial seems intolerable and is straining me to the limits of my endurance, I can make it at once both more acceptable and more readily sustained when, relaxing into it with my will's compliance, I bless God, I force myself to give thanks. It is not only for the laughter but also for the tears, for this very anguish, this sacramental moment heavy with woe, that I bless him. . . . I am not trying to escape from it, O my God; I am trying to take hold of it and use it as a sacrifice and an offering of love, for what else have I at this moment to give You? 'I will sing of the Lord because he is dealing so lovingly with me.' I have no feeling of this now, but when the dark pain has passed, or at least lessened, I realize that in the deep places of the spirit, God has indeed dealt lovingly with me for he knows me and my needs. . . . Even though I am out of tune, he has lifted me above my entanglement with the misery and helped to prevent me from centering myself in it, particularly in respect of my emotions.** Thanksgiving strangles self-pity. Easily we give thanks for any kindness, for delights, but giving it

---

*See also 41:3, Underhill.
**See also 120:3, St. Teresa of Avila.

supernaturally for hurt and pain produces a great richness of heart which uncovers the truth that in accepting God's will we do indeed choose our sure happiness.* Experience is gained by a progress of circles."

Sibyl Harton
Doors of Eternity
pp. 81-84

"People sometimes ask me if I have ever felt like losing my faith. No: my faith is always part of me. But faith is not a state of easy and calm security. It is an adventure of ceaseless battling with troubles; a peace of mind and a serenity indeed, but a costly peace and serenity in the midst of conflict. After all our world is a world of conflict, and faith is not an escape from it, but something which — in St. John's words — overcomes it. . . . My faith in God is most acutely tested by the experience of suffering which seems to have no special wrongdoing at base. Indeed belief that God is almighty and all-loving is strained for the sensitive Christian until he goes on to see the divine way of dealing with suffering in the Cross of Christ. There the answer comes. . . . Faith is a costly thing, valid only in terms of the challenge to a costly way of life. Those who possess it have found it not to be a way of escape from life's conflicts, but a way of meeting them with the certainty that the power of God and goodness will prevail."**

Margaret Duggan, ed.
Through the Year With Michael Ramsey
pp. 15, 39

"Job had believed God to be just and man's duty to be to walk in His ways. But it is no longer possible for one who is smitten with such sufferings to think God just (Job 9:22).
. . .
He has recognized, before this, the true God as the near and intimate God. Now he only experiences him through suffering and contradiction, but even in this way he does experience God. . . . 'As God lives, who has withdrawn my right' (Job 27:2). God lives and he bends the right. Now he can only ask to be confronted with God. 'Oh that one would hear me!' (Job 31:35). In the last instance, however, he merely means that God will again become present to him. 'Oh that I knew where I might find him!' (23:3). . . . The absurd reality of a truth known to man and a duality sent by God must be swallowed up somewhere, sometime, in a unity of God's presence. How will it take place? Job does not know this, nor does he understand it. He only believes it. We may certainly say that Job appeals from God to God. . . . The voice from the tempest is not only *a* voice but the voice of *Him who answers*, the voice of Him that 'heard' (31:35), and appeared so as to be found of him (23:3). In

---

*See also 59:3, Lewis.
**See also 108:1, Penelope.

vain Job had tried to penetrate to God through the divine remoteness; now God draws near to him. No more does God hide himself, only the storm cloud of his sublimity still shrouds him and Job's eye 'sees' him (42:5). God offers himself to the sufferer who, in the depth of his despair, keeps to God with his complaint. God offers himself to him as an answer. It is true that the overcoming of the riddle of suffering can only come from the domain of revelation: the revelation as an answer to the individual sufferer concerning the question of his sufferings, the self-limitation of God to a person, answering a person.''

Nahum Glatzer, ed.
Martin Buber: On the Bible
pp. 193-96

"It has been well said that earthly cares are a heavenly discipline; but they are even something better than discipline — they are God's chariots, sent to take the soul to its high places of triumph. . . . Everything that comes to us becomes a chariot the moment we treat it as such. And on the other hand, even the smallest of trials may be a Juggernaut car to crush us into misery or despair if we so consider them. It lies with each of us to choose what they shall be. It all depends not on what these events are but on how we take them. If we lie down and let them roll over us and crush us, they become Juggernaut cars; but if we climb into them as in a car of victory and make them carry us onward and upward, they become the chariots of God. . . . Joseph had a revelation of his future triumphs and reigning, but the chariots that carried him there looked to the eye of sense like dreadful Juggernaut cars of failure and defeat. Slavery and imprisonment are strange chariots to take one to a kingdom, and yet by no other way could Joseph have reached his exaltation. . . . The great point then is to have our eyes open to see in everything that comes to us a 'chariot of God,' and to learn how to mount into these chariots. We must recognize each thing that comes to us, as being really God's chariot for us and must accept it as from him. He does not command or originate the thing, perhaps; but the moment we put it into his hands it becomes his, and he turns it into a chariot for us. He makes all things, even bad things, work together for good to all those who trust him. All he needs is to have it entirely committed to him.''

Hannah P. Smith
The Christian's Secret of a Happy Life
pp. 250-51, 256

"As I have begun to crawl out of the slough of self toward Christ and others, I have realized that at least I can use my miserable days by trying to love his people and do his will. My own misery often sensitizes me to the signs of lonely agony in other lives which I could have missed otherwise. The positive acceptance of one's own suffering is a way of participating in a very real power God releases into the world, a power which allows other men to be strengthened to embrace and carry their own burdens as they see us carrying ours. Through this trying to do God's will, this increased sensitivity to others, and this possible release of power into the world, I have discovered what Frankl meant when he said that 'suffering ceases to be suffering in some way the moment it finds a meaning.' ''

Keith Miller
A Second Touch
pp. 78-79

"Born as pure potential, we need to grow and this growth is linked with pain and suffering. However strange it may seem, suffering is imperative for the preservation of life created from nothing. If animals did not feel hunger, they would make no effort to find food but would simply lie down and die. Similarly acute discomfort compels man to look for nourishment.''

Archimandrite Sophrony
His Life Is Mine
p. 33

"For whatever reason God chose to make man as he is — limited and suffering and subject to sorrows and death — he had the honesty and courage to take his own medicine. Whatever game he is playing with creation, he has kept his own rules and played fair. He can exact nothing from man that he has not exacted from himself. He has himself gone through the whole of human experience, from the trivial irritations of family life and the cramping restrictions of hard work and lack of money to the worst horrors of pain and humiliation, defeat, despair, and death. When he was a man, he played the man. He was born in poverty and died in disgrace and thought it well worth while. . . . He was not merely a man so good as to be 'like God' — he was God.''

Dorothy Sayers
Creed or Chaos
p. 4

New Illuminations:

On Jesus' Arrest and the Desertion by His Disciples

Matthew 26:47-56	Mark 14:43-52	Luke 22:47-54, 63-65

"From the moment of his arrest, Jesus knew that he was going forward to grapple alone with evil in the midst of darkness. 'This is your hour and the power of darkness' (Luke 22:53). St. John makes it clear that this was the hour towards which the whole of his ministry has all along been moving (John 8:20; 12:23-27). Philosophers through the ages have wrestled with the problem of evil; countless ordinary men and women have struggled with the fact of evil. The story of the Cross, as Christians have interpreted it, shows Jesus Christ grappling with the power of evil, naked, relentless, undisguised and in its totality. Here is a mystery before which the intellect eventually has to call a halt. Both God and evil are greater than ourselves. We cannot but be baffled when confronted with God and evil in mortal combat. Later on the Cross, in the soul and body of one Man, that conflict was to be fought out to a conclusion. There could be no draw, no treaty, no compromise, no co-existence. One side must win, and one side must be annihilated."

Douglas Webster
In Debt to Christ
pp. 47-48

"Jesus goes out in front of the troop which, with its torches and arms, wants to lay hands on him. He goes freely, spontaneously, to his passion. Jesus cures the servant whose right ear had been cut off by the sword of a disciple. Not only is Jesus unwilling that his disciple defend him by force — 'Let me at least do this,' he said (Luke 22:51: Goodspeed) — but he repairs the damage which the sword had caused. It is the only miracle which Jesus performed during his passion. . . .

"On two occasions when Jesus gave his name to the soldiers they drew back and fell to the ground. Their prostration means that Jesus is stronger than they, and that it is by his own free choice that he gives himself up. . . . The example of non-resistance that Jesus gave does not mean that he consents to evil nor that he remains merely passive. It is a positive reaction. It is the reply of love — which Jesus incarnates — opposed to the enterprises of the wicked. The immediate result seems to be the victory over evil. In the long run, the power of this love is the strongest. The Resurrection followed the Passion. It is the shedding of blood which has guaranteed the spreading of the Gospel. Is this a weak and vague pacifism? No, it is a burning and victorious flame. If Jesus at Gethsemane had asked his

Father for the help of twelve legions of angels, there would have been no Easter or Pentecost."

Monk of the Eastern Church
Jesus: A Dialogue with the Savior
pp. 149-50, 157

"Gethsemane is the place where Jesus is arrested by the band of his opponents under the leadership of Judas — a scene which, according to the description of the Gospels, finds Jesus prepared and the disciples unprepared. The picture presented by the account is not one of Jesus and his followers on one side and his enemies on the other. Rather it shows Jesus alone, and on the other side his enemies and all around the disturbed band of his disciples. . . . Jesus permits it. His final words according to the oldest record are 'Let the Scriptures be fulfilled.' The disciples flee."

Gunther Bornkamm
Jesus of Nazareth
pp. 162-163

"Now follow the eleven disciples through the waking nightmare that ensues. The earthly life story of the Incarnate Word is a straight course up the mountain; now he has almost reached the top — the Cross. Here the thicket is the densest, most wounding, and most blinding. . . . All that the eleven can see is failure. For as at the outset, the mystery of redemption is hidden in silence so now its climax is hidden in noise — malice of enemies. . . . The eleven are *in* Jesus through all this — have they not drunk his blood? And their suffering is a thousand fold enhanced by their personal failure at the crisis. There is nothing left in them but need of him whom they failed, who has been taken from them, whom they can never hope to see again. Self-sufficiency is dead and they are just an emptiness. So there is room in them at last for his free bounty, but of course they do not know that yet."

Sister Penelope
The Wood
p. 125

"We know that at one period the disciples confidently expected an earthly kingdom to be set up, and although their hopes became more and more deferred, yet his death came to them as a kind of end-of-the-world disaster, so that every loyalty was driven out by their fear and disappointment. . . . Despite his constant reminder that his kingdom was a spiritual kingdom, it appears that somehow they expected him to take the power and reign. In their hour of desolation, one betrayed him, one denied him publicly three times, and the others left him and fled (Mark 14:50).

"I am far from judging the disciples harshly, and I would be slow to suggest that you and I would have behaved any differently in the same circumstances, but I find the wholesale desertion at the end of Christ's life an almost certain indication that they could not understand this basic fact about God: he does not use force to accomplish his purpose. I hope I am not being unduly imaginative when I suggest that it must have crossed their minds many times in those last dark days that it would be the easiest thing in the world for God to intervene and prevent the murder of his perfect son. What a justification of his claims, what a demonstration of the power of light over darkness, what a rousing victory for the God who had visited his people! But no celestial rescue party left the clouds of heaven, no angel interfered in the final tragedy.

". . . It is, of course, easy for us to be wise after the event and to know that 'thus it must be.' But I think that we are still puzzled by the apparent inaction of God. . . . There is the universal longing for God to intervene, to show his hand, to vindicate his purpose. I do not pretend to understand the ways of God more than the next man, but it is surely more fitting as well as more sensible for us to study what God does do and what he does not do as he works in and through the complex fabric of this disintegrated world than to postulate what we think God ought to do and then feel demoralized and bitterly disappointed because he fails to fulfill what we expect of him. I am certain that God who is our Father and understands us perfectly has to teach us that he will no more interfere with other people's freedom than he does with our own (Luke 9:50, 54-55)."

J. B. Phillips
Making Men Whole
pp. 32-33

New Illuminations:

On the Trials, Mockings, and Scourging of Jesus

"There is little doubt about the actual attitude of the audience of Jesus, at least in general lines, from the account of the evangelists. The report merits historical acceptance since the outcome of the activity of Jesus is shown in precise historical data: the arrest of Jesus by the Jewish authorities, his delivery to the Roman tribunal, the process against him, and finally his execution on the cross. Several minor questions may be debatable, for instance, what was the status of Jewish legal proceedings against Jesus, how the guilt for this judicial murder is to be shared between Jews and Romans, and to what extent the people, the followers of Jesus and people who were not hostile to him, can be freed from all share in this guilt. . . .

"The people tend to believe more readily than their leaders, but they do not arrive at any decisive acceptance of the Messiah. They followed the Galilean healer and wonderworker, were astounded at his teaching of the law and listened eagerly to his preaching. But they had no understanding of his implicit Messianic claim . . . If we leave aside an attempt to proclaim a political Messiah after the multiplication of the bread (John 6:15), the opinion of the crowd continues to be divided, uncertain and undetermined, or the germ of belief is soon suppressed by the Pharisees and the fear of official authority. . . .

"The particular enemies of Jesus, the influential (Pharisee) and leading (Sadducee) classes in Jerusalem are thrown into stronger relief in the tactical and eventually successful measures they adopt against him. The tragic *denouement* of his conflict with the official leaders of Judaism (or simply with the 'Jews') manifests itself as an instance of that dark reality, described in the prologue, that the 'world' did not recognize the Logos at his advent, that 'his own' did not receive him (John 1:10 seq.). The 'elevation' on the cross, that takes the 'Son of Man' back into the glory of his Father and releases the energy of divine life for believers is a God-ordained necessity to raise all men to himself in his heavenly sphere."

Rudolf Schnackenburg
God's Rule and Kingdom
pp. 178-79

"Jesus' trial before the Jewish high court has been elaborated by the Gospels in the spirit of faith in Christ. The quite dramatically constructed report begins with the summoning of false witnesses who contradict one another. Jesus' own confession before the high priest that he is the Messiah, a confession made openly for the first time, forms its center. It ends with Jesus being sentenced to death for blasphemy. The account thus becomes a testimony to Christ in strong contrast to the rage and cruelty of his enemies. ('He was silent.')

"But the details are in contradiction to our reasonably reliable knowledge of Jewish procedure at court. . . . This procedure demands that capital crimes should be tried during daytime only, certainly not during festival times, and not be dealt with at a sitting of one day only. The immediate appearances of witnesses for the prosecution, moreover, who quote in distorted form a saying of Jesus', certainly genuine, about the end of the old temple and the building of a new one, would have been a serious breach of the law. Finally, there is not one single instance of a person every being accused of blasphemy and sentenced to death by the Jewish authorities because he claimed to be the Messiah. There is no mention of the abuse of the name of God. Moreover, in the case of blasphemy, the Jewish authorities would certainly have had the right to have had Jesus executed, for instance, to have him stoned (Acts 6:8ff.). But Jesus is not stoned but handed over to the high court by the procurator Pontius Pilate, and is crucified by him, a punishment which was the exclusive right of the Roman law court, and which was instituted for political crimes."

Gunther Bornkamm
Jesus of Nazareth
pp. 163-64

"There can be no doubt but that Jesus claimed an active role in the Final Judgment. The most significant passage is Jesus' profession before the Sanhedrin: 'Hereafter you shall see the Son of Man sitting on the right hand of power* and coming in upon the clouds of the sky' (Matthew 26:64). Several modern scholars regard this not as a statement of the advent of Jesus from heaven, nor as an implicit threat of the judgment upon his earthly judges, but as an announcement of his coming elevation to the right hand of God and of a divine justification — as vindication. . . . The reference to the Parousia is indisputable. The only problem in the answer of Jesus to the high priest arises from the word 'hereafter' in Matthew's text. Luke rendered it as 'from now on' and so changed and curtailed Jesus' reply. 'From now on will the Son of man sit on the right hand of the power of God.' "

Rudolf Schnackenburg
God's Rule and Kingdom
pp. 172-73

*See also 125:1, Ramsey.

"In the Gospels, we see the resentment of the powerful groups against Jesus growing and stirring and rising like a flood until it overwhelms him. And the main point of their accusation was just, though they did not realize it. What Jesus did and said implied, whether or not it explicitly claimed, that he was of God and from God and knew God in a way that no other man ever did or could. He claimed to know the very nature of God in a way that only an insider could know it. So they accused him of claiming to be the Son of God. 'We have a law and, according to that law, he ought to die because he has claimed to be the Son of God.' The irony of that statement is that men cannot allow God to be God, to be himself as he is without *their* control and consent. *That* God they will always kill. The killing of God is a permanent human activity."

Richard Holloway
A New Heaven
pp. 24-25

"Now there can be little doubt that whatever the real motive was, Christ seems to have been executed on a charge of insurrection and political conspiracy. The accusation which was written out and pinned above his head on the cross said that he claimed to be the king of the Jews a claim which was certainly political if interpreted in the obvious way. From what we can gather from his trial and appearances before Pilate, it was claimed that he spoke against Caesar; and he was executed by Pilate however cynically as having been charged by loyal leaders of Jerusalem's Religious Establishment with sedition. How seriously can we take this picture of Christ?

"Again we must try to use our historical imagination. The Palestine of the time of Jesus was politically volcanic. . . . At top were the Roman administrators who were, as a rule, happy to leave the local rulers to manage affairs, provided taxes were paid and the peace kept. But the mix in Palestine was too explosive. The ecclesiastical establishment and the Herods, the client kings of the Roman power, had a strong interest in maintaining the status quo. Change could not possibly be in their interest. It never is for the privileged, who have learned to live with and learn the system. . . .

"Below that level there was a seething market place of religious movements, some activist, some escapist, dedicated to the violent overthrow of the Roman occupation. We hear echoes of these movements and they must have provided a complicated background to the ministry of Jesus. There seemed to have been a few zealots, a group committed to violent revolution, among Jesus' followers. . . . Christ must have aroused the interest and expectations of many of these groups. . . . He *had* something that we now call *charisma*, leadership quality to an ultimate degree and an ability to use language itself as a weapon which he turned against the complacent and powerful who anxiously protected their own privileges. . . .

"There is no doubt that the political anxieties of the day contributed to his death, but it is impossible to cast him as a first century Che Guevara. We need not go to his trial to find our evidence. The trial accounts of the New Testament do not give us enough to go on, and some hold, anyway, that the accounts there do not square with what is known of legal procedure in those days. No, we must go back to what we know of his life and sayings, because it is there that we find the real refutation of the claim that Christ was simply a political revolutionary.

"In the first place, there was no strategic hate in Jesus. . . . On the contrary he reverses the process of group hatred by preaching love of the enemy and non-resistance toward those who would exploit us. . . . Secondly, there was no exclusive group loyalty in Jesus: he moved freely among every type of person: Roman soldiers, tax-collectors, the rabble of the city, and the rich and powerful from both the civil and religious establishments. Thirdly, he did not, as all revolutionaries do, preach a conspiracy theory to explain evil and suffering. The fault did not lie in the socio-economic structure but in the heart of man whence came all evil and its consequences. Jesus went to the root of our human dilemma: our nature and its taint of sin and alienation from God."

Richard Holloway
A New Heaven
pp. 28-30

"Pilate's pronouncement of the death sentence does not at all exclude the possibility that the Jewish authorities delivered Jesus as a political suspect into the hands of the Romans in order to get rid of the hated prophet from Galilee. This is how Luke and John present the matter, certainly correctly as regards the point. Pilate found himself considerably embarrassed by this as the records show. We have no reason to doubt this even though the tendency of the Gospels is to show the Procurator as a witness of Jesus' innocence, and thereby to exculpate Pilate, the representative of Rome, and at the same time, to make him into the involuntary instrument of public opinion aroused by the Jewish leaders. Pilate tried to extricate himself by offering to pardon Jesus, but the incited people insisted upon the liberation of the Zealot Barrabas instead of Jesus — Barrabas who was rightly sentenced for the crime of which Jesus was wrongfully accused. Jesus is thus delivered up to the derision of the Roman soldiery, whipped and led to the Crucifixion, forsaken even by his disciples."

Gunther Bornkamm
Jesus of Nazareth
p. 164

"We are stunned by the vision of a man who feels pain and betrayal but who with a child-like simplicity has handed over his life to his Father and does not need to fight for his life with the strategems of power and force because he has already given it away. We recognize the paradox: this is Gospel strength.

"With all this echoing in our hearts, don't we know we are being called to follow our Master? Jesus certainly was not naive. He knew what was in men's hearts. He saw what was coming. But he also trusted in his Father's love. As we inhabit the story, we gradually are brought face to face with our own strivings for power: the power of education, of age, or position. Here we hand ourselves over to the power of darkness. It is our refusal to trust in the Father the way Jesus did. Yet we know we are being called to follow in his way. It is no accident then that Jesus consistently chooses to be powerless. In the Gospel stories, our Lord challenges us to abandon our attempts to seize power and control, to freely choose to hand over control of our lives to the Father, with child-like simplicity."

Thomas Kane
"Powerless and Weak"

"It is possible to make generous allowance for the crimes of passion, but even the most callous can be aroused to indignation by cold, planned treachery. Yet in the Cross we find just this pattern of events being worked out around the human life of the Son of God. He is the victim of a plot. He is betrayed by a follower. And he submits to it. If we feel that life is unfair to ourselves or our friends, we are bound to recognize that it was even more unfair to Christ. If we complain because of injustice, we must remember that Jesus suffered because of injustice as even one of the dying thieves admitted. At the end of St. Luke's description of our Lord's trial before Pilate, there comes this remarkable summary: 'Pilate released the man they asked for, who had been put in prison for riot and murder, and *handed Jesus over to their will*' (Luke 23:25 — Goodspeed). Justice? The Cross certainly touches human life in its vast area of rampant injustice. We may not understand the Cross of Christ or the injustice of some people's circumstances, but we cannot say that the Cross is unrelated to them."

Douglas Webster
In Debt to Christ
p. 18

"God was executed by people painfully like us, in a society very similar to our own — in the over-ripeness of the most splendid and sophisticated empire the world has ever seen. In a nation famous for its religious genius and under a government renowned for its efficiency, he was executed by a corrupt church, a timid politician, and a fickle proletariat led by professional agitators. His executioners made vulgar jokes about him, called him filthy names, taunted him, smacked him in the face, flogged him, and hung him on the common gibbet — a bloody, dusty, sweaty, and sordid business. If you show people that, they are shocked. So they should be. If that does not shock them, nothing can."

Dorothy Sayers
The Man Born to Be King
p. 7

" 'Jesus is delivered up to their will.' The phrase which the Gospel uses in speaking of Pilate applies to me every time I personally cooperate with the tempter and every time I cooperate in another's sin. 'Dost thou betray the Son of Man with a kiss?' The kiss by which Judas betrays his Master is every prayer which I venture to say without rooting out from my heart all complacency toward evil."

Monk of the Eastern Church
Jesus: A Dialogue with the Savior
p. 104

New Illuminations:

On Jesus' Road to Calvary

"When they came to arrest Jesus, it was the middle of the night. We know he had not slept. We know he was in agony of uncertainty and apprehension. . . . In the hours that followed, he was dragged through six trials and was finally brought back to Pilate for final sentence. The detail as we have it may not be totally accurate, but there is no doubt at all that he was put through a most gruelling night. During these hours, he was beaten up at least twice and was bound, his arms pulled back tightly and roped painfully to his body. Immediately after Pilate had passed the sentence of death, he sent him away to be scourged. Scourged! The word for us has a cozy, almost domestic ring about it, suggesting little more than an energetic application of a little vim to a dirty pot. But there were few more painful ordeals than Roman scourging. The victim was stripped and he was either tied to a pillar in a bent position with his back exposed so he could not move, or he was stretched rigid upon a frame. The scourge was made with leather thongs studded with sharpened pellets of lead and pieces of bone. It literally ripped a man's back to pieces so that many lost consciousness under the lash and many emerged from the experience raving mad. After more sadistic horseplay by the soldiers, he was led away to be crucified.

"The procession to the place of execution always followed the same pattern. The criminal was placed in the center of a hollow square of four Roman soldiers. In front there walked a herald carrying a board on which the charge was painted. It was later pinned above the head of the victim. The criminal was taken to the place of execution by the longest possible way, through the busiest streets and through as many of them as possible, so that he might be a dreadful warning to others. As he went he was lashed and goaded. He was forced to carry at least part of his cross."

Richard Holloway
A New Heaven
pp. 43-44

"When our lord was at Nazareth, he went into the synagogue and read to the people and proceeded to give them a further explanation of what he had read. It roused their ire. The congregation rose up and began pushing him out of town, even threatening to pitch him off a high place. Then it was that he went through the crowd and went toward Capernaum. Here we witness the first showing of that innate courage of Christ which would lead inevitably to Golgotha*. . . . Resolution is a quality of character not

---

*See also 15:2, Stott.

mentioned much these days. It is ninety percent of all heroic action. . . . Consider how the courage and sheer heroism of Christ puts us to shame. He walked straight up to and through the denials of Peter, the treachery of Judas, the mockery of Pilate, the scourging and the Cross."

Richardson Wright
A Sower Went Forth
pp. 35-37

"The guards felt that they knew what the public wanted. They would not run any further risk of killing Jesus prematurely. When they saw how little strength there was left in him, they drafted a man from the onlookers to help him out. The chosen man's name was Simon from the beautiful city of Cyrene in upper Libya where a Jew was as good as anybody else among the Gentiles where he held equal citizenship with the Greeks who had founded the town. One minute before he was drafted, Simon was an unknown molecule swimming in the vast bloodstream of the human race. Suddenly a guard pointed a finger, snarled an order and the burly Cyrenian, seething with his bad luck, ceased to be a gawking spectator from a distant city and became immortal. Simon, the unknown Cyrenian, bent to help Jesus carry his cross. He had done no crime. His pleasure was spoiled. It was an aching nuisance to take such a load, and the way to the hill of Golgotha was such a long one. . . . Even with the strength of Simon the Cyrenian — who suddenly found himself taking a strange, mysterious liking to this convict and carried the cross with an utterly and inexplicable satisfaction — Jesus felt his knees buckle under, and for the third time he fell down. But his tormentors were not so worried now. Here was their destination. He had only to lug the cross up that final stretch of steep hill and there he would be! Calvary!"

Fulton Oursler
The Greatest Story Ever Told
p. 282

"Is the spirit of mourning really what the Cross is intended to elicit? Jesus turned to the women who bewailed and lamented on the road to Calvary and said, 'Daughters of Jerusalem, weep not for me but weep for yourselves and your children.' Christ does not want our pity. There is a fine passage in F. W. Robertson's famous sermon on the loneliness of Christ which is a corrective to all such sentiments: 'You degrade Christ's loneliness by your compassion for him! Adore if you will — respect and reverence that sublime solitariness — but no pity; let it draw out the firmer and manlier graces of the soul.' The Cross of Jesus claims our attention but not our pity. This is all that Jesus asks of his disciples on the eve of his Passion. 'Watch!' "

Douglas Webster
In Debt to Christ
p. 28

New Illuminations:

On Sacrifice I

"Sacrifice is as obscure in its origin as it is varied in its form. We do not know who offered the first sacrifice, nor what he meant by it; but this much is certain: the root idea which underlies sacrifice all over the world is *fellowship*. Sacrifice therefore exists primarily and essentially in God who, being both individual and social, is ever giving and taking in the depths of his own being. And creation was a further act of sacrifice because it was, and its continued being is, a further giving out of himself. That divine self-giving is to be answered on behalf of the whole creation by the conscious, willing self-giving of man who, made in his Maker's threefold image, can find no satisfaction save in his fellowship with him. Ultimately and ideally, then, sacrifice is the same as love, and it certainly has no essential connection with either suffering or sin. . . .

"The presence of evil in the world, by putting an obstacle in the way of this mutual self-giving between God and man, has introduced into sacrifice the element of suffering. Consequently, just so far as man has any sense of alienation from his God, to that extent also there enters into his practice of sacrifice the element of propitiation. . . . Since man is so constituted that he cannot express himself otherwise than through his body and other material means, sacrifice involves for him the use of a physical medium. A material gift must express his intention and if possible effect his desire."*

Sister Penelope
The Wood
pp. 46-47

"In the Old Testament, sacrifice was instituted because of sin. It was God's merciful provision for the salving of man's conscience. The sacrifices which were constantly offered symbolized the desire of man to be right with God. The offerer identified himself with the purity of the offering by the laying on of his hands. He is saying in effect, 'I would like to be pure like this, but I am not, so I offer this instead.' But the system was quite inadequate to meet the moral and spiritual needs of men. The victim was passive in character; being an animal it could hardly be otherwise. The purity was merely physical, 'a lamb without a blemish,' and therefore, non-moral. There was no personal bond between the offerer and the offering. So the sacrifices could never effect what they symbolized. The Epistle to the Hebrews discusses this problem more fully than any other book of the New Testament* (Hebrews 10:4-10)."

Douglas Webster
In Debt to Christ
pp. 84-85

"The concept of sacrifice, derived from the ancient Jewish sacrifices described in the Old Testament, was very prominent in the New Testament writers for their understanding of the salvation wrought by Jesus Christ. Our Lord himself used the language of sacrifice when at the Last Supper he spoke to the disciples about the new covenant in his blood and instituted the Eucharist as the memorial, or the recalling, of his death. . . .

"The word 'sacrifice' has come both in popular and religious use to be sublimated in ways far from its original history. It is used of giving something up, of making some unselfish gesture, of losing one's life, or simply parting with something. . . . As the Jewish systems of sacrifice developed, a certain rationality about their meaning became apparent. They witnessed to a deep feeling that as man approaches God something desperate needs to be done on account of the estrangement of sin. Man cannot easily slip into divine presence; man as a sinner cannot lightly approach the Holy God; hence the strange system of sacrifices. And the idea of offering something to God is therefore present. Perhaps the offering of an animal is in some half-conscious way felt to represent the offering of a life of the man bringing the sacrifice. But of that we are not quite sure. For all its ceremonial elaboration, the system could not conceal hints of an inner scepticism about its own validity. . . . But we also find in the Psalms that what God really requires is not sacrifice at all but moral obedience (Psalm 51:16-17). . . . No words ever uttered by a prophet could have been more awe-inspiring than the words of the prophet Micah (Micah 6:6-8)."

Michael Ramsey
Jesus and the Living Past
pp. 64-66

---

*See also 43:1, Hebert; 1:2 Du Bose.

---

*See also 1:2, Du Bose.

"Consider the strange theophany to Abraham's grandson Jacob at the ford of Jabbok. When deadly peril threatened him in consequence of his past sin against his brother, 'Jacob was left alone, and a man wrestled with him until the breaking of the day' — a man who would not otherwise leave hold of him, both lamed and blessed him, changed his name to Israel, God-persists, because Jacob had striven and prevailed *with God*. There are great depths of mystery here, but one thing surely we may take as certain. A man prevails with God when he takes the discipline God lays on him, however much he suffers in the struggle. Jacob as well as Abraham was a key man for the work of salvation, one of the primates whence the Savior was to spring. When he also responded, then indeed the day was breaking and the climax of God's age long persistence in his purpose was at hand."

Sister Penelope
The Coming
p. 85

New Illuminations:

On the Crucifixion of Jesus

Matthew 27:33-66	Mark 15:22-47	Luke 23:33-56

"By his act of faith and subsequent persistence in it, Abraham became the first stone of the bridge* which was to span the gulf between God and fallen man. Many centuries were to pass in the building of that bridge, stone by stone from either side, the action of God evoking the response of man until there should lack only the keystone to complete the arch. . . . As a bridge is made of stones, so is a nation made up of individuals. The Chosen People were not so much the bridge as the quarry whence its stones were hewn. . . . The history of the Chosen People is dominated by great individuals in whom the progress of the divine purpose comes to the surface and is visible; but for the most part the bridge, like the seed grows secretly. . . .

"Isaiah formulated his doctrine of the faithful remnant through whom the hope of Israel should be realized. . . . Like the underground stem of a virile plant, it sends up shoots at intervals which will never fail to bear fruit, though they may not always overtop the weeds among which they grow. . . . Under the yoke of Rome and the Herods, things looked black enough outwardly. But for all of that, or rather because of it, the bridge of which Abraham was the foundation was nearing its completion. History was converging on the faithful remnant, hidden like leaven in the lump of Herod's subjects. . . .

"In spite of the desperate present, they believed that God would again intervene in human history to put things right. . . . In this alone all who hoped at all were agreed. They all looked for God himself to act. . . . 'The Word was made flesh and dwelt among us,' God had acted.** He by whom all things were made had himself as man entered the created order. The keystone of the bridge was at last in being. . . . The New Testament is the record of God's placing the keystone in the bridge through the sacrificial life, death, and ultimate resurrection of his son — the Christ. . . . So John and Jesus, stone and keystone of the bridge were prepared for thirty years, one in the desert, the other in his home, and the eyes of those who looked for redemption in Israel turned to neither. . . . So great is the fury of the tempest of the Crucifixion that nobody sees that the keystone is quietly settling into place and *finishing the bridge.* . . . Jesus points to the bridge, of which he himself is the keystone, and says to the whole human race, 'This is the Way: walk in it.' "***

Sister Penelope
The Wood
pp. 42-125

*See also 78:2, Thielicke.
**See also 83:1, Penelope.
***See also 122:3, Phillips.

" 'So they took Jesus (the Delight of God) and he went out, carrying the cross by himself to a spot called the Place of the Skull, or in Hebrew, Golgotha. There they crucified him, one on each side and Jesus in the middle!' (John 19:17-18). The Delight of God crucified! He to be hanged in shame between two thieves that our eyes might see God's salvation which he had prepared before the face of all people; a light to lighten the Gentiles, and the glory of his people Israel: that we who sat in darkness might see a great light; that to us who sat in the region of the shadow of death, light might spring up."

Amy Carmichael
Thou Givest . . . They Gather
p. 202

"When they reached the place of execution, the cross was assembled. The upright beam was usually in place in its socket and the victim was forced to carry the cross beam. At this point it was customary to give the victim a drink of medicated wine mingled with gall, to help drug him for the pain that was to follow. Jesus refused the drink. Halfway up the upright beam of the cross there was a projected ledge of wood, called the saddle, in which part of the criminal's body rested, or the weight of his body would have torn the nails clean through his hands. At that moment the victims cursed and swore and shrieked and spat at their executioners. We are told by Luke that Jesus prayed, 'Father, forgive them for they do not know what they are doing.' Usually only the hands were nailed, the feet being loosely bound to the upright beams of the cross, and the criminal was stripped naked. But the real terror was yet to come. The real terror of the crucifixion was that it was a lingering death."

Richard Holloway
A New Heaven
pp. 44-45

"There is a phrase which the Greek Liturgy is constantly applying to God in Christ — 'O Lord and Lover of Men.' The whole religious movement of the drama of the Passion is gathered up in that. Re-enter that history and see what it means. Let us read and brood on the Gospel account of the Passion, all the curt notes crowded together. Detach them; take them separately; dwell upon them. The anointing by the woman of Bethany of One who never seemed more divine than now, accepting so peacefully the menacing web of events that begins to hem him in. And even that gesture of love spoiled for him by the sordid displeasure of his own disciples. All that stresses his isolation. And then the incredible beauty of that double manifestation of humble and generous service, the Last Supper and the Washing of the Feet, with their deep and selfless reverence and concern for our human weakness and need. And lastly, Gethsemane, the real crisis, the victory; nothing matters to him after that. . . . Because of that scene, at the very heart of human suffering we always find Christ, the Lord and Lover of men. We often feel we make such a mess of our suffering. We beg to be let off, and so we think we have failed God. Gethsemane is the answer of the Divine Compassion to that fear. . . . After that he comes with a strange serenity to the betrayal and Peter's denial.

"Think of these events as they were, crowded and driven together — the 'dense and driven passion' as Hopkins called it. . . . Think what each of these events meant, beating one after another on a soul unique in its sensitivity to evil, sorrow, love — completely awake to its own awful destiny and moving towards it in absolute loneliness and still at every point pouring itself out in loving care for men, self-given without hesitation to the vocation of sacrifice because it was the Lord and Lover of men, feeding and saving them ever since by the fruits of his self-given love.''

Evelyn Underhill
The Light of Christ
pp. 86-87

"The outline of the official story is the tale of the time when God was the under-dog and got beaten, when he had submitted to the conditions he had laid down and became a man like the men he had made, and the men he had made broke him and killed him. This is the terrifying drama of which God is the victim and hero. If this is dull, then what in heaven's name, is worthy to be called exciting? The people who hanged Jesus never, to do them justice, accused him of being a bore — on the contrary, they thought of him too dynamic to be safe. . . . That God should play the tyrant over man is a dismal story of unrelieved oppression; that man should play the tyrant over man is the usual dreary record of human futility. But that man should play the tyrant over God and find him a better man than himself is an astonishing drama indeed. Those who did hear it for the first time actually called it News, and Good News at that though we are apt to forget that the word Gospel ever meant anything so sensational.''

Dorothy Sayers
Creed or Chaos
pp. 5, 7

"Hanging on the cross, there came the taunts of the High Priests, 'Let Christ, the King of Israel, come down from the cross . . .'. And like a mocking echo of the people's cheers on Palm Sunday, only five days ago, from the cross beside him, 'Lord, remember me when you come into your kingdom.' Do you think that dying bandit saw into a spiritual Kingdom beyond death? Perhaps the royal answer showed him one.* But it is far more likely the thief himself, half delirious with agony, had remembered some rumor that had reached him in the condemned cell which prompted a wild hope in the Man beside him. In the end Jesus died with the fact of his royalty placarded above his head — 'Jesus of Nazareth, King of the Jews.'

"It never mattered much again that he had been born a king, as this world counts royalty. But it mattered terribly to Jesus of Nazareth while he lived. Perhaps kingship had to be his right, if he was to think it worth renouncing. Perhaps he had to let it come actually within his grasp on Palm Sunday before renunciation could be real. And then he took kingship — he took that golden symbol of all the lusts of the eyes and the lust of the flesh and the pride of life — and cruelly, deliberately, mercilessly, he nailed it to his cross. 'Don't be afraid; I have conquered the world' was what he had said before he went out to die. It was true. He was young and all the best that the world thinks it has to offer was within his grasp if only he would thrust aside the known purpose of God for his own human life — and for all the world beside. It all hung on that.

" 'Art thou a king, then?' 'For this cause came I into the world. For this I was born, that I might bear witness unto the truth.' That is the truth about the world and all the best that it has to offer — that taken just in themselves and sought for themselves, apart from God, instead of God, against God, these things are worth in the end just what he rated them at — death. 'I have *conquered* the world' before Good Friday began. And Good Friday proved it for all the world to see.''

Dom Gregory Dix
The Claim of Jesus Christ
pp. 55-57

"It is not the broad river that turns the turbine; it is the water rushing through the narrowed gorge. The latter does not create the power, either; there must be a turbine there. In personal life, what is the turbine? The clearest image of what it is is Jesus Christ on the Cross of Calvary. Life was certainly hemmed in for him. . . . Because God leaves men free, they are able even to close the Lord of the Universe out of His world. . . . The hands that were active in the healing of men were now nailed down to the Cross; feet that were accustomed to visit haunts of need were now securely

---

*See also 80:1, Holloway; 86:3, Webster.

held. He was not only hemmed in physically; he was closed in upon spiritually. Unresponsiveness was at its maximum all around. Pharisees and Sadducees who heretofore had been divided by their quarrels were united in their hate of him; Roman and Jew, generally at swords' points gladly collaborated for this deed. An atmosphere of hate and malice and cynicism almost engulfed him. He was bereft of his friends, even his closest ones. So great was his defeat that a few days later, on the road to Emmaus, two of his disciples could say, sadly, 'We had thought that it was he who would save Israel.' Yet from that Cross have streamed power and healing, light and salvation unto the ends of the earth. And his spiritual activity during those hours included also the immediate: He prayed for his persecutors;* He redeemed a dying thief for eternal life; He made arrangements with John for his mother's care. But supremely He reveals to us what it is that marks the difference, in the same circumstances of life, between frustration and spiritual power and confidence: 'Father, into Thy hands I commend my spirit.' "

James A. Pike
Beyond Anxiety
pp. 62-63

"For a long time now we are told darkness covered the earth. Then within the darkness Jesus spoke, 'My God, My God, why hast thou forsaken me?'** This is the first verse of the Messianic Psalm (22), which our Lord has pondered again and again and which he knew to be fulfilled in himself. He had no tinsel dreams of a Messiah who would rule by force. Our Lord knew that the Messiah must be a suffering Messiah, as he could only save suffering men through suffering. So when he said these words there was no falling from the perfect confidence in the Father. There is not the cry of one who doubted but of one who shared life's darkest problems, who experienced to the death life's direct pains. Nevertheless, he felt to the full the agony and the distress of the deepest spiritual temptation. In Incarnation and the Cross are the way in which God has come to us through the storm. . . . Hate brought him thorns and he turned them into the Crown of Life, and the worst day in his life's experience, the Friday that brought him murder and a death in the dark, he changed into the best day in his love's expression, so that we call it Good Friday.''***

Harry C. Griffith, ed.
A Gift of Light: A Collection of Thoughts from the Writings of Father Andrew
pp. 64-5, 70

"For Christ, his sacrifice was indeed a double agony; he felt it both as a man and as God. As man he identified himself with sinners, the whole human race beset and victimized by Satan; as God he was refusing Satan any rights whatsoever and resisting him to the uttermost. As God he was feeling the horror and repulsion that the Holy must always feel in the presence of sin; as man he was feeling the divine wrath and displeasure that the sinful must feel in the presence of the Holy. This is the heart of the Cross. It was this dread experience from which Jesus had shrunk in Gethsemane but to which he finally submitted himself. It was to be his alone, unshared, unknown and untold. . . . The only hint of its character is to be found in that bitter cry of dereliction from the Cross, where Christ exposed himself to the full force of sin and evil in order to break its power. While this was happening he felt cut off from God. . . . Here is God the Son himself actually feeling as sinners feel, bereft, forsaken, without hope, without God! This is the sense in which on the Cross Christ comes completely beside us to where we are. His Life and Death were an ever deeper entering into human experience, every human experience.''

Douglas Webster
In Debt to Christ
p. 48-49

"It is often overlooked how far reaching are the claims concerning Jesus and concerning the doctrine of God implied in the early preaching of the Apostles. It was 'that Christ died for our sins in accordance with the scriptures' (1 Corinthians 15:3). What does this tradition say and imply? It is about the Biblical theism which in Jesus had been finding fulfillment. The term Christ implies one who fulfills the purpose of the God of Israel, and the phrase 'in accordance with the scriptures' implies the same fulfillment. It is a message about the God in whom the Jews have long believed and about the climax and goal of his activity in history. This climax, fulfillment and goal is, staggering to say, the death by crucifixion of the Christ. Further the death by crucifixion has some relation to 'our sins.' Whose sins are involved? . . . Let it be noted that the death of Christ concerns the sins of men and women anywhere and everywhere, and a confrontation of judgment is clearly implied. This is a message about a universal significance in Jesus, and it is also a message about the God of the scriptures, his purpose and his vindication. The far reaching impact of the death of Christ is possible because the message goes on to tell of his subsequent resurrection, 'that he was raised . . .' It is by the presence and impact of the risen Christ that the message is preached with power, received with power and vindicates itself wherever the Christian message extends.''

Michael Ramsey
Jesus and the Living Past
pp. 39-40

---

*See also 100:2, Hooke.
**See also 118:2, Holloway.
***See also 46:1, Webster.

"The earliest Christian preaching had the death and resurrection of Jesus at the center. The belief in the resurrection included both the action of God in raising Jesus from the dead and the contemporary presence of Jesus as alive. This did not mean, however, that the crucifixion of Jesus belonged to the past alone, for it was continually emphasized that Jesus who is alive and contemporary is the Jesus who was once crucified. The crucifixion continued to be seen as a timeless confrontation between the judgment and compassion of God and the sinfulness of the human race. Both Baptism and the Eucharist emphasized the continuing significance of the death of Jesus. In baptism, converts were believed to be united with Jesus in his death, and the Eucharist was a showing forth of his death and a recalling of it unto the present time."

Michael Ramsey
Jesus and the Living Past
pp. 5-6

"When Jesus died, the veil of the temple was rent in two from the top to the bottom. It is St. Mark who records that, and one wonders what St. Peter thought when he first heard of it. The veil of the temple was the curtain that separated the Holy Place from the Holy of Holies, the innermost sanctuary of the Lord God. Nobody ever went through the veil except the high priest on the Day of Atonement, and then he went in alone bearing the blood of victims previously slain as offerings for sin. He did not stay there nor did he make a way for other people. He came out again, dismissed the scape-goat, the sinbearer, and then, having changed into the golden garments of his office, he reappeared before the expectant people, having ratified their covenant relationship with God *for one year*. Meanwhile the veil hung dark across the empty sanctuary; no eye could pierce it, no representative of man pleaded with God beyond it. But at the moment of Jesus' death, the veil was rent because to that which the Holy of Holies symbolized he, who was himself a scape-goat, sin-offering and priest, had made a way through. Moreover his sin offering was adequate and unrepeatable, for he was sinless. And we are still waiting for our High Priest to reappear in the glorious raiment of his office. . . .

"On Good Friday evening, his friends had only a dead Jesus to show their love, but that was better than nothing. So two men who had never before dared show him friendship openly, took his body down and buried it after the Jewish fashion. That is to say the tomb was a cave hewn out of a rock with a ledge for the body and a round stone to block the door. There was no coffin, but the body was wrapped from head to feet in long wide bandages with spices sprinkled between the folds; a separate cloth went round the head. It was done in a hurry, because the Sabbath was approaching. This therefore left a further chance for others who loved him to go and do a little more when the Sabbath was over — always supposing that they would get in. But it was only his body. He himself was dead and the light of light had gone out with him. They never dreamt that it had gone just around the corner into paradise. Nor did any, apparently, remember for their comfort that it is always the darkest hour that comes before the dawn."

Sister Penelope
The Wood
pp. 126-128

"Do you know Fra Angelico's wonderful picture of our Lord's desert in Hades which is called 'The Harvest of Hell'? It shows us the liberated soul of Christ passing straight from the anguish of the Passion to the delighted exercise of rescuing love. He comes with a sort of irresistible rush, bearing the banner of redemption to the imprisoned spirits of those who knew him not. There they are pressing forward to the mouth of the cave, the darkness, narrowness, unreality from which he comes to free them, free them at his own great cost. Nowhere, not even in his own Resurrection garden does he seem more victorious, more Divine. The awed delight of the souls he rescues is nothing besides the rescuer's own ecstatic delight. It is as if the soul released on calvary could not wait a minute, but rushed straight to the joy of releasing the souls of other men* (Matthew 27:52-53, 1 Peter 3:19-20). There is no hint of the agony and darkness through which he has won the power to do it. Everything is forgotten, the cost, the darkness, everything but the need the Rescuer is able to meet. . . . It was in the Passion, says St. John of the Cross, that Christ 'finished that supreme work which his whole life, its miracles and works of power, had not accomplished: the union and reconciliation of human nature with the life of God.'** Here we learn all that it means to acknowledge him as our Way and our Truth and our Life. I suppose no soul of any sensitiveness can live through Holy Week without an awed and grateful sense of being incorporated in a mystery of self-giving love which yet remains far beyond our span."

Evelyn Underhill
The Light of Christ
pp. 78, 81

---

*See also 121:3, Penelope.
**See also 70:1, Hooke.

New Illuminations:

On Sacrifice II: The Cross

"In the New Testament the word 'redemption' is often associated with the word 'blood': 'In whom we have redemption through his blood' (Ephesians 1:7). What this verse is saying is simply that the act of redemption was also an act of sacrifice. In redeeming us the Son of God offered himself in sacrifice. His was a redeeming death because it was a sacrificial death. His death was a sacrifice in that it was on *our behalf*. He allowed himself to be treated as a victim, both by man and by God."

Douglas Webster
In Debt to Christ
p. 84

"From the first days of the Christian Church animal sacrifices had no place whatever in its life. But instead of them, the Christians now spoke of Christ's own sacrifice as the ground of their new relation to God. . . . For Christ had fulfilled, abolished, superseded the old system not by attacking it or denouncing it but simply by replacing it by himself, his own life, death and resurrection; himself the true victim, himself the true priest. The old sacrifices were bulls and goats; Christ's sacrifice was that of his own life, his body, his will. The old sacrifices had no real moral effect. Christ's sacrifice had a cleansing power and enables Christians to make a true approach, offering themselves in union with him. The old sacrifices were a series of pathetic repetitions year by year. Christ's sacrifice once and for all opened the way for lives to be effectually consecrated to God. He sacrificed himself once in order that the sacrifice of human lives in and through him could continue forever*.

. . .

"The Apostolic writers likened Jesus to a series of images drawn from the Old Testament. Each of them is familiar in its Old Testament setting; what is new is likening each one to the mission and achievement of Christ. (1) Jesus is the Passover Lamb (1 Peter 1:19). Jesus did for the people of God whatever the passover lamb did for the old covenant. (2) He is the sin offering. The image is of the offering made once a year when the high priest entered the holy of holies taking with him a sacrifice designed to cleanse the holy places and the community. (3) Jesus is like the scapegoat who carries away the sins of the people into the uninhabited regions (1 Peter 2:24). (4) Jesus is the inaugural sacrifice, initiating the new covenant (Mark 14:24). This recalls the scene in Exodus 24 when, at the inauguration of the old covenant, sacrifices were offered and Moses dashed some of the blood over the people and some over the altar. (5) Jesus is the Lamb of God who takes away the sin of the

world. Where does that image come from? It does not seem to correspond to any Old Testament image, as the passover lamb was not regarded as taking away sin. Perhaps we have a new, complex Christian image in which several Jewish images are fused together (Isaiah 55:17) in a complete picture of Christ as the Lamb of God. . . .

"How are we to understand the Christian use of these images? There may be nothing remarkable about the use of the images themselves; but there are things strikingly remarkable about some of the uses made of them, and it is here that we may see the new and Christian phenomenon. First it is striking that Jesus is pictured both as the pure offering of the day of atonement and also as the sin-bearing scapegoat. He brings to the Father a pure and perfect offering of an utterly selfless and perfect obedience; and at the same time he takes on the burden of the world's sin, the total calamity of man's darkness, grief, and estrangement . . . going right into the 'uninhabited regions.' . . . Second, St. John in his story of the passion brings out that Jesus is, in the one event, both the sacrificial victim and the victorious king who reigns supreme. Yes, Jesus is dying as sacrifice, Jesus is dying as victim; but in the self-same scene, Jesus is a victorious king."

Michael Ramsey
Jesus and the Living Past
pp. 66-70

"In the passages of the Second Isaiah, the unmerited suffering of the Servant voluntarily endured is seen to end in death, by means of which those for whom and at whose hands he suffers are restored to fellowship. Thus the servant is offered for the sins of others but with this difference, that he willingly offers himself thus combining priestly and prophetical ideas of death which is at once a sacrifice and personal moral act.*

"Thus the servant transforms and sublimates all previous ideas of sacrifice existent among men. He reverses all human values by showing that suffering and death, the result of the Fall, are the very material of redemption when taken hold of and used by the obedient will of man. The pains of death thus endured become the birth-pangs of new life, both for him who dies and for those for whom he dies. So the Suffering Servant picture means far more than the prophet knew or we know: it unveils the heart of God himself, in whom sacrifice apart from sin exists eternally. It shows us that the only way evil can be got rid of is by

_____
*See also 48:1, Penelope.

_____
*See also 108:1, Penelope.

making it instrumental to good; and this can be effected only by the right use of suffering. When you suffer, as you must do whether you will or not, everything depends on how you take it. You can make it multiply evil or you can make it good in itself and productive of more good. The root of the matter is faith and love and obedience.''

Sister Penelope
The Wood
pp. 84-85

''As I think back over the years I have been preaching about the cross, I realize that I have almost always *moralized* it. I shudder as I think how I have trivialized the cross, instrumentalized it, made it a symbol for our need for discipline, our need to deny ourselves. All that is true enough, but it is not what the cross means. The cross is not a dreadful warning to us. . . . The cross is, simply and staggeringly, the sign and certain seal of God's unconquerable and unquenchable love for us. . . . We cannot destroy that love. If only we could really see it, the cross is God's answer to all those questions that torment us about our own evil and the evil and suffering of the world. It is God's answer to every anguished why that we utter. . . .

''Good Friday ought either to make us atheists or drive us to a scandalous and releasing insight into the very nature of God. The cross is either the last word of man, the final symbol of all the meaninglessness that stunts and crushes him, or it is the last word from God himself, speaking to us through our own anguish, comforting us through our own wounds. For the Church says that Christ, far from being forsaken by God, was God himself descending into the utmost depth of the human experience.* God was in Christ fully experiencing the Godlessness of his children. And how can words capture that insane and quivering paradox? God identifies with us even in our very atheism! So that when we say something happened which changed things for all time between God and man, we do not mean that it changed God's attitude toward us, that he was bought off by the blood of Christ. We mean that God changed our attitude to him by placarding his love for us in the cross of Christ. . . .

''Far from being an aloof and unconcerned observer of our anguish, who for divine sport has wound up his little universe and lets it run how it may, he is himself in it with us, endlessly trudging down all those roads that criss-cross history, rags on his feet, eyes dark with pain, endlessly moving up to Jerusalem to be put to death. . . . And the face we see beneath it all is the ravaged and lovely face of the Christ who struggles on through the world's Good Fridays,

traveling on and on, always setting his face to go up to Jerusalem and die for us.''

Richard Holloway
A New Heaven
pp. 46-47

'' 'Greater love than this no man hath, that a man lay down his life for his friends' (John 15:13). It demands a giving of oneself which continues right unto death. Golgotha is not a requirement of justice, but one of love. Master, I stand at the foot of your cross. I am bold enough to lift up my eyes to you and in this look cast on your sacrifice, I am learning that I did not know how to learn from the very words of the Gospel.

''Your feet are nailed to the wood. Your cross is the wine press where the true vine is pressed. Your arms are stretched out. They are open as an appeal to all men. Your head hangs low. You bow it in a motion of acquiescence. You have accepted and consummated God's will, therefore yours, in so far as it is also the Father's and the Spirit's. You bow your head as a sign of obedience to what the love of the Three requires towards men. At the same time your head is bowed towards those who are there below. It is bowed towards those who loved you, towards those who cried out: 'Crucify Him!'; towards those who suffer and linger on, groaning, towards those who seek without being aware of it. . . .

''Blood flows from your forehead, from your hands, and from your scourged body. It flows slowly in long streams; it is going to flow from your open side as though your heart were bursting under the pressure of your suffering love. The cup is poured out in a libation.

''The crown of thorns bruised your head. Woven in the form of a circle, those thorns are like the sins of men, gathered together and heaped upon you. All their sins are contiguous and bound together. . . . But around this head I see rays of light. A golden halo emanates from your blood stained head. This moisture gives its meaning to the painful vision. If I did not notice it, I would have only an incomplete picture of the Crucified. The Crucified is also Lord and Savior. . . . Master, your passion is not ended. Your wounds are still bleeding. They are still crucifying you this very day. Where? One has only to read the newspapers. Your body is tortured, crucified everywhere, at all times, in your human members.''

Monk of the Eastern Church
Jesus: A Dialogue with the Savior
pp. 158-61

''As I beheld Christ in silent majesty hanging upon his cross, I had a message for . . . all the disillusioned,

---

*See also 117:3, Father Andrew.

disappointed, bereaved, and out of heart: 'Behold me,' he said, 'Here I am dying in the dark, and I came to bring light to the world. I am dying at the hands of hate, and I came to bring love to the world. Death is closing in upon me, and I came to bring life to the world. But I remain true to my faith; dying in the dark, I believe in the Light, killed by hate I trust Love, with death closing in upon me I believe in Life. Do you then cling to your ideals; in any darkness still trust the Light, in all hatred still trust Love; and be sure that all consciousness be slipping from you and you yourself seem to be sinking into a void, eternal Life is yours.' So the message was given and the silence was full of peace.''*

Harry C. Griffith, ed.
A Gift of Light: A Collection of Thoughts from the Writings of Father Andrew
pp. 11-12

———————

*See also 24:3, Father Andrew.

———————

New Illuminations:

On Sin II: Borne by Christ to Die in Us by Faith

" 'The Son of Man came . . . to give his life a ransom for many.' The suggestion is that of slaves set free and so St. Paul speaks of our slavery to sin, to death, to the Law, and explains that as Christians we are now free. The idea itself is very simple. A slave cannot free himself. Someone else must do it for him; someone else must pay the price of manumission. We are slaves to sin, to the Law, and someone else must free us and pay the price. The price is Christ's death and he willingly pays it. God cannot overlook sin, not only because he is utterly holy, but because he is Love. Because God is almighty and omniscient as well as Love, his punishments are certain and cannot be avoided. God showed that fit punishment for sin is a cruel death. But because he loves, he himself took that punishment for us, showing what sin is and yet at the same time avoiding the necessity of punishing us. . . .

"We think of Christ as victor over sin, as well as victor over death. He came into the world to challenge the forces of evil, battled with human sin and with satanic enemies, and triumphed over all as he took his throne on the Cross. The essential point here is that Christ died on the Cross not only that we should escape the consequences of our sin, but he died to conquer sin itself. William Law puts it in these words: 'What is God's forgiving sinful man? It is nothing else in its whole nature but God's making him righteous again. There is no other forgiveness of sin but being made free from it.' The fundamental idea is that what Christ did *for* us, he did *in* us. The seed of Christ is planted in us at Baptism; there Christ is born in us, and our life in Christ is Christ's life in us. Our spiritual growth is the growth of Christ in us. He grows to maturity, and as we turn away from the temptations of the world, the flesh, and the devil, so is he being crucified in us; and each time we win a real victory there is a resurrection of Christ. His nature and spirit are born and formed in us, that we thereby may become new creatures. Christ is the atonement for our sins when, in and from him living in us, we have victory over our sinful nature."

Manassas
Go in Peace
pp. 31, 34-36

"Sin creates a disturbance in the moral order of the universe which cannot be ignored. If you throw a handful of sand into your watch, it won't go normally. It has to be cleaned. Now the dirty mess we have all made in God's world by our sin and selfishness has got to be cleaned up. We can't do it; God has to. God cannot turn a blind eye to all that

has gone wrong with his world through us. There would be no morality if good and evil were treated alike. Sin is something that has to be judged, confessed, removed. That is what Good Friday is all about. Jesus took upon himself this task, the weight and consequences and removing of human sin. The Cross is God himself in Christ clearing up our moral debts, satisfying what had to be satisfied, what we could never pay, what we could never do.

"In the last analysis the Cross is a disgusting business. Man has disgusted God by his behaviour. The wrath of God is the divine disgust. The Cross of Jesus is the place where that disgust and that burning love are both expressed — God himself in Christ stooping to clear up the mess. If you spill acid over your coat, you don't get rid of the marks with soap and water. If we litter the universe with moral evil, disobedience, cowardice, selfishness, we cannot get rid of the marks by trying to be better. Only blood cleanses this kind of thing: the blood poured out in generous love, the precious blood of Jesus, the quality and power of utterly holy sacrifice. . . .

"Christ's sacrifice is that of obedience. It is active and voluntary, it is morally perfect and it is personal. Through this sacrifice he both forgives sinners and deals with their sin. 'This is my blood of the covenant which is shed for many unto remission of sins.' "

Douglas Webster
In Debt To Christ
pp. 53-54, 85

"Few men know how to perceive the act by which the Lamb of God takes away sin and takes it upon himself. I [Christ] have taught you that I am present at your sinning — that my presence is both condemning and compassionate. Then I implore your gaze, your adherence. If you give them to me, the heart of the act is displaced. It is no longer sin which is at the center. All the evil forces are deflected. It is now I who hold the central position. In this second, you are freed. In this second is actualized what happened, when at Gethsemane and at Golgotha I assumed yourself and this sin. The crisis is no longer between you and sin. It is between you and me. From my heart a ray descends upon you. It draws you, takes hold of you, and your gaze reaches up to me because you allow your soul to follow the ray."

Monk of the Eastern Church
Jesus: A Dialogue with the Saviour
p. 114

"I was not born when you died. How can you be responsible for me? How can you die for me? 'You are a man; I died as Son of God and Son of Man. I am he through whom you were made. Your free will was my gift to you. It had become a fatal gift, not through my fault, but through the fault of you and all mankind. For love's sake, I made myself responsible for the use that you and all men make of my gift. You use it to bring death upon yourselves and one another. I will not leave you so that means my death too.' . . .

"If man had never sinned, there might have been a straight way through from mortal to immortal, mortal growing into immortality. . . . The question is will you wait till death comes to you against your will? Will you cling on to your private way, your private world, your mortal life, or will you yield it now?''

T. R. Milford
Foolishness to the Greeks
pp. 59-60

"Before ever Caiaphas and Judas and Pilate had acted, Jesus had *imposed* upon the terrible scandal of his death the character of a voluntary sacrifice for sin — the sacrifice of the Lamb of God that taketh away the sins of the world.

"That is the Eucharist — it is 'the *event* of Christ,' 'recalled,' not merely by men or before men but before God, in an action. 'As often as you eat this bread and drink this cup,' St. Paul told the first generation of Christians, 'you do proclaim the Lord's death till he comes' (1 Corinthians 11:26). . . . There your faith, your personal inward acceptance of the fact that 'he died for our sins' finds explicit all-embracing expression in an action. There your personal acceptance of the 'goodness,' which he rose to become 'in us,' is acted out in that gesture which brings the most fundamental identification with our whole selves possible in earthly life. . . . And this of necessity is a corporate act — the bread is broken that it may be distributed, the cup is given that it may be shared.

". . . Just as his act of voluntary self-sacrifice was the absolute opposite of self-regardingness that is the root of sin, so its reception into you in the Holy Communion is the death of sin in you. . . . Before you come to Communion, face your sins, detest them, resolve not to repeat them and pray earnestly to put them away for the future, not in vague general terms, but facing them individually. . . . When you have done that, never let the remembrance of your sins and the thought of your unworthiness keep you from your Communion. Of course, you are unworthy. That is why you must go to Communion. You need, and need desperately, the power of that risen life whose whole purpose is to become the *goodness* in us which we cannot, so to speak, stoke up for ourselves. Of course you have sins. That is why you must partake of the Body and Blood which is an antidote of sins.

You can go with a sure trust in him whom you will receive, if only you want to receive him to be the death of sin and the rising of goodness in you.

Dom Gregory Dix
The Claim of Jesus Christ
pp. 81-85

"The importance of the first Easter for the Christian practice and proclamation of sin's forgiveness is that it has shown that sin is not irretrievably a disaster, but that God can make something of it which is constructive and redeeming. If Jesus, the Messiah, had really been destroyed by the sin of men, then all he ever said about forgiveness would have been lost. John would have gone on hating Judas, and Peter could never have made an end of hating himself. In the Easter light it was clear that God had used the sins of all of them — whether the sins of weakness and ignorance or the sins of desperation and pride — to work the great blessing of Jesus' glorification as Saviour and Lord. . . .

"This is the reason why St. Augustine had the boldness to cry, 'O felix culpa' — O *happy sin*!* It is not the sort of cry one might expect from a genuinely penitent saint, and yet the Resurrection makes it altogether appropriate. The new life beyond forgiveness can find reason to rejoice even in one's sins.

". . . So, like St. Paul, we can 'give thanks in all things,' even in the knowledge of our sin, because Easter proved that human sin — far from destroying Jesus — was employed by God to release the power of his life into the hearts of all men everywhere.** John can forgive Judas, and Peter can forgive himself, and we can all despite our unworthiness and folly, be bold enough to claim fellowship with him as Master and Lord.

". . . When a man has died to self, that is to say, when he has faced the fact that nothing he does is quite honest enough, quite pure enough, quite sacrificial enough, quite wise or virtuous enough, to meet the demands life puts upon him, he is ready to find the meaning of his life in God and to discover that God alone can be trusted for results man could never foresee, for responses man could never earn, for triumphs man could never win by his own wit or power. To have been forgiven at the cross and born again in the power of Christ's Resurrection is to know that we owe our lives far more to God than to ourselves.''

John M. Krumm
The Art of Being a Sinner
pp. 114-117

---

*See also 110:3, Sayers; 119:3, Sayers.
**See also 71:3, Milford.

"It has been said, I think by Berdyaev, that nothing can prevent the human soul from preferring creativeness to happiness. In this lies man's substantial likeness to the Divine Christ who in this world suffers and creates continually, being incarnate in the bonds of matter. This doctrine of man leads naturally to the doctrine of sin. One of the really surprising things about the present bewilderment of humanity is that the Christian Church now finds herself called upon to proclaim the old and hated doctrine of sin as a gospel of cheer and encouragement. The final tendency of modern philosophies — hailed in their day as a release from the burden of sinfulness — has been to bind men hard and fast in the chains of iron determinism. The influences of heredity and environment, of glandular make-up and the control of the unconscious, of economic necessity and the biological development, have all been invoked to assure man that he is not responsible for his misfortunes and therefore not to be held guilty. Evil has been represented as something imposed upon him from without, not made by him from within. . . . I remember how an aunt of mine, brought up in an old-fashioned liberalism, protested angrily against having continually to call herself a 'miserable sinner' when reciting the Litany. Today, if we could really be persuaded that we are miserable sinners — that the trouble is not outside us but inside us — and that therefore, by the grace of God, we can do something to put it right, we should receive that message as the most hopeful and heartening thing that can be imagined."*

Dorothy Sayers
Creed or Chaos
p. 40

*See also 119:2, Krumm.

New Illuminations:

2 Corinthians 1:4-5   1 Peter 2:20-21; 4:12-14   Luke 9:23

"God's rewards are always out of proportion to our deserving. And we have to admit that some of us take a very long time to learn that there is no greater reward open to man than the privilege of being allowed to share Christ's cross. . . . St. Paul learned this lesson for himself and passed it on to us in Philippians 3:10: 'I want to know Christ in the power of resurrection, and to share his sufferings and even his death.' [Goodspeed]"

Joost de Blank
Uncomfortable Words
pp. 48-49

"We stand before the picture of utter self-abandonment, the uttermost expression of sacrificial love: the Cross. . . . To look at the Crucifix and then to look at our own hearts; to test by the Cross the quality of our love — if we do that unflinchingly and honestly, we don't need any other self-examination than that, any other judgment or purgation. The lash, the crown of thorns, the stripping, the nails — life has equivalents of all these for us, and God asks a love for himself and his children which can accept and survive all that in the particular way in which it is offered to us. . . . Only those who are willing to accept suffering up to the limit are capable of giving love up to the limit, and this is the kind of love which is the raw material of the redeeming life. Only those who place themselves in the hands of God without reserve and without fear are going to be used by him to save. We want a lot of practice before we can manage this. It will not come out of an easy-going religion. . . .

"What about the dreadful moment when a great test of courage, great suffering, a great bereavement faced us, and we knew we were for it and found the agony was more than we could face? . . . What about the sting, the lash of humiliation or disappointment, the wounds given by those we love best? Can we weave it all into the sacrifice of love?

"Here again, Christ does not go outside our ordinary condition. He hallows real life. Can we hallow it? Can we bear to let his light fall on our little fears, humiliations and pains and endure the chemical rays which can transform them into part of his sacrifice? Can we weave all that into the sacrifice of love, and what are we going to do with it if we can't? Our world is chaos without the Cross; but we never understand suffering until we have embraced it, turned it into sacrifice and given ourselves in it to God. . . . Then we see not torment and darkness, cruel physical pain and its results, but the peace of a Divine and absolute acceptance of selfless and abandoned love — suffering accepted and transfigured by the passion of redeeming love."

Evelyn Underhill
The Light of Christ
pp. 79, 83-85

"Perhaps you are given the task of living for others more than you ever did when life was secure. Could you really understand their needs if you yourself had not been plunged into these depths? Wounds must heal wounds. True helpers of their fellow men have always been those who were greatly hurt, who had to suffer great sorrows. Jesus could be our Pastor, our High Priest — only because he himself had to stand against the forces of love and death, and thus he could have sympathy with those who sit in the shadow of those powers."

Helmut Thielicke
Out of the Depths
p. 18

"If we really believe that the man who was nailed to the Cross of Calvary is our God, and hung there for love of us, we cannot wish that our following of him should not be a very costing thing.

"People often say, 'My mother was such a good woman: why should she have suffered?' or 'My boy was such a good boy: why should he have died?' It is a very natural thing to say, but when we find ourselves saying it, we should look at Jesus crowned with thorns, holiest of all, loveliest of all, and yet suffering more than all. His whole life as he lived amongst the people of his time was a beauty and a glory, a flame of love passing by, and yet he was crucified.

"It is our behavior in life, not so much what we do but how we do it, that marks us as the disciples of the Divine Master. Life is a great vocation, and Christ's disciples will put into it all they can of sacrifice, love, and labor. Christian character is the flower of which sacrifice is the seed. . . .

"If suffering went out of life, courage, tenderness, pity, faith, patience, and love in its divinity would go out of life too. Terrible as suffering is, none the less, it is the condition for some of life's greatest beauties even as the wounding of the shell is the condition for the pearl's appearing."

Harry C. Griffith, ed.
A Gift of Light: A Collection of Thoughts from the Writings of Father Andrew
pp. 30-34

"To respond to Christ's sacrifice is to be drawn near to the act whereby he redeemed us and also to recover through Christ the joyful meaning of our existence as God's creatures. . . . Is there in this world, dark, divided, bewildered, and bewildering any meaning, shape, purpose, clue, sovereignty? Our Christian answer is: Yes, there is meaning, shape, purpose, clue, sovereignty — and these are found in the death and resurrection of the Christ, in the way of living-through-dying.* It is through such sacrificial love that God's sovereignty is known, and evil is being overcome; and one day its victory will be complete. Such indeed is the Christian message: that in the life, death, and resurrection of Jesus Christ, God gives himself to mankind in utter self-giving love, sharing and bearing the world's calamity, so that in Christ and through Christ man and woman may be freed to give themselves to God, to one another, and to the service of the world."

Michael Ramsey
Jesus and the Living Past
pp. 74, 76

"Turning away from his family, his associate, his thriving business, his promising future, he [Otto Keller] set his will like a shaft of steel to do whatever God called him to do in serving Africa amid its agony. . . . He knew what it was to weep as they wept, to groan with hopeless agony as mothers groan who have no milk for their whimpering babes, to feel the utter hopelessness of a land and people perishing for lack of food and lack of loving care. . . .

"In the pain and pathos of famine relief, God had given my father an open entrance into thousands of African hearts. There he shared unashamedly in the suffering of Christ. And so in the outpouring of his own life, there was shed abroad the compassionate care of the living Lord. In one hand he brought maize meal, salt, beans and cups of cold water, in the other he bore the great good news of Christ's amazing love for these perishing people."

Charles Turner, ed.
Chosen Vessels
pp. 93-95

"In Jesus' suffering and death was wrought a transmutation of the concept of sacrifice. By a stupendous act of interiorization, sacrifice was translated from the sphere of exterior action to that of spiritual activity — an act which the Son of Man alone could make and present to man for his acceptance and practice.* We are held in awed wonder at the sublime majesty of this unique divine sacrifice, which alone leads man into a worship of God which is in spirit and truth. It is no surprise, though it is a miracle, that at this moment the veil in the temple is split, for there is now a newness of worship and vision beyond all foretelling and foreseeing.

". . . Standing now before the Cross, gazing at the crucified Lord, we cannot fail to recognize the centrality of his whole life and the purpose of this offering of himself, the total renunciation in the unity of body, soul, and spirit, in obedience to suffering and death. To acknowledge it as his destiny is to accept it in some sense as our own also; we are involved but whether as one on the far edge of the crowd or as one close to the Cross, whether as one blind or seeing, refusing or adoring, mocking or grieving, ah, there is the choice. . . .

"As far as the world is concerned the divine drama does not arrive at a static end with the death of the Incarnate God, not even with the ineluctable sequel of resurrection and ascension. For that freely willed obedience on Calvary of the Son of Man to his Father is a universal offering made not only to us but one in which we need to be found, to have our place. . . . But Jesus does not ask us to consider this intellectually, to look at the mystery from outside. We are enjoined to enter into his action.

". . . Do not merely remember what once and for all time I have done for you, but do something which will make your remembering immeasurably more interior, more penetrating, more vital. . . . The communication of the reality of Christ's sacrifice to each individual is visibly displayed in the Eucharistic dispensation of his Body and Blood. In union with him we plead it for the needs, especial and general, of the whole world. . . . And all our personal sacrifices, offerings, sufferings are united with his and taken up by him into the cup of his offerings. It is a doing of divine appointment, this glad and glorious sacrament of sacrifice and unity which makes us one with our God and one with each other."

Sibyl Harton
Doors of Eternity
pp. 67-73

"When the soul reflects what His Majesty is doing with it, and then turns to reflect upon itself, it realizes what little it is doing toward the fulfilment of its obligations and how feeble is that which it does do and how full of faults and failures. . . . He may perhaps answer the soul as he

---

*See also 46:4, Andrew.

*See also 71:2, Krumm.

answered someone who was very much disturbed about this, and was looking at the crucifix and thinking that she had never had anything to offer God or to give up for his sake. The Crucified Himself comforted her by saying that he was giving her all the pains and trials that he had suffered in his Passion, so that she should have them for her own to offer to his Father.* That soul, as I have understood from her, was so much comforted and enriched by this experience that she cannot forget it, and whenever she feels miserable, she remembers it and it comforts her and encourages her.''

St. Teresa of Avila
Interior Castle
p. 159

*See also 112:2, Harton.

'' 'There, but for the grace of God, go I' sounds pious, but it speaks not of compassion but of superiority. Compassion says, 'There, by the grace of God, I have been and I am.'* It is in this sense surely that we should understand St. Paul's words about Jesus: that God 'made him to be sin for us, who knew no sin.' So when our lot is cast with somebody who is finding his cross, his desert, his poverty overwhelming, we are on holy ground. . . . Our identification with the other person brings to our lives and to theirs the power, the joy, the victory which is already ours and all mankind's in Christ Jesus Our Lord.''

H. A. Williams
The True Wilderness
pp. 102-03

*See also 25:3, Theophan.

New Illuminations:

On the Resurrection of Christ

Matthew 28:1-10   Mark 16:1-8   Luke 24:1-12

"In the early days of Christianity, an 'apostle' was first and foremost a man who claims to be an eye witness of the Resurrection. They had known Jesus personally both before and after his death and could offer first-hand evidence of the Resurrection in addressing the outer world. The Resurrection and its consequences were the 'gospel' or good news which Christians brought. So the first fact in the history of Christendom is a number of people who say they have seen the Resurrection.

"It is very important to be clear about what these people meant. When modern writers talk of the Resurrection they usually mean one particular moment — the discovery of the Empty Tomb and the appearance of Jesus a few yards away from it. But this almost exclusive concentration on the first five minutes or so of the Resurrection would have astonished the first Christian teachers. In claiming to have seen the Resurrection, they were not necessarily claiming to have seen *that*. Some of them had; some of them had not. It had no more importance than any of the other appearances of the Risen Jesus. . . . But the 'Resurrection' to which they bore witness was, in fact, not the action of rising from the dead but the state of having risen; a state, as they held, attested by intermittent meetings during a limited period (except for the special, and in some ways different, meeting vouchsafed to St. Paul).

"The next point to notice is that the Resurrection was not regarded simply or chiefly as evidence for the immortality of the soul. On such a view, Christ would simply have done what all men do when they die: the only novelty would have been that in his case we were allowed to see it happening. But there is not in Scripture the faintest suggestion that the Resurrection was new evidence for something that had *in fact* been always happening. The New Testament writers speak as if Christ's achievement in rising from the dead was the first event of its kind in the whole history of the universe. He is the 'first fruits,' the 'pioneer of life.' He has forced open a door that has been locked since the death of the first man. He has met, fought, and beaten the King of Death. Everything is different because he has done so. This is the beginning of the New Creation: a new chapter in cosmic history has opened. . . .

"There are, I allow, certain respects in which the risen Christ resembles the 'ghost' of popular tradition. Like a ghost he 'appears' and 'disappears': locked doors are no obstacle to him. On the other hand he himself vigorously asserts that he is corporeal (Luke 24:39-40) and eats boiled fish. It is at this point that the modern reader becomes uncomfortable. He becomes more uncomfortable still at the words, 'Don't touch me; I have not yet gone up to the Father' (John 20:17). . . . These discomforts arise because the story the 'apostles' actually had to tell begins at this point to conflict with the story we expect.

"We expect them to tell of a risen life which is purely spiritual in the negative sense of that word: that is, we use the word 'spiritual' to mean a life without space, without history, without environment, with no sensuous elements in it. We also in our heart of hearts intend to slur over the *manhood* of Jesus, to conceive him, after death, simply returning into *Deity*, so that the Resurrection would be no more than the reversal or undoing of the Incarnation. We have thought (whether we acknowledge it or not) that the body was not objective, that it was an appearance sent by God to assure the disciples of truths otherwise incommunicabled. . . . On such a view, the body would really be a hallucition. . . .

"If the story is true, then a whole new mode of being has arisen in the universe. The body which lives in that new mode is like, and yet unlike, the body his friends knew before the execution. It is differently related to space and probably to time but by no means cut off from all relation to them. It can perform the animal act of eating. It is so related to matter, as we know it, that it can be touched, though at first it had better not be touched. It has also a history before it, which is in view from the first moment of the Resurrection; it is presently going to become different or go somewhere else. That is why the story of the Ascension cannot be separated from the Resurrection."*

> C. S. Lewis
> *Miracles*
> pp. 171-77

"Besides the language about Jesus being alive, there are references to the act whereby he was raised. . . . The raising is God's act. Thus to be a Christian is to 'believe in him who raised from the dead Jesus, our Lord' (Romans 4:24). . . . Both the empty tomb and the appearances of Jesus are properly parts of history, but it has been urged that the Resurrection itself, being beyond human scrutiny, cannot properly be described as history. It was an action of God indescribable in human terms yet made credible by known historical results. . . . The emphasis is upon the Resurrection as being not only a continuing life but a divine action. . . . Furthermore the primitive preaching and the Pauline,

---

*See also 125:2, Lewis.

Petrine, and Johannine writings concur in their certainty that there was a happening which was the effective cause of their faith in the living Jesus.''

Michael Ramsey
Jesus and the Living Past
pp. 30-32

"Just as Jesus' death, whatever its cosmic and timeless significance, was primarily his own immediate experience — the bringing to an end in himself all that had to be brought to an end — so his resurrection, whatever may have been its consequences in time and space, was primarily his own immediate experience — beginning in himself all that had to be made new, all the 'new creation.' . . .

"Thus we see converging here the two fundamental aspects of the resurrection, namely, the resurrection as the experience of Jesus and the resurrection as the act of God. From the moment when Jesus at his baptism experienced the inrush of the Spirit and became the channel of the power of the Kingdom,* there is to be seen a gradual revelation of the true nature of that power: every act of grace and healing was an act of God; each time the Son of Man forgave sins, the power of God** was active in forgiveness; and at the last, when power withdrew into itself, concentrating on the complete surrender of all into the Father's hands, strength was made perfect in weakness.*** The obedience of the Son was made perfect by the power of the Father in Resurrection, and the new creation came into being.''

S. H. Hooke
The Kingdom of God
pp. 151-152

"Starting on Easter Day a series of strange things began to happen. 'God has raised him to life again,' the disciples declared as they interpreted those happenings . . . It is as if Jesus' life of caring and his fundamental message that God is love were written on a document. Then by raising Jesus from the dead, God has, as it were, stamped the document with his great seal. He has ratified it and declared, 'This is utterly true.'

"Did it really happen? Did the disciples get it right? . . . The first indication is the courage of the early Christians when they spoke of their conviction that Christ was risen, and the love which grew out of that conviction. . . . Perhaps we may mention Paul in a letter to the Corinthians, he claims to have seen the risen Lord at his conversion on the road to Damascus. How was he changed from the violent persecutor into Paul, the missionary, whose life was packed with labors and dangers in the service of Jesus, the Lord whose resurrection was the focus of his gospel? 'If Christ was not raised, then is our gospel null and void, and so is your faith' (1 Corinthians 15:14).

"As for the evidence for the empty tomb, let me make two preliminary statements. First the gospels make it clear that Jesus' body was not merely resuscitated, reanimated, but rather was raised and in some way was transformed. That is the reason that the risen Christ was often not recognized at first sight and that he could appear and disappear in surprising ways. . . . Secondly, I do not find satisfactory the other explanations. I cannot think that a wild beast broke into the tomb and dragged the body away or that the women and the apostles found an empty tomb because they went to the wrong tomb, nor can I believe that a group of Jews stole the body, mutilated it or concealed it somewhere and then allowed the apostles to get away with their assertion that the Lord has risen from the tomb.''

Mark Gibbard
Apprentices in Love
pp. 60-63

" 'If Christ is not risen, all your faith is a delusion; you are back in your sins' (1 Corinthians 15:14). A familiar accusation against the Christian doctrine of the resurrection of the dead is that it is a presumptuous piece of self-conceit. That appears to be unanswerable unless the resurrection of Christ first of all does something about the problem of our sin. . . . George Bernard Shaw once thought that he had refuted the Christian doctrine of resurrection from the dead by the observation that he found the idea of an eternity of himself an intolerable one. Shaw had missed the point. The Resurrection was first of all the resurrection of Jesus Christ. It was not a reassurance that the fearful, squabbling, anxious apostles would go on like that forever. The Resurrection has to be able to make a difference in a man's inner life. . . .

"It is not good news to announce that God has provided a free bus trip to heaven. The Resurrection must have some power to transform man's arrogant, anxious, fearful self-centeredness into the trusting, loving compassion of Christ. . . . This transformation begins when the love of God, amazingly manifested at the Cross, is seen to have ultimate power and authority at the Resurrection. The Resurrection rescues the Cross from being a futile and pathetic gesture for it shows us what God can make out of sin and why; therefore we can dare to forgive it. We have already noted the audacity of Jesus to forgive sins. It astounded his contemporaries. His license to do it was finally given in the Resurrection.*

" 'If we be dead with Christ, we believe that we shall also live with him' (Romans 6:8). That speaks of a past event — a Christian's baptism into Christ's own self-renunciation and of a future consummation — the ultimate sharing of

---

*See also 12:1, Christiansen.
**See also 22:2, Nineham.
***See also 94:2, Bloom.

---

*See also 22:2, Nineham.

Christ's resurrected glory. But where, we may ask St. Paul do we stand right now? The answer is that we stand within the assurance of an ultimate victory but not yet in the full possession of it. We have seen through the pretenses of the evil which besets us — the demoralizing frustration, the anxious and fearful efforts to secure our own defenses and to insure our own reputation. We know how unreliable and self-defeating all such undertakings are. We are certain too about the ultimate possibility and power of an unquestioning faith in God's love and trustworthiness because we have seen in Christ's resurrection how fully he glorifies a life which puts its reliance in him alone. . . . The Christian man remembers once again him who had no other power at his disposal but the power of his faith and no other assurance to cling to but the courage of his hope in God, but who with these weapons met the enemy in decisive encounter, disarmed him and overthrew him utterly. . . . Within the context of this faith in Jesus Christ — God and man dying for our sins, raised for our justification — man's sorrow for sin does not deepen bitterness and increase alienation but leads out into a wider sense of identity with life and a surer confidence in its ultimate goodness. He finds a closer kinship with others who wrestle with sin's power.''

> John M. Krumm
> *The Art of Being a Sinner*
> pp. 112-113, 88-89

''*Resurrection is transfiguration reached through death.* With the Apostles who had met the full grown Man, his resurrection was the heart and center of the gospel; indeed the main requirement for Apostleship was to have seen him risen. For without the individual resurrection of the Second Adam, there is no resurrection for the first: the Fall has not been reversed, death is frustration, and God's original purpose for mankind can never be fulfilled. But glory be to God, Christ has been raised and by that fact the ultimate resurrection of all the dead has been guaranteed.* And when the dead have risen, they will be full-grown. . . . The general resurrection of mankind is the next-to-the-coping-stone of revelation. I say 'next to' because the resurrection itself is not the consummation of all things but only the essential prelude to it. In the Apocalypse the Church, mankind renewed in Christ, appears as the Bride made ready for her Bridegroom. She is called his wife in the same breath (Revelation 21:9), because in that last vision the marriage of the Lamb was actually come, and the reunion of man with God is about to be realized. The resurrection precedes this consummation; because the Bride-Church is not nubile until she is full-grown, the Second Eve is not a helpmate for the Second Adam till she is perfected, even as he.''

> Sister Penelope
> *The Coming*
> pp. 100-101

''Jesus lives! That is the first meaning of the Resurrection. . . . And this is the second: 'You now therefore have sorrow,' Jesus said to his disciples before he was taken from them in death. . . . Sorrow, because you can discern no meaning, no end to this insatiable universe which devours time and all its children. It is meaningless without the Resurrection. By the taking of Christ into his glory, God has given us a glimpse of his plan for his universe. He has, in Paul's words, let us in on his own secret purpose which is to reverse the inexorable process of decay, the running down of the universe, and to establish all things in Christ in a new creation that will know no more dying or separation, nor any tears but those of joy. . . .

''What then is left for us to do? Do we just wait for the return of Christ who is present in a hidden manner in the folds of history? Yes and no. Yes and no, because while he is glorified and has taken our dust into heaven, we are still caught in the dialectic of the dust we are and the glory that awaits us. . . . Yes this dust is bound for glory. Everything, every wounded child and every sparrow that falls to the ground in the cold of winter is, even now, being glorified. There is nothing else to say in Auschwitz or in the terminal ward of the cancer hospital or by the graveside on a dark Friday afternoon. There is only that. . . .

''This then is the final meaning of the Resurrection of Jesus Christ from the dead: it is a preview of the great future that awaits the whole of the created universe. That is why all the Easter hymns say that the Resurrection destroys death and sorrow, even 'world-sorrow,' and bids our hearts rise with Christ.''

> Richard Holloway
> *A New Heaven*
> pp. 60-62

''In the Christian Story, God descends to re-ascend. He comes down, from the heights of absolute being into time and space, down into humanity. But he goes down to come up again and bring the whole ruined world with him. . . . One may think of a diver first reducing himself to nakedness, then glancing in mid-air, then gone with a splash,

---

*See also 117:4, Underhill.

vanished, rushing down through green and warm water into black and cold water, down through increasing pressure into the death-like region of ooze and slime and old decay; then up again back to color and light, his lungs almost bursting, till suddenly he bursts the surface again, holding in his hand the dripping precious thing he went down to recover. He and it are both colored now that they have come up into the light.

"In this descent and re-ascent, everyone will recognize a familiar pattern: a thing written all over the world. It is the pattern of all vegetable life. It must belittle itself into something hard, small and deathlike, it must fall into the ground; thence the new life re-ascends."

C. S. Lewis
Miracles
p. 135

New Illuminations:

On Reconciliation: Justification, Redemption, and Salvation

| Matthew 20:28; 26:28 | Mark 14:24 | Luke 1:67-69; 19:10; 24:25-26 |

"A great deal of confusion has been caused by the fact that the English word 'atonement' has moved away from the sense it had when the Bible was translated, viz., reconciliation. The Hebrew word which lies behind it originally meant 'covering' or 'wiping out,' and it may have included the idea of an expiation that had to be made before the sinner could be acquitted, but it certainly did not imply anything like propitiation of an angry God. For, as scholars have pointed out, it is always God Himself who is regarded, in the Old Testament, as having appointed the ritual of sin-offering, in His desire for reconciliation, taking this merciful initiative because he does not desire the death of a sinner but his restoration.

"But when we come to the New Testament, we can go much farther than this. For the Greek word used to correspond to the Old Testament 'atonement,' means simply reconciliation. Moreover, the New Testament does not speak of God being reconciled to man but of man being reconciled to God, and of God as the Reconciler taking the initiative in Christ to that end. There are indeed three passages where we find another word in the English Bible: 'propitiation.' In 1 John 4:10, it is clear that the word does not mean anything like the appeasing of an angry God, for the love of God is the starting point. 'Herein is love, not that we loved God but that he loved us and sent his Son to be the propitiation for our sins.' The Pauline passage has been much discussed by commentators. 'Being justified freely by his grace, through the redemption that is in Christ Jesus, whom God has set forth as a propitiation through faith, by his blood . . .' (Romans 3:24f). Professor C. H. Dodd, who has made a careful study of the word, assures us that the rendering 'propitiation' is misleading and that the real meaning of the passage is that God has set forth Christ as 'a means by which guilt is annulled' or even 'a means by which sin is forgiven'. . . . It is just possible that we should translate the Greek word as 'mercy seat' or 'place of forgiveness.'

"But however we translate these terms borrowed from the Jewish sacramental system, it is quite plain that in the New Testament they undergo a transformation of the meaning because of the really extraordinary setting which is now given to them. We saw that even in the Old Testament usage the pagan meanings had been left behind because it was God Himself who was regarded as having mercifully appointed the ritual of expiation, though man had of course to supply the victim. But this is the amazing new fact when we come to the New Testament: that God even provides the victim that is offered, and the victim is His Son the Only Begotten. In short, 'it is *all* of God': the desire to forgive and reconcile, the appointing of means, the provision of the victim as it were from His own bosom at infinite cost. . . . There is in the New Testament no uniformity of conception as to how this sacrifice brings about the reconciliation. But in whatever way, it all took place because God so loved the world. Its background is the eternal love of God. . . . Moreover, there is in the New Testament a remarkable identification of the love of Christ which led him to the Cross and the love of God which sent or gave him. The identification is more striking because it is made so tacitly. When Paul is speaking of the great reconciliation, he speaks of the love of Christ and the love of God almost interchangeably. In discoursing of the love that was shown in the Cross of Christ, the New Testament is never able to stop short of tracing it up-stream to the eternal love of God dealing sacrificially with the sins of the world."

D. M. Baillie
God Was in Christ
pp. 187-89

"Jesus' death is the most positive thing he did in his earthly life. What then did he do by his death? Perhaps we can make it clearest by taking what is supposed to be a particularly theological phrase 'justification by faith.' I want to convince you of four things: (1) Everyone wants to be justified. (2) Nobody can attain it. (3) Only God can give it. (4) Everyone can receive it.

"Everyone wants to be justified, to be approved, to be in the right. If you are accused of a crime, this means being acquitted. It is the basis of self-respect. . . . This perfectly natural human desire is one of the powers that drives the world. It can deal with a certain amount of evil in the world, but there is a point beyond which it cannot go. It can deal with some kinds of ignorance, but can we be reconciled to one another this way? The impossibility of justifying ourselves is where the Old Testament leaves us. The lesson that was learned by the Jews was that though they might satisfy each other, though they might be successful by other people's standards, the only thing that really mattered was how they stood with God. . . . Israel alone through its experience of worldly failure and supreme faith in the living God, could appeal away from the judgment of history, to the highest judge of all. The Greeks might think Israel silly, the Romans might despise them as a subject nation, but God must accept them as his faithful people and he must show them to be right. All through the prophets runs the promise that he will do so. This is the crisis of holiness. It is the crisis of all human religion and morality. . . .

"Now can we take all these varied hints together, and use them to understand what Jesus did? To begin with he lived and died as a Jew, as a perfectly faithful Jew, as more than just *a* Jew, as the Christ, the destined king and leader of the Jews. He saw that if his people were to be what God intended, they must share their treasure with the publicans and sinners, and lose their national identity for the sake of saving the world. That is the one thing they could not do. So he did for them what they could not do themselves. Already in the Old Testament there had been times when a few, only a very few, a remnant of the faithful, had saved the nation by their faithfulness. . . . Jesus undertook to forgive in the name of Israel and of Israel's God the publicans and sinners who let down the side, the Romans who oppressed, the Greeks who mocked, the Pharisees who misunderstood, the priests who compromised — everyone, everyone who was contributing to the defeat of the divine purpose. He could only do that by taking upon himself the consequence of all that wrongness, and offering to be henceforth responsible for everything they did and were.''

T. R. Milford
Foolishness to the Greeks
pp. 52-56

"The work of Jesus Christ in saving the world and redeeming mankind is like creation: it is a fact and mystery. It is a fact: men and women know they have been changed by it. . . . In proclaiming the fact of our salvation through Christ, the New Testament uses certain metaphors, certain communication devices, which do not contain the mystery, but which set going a reaction, a recognition in the minds of the listeners. . . . The First Letter of Timothy (2:6) uses the image of slavery: humankind was enslaved, but Christ's death has bought our release, ransomed us. Writing to the Romans, Paul describes us as enemies of God whom Christ has reconciled, and in the letter to the Ephesians, he widens that claim to describe a peace which has been won between man and man as well as between God and man. There are other metaphors, such as the great metaphor of Justification or Acquittal, a legal metaphor which proclaims that Christ won a verdict of innocence for all us guilty ones.

". . . There have been three great models offered to explain our salvation, three great theories, though frequently their protagonists have treated them as infallible truth. We can learn something from each of them. Each emphasizes an important fact of salvation doctrine. . . . The earliest theory sees mankind as a land which has fallen into enemy hands. We belong to God; he is our rightful ruler and king, but his rule has been usurped by the great enemy of God, the devil, the present Prince of the World. He has usurped God's rule and holds us in bondage. He has colonized us, and we live in bondage to his imperial rule. Like the Israelites in Egypt, we are slaves, held fast in bitter bondage, bound under the heel and tyrannous jurisdiction of the devil. And Christ is the great liberator. He comes forth from God to do battle against the devil. Like a commando from the Almighty, he comes in disguise as an undercover agent, to deceive and confuse the devil. He comes right into enemy territory and begins a campaign of sabotage*. . . . Then he

moves toward the great and final encounter: he takes on Death the last enemy.* He submits to that and destroys it from within, shattering its grisly power over men. The final sign of that victory is the Resurrection: that is the great moment, the hoisting of the colors of God over his wounded creation. . . .

"The second theory is one which many find congenial. It is particularly dear to the hearts of Evangelicals and our friends in the Salvation Army. It has enormous power and has won many souls for Christ. This theory emphasizes man's personal sinfulness rather than his captivity to the devil: it is private rather than corporate. It is concerned with individual souls rather than with mankind as a whole. It sees his state not so much as an invasion from Satan, but as an act of willed collaboration on his part. We have sold ourselves into bondage because of our willfulness and sinfulness. We cannot redeem or ransom ourselves. We have no savings left, nothing that we have not pawned or mortgaged. But Christ acts as our substitute. He pays our ransom by giving himself. He swaps himself for us. . . . The great strength of this theory is that it takes human sinfulness seriously. Its weakness is that it can be expressed in such a way that it drives a strange wedge between God and Christ; whereas the witness of the New Testament is that 'God was in Christ' and that our salvation was won for us *by* God *through* his Son, and not *from* God *by* his Son.

"The third great theory sees the work of Christ as having its effect by changing people's attitudes as they think about and contemplate the great and loving sacrifice of Christ. As we study how he lived, our very understanding of God is altered, because the life and death of Jesus shows us what God is like. He is our servant and our victim. He rescues us, ransoms us from the bondage of anxious selfishness not by an act of power and overwhelming justice, but by an act of self-emptying love. He *woos* us, this God of ours. He defeats us by the lengths to which his love will go. . . . He spares not his own Son, the very desire of his heart, his very heart itself. God was in Christ offering us the ultimate proof that we are his, that he really loves us and will never forsake us, no matter how furious and self-destructive *our* rejection of *him* is. He absorbs it all — all our hate and all our sorrow; he bears it in his own body on the tree; he takes it upon himself. The Cross is the final example of God's love: it is the action which finally secures our release from our own fears and loneliness; the proof that God is still for us even though we are against him.''

Richard Holloway
A New Heaven
pp. 34-39

"*God has acted*. On the Cross, God was doing as well as saying. If we want one single Biblical word for this, it must be the word 'redemption,' and if we want a modern equivalent, the nearest we can get is 'rescue.' God's action in the Cross is not a grandiloquent display of power or love;

---

*See also 61:2, Penelope.

---

*See also 46:3, Lewis.

it is a rescuing action reaching down to the deepest point of man's need, of every man's need. Notice some of St. Paul's uses of this word:

'Christ redeemed us from the curse of the Law, having become a curse for us' (Galatians 3:13).

'When the fullness of time came, God sent forth his Son, born of a woman, born under the Law, that he might redeem them which were under the Law' (Galatians 4:4, 5).

In the minds of his original readers, the idea of a redeemer would conjure up a picture of a great benefactor liberating prisoners of war or emancipating slaves, even, if necessary, by paying some ransom price for them. This says St. Paul is what Christ has done for men through his Cross. He has set them free from bondage to sin. . . . Christ has effected God's purpose for the race.''

Douglas Webster
In Debt to Christ
pp. 83-84

''In speaking of Christ's supreme act of reconciliation, we are, of course, talking of something that can never be repeated. . . . We can and should reproduce the works of Christ since the power and the motive are supplied by his unchanging love, but we are in no position and never could be in a position to build a bridge of reconciliation between the holiness of God and the sinfulness of man. . . . It is necessary to stress the *fact* of reconciliation achieved by Christ on the Cross. It is of central importance that at the Cross we are face to face with an action which could only be initiated and carried through by God.

''Jesus himself very rarely called men sinners, and he certainly did not attempt deliberately to arouse a sense of guilt. Nevertheless it is universal for a human being, when he awakens on the God-ward side, to experience a sense of guilt. There are many pathetic and desperate attempts to close the gap that man's sin has made between himself and God. And millions have found that what we feel ought to be done, but what we know we could never do, *has been done* through Christ's mysterious sacrifice. At the most, the human soul can only construct a desperate bridgehead towards God, but the gulf remains unspanned. But in Christ we sense intuitively, even perhaps irrationally, that the bridge has been well and truly built, and that, through him, we have access to the Father*. . . . To an infinitely great and permanent degree, the unique sacrifice of Christ has changed

*See also 117:1, Penelope.

the relationship between man and God. Men may be slow and blind or obstinate and rebellious, but the reconciliation is potentially true already.''

J. B. Phillips
Making Men Whole
pp. 38-41

''The truly human instinct to offer life itself as the only sacrifice really worthy of God was fulfilled by the offering of Christ upon the Cross. His offering was not one of bulls or goats; he brought no substitute, no representative, rather he offered himself in perfect fullness of his ideal manhood — a life surrendered at every point, that passed under the harrow of the Passion, through the agony of the death upon the Cross — not a momentary but a constant offering. He lives as sacrifice as well as priest. His ascended life is a perpetual offering. In him manhood stands offered and accepted before the throne of God.

''Since the end of all priestly work is fellowship with God, Jesus brings the fellowship of man to rest in God. His sacrifice becomes our peace. That life which he brought victoriously through death is not only offered perpetually in the courts of heaven and pleaded constantly on the altars of his church on earth, but it is also imparted to us in sacraments which he has lovingly devised. Jesus fulfills all priesthood and mediates to us that endless life which is the goal of human destiny — eternal fellowship with God. By him, through him, and with him we dwell in God and he in us.''

F. W. Drake
The Spirit of Glory
pp. 97-98

''The insistence on the reign of God as the principal concept of salvation must be regarded as an original contribution of Jesus. In rabbinical thought salvation is 'the consequence of the reign of God but not the reign itself.' With Jesus, it is made the very marrow of salvation and it gives his gospel a great unity and concentration. He proclaims God's salvific will and redeeming mercy as a present reality in his concept of the royal reign of God and he makes it the ultimate motive for longing for salvation: a share in the fully developed and imperishable reign of God which brings the fullness of beatitude to the redeemed.''

Rudolf Schnackenburg
God's Rule and Kingdom
p. 94

New Illuminations:

On the Post-Resurrection Appearances of Christ

Matthew 28:9-15	Mark 16:9-13	Luke 24:13-44	Acts 1:1-5

"Whether called gospel, book or narrative, the works written by Mark, Matthew and Luke are above all literary expressions of the theological convictions of their authors, and often divergent details of their stories become important to us as indices of these theological convictions. The consequence of this view of the gospel is both immediate and far reaching. Now we no longer ask ourselves, did Jesus appear as risen from the dead to his disciples not at all (so Mark), or in Galilee (so Matthew), or only in Jerusalem and its environs (so Luke)? Instead we ask ourselves, what is Mark trying to say to us by deliberately omitting appearance stories, or Matthew by locating the major appearance in Galilee, or Luke by limiting appearances to the Jerusalem area? . . . For far too long we modern readers of the gospels have allowed our attention to be diverted from the true intention of the gospel narratives by constantly asking the historical question, what is it that the gospel writer is challenging us to accept or deny by means of this particular narrative? . . .

"Luke has appearances to the two disciples on the Emmaus road, and to the disciples as a group, and the Jesus who appears is still a very human Jesus.* In Luke's gospel, with his attention fixed on the ministry of Jesus, the appearance stories are appearance stories; and the teaching of Jesus to his disciples is brief, and the reference to the ascension is minimal. But in Acts 1:3-11, the appearance story is really the further ministry of Jesus as Jesus risen from the dead with his disciples, and the description of the ascension is much more elaborate. But now the attention of Luke is upon the early church and upon the necessity of fulfilling the instructions of the risen Lord to its first readers."

Norman Perrin
The Resurrection
pp. 5-6, 73

"After his resurrection Jesus suddenly appeared in the midst of his disciples. He does not linger over long reproaches on their infidelity and unbelief. And they do not waste time over long excuses or explanations. Everything happens so simply, so familiarly: 'Have you here anything to eat?' They offered him a piece of broiled fish and a honeycomb. Life goes on again in normal conditions, at the very point where it had been interrupted.

"When I have betrayed and abandoned Jesus, it is not necessary that I anxiously look for and prepare the conditions for my repentant encounter with the Master. I must

only reintroduce Jesus into my daily life, put him in the present context, involve him in the difficulties and hopes of the moment. The gesture is sufficient, by which we offer Jesus his share of the fish and honey which are daily nourishment. Right away Jesus is going to resume his place at our table and share our life again. That will come about in an instant; but as far as we are concerned it must be done in humility and repentance. The exterior attitude will be simple and easy. Yet it must be characterized by an interior prostration.

" 'After that, he appeared in another shape . . .'(Mark 16:12). After his resurrection Jesus appears to those who have known him, but under new forms so that they do not recognize him at once. Mary, near the sepulchre, took him for the gardener (John 20:20, 15). On the road to Emmaus, the two disciples took him for a traveller. The apostles who were fishing did not know who this stranger was standing on the shore of the lake until John says to Peter: 'It is the Lord' (John 21:4, 7).

"Why all these changes in our Saviour's appearance? Jesus wants to indicate that his physical presence is no longer localized, as it was before his resurrection, in a definite place, bound to a specific form. His presence is no longer limited. It has become universal as to place and form. His glorified body can be approached everywhere by everyone."

Monk of the Eastern Church
Jesus: A Dialogue with the Saviour
pp. 176-178

"In Eastertide, we may consider the Resurrection appearances of our Lord, and how they bring us solutions of life's problems. His first appearance is to a watcher by a tomb. Mary Magdalene is not only a type of the artistic temperament, the lover of beauty, but, as she kneels by the sepulchre, she is the type of the mourner out of whose life all that is worth living for is gone. When she knew for the first time what it was to be loved with a pure love, the whole of her life was changed, and she saw a glory in life that she had never seen before. But when she had seen that love die in the dark, as she sobbed by that garden tomb it must have seemed that the whole of life was a complete betrayal, that the best one could say about it was that it was a garden with a tomb in it, into which sooner or later every fair thing would go.

"Surely faith and hope were left behind that day, when love knelt by the tomb of Christ in the garden, or did she remember those words spoken by another tomb, 'Said I not unto thee that if thou wouldst believe, thou shouldst behold

*See also 123:2, Kelsey.

the glory of God?' (John 11:40). We do not know, but this we do know, that to her, the mourner, came the risen Christ with the revelation of the continuance of personality after death.''

Harry C. Griffith, ed.
*A Gift of Light: A Collection
of Thoughts from the Writings of Father Andrew*
pp. 46-47

"We watched him die, hoping until the very end for some miracle. But they took his body down and carried it away. He had died on Friday. Now it was Sunday and we were going home to Emmaus to see if we could find some reason to go on, a way to pick up the pieces and go on living. . . . We were half way home when a stranger caught up with us. I don't know where he came from, but we were so deep in our own thoughts that it was no wonder we didn't see him until he was along side. . . .

"And then the stranger began to talk about the scriptures. I could hardly believe my ears. This man knew the writings better than anyone I ever heard except one. My heart simply burned, hearing the way he talked. I had heard only one other person talk like that ever before, and he was dead. This man had the same kind of fresh point of view. He said that we had misunderstood the prophets, and that one never really wins through strength but through weakness. The Messiah, he said, would naturally have to die before he could be glorified. It made such sense. He spoke of the suffering servant, of dying to rise again. He showed us how this theme kept occurring through the books of scripture from Moses right through the prophets.

"The whole of the law and the prophets became luminous. My spine tingled as I listened. Then we started to turn off the road toward a little village, but the stranger seemed about to walk on. I called to him, 'Sir, why don't you stay here at the inn with us.' He seemed happy to be invited. He nodded in agreement and came in with us. The inn-keeper showed us where to wash and then fixed a table for us. The servant brought loaves of bread and set a jug of wine and cups on the table. The stranger sat down quite casually at the table. He reached over and took some bread. It was unusual for a guest and stranger to reach for food or drink first, but somehow I did not think it strange — the order of things just seemed to be different. Then he said a blessing. Somewhere I had heard a blessing like that once before. Then he broke the bread and gave it to us.

"I was looking at his hands, and suddenly I saw them. There was a print of nail in each hand. A shudder of joy passed through me. . . . My eyes traveled from the hands to the face . . . and the man was a stranger no longer. It was Jesus, the very one I had loved so much, who had accepted and understood me when no one else had ever tried. He looked at me with an expression that I wish I could describe . . . it was a mixture of joy and confidence, of compassion and friendship. There was a touch of humor in the slight smile upon his lips. I reached out my hands in amazement, with joy and yet bewilderment, and then he vanished.

"Suddenly the joy burst through me as if a dam had broken. I felt as though I had truly been carried to the heart of love. It was strange that his disappearance did not make me sad. His disappearance was part of his victory, victory over space and time and everything. His vanishing meant that he was always present, always there.''*

Morton Kelsey
The Other Side of Silence
pp. 258-260

"When the two friends, their supper unfinished, reached Jerusalem with their news, they were met with the tidings that Peter also had seen their Lord. While they yet spoke there was Jesus in the midst of them. 'But,' says St. Luke, 'they were startled and frightened and supposed that they saw a spirit.' Their faith in his Christhood and in the fact that he lived stopped short, as yet, of bodily resurrection. They believed themselves to be in the presence only of a ghost.

"We can hardly be wrong in taking this story of Luke's as a complementary version of that dated by St. John at the same time. It is the glory of the resurrection narratives that they agree completely in regard to the main characteristics of the appearances, and differ in details exactly as the accounts of independent witnesses always do differ, because no two minds register quite the same impressions. This appearance to the ten apostles and apparently to some others on the evening of Easter Day is really the central one of all, because in it the purposes and consequence of the Resurrection are most clearly manifested. Our Lord is confronted with the nucleus of his seed, the foundation of his church; and his first care is to establish them. Accommodating himself to their needs, he gives them the utmost sensible proof of the reality of his risen body, and of its identity of that with which he suffered. *But he does not explain it.* Then as now, it is the fact of the resurrection that is important, not its manner; we still do not know the laws that govern risen bodies. . . .

"But to return to Easter evening. The Lord elicited from his apostles faith in his Resurrection, but he did not say one word about the past. In his message to them by the woman that morning, he had already, for the first and only time on record, called them his *brethren*. Yet it was not as brethren that they had behaved when they departed from him in Gethsemane. It was as much as to say, 'That was not the real you; I know you better than that'; and by his

---

*See also 123:1, Perrin.

318

faith in them, he generated theirs in him. And by that faith they were justified, that is, accounted righteous by reason of that which in itself was his gift, part of the free bounty that his tremendous, forgiving, trusting love was pouring into them. Here then is the new covenant in action, the covenant of grace.''

Sister Penelope
The Wood
pp. 134-36

"When they return to Jerusalem, the disciples tell 'how he was known to them in the breaking of the bread' (24:35). This is undoubtedly a reference to the Eucharist. Luke is telling his readers that the risen Lord can be known to them, as he became known to these two disciples in the Eucharist. The evangelist is concerned to build a bridge as he was in his ministry — and as he can be known as risen — and the reader that reads his two-volume Luke-Acts. So he constantly represents Jesus at prayer, attending the synagogue 'as his custom was' (4:16), being led and guided by the Spirit of God, and so on — all things which in their turn the apostles do and experience in Acts, and all things which the believer can do in the Christian community.''

Norman Perrin
The Resurrection
p. 65

"Christ himself assumed manhood's perfection — perfection in the sense of full development, as well as in the sense of sinlessness — for the first time at the Transfiguration, in the sight of Peter, James, and John. The Greek says, 'He was *metamorphosed* before them.' Metamorphosis, change in form at different stages on the way to perfection, is common in the natural world, the most familiar instance being that of the creature which ends up as a butterfly, after being successively an egg, a caterpillar, and a chrysalis. The Transfiguration of Christ suggests that Man also is a metamorphic creature, and that properly he passes through two preparatory stages only before his reaching of his full development, the pre- and post-natal. For the teaching of the Bible is that death, for Man, is the result of sin; the state of being dead is the third stage put in between the second and last, as a remedial penalty for sin. And the fact that our Lord deliberately reverted to his mortal form on the Mount,* and went thence to Jerusalem to die in it, demonstrates the truth of his own saying, 'No man taketh my life from me; I lay it down of myself. I have power to lay it down, and I have power to take it again' (John 10:18). For after death he passed again to his perfection, this time

---

*See also 48:1, Penelope.

finally. In that perfected body, that yet bore the marks of what its larval form had borne on Calvary, he was touched and handled, as well as seen and heard, by many of his friends during the forty days (Acts 1:3). All that we know of Manhood perfected, Man in his final form, that perfect form that God intends us all to reach, all that St. Paul, for instance, teaches about the risen body and its relation to the former earthly one, is based on their direct first-hand experience of the risen Lord in A.D. 29.''

Sister Penelope
The Coming
pp. 45-46

" 'But some one will ask: How can the dead be raised? With what kind of body will they come back? Senseless man! What you sow is not brought to life unless it dies. And what you sow is not the body that is to be, but a bare grain, perhaps of wheat or something else . . .' (1 Corinthians 15:35-37). . . . The death of seed is only the condition of its passing into a more perfect existence. The image is a common symbol in the ancient world for survival and resurrection, both in the mystery religions and in Rabbinic Judaism. Paul's immediate source is probably a saying of Jesus which we find reflected in John 12:24, 'Unless the grain falling into the ground dies . . .' The grain that is sown is not what it is to become, but a simple grain. . . . Likewise, the body will not have the same qualities as it had here below. But neither is the transformation of the identical body impossible to God. If there is such a variety already observable in creation, why should God's power be limited to the kind of bodies we can see? It is important to observe that Paul reduces the whole question to the first cause. He does not of course say that the transformation of the grain is miraculous; but it is an effect of God's will, his gift. So too, the body may be entirely corrupt; God cannot only restore it but elevate it to a superior state. . . . From a state of dishonor, humiliation, and sordidness, the body rises in glory, which here is not just honor, but a quasi-physical splendor, light, brilliance. As Jesus at the Transfiguration appeared in glory, so the bodies of Christians at the final resurrection will be made conformable to Christ's glorious body. . . .

"From being a natural body, it becomes a spiritual body. We use the term 'natural' here to describe this body animated by the human soul (psyche), i.e., a principle of life proper to it, yet still for all that quite limited to merely human horizons. This very same body at the resurrection will be animated and totally penetrated by a new principle of life, the pneuma or Spirit which will perfect and elevate it, as it does even now to a limited extent. The transformation then, however, will flow over completely into the physical, transforming it. . . .

"Spirit means the active creative power of God. Hence a 'spiritual body' means a body in which the creative and life-giving power of God has become totally operative. In the case of the first creation, it was by God's breath, his pneuma or Spirit, that man became a living being. His same divine power now exerted upon the deceased person not only restores the natural life but charges it with a new and divine vitality which the first creation did not know. The risen body is not a ghost; it is real matter enjoying a superior and definitive state of being."

George T. Montague
The Living Thought of St. Paul
pp. 131-33

New Illuminations:

On Christ's Commission to His Disciples

Matthew 28:16-20	Mark 16:14-18	Luke 24:45-49	Acts 1:6-8

"I shall have the occasion to use the word *myth* in connection with the resurrection narratives, and by implication in connection with other biblical narratives. It is one of the tragedies of the contemporary discussion of biblical texts that the word *myth* has come to carry the negative connotation of something opposed to fact, something not true, such as a fairy story about the gods. The truth is that myths are the narrative expression of the deepest realities of human experience. Myths are ideas people live by and for which they are prepared to suffer, to kill and be killed. I was born and brought up in England and I can testify to the force of the myth of the English gentleman, of something being 'simply not cricket.' There have been many occasions when that myth motivated me to one action rather than another. . . . I would call the story of 1776 the foundation myth of American origins; and in saying this, I would regard myself as making the strongest and most positive statement I can about the story. By means of this story and the subsequent working out of its consequences in the history of the American people, the multitudinous immigrants of diverse origins have created the possibility of a genuine existence in one community as Americans. . . .

"The matter is no different with regard to the gospel narratives in general or the resurrection narratives in the gospels in particular. . . . The functioning adequacy of these narratives as the foundation myth of *Christian origins* affirm what it means to say 'Jesus is risen!' . . . When I use the word *myth* I am making no judgment about the historicity of the resurrection. The great biblical myths, including that of the resurrection, are like the myth of 1776 in that they are a mixture of mythicized history and historicized myth. The proportions of this mixture are for the hard-nosed historian to determine, if he or she has the data to make that determination, which in the case of the resurrection he or she does not. But the functioning power of the narrative as *myth* is dependent upon the ability of the narrative to provide the structure and cohesion of a particular human group — in this instance of Christians."

Norman Perrin
The Resurrection
pp. 9-13

"In the second part of the resurrection narrative, Jesus makes a speech which is, in effect, a major statement of the Lukan theology. It begins with a restatement of the need to interpret the Christ event in the light of scriptures. 'Thus it is written that Christ should suffer and on the third day rise from the dead.' For Luke to say that the Christ should 'rise from the dead' is to say that he should 'enter his glory.' This is an important insight into Luke's understanding of the resurrection.

"The speech of the risen Jesus then continues with a statement of the Lukan understanding of the foundation myth of Christian origins, 'that repentance and forgiveness of sins should be preached in his name to all nations, beginning from Jerusalem.' The evangelist Luke has an understanding of the Christian Church, and of the situation of the Christian believer in the world, every bit as distinctive as that of the evangelist Matthew, and quite different from it. Like Matthew, he faces the problem of finding a means of self-identity for the fledgling Christian community which could no longer identify itself in terms of the Jewish foundation myth — the religion of verbal revelation, the Torah, and of obedience to that revelation as authoritatively established by the rabbi. . . . But whatever the particular historical and cultural reasons might be, clearly the community or communities out of which and for which Luke wrote were desperately in need of a distinctively Christian foundation myth. I am not claiming that the evangelist recognized this need and self-consciously set out to meet it; what I am claiming is that this need has shaped his understanding of the story of Jesus and the apostles, whether consciously or unconsciously.

"For Luke the heart of the matter lies in the idea of a sacred center, a *place* where God is to be found and known. Luke is heir to a tradition in which Jerusalem was what one might call 'the navel of the universe,' the place above all others where God was to be found and known, the place above all places sacred and inviolable as the holiest of all places. . . . But Jerusalem fell to the Romans in the Jewish War of A.D. 66-70. The inviolable was violated. Indeed Hellenistic Judaism perished in the convulsions which followed. But Hellenistic Jewish Christianity survived. It survived because it found a new sacred center in the Christian movement itself; the life of Jesus became the navel of the universe, the place where God was particularly to be found and known. . . .

"The members of the movement relate to the sacred time of Jesus, and wherever the gospel of repentance and the forgiveness of sins is preached, *there* is 'the navel of the universe.' . . . Moreover the believer was bound to Jesus by one further factor: the believer was empowered by that same Spirit which had empowered Jesus himself. This is the import of the last element in this speech of the risen Lord to his disciples: 'You are witnesses of these things. And behold, I send the promise of my Father upon you; but stay in the city until you are clothed with power from on high.'

"Now we can see why Luke resolutely locates all the resurrection appearances in or near Jerusalem. For Matthew the foundation myth climaxes in the commissioning of the disciples to form the Christian Church, and he believes that this took place in Galilee in fulfillment of the promise of Jesus to his disciples that they would see him in Galilee. But for Luke the essence of the myth is the fate laden progress of Jesus to Jerusalem, and of the gospel from Jerusalem to Rome. So the resurrection appearances take place in Jerusalem where the disciples/apostles must stay until they begin the progression from Jerusalem to Rome. The needs of the myth demand it."

Norman Perrin
The Resurrection
pp. 67-70, 76

"There is no longer any question of any claim on God, such as under the Old Covenant was felt to accrue from observance of the law. The sufficiency is all on God's side, and men have nothing apart from what he gives. The water-pots are full indeed now, full of life-giving wine, but it is against the law of the universe for anything to be self-contained. The apostles are called to be not only pots but pipes. They are the first installment of God's irrigation system for this dried-up world. So Jesus, who by taking the manhood into God has made it the inexhaustible reservoir of life for all creation, pronounces to these newly shriven penitents their commission: 'As the Father has sent me, even so I send you . . .'

"Thus as members and extenders of the New Humanity, the apostles take their unique place in the line directly after the Head. . . . Putting together the closing verses of St. Matthew and St. Luke and the opening verses of Acts, you find connected with the Ascension two commands, to wait and to go; two promises, of the Holy Spirit and of the Lord's return, and one statement of present and abiding fact, 'Lo, I am with you always to the close of the age.' "

Sister Penelope
The Wood
pp. 136-137

New Illuminations:

On the Ascension of Christ

Mark 16:19   Luke 24:50-53   Acts 1:9-11

"The ascension is the withdrawal into eternity of Jesus' *living* manhood, bearing to the throne of God the manhood he had taken 'for us men and for our salvation' from the very substance of his mother Mary. The account in Acts 1 describes how, as his apostles watched, 'He was raised up from the ground and a cloud received him from their sight' (Acts 1:9). The 'cloud' is the *Shechinah* — the cloud which in Old Testament Scripture and Jewish tradition hides the very presence of God. (There is no need to think of an Ascension of many millions of miles to a physical heaven!) It is an acted parable, an intimation to the Apostles, still overjoyed at the recovery of their Master, that this is his last resurrection-appearance in this world, and of where they must now seek him and find him, the man they loved and knew — in the very being of God himself."

Dom Gregory Dix
The Claim of Jesus Christ
p. 72

"The account of the Ascension presents difficulties only if we treat it as a literal description. Like the narrative of the Day of Pentecost, which follows shortly after, it is a pictorial representation of an event which is essentially incapable of prosaic description. . . . When the post-Resurrection appearances ceased, giving place to a new development in the situation, there was no other way open to first-century writers of expressing the conviction that the Christ, having triumphed over death, still lived in the perfect relationship to God which he had always enjoyed, but was now freed from the limitations of time and space which the Palestinian ministry had imposed upon him."

William Neil
The Message of the Bible
p. 108

"The last appearance of our Lord was such as showed plainly no more were to be expected. Like so many things, this appearance was both history and symbol; and the Creed expresses it by saying that 'he ascended into heaven and sitteth at the right hand of God.' Historically the Apostles witnessed a visible ascent of the Lord from a mountain-top until a cloud received him out of their sight. Symbolically the Ascension betokened the mystery already consummated on Good Friday — that is, the arrival of the perfected Manhood

at its home in God. However certain you may be that heaven is a state and not a place, you may still learn a great deal about heaven from contemplating *the* heavens and the place of our little earth in that vast organic unity. Think of God as himself enwrapping the universe rather than as resident in any part of it, by all means; but do not regard the language of the Creed as childish. . . . If you define heaven as where God reigns undisputed and adored it is easy to see in what sense the Word 'came down' from heaven, taught us to pray that the Father's kingdom might 'come' on earth as it is in heaven,* and himself 'ascended' hither to reign at his Father's right hand. But do not cavil at the metaphors, for you will find no better."

Sister Penelope
The Wood
p. 137

" 'Jesus is Lord.' That is the faith which we proclaim on the lovely festival of the Ascension — Lord in his sovereignty, Lord in his presence.

"It was indeed for the advantage of his disciples, and for our advantage that he went away. And throughout the life of a Christian, this law of gain through loss, will often recur. . . .

"For the biblical writers and for much Christian thought in post-Biblical times, heaven or the other world was a place beyond the sky. Thither Christ had gone up at his Ascension, and there the saints reigned with him in dazzling light. It was another world related to this world astronomically, which really meant that it was part of this world.

"Yet within this language of locality, just because it was language about God, there was something that transcended locality altogether: the supremacy of Christ everywhere, and the union of Christians with God through him. The right hand of God meant no local activity, but a symbol of God's sovereign power.** The Ascension of Christ meant a presence unrestricted: if he is here, he is there; if he is there, he is everywhere. God being 'above' meant a relationship no less describable as 'within.' The spatial conception of the 'other world' lingered, but the heart of Christian belief knew from the beginning that it was only using symbols for the God-Christ-mankind relationship beyond locality. So that the 'otherness' of the other world is not that of a structure standing over against the world. It is the otherness of

*See also 59:2, Lewis.
**See also 114:1, Schnackenburg.

man's life with God, invisible, present already and leading to a destiny after death.''

Margaret Duggan, ed.
Through the Year With Michael Ramsey
pp. 84, 100-01

"Our Lord's Ascension is also his accession to the throne of God. Taking his royal power, he brings in the New Age, bestows the Holy Spirit as his gift for men, judges, though not yet openly, expects till all his enemies on earth be overcome. All that he does as King. As Shepherd, he goes before his flock to lead the way; as the Ark of God's indwelling, he is uplifted to his resting-place; as Bridegroom, he goes to prepare a place for his Bride. Whichever way you look at it, the Ascension from the Mount of Olives, tremendous, glorious climax though it is, is only a stage in his one coming to the Father, not its consummation, though it prefigures it. We pray in the collect for Ascension Day that we may in heart and mind thither ascend, whither our Saviour Christ is gone before. That, for the present, is all we can do. But let us not forget that we are destined eventually to ascend to heaven in our bodies, our final risen bodies, too.''*

Sister Penelope
The Coming
p. 31

_____

*See also 105:2, Penelope.

"All the accounts of the Ascension suggest that the appearances of the Risen Body came to an end. Some describe an abrupt end about six weeks after the death. And they describe this abrupt end in a way that presents greater difficulties to the modern mind than any other part of Scripture. For here, surely, we get the implications of all those primitive crudities to which I have said that Christians are not committed: the vertical ascent like a balloon, the local Heaven, the decorated chair to the right of the Father's throne. 'He was caught up into the sky' says St. Mark's Gospel, 'and sat down at the right hand of God.' 'He was lifted up,' says the author of Acts, 'and a cloud cut him off from their sight.' . . .

"Can we then simply drop the Ascension story? The answer is that we can do so only if we regard the resurrection appearances as those of a ghost or hallucination. For a phantom can just fade away; but an objective entity must go somewhere — something must happen to it*. . . . The records represent Christ as withdrawing into some different mode of existence. It says — he says — that he goes 'to prepare a place for us.' This presumably means that he is about to create that whole new nature which will provide the environment and conditions for his glorified humanity and, in him, for ours. . . . That is the picture — not of unmaking but of remaking. The old field of space, time, matter and the senses is to be weeded, dug, and sown for a new crop. We may be tired of that old field: God is not.''

C. S. Lewis
Miracles
pp. 177-79

_____

*See also 121:1, Lewis.

New Illuminations:

ROMANS

3:24f/122:1 Baillie
4:24/121:1 Ramsey
5:1-2/80:2 Ramsey
5:8/64:3 Jones
6:8/121:2 Krumm
7:1-4/83:2 Nee `
7:4/83:2 Nee
8:3/83:1 Phillips
8:11/105:3 Montague
9:15, 18/78:2 Ward
11:16/72:1 Jeremias
12:2/59:1 Allen
12:16/63:2 Theophan
13:10/83:2 Phillips
13:10/63:3 Milligan
14:13b, 21b/87:1 Laubach

1 CORINTHIANS

2:9/28:2 Allen
3:12-15/86:2 Milligan
3:14/86:3 Bornkamm
7:29, 31/47:2 Schnackenburg
11:23-26/108:3 Montague
12:12-31/55:1 Kunkel
15:10/80:2 Briscoe
15:3/117:3 Ramsey
15:14/121:2 Krumm
15:26/70:3 Sophrony
15:31/46:1 Webbe
15:35-37/123:3 Montague

2 CORINTHIANS

1:8/39:1 Miller
4:6/57:1 Mascall
12:9/94:2 Bloom

GALATIANS

2:20/3:1 Kunkel
2:20/80:2 Holloway
3:13/122:3 Webster
3:21b-26/83:2 Phillips
3:24/83:1 Penelope
4:4, 5/122:3 Webster
5:22-23/27:1 Underhill
5:22-23/67:2 Drake
6:2/93:2 a Kempis

EPHESIANS

1:7/118:1 Ramsey
2/83:1 Phillips
2:8-9/21:2 Tugwell
2:10/24:2 Payne
3/57:1 Sophrony
4:11-12/37:1 Chambers
4:15/70:3 Neil
6:10-11/61:2 Pardue
6:17/70:3 Sophrony

PHILLIPIANS

2:5/59:3 Lewis
3:6/21:1-2 Tugwell
3:10/120:1 de Blank

COLOSSIANS

1:26/90:2 Phillips
2:9/23:1 Penelope
2:13/79:3 Wedel

1 THESSALONIANS

4:13-18/105:2 Montague
5:5/105:1 Montague

1 TIMOTHY

2:6/122:2 Holloway

2 TIMOTHY

1:6/89:3 Pardue
2:19/27:2 Beaufoy
3:15/84:1 Ward
3:16/84:1 Thielicke

HEBREWS

9:14/67:2 Drake
10:8-10/116:1 Webster
11/89:1 Neil
11:6/89:3 Williams
12:26-28/27:3 Phillips Bible

JAMES

1:13-14/13:1 Kunkel
2:18/7:2 Andrewes
3:17/25:5 Sophrony
4:7/64:1 Stott

1 PETER

1:12b/57:1 Sophrony
2:20-21/31:1 Phillips
3:19-20/117:4 Underhill
4:14/67:1 Drake

2 PETER

1:19/7:2 Andrews

1 JOHN

1:8, 10/64:1 Stott
3:2/37:1 Phillips
3:4/64:1 Stott
4:10/122:1 Baillie

REVELATIONS

3:7/42:1 Schnackenburg
3:20/108:3 Monk
6:11/76:2 Jeremias
19:17/23:1 Jeremias
21:9/121:3 Penelope